CASPIAN

SEA

LAKE
VAN

LAKE
URMIA

Tepe Hissar

e Gawra
chiyah
ird Ali Agha
Jarzi
Palegawra
la Balka
Karim Shahir
Jarmo
Hazar Merd
Matarrah

DARYA-YI-NAMAK

Samarra

IRAN

Sialk

TIGRIS
OPOTAM
Jemdet Nasr
IA
Susa

Uruk
i Muhammed
Al. Ubaid
Eridu

PERSIAN

GULF

THE GREATNESS THAT WAS BABYLON

The
Greatness that was
BABYLON

*A sketch of the ancient civilization
of the Tigris-Euphrates valley*

by

H. W. F. SAGGS

HAWTHORN BOOKS, INC.
PUBLISHERS, NEW YORK

Contents

List of illustrations   xi

List of line illustrations in text   xv

Foreword   xvii

PART I

GENERAL AND POLITICAL HISTORY

Chap. I.   Mesopotamia before 2000 B.C.   3

Mesopotamia defined: Old Stone Age: Neolithic Revolution: Karim Shahir: Jarmo: *Hassuna* culture: *Samarra* culture: *Halaf* culture: earliest settlement of south Mesopotamia: *Eridu* culture: *Hajji Muhammad* phase: *Ubaid* culture: origin of cities: *Uruk* culture: *Uruk* IV period: origin of writing: temples and religion of *Uruk* period: cylinder seals: *Jemdet Nasr* culture: Mesopotamian influences in Egypt: religion of *Jemdet Nasr* period: metal utilization: *Early Dynastic* period: Sumerian origins: Flood legend: dynasties of Erech and Kish: early Sumerian political and social organization: *En* and *Lugal* functionaries: fortification of cities: Semitic infiltration: earliest written documents: Dynasty of Lagash: First Dynasty of Ur: economics of Sumerian city-states: Urukagina's reforms: Lugalzagesi of Umma: Sargon of Agade: Naram-Sin: Gutian period: Gudea of Lagash: Third Dynasty of Ur: Amorite invasion: collapse of Third Dynasty of Ur.

2.   Babylonia and Assyria, circa 2000–1350 B.C.   60

Ishbi-Erra and the kingdom of Isin: kingdom of Larsa: First Dynasty of Babylon: Mari and its archives: Assyria: trade between Assyria and Asia Minor: Yasmah-Adad: unification of Babylonia: achievements of Hammurabi:

Cassites: sack of Babylon: Hittite kingdom: Hurrian influences in Mesopotamia: kingdom of Mitanni: Cassite dynasty: Assyrian independence: end of kingdom of Mitanni.

3. The Rise of Imperial Assyria   83

Ashur-uballit: weakness of Babylonia: Babylon captured by Tukulti-Ninurta I: Assyrian decline: Second Dynasty of Isin: Nebuchadrezzar I: Aramaean pressure on Assyria: conquests of Tiglath-Pileser I: thriving trade: intensified Aramaean pressure causes Assyrian decline: crystallization of Aramaean kingdoms: improving trade in Assyria: conquests of Adad-nirari II: *limmu* lists and chronology: Ashur-nasir-pal's military and administrative achievements: Shalmaneser III: consolidation of Assyrian position in the west: Assyrian use of Syrian craftsmen: rebellion against Shalmaneser III: Shamshi-Adad V: attack upon Babylonia: Semiramis: Adad-nirari III: mounting pressure from Urartu: Assyrian loss of trade routes: revolt in Assyria.

4. Assyrian Supremacy   105

Situation in Assyria at accession of Tiglath-Pileser III: administrative reforms: settlement of Babylonia: action against Urartu: action in Syria: Ukin-zer's rebellion in Babylonia: Shalmaneser V: siege of Samaria: Sargon: Merodach-baladan seizes throne of Babylonia: rebellion in Syria and Palestine: pressure on Assyria from the north: invasion of Urartu: settlement of Babylonia: military and diplomatic relations between Mushku (Meshech) and Assyria: Cimmerian hordes threaten the civilized world: Sennacherib: rebuilding of Nineveh: insurrection in Babylonia: conflict with Elam: sack of Babylon: civil achievements of Sennacherib: murder of Sennacherib: Esarhaddon's succession: defeat of rebels in Babylonia: northern provinces lost to Assyria: rebuilding of Babylon: arrangements for succession at Esarhaddon's death: invasion of Egypt: Ashurbanipal: new attacks upon Egypt: sack of Thebes: Psammetichus expels Assyrian garrisons from Egypt: friction in Babylonia: decline of Elam: Assyrian intervention in Elamite succession: civil war in Babylonia: capture of Babylon and suicide of Shamash-shum-ukin: Assyrian sack of Susa: death of Ashurbanipal: chronology of final years of the Assyrian empire: Nabopolassar assumes kingship in Babylonia: alliance with the Medes: Egyptians support Assyria: capture of Ashur: fall of Nineveh.

5. Neo-Babylonian Empire   140

Final defeat of Assyria and allies at Carchemish: siege and capture of Tyre: policy of Nebuchadrezzar: Amel-Marduk: Jehoiachin of Judah: Neriglissar: campaign in Asia Minor: Nabu-na'id: attempted economic and religious reforms: Harran: Nabu-na'id transfers court to Western Arabia: Cyrus: attack upon Babylonia: capture of Babylon: death of the old civilization of Babylonia.

PART 2

SOCIAL AND CULTURAL HISTORY

6. The Foundations of Babylonian Society and the Babylonian Way of Life   157

Origins in *Uruk* culture: canal-making and irrigation as social forces: theory of 'primitive democracy': effect of Semitic infiltration upon Sumerian society: religious theory underlying the Sumerian city-state: land tenure and economic organization: transport and communications: the *Ensi*: temple-estate personnel: slavery: adoption and child care: holidays: food and drink : housing and house equipment: sewage disposal: town planning: water supply: clothing: hair styles: marriage and sexual relations: education: sports and pastimes: music: health and psychology: dreams: social misfits: treatment of animals.

7. Law and Statecraft   196

Respect for rule of law in ancient Mesopotamia: economic justice a concern of the king: laws of Ur-Nammu: laws of Lipit-Ishtar: *ana ittishu*: laws of Eshnunna: laws of Hammurabi: the Assyrian laws: administration of justice: the Ordeal: international law: treaties and diplomacy.

8. Administration   233

Third and second millennia: end of *Early Dynastic* period: period of Third Dynasty of Ur: Old Babylonian period.

New Assyrian period: efficient administrative system: Assyria not considered barbarous by contemporaries: relation of smaller states to Assyria: tortures: imperial administrative correspondence: governors and their

subordinates: communication system: local city administration: taxation and tribute: civil order: the Assyrian
army.

New Babylonian period: decentralization of power:
temple administration at Erech: temple estates: *shirke*:
royal share of temple revenues: New Babylonian provincial administrative policy.

9.   Trade and Economics   269

Foreign trade: prehistoric period: *Protoliterate* and
Early Dynastic periods: connections with Egypt and India:
maritime trade *circa* 1900 B.C.: trade with distant regions
under the Agade dynasty: trade with Asia Minor *circa*
1900 B.C.: theory that ancient Mesopotamia lacked a
'market economy': Syria in international trade: merchant
colonies: trade routes through Urartu, Syria and Iran:
attempts of New Babylonian kings to gain new trade
routes.

Internal trade: the *tamkarum* or merchant banker: loans:
commercial contracts: dishonesty: transport of goods:
real estate transactions: revendication: concern of Assyrian kings with internal prosperity: temple and private
trading in New Babylonian times.

10.   Religion   299

Sources for our knowledge: was Babylonian religion
Semitic?: animism: demons: exorcism: sympathetic
magic: *Shurpu, Maqlu, Utukki Limnuti* and other texts
concerned with demons and magical rituals: demons in
the New Testament: good demons: witchcraft: taboo:
omens: prevention of ill consequences of omens: prayer:
henotheism: the pantheon: Anu: Enlil: Ea: Sin:
Shamash: Ishtar: Adad: Ninurta: Nergal: Fire-gods:
Marduk: Nabu: Ashur: Dagan: the service of the gods.

Types of cult functionary: *En*: *Erib-biti*: *Mashmashu*
and *Ashipu*: *Kalu*: *Naru*: *Sheshgallu*: *Shangu*: *Baru*:
Sha'ilu: eunuchs: *Entu*: *Qadishtu*: temple prostitution as
described by Herodotus: offerings to the gods: sacrifices.

The temple complex: the ziggurat: Tower of Babel:
shrine of the god: making a divine statue: divine processions.

11.   The King   359

Mesopotamian concept of kingship: origin of kingship:
'divine kingship': royal substitution: the king responsible
for building and restoring temples: restoration of a

temple: reports to the gods: canal-making a royal duty: the king as protector of the weak: 'royal tombs' of Ur and theories concerning them: the Sacred Marriage: the *Akitu* festival: the New Year festival at Babylon: 'cone-smearing'.

12. Literature   390

Epic of Gilgamish: Atrahasis: Epic of Adapa: Epic of Creation: other creation myths: Nergal and Ereshkigal: Descent of Ishtar: Myth of Zu: Etana: legends of Sargon of Agade and Naram-Sin: Epic of Tukulti-Ninurta: Wisdom literature: Sumerian proverbs, precepts, maxims and tensons: edubba compositions: schools: Poem of the Righteous Sufferer: Babylonian Theodicy: Dialogue of Pessimism: Counsel of Wisdom: Akkadian proverbs, precepts, maxims and anecdotes.

13. Mathematics and Astronomy; Medicine; Chemical Technology; Art   445

Mathematics: numeration and number symbols: place-value notation: mathematical texts: Babylonian quadratic equation: geometrical text.

Astronomy: relation to astrology: astronomical observations: intercalation: ephemerides.

Medicine: medical practitioners: diagnostic and prognostic texts: prescriptions: surgery.

Chemical technology.

Art: decorated pottery: sculpture: inlay: Assyrian bas-reliefs: carved ivory: painting: metal-work.

14. Legacy and Survival   483

Channels for transmission of elements from Mesopotamian civilization: Mesopotamian elements in the Bible: astrology: the zodiac: horoscopes: astronomy: numeration: time division: vocabulary: architecture: symbols in religious art: literature, literary forms, folk-lore: nominal monogamy.

Bibliography   505
Chronological Tables   531
Index of Biblical references   537
Subject Index   539
Index of Proper Names   551
Index of Sumerian, Akkadian, Hebrew and Greek words 561

List of Illustrations

BETWEEN PAGES 108 AND 109

1   White temple at Warka
2A Cone mosaics from Warka
2B Silver model of a boat, from the 'royal tombs' of Ur
3A The ziggurat of Ur
3B Ruins of ziggurat of Borsippa (modern Birs Nimrud), possibly the original 'Tower of Babel'
4A Ruins of ziggurat of Dur-Kurigalzu (modern Aqarquf)
4B Ruins of processional way at Babylon
5   Lion head in copper, with bitumen core (from Ubaid)
6   The Ishtar Gate (reconstruction)
7   Harp (restored) from the 'royal tombs' of Ur
8A Alabaster vase from Warka
8B Early Sumerian dress (carving on a stone mace-head)
9A Cattle trough from Jemdet Nasr (early third millennium)
9B Gaming board from Ur (first half of third millennium)
10 The god Imdugud ('Severe Wind') with stags; an early Sumerian monument probably concerned with fertility
11A Cult objects, usually described as a lamp cover, in the form of intertwined snakes (late third millennium)
11B Inlaid panel from Ur (first half of third millennium), showing religious representations related to a fertility cult
12 War scene from the 'Standard of Ur' (first half of third millennium)
13A Lavatory, with remains of seat of bitumen (third millennium)
13B Main drain of a palace (third millennium)
14 Head of Sargon of Agade
15A Window grille (third millennium)
15B Bronze 'frying pan'
16A Rock relief of Naram-Sin in Qara-Dagh range, Iraq (circa 2280 B.C.)
16B Stele of Naram-Sin (circa 2280 B.C.)

BETWEEN PAGES 220 AND 221

17 Head from Warka (third millennium)
18A Bronze foundation deposit representing a Sumerian ruler bearing the head-pad at the building of a temple

xi

18B Head of a Sumerian in diorite (end of third millennium)

19 A goddess holding vase, for use as a fountain (from Mari)

20 A Sumerian official

21A Babylonian boundary stone (late second millennium B.C.)

21B Cast of the stele of Hammurabi (early second millennium B.C.)

22 Part of a cuneiform tablet (from Nineveh, first millennium B.C.), bearing the end of the Flood story from the *Epic of Gilgamish*

23 Obverse of a cuneiform tablet inscribed with geometrical exercises (early second millennium B.C.)

24 Reverse of a cuneiform tablet inscribed with geometrical exercises (early second millennium B.C.)

25 Inscribed cone of Ur-Bawa (*circa* 2200 B.C.)

26A Old Babylonian cuneiform tablet and envelope; a contract for the sale of land

26B Cuneiform tablet (*circa* 600 B.C.) bearing a map of the world.

26C Cuneiform tablet with Egyptian endorsement

27A Impression of cylinder seal, showing Maltese crosses

27B Inscribed clay model of an internal organ, for use in divination

28 King Ashur-nasir-pal II

29 King Ashur-nasir-pal II

30 An Assyrian god

31 Assyrian religious ceremony of the first millennium B.C. involving the king

32 The Assyrian king in a cult scene before stylized sacred tree

BETWEEN PAGES 332 AND 333

33A Scenes from the bronze gates of Shalmaneser III (ninth century B.C.)

33B Scenes from the bronze gates of Shalmaneser III (ninth century B.C.)

34 Assyrian forces and [bottom register] prisoners-of-war

35 Relief on an obelisk of Shalmaneser III showing [top section] Jehu of Israel offering tribute

36 Foreigners bringing tribute to Assyria (from an Assyrian bas-relief)

37 Esarhaddon with captive Egyptian kings

38 Wild horse hunt (from an Assyrian bas-relief)

39 Herd of gazelles (from an Assyrian bas-relief)

40 Lions released for the hunt (from an Assyrian bas-relief)

41 Hunting dogs, and man with nets (from an Assyrian bas-relief)

42 The deer hunt (from an Assyrian bas-relief)

43A Dying lion (from an Assyrian bas-relief)

43B Paralysed lioness (from an Assyrian bas-relief)

44A Hunting dogs (from an Assyrian bas-relief)

44B Hunting scene (from an Assyrian bas-relief)

45 Assyrian archer and squire (from an Assyrian bas-relief)

46A Assyrian tortures (from an Assyrian bas-relief)

46B Assyrian siege craft, showing prototype of the military tank (from an Assyrian bas-relief)

47 Battle scene (from an Assyrian bas-relief)

48 Assyrian slingers (from an Assyrian bas-relief)

BETWEEN PAGES 444 AND 445

49 The high-priest and goddess escort the king to the Sun-god sitting in his shrine behind the sun-disk (first millennium B.C., probably copied from a more ancient monument)

50A The rising of the Sun-god; a cylinder seal impression

50B Mythical hero [Gilgamish?] with lion; a cylinder seal impression

51A Boxing, possibly as a cult act (from a plaque)

51B Copper stand in the form of wrestlers (third millennium)

51C Cult scene of questionable nature (from a plaque)

52 Musicians (from an Assyrian bas-relief)

53 Colossal human-headed lion, representing a good genie guarding an Assyrian palace

54A Face of Humbaba, an ogre mentioned in the *Epic of Gilgamish*

54B Lamashtu, a dreaded female demon (from an amulet)

55 A Babylonian devil

56A Babylonian monster (*circa* 1900 B.C.)

56B Amulet, showing gods associated with mythical beasts

57A The wind-demon Pazuzu, with [top register] exorcist priests in animal head-dress (an alabaster amulet from Babylon, first millennium)

57B Detail from reredos by Jacques de Baerze (*circa* 1300 A.D.), showing astral symbols and demons possibly deriving ultimately from ancient Mesopotamia

58A Rein-ring from Ur (third millennium)

58B Weight in form of a lion (first millennium B.C.)

59 Brazier (from Nuzi)

60A A carved ivory; a lady [perhaps a cult-woman] at her window

60B A carved ivory

61A Winged ibex (Achaemenid period)

61B Bronze dragon's head from Babylon (sixth century B.C.)

62 Jewellery of ancient Mesopotamia

63 Carved limestone floor from doorway of an Assyrian palace

64 The Gebel el-Arak knife, with carved handle showing ship of Mesopotamian type in Egyptian art (early third millennium)

Colour Plates

(*Facing page* 378) Ram from Ur (first half of third millennium) in gold foil, shell and lapis lazuli.

(*Facing page* 480) Carved ivory embellished with gold and precious stones, from Nimrud (eighth century B.C.)

ACKNOWLEDGEMENTS

The sources of the plates are as follows:

Courtesy of the Trustees of the British Museum: colour plates *opposite* pages 378 *and* 480 and plates 2B, 5, 7, 8B, 9A, 9B, 10, 11B, 12, 18A, 20, 21A, 22, 23, 24, 25, 26A, 26B, 26C, 27A, 27B, 28, 29, 30, 31, 32, 33A, 33B, 34, 35, 36, 38, 39, 40, 41, 42, 43A, 43B, 44A, 44B, 45, 46A, 46B, 47, 48, 49, 50A, 50B, 51A, 51C, 52, 53, 54A, 54B, 55, 56A, 56B, 58A, 60A, 60B, 62, 63

Courtesy of Penguin Books Ltd.: plates 1, 2A, 6, 8A, 16B, 17, 19, 51B

Courtesy of Joan Saggs: plate 4B

Courtesy of Monsieur le Conservateur du Musée du Louvre: plates 11A, 18B, 58B, 61A, 61B

Courtesy of the Oriental Institute, University of Chicago: plates 13A, 13B, 15A

Courtesy of the Department of Antiquities of the Republic of Iraq, and Professor D. J. Wiseman: plate 14

Courtesy of the University Museum of the University of Pennsylvania: plate 15B

Courtesy of the Mansell Collection: plates 16B, 21B, 64

Courtesy of the Berlin Museum, and Professor D. J. Wiseman: plate 37

Courtesy of Dr. O. R. Gurney and the late Professor D. S. Rice: plate 57A

Courtesy of Monsieur le Conservateur du Musée des Beaux-Arts, Dijon: plate 57B

Courtesy of Harvard University Press: plate 59

Author's photographs: plates 3A, 3B, 4A, 16A

Line Illustrations in Text

	Page
The earliest pictographs	23
Drinking tube	173
Brewing	174
Milking scene	174
Clay whistle	190
Inscription on Pazuzu amulet	304
Ishtar symbol	334
Adad symbol	335
[Geometrical figure]	453
Ionian column and its ancestor	496
Assyrian sacred tree	497
Cross in form of sacred tree, after a brass in an English cathedral	498
Mosque of Samarra	499
Intertwined serpents in Islamic art	500

Foreword

THERE is in English, so far as I am aware, no book which gives an up-to-date account of the civilization of Babylonia and Assyria as a whole. In this work I have attempted to make good this deficiency, addressing myself particularly to the general reader and to students in their final year at school or their first year at university. No previous knowledge of the subject is assumed beyond such biblical knowledge as any reader interested in the broader aspects of human history may reasonably be expected to possess.

It is hardly necessary to point out that in an introduction to such a vast field of human activity, much of interest and importance has had to be omitted or dealt with cursorily. In making my selection of topics I have attempted to emphasize those aspects of the subject, such as economics or administration, which are little touched upon in older works, and to omit, or to give only a slight account of, such matters as have been adequately treated. Thus Mesopotamian art, of which there is a lucid account in H. Frankfort's *The Art and Architecture of the Ancient Orient* (1954) and which has been the theme of some later works, is limited to a few pages, whilst the fascinating history of Mesopotamian excavation has been omitted altogether in view of the many excellent popular accounts of the subject from A. H. Layard's *Nineveh and its Remains* (1849) to M. E. L. Mallowan's *Twenty-five Years of Mesopotamian Discovery* (1956). No apology is made for the fact that two long chapters out of fourteen are given to aspects of religion; odd though it may appear to our present Man-centred age, this still represents considerably less than a just proportion in the life of the ancient world. Purely for considerations of space, some topics have had to be omitted which I would gladly have included: amongst them I may mention several religious themes (such as burial rites and ideas of the

Afterlife, the problem of incipient henotheism, and the 'seculariz-ing tendency' discussed in a recent article by W. von Soden), and such diverse matters as agricultural practice, metal technology, and the tactics of Assyrian armies in the field.

The reader should not be deceived by the apparent confidence with which precise dates have been offered at many points from the mid-third millennium onwards. Mesopotamian chrono-logy is still a very controversial subject, and for the third and second millennia there are three main systems current. My own dates represent an attempt to utilize the system originally worked out by Professor Sidney Smith and slightly adapted by M. B. Rowton in the light of later research. It should be emphasized that though (it is hoped) the dates given are correct *relatively* – that is, are consistent with each other – there is a possible error in the *absolute* datings of a century either way at the beginning of the third millennium, reducing to about ten years by the end of the second. Most dates for the first millennium can confidently be given (as is explained within the book) to within a year.

A word of explanation may be desirable with regard to the transliteration of proper names. Where a biblical or classical form is current, this is generally employed. In other instances, in order to spare the non-specialist reader the distraction of a series of diacritical signs, the precedent of the English versions of the Old Testament has been followed in representing ṣ, š, ṭ and ḫ (the 'ch' sound in Scottish 'loch') by s, sh, t and (in most cases) h respectively, and in omitting the glottal stop except where (as in Nabu-na'id) its omission would suggest a false pronunciation. A slight inconsistency has been accepted by transcribing the ḫ sound by kh (not h) in such a name as Arrapḫa, where Arrapha might suggest a pronunciation Arrafa. Wherever the form of a proper name leaves (in the light of the above ex-planation) any doubt as to the accurate transcription, the exact form is given in square brackets in the Index of Proper Names after the form employed in the text.

The translations are, except where otherwise indicated, my own renderings of the original text into (I hope) English which accords with modern idiomatic usage. Restored words or passages about which there can be no doubt are not specially marked. Round brackets within translations denote words implied but not verbally represented in the original, whilst square brackets enclose an explanatory remark; bracketed question-marks indicate an element of doubt in the translation of the words concerned.

Biblical quotations are mostly from the Revised Version, although in some cases, where the Victorian revisers wantonly mauled the Jacobean English of the Authorised Version without producing a more accurate rendering, the older translation has been preferred.

H. W. F. SAGGS

Epiphany, 1962

PART 1

GENERAL AND POLITICAL
HISTORY

I

Mesopotamia before 2000 B.C.

ONE of the difficulties in discussing the ancient civilization of Mesopotamia lies in the geographical terminology. 'Mesopotamia' itself is ambiguous: to some, acquainted with British operations in the Near East in the First World War, it means the region between and around the Euphrates and Tigris from the Persian Gulf to Mosul; to others, at home in the classics, it implies an area at the north-west end of this. When used in this work, 'Mesopotamia' is intended to be taken in the former sense. 'Iraq' is equally ambiguous: it can be (and in this book is) used anachronistically with reference to ancient times to mean the whole of the region included in the modern state of that name; but for Arabists it can have a more limited sense. 'Babylonia' and 'Assyria' are convenient terms: properly they denote the principal southern and northern kingdoms in the area under discussion from the second millennium onwards, but they are frequently used more loosely for the southern and northern parts of the area without reference to political entities and of a time before Babylon existed. Sumer means the southern and Akkad the northern part of Babylonia.

In some passages, especially in the earlier part of the cultural history, there is little or no logical justification for treating events in Iraq in isolation from the surrounding areas. A general limitation to the more restricted area has, however, been dictated by considerations of space, and it has only been possible to cast passing glances at events and developments in the peripheral areas.

In Iraq, as in many other parts of Europe and Asia, it is now possible to trace human occupation back to the stage of development generally known as Palaeolithic or Old Stone Age, at which Man still subsisted through hunting and food-gathering, before he began to live in settled communities and control his food supply by the domestication and herding of animals and the growing of cereals. The present evidence for this stage in Iraq is not extensive, being confined to a few sites in the highlands. However, though the evidence is sparse, it is enough to establish the presence of Man in Iraq (as also in the peripheral areas) from a period which, as a very rough guide, may be put at between one hundred and one hundred and fifty thousand years ago.

At that period the northern part of Iraq presented a very different landscape and fauna from that to be found in the area now. Throughout historical times the region which includes Iraq has always been, as it remains today, so deficient in rainfall that in many parts it is virtually uninhabitable away from the river valleys. This was not always its climate. About a hundred thousand years ago, when glaciers covered a large part of northern Europe, the whole area from the Atlantic coast of North Africa and across the Near East to Iran enjoyed a far more abundant rainfall. Thus at that time the whole region was a kind of vast park, with plant life sufficient to support a wide range and plentiful supply of animals; among this extensive fauna was a very rare food-gathering biped – the creature we know as Palaeolithic Man. Evidence for human occupation in Iraq at this ancient period comes from a cave site at a place called Barda Balka, where stone tools have been discovered of types which can be related to those found elsewhere in Asia and Africa. Alongside these man-made tools are the remains of animals such as the elephant and great deer, which must at that time have been much commoner in the region than Man himself.

Human occupation in Iraq towards the end of the food-gathering era is represented by remains in caves at Zarzi and Hazar Merd in the Kurdish hills in the Sulaimania *liwa*, associated with flint industries classified respectively as Aurignacian and

Mousterian; a third cave site, Palegawra, in the same area, may be a little later. The examination of animal bones from these sites shows that at this time, just before the sociological and economic change now often called the Neolithic Revolution, Man fed himself to a large extent by hunting the larger mammals, his prey including wild horses, pigs, sheep and goats, deer and gazelles. By this time Man knew the use of fire, and no longer ate his meat raw.

Until Carbon-14 analysis or other techniques provide some more definite indication, the period of the earliest human habitation of the caves just mentioned cannot be given with confidence to within thousands of years: as a very rough guide, however, one may date the human societies represented by these sites at about 10000 B.C.

The transition to an economy based on the cultivation of crops, particularly cereals, and the domestication of animals probably began, so far as can be judged from the present evidence, in the Near East in the eighth millennium B.C., in the area between Palestine and the Zagros range. With the recession of the polar ice-cap at the end of the last Ice Age the course of the Atlantic rain-winds moved northwards, and the Near East became increasingly arid. In this area wheat and barley grew wild, and the wild ancestors of dogs, goats, sheep, cattle and pigs were found. Man in this region was now forced, as a condition of survival, to engage in food production; gradually he descended from the highlands, since the increasing scarcity of wild food-plants and the game on which he had preyed no longer permitted him to live by simple food-gathering. Like all later revolutions, this change was doubtless a painful one for those directly concerned: it is perhaps remotely reflected in stories of the loss of the Golden Age to be found in many mythologies, and best known from the Old Testament tale of the expulsion from the Garden of Eden, after which Man, for whom hitherto every creature and the fruit of every tree had been freely available for food, could now only eat bread in the sweat of his brow.

The period covered by this so-called Neolithic Revolution amounted to several thousands of years; for the Near East, where it began, we glean our knowledge of it from a substantial number of sites extending from Palestine to Iran and from Anatolia to South Arabia. From the nature of Man's changed way of life, such sites are typically no longer cave dwellings (although Neolithic Man may well have continued to use caves in some circumstances as some Kurds still do in the same area today) but open sites: from the combination of their favourable position and human conservatism it happened that many such sites were subsequently occupied for many centuries or millennia – well into historical times in some cases, and to the present day in more than one – so that the neolithic remains form the bottom layer of a considerable mound of debris of human occupation. Such a mound, composed of the remains from various periods of occupation in superimposed strata, is commonly called, according to the language current in the locality, a *tell* or *tepe*. Because of the difficulty and expense of opening a major *tell* to the depth and extent necessary to reach and assess the neolithic evidence, the greater part of the information so far available comes from sites which were not occupied in historical times. A notable, though by no means the only, exception, is Jericho (Tell es-Sultan), which would also have the distinction of being one of the earliest known neolithic settlements, if the dating proposed by its excavators, but disputed by some other archaeologists, is accepted. According to its excavators (on the basis, amongst other things, of radiocarbon analysis of two samples) it was settled at about 7500 B.C. and by 6800 B.C. had grown to the size of a town of nearly ten acres with a population estimated at two thousand. The houses were of mud-brick, with floors of beaten mud and roofs perhaps of tree branches plastered with mud. The dead were buried under the floor in a remarkable cult in which the skulls had the features restored in plaster (a practice followed in parts of Melanesia up to modern times, though no direct relationship is suggested) and were then buried separately from the bodies.

With the deliberate cultivation of food-plants and the domestication of animals and (until our own day) unlimited land, came the possibility of a considerable increase in population. Village societies grew up, in which families united in food production and defence; and the consequent relative security of food supply gave leisure which permitted some measure of specialization. Two aspects of this specialization with almost immeasurable consequences for the subsequent activities of Man were the development on the one hand of the arts and on the other of a social group professionally concerned with the religious response of Man to the pattern imposed on his life by the agricultural cycle.

Some evidence for the beginning of the practice of harvesting cereals comes from the Mount Carmel region from cave sites of the very end of the Old Stone Age. Here have been found sickles, consisting of flint teeth set in a bone haft, used by the people known as Natufians. Examination of the edges of the flint blades indicates that they were employed for cutting the stalks of cereal plants. This may, however, only have involved the harvesting of wild wheat and barley native to the area and need not imply deliberate cultivation; certainly the Natufians had none of the usual domestic food-animals, though there is evidence that they did tame dogs.

Unless the very early date claimed for the neolithic settlement at Jericho is finally confirmed, the earliest evidence of the beginning of a definite change from food-gathering economy to food-producing comes from an open site of about two acres at Karim Shahir (east of Kirkuk), which was occupied for a short time only in the region of 7000 to 6000 B.C. Here half the animal bones found were of species, such as the goat, sheep, pig and some kind of horse, which, if not actually already domesticated, were shortly to become so. In addition stone sickle blades, querns and hoes were found, suggesting the practice of certain agricultural operations, though so far no grain has been identified from the site. Stone floorings, hearth-stones and what seems to have been a storage pit were also discovered; architectural details of the type of house to which these belong remain uncertain.

Karim Shahir marks an early stage in transition and can hardly yet be regarded as a neolithic village: indeed, there is nothing to prove that occupation was more than seasonal. A gap remains to be filled in the culture sequence and time lapse between this and the later site of Jarmo (also east of Kirkuk), which has been dated by Carbon-14 analysis to 5000 B.C. or a little later. (Those who accept a date of 7500 B.C. for the neolithic settlement at Jericho would need to date Jarmo at 6000 B.C., the evidence of Carbon-14 analysis notwithstanding.) On this site were found rectilinear houses comprising several rooms. The walls and floors were of *pisé* (compressed clay) with stone foundations, and there were built-in clay ovens with chimneys, and clay basins in the floors. There were figurines in clay (mostly unbaked) of animals as well as of a mother-goddess: the mother-goddess represented by such figurines seems to have been the central figure in neolithic religion, in which fertility and increase were of supreme importance to society. In addition there were found beautifully smooth limestone bowls, ornaments (principally bracelets and beads) and flint tools, a large proportion of the latter being microliths, which are typical of the neolithic period. It is only in the later stages of occupation at Jarmo that pottery is found, and the absence of any trace of the earliest stages of pottery-making is against any supposition that this important development originated here. This negative evidence is not, however, conclusive, for it must be remembered that the earliest stages of pottery would probably consist of a clay lining to a wicker-work basket, and of this traces would hardly be likely to survive.

By the Jarmo period almost all the animal bones found – over 90 per cent of them – are of domestic or domesticable species, such as the domestic goat (distinguishable by the shape of its horns from the wild mountain-goat), the sheep, the pig, the horse, and cattle: it has been suggested that since agriculture had already begun the ox may already have been used for drawing the plough at Jarmo, but against this is the fact that on certain of the earliest cylinder seals, from nearly two millennia later, it is humans who are depicted as dragging the primitive plough. At least two kinds of wheat (represented by carbonized grains of Einkorn and of an ancestor of emmer) were in use at Jarmo, as well as some kind of field pea: the use of cereals can also be established by the presence of querns, mortars and winnowing trays. Barley, so important afterwards in Mesopotamia, does not appear to have been found at Jarmo, and it may only have come into cultivation later as a dominant weed in wheat fields, as oats and rye at much later periods certainly did. The cereals used at Jarmo would be parched in the ovens, then ground and eaten as a gruel or made into a dough which was cooked into unleavened biscuits. Beer would have arisen from the fermentation of stale gruel.

That the remains of Jarmo are those of a permanent village is beyond doubt, since there is a sequence of eight floor levels, indicating habitation through at least eight generations. Another neolithic site in Iraq, Mulaffa'at between Mosul and Erbil, is more primitive than Jarmo in the remains of its material culture and perhaps a little earlier, but nevertheless represents a fully established village site. Gird Ali Agha, north of Erbil, is later than Jarmo but still shows no clear links with the first of the well-defined cultural stages, that of *Hassuna*.*

Between the stage of human development represented by Jarmo and the relatively advanced civilization now datable to around the beginning of the third millennium B.C. one finds substantial technological progress in several spheres of activity. Some archaeologists, taking the view that the extensive developments involved cannot be compressed within a maximum of two thousand years, argue that if the Carbon-14 dating of the Jarmo settlement is beyond question, the settlement itself must have been a backwater out of the main stream of development, and represented a cultural stage which elsewhere had already been superseded a millennium before. Against such a view, however, is the presence of obsidian at Jarmo: the nearest source of this stone is Anatolia, several hundred miles away, so that Jarmo must have had some kind of trading relations with the outer world, and thus can hardly be supposed to have remained in cultural isolation in other respects. One is thus driven to the conclusion that cultural development after this period was far more rapid than has hitherto been supposed.

Leaving Jarmo apart, the earliest type of settlement in the main stream of cultural development in prehistoric Iraq is that known as *Hassuna*, named from a site west of the Tigris not far south

* Where a place-name is printed in italics, it is being used not of the particular site but of the culture (or 'assemblage') named after that site and in most cases represented at a number of other sites also.

of Mosul. In addition to the site which gave the culture its name, settlements forming part of the same early stage have been found at Matarrah (south of Kirkuk), Nineveh, Arpachiyah and elsewhere.

A number of phases can be distinguished in the *Hassuna* culture. The first settlement at Hassuna itself had clearly developed beyond the earliest stages of food production, as one sees from the presence of querns, stone tools which were probably hoes, and pottery, including storage jars for corn. It was still, however, typically neolithic in the sense that, except for importing obsidian, it remained a closed and self-supporting economic unit. Moreover, it was not only neolithic but early neolithic, since the presence of sling-bullets of clay indicates that hunting still played a substantial part in the provision of the food supply. The tools suggest that the form of agriculture practised was that known as hoe-culture, and as this generally exhausts the soil fairly rapidly, requiring the primitive communities practising it to take up a new site from time to time, it is likely that the early neolithic *Hassuna* communities were still nomadic to some extent.

After this first phase of neolithic occupation at the *Hassuna* sites a long period of continuous occupation succeeded, suggesting that more efficient agricultural methods, in particular fallowing, were in use, whereby the rapid destruction of the soil's fertility was prevented. Subsequent developments included the origin of the typical oriental house: this consists of a number of rooms grouped round a central courtyard, and houses of this plan are still found in Iraq. In the *Hassuna* period socketed stones were provided on which doors could pivot. Clay ovens for baking bread are found, and for the harvesting of corn crops there were sickles consisting of flint flakes bedded on to a wooden base by means of bitumen. Metal was not yet in use.

Decorated pottery, which is important not only aesthetically but also because it provides a convenient tracer for the culture with which it is associated, had its origins in the *Hassuna* period. Pottery similar to *Hassuna* archaic painted ware has been found as far afield as the Amuq in Syria and Mersin on the coast of Cilicia, and this suggests that the *Hassuna* settlements from their beginning were part of an extensive cultural group: a connection with Iran has also been mooted. Trade certainly developed during this period and in addition to obsidian other semi-precious stones, such as turquoise and malachite, used for making beads and amulets, came to be imported, no doubt alongside more perishable goods of a kind unlikely to reveal their former presence to the archaeologist.

The religious ideas of the *Hassuna* period are reflected in the existence of clay figurines of the mother-goddess, as well as infant burials in jars, possibly foundation sacrifices for buildings. The presence of vessels associated with burials and possibly containing food and water, hints at a vague belief in some kind of survival after death.

Contemporary with the latter part of the *Hassuna* culture was a distinctive pottery bearing geometrical designs and stylized animals. This is known as *Samarra* pottery, from the famous site on the middle Tigris at which it was first discovered in 1911. It has since been recognized at a few other sites on the middle Euphrates and in the north, including Nineveh (level 2b). There is still much doubt as to its exact chronological position in the cultural sequence, whilst there is a difference of opinion amongst archaeologists as to what is to be included in the category 'Samarra pottery'. It has not been related to distinctive features in other spheres of activity, such as architecture, metallurgy or with any great confidence) burial rites, and R. J. Braidwood remarks that *Samarra* ware represents neither a 'culture' (a word he dislikes in such contexts) nor even (applying the word he favours) an 'assemblage'; for Braidwood (whose evaluation of the evidence carries weight), *Samarra* ware is little more than a mere style of painted pottery. With these reservations, it may be mentioned that there are archaeologists who would see some relationship between the culture associated with *Samarra* pottery and contemporary Iranian civilization. In the first place, there is much in common between the designs of the *Samarra* pottery and those of the pottery from certain Iranian sites. Also, though the evidence from burial rites is scanty, for what it is worth it does seem to support the theory of a connection between Iran and the people associated with the *Samarra* pottery. The latter appear to have buried their dead in the extended dorsal position (in plain English, flat on their backs), and this was the burial position practised by the people of the *Ubaid* culture (see below), who are generally accepted as being of Iranian origin. Against the latter point, however, it may be mentioned that there is compelling evidence (see below, page 18) specifically dissociating the *Samarra* and *Ubaid* cultures. No structure of the *Samarra* period (of which the builders employed large unbaked bricks) has yet been excavated in such a way as to enable a comparison of the architecture to be made with that of buildings from other prehistoric cultures. As to the religion of the *Samarra* people, all we can say is that, as with all these prehistoric cultures, such scanty evidence as we have indicates that the religion was largely concerned with fertility cults associated with the mother-goddess, and heavily permeated with magic.

A new and beautiful pottery, of a buff colour with decorations in red, white and black, marks the advent of the *Halaf* culture, named after the site of Tell Halaf on the Habur at which it was first found. It seems clear that the people who made this fine pottery also brought certain other advances in technology. A wider range of cereals and domesticated animals was utilized, whilst the presence of spindle whorls proves the existence of a textile industry. Whilst stone remained the normal material for tools, there now occur beads, pins and even a few implements made of copper. The technical perfection of the pottery makes it certain that proper kilns existed, in which very high temperatures could be achieved, and, indeed, remains of such kilns have actually been found at Arpachiyah and Carchemish. It is possible, in view of the technical skill required in the manipulation of such kilns, that the potter was already a specialized full-time craftsman.

It is probably from the *Halaf* period that the invention of wheeled vehicles dates. This is indicated by the fact that what appears to be a chariot is painted on a *Halaf* vase.

As to religion, there was certainly some kind of belief in an Afterlife, for with the dead were buried pots, ornaments and implements, which must have been intended for the use of the deceased in the Afterworld. Clay figurines of 'mother-goddess' type bear witness to the practice of fertility cults.

There is ample evidence for trade between communities at this period. A community, said to belong to the *Halaf* culture, was engaged in quarrying obsidian at a site near Lake Van, and obsidian was widely used in all *Halaf* villages. Moreover, at the *Halaf* settlement at Chagar Bazar on the Habur (in north-west Mesopotamia) there was found the shell of a shell-fish which can only have originated in the Persian Gulf.

In the *Halaf* villages – which might now perhaps be more properly called small towns – cobbled streets are found. Little is known about developments in domestic architecture: there are some very striking buildings – circular structures with a domed roof and a long rectangular chamber attached, and now generally referred to as *tholoi* – but whatever their function may have been they were hardly private houses. These *tholoi* are of particular architectural interest in that the domed roof shows that the *Halaf* people had mastered the principle of the vault. With an exception at *Tepe Gawra*, where they continued into the *Ubaid* period, buildings of this type are never again found after the *Halaf* period, and in view of the intense conservatism of human beings in all matters concerned with religion, this could be taken to indicate that these structures had a secular rather than a religious purpose. It is equally possible, however, that they did have a religious function and that their total disappearance is to be explained on the assumption that they were associated with a cult which the succeeding *Ubaid* people deliberately eradicated. That the *Ubaid* people differed strongly from their predecessors in matters of religion is shown by the fact that they eliminated from their art all traces of representations of humans or animals, although such representations are commonly found in the cultures which preceded them.

The *Halaf* culture probably arose in Assyria, where its development can be traced through a number of stages. At its fullest extent it reached to the coasts of Syria and Cilicia, into Armenia and southwards as far as Samarra, but the fact that it appears fully formed and sometimes mixed with features from other cultures shows that none of these can have been the place of origin. A negative piece of evidence as to the ultimate place of origin of the *Halaf* people is provided by the fact that no trace of the culture is found in Iran, but other than this the problem provides a fertile field for guessing. The *Halaf* people were probably not invaders dispossessing an earlier cultural group; the distribution of their culture as at present known is very similar to that of *Hassuna*, and this indicates that the general pattern of relationship between settlements across the area was not seriously disturbed by their arrival.

It is at about this period that occupation of southern Iraq began, and evidence is available from the prehistoric period of a number of distinct strata of population, distinguishable by such physical remains as their pottery, manner of burial and types of building. When we come into the light of history shortly after the beginning of the third millennium, it is possible to recognize at least three ethnic and cultural elements in Babylonia. First in importance from the point of view of later developments were the Sumerians, to whom the origin of the Mesopotamian civilization is generally attributed. Also there were already Semites, whose ethnic and cultural influence continually increased in consequence of peaceful trickles or violent irruptions of their congeners from the west. In addition to these there must have been a third element, since the names of many of the Sumerian cities belong to a language which is neither Sumerian nor Semitic, whilst there are a substantial number of common words in the Sumerian language which are neither Sumerian nor Semitic in origin. It is therefore a challenge to attempt to identify these different groups with the various prehistoric groups which can be traced by pottery in south Iraq from the fourth millennium. At present no generally accepted conclusions on this matter have been reached.

Up to very recent times it has been held that all of southern Iraq, from well north of Baghdad, has been built up since palaeolithic times by the annual silt deposits of the Tigris and Euphrates: the most southerly part, from Ur and Eridu south-eastwards, was believed to have become habitable only by neolithic times. This view has now been attacked by geologists, who argue that the whole Tigris-Euphrates basin is sinking at approximately the same rate as the deposit of silt, and that during the Pleistocene period, far from the Persian Gulf having receded, it has in fact extended north-westwards, covering what was formerly land. However that may be, the occupation of southern Iraq was relatively late compared with other parts of the Near East, and there is no trace of palaeolithic or (except in so far as the settlements about to be mentioned may be so described) neolithic occupation: a single palaeolithic scraper found in an ancient lake-bed near Kerbela had almost certainly been washed down in ancient times by the Euphrates. Palaeolithic Man preferred mountain regions where natural caves gave shelter in the neighbourhood of the pasturelands where he might find beasts of the chase, whilst Neolithic Man did not go farther into the marshy plains than where rainfall was adequate for agriculture. Whether or not it was overpopulation of the lands to the north which ultimately compelled the colonization of Babylonia by forcing some of the northern farmers to go farther afield is still in dispute. Some authorities consider it more probable that the original immigration came from Iran, where climatic conditions up to the fourth millennium B.C. approached those of south Mesopotamia far more closely than they do today: Iran was not yet an arid salt desert, and rivers without an outlet must have provided swamp conditions not wildly dissimilar from those existing then (and now) in southern Iraq.

The earliest settlement in south Babylonia, at the site called Eridu by the Sumerians a thousand years later, corresponds in time to the *Halaf* and *Samarra* era farther north. The excavators of Eridu distinguished nineteen strata of ancient occupation, and found that the oldest stratum (XIX) was on virgin soil. On the basis of pottery and architecture they treated strata XIX–XV as representing a single cultural phase, which they designated *Eridu*.

The place of origin of the first *Eridu* settlers remains open to discussion. If, as some think, they were in fact proto-Sumerians, Sumerian tradition could be taken to suggest that they came from the south-east. There is (at least at present) no archaeological evidence to support such a view, though it is claimed that remains of ancient cultivation are visible to aerial photography beneath the northern end of the Persian Gulf, and this might be the missing link. Some authorities, as mentioned above, connect the *Eridu* folk with the highlands of Elam, whilst others treat them, on the basis of affinities which their pottery shows with *Halaf* and *Samarra* ware, as a southward migration of peasants of the *Halaf* and *Samarra* cultures. Professor Gordon Childe considered that the *Eridu* culture was simply the earliest form of the succeeding *Ubaid* civilization, and it has been argued in detail that pottery, building methods and religious customs show such continuity from the *Eridu* to the *Ubaid* period that there is no need to postulate any cultural break between the two.

The *Eridu* settlers must from the beginning have formed a farming community, although fishing may also have been prominent in their economy. From the very first, climatic conditions must have forced these incomers to engage in drainage operations, canal-making and work on irrigation; this had wide-spreading social consequences, since it necessitated the co-operation of men in much larger units than the typical neolithic village, and so prepared the way for the characteristic city-state of the third millennium.

A small shrine of unbaked brick was erected by the earliest settlers at Eridu itself, and the spot must have acquired special sanctity, for a series of at least twelve further temples were subsequently built or rebuilt in prehistoric times on precisely the same site; temples were also built on the same site within the historic period.

There is another prehistoric culture (or, as some would prefer to say, 'assemblage') in south Iraq, which has been variously interpreted. This one is designated *Hajji Muhammad*, from the site near Warka at which its distinctive pottery was first noticed. It has now been recognized at a number of southern sites, and it may be an early stage of the notable *Ubaid* culture which succeeded it.

The *Ubaid* culture marks a new and most important phase in the proto-history of Mesopotamia. Although ultimately achieving a considerable extension to the north, as far as the upper Tigris and Habur, where it supplanted the *Halaf* culture, it appears to have reached its highest development in southern Babylonia. This culture was a highly efficient peasant economy based on irrigation. The commonest raw material – namely, clay – was regularly used for such things as sickle blades, nails and bricks, but stone remained in use for tools and certain vessels: one assumes, in view of human conservatism in matters connected with religion, that the vessels in question were those employed in the cult. Was metal used? Contrary views have been expressed, but despite a suggestion that axes of baked clay were models of real implements made of copper, of which all traces have vanished in the wet soil, so many of them have been found that it seems almost certain that the clay tools were not models but the real thing. Either the people of the *Ubaid* culture were unacquainted with metal in their place of origin (generally taken to have been Iran), or they were unable to organize the necessary trade to obtain it from their old sources after migrating to their new home. However, baked clay tools may have appeared quite satisfactory for the purposes of the *Ubaid* people, for the fine clay of Babylonia will vitrify relatively easily and then forms a product of such hardness that it is difficult to smash it even with a hammer.

The length of time during which the *Ubaid* culture endured is indicated by the existence of six or seven successive temples of the *Ubaid* period in the town of Eridu, but to convert this into an absolute period of time involves disputable assumptions. Mudbrick buildings quickly crack and crumble, and Professor Gordon Childe's assumption of an average of a century for the life of each temple is probably excessive, as even for the first millennium B.C. we find mention of temples collapsing within forty years. Thus the figure of six hundred years that Gordon Childe arrives at for the time span of the *Ubaid* culture might well need to be halved.

In the town of Eridu the temple, still on the site originally chosen for their shrine by the first *Eridu* settlers, was by *Ubaid* times a buttressed building on a platform. The plan, a long central nave with rooms leading off each side, conformed to the general plan of the later Sumerian temples. To judge by the remains of fish bones in the sanctuary of Eridu, offerings of fish were made to the god; that fish should be offered to the god is an indication of the importance of fishing in the economy either at that time or possibly (in view of human conservatism in religious matters) at a rather earlier period. The fish offerings would also suggest that the god of Eridu was a water-god in the *Ubaid* period, as he certainly was in historical times. This is a hint that some aspects of the later Sumerian culture already existed; indeed, the general development of temples in *Ubaid* times indicates that the form of society characteristic of later Sumer, in which the god was the owner of the land and his temple the focus of the community, had already come into existence.

The spread of *Ubaid* culture northwards was, once it began, rapid and extensive, since in most places *Halaf* art was cut off in full bloom, certain characteristic religious symbols in the art disappearing suddenly without any period of decadence. None the less, the *Halaf* people were not completely eliminated, for at the site of Tepe Gawra (near Mosul), one of the places in which a northward extension of the *Ubaid* culture is attested, there were found the *tholoi* buildings characteristic of the *Halaf* people. Also, despite the general absence from *Ubaid* art of any representations of humans or animals, there were animal and human figures in the pottery decoration of Tepe Gawra at the end of the *Ubaid* period.

Except for the instance just mentioned, all trace of human or animal figures in the pottery decoration of the *Ubaid* period was absent during the whole of its extent in time and space: this suggests some kind of taboo on representations of human or animal likeness similar to that so strongly held amongst the ancient Hebrews and later Moslems. The *Halaf* and *Ubaid* peoples were also very much at variance in their use of amulets and figurines: mother-goddess figurines, so common at *Halaf* and *Samarra* sites, are totally lacking in *Ubaid* levels at Eridu, though attested at some other *Ubaid* sites.

Such facts, indicating a striking difference in religious conceptions, are very strongly against any suggestion that the original *Ubaid* people were migrants from the *Halaf-Samarra* culture.

Although the *Ubaid* expansion represented the first unified civilization of the whole of Mesopotamia and surrounding lands, with cultural relationships which can be traced from the Indus valley to Egypt with other communities of a basically similar type, it remained essentially a peasant society living in villages built of unbaked brick: stone was very rare and used only for doorways, pavings and fireplaces. Drains lined and covered with stone were also in use.

The religious conceptions of the *Ubaid* people are attested by their graves, of which the furnishings reflect some belief in an Afterlife, and by figurines. The figurines (all of females) are of two types, one human-headed and the other grotesque: the latter type perhaps points to a belief in demons.

The *Ubaid* civilization was the one stage of prehistoric development which can properly be regarded as a unitary culture over the whole of Mesopotamia: the phases succeeding it show some marked differences between the developments of north and south. Some scholars would regard the culture of the *Ubaid* people as representing the earliest evidence of the Sumerians of the next millennium; a difficulty in accepting this is that the Sumerians as we know them never occupied an area anything like that covered by the *Ubaid* culture.

In southern Iraq, the later Sumer, the next cultural stage introduced a revolutionary change, the creation of cities, and to describe this it is necessary to run ahead of developments in the north. The aggregation of communities in the south into cities was almost certainly dictated by the rivers: to control and utilize them effectively needed co-operation on a larger scale than small isolated primitive villages could provide. A similar development occurred in the two other ancient river-valley civilizations – those of the Nile and of the Indus – but present archeological indications are that it took place earliest in Mesopotamia and that some of the consequent aspects of material progress spread from there eastwards and westwards. The phase in question, known as *Uruk*, was first recognized at Warka (of which the ancient name was Uruk, the Erech of *Genesis* x. 10) and Tello (ancient Lagash), and has since been found represented at Eridu, Ur and Tell Uqair (about forty miles south of Baghdad). Warka, the site from which this phase is best known, is particularly important as an excavation site for two very different reasons. In the first place, it has great significance from the fact that it appears to have been the very centre of early Sumerian civilization. Secondly, the excavations there have been the outstanding example in Iraq (where some of the alleged archaeology has been little more than museum-assisted treasure-hunting) of scientific archaeology, for which great credit is due to successive German scholars, in particular Dr. H. Lenzen.

In archaeological excavations the strata are generally (though not invariably) numbered from the top downwards, so that the lowest number denotes the latest period and the highest the earliest. At Warka the earliest phases (strata XVIII to XV) represent *Ubaid* (more precisely *Ubaid* I) occupation: by the end of this period the use of baked bricks for building was known, though not yet extensively employed. The pottery of strata XIV to IV (some archaeologists would draw the line at V or VI) forms a homogeneous group, such that these strata are taken as a whole to represent a distinct period in Mesopotamian protohistory, and called *Uruk*. The *Uruk* period does not appear to mark the imposition of a totally new stratum of population upon that of *Ubaid*, since, for instance, the early *Uruk* temples at Eridu continued the architectural tradition of the preceding *Ubaid* period; moreover, the evidence from Warka itself shows that there was some overlap, pottery typical of the *Ubaid* period appearing in strata XII–VII, though no longer as the principal type. This later *Ubaid* pottery is referred to as *Ubaid* II.

As the evidence of Eridu shows, the earliest temples of the *Uruk* period carried on the building traditions of the preceding *Ubaid*, employing as their material sun-dried brick. Gradually, however, the *Uruk* temples developed in size and magnificence; by the end of the *Uruk* period they had become striking features of the Mesopotamia landscape, visible to great distances across the flat Sumerian plain and proclaiming afar the wealth and splendour of the city god. Colour added to the impressive effect: by stratum VI the walls and columns of temples were decorated with clay nails, their heads painted red, white or black, arranged in mosaic patterns (see plate 2A).

A temple of level V shows an important innovation. It was built with a foundation of blocks of limestone on a bed of *pisé* (rammed clay), and this has been taken as indicating the arrival of a mountain race familiar with techniques of stone-working. There is other evidence suggesting foreign infiltration, for the *Uruk* period (not only level V) undoubtedly brought a considerable number of innovations, including new pottery shapes, the potter's wheel, and the introduction of the bow. Though the use of metals was already known to the people of the *Halaf* culture and the northern extension (though not the original southern settlements) of *Ubaid*, it was not until the *Uruk* period that metal came into general use, copper implements being found from stratum XI onwards. If these changes are based on foreign infiltration the evidence points to at least two new elements, the main one giving the colour to the *Uruk* period as a whole, and a subsidiary mountain race whose arrival is marked by the limestone temple of stratum V and the invention of writing in stratum IVa (or IVb – differing views on this are held by different scholars). It has been suggested, on the basis chiefly of the relationship of the new *Uruk* pottery to certain types found in Palestine and Syria, that the main new racial element was Semitic, but this conclusion – though not necessarily wrong – goes beyond the present evidence. The mountain race could be the people later known as Sumerians, but this again is not finally proved.

The period represented by the stratum *Uruk* IV (sub-divided by archaeologists into IVc, IVb and IVa in order of age) is of particular interest because in it (more precisely in *Uruk* IVb or IVa) we meet the most striking of the inventions due to the *Uruk* people – writing. The invention of writing represents a real advance in civilization, whereas change in pottery type, commonly used as the basis of nomenclature for the prehistoric and protoliterate cultures, need not. For this reason the term *Proto-literate* is now frequently employed to designate the whole period into which the invention of writing falls: it is used in this work when it gives rise to no ambiguity. Its undoubted convenience is impaired by the fact that different scholars give the term different meanings, all equating its end with the stratum *Uruk* III (otherwise referred to, with *Uruk* II, as *Jemdet Nasr*), but variously placing its beginning anywhere between *Uruk* VIII and V.

There are those who argue that the *Uruk* writing as we first meet it in the stratum IVa (or IVb) has antecedents still unknown to us: this is a possibility but no conclusive evidence has yet been adduced in support of such a theory, and it will not be considered further. The origin of writing was lowly. It arose not as the servant of religion (except indirectly), not as the vehicle for transmission of history or literature or noble thoughts, but simply in connection with the prosaic task of keeping the temple accounts. Outline pictures of the objects concerned, together with marks for numerals, were scratched with a reed on the most readily available Mesopotamian raw material – a handful of wet clay. Numerous examples have been found from stratum IVa at Uruk. The identity of the objects depicted is in many cases quite obvious. It is the fact that in some cases the objects drawn are already simplified and stylized which is the chief reason for supposing that writing when we first meet it at this period had already come some way from the original pictorial stage. Furthermore, a surprising number of the pictographs represent objects, such as wild beasts, which it can rarely have been necessary to refer to in temple inventories, and this indicates that already some of the signs represented other meanings than the concrete objects they originally depicted. Examples of a few of the pictographs of the earliest writing are shown opposite.

Clay ever afterwards in the Mesopotamian culture remained the most common writing material, whilst associated with the deity concerned with the scribal art was the reed, the plant generally used for the stylus. Since clay when dried, and especially when baked, is virtually indestructible, the soil of Iraq contains vast numbers of these inscribed lumps of clay spanning the whole period from just before 3000 B.C. to the final extinction of this means of writing, at about the time of Christ. The shape and size of such pieces of inscribed clay (known as 'cuneiform tablets', although for the earliest form of writing the term 'cuneiform' is

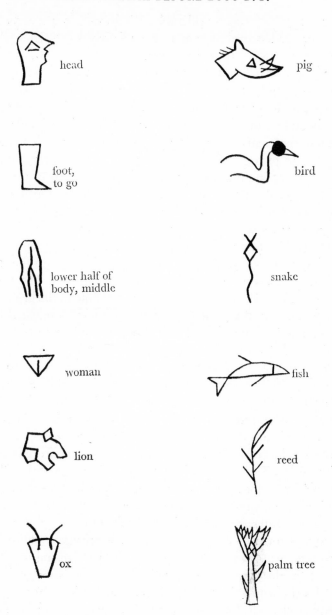

head

pig

foot,
to go

bird

lower half of
body, middle

snake

woman

fish

lion

reed

ox

palm tree

The earliest pictographs

23

not appropriate) vary considerably. Whilst some of the early ones are more or less oval or round, like a flattened bun, later tablets are almost always roughly rectangular. The dimensions range from about match-box size to the size of a blotting pad, though most commonly the tablet is small enough to be held in the hand.

Because the earliest form of writing was wholly pictographic, and because a written language cannot be analysed unless the writing represents morphological or grammatical elements in addition to pictographs, it is impossible to know with certainty what type of language was spoken by the inventors of the *Uruk* writing. At the time when the writing had developed to the stage at which grammatical elements are recognizable, the language being written was certainly Sumerian.

The architecture of the late *Uruk* period also shows interesting developments which give rise to many problems, and the stone temple of stratum V at Uruk has been mentioned. The period *Uruk* VI–IV marks a very significant development, the beginning of the ziggurat, the great stepped tower which dominated later Mesopotamian cities, and of which one example has lived on in Jewish and Christian tradition as the 'tower of Babel'. The earliest example at Uruk consists of a high terrace about an acre in extent, built of *pisé* and unbaked bricks, with its corners orientated north, east, south and west, and rising forty feet above the plain. Access to the top was gained by a stairway or a ramp. On top of part of the terrace stood a temple, covered with whitened plaster, and from this circumstance commonly referred to as 'the White Temple' (see plate 1). The basic design of the White Temple was a long rectangular chamber running north-west to south-east, with rooms opening off on the two long sides. The monotony of the exterior walls was broken by a series of vertical recesses, a form of ornamentation which became traditional in Mesopotamian temples. A temple of a similar plan and on a high terrace (in this case in two stages) occurs at the same period at Tell Uqair, whilst the famous ziggurat of Ur (see plate 3A) also appears to have had its origin in the *Uruk* period. Valuable assistance in deducing the actual appearance of such buildings is provided not only by the remains of the foundations but also by fragments of stone models of buildings found at Warka.

There are a number of other temples at Warka from the *Uruk* IV and III–II (*Jemdet Nasr*) periods, but little is known of the actual form of worship at this time. One of the more imposing temples was a building of cruciform internal plan with three separate *cellae* at the head of the cross, which may indicate the worship of some form of trinity of deities: here neither altar, offering table nor podium has been found. Dr. H. Lenzen has pointed out that during the late *Uruk* period temples existed in pairs, which strongly suggests the worship of a divine couple. Throughout the whole of the historical period the effective supreme deity at Uruk was Innin, whose name also occurs (possibly from false etymology) as Inanna, which in Sumerian means 'Lady of Heaven': whether the name in either form was used in the *Uruk* period is problematic. In the historical period this goddess was in some cases associated with her father An or Anu, but most commonly with Dumuzi (Tammuz of *Ezekiel* viii. 14; see below, pages 377 ff.), a chthonic deity prominent as a god of vegetation from archaic times. Though the actual name Dumuzi certainly does not occur until well into the third millennium, a fertility god with his characteristics was the focal point of a cult from much earlier times. It is thus at least a strong possibility that the divine pair worshipped at Warka in the late *Uruk* period comprised the two fertility deities who later became known as Dumuzi and Innin.

However, though something can be learnt about contemporary religion in the *Uruk* period from temple architecture, as well as from burial customs, these are no longer – from towards the end of this period – the only significant evidence. We can also learn something from another invention due to the *Uruk* people, namely, the cylinder seal. This invention, of wide application in later Mesopotamian civilization, ante-dated the invention of writing; in precise archaeological terms its origin was in the *Uruk* V period. The stamp seal, known since the *Halaf* period, now began to be replaced by the new invention. The cylinder seal, in the form of a small cylinder of semi-precious stone usually not bigger than a man's thumb, was engraved with a design which by rolling could be transferred to wet clay; for examples from later periods see plates 27A and 50A, B. The original purpose was to protect property. A treasured object would be placed in a vessel which would be covered with a cloth or skin tied on by a cord. A layer of clay would be spread over the cord and the seal design then rolled across it. By this means the magical efficacy of the religious, cultic or mythological scene on the seal was thought to be placed over the vessel; it obviously also made it impossible to tamper with the vessel without the owner's knowledge, but this was probably a secondary consideration. The invention of the cylinder seal apparently took place at Warka itself, since at no other site of the *Uruk* culture are such seals found before the *Jemdet Nasr* period.

Although the scenes on the cylinder seals of the *Uruk* V and IV phases give evidence concerning contemporary religion, it is far from easy to decide what these scenes actually mean. Animals are frequently represented, and in some cases certainly involve religious symbolism; thus, for instance, there is one seal in which two moufflon rams, intertwined serpents and an eagle with outspread wings all occur together in an heraldic composition, and this could not possible depict an actual scene. Perhaps the commonest scene is that of foliage with two animals placed antithetically, one on either side. This scene is generally considered to symbolize the fertilizing activity of the god Dumuzi, to whom the other symbols mentioned are also related. The symbol of the mother-goddess also occurs. On other seals of the period there are representations of ritual scenes, involving either offerings of fruit, vegetables or meat to the gods, or activities in connection with the flocks and herds sacred to the gods.

The *Jemdet Nasr* period, as the stage corresponding to strata III and II at Warka is still often called, immediately followed the phase of the *Uruk* period in which writing is first found, and most scholars consider the later phase a direct extension of the earlier. It was an age of expansion. Inside south Mesopotamia (Babylonia) the growth from village to city had been occurring in the southernmost part (Sumer) from the *Ubaid* period onwards, and is well attested from Eridu, Ur and Erech. During the *Uruk* period this development was very marked in Sumer. However, up to the time of *Uruk* IV the northern boundary of this development seems to have been Uruk (Erech) itself: in the central and northern part of Babylonia communities (with isolated exceptions) continued to live in small villages. In the *Jemdet Nasr* period this situation changed, perhaps as a result of some improvement in irrigation techniques, and cities began to develop in central and northern Babylonia as well, Nippur, Kish and Eshnunna (on the Diyala) being outstanding examples. A temple of the *Jemdet Nasr* type has even been found as far north as Tell Brak on the Habur, though since other contemporary sites in northern Mesopotamia show no trace of *Jemdet Nasr* pottery the remains at Tell Brak probably derive from a colony transplanted from the south rather than from cultural expansion in the more general sense.

Abundant evidence of Mesopotamian cultural influence is found at this time in Egypt. Significant is the fact that cylinder seals (a specifically Mesopotamian invention) occur there, together with methods of building in brick foreign to Egypt but typical of the *Jemdet Nasr* culture. In Egypt also at this time Mesopotamian motifs and objects are represented in art, a striking example being a boat of Mesopotamian type found carved on a knife handle (see plate 64 and compare the boats of plates 2B and 33B). There are some peculiar Egyptian pots which may show Mesopotamian influence, whilst the principle of writing (though not the technique) was certainly taken over by the Egyptians from Mesopotamia. The obvious point at which the Sumerians (assuming this to be what the people of the *Jemdet Nasr* culture were) and Egyptians might have met at this time is Syria, but there are archaeological objections to such an explanation, the main one being that Syria at this time does not show either the Egyptian or Mesopotamian influence which on such a theory one would expect to find. It seems more likely that it was on the coast of either South Arabia or Somaliland that Egyptian and Mesopotamian traders met at this time, probably in quest of incense for the cult.

Cultural expansion in the *Jemdet Nasr* period also affected the regions east and north of Mesopotamia. Inscribed tablets showing Mesopotamian influence occur at this time at Susa and Sialk in

Iran, whilst cylinder seals have been found as far afield as Troy, and at a site (Tepe Hissar) near the south-eastern corner of the Caspian Sea.

In southern Mesopotamia itself cylinder seals, now becoming more abundant, present fuller pictorial information about the cult than is available for the preceding phase, though precisely how the information is to be interpreted is much in dispute. The chief point at issue is the extent to which Dumuzi, or rather an earlier prototype of this fertility and pastoral god, is to be seen as the principal figure. The goddess Innin, the female fertility deity and specifically the city-goddess of Uruk, is now certainly repre-sented on the seals, not anthropomorphically (as possibly in the mother-goddess figurines of earlier periods) but by means of symbols known from the historical period to have been associated with her.

In addition to the abundant cylinder seals of the *Jemdet Nasr* period there exist a number of larger objects bearing scenes represented in relief, which provide us with some further insight into the religion of this ancient time. An object of great impor-tance in this connection is an alabaster vase more than three feet tall from Warka, with scenes carved in relief in four registers which diminish in size from top to bottom (see plate 8A). The two lowest bands depict ears of barley, date palms, sheep and rams – that is, the plants and animals upon which civilized man depended and through which the fertilizing deities showed their favour. The next band shows men, naked as befitted a worship-per before a deity, bringing offerings to the gods. The highest and broadest band of relief shows the goddess, or a priestess representing the goddess, standing, clad in a robe and a peculiar headdress, before the symbols which are known in later times to have represented the fertility goddess Innin. The goddess, or her representative (if that is how the figure is to be taken), is receiving a basket of fruit: behind her are other gifts. The whole series of bands has been interpreted as relating to the Sacred Marriage at the New Year Feast (see below, pages 382 f.), upon which the fertility of the land depended. Whilst such a specific explanation of the scenes may be questioned, there can be no doubt that the whole was concerned with fertility cults. The same is true of the kind of scene carved in relief on a stone trough of the *Jemdet Nasr* period (see plate 9A): here the hut is obviously a cult hut sacred to Innin or her prototype, for the objects projecting on each side of the hut and the one to the extreme right of the relief are the symbols of the fertility goddess. The whole scene was probably connected with a cult intended to give fecundity to the flock.

As to material culture, we are not very well informed, for because most of the excavation bearing on this period has been in temple areas, not many tools or articles of household use have come to light. The range of metals in use was becoming more extensive and now included gold, silver, lead and copper. A fragment of an iron tool was also said to have been recovered, but no more information than that was forthcoming about it. Weapons in use now included the bow, the mace and the spear: a copper spearhead was found from this period at Ur, and a copper dagger blade at Fara.

Amongst other metal objects found from this period were what A. L. Perkins (*The Comparative Archeology of Early Mesopotamia*, (Chicago, 1949), page 148) describes as 'two little copper spoons with long handles (probably for cosmetics), the handle of one being twisted in cable fashion, and a heavy two-pronged copper instrument fixed to a wooden handle.' Fish-hooks, nails, chisels and various unidentified tools, all made of copper, were also found. Copper was also employed for vessels, mostly shallow bowls.

Woven cloth was used by this period, for traces of it have been found on an animal amulet of copper.

This brief account of the *Uruk* and *Jemdet Nasr* periods (otherwise known collectively as *Protoliterate* or *Predynastic*) applies only to developments originating in the south of the land, in what was later Sumer and part of Akkad. It is clear that the north had no original part in these striking advances, which only reached there either by colonization (as apparently at Tell Brak, the sole northern site which shows close relationship with the south in this period) or more slowly by cultural diffusion. Writing does not appear during this period at any site north of the Diyala, whilst the pottery type known as *Jemdet Nasr* is also lacking. It seems odd that the *Jemdet Nasr* expansion, whilst affecting Egypt and Iran, scarcely touched northern Mesopotamia. The explanation may be that there was a flourishing (though less advanced) rival culture in the north, for there occurs at this time a characteristic pottery widespread in the north but (with two possible exceptions) not found at all in the south. Furthermore, it would appear that the form of religion in the north differed from that in the south, for at northern sites the presence of a number of sanctuaries points to the existence of a pantheon rather than, as is supposed for Uruk, a divine couple.

A significant fact is that one of the temples (the 'Western Temple' of level VIIIc) at Tepe Gawra, one of the principal northern sites, was subsequently used for secular purposes as a storehouse. This seems to be a unique event in the history of Mesopotamian religion, and may indicate that the possession of Tepe Gawra changed hands from one group of population to another which, though it had much the same material culture, had a different religious tradition and so subsequently perpetrated the deliberate desecration of a building associated with a despised cult.

Following the *Protoliterate* comes a period known as *Early Dynastic*, divided into sub-phases I, II and III (I in this numeration being the oldest). This term is used to denote the time in which city-states flourished throughout Babylonia. It begins with the end of the *Jemdet Nasr* period, when writing becomes intelligible to us, and covers a span, variously estimated at between three and six centuries (in this book taken as four, *circa* 2800–2400 B.C.), ending with the rise of the first empire, that of Sargon of Agade. In the *Early Dynastic* period a people called the Sumerians come into prominence, and it was to them that the city-state organization was due. As to the origin of these people there is a great division of opinion between scholars as to which of the cultures preceding the *Early Dynastic* represents their first appearance. The *Early Dynastic* period represents a flowering of the *Uruk* and *Jemdet Nasr* cultures, and as it is already possible to see in the *Jemdet Nasr* period some of the main economic and religious features of later Sumerian civilization, few scholars would seriously question that the *Jemdet Nasr* culture was predominantly Sumerian. Between the *Jemdet Nasr* and *Uruk* cultures there is such a strong line of continuity that the latter also is generally (with a few dissenters) regarded as Sumerian, and it is on the period before this, when the *Ubaid* culture was superseded by the *Uruk*, that the argument chiefly turns. The *Uruk* period marks, as has been seen, some striking advances over the *Ubaid*, but none the less there is some continuity in such matters as temple architecture and perhaps the cult. Thus authorities, according to whether they rate more strongly the cultural breach or the continuity, either regard the *Uruk* phase as marking the arrival of intrusive Sumerians into a land already enjoying the thriving *Ubaid* civilization, or else treat it as a development within the *Ubaid* culture, which is then seen as itself the creation of the ancestors of the historical Sumerians. A point which favours the former theory is that a number of the oldest Sumerian cities, which were originally founded in the *Ubaid* period, bear names which are non-Sumerian: Lagash or Shirpurla (modern Tello) is an example.

There are many theories, but no certainty, as to the original home of the Sumerians. The difficulty and obscurity of their agglutinative tongue has led to it being compared, in most cases quite unscientifically, with several dozen other languages, ranging from Chinese and Tibetan through Dravidian and Hungarian (a current favourite for amateurs!) to the remoter languages of the African continent, of American Indians and of the Pacific Islands. Basque has not been overlooked, whilst a Jewish scholar, of great erudition but not exempt from the human weakness of racial prejudice, long put it on the level of Volapuk by maintaining that Sumerian had never existed at all as a natural living language but was an artificial creation of Semitic Babylonian priests. What is certain is that the language is unrelated to either Semitic or Indo-European, is agglutinative in structure, and probably tonal. It is, however, now generally recognized that language has no essential connection with racial origins, and no scholar of repute would now seek to solve the problems of Sumerian origins on the basis of language alone. Physical anthropology provides some evidence on the basis of cranial remains, but the interpretation of this evidence is still highly controversial.

The discusion of the place of origin of the Sumerians must still start with the assumption that, wherever they came from in the first place, it was not Sumer. This has been challenged, but the challenge has not been supported by any cogent argument. The land of Sumer had, in fact, no indigenous inhabitants: though the older hypothesis that the land did not rise from the Persian Gulf till the fifth millennium is now regarded as false, the archaeological fact is indisputable that no remains of human culture exist in south Babylonia earlier than the *Eridu* period, datable perhaps to about 4500 B.C. or a little later.

As to the direction from which the Sumerians came, theories have been very diverse. Ancient tradition, transmitted through Greek, speaks of a fish-man Oannes who swam up the Persian Gulf, bringing with him the gifts of civilization. This tallies with Sumerian ideas as we know them from cuneiform documents, since the god of wisdom, Enki (to give him the name he bore in Sumerian contexts, Ea being the name used by the Semites) was associated with the waters. Moreover, Enki was also tutelary deity of Eridu, an ancient city on the banks of a lagoon of the Persian Gulf, already mentioned as one of the sites of the earliest occupation of southern Babylonia and according to Sumerian documents the first of five cities existing before the Flood. All this tradition has been taken as pointing to a settlement of Sumer by sea from the south-east up the Persian Gulf. Furthermore, Tilmun, of which the identity with Bahrein is now generally accepted, is of great importance in the earliest stratum of Sumerian religion, and it has been suggested that it represents a Sumerian cultural centre earlier even than Eridu. This likewise would imply that the Sumerians entered Mesopotamia by way of the Persian Gulf. There is, however, at present no archaeological evidence to support such a theory, although excavation is going on in Bahrein and should ultimately give a decision one way or the other.

The prevailing view, based on the main stream of tradition in ancient Sumerian literature (particularly the epics) and on the widespread cultural links between Sumer and Iran (in particular Elam) in the late prehistoric and protohistoric periods, is that the Sumerians came into south Babylonia from the east or north-east. The importance of the ziggurat in Sumerian religion has also been taken as evidence that the original home of the Sumerians was mountainous, but this is a dubious line of argument, as the ziggurat represented the Cosmic Mountain and was related not to a particular area but to a cosmology held in the ancient world, with various modifications, from Egypt to China.

Others would attempt to relate Sumerian origins to the early culture of the Indus valley or of south Baluchistan, or both. The people of the Indus valley (*Harappa*) culture, whose writing has not yet been deciphered, *may* have been related to the pre-Indo-Aryan Dravidians, now found in south India; and the theory of an actual ethnic link between the Sumerians and the Harappans has particular attraction for those who have the eye of faith to see a linguistic relationship between Sumerian and Dravidian. There is indisputable evidence, in the form of art motifs and material objects characteristic of one civilization found at sites of the other, of trade relations in the third millennium between the Sumerians and the peoples of the Indus valley or Baluchistan. Moreover, representations of cult-scenes involving Indian humped bulls have been found at Ur and Susa; these suggest that there were actually enclaves of Indian merchants in south Mesopotamia and Iran who needed the consolations of their own religion. From this third millennium evidence there has been extrapolated a theory of a relationship between Sumerians and Dravidians dating from the *Uruk* period and going back beyond a commercial and cultural connection to an ethnic and linguistic link; this is an attractive view for which the one thing at present lacking is proof.

An attempt has also been made to combine all the traditions and archaeological evidence into one theory by postulating two waves of Sumerians coming from the east, one travelling by sea to the Persian Gulf and the other overland by way of Iran, with another group of the same people migrating eventually to the Indus valley. Whilst it is impossible to say finally that there could have been no ethnic movements on these lines, there is no evidence at present to prove that there was. Early contacts with India, like those with Egypt, can be adequately explained as due to trading relations and do not necessarily imply large scale racial movements, whilst a common origin for Dravidians and Sumerians or even a close relationship between them cannot be said to have been made out. The most one can safely conclude at present is that the Sumerians came from somewhere east of Babylonia.

The *Early Dynastic* is the period in which, even though the documentation is still relatively scanty and often doubtful of interpretation, we may consider ourselves to have passed from prehistory to history. In it the distinctive characteristics of the Sumerian city-states appear, reach their full development, and finally begin to pass into decay, whilst traditions become attached not only to particular city-states but to historical individuals. Widely differing opinions are held as to the relative value of the various kinds of evidence about this time. The most reliable evidence is certainly that of archaeology, but this is sometimes difficult of interpretation and often entirely lacking at the most tantalizing point. Sumerian tradition, in the form of a composition known as the *Sumerian King List*, dating in its present form from the early second millennium but incorporating older material, is explicit about the dynasties in Sumer in the third millennium, though the compiler worked with the erroneous idea that every dynasty governed the whole of Sumer and Akkad and began and ended in a military victory or defeat. Certain other Sumerian literary traditions preserve memories, of disputed value, of third millennium history and personalities. Almost worthless as an independent source are the traditions transmitted in Greek literature from the third century B.C. work of the Babylonian priest Berossus.

The Sumerians, like the Hebrews (who borrowed the story from Babylonia), had a tradition of a Flood.* The *Sumerian King*

* The oft-asserted claim that Sir Leonard Woolley discovered evidence of the biblical Flood at Ur goes wildly beyond the facts. If the silt layer found by Woolley had been the deposits of a flood of the magnitude of that mentioned in the Bible, a similar silt layer would necessarily have existed at a corresponding

List mentions five cities as existing before the Flood: Eridu, Bad-tibira, Larak, Sippar and Shuruppak. Eridu was undoubtedly, as we have already seen, of great antiquity, and Shuruppak probably goes back to the *Ubaid* period. Sippar has been the scene of tablet-mining rather than archaeological excavation and nothing is definitely known yet about its earliest levels. Larak is unidentified, whilst Bad-tibira, probably modern Tell Madineh, has not been excavated. The actual statement of the *Sumerian King List* concerning these cities begins:

> When kingship was lowered from heaven the kingship was in Eridu. In Eridu Alulim became king and reigned 28,800 years. Alalgar reigned 36,000 years. Two kings reigned 64,800 years. I leave the subject of Eridu; its kingship was carried to Bad-tibira . . . .

The account goes on according to this formula. One of the kings of Bad-tibira was 'Dumuzi, a shepherd', who reigned 36,000 years. The relation between this misty ruler and the fertility and pastoral god of the same name is enigmatic: what is clear is that the fertility and pastoral god was worshipped long before he received Dumuzi as his principal name. At the end of the account of the five pre-diluvial cities the *Sumerian King List* sums up:

> Five cities were they. Eight kings reigned 241,200 years. The Flood swept thereover.

It may be mentioned here that the earliest part of this tradition, that concerning Eridu, probably relates to a time substantially before the *Early Dynastic* period as we have defined it. This conclusion seems necessary from the archaeological evidence, which shows that there was no important occupation of Eridu after the *Uruk* period and very little after the *Ubaid*.

level in every Sumerian city. This is not the case; even sites quite close to Ur fail to reveal a flood stratum at the appropriate level.

Quite apart from the crucial objection mentioned, Woolley's explanation of the facts is not the only possible one. The Euphrates has frequently changed its course, and Woolley's silt stratum might well be the sediment of the river bed itself at some period. Furthermore, whilst the stratum in question certainly consists of detritus originally brought down by a river, there seems to be no proof for Woolley's specific claim that it was deposited in its present position by water: it may thus simply represent an ancient sand dune. What is certain is that if the stratum in question was actually laid by a flood, it was a purely local flood.

The two first dynasties after the Flood, when once again 'kingship was lowered from heaven', were, according to the *Sumerian King List*, those of Kish in the north of Babylonia and Erech in the south. The alleged change from Eridu, the most ancient city, to Erech as the main seat of civilization in the south is amply borne out by the archaeological evidence, since Eridu was practically abandoned long before the *Early Dynastic* period, probably because of the salting up of the soil in consequence of faulty irrigation techniques. This change from Eridu to Erech as the cultural centre in the south is also reflected in an ancient myth. According to this myth Innin, the goddess of Erech, went to the Abzu, the shrine of her father Enki in Eridu, where Enki provided fitting entertainment. Drinking freely, in the Sumerian fashion, of his own good wine, Enki became filled with generosity and proceeded to heap upon Innin more than a hundred gifts, comprising all the basic concepts of Sumerian culture and including such things as kingship, justice, truth, falsehood, ritual prostitution, music, a number of crafts, wisdom and understanding. Innin loaded them into a boat and, despite steps taken by the repentant Enki to try to recover his gifts when the effects of the drink had worn off, managed to get the precious objects safely to Erech.

As archaeology shows, Erech was already of great importance in the *Protoliterate* period, but the evidence only informs us upon general trends. When we reach the *Early Dynastic* period, a lucky chance makes it possible for us to visualize at least a shadowy picture of actual events in Erech and to some extent elsewhere in Mesopotamia. We owe this to the fact that a school of epic writers arose in Erech, whose poems, known to us in copies from the beginning of the second millennium, incorporate in a less bald form than the *Sumerian King List* the early traditions of that city and its rulers. These epics relate to the *Early Dynastic* II period or the beginning of *Early Dynastic* III.

Another literary source relates, in an even more nebulous fashion, to an even earlier period. These are the myths, the tales of the behaviour and exploits of the gods, which are generally thought to reflect the sociology of the time at which Sumerian society crystallized in the city-state, that is, in archaeological terms, *Early Dynastic* I or even *Jemdet Nasr* (late *Protoliterate*).

Th. Jacobsen of Chicago, in two penetrating studies, has employed these myths and epics, in conjunction with the archaeological evidence, to give a picture of political and social organization and development in Sumer during the *Early Dynastic* period. There are (regrettably) fashions in the study of ancient society as in everything else, and Jacobsen's view of *Early Dynastic* Sumerian society, which reigned almost unchallenged for two decades, is now being assumed to be invalid, although (except for some acute criticisms by A. Falkenstein, which may require Jacobsen's original statement to be modified to some extent) no one has disproved his arguments as a whole and no significant new evidence has come to light. Jacobsen's general line of approach is therefore utilized here.

According to Jacobsen's arguments, in earliest Sumerian society ultimate sovereignty resided in a general assembly of all citizens – probably including women as well as men – who came together to decide upon action when some emergency threatened. All citizens could speak but the opinions of some, particularly the older men, naturally carried greater weight than that of others. Discussion continued until virtual unanimity was reached: there was no question of taking a majority vote. The final decision was formally announced by a small group called 'lawmakers'. (The anthropologist K. C. Rosser has studied the social structure of a village in the Himalayas, and found there a method of reaching decisions almost identical with that postulated by Jacobsen for archaic Sumerian communities.)

Amongst the recurrent decisions which the assembly had to make was the choice of an official called in Sumerian *En*, a word which later came to mean 'lord'. In the early *Early Dynastic* period this person was primarily a cult functionary, being the consort of the deity (male or female according to whether the city-deity was goddess or god), and living in sacred quarters, called the *Egipar* (in Akkadian *Giparu*), attached to the temple. It was the *En* who originally played the vital role in the Sacred Marriage upon which the fertility of the city-state depended. In cities (such as Erech) in which the *En* was a male, his secondary administrative functions in connection with temple lands gave him great political importance and he at one stage became virtually the ruler: the *En* Gilgamish (see below, pages 39, 391) is an instance of this. Very early there came about some division between the priestly and secular functions of the *En*, and already by the middle of the *Early Dynastic* period he had taken up residence in a special palace, where he soon came to have an extensive household which included scribes, cooks, butlers, craftsmen, musicians and the usual kinds of court functionaries. By the end of the *Early Dynastic* period the actual ruler was, as the Lagash texts show, no longer the *En* but an official, originally concerned with agricultural operations, who bore the title *Ensi* (see below, page 44). Cultic duties were delegated to a special priest or priestess.

In the event of attack from outside the assembly had to choose a war-leader or king (Sumerian *Lugal*, meaning literally 'great man' or 'great householder'): his place of residence was not in the temple and he may be considered in his origin as being a secular officer. The office of neither *En* nor *Lugal* was originally hereditary or permanent, that of the *Lugal* at least being granted only for the duration of the emergency.

Jacobsen considers that this pattern of what he calls 'primitive democracy' was ultimately extended from the city-state to the land of Sumer, when it came to be regarded as a political entity. His main argument is the peculiar position in later history of Nippur, the city of the god Enlil. This city must at some very early period in the development of Sumerian culture have had some peculiar importance, for throughout Sumerian history kings of the various city-states derived their authority primarily from recognition, not by their own city-god, but by Enlil of Nippur. Also the Sumerian word for 'Sumer' probably originally denoted 'Nippur'. Such facts could be easily explained if Nippur had at some early period held a hegemony over the whole of Sumer, but there is no proof of such a situation either from tradition or from the archaeological evidence. It has therefore been suggested that Nippur owed this special status to having been at some very early period the sanctuary to which the notables of all the Sumerian cities resorted to elect a war-lord in times of emergency: such a stage in the development of political organization is well known in some other cultures. The date at which it may have occurred in Sumer must have been after the rise of Nippur as a large city, which occurred in the *Jemdet Nasr* period, and not later than *Early Dynastic* II, when the widespread occurrence of city walls could be taken to indicate that the Sumerian cities were in a state of potential mutual hostility, or at least all making separate arrangements for defence against an external enemy. Jacobsen would relate the formation of the supposed Nippur League to the pressure of invading Semites who were, by means of the concerted action taken, diverted to the less well-defended north. In support of this hypothesis there is plentiful evidence of Akkadian (Semitic) occupation in the Diyala region from the *Early Dynastic* II period onwards, and this wave of Semites may first have appeared in Babylonia in *Early Dynastic* I.

Jacobsen points out that the *En* or *Lugal*, once appointed, would attempt to perpetuate the position temporarily granted him, even after the emergency was over, and also that the functions of *En* and *Lugal* would tend to become vested in the same man. This tendency to the growth of permanent kingship is depicted in a myth concerning the warrior god Ninurta. The myth shows him maintaining a permanent body of troops with which he goes raiding beyond the borders of the state, whilst within the state he accepts the position of redresser of wrongs. He would tolerate no opponent and when, in the myth, the plants meet in assembly to choose themselves a king, Ninurta destroys his potential rival in battle and liquidates the opposition.

None the less the *Lugal* or the *En*, even when he had made his office a permanency, was by no means an absolute ruler. Gilgamish, for example, the powerful semi-legendary *En* of Erech, when he wished to make war with Agga of Kish, first consulted the Elders, who are specifically described as 'counsellors' and were probably the heads of family groups. When these opposed him, it was not until Gilgamish had called together a general assembly of all male citizens (females no longer participated) and obtained their consent, that he was able to proceed with the measures he had planned.

This stage, in which the *En* is a permanent but not absolute ruler, may be related to the *Early Dynastic* II period or the beginning of *Early Dynastic* III, in which all the Sumerian epics may be placed. Whereas myths centre around gods, epics concern human or part-human heroes, such as Enmerkar and Gilgamish. One of these tales gives an account, tantalizingly obscure it is true, of trade at this early period between Erech and a city in the mountains of Luristan (western Iran). Enmerkar, the *En* of Erech, wished to build and beautify with lapis lazuli a shrine to his patroness the goddess Innin: she was also his great-aunt, and the close relationship of the hero with the great goddess suggests that the tale comes from early in the Epic period. In furtherance of his pious intention Enmerkar sent to the ruler of Aratta, which lay to the east over seven mountain ranges, demanding the sending of lapis lazuli and timber, and dispatching to him a donkey caravan laden with barley which the soil of Sumer so bountifully yielded: the appearance of the string of laden asses winding through the mountains is aptly likened to a line of ants filing from their hole. The *En* of Aratta also claimed to be under the protection of Innin, and the poem thus reflects a tradition of a common religious and economic culture covering the whole region from the Euphrates to the mountains of Iran – a view supported by the archaeological evidence of the material culture of this region at the time. It may be significant that in the dispute which developed between Enmerkar and the *En* of Aratta organized warfare does not appear to be envisaged as the final solution. This again conforms with the archaeological evidence, since it was not until the *Early Dynastic* II period that the fortification of cities, with its implication of the existence of inter-state warfare, became general. This very development is ascribed in another epic to Enmerkar's third successor, Gilgamish, builder of the great outer wall of Erech. Although the territory of Erech had been (according to the epics) overrun by Semitic nomads as early as the reign of Enmerkar (see below, page 41), it was only in the time of Gilgamish that siege warfare between cities first occurred: the actual circumstance, as we learn from yet another epic, was that the walled city of Gilgamish was attacked by Agga, king of Kish.

It was Kish – according to the *Sumerian King List* – which was the seat of the first dynasty in the north of Babylonia after the Flood. This city has been excavated to virgin soil, and apart from some neolithic remains which have not been related to any of the early cultures of Mesopotamia, the earliest phase of occupation was in the *Jemdet Nasr* period. The old neolithic site was at that time resettled, probably in the course of the Sumerian expansion consequent upon the technological advances of the *Uruk* period, though it is notable that the cultural background at Kish was not purely Sumerian. Even some of the earliest rulers of the Kish dynasty bore Semitic names, whilst there are features of the art and architecture of the city which indicate a tradition divergent from that in the southern cities. Such facts could be explained on the supposition that towards the end of the *Jemdet Nasr* period a wave of Semites infiltrated from Arabia or Syria, establishing Kish and Mari (a city on the middle Euphrates, for which corresponding evidence is available) as their principal centres. Such Semitic invaders are actually mentioned in the epic literature, in which at one point Enmerkar, *En* of Erech, is hard pressed by the Martu (the Sumerian designation for an early group of Semites from the west) who were overrunning the land. However, these Semitic invaders rapidly became Sumerianized by contact with the more highly civilized dwellers of the land, so that most of the later rulers of Kish have Sumerian names. The period of assimilation, and perhaps the contempt of the sophisticated Sumerian city-dweller for the nomadic barbarians pressing into his land, and destined to inherit his culture, are reflected in a Sumerian myth. In this myth the god Martu, who bears the name by which the Semitic nomads were known, seeks the hand in marriage of the Maid of Kazallu (a northern Sumerian city). This leads a relation of the Maid to point out to her that Martu 'eats raw meat, during his life has no house and after death lies unburied'. The Maid was undeterred, however, and the marriage – representing the fusion of races – took place.

Kish was certainly the most important centre of northern Babylonia in the *Early Dynastic* period, and afterwards, even when it was no longer an independent dynastic capital, its name was included in the titles of any ruler who claimed dominion over the whole of Babylonia. Jacobsen makes the interesting suggestion that Agga, king of Kish, was already in a position to exercise some form of suzerainty over city-states farther south, and that in the war between Agga and Gilgamish the latter was technically a rebellious vassal. The attempt at creating a political unit greater than the city-state could be expected as a consequence of the growth in royal power. The king would establish in his various cities royal households in which the servants bore allegiance only to the king and not to the town in which they served. There is some evidence to support this theory of the course of events from contemporary economic documents, which by the early *Early Dynastic* III period (in which, or shortly before in *Early Dynastic* II, Agga and Gilgamish are probably to be placed) are to some extent intelligible to us, and sufficiently explicit to fill in some details of contemporary life.

Archaic tablets have been found at a number of sites, and may here be listed in the following approximate chronological sequence, from oldest to latest:

    i stratum IVa at Erech (period *Uruk* IVa), (apparently contemporary with these was a single limestone tablet from Kish bearing pictographs),

    ii strata III and II at Erech; tablets from the sites Jemdet Nasr and Tell Uqair (period *Jemdet Nasr*),

    iii tablets from Ur (period *Early Dynastic* I),

    iv stratum I at Erech; tablets from Fara (period early *Early Dynastic* III).

Doubt as to the language of composition is possible only with the *Uruk* IVa tablets, and even here the pictographic writing makes it possible to offer a reasonable guess at the contents in some cases. The earliest writing which can be proved to be Sumerian comes from the *Jemdet Nasr* period and is a group (several times repeated) of three signs, which we may represent by X-Y-Z. The two signs X-Y can be recognized, from their virtual identity with forms found in Sumerian later in the millennium, as the name of a god, 'Lord Air', read in Sumerian as EN.LIL. This identity does not, however, in itself prove that the signs X-Y were read as Sumerian, since EN.LIL could conceivably itself be a literal translation of a phrase, denoted by the same signs, in an earlier language. Z, ◅━◅, is recognizably the picture of an arrow, but as there are few contexts in which 'Lord-Air arrow' would make sense, one must look for a language in which the word for 'arrow' has a homonym more appropriate here. Such a language is Sumerian, in which TI (of which the written representation in later periods is clearly derived from the pictogram we have called Z) meant both 'arrow' and 'life' or 'live'. Reading the sign Z as TI, with its second sense, does give a meaningful phrase, since 'Enlil, give life!' represents a proper name of a type very common throughout Sumerian and Babylonian civilization. The group X-Y-Z is therefore to be read as Sumerian, EN.LIL.TI, establishing this as the language of texts of the *Jemdet Nasr* period.

The intelligible archaic tablets from this time onwards are of two main kinds which, if one had to give them a label, could be respectively called 'economic' and 'literary'. The term 'literary' is, however, at this stage rather pretentious, since tablets of this class consist simply of lists of objects, for example, kinds of fish, birds, animals, plants, gods, forming a kind of primitive lexicon. The main source of such 'literary' tablets so far has been Fara (the site of ancient Shuruppak, the home of the Babylonian counterpart of Noah), but a few of this type are also known from the other sites. It is, however, not these 'literary' texts but the 'economic' ones which are revealing as contemporary evidence of the early *Early Dynastic* III period. Some of these texts are the records of a palace at Fara, and mention large numbers of personnel of all kinds. As Jacobsen points out, the numbers in some categories appear impossibly high if an actual palace staff is in question: there are for instance one hundred and forty-four cup-bearers and sixty-five cooks. This makes it look very much as though the documents actually concern military personnel organized on the basis of a household. This interpretation is confirmed by the fact that the records from this palace also contain references to the repair of war-chariots and lists of troops going to battle. This goes to support the conclusion that by the early part of the *Early Dynastic* III period kings had developed to a position in which they could maintain standing garrisons in key cities.

It is equally clear, however, as the epic of *Gilgamish and Agga of Kish* shows, that the balance of power in favour of the suzerain was still very precarious, and that a single city might successfully challenge him. By the time the first historical inscriptions begin (towards the middle of the *Early Dynastic* III period) the attempt of Kish to wield a wider suzerainty had definitely failed, and Sumer consisted of a large number of small independent kingdoms and city-states.

Within the Sumerian city-states as we first meet them in the historical inscriptions, each state had its own ruler called the *Ensi*, a title which seems originally to have denoted the leader who organized the population for the seasonal agricultural operations; the title *Lugal* (king) was only applied to a ruler who in addition to ruling his own city exercised some kind of hegemony over other city-states. The names of a number of the early rulers of city-states are known, some from the *Sumerian King List*, others from inscriptions (generally dedications in temples) of the rulers themselves, but the city from which we are best informed in this respect is Lagash. From affairs in this city-state we learn a great deal concerning Sumerian life and history from about the middle of the third millennium onwards.

The site of Lagash, now known as Tello, is still set in the midst of a most fertile region criss-crossed with irrigation canals fed from the Shatt-el-Hai, a canal connecting the Tigris and Euphrates. In antiquity this same canal, together with another called the Lumma-girnun, ensured to Lagash not only bountiful crops but also a thriving river-borne trade and in consequence considerable material prosperity. Such economic and social stability ensued as to provide conditions in which a dynasty founded by a certain Ur-Nanshe was able to rule in unbroken succession through six reigns for over a century.

A neighbouring city, Umma, also on the Shatt-el-Hai, lay to the north of Lagash on the other side of the Lumma-girnun. The direction of flow of the Shatt-el-Hai being from north to south, Umma was in a position to interfere with the water supply of Lagash, and this gave rise to conflict between the two cities on a number of occasions. It is the documents recording the circumstances of such events which provide our first substantial historical narratives, beginning in the period shortly after 2500 B.C. The earliest of these are some inscriptions of Eannatum (third ruler of the dynasty), notably a stone relief set up to mark his defeat of Umma: the monument is known as the Stele of the Vultures from the gory details shown of carrion birds fighting over the entrails of the slain after the battle in which Eannatum led his city to victory. A little later a cone-inscription of Entemena, Eannatum's nephew, gives a history – no doubt one-sided – of the conflict between Umma and Lagash for several generations up to his time.

Such records also provide some hints of the wider aspects of Sumerian political organization, supplementing what we know from the *Sumerian King List* and inferentially from literary and economic texts. Inscriptions of both Eannatum and Entemena mention an earlier occasion of dispute at which a certain 'Me-silim king of Kish' had acted as arbitrator, settling the terms of peace and setting up a boundary stone between the territories of the two cities: clearly he exercised some kind of hegemony. The exact date of Me-silim is not known, but he was certainly an historical personage, probably a century or more earlier than Eannatum, for two dedication inscriptions of his are known from Lagash and Adab. It is unlikely, partly for chronological reasons and partly because his name does not occur in the *Sumerian King List*, that Me-silim was king of Kish itself at the time of that city's attempted suzerainty over Sumer. More probably he was king of some other city-state who had gained control of at least part of Akkad and had in consequence been invested by Enlil of Nippur with the ancient and splendid title 'king of Kish'. This would indicate other temporarily successful attempts at wielding hegemony over the whole of Sumer after the time of Agga of Kish.

Another city which may have exercised some temporary

hegemony is Ur. A dynasty of Ur is mentioned in the *Sumerian King List* at a period corresponding to that called *Early Dynastic III* in archaeological terminology. Some of the rulers of this dynasty (which is referred to as the First Dynasty of Ur) are known from contemporary inscriptions. From the beginning of this period come the 'royal tombs' of Ur (see below, pages 372 ff.), spectacular in their contents and significant for the history of religions, though of no great importance for our knowledge of political or social history.

The government of the Sumerian city-states at this time was theocratic. Almost all the city lands belonged to the temple, and the *Ensi* was the bailiff of the city deity; he and his family administered the temple estates, with a hierarchy of officials beneath them. It is likely that the *Ensi* had originally been elected by the free citizens, but by the middle of the third millennium the office had, at least in Lagash where we know the situation most fully, become hereditary.

The temple lands were divided into three categories, of which some account is given below (see page 165). One of the categories consisted of land let out on a share-cropping basis, a rent equivalent to one-third of the crop being paid, one-sixth of it in silver and the rest in kind. Although private property in land was very rare until nearly the end of the third millennium, this economic system in Lagash permitted the accumulation of wealth in private hands. At the same time, the military exploits of Lagash under Eannatum greatly strengthened the power of the *Ensi* as an individual, the prestige of Eannatum himself being so great that he was admitted to the Sumerian pantheon. These trends upset the equilibrium of the original economy, and changes took place which to at least one section of the population appeared as abuses. Since the economic system contained elements both of state socialism and of capitalism, it is possible, according to political preference, to see these abuses as the natural consequence of either the one or the other. The main complaints were two: the *Ensi* was treating the temple lands and the god's possessions as his own private property, and citizens were subject to excessive taxes, levied both by the *Ensi* and by the temple officials, on all aspects of life and death.

Taxes were, for instance, levied on cattle, fisheries, sheep-rearing, divorce and burial. The economic developments also produced a class of rich men, who by judicious loans were able to oppress the poor, the wealthy man making the poor man a loan and then foreclosing at an inconvenient time, taking in settlement an animal or other goods of the debtor of value far exceeding the amount of the loan.

Possibly as one consequence of the economic disruption in Lagash, the Ur-Nanshe dynasty came to an end; towards its end there can be seen, tied up with the economic changes, an interesting sociological trend, that is, the rise of a secular power distinct from the religious authority, and this is reflected in subsequent political developments. There was, according to the Soviet scholar I. M. Diakonoff (*Revue d'Assyriologie*, 52 (1958), page 12) a struggle between, on the one hand, the priests and aristocracy (standing for the autonomy of the temple estates), and on the other the *Ensi*, who attempted to strengthen his control by annexing the temple estates. It is an anachronism and over-simplification to speak, as some scholars have done, of 'clerical' and 'anti-clerical' parties in the dynastic changes which follow.

Urukagina, one of the men who came to power in this period, thirteen years after the end of the Ur-Nanshe dynasty, attempted to take steps to deal with the abuses which had arisen and to restore the conditions of older times. In an inscription he records the abuses (from which the details given above are taken) and lists the reforms carried out to reduce the exorbitant nature of the taxes and the victimization of the economically weak:

> An appointed priest may no longer go into the garden of a villein and fell a tree or take away the fruits.
> If a villein has a fine ass which bears a foal, and his Patron says: 'I will buy it', if, (in the case) when the man is willing to sell, he [the villein] tells him [the Patron], 'Weigh out a satisfactory amount of silver', or if he [the villein] is unwilling to sell, the disgruntled Patron may not beat him.
> If a villein makes a fish-pond, no-one of the gentry class may take away his fish.

In another paragraph the overseers of shepherds and fishermen were prohibited from taking an income direct from the produce of their subordinates instead of obtaining it from the temple administration. Figures are also given for the reduction in taxes in connection with such matters as marriage, divorce and burial. A fiscal reform was also made in connection with sheep-rearing. However, these reforms did not give Lagash the desired economic strength and stability, and Urukagina fell a victim to the rivalry which always existed between Lagash and the neighbouring city of Umma, whose king, Lugalzagesi, finally overthrew Lagash, shortly after 2400 B.C.

Lugalzagesi embarked upon a policy of military conquest which ultimately brought the whole of Sumer under his control, with Erech as his capital. He was not only supreme within Sumer, but claimed to wield influence far beyond his own borders, 'from the Persian Gulf along the Tigris and Euphrates to the Mediterranean', so that 'all the dependent rulers of Sumer and the *Ensis* of all independent countries bowed to his arbitration in Erech'. Jacobsen points out that though this is an idealized picture, not necessarily fully according with political realities, it does indicate that the ideal was internal peace under a suzerain powerful enough to check all rivalry, and external peace through a ruler sufficiently influential to be acceptable as an international arbitrator. Lugalzagesi's political expansion obviously represented no new phenomenon. There had been since the time of Agga of Kish a number of fleeting attempts at hegemony over wide areas. A ruler of Ur contemporary with Ur-Nanshe exercised control over cities at least as far north as Nippur, whilst there is evidence that during the reign of Eannatum the forces of Mari on the middle Euphrates penetrated almost as far south as Lagash. Lugalzagesi finally attempted to obtain direct control of the whole of Babylonia by subjugating Kish, once again the predominant city in north Babylonia. He may have succeeded temporarily, as the *Sumerian King List* represents this as a change of dynasty, but he himself was shortly afterwards overthrown by Sharrum-kin (Sargon), the former vizier of a king of Kish.

Sharrum-kin is a Semitic name and the dynasty he founded

was a Semitic dynasty. There is an Arabic proverb which says: 'The desert is the cradle of the Arab, and Iraq his grave.' This recognizes the fact that throughout history successive waves of Semites from the desert have been driven or drawn to the fertile valleys of the north-east, there to be assimilated into the civilization of the settled peoples. Reference has been made to evidence for this process earlier in the third millennium, and it was still taking place at the time of Sharrum-kin (2371–2316 B.C.). Earlier writers have seen subsequent developments in terms of a racial struggle between Semites and Sumerians, but this does not accord with the facts. Texts from before the time of Sharrum-kin contain lists of personal names of which about half are Sumerian and half Semitic, which suggests that the two ethnic groups were living peaceably side by side. There is no evidence at this time of anything in the nature of a Semitic 'invasion', and such Semites as did come in from the desert probably came as individual families, settling in the Sumerian cities and rapidly adopting Sumerian culture and a loyalty to the particular city-state to which they had attached themselves. For geographical reasons Semitic influence arriving in this manner was likely to be stronger in the northern part of the country than in the south, and the sociological and linguistic influence of Semites would be felt there sooner. Thus some – but only some – of the rulers of Kish of this period bore Semitic names, whilst the last king of Kish, of whom the Semitic Sharrum-kin had been the vizier, bore a name that was Sumerian. As a strong piece of evidence for lack of any kind of racial prejudice, it may be mentioned that the statue of the Sumerian king Lugalzagesi in the temple of the Sumerian god Enlil in the holiest of Sumerian cities, Nippur, was inscribed not in Sumerian but in the current Semitic language, Akkadian. Sharrun-kin's own city was Agade (still unidentified), which he personally had founded, possible originally as an administrator under the king of Kish. When the *Sumerian King List* mentions this city in relating Sharrum-kin's defeat of Lugalzagesi, it simply states that 'Uruk was smitten with weapons; its kingship was carried to Agade', with no suggestion of any change beyond the transfer of suzerainty from one city-state to another. Sharrum-kin himself claims that it was Enlil – the great Sumerian god – who judged his case with Lugalzagesi, whilst Sharrum-kin's titles show that the principal deities with whom he had relations were Sumerian.

The dynasty founded by Sharrum-kin (more commonly referred to as Sargon of Agade), though it endured for little more than a century (2371–2230 B.C.), left a permanent imprint on Mesopotamian history. Sargon's policy was to destroy the walls of cities within Babylonia, thus depriving potential rebels of strongholds, to appoint only citizens of Agade to high administrative positions, backed with reliable garrisons, and to take members of local ruling families to his capital as hostages. He thereby weakened local autonomy and prepared the way for later centralized control of the land.

Sargon himself gained control not only of all Sumer and Akkad but of much of the rest of the Near East as well. Under his rule international trade flourished, at least from the Mediterranean coast to the Persian Gulf (see below, page 277). Later literary tradition, however, accords Sargon a more extensive empire, including Asia Minor. There is a text of this *genre*, long known, which refers to an expedition made by Sargon to protect from the local king a Mesopotamian merchant colony at Burushkhanda in Asia Minor: a more recently identified poetical text dating from about 1800 B.C. appears to give an earlier and independent account of the same incident.

Literary tradition has attached itself strongly not only to Sargon but also to his third successor and grandson, Naram-Sin (2291–2255 B.C.), who is mentioned not only in literary tradition but also in a number of omens and proverbial sayings, most of which are tantalizingly obscure. As an example, one such contains the passage:

> The east wind is a wind of prosperity, the friend of the divine Naram-Sin . . . ,

which probably incorporates a tradition, meaningless to us, concerning an incident in some campaign. In the case of this ruler also, archaeological evidence, as well as Naram-Sin's own inscriptions, lend some support to the later literary tradition. According to his own inscriptions, Naram-Sin effected the military defeat of Mani of Magan, a claim which indicates that he controlled the whole of the western coast of the Persian Gulf at least as far as Oman. A poetic composition of some centuries later extols the magnificence of Naram-Sin's times, speaking of

> mighty elephants and apes, beasts from distant lands, abounding in the great square (of the capital):

this suggests trade relations with India. In the north-east Naram-Sin penetrated into what are now the Kurdish hills, quelling, at least temporarily, the hill-tribes, then known as the Lullu, and setting up a great relief, carved high in the face of the rock, which still exists, though much damaged (see plate 16A). To guard the route into Asia Minor he built a great castle at Tell Brak, and it is likely that there was another such garrison at Nineveh. A stele of his has been found as far north as Diarbekr on the borders of Armenia. Indications are that this most able ruler sought to give some kind of central administration to an empire transcending a collection of individual city-states; literary tradition, supported to some extent by inscriptions from the time of Naram-Sin himself, mention that precious wares flowed into Agade from all quarters, whilst city administrators sent in their monthly and yearly tribute.

It was probably Naram-Sin's imperialism which, in Sumerian eyes as well as in fact, led to the downfall of his dynasty. Literary tradition is ambivalent towards Naram-Sin: he is treated not only as a great hero but also as an ill-fated ruler. (It should be mentioned that Dr. O. R. Gurney of Oxford has adduced evidence in the light of which the last statement may be questioned.) Naram-Sin's own inscriptions mention a general rebellion of the principal cities of Sumer and Akkad, including Kish, Uruk and Sippar, whilst the tradition mentions that the goddess Innin decided to abandon the capital, Agade. The immediate cause of the withdrawal of divine favour is now known. A Sumerian text, recently put together from a number of fragments in various museums, describes in the opening lines the early splendour and wealth of Agade, to which came peoples from all quarters bearing their tribute. The impious deed of Naram-Sin brought this to an end, for he allowed his troops to desecrate, sack and loot the *Ekur*, the great temple of the great god Enlil in the holiest of Sumerian cities, Nippur. All was now at an end for Naram-Sin and Agade, for the furious Enlil brought down from the hills upon the fertile land a barbarous race, the Gutians. These savages disrupted communications and trade, upset and ruined the irrigation system, which always required careful, constant and centralized control, and produced famine and death throughout the land. To turn aside Enlil's wrath from Sumer and Akkad as a whole, eight of the senior gods undertook that Agade should itself be destroyed in requital for the violation of Nippur, and achieved the complete and enduring desolation of Agade by a curse reminiscent of Isaiah's much later execration of Babylon (*Isaiah* xiii. 19-22).

The consequences of Naram-Sin's policy of centralized government from Agade were not so sudden and catastrophic as the Sumerian poem suggests, and although Gutian raids on Mesopotamia may well have begun during the reign of Naram-Sin, it was not until the time of his son and successor Sharkalisharri that the central authority definitely broke down.

It had been plausibly argued that, in fact, the Gutians were neither the sole nor the deciding factor in the downfall of the Agade dynasty. Under the rulers from Sargon to Naram-Sin the cultural and military achievements of Agade had been felt from the Mediterranean coast and Asia Minor across the whole Near East to Susa and Oman, whilst economic relations had extended even farther, in the west to Cyprus and eastwards as far as India. There is no indication in contemporary inscriptions that the Gutians were recognized as a menace sufficiently serious to disrupt this situation, and this can hardly be due to deliberate suppression of the truth, since conflict with rebellious city-states and the Lullu is freely mentioned. Anubanini, king of the Lullu, spoken of in a later legend as a scourge of the land, had sufficient power to be able to set up a victory stele on his own account: the fact that this was written in Akkadian incidentally testifies to the widespread cultural influence of the empire of Agade, even amongst its enemies.

Other non-Sumerian and non-Semitic peoples were also in evidence at this time, in particular the Hurrians, who became of high importance later on, in the middle of the second millennium. There were already Hurrian workers at Nippur in the Sargonic period, concerned with manufacturing garments: these people were probably prisoners-of-war taken in the Zagros mountains. Hurrians are now known from their own inscriptions to have been already in the Sargonic period settled in northern Mesopotamia, where they may well have exerted pressure against the south. A coalition of peoples in the west also came into military conflict with Naram-Sin, inflicting upon him a severe defeat.

It was this combination of pressures which finally dislocated the central administration of Agade and left the land powerless against the invaders from the hills. A period of anarchy succeeded, which the *Sumerian King List* summarizes in the words 'Who was king? Who was not king?'. With the breakdown of central administration government no doubt reverted to individual city-rulers, who in some cases may have been able to administer a rather larger area than their own immediate territory: one such case was Erech, to which the *Sumerian King List* ascribes a short-lived dynasty between that of Agade and the Gutians.

A list of twenty-one so-called kings of the Gutian period is given in the *Sumerian King List*, but in view of their extremely short reigns (only one exceeded seven years and about half of them were three years or less) it seems likely that they were chiefs appointed for a limited term of office. Later tradition emphasizes the barbarity of the Gutians, and if their social organization was primitive it is likely that kingship as a developed and permanent institution had not yet arisen amongst them. Some of the later names in the list of Gutian rulers are Semitic, which indicates that assimilation of the barbarians was taking place, whilst a few dedication inscriptions show that they had adopted the religious cults of the land. The Gutian period, which may be taken as beginning at about 2250 B.C., just after the reign of Naram-Sin, was certainly at an end by 2120 B.C.

The later civilized peoples of Babylonia remembered the period of Gutian domination with abhorrence, as a time of barbarism, when the gods were not respected and temples were plundered and neither women nor children spared. The impact of the Gutians was felt most severely in the northern part of the land, Akkad, whereas in Sumer several of the old city-states, although they may have suffered material damage in the first wave of barbarian invasion, remained virtually autonomous. One of the cities which suffered least seems to have been Lagash. This city, destroyed by Lugalzagesi of Umma at the beginning of his climb to ascendancy over Sumer, had been rebuilt during the prosperous days of the Agade dynasty, and no doubt regained much of its old importance as a river-port. It was now able to recover much of its past splendour, particularly since with the destruction of Agade its principal rival as a terminal for sea-borne trade up the Persian Gulf had been removed. In the absence of a strong central government the *Ensis* of Lagash were able to extend their authority beyond their own city-state, forming a new dynasty, known in some detail from the inscriptions of the rulers themselves though unmentioned in the *Sumerian King List*. The best-known ruler of this dynasty is the fourth, Gudea, as to whose activities we have much information from his many extant inscriptions. Gudea's authority extended well beyond Lagash: he claimed to be suzerain to Nippur and Erech, and even undertook a campaign to loot the Elamite city of Anshan. His inscriptions, though principally concerned with his piety in the building or restoration of temples and the fulfilment of his duties to the gods, contain numerous references to trading expeditions. He claims that 'Magan, Meluhha, Gubi, and Tilmun brought tribute; their ships came to Lagash with timber'. Stone, bitumen and gypsum were brought in shiploads for the building of the temple of Ningirsu, whilst other goods brought from abroad by Gudea included diorite from Magan, cedarwood from the Lebanon, copper from Kimash, and gold from Hahu; the latter was probably in Asia Minor, and Kimash in the mountains of western Iran.

Gudea was succeeded by his son and grandson, but during the latter part of this period Lagash came under the suzerainty of other city-states which were re-emerging as independent powers.

Utu-hengal of Erech (2120–2114 B.C.) defeated the last of the Gutian rulers, and was duly recognized at Nippur as 'King of the Four Regions' (a title first employed by Naram-Sin), and was included in the *Sumerian King List*. This marks the re-emergence of the system of centralization of government employed by Naram-Sin; subordinate city-states were ruled through governors, who recognized Utu-hengal as overlord. One such governor was Ur-Nammu of Ur, who subsequently became an independent ruler (2113–2096 B.C.). This ruler founded a celebrated dynasty under which, through extension of the system of centralized control, there developed a highly organized empire, more compact than that of Sargon of Agade, which endured for over a century (2113–2006 B.C.).

The period of the Third Dynasty of Ur, as this is called, shows Sumerian civilization in its most fully developed form. Though tablets in vast numbers – in the region perhaps of fifteen thousand legal, administrative and economic documents already published, and perhaps a hundred thousand or more counting those excavated but unpublished – are known from the period of the Third Dynasty of Ur, our knowledge of this time is not in corresponding detail, largely because the documents are written in very condensed phraseology and are full of technical words upon which the exact sense turns but which scholars can at present understand only very approximately. Direct archaeological evidence witnesses to a considerable material prosperity at this time, in that almost everywhere traces of building activity are discernible. Ur-Nammu himself, founder of the dynasty, built or rebuilt temples in many of the ancient cities, including Erech, Lagash, Nippur and Eridu, but his most striking work was at his capital, Ur. Here he rebuilt, in honour of the Moon-god Nanna, the ziggurat, a great rectangular stepped tower in three (some would say only two) stages, about two hundred feet by one hundred and fifty at the base and perhaps seventy feet or so high, with a shrine on top. This ziggurat, restored by later kings and finally uncovered from 1923 onwards by Sir Leonard Woolley, still stands as a monument to the piety of Ur-Nammu (see plate 3A). Ur-Nammu's successors likewise engaged in works of piety, and from chance

references on tablets of the period it is possible to make some
interesting economic calculations in connection with one of the
temples. The particular one in question was built in the reign
of Ur-Nammu's third successor, Shu-Suen, for the god Shara at
Umma; although by no means the largest in Sumer, it was
at least seven years in building. Nearly nine million large
and seventeen million small bricks went into its construction,
and as a tablet informs us that a worker's brick production was
eighty a day, the making of the bricks alone, it has been
calculated, would have occupied a thousand men for nearly
a year.

Temple restoration was not the only constructional activity
of Ur-Nammu and his successors. In the interests of a thriving
agriculture and trade Ur-Nammu dug many canals, and restored
Ur's sea-borne trading connection with Magan. As a further
achievement he claims to have re-established civil order and
security in the land; this had become notably absent wherever
the Gutian invaders had destroyed the ancient regime. Ur-
Nammu's claim is substantiated by the fact that fragments
of a collection of laws promulgated by him have been
recovered.

The administrative system introduced during the rule of this
dynasty minimized the risk of rebellion by careful control of the
Ensis, who became governors rather than ruling local dynasts.
The control of garrisons was taken out of their hands, whilst
the danger of an administrator acquiring too much power
through strong local ties was reduced by the practice of posting
such officials from one city to another. The king was kept informed of affairs within his cities by a system of royal messengers,
whilst relations with princes beyond the empire were maintained
through diplomatic representatives.

Ur-Nammu was succeeded by his son Shulgi (2095–2048 B.C.),
who in his long reign further increased the extent and splendour
of the empire of the Third Dynasty of Ur, military expeditions
being undertaken outside Babylonia, as a result of which both
Elam and Assyria came within his economic control. The peoples
on the eastern frontier were kept in order by a combination

of punitive expeditions and marriage alliances between Sumerian princesses and local rulers. Shulgi, like his father and his successors, also engaged in temple building. Two of his sons, Amar-Suen (2047–2039 B.C.) and Shu-Suen (2038–2030 B.C.), successively followed him, after serving apprenticeships as governors of cities during their father's lifetime. It is during these reigns that we have indications of a new wave of Semitic infiltration from the west. This time it took the form not of single peaceful families of migrants but of armed incursions of whole tribes, for security against whom Shu-Suen built a defensive wall-system. This new invasion shortly brought disaster to the empire of the Third Dynasty of Ur; though it was not upon Shu-Suen but upon his successor, Ibbi-Suen (2029–2006 B.C.), that the disaster fell.

Ibbi-Suen came to the throne whilst still a youth, and the continuance in office of most of the previous senior officials shows that there was no immediate change of policy. Taxes (in the form of cattle) flowed in from the various parts of the empire, and two Sumerian literary compositions had their origin in the early part of Ibbi-Suen's reign, which suggests (if it is true that in antiquity literature and national well-being went hand in hand) that calamity had not yet fallen upon the land. Then gradually, after his second year, in city after city Ibbi-Suen's authority ceased to be recognized: this is shown by the fact that the legal and administrative documents from these places are no longer dated by Ibbi-Suen's official year-formulae.* Another indication of the breaking up of the empire is that after Ibbi-Suen's sixth year the *Ensis* of the various cities of the empire no longer made their normal deliveries of beasts for the offerings for Nanna, tutelary deity of Ur. That a military threat was recognized is shown by the fact that the date-formula for Ibbi-Suen's sixth year mentions the repairing of the defences of the key cities of Nippur and Ur.

Information upon the course of events is provided by a broken

---

* A year-formula was a means o ʃdating legal and administrative documents. Each year a short sentence, relating to some currrent event, was promulgated by the king – technically, by the god – and the year would be known by this. Some typical formulae are '[The town] Simurru was destroyed', 'He made the ritual drum [called] Nin-igizi-barra for [the goddess] Inanna', 'He made the heavenly throne for [the god] Nanna.'

letter to Ibbi-Suen from a certain Ishbi-Erra, a foreigner from Mari who had taken service with Ibbi-Suen and who at the collapse of the empire became king of Isin. Ishbi-Erra refers to the fact that he had been charged with buying grain in the region of Isin and Kazallu (two cities of Akkad) and reports that he had bought a large quantity (144,000 *gur* or about 10,000 tons) at the favourable price of half a shekel of silver per *gur*, but that the price had now doubled. He also had the less welcome news that the Amurru (Amorites, the people from the western desert) were forcing their way into the country, taking the fortresses one by one, and that he was unable to forward to Ur the grain which he had bought: he suggested that he might be placed in charge of Isin and Nippur, a suggestion to which the king agreed.

The cheapness of the corn bought by Ishbi-Erra indicates that the Amorite breakthrough occurred just after harvest. Ur obviously relied largely on imported grain, which Ishbi-Erra had been unable to forward; the capital was thus in a particularly desperate position, as Ibbi-Suen's reply to Ishbi-Erra shows, for he offered to pay double price for the corn if only his official could get it to Ur. As a result of this situation inflation set in in Ur, and became so severe that in the seventh and eighth years of Ibbi-Suen barley and fish were selling, according to the account tablets, at fifty to sixty times the normal price. As a result of the loss to the Amorites of the corn lands, inflation and famine doubtless occurred elsewhere in Sumer, and later omen literature refers to risings and rebellions against Ibbi-Suen. After his seventh year it appears from the disuse of his date-formulae that Ibbi-Suen was no longer recognized at Nippur, the city of the god Enlil, by whom kingship was bestowed.

Ibbi-Suen's empire had thus crumbled away until it consisted of little more than the city-state of Ur; even if the governors of certain other regions retained a personal loyalty to Ibbi-Suen, they were unable to give any effective support. Ishbi-Erra apparently came into this category, remaining loyal to Ibbi-Suen as long as possible, for not before the twelfth year of Ibbi-Suen did he begin to issue his own date-formulae as ruler of Isin.

With the collapse of the central authority in Sumer and Akkad.

the land faced a further menace, the ever-recurring threat from the mountain dwellers to the east. For several years before the end of Ibbi-Suen's reign, the land had been subject to raids by peoples from Elam, and two successive date-formulae of Ishbi-Erra of Isin, referring to victories over such people, indicate that central Babylonia as well as the south was affected: it has indeed been suggested that the Elamites were allies of Ibbi-Suen, attacking rebellious cities, but the subsequent fate of Ur does not make this probable. In the twenty-fourth year of Ibbi-Suen's reign a group of peoples from Elam made an attack on the land, in the course of which Ur was destroyed and Ibbi-Suen himself transported to Elam. So finally vanished the last relics of the Third Dynasty of Ur. At Ur itself an Elamite garrison was left on the ruins of the devastated capital, and not finally expelled until Ishbi-Erra was in a position to consolidate his kingdom.

2

Babylonia and Assyria, circa 2000-1350 B.C.

ALTHOUGH the disappearance of the Third Dynasty of Ur marks the end of the Sumerians as an independent and distinct political entity, it would present a totally false conception to speak of the 'defeat' of the Sumerians. There is no evidence of a conscious realization in the ancient world of a conflict of Sumerian *versus* Semite, and the political events of this time were the result and not the cause of sociological and cultural changes which, though only then becoming clearly apparently, had been in progress for decades or centuries.

At the end of the third and the beginning of the second millennia B.C. there was a movement of West Semitic peoples eastwards into central Mesopotamia and Babylonia. Already under the empire of the Third Dynasty of Ur there was a considerable amount of peaceful penetration into Babylonia, as the presence of West Semitic names in lists of temple personnel clearly shows. This movement continued for about two centuries and left a lasting mark on the culture of the area, in its political, religious and social aspects. The immigrants concerned, referred to by modern authorities variously as East Canaanites, West Semites or Amorites, settled in a number of ancient centres where they formed kingdoms which showed some important differences from the earlier Sumerian temple-states as well as from the latest independent Sumerian political unit, the empire of the Third Dynasty of Ur. One of the main differences was in the conception of land tenure. In the original pattern of Sume. city's land all belonged to the local god, whilst conseption land could be owned by the clan, the private citizen. (Soviet assyriologists do not accept th. of the original conception of land ownership in Sumeria.

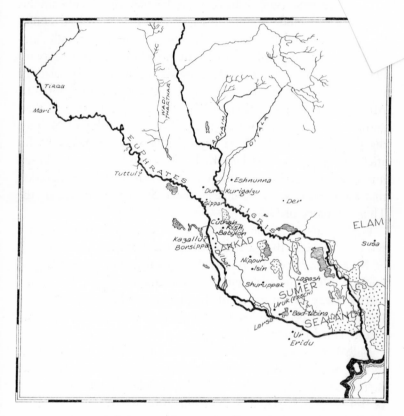

Babylonia in the second millennium B.C.

Well before the sack of Ur a number of rulers of city-states had acquired an independent position, amongst others the *Ensi* of Eshnunna on the Diyala, and apparently the ruler of Der, a city near the Elamite frontier. The city-ruler who finally achieved a temporary supremacy, and whose dynasty was in some senses the heir to the Third Dynasty of Ur, was Ishbi-Erra of Isin, whose reign may be taken as 2017–1985 B.C. The chronology of Ishbi-Erra's rise to supremacy is, however, far from clear: he continued to recognize the authority of the king of Ur longer than a number of other city-princes and certainly seems not to have acted as an independent ruler of Isin before the twelfth year of Ibbi-Suen. Within the next two or three years he was able to extend his authority to include Nippur, the city vital for control of Sumer. Little is known of the events of the following years, though date-formulae refer to works of fortification and hint at struggles with Elamite invaders and the establishment of diplomatic relations with a number of the nomadic tribes pushing into Mesopotamia. After the final destruction of Ur, the general picture is that, perhaps partially as a consequence of his guardianship of Nippur, the legitimacy of Ishbi-Erra's supremacy was recognized as far afield as Arrapkha (modern Kirkuk) in the north and Tilmun (modern Bahrein) in the south, which gives force to the suggestion that Ishbi-Erra was regarded as the heir to the empire of the Third Dynasty of Ur.

Eight years after the destruction of Ur, Ishbi-Erra was in a position to expel the garrison which had been left on the ruins; he later rebuilt the city, re-installing the statue of the Moon-god Nanna, Ur's tutelary deity, which the invaders had earlier carried away to Anshan. This further strengthened the claim of Ishbi-Erra to be considered the legitimate successor of the kings of the Third Dynasty of Ur.

Ishbi-Erra was succeeded in the direct line for four generations, by rulers of whom for the most part little is known. There are indications that during the earlier part of the period the kingdom of Isin was consolidated and extended, some outlying states, such as Der, hitherto independent, becoming subject. Law and civil order were enforced over the region controlled from Isin, and conditions for a restoration of the internal and foreign trade which had flourished in the Third Dynasty of Ur period began to re-appear. The first hints of a setback come from the reign of Ishbi-Erra's third successor, Ishme-Dagan (1953–1935 B.C.), who had to put down some kind of civil unrest, which involved, according to a hymn, the partial destruction of Nippur, although he certainly retained control of this key city, as well as of Ur, Erech and Eridu, together with Der and much of north Babylonia. The details of these troubles are obscure. Waves of Beduin* were still thrusting in, and are specifically mentioned in the hymn on the destruction of Nippur. The first stirrings of the kingdom of Assyria are noticeable within this period, and soon afterwards (*circa* 1900 B.C.?) its prince, Ilushuma, whose reign was in part contemporary with that of Sumu-abum of Babylon, made a raid into Babylonia, probably down the east of the Tigris, in the course of which he took Der and claims to have 'freed' Ur and Nippur. This reference to the 'freeing' of Nippur and Ur probably refers to the driving out of Beduin invaders, with whom Isin was unable to cope. Der was important to Assyria as the main city on the trade-route from Elam along the east side of the Tigris, whilst Ur was the main sea port for the whole of Mesopotamia. It is therefore understandable that the Assyrians in the hinterland, directly dependent upon these places for their trade, should be concerned to have them in reliable hands. A beneficiary of Isin's weakness was the city-state of Larsa, on the Euphrates between Erech and Ur, of which the rulers later managed to carve out an independent kingdom in the south: the process was beginning at this time, since in a contract from Lagash an oath is taken not by Ishme-Dagan of Isin (the nominal suzerain) but by a man known to have been the ruler of Larsa.

Ishme-Dagan is referred to in literary compositions as a king who 'set law in the land', a phrase which may have referred to the promulgation of legislation, though at present the only collection of laws known from this dynasty is that of his successor, Lipit-Ishtar, of whose laws fragments have been found at Nippur and Kish. Lipit-Ishtar himself speaks of the 'freeing' of citizens of certain cities, and this probably refers to social reforms concerned with manumission from slavery.

Politically the fragmentation of the Isin kingdom, which began

* This term is of course an anachronism in such a context. It is, however, a convenient description, provided it is remembered that it is intended to denote here not fully nomadic peoples using camels, but semi-nomads dependent upon asses for transport.

in the reign of Ishme-Dagan, was strongly marked at the time of Lipit-Ishtar. Details of events are very ill known, but Larsa emerges as a definite rival, and date-formulae mention a number of military operations by Larsa's king, Gungunum (1932–1906 B.C.). Notable amongst these operations was the capture of Ur, by which Larsa gained control of the foreign trade from Bahrein which passed through that city. There was also much building activity. It is interesting to notice that religious unity in Babylonia transcended political fragmentation: not only were daughters of both Ishme-Dagan and Lipit-Ishtar high-priestesses of Nanna in Ur under the rule of Gungunum, but also the successor of Lipit-Ishtar of Isin actually made dedications in that city regardless of it being politically under Larsa.

The successors of Gungunum extended their power by military measures towards north Babylonia, ultimately absorbing a number of cities, in particular Nippur and Erech, which had formerly belonged to Isin. Of greater ultimate significance than military victory was, however, the attention which the rulers of the Larsa dynasty bestowed on the the irrigation system. Gertrude Bell applied to Iraq the saying 'he who holds the irrigation canals, holds the country', and to judge by their activity in this respect the kings of Larsa seem to have been well aware of this truth. It is even possible that disregard of this principle may have contributed to the collapse of the empire of the Third Dynasty of Ur, since from the latter part of that period, whilst vast programmes of temple building were carried out, we hear far less of public works on canals.

The second successor of Gungunum, Sumu-ilum, was contemporary with the beginning of the famous dynasty commonly known as the First Dynasty of Babylon (1894–1595 B.C.). Under the Third Dynasty of Ur Babylon had been a small city ruled by an *Ensi*, but it is not known whether it was subsequently part of the region ruled by the kings of Isin. Nor have we at present much satisfactory information about the founder of the First Dynasty, Sumu-abum. His name, and some sociological features of the kingdom he established, indicate that he was of West Semitic origin, but whether he had, like Ishbi-Erra earlier, formerly been in the service of another Mesopotamian state or whether he conquered Babylon direct from the desert is at present unknown, though a cult favoured by him suggests some relationship with Isin. Much of his fourteen-year reign was spent in the strengthening of Babylon by fortifications and by the subjugation, by military or diplomatic means, of a number of other cities in the area, notably Kish and Sippar.

The simultaneous expansion of Larsa in the south and Babylon in the north inevitably led in the end to conflict between these two powers, but it would be an over-simplification to regard a struggle between these two city-states as the key to the history of Mesopotamia during the succeeding century. From Mari on the Euphrates to the Diyala and the Elamite border a considerable number of other city-states still existed which, though destined ultimately to be absorbed by Babylon or Larsa and finally unified under Hammurabi, for the present enjoyed, in varying degrees, independence and the possibility of territorial expansion. The pressure of infiltrating Semitic tribes towards the end of the period of the Third Dynasty of Ur had resulted in the establishment of Amorite rulers in many of these city-states. With possession of the central shrine of Nippur passing back and forth between Isin and Larsa, no state could now properly be regarded as sole legitimate ruler of Babylonia.

Larsa itself suffered a serious setback when it was invaded by the armies of Kazallu and Mutiabal, the last ruler of Gungunum's dynasty being driven from the throne. The invading armies were defeated and the power of Larsa restored by Kudurmabuk, a sheikh with an Elamite name and strong Elamite affinities, though probably of Amorite descent; he set his own son, Warad-Sin, upon the throne. Isin meanwhile continued to decline in importance; and finally it was conquered and its dynasty brought to an end by Rim-Sin (1822–1763 B.C.) of Larsa, brother and successor of Warad-Sin. Rim-Sin attached the greatest significance to this event, which made him sole ruler of middle and south Babylonia and legitimate heir to the titles of the kings of the Third Dynasty of Ur: the last thirty years of his sixty-year reign were dated by this event.

Larsa's defeat of Isin fell at the very end of the reign of Sin-muballit (1812–1793 B.C.), Hammurabi's father. Although not a few independent states yet remained, notably Mari and Eshnunna, this was a critical development, in that it represented the elimination of the remaining buffer between the two rising powers, Babylon and Larsa. Hammurabi (1792–1750 B.C.) thus came to the throne with an apparently powerful and expanding state extending from his borders to the Persian Gulf and Elam. His ultimate success in gaining control of all Babylonia is perhaps a tribute as much to his administrative and diplomatic skill as to his military achievements.

We get a picture of the vigorous diplomatic activity of this time from documents found at Mari, today represented by the site of Tell Hariri in eastern Syria. The occupation of this city, important as a stage on the trade route up the Euphrates between the Persian Gulf and the Mediterranean, goes back to at least the *Jemdet Nasr* period. The site, excavated by French archaeologists between 1933 and 1938, seems to have been at the peak of its importance at the beginning of the second millenium B.C. The excavations yielded many important finds from this period. Besides important sculptures, wall paintings and bronzes, the site produced much information on palace and temple architecture; all of this bore witness to considerable material prosperity. The most important of all the finds from Mari was, however, a collection of well over twenty thousand cuneiform tablets, mainly letters and administrative and economic documents. These tablets, still in course of publication, are shedding a strong beam of light on events in the Near East at the beginning of the second millennium B.C. Mari was particularly significant at this period since, as the most westerly of the old Sumerian states, it was both the first to feel the effects of any wave of Amorite pressure and also the first to exert a civilizing effect upon such invaders. Thus Ishbi-Erra, founder of the dynasty of Isin, and racially an Amorite, is referred to as 'the man of Mari', indicating that he had earlier been in the service of that state.

The Mari dynasty concerned in the archives mentioned was founded by a certain Ishtup-Il at the same period, and as part of the same racial movement, as the dynasties of Isin, Larsa, Assyria and Babylon. Briefly the regnal history of Mari is one of patrilineal descent, interrupted by a period of foreign domination, when Shamshi-Adad of Assyria put in one of his sons as sub-king. The native dynasty afterwards regained Mari, but was brought to an end by the final conquest of the city by Hammurabi of Babylon in his thirty-fifth year. The archives fill out this bare historical framework with a remarkably detailed picture of public administration, political intrigue, and the work of officialdom during the period. We frequently read of the dispatch of ambassadors, whilst the correspondence between the various Amorite rulers which we find in the Mari letters is full of references to troop movements, the units concerned being numbered in thousands rather than hundreds. Ration lists for officers and troops enable an estimate to be given of the forces present in Mari, which amounted to a minimum of ten thousand in the state, of which four thousand were in the garrison at the capital. The duties of such troops were largely concerned with protection of the settled populations against marauding semi-nomads. Yasmah-Adad of Mari, writing to Ishme-Dagan, his brother and his senior, explained that of a thousand troops five hundred had been put to guard the town and the other half to guard the cattle. Economic as well as military and political co-operation was practised by the Amorite rulers. The sub-king of Mari, when pasture was scarce in his own territory, sought from the sub-king of Qatna permission to have his flocks pastured with the flocks of Qatna, a request to which the sub-king of Qatna acceded.

A situation of coalitions and counter-coalitions is explicitly referred to in another document from Mari which says:

> There is no king who of himself alone is strongest. Ten or fifteen kings follow Hammurabi of Babylon, the same number follow Rim-Sin of Larsa, the same number follow Ibal-pi-El of Eshnunna, the same number follow Amut-pi-El of Qatanum, and twenty kings follow Yarim-Lim of Yamhad.

The date of this letter is obviously earlier than Hammurabi's thirtieth year, in which he effected a decisive defeat of Rim-Sin, and it must be later than his tenth year, since before that time the list of major kings would certainly have included Shamshi-Adad of Assyria. Shamshi-Adad, one of the greatest of the kings of Amorite origin, made Assyria temporarily one of the most powerful of Mesopotamian states; certainly he survived to Hammurabi's tenth year, since a document exists, dated in that year, in which an oath was sworn jointly by Shamshi-Adad and Hammurabi.

The continuous history of the geographical region (not the political state) of Assyria – in the earliest period known as Subartu – goes back at least to the period of the *Halaf* culture, of which it was the centre and probably the cradle. This culture was superseded by a form of that known as *Ubaid*, of southern origin; in consequence what was basically one culture came to extend over the whole of Mesopotamia. Sumerian civilization ultimately reached Assyria, probably several centuries after its first rise in southern Babylonia, and a temple of the *Early Dynastic* period has been excavated at Ashur. The *Assyrian King List* from Khorsabad hands on the tradition concerning Assyrian rulers, and according to this the first seventeen, in the pre-Sargonic period (i.e. before 2370 B.C.), were apparently nomadic chieftains, since they are specifically described as dwellers in tents.

Subsequently the land of Assyria formed part of the empire of Sargon of Agade, and then of that of the Third Dynasty of Ur; the collapse of the latter empire gave to Assyria, as to other constituent city-states, the possibility of independence. For part of the ensuing period we have quite extensive information concerning Assyrian trade with Asia Minor, thanks to an archive of over three thousand texts obtained during the past half-century by legitimate excavators and illicit diggers at Kultepe in the heart of eastern Asia Minor. Kultepe represents the site of ancient Kanesh, and here, known to us from the period 1950–1800 B.C., lived a colony of Assyrian traders. Arguments have recently been put forward suggesting that the region was actually under the military control of Assyria, but the positive evidence is very scanty and there are difficulties in supposing an Assyrian empire at this time extending farther north than at any other period in history. It is more likely that the merchant colony, which had its own municipal organization and legal system, was an enclave under the protection of a native king: the institution of the foreign trading colony enjoying protection and special privileges was very common in the ancient world in the second and first millennia, and is indeed referred to more than once in the Old Testament.

Trade between Kanesh and Ashur (referred to in the documents as 'The City') was by means of caravans of donkeys of up to two hundred beasts; some details of this trade and its organization will be found below on page 218. Trade between Anatolia and Mesopotamia may well go back substantially beyond the period to which the extant documents relate, and, indeed, this is suggested by the late tradition (see above, page 50) telling how Sargon of Agade led a military expedition to the assistance of a merchant colony suffering oppressive treatment in Asia Minor.

The wealth accruing to Assyria from such trade put it in a very strong position during the period of fragmentation following the collapse of the empire of the Third Dynasty of Ur. Ilushuma, the earliest known Assyrian ruler of this time, was strong enough to make a successful raid into Babylonia east of the Tigris, in which he captured Der, a city on the Elamite border sited at the western end of one of the trade routes across Iran. Ilushuma also thrust across the Tigris to make some very problematic interference – described literally as 'setting the freedom' – in the affairs of Ur and Nippur: this may (as has been mentioned earlier) conceivably have related to an attempt to protect the vital southern port of Ur against a new wave of Beduin invaders. Ilushuma was succeeded by his son Irishum I (late twentieth and early nineteenth century B.C.) and great-grandson Sargon I of Assyria (soon after 1860 B.C.), both of whom enjoyed considerable prestige. Assyrian prosperity and power did not long survive these rulers, however, for the circumstances which had brought them about shortly came to an end. The Indo-European tribes were already stirring beyond the Caucasus in Eastern Europe, and at about this time the Hittites began to thrust into Anatolia from the north-east. As a result of such racial movements the older political organization of Asia Minor was thrown into chaos, and Assyrian trading relations with Kanesh necessarily came to an end. Assyria entered upon a period of decline. The *Assyrian King List* mentions a king Naram-Sin, who may conceivably have been the Naram-Sin who is known as ruler of the state of Eshnunna on the Diyala. This would suppose an actual conquest of Assyria by Eshnunna, but there is at present no mention of such an event from documents from Eshnunna, though they do indicate that in the early second millennium B.C. Eshnunna was a powerful and expanding state. However, if Assyria was actually subject to Eshnunna, this situation was of brief duration, and the state ultimately fell into the hands of yet another Amorite chieftain, the energetic and able Shamshi-Adad (*circa* 1814–1782 B.C.). As with most of the founders of Amorite dynasties, very little of moment is known of his antecedents. His father was a certain Ila-kabkabu, ruler of a small Mesopotamian state, who was at first allied with Yaggid-Lim, one of the first Amorite kings of Mari, but subsequently engaged in hostilities with him. After Shamshi-Adad had made himself secure on the throne of Assyria, a palace revolution occurred in Mari, in which king Yahdun-Lim, son of Yaggid-Lim, was killed. There is no proof that the revolution was engineered by Shamshi-Adad, but as he was the ultimate beneficiary of it he is open to the strongest suspicion. The crown prince, Zimri-Lim, fled for refuge to the kingdom of Yamhad in the Aleppo area, and Shamshi-Adad assumed control of the powerful and wealthy state of Mari, installing his younger son, Yasmah-Adad, as sub-king: his older son, and subsequently his successor on the throne of Assyria, was already sub-king of a state called Ekallatim. Yasmah-Adad seems to have been a young man of many engaging qualities, high amongst them loyalty to his father and senior brother, but not possessed in any large measure of administrative ability.

Some of Yasmah-Adad's correspondence makes amusing reading, and quite frequently it happened that his older and more able brother had to help him out of scrapes. In one letter his father rebuked him vigorously for his discourteous treatment of some persons of royal blood. In another, Yasmah-Adad writes to his father, quoting the latter's contemptuous words to him: 'You're not a man! You haven't a beard on your chin! How long are you going to be unable to administer your estate?'. Elsewhere Shamshi-Adad criticizes Yasmah-Adad for always wanting advice about managing the matters entrusted to him, and holds up Ishme-Dagan as an example of the way in which a sub-king should behave. On another occasion Yasmah-Adad had had the audacity to ask his father to add to his territory the city of Shubat-Shamash. The impudence of this had annoyed Shamshi-Adad who – according to Ishme-Dagan in the letter he wrote to Yasmah-Adad to smooth things over – had commented angrily: 'He hasn't put Mari and Tuttul on a sound basis yet and now he wants Shubat-Shamash!'

Yasmah-Adad's kingship of Mari did not long survive his father's death in Hammurabi's tenth or eleventh regnal year. Zimri-Lim, heir of the former Mari dynasty, emerged from his refuge in the west, and with the backing of the three powerful states of Yamhad, Eshnunna and Babylon was able to oust Yasmah-Adad after a reign which altogether had lasted seventeen years.

The reasons which led Hammurabi of Babylon and the king of Eshnunna to transfer their support from Assyria to the earlier Mari dynasty are not clear. As at many other periods of history, wherein a condition of tension has existed in an area containing a large number of states, amongst which none had a decisive advantage over the others, fresh alignments of powers were constantly taking place amongst the Amorite states, and personal loyalties and antagonisms as well as obvious immediate political advantage may well have come into consideration. Subsequently Eshnunna left the Yamhad-Mari-Babylon coalition and engaged in warfare against them in alliance with its eastern neighbour, Elam, and the north Mesopotamian state of Andariq. By Hammurabi's twenty-ninth year Zimri-Lim, possibly recognizing the now powerful Babylon as the greatest danger to his independence, joined against his former ally Hammurabi in a coalition headed by Elam and Eshnunna. Hammurabi defeated this coalition and established himself decisively as the major power in the area. Since Rim-Sin of Larsa had long controlled virtually the whole of southern Babylonia, two powerful kingdoms were now face to face. In the following year Hammurabi overthrew Rim-sin, thereby making himself sole ruler of Babylonia (1763 B.C.). There still remained some independent outlying city-states, and these Hammurabi defeated in the following three years, his last major objective being the capture of Mari. Zimri-Lim became a vassal of Hammurabi, but a year later a revolt broke out and Hammurabi was compelled to destroy the walls of Mari and to remove Zimri-Lim.

The political and military activities of Hammurabi had thus converted a city-state into the centre of an empire, and Hammurabi's subsequent administrative achievements matched his military success. These achievements are best known from the collection of laws promulgated by him, and from voluminous correspondence with his regional officials.

The prologue to the *Laws* (on which see pages 206 ff.) gives some indication of Hammurabi's policy, describing how the gods called him,

> Hammurabi, the reverent god-fearing prince, to make justice appear in the land, to destroy the evil and the wicked that the strong might not oppress the weak, to rise like the Sun-god over the Black-headed Ones [i.e. humans] to give light to the land,

and how, at the command of the god Marduk, he

> set forth truth and justice throughout the lands and prospered the people.

Hammurabi details his piety, describing the propriety of his relationship to the shrines of the great gods in the major cities of his realm, Nippur, Eridu, Babylon, Ur, Sippar, Larsa, Erech, Isin, Cuthah, Borsippa, Dilbat, Lagash, Mari, Agade, Ashur, Nineveh and others. That his boast had considerable justification becomes clear from the details of his correspondence: no detail was too small, and no official too important, for Hammurabi to be able to give clear-cut decisions and orders in the interests of good government. A high official who had been instructed to clear out a canal near Erech and had been tardy in the matter was ordered to have the work completed in three days and to report. Accusations of land-snatching were investigated and justice served. When an accusation of bribery reached the king a letter was sent ordering investigation of the matter and, if the case were made out, confiscation of the bribe and dispatch of the defendants and witnesses to Hammurabi. It was the king also who gave orders for the intercalation of a month to bring the calendar, based on lunar observation, into line with the vernal or autumnal equinox. A vigorous policy of canal-building, to bring agricultural prosperity to his land, was also prosecuted by this ruler. The details of administration and social organization in Hammurabi's kingdom are dealt with elsewhere.

Hammurabi welded into one kingdom the many city-states of Sumer and Akkad, and gave the whole land one language for administration and business (Sumerian continued to be used liturgically as long as Babylonia endured), and one legal system. Some would also add that he gave to Babylonia one pantheon, with Marduk, the god of the city of Babylon, at its head; but it has been argued against this that Marduk did not become national god of Babylonia till well after the time of Hammurabi.

The sociological pattern imposed upon the land by Hammurabi continued to be felt until the end of Babylonian history: his military achievements, however, did not long survive Hammurabi himself. Racial movements caused by the stirring of the Indo-European tribes beyond the Caucasus have already been referred to, and the effects of southward migration of these peoples now began to be felt farther afield. Early in the reign of Hammurabi's son Samsu-iluna (1749–1712 B.C.), a Cassite army made a raid from the Elamite border, and though subsequently repelled by the Babylonians, succeeded in conquering Ur and Erech. These Cassites, who later established a dynasty which ruled Babylonia for several centuries, were a people who came from the Zagros hills. Although their language is not yet definitely assigned to any well-known group, some features of their pantheon indicate that they had been in cultural contact with Indo-European peoples; this latter fact suggests that their emergence at this time was due to pressure from the Indo-Europeans stirring in the north. Personal names in business documents of the next century or more show

73

that a steady peaceful infiltration of Cassites into Babylonia continued to take place.

In the twenty-eighth year of Samsu-iluna there was a revolt in the south of Babylonia (the marsh country known as 'the Sealands') which he was unable to suppress, and so arose the so-called 'Dynasty of the Sealands', which continued to control a region approximating to the ancient Sumer for more than two hundred years, outliving, indeed, the First Dynasty of Babylon. The political history of Samsu-iluna's successors, Abi-Eshuh (1711–1684 B.C.), Ammi-ditana (1683–1647 B.C.), and Ammi-saduqa (1646–1626 B.C.), was largely a matter of small scale border campaigns and work on defensive walls, perhaps indicating an awareness of the possibility of sudden attack.

The end of the First Dynasty of Babylon represents one of the landmarks of ancient history, and introduces in catastrophic manner some peoples who played a leading part in the history of the succeeding centuries. Suddenly in 1595 B.C., the thirtieth year of Samsu-ditana (1625–1595 B.C.), the final king of the dynasty, Mursilis I, the fourth ruler of the Hittite empire, swept out of Asia Minor into Syria (where he took Aleppo), and down the Euphrates, sacking Mari on his way. The conqueror reached Babylon, which he plundered and burnt, and then returned to his capital, apparently as suddenly as he had come, but too late to crush a court conspiracy which led to his assassination. His sojourn in Babylon had, however, been long enough to disrupt government and administration there, and Babylonia fell an easy prey to a horde of Cassites who, after the Hittites had retreated, swept down from the mountains to the north-east.

Passing mention has already been made of the arrival in Asia Minor of the Hittites. The earliest inhabitants of Asia Minor, now commonly known as 'Hattians', from the name 'Hatti' which they gave to their land, spoke dialects which were not Indo-European, and the Indo-European speakers seem to have begun to arrive in the area in the first century of the second millennium. Evidence for this comes from the documents of the Assyrian merchant colony at Kanesh, in which the non-Assyrian personal names include a few which may be interpreted as Indo-

European. Before the coming of the Indo-European Hittites, the land comprised ten or so small kingdoms, amongst which Burushkhatum (Burushkhanda) held first rank, but virtually no contemporary native records remain from the Hattian period, though there are later records which may incorporate genuine Hattian tradition.

After the period of confusion resulting from the incursion of Indo-European invaders into the region of the Halys, one of their princes, a certain Labarnas (after 1700 B.C.), carved out a kingdom for himself, which, according to Hittite tradition, he rapidly enlarged by military successes until he had made the sea his frontiers. Princes of the royal family were appointed governors of the major cities. The capital of Labarnas was a city called Kussara (still unidentified), but his son transferred his capital to Hattusas, a stronghold in the bend of the Halys, and changed his own name to Hattusilis. We have a certain amount of information as to the social organization of the country at the time of Hattusilis I (*circa* 1650 B.C.) from the record of a speech made by this king on the occasion of his adopting an heir, Mursilis I. This indicates that government in the Hittite kingdom was at this time essentially restricted to a noble and closed caste ruling over the indigenous population and alone concerned in military activities and the central administration of the state. The common man was free, though liable to forced labour for the benefit of the state.

Under Hattusilis I the Hittite kingdom expanded to the south and east and stretched out over the Taurus to the fertile plains of northern Syria. Yamhad, the powerful state centred on Aleppo, which had given refuge to Zimri-Lim of Mari when a fugitive from Shamshi-Adad and had subsequently been an erstwhile ally of Hammurabi of Babylon, was temporarily reduced to vassalage by Hattusilis, though subsequently it recovered its independence. Mursilis I, the adopted heir of Hattusilis, repeated his predecessor's exploits in Syria, finally destroying the city of Aleppo. It was then that he made the famous raid down the Euphrates which ended in the destruction of Babylon and the elimination of its First Dynasty. However, despite the striking military achievements of which the Hittite ruling caste was capable, its social organization lacked stability, and the victorious Mursilis, who himself had been adopted as heir after an unsuccessful insurrection by the former crown prince, returned with his plunder from Babylon only to be assassinated by his brother-in-law, Hantilis.

The Hittite devastation of Babylon had left the land wide open to the hordes of the Cassites, a racial group from the Zagros. Individual Cassites are found in Babylonia already during the early part of the First Dynasty, and it has been mentioned (see above, page 73) that Hammurabi's successor had a clash with Cassite military forces east of the Tigris. From this time onwards Cassites began to settle in the north-east of Babylonia under their own kings, and it was one of these rulers, Agum II (Agukakrime), who came to settle as king of Babylon after that city had been plundered by Mursilis. He apparently managed to extend his authority up the middle Euphrates as far as the kingdom of Hana, and also claimed the kingship of Gutium in the hills east of Assyria.

With the Hittite sack of Babylon and the Cassite invasion the political achievements of Hammurabi had been finally brought to an end. Babylonian culture, however, continued to exercise a vast influence throughout the Near and Middle East. Not only did the Cassite kings adopt the language and cuneiform script of Babylonia, but dialects of Akkadian were widely employed for official business far outside Babylonia and Assyria. A fortunate discovery at the end of last century by a peasant woman at El Amarna* in Egypt revealed some of the diplomatic correspondence which had passed around 1400 B.C. between the kings of Egypt on the one hand and the kings of the Hittites, Mitanni, Assyria and Babylonia and princes of various cities in Syria and Palestine on the other; almost throughout the language is Akkadian – albeit in some cases heavily influenced by the native tongue of the writer – so that it was clearly the recognized language of civilized intercourse between nations. Even in Ugarit in Syria, where a quite distinct Semitic language was spoken, and where a distinct alphabetic system of cuneiform writing had been invented (this

* Often wrongly called Tell el Amarna, on the incorrectness of which see Sir Alan Gardiner, *Egypt of the Pharaohs* (1961), page 220.

being employed above all for the native Canaanite literature), Akkadian was used to a considerable extent for juridical texts.

At the same time that Babylonia fell under the control of the Cassites, Assyria and much of the rest of the Near East south of the Hittite area was coming under the waxing influence of yet another racial and cultural group, the Hurrians. These people, long known in the Old Testament as the Horites or Horims* (*Genesis* xiv. 6; *Deuteronomy* ii. 12), spoke a language having no recognized affinities except the later Urartian. They must have reached the mountains north of Assyria, presumably from the Caucasus region, in the second half of the third millennium, before the Agade period; two inscriptions of the Agade period, one in Akkadian and one in Hurrian, show that there was already a Hurrian kingdom centred on the city of Urkish in the Habur region west of Assyria. This early Hurrian kingdom was, how-ever, probably an isolated and special case, since the documents from other cities, such as Nuzi, Arrapkha and Tell Brak, which were later leading centres of Hurrian influence, show at this early period only the slightest trace of Hurrian elements in the personal names. The southward migration was still under way during the Third Dynasty of Ur, and documents of that period show heavy Hurrian influence in the personal names occurring in documents from Dilbat, not far from Babylon, suggesting the presence of a colony there. At the beginning of the second millennium the evidence of personal names shows the presence of Hurrians over a wide area. They can be traced in the documents of the Assyrian colony in Cappadocia, and are strongly represented in Nuzi and Arrapkha in the Kirkuk area east of Assyria, and in the Syrian cities of Qatna, Alalah and Ugarit. At Mari a number of ritual texts in the Hurrian language have been found.

Mursilis I, in his thrust to Babylon, had encountered hostile Hurrian princes on the upper Euphrates. These were peripheral to the central area of Hurrian power, which in the mid-second millennium was the Habur region. After the murder of Mursilis, dynastic confusion seriously weakened the Hittite state for several generations, and it was during this time that there arose the

* *sic* in A.V. of *Deuteronomy* ii. 12.

important state of Mitanni with these Hurrians as its nucleus. This state at its greatest extent stretched from Lake Van to the middle Euphrates and from the Zagros to the Syrian coast.

The kings of Mitanni bore not Hurrian but Indo-European names, whilst the old Indian gods Mitra, Varuna, Indra and the Nasatiyas were worshipped. In Hurrian documents, particularly those concerned with horses and warfare, technical terms occur which have cognate forms in Indo-Aryan. It is also significant that unlike all the earlier peoples of the Ancient East, amongst whom burning of the corpse was rare and sometimes regarded as a horror transcending death itself, burning was the proper mode of disposal for the bodies of the early Mitannian kings. All this points to the presence of an Aryan warrior caste ruling over a largely non-Aryan population. There is some evidence of the same kind, though less cogent, pointing to the presence of Indo-Aryan elements amongst the Cassite ruling caste also.

Our main knowledge of the state of Mitanni comes from the Egyptian diplomatic archives (on cuneiform tablets) found at El Amarna (see page 76); though these begin only after 1450 B.C., it is clear that by that time the Mitannian rulers represented an established dynasty. A number of earlier Hurrian princes, bearing Aryan names, are in fact mentioned in certain texts containing legendary material, and these may represent some of the early kings of the Mitannian dynasty. The first Mitannian king of whom we have sound historical knowledge is, however, Parattarna, who appears just after 1500 B.C. as the ruler of a powerful kingdom controlling vassal states in Syria and in a position to stand as an equal with Egypt and Hatti. The next prominent Mitannian ruler was Saussatar, a contemporary of Tuthmosis III of Egypt (1490–1436 B.C.), with whom he had diplomatic relations, despite the fact that Tuthmosis in his numerous campaigns into Syria came into conflict with a number of local Hurrian rulers, thereby encroaching on the Mitannian sphere of influence in the south-west. Saussatar's successor, Artatama, gave a daughter in marriage to Tuthmosis IV (1413–1405 B.C.), creating a relationship which involved an alliance between the two; and a similar relationship was created between

78

the successors of the two kings, Amenophis III (1405–1367 B.C.) and Shuttarna II (end of reign by 1390 B.C.). Under these kings Mitanni still controlled Assyria, and Artatama was apparently able to employ an Assyrian deity, Ishtar of Nineveh, to increase his credit at the Egyptian court; a letter to Amenophis III from Artatama's grandson Tushratta, announcing that Ishtar of Nineveh had expressed a desire to visit the Egyptian court again, refers to a former visit of the statue in the time of one of Tushratta's predecessors. Obviously Ishtar of Nineveh had a high reputation internationally, which must certainly have reflected lustre upon her guardians.

Meanwhile the Cassite dynasty in Babylonia had consolidated its position and succeeded in once again unifying the country and in protecting it from the pressure of Assyria (now under Mitannian vassalage) and Elam. In domestic policy Cassite government seems to have been, to judge by the extant economic documents, mild and unoppressive. One of the factors which most affected the reaction of the ancient city-states to a king was his attitude to the prescriptive rights of their citizens, involving in many cases exemption from taxes or corvée duties. Extant charters promulgated by the Cassite kings indicate that they were liberal rulers in this respect, and the apparent absence of native risings may well have been related to this liberality. It may also help to explain the relative ease with which the Cassites were ultimately able to displace the Sealand dynasty. From the First Dynasty of Babylon to the end of Babylonian history the possibility of administering the southern half of Babylonia depended to a considerable extent upon the co-operation of a few key cities, notably Erech and Ur, and the economic and administrative policy of the Cassites may well have influenced these cities in their favour before a military coup was ever attempted: these southern cities were certainly subsequently treated with honour by the Cassites, some of whose kings undertook building operations and other works of piety there. The actual military conquest of the Sealands was effected by Ulamburiash, during the reign of Kashtiliash III, his older brother. Ulamburiash, after serving as viceroy or sub-king in the Sealands, succeeded to the Cassite throne in about 1450 B.C., and in doing so re-united Babylonia after a partition lasting over two hundred years. Discord did, however, break out again later, requiring Agum III, the son and successor of Ulamburiash, to undertake a further campaign against the Sealands.

By the time of Kara-indash, the successor of Agum III, Babylonia was of sufficient importance to warrant an exchange of ambassadors with the Egyptian court, whilst an alliance is indicated by the sending of a Cassite princess to join the harem of Amenophis III.

The three successors of Kara-indash are, like him, named in the El Amarna correspondence, the second of these successors, Kurigalzu I, being the most important of the Cassite kings. He maintained good relations with Amenophis III and was in a position to undertake a successful campaign against Elam; this power was anciently associated with Sumer, and was always, in times of Babylonian weakness, apt to involve itself in affairs in southern Babylonia. Kurigalzu, however, took the initiative and remained firmly in control in that area, where he engaged in temple restoration and similar works in Erech, Ur and Eridu. The work for which he is best known to posterity is the fortified new capital built by him; the remains of this are to be found at Aqarquf near Baghdad, the ziggurat (see plate 4A) being a prominent feature of the landscape and one of the essential sights for any tourist in Iraq.

The strong position of Kurigalzu owed something to the fact that Mitanni had by his time been seriously weakened by a combination of events. After the murder of Mursilis I the dynastic confusion and political and military weakness of the Hittites had at first permitted Hurrian princes to gain control of much of north Syria, from where raids were made into Hittite territory, whilst the kingdom of Mitanni proper, closely allied with Egypt, appears to have controlled certain areas of Hittite border-lands. This situation ended with the accession about 1375 B.C. of the vigorous ruler Shuppiluliuma, the beginning of whose reign approximately coincided with a dynastic crisis in the Mitannian succession. At the death in about 1390 B.C. of Shuttarna II, son and successor of Artatama, who like his father had been closely linked with Egypt, the kingdom was split by civil war, and the heir was murdered by an anti-Egyptian party. The next son, Tushratta, ultimately managed to assert himself as king of Mitanni, but the earlier Hurrian homeland, south of Lake Van, broke away forming a separate kingdom under a younger brother of Tushratta, another Artatama. Artatama received support from Shuppiluliuma in an unsuccessful invasion of Mitanni proper, whilst Tushratta revived the old alliance with Egypt. Unfortunately for Mitanni, the religious conflicts which came to a head in Egypt in the reign of Akhenaten (1367–1350 B.C.) were already serving to deflect the royal attention from foreign affairs, and Tushratta seems to have obtained very little Egyptian support in the course of the events which followed.

Warfare broke out between Tushratta and Shuppiluliuma, who invaded north Syria, gaining control of a number of Hurrian states in Syria, erstwhile vassals of Mitanni or Egypt. It is curious that the land of Mitanni was never directly attacked by Shuppiluliuma, and it has been suggested that this was a matter of deliberate policy dictated by the desire to avoid action which might unite the lesser Hurrian princes on the side of Mitanni. After a troubled reign, towards the end of which he regained much of the territory west of the Euphrates lost in his early days, Tushratta was murdered (*circa* 1350 B.C.) by a son, acting for the party supporting Artatama, who thereupon claimed the kingship of Mitanni. A younger son of Tushratta, Mattiwaza, managed, however, to escape, and, after an abortive attempt to secure sanctuary in Babylonia, fled to throw himself upon the mercy of Shuppiluliuma, who was then in the strong though potentially embarrassing position of having both the legitimate and usurping claimants to the throne of Mitanni dependent upon him.

A beneficiary of the troubles which had fallen upon Mitanni was Assyria. For a time Assyria had been in thrall to Mitanni, but the disputed succession at the death of Shuttarna II, when Artatama seems to have encouraged an attack on Tushratta, allowed it to recover a measure of independence. Burnaburiash II, the second successor of Kurigalzu I on the throne of Babylon, after resuming relations with Egypt which had been allowed to lapse, complained when Ashur-uballit I of Assyria had an independent ambassador accepted at the Egyptian court, and this suggests two things. These are, firstly, that Assyria was re-emerging as a state of international importance, and secondly, that Babylonia was attempting, unsuccessfully, to replace Mitanni as the suzerain of Assyria. However, the fact of Assyria's re-emergence had to be accepted, and an alliance between Babylonia and Assyria was brought about by the marriage of a daughter of Ashur-uballit to the second Kara-indash, the son and heir of Burnaburiash II. Assyria had thus become a power to reckon with, and it may have been Shuppiluliuma's recognition of the need for a reliable buffer against this re-awakening state which led him finally to assist Mattiwaza, the rightful heir of Tushratta, who had been cooling his heels at his court for ten years, to regain by force of arms the throne of Mitanni, now reduced in size and importance by the loss of Carchemish to a Hittite sub-king.

Three further Hurrian princes of Mitanni (in its reduced form generally known as Hanigalbat) are known, but the epoch of Mitanni was past. Shattuara I was defeated and made vassal by Adad-nirari I (1307–1275 B.C.), whilst his successor revolted only to be conquered afresh. The kingdom of Hanigalbat was finally brought to an end and made into an Assyrian province when Shalmaneser I (1274–1245 B.C.) conquered the last king, Shattuara II. This conquest is of some sociological interest in that over 14,000 prisoners were deported: this marks an early instance of the deportation policy later extensively operated in the Assyrian empire.

3

The Rise of Imperial Assyria

IN the Mitannian period the fortunes of Assyria, which had emerged to temporary prominence in the time of Shamshi-Adad, had sunk to a very low ebb. With the decay of Mitanni Assyria once again became a force in international politics, and the reign of Ashur-uballit I (1365–1330 B.C.) may be taken as marking the beginning of the long process by which Assyria ultimately rose to supremacy in the Near East. As the result of the marriage of his daughter to Kara-indash,* the son of Burna-buriash II (1375–1347 B.C.) of Babylonia, Ashur-uballit brought about an alliance between Babylonia and Assyria; this alliance, by which Babylonia was able to obtain Assyrian backing to deal effectively with the Sutu (troublesome nomads who infested the middle Euphrates region and harassed both states with border raids), continued after the death of Burnaburiash. Yet though the Babylonian dynasty was now related to the Assyrian, Babylonian support for a pro-Assyrian policy was by no means unanimous and soon a revolt broke out in Babylonia, in the course of which the legitimate successor was killed and replaced by a usurper, Nazi-bugash. Ashur-uballit of Assyria was, however, in a position to make a vigorous and effective intervention, liquidating the anti-Assyrian party at the Babylonian

* The name also appears as Kara-hardash. There are discrepancies between two cuneiform accounts of these events, and it is not clear whether or not this person was ever king of Babylonia.

83

court and installing Kurigalzu II (1345–1324 B.C.), as king.

The good relations between Babylonia and Assyria did not outlive Ashur-uballit, and upon the accession of Enlil-nirari (1329–1320 B.C.) to the throne of Assyria war broke out, possibly as a result of Kurigalzu II – a direct descendant of Ashur-uballit of Assyria – claiming the succession in Assyria for himself. The war was indecisive, but seriously weakened Babylonia, so that it was unable to prevent an Elamite raid which possibly reached Babylon itself and the neighbouring city of Borsippa. Assyria was left in a stronger position, and Arik-den-ilu (1319–1308 B.C.) won victories over the peoples to the east and north of Assyria. At this time there is the first evidence of a new wave of invaders from the west, known as the Ahlamu, Aramaeans closely associated with the Sutu already mentioned; Arik-den-ilu inflicted a military defeat on these Ahlamu, taking much spoil. His son Adad-nirari I (1307–1275 B.C.) further extended the influence of Assyria, winning victories over the Cassite Nazi-maruttash and over the regions to the north. Hanigalbat, which had been in a state of vassalage, now, under Hittite influence, rebelled, bringing down upon itself a punitive campaign. Shalmaneser I (1274–1245 B.C.) found it necessary to solve the problem of the western border by incorporating Hanigalbat into Assyria as a province, with the deportation of many thousands of the population. He secured the northern frontier, at least for the time being, by a defeat of the newly emergent power of Uruatri (Urartu), first mentioned in this reign; this power, probably at this time a confederation of tribal chieftains and princedoms rather than a single kingdom, was in the eighth century to become the primary rival of Assyria. It was under Shalmaneser I that Kalhu (Calah of the Old Testament), the later capital city, was founded.

A rapid decline set in after this period. Tukulti-Ninurta I (1244–1208 B.C.) began his reign in the Shalmaneser tradition, with conquests accompanied by extensive deportations in the west and north, including the Nairi lands, south-west of Lake Van. Even more spectacular was his conquest of Kashtiliash IV (1242–1235 B.C.), by which he brought Babylonia under Assyrian rule for the first time: a propaganda poem, know as the *Tukulti-*

Ninurta Epic (see page 429) was written to recount this exploit
from the Assyrian point of view. Tukulti-Ninurta's policy in the
south was first to establish Assyrian administrators in Babylonia
proper, and then deal militarily with peripheral territories from
Mari and Hana to the Elamite border. Tukulti-Ninurta carried
away the statue of Marduk from Babylon to Ashur, and it has
been suggested that, paradoxically, Tukulti-Ninurta's conquest of
Babylon was ultimately a victory of Babylonian culture over
Assyrian, in that it damaged Assyrian unity of purpose by leading
to dissension in Assyria between those who wished to adopt
Babylonian religion and those who wished to follow the simpler
paths of their forefathers. Thus, an *akitu* ritual found at the city of
Ashur relates not to the national god Ashur but to Marduk of
Babylon. However, a recent study has shown that the undoubted
increase in the use of the element 'Marduk' in Assyrian personal
names at this time was part of a general trend of developing
cosmopolitanism, in consequence of which a number of other
gods besides Marduk received increased popular recognition.

Later in the reign of Tukulti-Ninurta a rapid and as yet un-
explained change of policy occurred on the part of this king,
whose military activities entirely ceased. One can make various
speculations as to the cause of this state of affairs, but it is likely
that the military expansion during nearly a century was proving
a severe economic strain. It is also possible that racial movements
at this time, of which the Philistine entry into Palestine was a
part, and which was the immediate cause of Hittite collapse, may
have contributed to Tukulti-Ninurta's inertia by cutting off the
Assyrian sources of metal. Whatever the effective cause, it
ultimately produced such internal stress that revolt broke out,
and Tukulti-Ninurta died at the hands of a son, Ashur-nadin-apli
(1207–1204 B.C.). Assyria now entered upon a period of such
weakness that the two successors of Ashur-nadin-apli were actually
vassals of Babylonia. This state of vassalage was, however, short-
lived, and an anti-Babylonian revolt brought to the throne yet
another son of Tukulti-Ninurta, Enlil-kudur-usur (1197–1193
B.C.), who led an attack upon Babylonia. As a result of a mis-
translation it was formerly held that both the Assyrian king and the

Cassite ruler fell in battle. This has now been shown to be a false interpretation of the text concerned, but what actually happened is not altogether clear. The crucial passage, as translated by H. Tadmor (*Journal of Near Eastern Studies*, XVII (1958), page 131), says:

> Enlil-kudur-usur, king of Assyria and Adad-shum-usur, king of Babylonia, battled. While Enlil-kudur-usur (and) Adad-shum-usur ... were engaged in battle Ninurta-apal-Ekur the son of Ili-ihadda, a descendant of Eriba-Adad, returned to his land [Ashur]. He summoned his big army and came to Ashur in order to conquer it. A fire broke out in the camp of Adad-shum-usur; he turned and went back to his country.

Part of the same sequence of events is mentioned in the *Assyrian King List*, which reads:

> Ninurta-apal-Ekur ... descendant of Eriba-Adad, went to Karduniash [i.e. Babylonia]; he came up from Karduniash, he seized the throne [of Assyria], and ruled three [or, according to a variant reading, thirteen] years.

Dr. Tadmor interprets the two pieces of evidence as follows. Ninurta-apal-Ekur, an Assyrian nobleman and a distant descendant of Eriba-Adad I, was living in Babylonia, backed by the Cassite king. He advanced with the Babylonian army and during the campaign he managed to muster an army of his own and seized the Assyrian throne. A conflagration in the Babylonian camp caused the Babylonians to break off the attack on Assyria and return home.

Ninurta-apal-Ekur reigned over Assyria from 1192–1180 B.C. Assyria itself, though secured from nominal dependence upon Babylonia, was at this time reduced geographically to its narrowest limits; it consisted of no more than the homeland proper, and Ninurta-apal-Ekur's son and successor, Ashur-dan I, did not claim the title of king but contented himself with that of Prince (*Ishshaku*, an Akkadianized form of the old Sumerian word *Ensi*). The lands east of Assyria have always, up to our own day, been subject, in the absence of a strong administrative authority, to pillage and looting at the hands of tribesmen from the hills. Some of the hill country in question, east and south of the Lower Zab, had formerly been controlled by Babylonia, which was thus in a position to guard the security of the trade routes; but Tukulti-Ninurta's attack upon Babylon had seriously weakened the southern kingdom and produced internal tensions which led to the overthrow of the Cassite dynasty and its ultimate replacement, after a period of confusion, by a national Babylonian dynasty in Isin. In such a situation Babylon was unable effectively to protect the lands in the region of the Lower Zab, and with the trade routes upon which it depended subject to dislocation from marauding tribesmen from the hills, Assyrian commerce must have fallen into a desperate situation. It was probably for this reason that Ashur-dan I, and possibly his father before him, undertook military activities in the lands beyond the Lower Zab.

The new dynasty in Babylonia, generally known as the Second Dynasty of Isin, consolidated its position during the long reign in Assyria of Ashur-dan I (1179–1134? B.C.), and at the death of the latter seems to have been in a position to meddle in the Assyrian succession. It thereby secured a brief reign of its protégé Ninurta-tukulti-Ashur, who restored to Babylon the statue of Marduk which had been in Assyrian possession since the time of Tukulti-Ninurta.

Little is known about the early kings of the Second Dynasty of Isin before the reign of the most important of them, Nebuchad-rezzar I, ruler from 1124 to 1103 B.C. By his time the central administration in Babylonia was fully in control of events throughout the homeland, and he was in a position to turn his attention to foreign affairs. As always in times in which a strong central government was lacking, Babylonia had long been subject to raids from Elam, in the course of one of which a statue of Marduk had been taken from Babylon. Nebuchadrezzar defeated the forces of Elam, recovering the statue of Marduk and bringing back captive the statue of an Elamite god. To the north-east he dealt with the Lullubi* in the Qara-dagh area, who had been a

* The names and geographical area strongly suggest that this people and the Quti (see page 88) were the descendants of the Lullu and the Gutians of the third millennium, referred to on page 52.

scourge of Babylonia since at least the time of Sargon of Agade; he also attacked some Cassites in the mountain area, presumably some of the original stock which had never descended to settle in Babylonia. Babylonian suzerainty over Assyria also continued during part of his reign until the able ruler Ashur-resh-ishi (1133–1116 B.C.), finally secured independence for the northern kingdom.

By this time pressure of Aramaeans pushing in from the west was being felt both by Assyria and Babylonia. The immediate effects were, however, more serious for Assyria than for Babylonia, since in encroaching upon the Habur region these Aramaeans threatened the security of the Assyrian trade routes leading to the Syrian coast and Anatolia. The vigorous Ashur-resh-ishi undertook a successful campaign against the Ahlamu, the branch of the Aramaeans in this area, and in an inscription he describes himself as 'the one who crushes the widespread forces of the Ahlamu'. Trade routes along the eastern border were similarly threatened by hill tribes, and here Ashur-resh-ishi undertook campaigns against the Quti and the Lullubi; it is probably in this region that Assyrian and Babylonian interests came into conflict over the question of spheres of influence. This resulted in the Babylonian king attempting an invasion of Assyria from the south – an attempt which ended in a complete Assyrian victory.

Ashur-resh-ishi was succeeded by an equally able son, Tiglath-Pileser I (1115–1077 B.C.) whose exploits are known in some detail from a large clay prism. It was this king who established the main lines of the policy of frightfulness followed by later Assyrian kings. It presents, however, a very one-sided picture to think of the Assyrians as butchers falling upon harmless villagers going about their own peaceful business. In fact, there were at this time large scale racial movements in progress which, if not checked, might well have destroyed, or drastically altered the course of, Mesopotamian civilization. Iron had by this time come into general use, and the main source of this vital metal for the whole of the civilized world was in a certain area of the Hittite kingdom. Into the region east of this there had thrust from the north a horde of people called the Mushku, known from the Old Testament as

Meshech. Shortly after the accession of Tiglath-Pileser a large group of this people, numbering twenty thousand, pushed south-wards, invading the Assyrian province of Kummuh. Tiglath-Pileser reacted energetically, marching north-westwards to the Tur Abdin and attacking the invaders there, defeating them decisively and then marching eastwards across Kummuh to deal with elements of the native population which had come to the assistance of the northern invaders. In campaigns of subsequent years Tiglath-Pileser extended and strengthened his control over the region to the north, north-west and north-east of Assyria, ultimately getting farther into Asia Minor than any of his predecessors. Having settled these areas, he was then in a position to go west to the Syrian coast, to obtain timber and the other benefits of trade with the Phoenicians. Gubla, Sidon and Arwad quickly paid tribute, and Tiglath-Pileser gives an account of a sea trip on which he was taken, in the course of which a *nahiru* (some kind of whale?) was caught and given to him. A similar compliment was paid him by the king of Egypt who sent a present of a live crocodile.

Although he had been able to check the menace from the north, Tiglath-Pileser still had, like his successors for generations, continuous trouble with the hordes of Aramaeans pressing in from the west. Many references have already been made to pressure of peoples from the desert, and it has always been a recurring problem which affected all the lands of the fertile crescent: the migration of Abraham and the invasion of Palestine under Joshua are both parts of this same phenomenon. However, the pressure was particularly severe on the western borders of Babylonia and Assyria at the end of the second millennium, and the specific reason for this remains to be explained. Just before 1200 B.C. the Hittite power collapsed before an invasion by land and sea of a group of peoples out of eastern Europe, of whom the Philistines were a part. Ramesses III of Egypt inflicted a naval defeat on them, keeping them out of Egypt, but they secured control of Syria and Palestine, with results illustrated by the *Book of Judges*. This may well have led to tribal movements away from Palestine which would accentuate the pressure farther eastwards. There are also indications that it was at about this time that the kingdom of Saba (the biblical Sheba) took its rise, and this may in turn have caused some of the southern tribes to move northwards.

The precise relations between Assyria and Babylonia during the reign of Tiglath-Pileser I is uncertain. There were raids in both directions, and the Assyrians may have gained some border territory, but there is no indication that Tiglath-Pileser ever attempted to conquer Babylonia. There would, indeed, have been little or no advantage to Assyria in so doing. All the principal trade routes of Western Asia were in Assyrian hands and trade flowed uninterrupted, with great profits to Assyria as the middle-man, from the Phoenician sea-coast and the ports of north Syria to Babylonia.

The material prosperity which ensued from this thriving trade enabled Tiglath-Pileser I to engage in munificent works of temple-buildings and restoration, ensuring for him a legacy of high respect from his successors.

The Aramaean pressure already so evident intensified after the reign of Tiglath-Pileser I, and his successors inherited national decline and disaster. Tiglath-Pileser's immediate successor was his son, Asharid-apal-Ekur II, but he reigned for only a year, to be followed by Ashur-bel-kala (1074–1057 B.C.), who is known to have undertaken campaigns against both Urartu and the Ara-maeans: it is interesting to notice that despite the racial conflict the gods of the Aramaeans were admitted to the Assyrian pan-theon, for this king invoked 'the gods of the land of Amurru' against anyone who destroyed an inscription of his. As happens with men faced with a common threat, Ashur-bel-kala enjoyed good relations with his Babylonian contemporary, Marduk-shapik-zer-mati (1080–1068 B.C.). The latter, under attack from a confederacy of Aramaean chiefs, went to the Assyrian capital to seek military aid (which Ashur-bel-kala was apparently unable to provide), but on his return found Babylon already occupied by the invaders. Ashur-bel-kala was in no position to upset the situation, and recognized the usurping Aramaean king, Adad-apal-iddinam (1067–1046 B.C.), with whom he made a marriage alliance. Increased Aramaean pressure and interference with the trade routes probably led to economic difficulties and social unrest, and Ashur-bel-kala's reign was marked by a rebellion, whilst at his death the legitimate succession was interrupted.

For over a century the situation in Assyria and Babylonia is very obscure, although the sequence of kings is known. This was a period of great stress. The dislocation was so bad that a chronicle relating to about 990 B.C. records that 'for nine years successively Marduk did not go forth, Nabu did not come', that is to say, the New Year Feast, at which Marduk of Babylon went out of the city to a shrine called the *Akitu*-house (see below, page 384) and Nabu of Borsippa visited him on his return to the city, was not carried out. As this was the central event of the Babylonian year, this record indicates that the administration was completely disrupted at this time. Assyria likewise suffered, and under Ashur-rabi II (1010–970 B.C.) the Assyrian settlements on the middle Euphrates were lost to the Aramaeans, although farther north the same king was able to undertake an expedition to the Amanus.

The Aramaean racial movement which had caused so much dislocation in Assyria and Babylonia lost momentum after about 1000 B.C., and the tribes began to consolidate into a number of small states. In Palestine the Hebrew tribes, which although not Aramaean yet contained an Aramaean element, crystallized at the same time and as part of the same process into the two kingdoms of Israel and Judah; and we also read in the Old Testament of other, more purely Aramaean, states, such as Damascus and Bit-Adini ('the house of Eden', properly to be rendered 'Beth-Eden', of *Amos* i. 5).

The presence of these many small and often mutually hostile groups in the Euphrates valley must initially have imposed considerable hardship upon the Assyrians, in that there was no power able to keep open the trade routes upon which the Assyrian way of life depended, whilst the multitude of separate territories through which the caravans had to pass involved a great burden of customs duties upon the merchandise they carried. In Babylonia tribesmen had been able to pass through the lands between the great cities and settle on the eastern bank of the Tigris, whilst the southern marsh area, the 'Sealands', was occupied by the Kaldu, a people related to the Aramaeans, and these were in a position to interfere with sea-borne trade up the Persian Gulf. With the gradual settlement of the Aramaean tribes, their consolidation into settled states and their recognition of the connection between their own prosperity and unhindered international traffic, trade once again began to flow across Syria. One can best visualize the changed situation by comparing the turbulent state of affairs represented in the *Book of Judges* with that under Solomon two centuries later.

Thus in Assyria the new dynasty founded by Ashur-rabi II at the beginning of the tenth century faced slowly improving conditions. Ashur-dan II (933–912 B.C.), of this dynasty, son of a little-known Tiglath-Pileser II (966–935 B.C.), relates in an inscription how he rebuilt the 'Craftsmen's Gate' in Ashur, first erected by the celebrated Tiglath-Pileser I and subsequently allowed to fall into ruins. As this was the main gate in Ashur for traffic with the west, this implies an improvement in trade connections in that direction.

It was, however, under Ashur-dan's son, Adad-nirari II (911–891 B.C.), that Assyria once again entered upon a period of conspicuous economic and military expansion. In accordance with customary Assyrian strategy his first campaign was directed to the lands south of the Lower Zab. As happened earlier when Ashur-resh-ishi undertook campaigns in the same direction, this brought Assyria into collision with Babylonia, whose king was attempting to establish his authority beyond Babylonia's northern borders, in the Jebel Hamrin area south of the Lower Zab. The Assyrian king was able to clear the Babylonian army from this region and annexed – together with towns farther south – the vital city of Arrapkha, which as an important garrison town was always a key to Assyrian control of the hill country beyond its eastern borders.

With the eastern and southern borders secure, Adad-nirari was now able to turn to the provinces west of the Tigris, where much of the region still remained in the hands of Aramaean tribesmen and their confederates. He was able to compel these nomads to recognize his suzerainty formally by the payment of tribute: at the same time a number of towns along the middle Euphrates, formerly Assyrian possessions, were taken, refortified and used to protect the trade routes.

A little farther north, around Nisibin, in the area then known to the Assyrians as Hanigalbat, was one of the many small kingdoms which had crystallized as the movement of Aramaean nomads lost their impetus. These people, known as the Temanites (probably unconnected with the biblical 'Teman', which was part of Edom) proved an obstinate enemy. In several vigorous campaigns, in which all the resources of Assyrian siege warfare were employed, Adad-nirari wiped out this independent kingdom city by city, finally taking the king captive to Assyria, after various local princes of the area had met that fate. Adad-nirari subsequently extended Assyrian control to the banks of the Habur, taking Guzana (Gozan of 2 *Kings* xvii. 6 and elsewhere, later the capital of an Assyrian province and today Tell Halaf) and making its prince a vassal. Other local city princes along the Habur were likewise compelled to recognize Assyrian sovereignty by the payment of tribute; by such means Adad-nirari secured control of the Habur along its whole length, gaining security for his western borders. His southern borders were guaranteed by treaty with the Babylonian king, concluded after the military conflict of the two powers at the beginning of Adad-nirari's reign. The treaty document is commonly known as the *Synchronous History*: this name derives from the fact that as the basis for the peace settlement it gives a chronological account of the boundary disputes between the two powers in the past. This document is thus a valuable source for arriving at the chronology of the period prior to Adad-nirari II.

Another group of documents valuable for establishing Assyrian chronology begins in this reign. These are the *limmu* lists. At the beginning of a reign the New Year Festival at the capital was presided over by the king, and in subsequent years by the high royal officials in turn. During his period of office the official concerned was called the *limmu* and the year in Assyria was dated by this: dates on legal documents were given in the form 'in the *limmu* year of So-and-so'. Lists of these *limmus* have been found, enabling the complete series to be established from the beginning of the ninth century to nearly the end of the seventh century B.C. Many of these entries are accompanied by brief references to campaigns or other events; by good fortune the entry for one particular year mentions an eclipse of the sun in a certain month, and as the date at which this event took place can be calculated precisely by modern astronomers, this fixes one year exactly. Through this one certain year the whole series of more than two and a half centuries can be fixed. Thus during most of the first half of the first millennium B.C., beginning with Adad-nirari's reign, events can be accurately dated to within a year.

In Adad-nirari's reign tribute flowed in from vassals in the form of chariots, corn, horses, golden vessels, wine and food in general, cattle and sheep. This increased wealth was, however, not squandered but, at least in part, applied to the economic development of Assyria. Adad-nirari specifically states:

> I built administrative buildings throughout my land. I constructed irrigation machines throughout my land. I increased grain stores over those of former times. ... I increased the number of horses broken to the yoke. ...

It was probably also Adad-nirari who, in an inscription in which the name of the writer does not appear, claimed to have imported Bactrian camels into Assyria and bred them in herds.

The entente with Babylonia seems to have facilitated trade with the south, for another inscription relates to the rebuilding of the quay wall at Ashur, obviously in the interests of riverine transport: a similar quay wall of huge blocks of stone from rather later has been uncovered at Nimrud (see below, page 181), and there is no doubt that there was at certain periods a flourishing river-borne traffic at the Assyrian capital.

For the next sixty years Assyrian kings followed a consistent policy of consolidating the work of Adad-nirari. The security of central Assyria demanded the control, by garrisons and conquest, of the hill peoples to the north and east, and also of the trade routes into Cappadocia and to the Mediterranean. Implementation of these desiderata inevitably led sooner or later to a change in status of the outlying territories from tribute-paying vassals to provinces fully incorporated into the empire. Adad-nirari's son and successor, Tukulti-Ninurta II (890–884 B.C.) employed his first four years in campaigns against the Nairi country, south-west of Lake Van, ultimately succeeding in subjugating the king of Nairi and making him a vassal of Assyria, bound by oath and responsible for supplying horses for a force of light cavalry, now for the first time being introduced into the Assyrian army. Later in the same year Tukulti-Ninurta was able to deal with the mountainous region east of Assyria, gaining security for the area between the Upper and Lower Zab. This cleared the way for an expedition southwards down the region east of the Tigris, which he undertook the next spring. The reigning dynasty in Babylonia was so very weak that Tukulti-Ninurta was able to get right to Dur-kurigalzu (modern Aqarquf, near Baghdad) and to Sippar without apparently arousing Babylonian opposition. From Sippar the Assyrian army proceeded, still apparently unopposed, across to the Euphrates, beating the bounds of Assyrian territory up to the Habur. He then went northwards along that river as far as Nisibin, receiving tribute from local rulers on the way. In a short final diversion he made a raid upon Mushku in Asia Minor. In internal affairs Tukulti-Ninurta continued the policy of Adad-nirari, assisting agricultural development and corn production by irrigation and forced settlement of population.

Tukulti-Ninurta's son, Ashur-nasir-pal II (883–859 B.C.) (see plates 28, 29), has generally been castigated by modern commentators for the frankness and apparent relish with which he relates the brutalities he inflicted on the conquered, and in the heat of moral indignation his undoubtable administrative achievements have been largely overlooked. Ashur-nasir-pal's first activities were in connection with the mountain areas to the east, where he extended Assyrian control among the mountain folk and secured recognition of Assyrian suzerainty by people hitherto outside the Assyrian orbit: two subsequent campaigns were necessary to bring Zamua (the highly defensible Sulaimania valley, of which the passes can very easily be closed) into subjection. To the north-west of Assyria proper, in the Kashiari mountains, lay an area which had once belonged to Assyria but had long ceased to recognize the central government. This region Ashur-nasir-pal now took, creating a new administrative district centred on Tushkhan (modern Karkh), where Assyrian colonists were settled: a subsequent rebellion in the area was visited with dire reprisals in the offending districts.

In the west there had emerged another powerful Aramaean state, Bit-Adini (see above, page 91), with its capital at Til-barsip (modern Tell Ahmar), south of Carchemish. At the beginning of Ashur-nasir-pal's reign this state stirred up trouble amongst the Assyrian tributaries along the Habur and upper Euphrates, the focal point being the city of Suru in Bit-Halupe, where a puppet king from Bit-Adini had been set up. Prompt and vigorous action by Ashur-nasir-pal secured the submission of the insurgents, and the capture of the pretender. The list of loot removed from the palace and temples of the defeated city gives some idea of the wealth of the riverine Aramaean states: in addition to the usual items of cattle and sheep, silver and gold, there are mentioned vessels of bronze, iron and lead, precious stones, unguents, textiles of wool and linen, and cedar and other aromatic timbers. The rebel leaders suffered death by impaling, flaying alive or by immurement in a wall, and these severe measures secured peace for the area for five years. Then trouble arose from the opposite direction, Nabu-apal-iddin of Babylonia sending a force of three thousand troops to assist the rebellious Suhu tribe on the middle Euphrates, which moved up-river to take the stronghold of Suru as a base. The main Assyrian army, at the time in the province of Kummuh, made a rapid march down the Habur, and inflicted a severe defeat on the insurgents in a two-day battle, the political effects of which were felt, according to the claim of Ashur-nasir-pal's annals, far afield:

> I established power and might over the land of Suhu. The fear of my dominion extended to the land of Karduniash [north Babylonia], and the chilling terror of my arms overwhelmed the land of Kaldu [Chaldaea, south Babylonia].

However, in the following year there was another rebellion in the area, though it was easily crushed: Bit-Adini may have been behind this latter rebellion, for in the succeeding year Ashur-nasir-pal made an attack upon one of its cities, compelling the recognition of Assyrian suzerainty. This opened the way to the Syrian coast, and in the following year the Assyrian army marched, virtually unopposed, to the Mediterranean, by way of Carchemish and the Orontes, receiving tribute from the small states *en route* and from the coastal cities as far south as Tyre.

For the remaining fifteen years of the reign of Ashur-nasir-pal the empire enjoyed a considerable measure of peace and stability. Only one campaign is recorded, that of 866 B.C., when action was necessary against insurgents in the Kashiari hills, a region highly susceptible to pressure from the potentially powerful state of Urartu (biblical Ararat, later Armenia).

In domestic policy Ashur-nasir-pal's most notable achievement was the founding of his new capital at Kalhu (biblical Calah, modern Nimrud), which was ceremonially opened in 879 B.C. A stele discovered at Nimrud in 1951 describes this event, and other aspects of his domestic policy, in detail. The town was largely settled with peoples captured and deported in his various campaigns. Irrigation projects were carried out to increase the fertility of the region, and gardens were planted with a large range of plants and trees collected by the king in the course of his campaigns. Temples were built and ornamented, and a zoological garden established in which the king housed and bred herds of bulls, lions, ostriches and apes. Wild elephants were presented to him by his governors, all these beasts, except the apes, being destined to be cut down by the king in the ceremonial hunt. The dedication of Calah was marked by a huge feast in which nearly seventy thousand people, workers, male and female, government officials and representatives of tributary and subject races, came together for ten days of rejoicing.

Shalmaneser III (858–824 B.C.), Ashur-nasir-pal's son and successor, continued and consolidated the work of his father. The early years of his reign were directed to strengthening the Assyrian position in the west: in his first year Shalmaneser made an expedition, apparently unopposed, to the Mediterranean coast. At this stage Bit-Adini, which Ashur-nasir-pal had made tributary, was attacked by Assyria and brought under more direct control. Whether Shalmaneser's attitude was due to some overt hostile action on the part of Bit-Adini, or whether it resulted simply from a recognition of a potential danger, is not known. Certainly Bit-Adini could command considerable military resources, for it took three campaigns before Shalmaneser was able to capture the king and royal family. In the course of the same campaigns Shalmaneser re-asserted Assyrian control over the regions immediately to the north, where there had been an extension of Urartian influence.

The defeated Bit-Adini was now re-settled and organized as an Assyrian province, Assyria thereby acquiring a firm control over the important trade routes along the upper Euphrates to Cilicia and Asia Minor. This was a serious threat to the rich and powerful trading states of Syria, which proceeded to form an anti-Assyrian coalition headed by Adad-idri* (the biblical Ben-hadad) of Damascus, and including contingents from Israel and Ammon. A full-scale attack on the Assyrian army near Qarqar proved disastrous to the Syrians, their losses totalling, according to the most modest Assyrian claim, fourteen thousand out of a total of seventy thousand under arms.

Assyrian policy now suffered a temporary diversion, action becoming necessary in Babylonia where rebellion had broken out against the Assyrian-supported native king. It is clear that by this time the whole of southern Babylonia was already in the control of local Chaldaean chieftains, and Shalmaneser found it necessary to make a show of force against these tribesmen, to compel acknowledgement of suzerainty by the payment of tribute.

Shalmaneser now turned his attention to the west. In 849 B.C. the last of the nominally independent states on the upper Euphrates, Carchemish, already a tributary, was brought under direct Assyrian rule. The Syrian coalition farther west remained, how-

* An alternative reading proposed for this name would make it much nearer to the biblical form.

ever, a serious threat to the Assyrian position in the area, and despite a number of small Assyrian successes in the next four years, in the last campaign of which a huge Assyrian army of one hundred and twenty thousand was put into the field, no conclusive defeat of the coalition proved possible at this time.

Four years later, when Shalmaneser again directed the main weight of Assyrian power against the west, the situation had changed; by that time two of the leading personalities of the Syrian coalition, Ahab of Israel and Adad-idri of Damascus, had died, the latter murdered, according to the Old Testament narrative (2 *Kings* viii. 15), by his servant Hazael, who then usurped the throne. With the death of Adad-idri the coalition had fallen apart, and the *Second Book of Kings* gives a picture of the dynastic and inter-state intrigues and conflicts which followed. Hazael, without an ally, lost sixteen thousand men and much of his territory, though Damascus itself was not taken; Jehu of Israel (see plate 35) and the kings of Tyre and Sidon paid tribute to Shalmaneser, whilst Egypt showed a friendly interest by a gift of dromedaries, a hippopotamus and other exotic animals. During the eight following years Shalmaneser was largely engaged in consolidating his position in the west: he extended his authority north-westwards over Tabal (biblical Tubal) and Que (Cilicia), making them tributaries. In central Syria he inflicted a further defeat and loss of territory on Hazael.

Assyria was thus in complete control of Syria and of all the trade routes into Asia Minor. Iron production, still largely a monopoly of Asia Minor, thus became subject to Assyrian control, just as timber production was in the Lebanon and as the silver mines were in the Amanus. Syrian craftsmen and artists were likewise at the disposal of Shalmaneser, and many of them were transported to the Assyrian cities; this recalls the way in which in the previous century Solomon had employed craftsmen from Tyre and Gebal (classical Byblus north of Beirut) as carpenters, masons and bronze-smiths in building his palace and temple (1 *Kings* v. 18, vii. 13, 14). Vast quantities of carved ivories have been found in the excavations at Nimrud (Calah), especially in the fortress built by Shalmaneser in the lower city, and it has now been established that these were the work of Syrian craftsmen. Fortifications built by Shalmaneser are also known in the city of Ashur, and these reveal the use of methods first introduced to Mesopotamia at that period but always followed in later times: these may have been influenced by Syrian practice, for certainly the science of fortification was well developed in the Syrian cities, several of which were able to withstand repeated sieges. The famous 'bronze gates' of Balawat – metal bands on gates, decorated in repoussé work with scenes from Shalmaneser's principal campaigns (see plates 33 and 34) – may likewise owe something to metalworkers of the type of Hiram of Tyre in the previous century, who 'was filled with wisdom and understanding and cunning, to work all works in brass [i.e. bronze]' (I *Kings* vii. 14).

Apart from a minor disturbance in the west, when Assyria reacted vigorously to avenge a loyal vassal slain in an insurrection, the remainder of Shalmaneser's military activities were concerned with the north and east. Urartu, itself probably by this time already under pressure from barbarians from the north, was a growing threat to Assyria, not so much in the region where the two kingdoms marched as in the extreme north-west and extreme east, where the two empires were in competition for the control of vital trade routes, in one case that from Syria into Asia Minor and in the other that coming from India and China across Iran. Thus Shalmaneser's remaining campaigns consisted of inconclusive clashes with the forces of Urartu, and punitive expeditions against reluctant tributaries in the Kurdish hills and Iran.

The final years of Shalmaneser's long reign were marked by a great rebellion in the homeland. In the Mesopotamian conception, as also (as Sir James Frazer exhaustively established) in many other parts of the world, kingship was regarded as a function, often semi-divine, bestowed by the gods for a limited period, and able to be withdrawn at the will of the gods. In many parts of the world the king was put to death when he ceased to exhibit sexual vigour, and in Babylonia the king made an annual token surrender of his kingship to the god. There was no such annual surrender in Assyria, but it has been suggested that the term of kingship there was nominally limited to thirty years. This is suggested by the circumstances in which the king acted as *limmu* official (see above, page 93). The king always acted as *limmu* at the annual festival in the first full year of his reign, being represented in other years by a sequence of high officials. Shalmaneser III officiated not only at the beginning of his reign but again in his thirty-first year, which suggests that he was formally commencing a second term of kingship. It was shortly after this that Ashur-danin-apli, a son of Shalmaneser, led a rebellion which secured extensive support, including that of the important and ancient cities of Nineveh, Ashur and Arbailu (modern Erbil). The matter cannot be proved, but there may have been some direct connection between the renewal of Shalmaneser's kingship and the insurrection.*

The son accepted by Shalmaneser as his successor was Shamshi-Adad V (823–811 B.C.), who was engaged in the early years of his own reign, as well as before his father's death, in putting down the widespread rebellion led by Ashur-danin-apli. He finally established his position with help from the king of Babylonia, whose suzerainty he was compelled to admit in a formal treaty. Once Shamshi-Adad had, with Babylonian assistance against the rebel cities, gained control of his land, his first three campaigns were directed against the northern and north-eastern regions. Urartu continued to constitute a growing threat, and much of Shamshi-Adad's military activity in these years was directed to securing a suitable pro-Assyrian attitude from the chieftains of the Nairi lands, which formed a buffer south-west of Lake Van. Farther east a new racial movement was complicating the situation. Here the Medes, a branch of the Iranian people first mentioned in the reign of Shalmaneser III, had recently migrated into the area south-east of Lake Urmia. A show of force against the Median towns secured a wholesome respect for Assyrian authority, substantial loot, and the ready payment of tribute by the other small states of the eastern area.

* It is an interesting parallel, though not necessarily a significant one, that it was when the present Emperor of Ethiopia had just completed thirty years of his reign that there was an abortive revolution in 1960 aimed at replacing him by his son.

Shamshi-Adad was now in a very different position from when he had had need of Babylonian help to put down rebellion in his own cities. He was now strong enough to turn his attention southwards from Nairi, marching down the Tigris to the territory from which the Cassites had earlier descended upon Babylonia, which was traditionally recognized as being in the Babylonian sphere of influence. Having conquered this area and deported the population, Shamshi-Adad crossed the Diyala into the eastern part of Babylonia proper, where he proceeded, according to his own account, to devastate the whole border area, looting, burning the towns and cutting down plantations. The king of Babylonia, Marduk-balatsu-iqbi, the successor of the one who had assisted Shamshi-Adad to gain his throne, was now understandably alarmed, and organized a coalition of Elam, Namri (a state north of Elam and not to be confused with Nairi), the virtually autonomous Chaldaean tribes of south Babylonia, and some of the remaining Aramaean tribes east of the Tigris. The Babylonian coalition was however defeated in a pitched battle, and it appears that the following years saw Assyrian military activity in central and southern Babylonia. Shamshi-Adad offered sacrifices in the city of Babylon itself in 811 B.C.

It is not clear what prompted Shamshi-Adad's attack upon Babylonia, nor what advantages he hoped to achieve. There is no reason to suppose that Babylonia in any sense represented a military threat to Assyria, either alone or as a potential ally of Urartu. The Assyrian action may have been concerned with trade routes. The Kaldu (Chaldaean) tribes clearly had a very strong grip on the south of Babylonia at this time, and according to the *limmu* lists Shamshi-Adad conducted a campaign against that particular area. The cities of southern Babylonia had in earlier times been, as they were later again to be, of considerable importance as entrepôts for trade from India and Arabia passing northwards *via* Oman and Bahrein (Tilmun). At a later period racial movements in northern Iran certainly dislocated the trade routes in that area and led to the use of routes through south Iran (Elam) and Babylonia: it is thus possible that the Median incursion was already producing this effect, and that Shamshi-Adad was attempting to acquire control of the trade route from the southern ports through Babylonia and along the Tigris. There is, however, at present no proof of this, though it may be noted that Shamshi-Adad's successor, Adad-nirari III, specifically claims to have made the kings (that is, the sheikhs) of Kaldu his vassals, imposing tribute and taxes upon them.

An inscription reveals that Adad-nirari III did not ascend the throne until the fifth year of his nominal reign, which gives grounds for supposing that his mother, Sammu-ramat, was regent after the death of Shamshi-Adad. This lady, whose name and story are preserved in mutilated form in the Greek Semiramis, was obviously a very important person, for she had a memorial stele at Ashur along with those of kings and high officials of Assyria, whilst she is (quite exceptionally for a woman) mentioned along with the king in a dedication inscription.

The reigns of Adad-nirari III (810–783 B.C.) and of his son Shalmaneser IV (782–772 B.C.) witnessed a great increase in the power of Urartu, and there were a number of clashes between the two powers, particularly in the Median area. In the north-west also, Urartu made substantial encroachments on territories previously controlled by Assyria, in particular Melid. This encouraged the defection of other north Syrian states, and a re-organized coalition, which included Damascus, Que, Gurgum and Sam'al, attacked the pro-Assyrian state of Hamath (well-known from the Old Testament). Adad-nirari gave prompt assistance to his loyal vassal, in a series of campaigns first driving a wedge between the northern allies and Damascus, and then making a direct attack upon the latter, which surrendered and paid a rich tribute. The other states of Syria followed suit in accepting the suzerainty of Adad-nirari. Urartian pressure in the west thus had the result of moving Assyria's main centre of control in Syria southwards. An incidental result, referred to in the Old Testament (2 *Kings* xiii. 24–25), was that, as a result of the weakness of Damascus, Jehoash of Israel was able to regain certain border territories taken from Israel during the period of supremacy of Damascus.

Urartian advances along almost the whole of the northern

frontier of Assyria continued during the years succeeding the reign of Adad-nirari III, and, in the absence of a ruler of his calibre to minimize the consequences of this trend, Assyria suffered severely. Urartu gained a firm grasp on the regions immediately south of Lake Urmia and so controlled the trade routes from northern Iran. More serious still was the situation in the west, where the Urartian thrust dispossessed Assyria of almost the whole region north and west of Carchemish, thereby taking from Assyria control of the metal trade of Asia Minor. Besides the economic consequences, this must have had a direct effect upon the military efficiency of Assyria, since almost the whole of the area upon which Assyria depended for the supply of horses was now in Urartian hands. The economic effects of the cutting of the routes into Asia Minor led to disturbances in Syria, and a number of campaigns were undertaken against Hatarikka (biblical Hadrach), Arpad and Damascus. It is during this period of Assyrian weakness that the reign of Jeroboam II of Israel is to be placed: the lack of any strong central control enabled him to extend his borders at the expense of Hamath and Damascus (2 *Kings* xiv. 25–28). There was also trouble from the districts along the Tigris south of Assyria proper, whilst within Assyria itself the economic distress arising from the cutting of trade led to revolts in a number of cities. In 746 B.C. there was a revolt in the capital itself, Calah, and Ashur-nirari V, the last of the three kings following Adad-nirari III, was murdered with the whole of the royal family.

The revolution which overthrew the old royal family brought to the throne the most able Assyrian ruler for over a century. Of the antecedents of Tiglath-Pileser III, the Pul of the Old Testament, little is known. In one inscription he claims descent from Adad-nirari III, and there is no good reason to question the claim. His name 'Pul' was used not only in the biblical *milieu* but also in Babylonia, and the suggestion has been made that this was his own personal name, the name of Tiglath-Pileser being a throne-name adopted at his accession as portending his intention to follow in the steps of the all-conquering ruler who first bore that name.

4

Assyrian Supremacy

WHEN Tiglath-Pileser III came to the throne Assyria was in a difficult, even desperate, military and economic situation. Control of much of the western territories had been lost. Babylonia was virtually in a state of anarchy, and the mountain regions to east and north of Assyria were largely in the control of Urartu. The succeeding forty years saw Assyria recover and consolidate control of all its old territories and re-establish itself firmly as the pre-eminent military and economic power of the Near East. These striking changes did not result from any cardinal improvement in the external situation – for indeed pressure from the north intensified during this period – but may be laid very largely to the credit of the administrative reforms undertaken by Tiglath-Pileser in re-organizing his civil service and the provinces. The provinces were in some cases reduced in size, in the interests both of efficient administration and also of pre-venting the acquisition of a dangerous measure of power by provincial governors. The re-organized provinces in turn were sub-divided into smaller areas under the control of lesser officials, who were generally speaking responsible to the governor but who had the right to make complaints and representations directly to the king: this was a useful safeguard and check upon the efficiency and loyalty of the provincial governors. A system of posting-stages (for the introduction of which the Persians have generally been given the credit) was organized across the empire, enabling the rapid passage of messengers between the king and his governors; the latter were also required to make regular reports themselves on the affairs of their provinces. In the buffer-states beyond the Assyrian provinces Tiglath-Pileser and his successors used the system of appointing a representative to watch Assyrian interests at the Court, control being exercised indirectly through the local royal family. Such local ruling families, provided they paid the tribute for which they were responsible and accepted the direction of the Assyrian Resident in matters of foreign policy and trade, were assured of the backing of the imperial power in the event of internal revolution or enemy attack: examples of this may be seen in the Old Testament, as for example when Ahaz of Judah, threatened by a coalition of Syria and Israel, appealed, not in vain, to Tiglath-Pileser (2 *Kings* xvi. 7–9).

Tiglath-Pileser's first military concern was the settlement of his southern border, where the Aramaean tribes along the Tigris had been giving trouble since the early years of Ashur-dan III (771–754 B.C.). The tribal lands of Puqudu (biblical Pekod), east and north of modern Baghdad, were conquered, re-settled and made part of the province of Arrapkha, which now became a long sausage-shaped territory right down the eastern side of the Tigris, and the key to the Assyrian control of Babylonia. The tribal areas farther to the south-east, between Babylonia proper and Elam, were made into a separate province under Assyrian administration. Such action strengthened the position within Babylonia itself of the native king, Nabu-nasir, with whose authority west of the Tigris Tiglath-Pileser did not interfere. Nabu-nasir maintained civil peace and a pro-Assyrian policy within Babylonia until his death in 734 B.C. Tiglath-Pileser was thus relieved of the anxiety of disturbances in the south, and was able to turn his attention to the main adversary of Assyria, Urartu. The general lines of the events of the following years can be reconstructed from the somewhat fragmentary annals of Tiglath-Pileser, whilst illuminating details are here and there supplied by the dispatches sent to the king from his generals, governors or intelligence officers on the Urartian borders. The sequence of events is at some points rather uncertain because of the difficulty of knowing in what order to piece together the fragments of the annals.

The counter-pressure upon Urartu began with an expedition into the Namri lands, the region north of Zamua (modern Sulaimania *liwa*), itself north of ancient Elam. The Assyrian army met with no Urartian forces (suggesting that the intelligence and communication system of Urartu fell far short of its Assyrian counterpart in efficiency) and was able to mop up piecemeal the opposition shown by local native leaders. Local rulers who came to terms with Tiglath-Pileser were left in place as vassals, subject to the payment of tribute, whilst other territories were placed under the direct rule of Assyrian officials and re-populated with tribesmen from east of Babylonia. However, the raid had alarmed Sardur of Urartu, who proceeded to organize a strong anti-Assyrian coalition in the West. The Assyrian intelligence and communication system proved more reliable than the Urartian had been in the previous year, and Tiglath-Pileser, his army now well equipped and supplied as a consequence of the vast numbers of horses, mules, camels, and cattle captured in his expedition to Namri, in which he had also acquired at least fifteen tons of copper, marched against the forces in the west. The Assyrian army apparently ambushed the forces of the coalition, which met with a disastrous defeat. Vast numbers of prisoners were taken – according to the annals nearly seventy-three thousand – though Sardur himself, by fleeing from his camp by night and leaving behind all his possessions, even his jewellery and personal seal, managed to escape and cross the upper Euphrates into his own land.

Those states not implicated in the coalition hastened to pay tribute to Tiglath-Pileser. The following years were spent in consolidating the Assyrian position in the west, where extensive administration changes were made; a number of kingdoms which had previously had the status of vassals but which had proved unreliable were converted into Assyrian provinces under direct rule. Isolated trouble spots remained, and during the following three years a number of anti-Assyrian activities in Syria are referred to both in the annals and in the royal correspondence. Such activities ranged from overt military action to local rioting against unpopular economic measures. A letter to Tiglath-Pileser from the Assyrian official putting affairs in order in the commercial sea ports of Tyre and Sidon gives an instance of the latter. The Assyrian authorities had imposed a tax upon the timber brought down to the quays from the Lebanon, whereupon the outraged citizens had rioted and killed the Assyrian tax collector. The Assyrian military governor reacted energetically, bringing into the towns concerned a contingent of Itu'a troops, a tough tribal body used for police duties amongst troublesome urban populations: the presence of these troops, so the writer tells the king, 'put the people into a panic'. When the lumber merchants had been sufficiently impressed by the demonstration, the Assyrian official instructed them to carry on with felling as before, but put an embargo upon export to Egypt or the Philistine cities.* This event may be referred to in *Isaiah* xxiii. 5. The contemporary kings of Judah and Israel, respectively Azariah and Menahem, were both involved in disturbances at this time, and 2 *Kings* xv. 19–22 describes how Menahem imposed a capital levy to pay the fine of a thousand talents of silver exacted by Tiglath-Pileser III (Pul).

It appears that in the following years Tiglath-Pileser III himself remained in Syria using this as his base, whilst units of his army were engaged in the north and north-east following up the Assyrian victory over Sardur. The Nairi lands south-west of Lake Van and north of the old province of Tushkhan, and the tribal area on the upper reaches of the Great Zab, were once again conquered; this time they were subject to the policy, extensively employed by Tiglath-Pileser III, of deportation of the native population and re-population of the land by captives from other parts of the empire. The whole region was placed under Assyrian governors.

The withdrawal of part of the Assyrian army must have given the petty rulers of Syria and Palestine a false idea of Assyrian strength, whilst economic measures of the type reflected in the

---

* The reference is to Ashdod, Gaza and the other towns of the coastal plain of southern Palestine, formerly the centre of Philistine power and still in the late eighth century occupied, according to 2 *Kings* xviii. 8 and 2 *Chronicles* xxviii. 18, by people designated as 'Philistines'.

1　White temple at Warka

2A Cone mosaics from Warka

2B Silver model of a boat, from the 'royal tombs' of Ur

3A The ziggurat of Ur

3B Ruins of ziggurat of Borsippa (modern Birs Nimrud), possibly the original 'Tower of Babel'

4A   Ruins of ziggurat of Dur-Kurigalzu (modern Aqarquf)

4B   Ruins of processional way at Babylon

5 Lion head in copper, with bitumen core (from Ubaid)

6   The Ishtar Gate (reconstruction)

7   (*opposite*) Harp (restored) from the 'royal tombs' of Ur

8A Alabaster vase from Warka

8B Early Sumerian dress (carving on a stone mace-head)

9A Cattle trough from Jemdet Nasr (early third millennium)

9B Gaming board from Ur (first half of third millennium)

10   The god Imdugud ('Severe Wind') with stags; an early Sumerian monument probably concerned with fertility

11A Cult object, usually described as a lamp cover, in the form of intertwined snakes (late third millennium)

11B Inlaid panel from Ur (first half of third millennium), showing religious representations related to a fertility cult

12   War scene from the 'Standard of Ur' (first half of third millennium)

13B Main drain of a palace (third millennium)

13A Lavatory, with remains of seat of bitumen (third millennium)

14   Head of Sargon of Agade

15A Window grille (third millennium)

15B Bronze 'frying pan'

164. Rock-relief of Naram-Sin in Qara Dagh, near Iran-Irin.

embargo on the export of timber southward from Lebanon may have created some hardship. In 734 B.C. there was trouble in south Palestine, where according to 2 *Chronicles* xxviii. 16–21 a coalition of Edom and the Philistine cities attacked Judah under Ahaz, whilst farther north an anti-Assyrian coalition was formed between Syria and Israel. According to the consistent story of the Old Testament (2 *Kings* xvi. 5–9 and the passage quoted from the *Book of Chronicles*) Ahaz maintained a pro-Assyrian policy throughout and called to Tiglath-Pileser for assistance. This was given, the Assyrian king easily disposing of the opposition from the Philistine cities and Syria, and intervening in Israel to replace king Pekah by Hoshea. The *Book of Chronicles* complains that Ahaz had to make a payment to Tiglath-Pileser despite his loyalty, a statement confirmed in part by the annals; it seems likely, if the account in the *Book of Chronicles* is otherwise reliable, that the payment demanded was what was known as *kitru*, that is, a payment for the military assistance given to a vassal in trouble.

Trouble broke out in a fresh quarter in 734 B.C., at the death of the pro-Assyrian king of Babylonia, Nabu-nasir. The Chaldaean tribes had already been in virtual control of all the Sealands (the southernmost part of Babylonia) for nearly a century, and were gradually extending their control up the Euphrates and Tigris. In the confusion which broke out on the death of Nabu-nasir, Ukin-zer, head of the Chaldaean tribe of Bit-Amukkani, revolted against the legitimate pro-Assyrian successor, Nabu-nadin-zer (734–732 B.C.), and ultimately seized the throne. The non-Chaldaean tribes east of the Tigris in north Babylonia remained loyal to Assyria, as did also (in general) the native Babylonians, although the usurper had seized the capital itself. A letter is extant giving an account of a parley at the gates of Babylon between Assyrian officials and the people barricaded within; it is curiously reminiscent of the interview between the Rab-shakeh official and the ministers of Hezekiah at the siege of Jerusalem in 701 B.C. (2 *Kings* xviii. 17–36). There is some indication that Assyrian diplomacy succeeded in sowing discord between the sheikhs of the Chaldaean tribes, thereby neutralizing part of their forces, including those of Marduk-apil-iddina, an ambitious and able leader who was later to head a rebellion himself and who occurs in the Old Testament under the name of Merodach-baladan (*Isaiah* xxxix. 1). In dealing with Ukin-zer Tiglath-Pileser's strategic planning revealed its value. The attack was directed from the province of Arrapkha, the Assyrian army by-passing the concentration of cities at the neck formed by the convergence of the Euphrates and Tigris, and entering Babylonia across the Tigris from a point farther south. Loyal tribesmen were set to guard the routes whilst the army moved westwards to the Babylonian cities. Babylon was taken from the insurgents, who fled to Sapia, the chief city of the Bit-Amukkani tribe, deep in the marsh country on the lower Euphrates. An Assyrian army pursued Ukin-zer, besieging him in his city and devastating the territory of Bit-Amukkani and the other insurgent Chaldaean tribes, Bit-Shilani and Bit-Sa'alli. Merodach-baladan and the other sheikh who had come to terms with Assyria had their tribal territories spared. The whole affair occupied three years. Babylonia was now placed under the hands of Assyrian administrators and in 729 B.C. Tiglath-Pileser himself 'took the hands of the god' in the New Year ceremony at Babylon, thereby being formally invested by the national god Marduk with kingship over Babylonia; no Assyrian king had held the kingship of Babylonia for over four and a half centuries. Tiglath-Pileser died in 727 B.C., leaving Assyria in control of an empire extending from the Persian Gulf to the borders of Egypt and including a substantial part of Anatolia and Cilicia.

Assyrian military operations as far south as Gaza, coupled with the dislocation of Egyptian trade by the Assyrian embargo upon export of timber to Egypt from the Lebanon, constituted a threat to Egypt. By the time of the short and ill-documented reign of Shalmaneser V, Tiglath-Pileser's successor, the Egyptians had embarked upon a diplomatic counter-offensive, attempting to subvert the petty kingdoms of Palestine and south Syria. Hoshea of Israel was implicated, bringing down upon himself attack by Shalmaneser (2 *Kings* xvii. 3–5). The capture of the Israelite capital Samaria after a three-year siege was followed by the usual policy of deportation (2 *Kings* xvii. 6), in which the 'ten lost tribes of Israel' – the fate of which has given play to much sterile fancy – were moved to the province of Guzanu (Gozan) and to the region south-east of Lake Urmia.

The actual capture of Samaria, attributed in the Old Testament to Shalmaneser, was claimed by his successor, Sargon. Possibly the latter had been the general directing the operation on behalf of Shalmaneser.

The beginning of the reign of Sargon (721–705 B.C.) was marked by fresh trouble in Babylonia. There the sheikh of the tribe of Bit-Yakin, Merodach-baladan, a brilliant diplomatist, as 2 *Kings* xx. 12 ff. (relating to a later period) shows, had worked himself into a very strong position. He had made himself paramount sheikh of the Chaldaeans, secured the support of the Aramaean tribes in Babylonia, and arranged an alliance with Elam, the old rival of Babylonia in southern Iran; immediately upon Sargon's accession Merodach-baladan entered Babylon and claimed the kingship of the country by 'taking the hands of Bel' at the New Year Feast of 721 B.C. The Assyrian army apparently attempted to repeat the manoeuvre down the east of the Tigris by which Ukin-zer had been defeated, but on this occasion was confronted by the Elamite army at Der. An engagement ensued and the Assyrian army, though unbroken, was unable to cross into metropolitan Babylonia and had to return to Assyria. With his hands full in other quarters Sargon was compelled to leave Merodach-baladan undisturbed as king for ten years. During this time the economy of the great cities in Babylonia suffered severe damage, the tribes-men interfering with the free flow of trade and practising various extortions upon the towns; Chaldaean control was highly unpopular with the great cities of Babylonia and down to within a few years of the final extinction of Assyria itself these cities were contantly appealing to the Assyrian king for assistance against the havoc wrought by Chaldaean tribesmen.

The immediate cause which compelled Sargon to leave Babylonian problems unresolved was that rebellion had broken out in Syria. This came very conveniently for Merodach-baladan, but that he was behind the affair, as he was in the similar case related in the *Second Book of Kings* (2 *Kings* xx. 12–17), cannot at present be proved. The rebellion was headed by Hamath, the sole remaining independent princedom in Syria: Sargon met and defeated the rebels at Qarqar in 721 B.C., and in sequel converted Hamath into an Assyrian province. In a little tributary state farther south the statesman and prophet Isaiah pointed out the lesson to be drawn from these events, regarding Assyria as the whilom instrument of God:

> Ho Assyrian, the rod of mine anger, the staff in whose hand is mine indignation! I will send against him a profane nation, and against the people of my wrath will I give him a charge, to take the spoil and to take the prey, and to tread them down like the mire of the streets. (*Isaiah* x. 5–6.)

Gaza, with some timorous backing from an Egyptian general named in the Old Testament as 'So' (2 *Kings* xvii. 4), was also involved; but in an engagement at Rapihu the Egyptian general (according to the Assyrian account) ignominiously ran off, leaving the king of Gaza to certain capture and probable torture and death. Possibly it was with this incident in mind that the Rab-shakeh made his mordant comment upon the value of Egyptian alliance:

> Thou trustest upon the staff of this bruised reed, even upon Egypt; whereon if a man lean, it will go into his hand, and pierce it: so is Pharaoh king of Egypt unto all that trust on him. (2 *Kings* xviii. 21.)

Apart from an abortive attempt by the city of Ashdod, on the coast of southern Palestine, to organize with vague Egyptian backing an anti-Assyrian coalition in 712 B.C. in concert with Judah, Edom and Moab, Sargon had no further trouble from Palestine. Isaiah refers (*Isaiah* xx. 1–6) to the capture of Ashdod by the Assyrian Commander-in-Chief, and points out to the people of Jerusalem the futility of looking to Egypt for military support against Assyria.

As with Tiglath-Pileser, the major problem of Sargon was the pressure from the north. Urartu, the history and culture of which are gradually becoming known as the result of Turkish and Russian excavations and which proves to have been one of the great powers of the ancient East, was itself under intense pressure from migrating Iranian tribes moving south and west from the steppes of Russia. One body of these migrants had already settled by the reign of Sargon, forming a kingdom of some importance known as Zikirtu, east of Lake Urmia. The main body was, however, the Medes, still loosely organized on a tribal system under a large number of semi-independent chieftains. Rusas I (733–714 B.C.), the energetic son and successor of the Sardur defeated by Tiglath-Pileser III, attempted, with a good deal of success, to come to terms with three Median chieftains, securing their military support against Assyria and also, it must be supposed, their co-operation in keeping open (in return for the subsidies usual in such cases) the trade routes from farther east which were essential to the prosperity of Urartu. At about this period the main route from Iran came up the western shore of Lake Urmia, east of Lake Van to Erzerum (where eighth-century Urartian bronze objects have been found) and on to Trebizond on the Black Sea, which, according to tradition, was founded in 757 B.C. Urartu was certainly enjoying the benefits of trade with Iran and perhaps India: this is indicated, according to authorities on technology, by objects mentioned when Assyria sacked some of the Urartian cities in 714 B.C. There is a possibility that Urartu may (through intermediaries) have had trading relations with lands beyond Greece, since allegedly Urartian bronzes are found in Etruscan tombs. One scholar goes so far as to suggest, on the basis of art motifs, that silk caravans reached Urartu all the way from China. Some of the trade taking the northern route through Erzerum and Trebizond had probably earlier passed across Assyria to the Mediterranean ports; the desire to cut the Urartian route and re-divert this trade, and the concomitant commercial prosperity, into the old channels may be seen as one reason for Sargon's subsequent campaigns in the region.

South of Lake Urmia, between Assyria and the territories of 'the mighty Medes', lay the lands of the Mannaeans (the Minni of Jeremiah li. 27), Assyrian tributaries. Shortly after the accession of Sargon trouble arose in the eastern part of this region, fomented by the king of Zikirtu, behind whom, in turn, was the shadow of

Rusas. Sargon dealt with the rebels, but the trouble recurred after two years, when Rusas engaged in overt military action. Sargon again reacted vigorously, and having disposed of the rebels appointed Ullusunu as king of the Mannaeans. Two years later, Ullusunu was attacked, through internal intrigue and external military action, by Urartu, but again Sargon was equal to the situation, giving Ullusunu all necessary aid and making a punitive raid over the southern borders of Urartu. In addition to these repeated interventions by Urartu in the affairs of a loyal Assyrian vassal there were pin-pricks in the form of frontier clashes; to deal with the problem, plans for a large-scale invasion of Urartu were laid. Intelligence reports streamed in to the Assyrian king, from Assyrian officials and from foreign spies. One writer suggested that the king should make a direct attack upon Urartu, and seemed confident that the capital Turushpa would fall to Assyria. Another letter spoke of an insurrection inside Urartu, and expressed the view that the tribes concerned would be pro-Assyrian in the event of an invasion. An invasion was evidently expected, for a disaffected informant from Urartu spoke of 'when the forces of the King of Assyria come for the third time'.

The forces of Sargon made the planned major demonstration against Urartu in the summer of 714 B.C. The itinerary and events are known in some detail from a famous report on the affair, drafted in the form of a letter to the god Ashur (see below, page 370). Sargon took his armies into the province of Zamua (see above, pages 95, 107), from where he marched northwards to the territory of his loyal vassal, Ullusunu the Mannaean, which he proposed using as a base against Zikirtu and Urartu. Sargon then led his forces eastwards to the territory of Zikirtu, where he captured and destroyed the principal fortified cities, doing this without opposition as Metatti of Zikirtu had gone forth to join up with the Urartian army and defend the passes. Sargon now turned westwards again, and learnt that the main Urartian army and its allies were defending a low pass in the mountains. At this point, as later with Alexander the Great in India, Sargon's forces, tired from the hardships of the campaign in difficult country, appear to have come very near to mutiny.

Unable to rely on the discipline of his main army, Sargon led an attack with his personal bodyguard and household troops on one wing of the opposing force, which he shattered. Thus heartened, the main Assyrian army fell upon the Urartian coalition, breaking their lines and causing panic. The Urartian general led his own force in a hurried but disciplined retreat, but the other contingents, now a leaderless and terrified rabble, fled in disorder over the mountains, where great numbers perished from the severe climatic conditions. The defeat and flight of the main Urartian army was a shock to Urartian morale, and Sargon was able to penetrate, with negligible opposition, deep into Urartian territory. Rusas left his capital Turushpa (which Sargon apparently did not venture to attack) and took to the mountains, where, according to Sargon, he eventually died of grief:

> He took to bed like a woman in confinement; he refused to let food or drink touch his mouth; he brought on himself an incurable illness.

The central administration of Urartu having apparently broken down, Sargon was able to march north of Lake Van, looting and destroying without opposition as he went. On the return journey from the north towards Assyria a solitary ruler, Urzanu of the Urartian city-state of Musasir, failed to give formal recognition to Sargon as overlord. Despite the city's remote situation and difficult approaches, through forests and mountains, Sargon found it necessary to make an example of Musasir, holy city though it was. Allowing his main force to continue on the way to Assyria, Sargon led a contingent of a thousand cavalry against the city, meanwhile issuing a general decree to Assyrian officials throughout the northern area that the flight of the prince of Musasir should be prevented. The reason for this instruction, and the necessity for taking action against Musasir at all, becomes clear in what follows. The city was a great cult-centre of Haldi, the national god of Urartu, and Sargon arrived to find a coronation feast in progress at which Haldi was appointing a successor (perhaps the prince of Musasir) to the vacant kingship of Urartu. The god himself and his consort were taken captive, the citizens deported, and a vast treasure of precious metals and bronzeware taken back to Assyria.

Though the Urartian capital was not taken, and though, according to an Urartian inscription giving the other side of the picture, Rusas (before succumbing to the fatal illness attributed to him by Sargon) made a successful counter-attack to regain Musasir, yet Sargon's expedition was effective in that, except for intrigues in the Tabal region (Tubal of *Ezekiel* xxxviii. 2, 3, etc.), there was no further trouble instigated by Urartu during the following twenty years or more.

Sargon was now free to deal with Babylonia. Ten years of tribal rule and dislocation of trade had served to render the inhabitants of the great cities very ready for Assyrian intervention, whilst internal affairs in Elam now paralysed the Elamite king's power to react. Sargon carried out the usual strategy of attack down the east of the Tigris; this forced a southward retreat of the Chaldaean army, whereupon the cities of north Babylonia took the opportunity of opening their gates and welcoming Sargon. Sargon duly 'took the hands of the god' at the New Year Festival in Babylon, but adopted the old title 'vicegerent (of the god)' rather than 'king' in Babylonia. Merodach-baladan's territory was overrun and his principal fortress captured; he himself, upon making submission to Sargon, was reinstated as chief of the tribe of Bit-Yakin.

Meanwhile intelligence reports reaching Sargon suggested that the successor of Rusas, Argistis, was planning an attack upon Assyria, though in fact the army he was raising may have had another purpose. In any case, in the event it had to be employed for another purpose: in 707 B.C. a great horde of barbarians, the *Gimirraya* (biblical Gomer of *Ezekiel* xxxviii. 6, etc., classical Cimmerians) entered Urartu from the north, defeated Argistis in his attempt to stop them, and passed westwards to Cilicia. Here they came into territory controlled by Assyria, and it is appropriate here to summarize briefly the course of events in this area during the reign of Sargon.

By the early years of Sargon, the interests of Mushku (biblical Meshech, classical Phrygia), a powerful state in south-east Asia Minor, were beginning to come into conflict with those of

Assyria. In 718 B.C. Mushku seems to have been behind a revolt by Carchemish (as a consequence of which the latter was made into an Assyrian province), and in 716 B.C. Sargon took military action against Mushku on the pretence of an encroachment by the latter on territories of the province of Que. After Sargon's successes against Urartu, the latter, thwarted in the east, sought to establish a network of alliances in the west, and succeeded in making common cause with Mushku and in subverting the allegiance of Sargon's principal vassal amongst the princes of Tabal. Sargon was able to deal with this rebel, but Mushku's apparent readiness to give at least moral support to disloyal vassals of Assyria, plus the pressure of Urartu, still proved too strong an unsettling force for some Assyrian tributaries, and in 712 B.C. there was another revolt. The offending territory was brought under direct Assyrian administration, and this and Tabal were fortified as a long wedge separating Mushku and Urartu. In 709 B.C. an attack was made upon Mushku from Que. Possibly from the motive of *Realpolitik*, or because Assyria had shown that all the trade routes from Syria into Asia Minor were firmly in its hand, or perhaps even as a result of the first rumblings of the Cimmerian invasion, the foreign policy of Mushku suddenly changed in favour of Assyria. Its king, Mita (Midas to classical authors), sent a present and sought to make a treaty of friendship with Assyria. Sargon was delighted, and in a letter written by him to his emissary in charge of negotiations, almost certainly his son Sennacherib, he asked that Mita should be informed of his pleasure.

This was the situation when the swarm of Cimmerians appeared in the north-west after the vain attempt of Argistis to stop them. Archaeological evidence points to Calah (still an important administrative centre although during the latter part of his reign Sargon made a new capital farther north at Dur-sharrukin) having been the scene of violent destruction at some time in the last decade of the eighth century B.C. This could be taken as evidence – though there seems to be nothing else to support the hypothesis – of a surprise Cimmerian raid on one or more of the great Assyrian cities. Sargon marched to Tabal in 706 B.C. and met the Cimmerian hordes in battle. Some very enigmatic evidence from a letter has been taken to show that Sargon finally fell in battle, but this conclusion is not undisputed. Whatever the manner of Sargon's death, he certainly died in 705 B.C., and the barbarian hordes moved away into the interior of Asia Minor at the same time.

Sargon's successor, his son Sennacherib (704–681 B.C.), had already had experience as an administrator and soldier on the northern frontier, and a number of reports from him to his father are extant, detailing developments in that area. Thus the fact that Sennacherib took no further action along the northern frontier at his accession is to be explained not as a failure by the son to comprehend the problem, but as the consequence of the father's success in dealing with it.

Profiting by the favourable military situation bequeathed to him by Sargon, Sennacherib's first work – and his most enduring – was the rebuilding of the ancient city of Nineveh and its adoption as the capital: such it remained until the overthrow of the Assyrian empire. Dur-sharrukin (modern Khorsabad), which Sargon had planned and built as a capital and moved to in the final years of his reign, was employed after his death only as a fortress.

The imperial peace was broken after two years by an insurrection in Babylonia. For reasons which can only be the subject of speculation, Sennacherib had omitted to 'take the hands of Bel' in Babylon to mark his assumption there of the kingship or vicegerentship. Merodach-baladan, who had remained faithful to his suzerain Sargon after his reinstatement in 710 B.C., considered the time opportune to make another bid for the kingship of Babylonia. The Chaldaean and Aramaean tribes were behind him, he was assured once again of the support of Elam, and he now put out feelers for a more widely based coalition against Assyria: it is in the years preceding the rebellion of 703 B.C. that the embassy of Merodach-baladan to Hezekiah (*Isaiah* xxxix) must be placed.

At the New Year Festival of 703 B.C. a native Babylonian, possibly nominated as an Assyrian puppet, officiated as king. Merodach-baladan promptly moved with his troops to the capital, deposed the official king, and proceeded to prepare the area of the northern cities against the Assyrian attack which would inevitably ensue. Merodach-baladan's main military formations were Elamite troops, of which a picked body were stationed as an advance post at Cuthah to hold up Sennacherib's advance, the main body being based at Kish. Sennacherib out-generalled the Elamites by sending an advance party to cut off Kish from Cuthah, whilst his main army took Cuthah by storm. The main Assyrian army then met and broke up the allied forces at Kish, and the cities of northern Babylonia were once again in Assyrian hands. Babylon received Sennacherib, as it had done his father, with enthusiasm; and the friendship was reciprocated, as looting by the Assyrians was restricted to the palace of Merodach-baladan.

The Assyrian army then proceeded to subjugate and de-fortify the whole of the Chaldaean area, which by this time was virtually the whole of southern Babylonia. The Chaldaean area was left under Assyrian officials, whilst northern Babylonia was placed under a native Babylonian king, Bel-ibni, one of the many foreign princes who had lived as hostages at the Assyrian court and been educated in readiness for such a situation.

A rebellion which Merodach-baladan had possibly intended to coincide with his insurrection in Babylonia broke out in Palestine in 701 B.C., Hezekiah of Judah being implicated (2 *Kings* xviii. 13 ff.), though against the advice of the greatest of his counsellors, Isaiah. Hezekiah was at this time the most powerful of the petty kings of Palestine, and according to 2 *King* xviii. 8 had established some measure of suzerainty over the Philistine cities, and had also (*Isaiah* xxx. 1–5) once again sought alliance with Egypt. Loyal rulers in the Philistine cities were overthrown, one of them, Padi of Ekron, being incarcerated in Jerusalem. A strong Assyrian force overran Palestine, defeated the Egyptian troops at Eltekeh, took the rebel cities (with the exception of Jerusalem), and rewarded loyal vassals in the Philistine cities with the grant of territories formerly belonging to Judah. Possibly because developments in Babylonia necessitated the early return of Assyrian forces to the homeland, Sennacherib did not press the siege of Jerusalem, and Hezekiah's city was spared by his submission and payment of a heavy indemnity.

In Babylonia, no sooner did the main Assyrian army withdraw than Merodach-baladan returned to his tribe and began again his intrigues with Elam and the Chaldaean and Aramaean tribes. Bel-ibni, lacking control of adequate armed forces, was unable to maintain effective government of the land, and in 700 B.C. it was necessary for an Assyrian army to make another incursion into Chaldaean territory, and a punitive raid over the Elamite border. Bel-ibni was removed, and Ashur-nadin-shum, a younger son of Sennacherib, appointed in his place.

Ashur-nadin-shum reigned in Babylonia for six years. Merodach-baladan died shortly after his accession, but Elam remained a constant threat to the tranquillity of the Sealands, serving as it did as a sanctuary for the disaffected section of the tribe of Bit-Yakin. To deal with this dangerous nuisance, the Assyrian authorities finally decided upon a direct attack by sea upon the Elamite area concerned. Sennacherib had settled Syrian craftsmen in Nineveh, and these he ordered to build a fleet of ships, which were sailed down the Tigris by sailors from Tyre, Sidon and Cyprus, transferred to a canal leading to the Euphrates, and brought down the Euphrates to the head of the Persian Gulf. Troops were embarked and taken over to the coast of Elam, where despite an awaiting concentration of Chaldaeans and Elamites they secured a bridgehead. From here they made a raid, destroying and looting the Elamite cities of the neighbourhood and taking prisoner what remained of the troublesome tribe of Bit-Yakin.

The claim in Sennacherib's annals that by his raid he had 'poured out terror over the broad lands of Elam' was belied by events. Elam reacted energetically. While Sennacherib's forces were still in the south, a raid was made by Elam across the Tigris into metropolitan Babylonia, where the Elamite king captured Ashur-nadin-shum at Sippar and set up as king of Babylonia in his place a native Babylonian by the name of Nergal-ushezib. In the middle of 693 B.C. the Assyrian forces, cautiously returning from the south, made contact with Nergal-ushezib at Nippur and defeated him, but no mention is made in the annals of any attempt to deal with the city of Babylon, where another Chaldaean leader, Mushezib-Marduk, proceeded to make himself king with

Aramaean support. After more than two seasons campaigning in the Sealands the Assyrian forces no doubt needed to return to base for re-equipment, and no immediate attack was made on Babylon. Instead, recognizing that Elam was now the decisive factor in Babylonian politics, Sennacherib undertook action to neutralize this danger. In 692 B.C. an Assyrian attack was made against Elam from the province of Der, to which conquered Elamite territories were now annexed. Climatic conditions dislocated an attempt to penetrate into Elam proper. In Babylonia Mushezib-Marduk declared his hand, refused to acknowledge the authority of the Assyrian governor, and raised a rebellion, which, however, the local Assyrian authorities were able to contain. Escaping to Elam, he returned with an army, had himself proclaimed king in Babylon, and following the policy of Merodach-baladan sent a considerable bribe to Elam from the temple treasuries with a request for military assistance. The assistance was forthcoming. The king of Elam mustered a great army from his own land and from the disaffected vassals who had formerly owed allegiance to Assyria, and joined forces with the army of the Chaldaeans. This great force marched northwards into the province of Arrapkha, and met the Assyrian army at Halule on the Diyala. The annals of Sennacherib give a graphic picture of the slaughter which ensued. Assyrian chargers wading through blood; the plain littered with mutilated bodies of the slain, hacked to bits for the sake of their rings and bracelets or for mere blood-lust; terrified horses dragging chariots of the dead – with such strokes the annals describe the carnage.

Though claiming a victory, however, the Assyrian army suffered such losses that it could not follow up its advantage during the succeeding year. In 689 B.C. internal affairs in Elam took a turn which kept the ruling house fully occupied, and the Assyrians, having made good the losses at the battle of Halule, were able to deal with Mushezib-Marduk. The Chaldaean forces retreated into Babylon, where they stood siege for nine months, finally succumbing to famine and disease. The Assyrian army entered the city, and departing from previous policy, looted and sacked it. The god Marduk – that is to say, his statue – was taken captive to Assyria, and Sennacherib assumed the title of 'King of Sumer and Akkad' (i.e. south and north Babylonia). There was no further trouble in Babylonia for eight years.

Along his northern frontiers, Sennacherib, as a consequence of his father's activities, his own first-hand experience in the region, and the knock the state in question had taken from the Cimmerians, had no trouble with Urartu. Some disturbances in the region of Que in the north-west in 696–5 B.C. may have been due to odd pockets of the Cimmerians remaining after the defeat of the main body by Sargon. On the eastern frontier Sennacherib, after the campaign against Merodach-baladan in 703–2 B.C., annexed certain territories, formerly independent or of vassal status, and fortified certain cities in the area against Elamite attack.

In his domestic policy Sennacherib is notable for his building activities and his interest in certain technical problems. He it was who rebuilt Nineveh, cutting new streets, enlarging squares, diverting water-courses and building great stone flood-defences to protect his new palace. Around the palace a great park was laid out 'like Mount Amanus, wherein were set all kinds of plants and fruit-trees such as grow in the mountains and in Chaldaea'. Beyond these botanical gardens were orchards, and to irrigate all this greenery a canal was cut for six miles. Sennacherib subsequently laid out further extensions to his botanical gardens, with 'all the plants of the land of Syria, myrrh plants, whose luxuriance was greater than in their native habitat, and all kinds of mountain vines'. He further extended the water supply and by means of dams created a large artificial marsh, which he then stocked with water-fowl, wild pigs and deer in imitation of the natural fauna and flora of south Babylonia. Substantial remains of one of Sennacherib's engineering works still exist – an aqueduct for carrying water over the bed of a wadi. This aqueduct was over three hundred yards long, twenty-four yards wide and contained half a million tons of rock. (For a fuller description see below, page 181.) Sennacherib describes his work in inscriptions on the aqueduct, saying 'I had a canal cut to the meadow-lands of Nineveh. I caused a bridge of limestone blocks to span deep-cut wadis, and let those waters pass over upon it'. A project of Sennacherib for supplying the city of Arbailu (Erbil) with water is also known. Sennacherib's interest in technical processes is shown by his claim to have invented new techniques in bronze casting: 'I ,Sennacherib, through the acute intelligence which the noble god Ea had granted me and with my own experimenting, achieved the casting of bronze colossal lions open at the knee, which no king before me had done. . . . Over great posts and palm-trunks I built a clay mould for twelve colossal lions together with twelve enormous colossal bulls . . . and poured bronze therein as in casting half-shekel pieces'. The reference is to the application of the *cire perdue* process to very large objects; the process itself had been in use as early as the early third millennium.

In 681 B.C. Sennacherib suffered a fate common amongst oriental monarchs, being murdered in Babylon by his sons. According to the biblical account (2 *Kings* xix. 36–7) this happened shortly after his return from a further campaign in Palestine, but no record of such a campaign exists in the Assyrian sources. The legitimate successor, nominated by Sennacherib and already formally accepted by the gods and the nobles of Assyria, was Esarhaddon. This prince had already had considerable experience at the time of his father's murder, since Sennacherib had placed him in supreme charge of Babylonia after the sack of Babylon in 689 B.C. His experience stood him in good stead. He delayed only to secure the formal approval of the gods, and then, without waiting to go through the usual procedure for equipping and provisioning his army for a long campaign, moved swiftly against the parricides from a westerly direction; the direction from which Esarhaddon came would accord with (though it does not positively substantiate) the biblical suggestion of Assyrian military activity in the west shortly before Sennacherib's death. The main Assyrian army prepared to oppose Esarhaddon in the Nisibin area, but at the approach of Esarhaddon dissension broke out amongst their forces, part of them, having learnt of an oracle of the goddess Ishtar favourable to that prince, declaring for him. The parricides fled into Armenia (Urartu), and Esarhaddon, now supported by the whole army, was accepted by the people of

Assyria. With Esarhaddon securely in the saddle, a purge of the army followed, those implicated in the revolt suffering the usual fate.

The period of unrest which marked the succession gave an opportunity for the current chief of the tribe of Bit-Yakin in Babylonia to assert his independence by an attack upon the Assyrian governor, whom he blockaded in the city from which he administered the southern kingdom. As soon as affairs in Assyria were settled, Esarhaddon ordered an attack upon the rebels from the Assyrian provinces east of the Tigris. The rebel chief fled to the old ally of Bit-Yakin, Elam, only to find that a change of foreign policy had accompanied a change of king in that land: the fugitive was promptly put to death in Elam. The brother of the late chief made submission to Esarhaddon and was installed as vassal prince over the whole of the Sealands. Two years later the other major Chaldaean chief, the prince of Bit-Dakkuri, which occupied territory up the Euphrates as far as Borsippa, and which had encroached on territories belonging to the citizens of Borsippa and Babylon, was also replaced by a vassal acceptable to Assyria.

Meanwhile Esarhaddon was faced with problems in the west and north-west. People of a new racial element were now over-running much of the territory of Urartu. This new element was the Scythians, known in cuneiform sources as Ashguzaya and in the Old Testament (*Jeremiah* li. 27 and elsewhere) as Ashkenaz. (The latter represents Hebrew consonantal '*šknz*, an ancient 'misprint' for '*škuz*, to be pronounced Ashkuz.) There is some evidence that Esarhaddon made a marriage alliance with one of the Scythian princes. Probably under pressure from these Scythians, groups of Cimmerians again appeared in the area of Tabal and the province of Hilakku. In 679 B.C. the Assyrian governors undertook successful action against them, but the pressure intensified and by 673 B.C. they were threatening the province of Shupria. By the end of the reign of Esarhaddon the provinces of Hilakku and Tabal were definitely lost.

The trouble in the west was centred on Sidon, whose king revolted in alliance with Sanduarri, a ruler of some cities on the

Gulf of Antioch. Esarhaddon captured and executed both kings
and sacked Sidon, founding on a new site nearby an Assyrian
fortress; as an object-lesson to prospective rebels he formally
dedicated the fortress in the presence of twenty-two kings of
western lands. To secure peace on the desert side of the western
provinces, where the king of the Arabs had just died, and possibly
with a view to securing the friendship of the tribes in the Sinai
Desert on the route to Egypt, Esarhaddon in the following year
sent a force to set the Assyrian nominee firmly on the throne, in
consideration of payment of a heavy tribute.

In Babylonia, Esarhaddon's first-hand knowledge of the situation and conciliatory policy produced a situation favourable to
Assyria. Babylon, devastated by Sennacherib, had probably
begun to be rebuilt by the end of his reign, and considerable work
of restoration was carried out by Esarhaddon. An inscription
describing the restoration amusingly illustrates how a divine
decree could be circumvented. At the sack by Sennacherib the
god Marduk, presumably through the priest at some divination
procedure, had written down 'seventy years as the measure of
the city's desolation'. The inscription claims that the god, having
got over his pique, 'turned the tablet upside down and ordered
the city's restoration in the eleventh year'. The meaning is
perfectly clear in the sexagesimal system of Babylonian writing,
where I (cuneiform 𒁹) represents 'one' or 'sixty'. The cuneiform
equivalent of IX thus denotes seventy, but turned about it reads
XI, that is, eleven.

An efficient administration in Babylonia contributed to the
well-being of citizens, and exiles returning after the chaos of the
Chaldaean troubles were reinstated in their property if they
could prove their claims. The Assyrian position in Babylonia was
so secure that in 676 B.C. it could be used as a base for an expedition
as far as the edge of the Salt Desert in Persia, where a number of
native kings were made tributary. An Elamite raid on central
Babylonia in the following year met with no answering revolt,
and was of only transitory significance.

In the north-east the Assyrian hold on the Mannaeans south
of Lake Urmia appears to have been weakened, as a result of the

infiltration of Scythian and Cimmerian* elements into the area, and certain Assyrian strongholds were definitely lost. The loss of the supply of horses from this area, upon which the Assyrian army so largely relied, may serve to explain the Assyrian thrust into previously unpenetrated territory in Persia, as well as an increasing interest in affairs in Media, where Esarhaddon gave assistance to a number of chiefs against rebel movements. There have recently been excavated and published parts of the largest cuneiform tablets yet known (eighteen inches by twelve inches), which give the text of a series of treaties with Median rulers. The object of the treaties (which, though at present known only from the version relating to the Median princes, were probably drawn up with all the vassal rulers of the empire) was to regulate the succession to Esarhaddon. Probably recollection of the circumstances of his own succession inclined Esarhaddon to this course.

Esarhaddon had six sons, of whom the first-born died at an early age. Amongst the survivors two, Shamash-shum-ukin and Ashur-ban-apli (Ashurbanipal), were generally regarded as having a claim to the succession: it is not clear which was the older, nor indeed can the possibility be excluded that they were twins. At a great assembly in Nineveh in 672 B.C. Esarhaddon, having previously obtained the approval of the gods and the assent of the family council, proclaimed Ashurbanipal as Crown Prince of Assyria and Shamash-shum-ukin as Crown Prince of Babylonia. The governors of the provinces and the vassal rulers were required to take oaths to recognize the settlement, the vassals at least ratifying the oath in a treaty in which they are reminded:

'When Esarhaddon king of Assyria dies, you will seat Ashurbanipal the Crown Prince upon the royal throne; he will exercise the king- ship and lordship of Assyria over you. You will protect him in country and in town; you will fight to the death for him. . . . You will not be hostile to him nor enthrone any of his older or younger brothers in his place . . . Should Esarhaddon, king of Assyria, die whilst his sons are minors, you will help Ashurbanipal the Crown

* For the cuneiform and biblical terminology applied to the Cimmerians (Kimmerioi) of Greek writers, see above, page 116.

Prince to take the throne of Assyria and you will help to seat Shamash-shum-ukin, his coequal brother, the Crown Prince of Babylon, on the throne of Babylon . . . .'

The details of the succession were promulgated during a brief period of calm in the empire shortly before Esarhaddon embarked on a new and far-reaching development of imperial policy. In 675 B.C. Tarqu of the Ethiopian dynasty ruling in Egypt (the 'Tirhakah king of Ethiopia' of 2 *Kings* xix. 9) led the king of Tyre into an anti-Assyrian intrigue, and Esarhaddon, deciding to strike at the root of the trouble, had crossed the Egyptian border although further progress was prevented by a sandstorm. In 671 B.C. an organized invasion of Egypt was put under way, Tarqu's army was routed in a set battle, and Memphis was besieged and taken. Tarqu himself escaped to Thebes or somewhere farther south. The princes of all Lower Egypt, including the pre-eminent one amongst them, Necho of Sais, now hurried to acknowledge Esarhaddon's suzerainty. Assyrian officials were appointed as representatives of Esarhaddon's interests within the territories of the native rulers, and Esarhaddon proclaimed himself king of Upper and Lower Egypt and Ethiopia – a claim in which he exceeded the truth. The lie is repeated in a sculptured monument set up at Zenjirli during Esarhaddon's return to Assyria: this shows the Assyrian conqueror holding cords which pass through the lips of two kneeling figures, one being the king of Tyre and the other a recognizably negroid figure representing Tarqu (see plate 37). In fact, Tarqu was still at liberty and in a position to exercise considerable influence. As soon as the main Assyrian army was well clear, Tarqu returned, induced some of the princes of Lower Egypt to renounce their new suzerain, and re-took Memphis. Esarhaddon set out in 669 B.C. to march to Egypt to deal with the situation, but died on the way.

Upon the death of Esarhaddon the carefully planned arrangements for the succession went smoothly into effect, both brothers taking their thrones. There was little outward indication that the end of the reign of Ashurbanipal would see the empire plunging to disaster, for geographically the empire was now at its greatest extent. None the less factors applying at this time can be seen which serve to explain the sudden collapse. First in significance was the situation along the northern frontiers; here the order established by Tiglath-Pileser III and Sargon II and largely maintained by Sennacherib had to an alarming extent broken down. With hordes of Cimmerian and Scythian barbarians roaming over Asia Minor and the territories of Urartu, trade with the northern region must have been at a standstill, and one of the principal sources of iron was cut off. The numerically powerful Median tribes – generally described in the annals of Tiglath-Pileser III and Sargon II as 'the mighty Medes' or 'the widespreading Medes' in recognition of their wide geographical extent – were now settling and coalescing into powerful units which ultimately became a kingdom able to meet the military might of Assyria on equal terms; and their confederacy must have deprived Assyria of another important source of metals and horses, and cut the routes bringing spices and semi-precious stones from India. Babylonia, though at present pacified with an administration based on the old city-states of the north, contained a vigorous new element, the Chaldaean tribes. These controlled, whether independently or under Assyrian suzerainty, almost the whole of southern Babylonia as well as substantial areas in the north, and in the course of the recurrent rebellions since the time of Ukin-zer had learned from the Assyrians much of the science of warfare and from the native Babylonians the arts of peace.

At the beginning of his reign it fell to Ashurbanipal to fulfil the arrangements for the attack planned upon Tarqu, but as a result of Ashurbanipal's other commitments, such as the settlement of a treaty by which the king of Tyre made his submission, the installation of Shamash-shum-ukin as king of Babylonia, and a punitive campaign in the Cassite area, Tarqu ruled undisturbed in Egypt for three years. In 667 B.C. a strong Assyrian army, with contingents from Syria, Phoenicia, Palestine and Cyprus, marched into Egypt. Tarqu was defeated, and withdrew to Thebes, and once again Memphis was in Assyrian hands. A subsequent attempt at rebellion in favour of Tarqu was made by the native princes, led by Necho, but Assyrian forces arrested the ringleaders and quashed the conspiracy. In view of the necessity of using acceptable native princes for the administration of a country such as Egypt, with a venerable and efficient bureaucratic system, the captured princes were used with clemency and after being taken to Nineveh to be loaded with gifts and favours and no doubt to enter into treaty-relation, they were returned to their posts.

Another attempt by the southern dynasty to regain Lower Egypt was made at the death of Tarqu in 664 B.C. His nephew Tanuatamun marched down the Nile as far as Memphis, where he repelled the Delta princes loyal to Assyria, who had come to oppose him. Ashurbanipal responded promptly, and an Assyrian army again entered Egypt in 663 B.C. The loyal princes of the Delta paid homage, whilst Tanuatamun, like his uncle before him, hurriedly fled. The imperial army moved southwards, on this occasion going as far as the ancient capital Thebes, which was taken and sacked. This event made a vivid impression throughout the Mediterranean regions, and the prophet Nahum half a century later refers to the fate of the city, under its Hebrew name of No-amon:

> Art thou better than No-amon, that was situate among the rivers, that had the waters round about her? . . . Ethiopia and Egypt were her strength, and it was infinite; . . . Yet was she carried away, she went into captivity; her young children also were dashed in pieces at the top of all the streets: and they cast lots for her honourable men, and all her great men were bound in chains (*Nahum* iii. 8–10).

During this period of conquest in Egypt, Assyria seems also to have undertaken some minor military engagements in the north-west. The Cimmerians, deflected from Syria by Sargon, were now themselves under pressure, both from the Scythians to the east and from Indo-European invaders from Thrace. They had already overrun the territory of Mushku (that is, Phrygia) and now began to press upon the kingdom of Lydia. Probably as a consequence of the same renewed pressure, the rulers of Tabal and Hilakku, territories which had ceased to be Assyrian provinces during the reign of Esarhaddon, now hastened to put themselves under the protection of Ashurbanipal. Gyges of Lydia sent an embassy to Ashurbanipal seeking, at the advice of his god given in a dream, friendship and military assistance against the Cimmerians. This seems to have been forthcoming, for Gyges was able to inflict a defeat upon the Cimmerians and after the campaign sent some of the spoil to Nineveh (*circa* 663 B.C.). However, the common commercial interests of Lydia and Egypt, both of them Mediterranean sea powers, led Gyges to support Psammetichus, son of Necho, in his expulsion of the Assyrian garrisons in the 650's. In consequence Assyrian support for Gyges was no longer forthcoming in Asia Minor, and in 652 B.C. (or, it has been argued, a little earlier) Gyges fell to a new Cimmerian attack. Their attempt to invade north Syria was, however, defeated by the Assyrian forces in the Cilician area.

The year of the sack of Thebes (663 B.C.) also saw the death of Necho, in whose place as prince of Sais the Assyrians appointed his son Psammetichus. Psammetichus, no doubt largely as a result of the favour of Assyria, gradually acquired a position amounting to supremacy over the other Delta princes, contrary, so Herodotus relates, to an ancient agreement. According to Herodotus an oracle foretold that vengeance would befall Psammetichus in the form of the Men of Bronze from the sea. Herodotus explains that the reference is to pirates from the lands of Greece and Asia Minor landing on the shores of Egypt, and describes how in the event Psammetichus made friends with the invaders for his own ends. In plain fact, the Men of Bronze were mercenaries from the coastal lands along the north of the Mediterranean, especially from Lydia. With their assistance Psammetichus was able to expel the Assyrian garrisons from Egypt between 658 and 651 B.C.

Not surprisingly, in view of the Assyrian reluctance to record unavenged defeats, no details are given in the annals of Ashurbanipal of the details of the enforced withdrawal from Egypt. Certainly, owing to events in Babylonia, Assyria was unable to make the vigorous reaction which would normally have been expected.

The tensions in Babylonia, quiescent under Esarhaddon, appeared again under Shamash-shum-ukin, and paradoxically were in the end intensified by the measures Esarhaddon had

taken to minimize them. Babylonia was, it is true, under the
kingship of Shamash-shum-ukin, but most of the Assyrian
governors were responsible to his brother Ashurbanipal, king of
Assyria. The imperial correspondence provides many instances
of the fact that Assyrian governors and other officials most
conscientiously refused to regard orders other than those coming
through the proper channels and ultimately emanating from the
king of Assyria; thus in the time of Esarhaddon a report was
made that a certain person in Babylonia holding fugitives refused
to hand them over 'without either the king's personal representative or a message bearing the royal seal'. This kind of attitude
gave many opportunities for friction in circumstances where an
Assyrian official, not having received instructions from Ashurbanipal, disregarded, or acted in direct disobedience to, orders
given by Shamash-shum-ukin. A letter exists in which Shamash-
shum-ukin, writing to his brother, mentions that he was obliged
to countermand his own orders. However, the diarchy worked
for at least twelve years, during which time Ashurbanipal was
able finally to cripple the major potential and actual enemy of
Babylonia, Elam.

The ancient kingdom of Elam was now, under the pressure of
Iranian new comers, rapidly breaking up. The racial group later
to be known as the Persians had settled to the north-east of the
kingdom, where they were virtually independent, whilst the
governors of some of the eastern provinces had made themselves
virtually autonomous. The kingship was as disturbed and subject
to sudden change as that of Babylonia had been since 734 B.C.,
but whether this was a symptom or a contributory cause of the
decline is not clear.

After various minor clashes, war broke out between Elam and
Assyria and in 655 B.C. the Assyrians overran the country, took
the twin capitals, Madaktu and Susa, and installed a pro-Assyrian
member of the royal house as king. Ashurbanipal's governors and
spies now began to send him alarming reports: Shamash-shum-
ukin was plotting against Assyria. This change of attitude was
related to developments in Elam, since whilst that country was
a threat to Babylonian security there was an overriding unity of

interests between the administrations of Ashurbanipal and Shamash-shum-ukin. This factor had now disappeared, and moreover Ashurbanipal seems to have made a mistake in his choice of a prince for appointment to the Elamite throne. Of this prince Shamash-shum-ukin had written to his brother to say: 'Speaking for myself, I am afraid of this Ummanigash, the Crown Prince; . . . he is dangerous'. Shamash-shum-ukin's appraisal of the man proved justified. He pursued the old policy of allying himself with the Chaldaean tribes, and as the tribesmen by this time had considerable support in Borsippa and Babylon Shamash-shum-ukin himself was drawn into the intrigue. The alliance was also welcomed by Psammetichus of Egypt, who was engaged in expelling the Assyrian garrisons from his country; and the desert Arabs were also involved. The actual conflict broke out in 652 B.C., when an Elamite army moved against northern Babylonia, whilst Shamash-shum-ukin attacked the great cities held by Assyrian garrisons. The Elamite army was defeated, and an internal revolution brought another change of king and immobilized the Elamite force for a year during the reorganization. The Assyrians seized the initiative, cleared south Babylonia of organized Chaldaean forces, and put Borsippa and Babylon, held by Shamash-shum-ukin, under siege, thereby cutting communications between the principal partners in the alliance. In 650 B.C. an attempt by an Arab force to break the siege of Babylon failed, as did a diversionary raid on the eastern border of Palestine. Meanwhile the situation in Elam continued to deteriorate, and in 649 B.C. open civil war broke out. Three distinct claimants to the throne now sought Assyrian backing, but the anti-Assyrian party seized control and appointed their own nominee. In consequence of the internal dissension in Elam no effective military support was given to Shamash-shum-ukin who, blockaded in Babylon, defended that city until famine compelled surrender in 648 B.C.: conditions had become so appalling that the defenders had resorted to cannibalism. To avoid the indignities which would otherwise have been inflicted upon his dead body, Shamash-shum-ukin destroyed himself by casting himself into the flames of a conflagration. The palace of the dead king was looted and any surviving rebel leaders hunted down and destroyed, their bodies being cut up and 'fed to the dogs, the swine, the wolves, the vultures, the birds of heaven and the fish of the deep'. Ashurbanipal himself occupied the throne of Babylon for a year, but for the rest of his reign ruled through a sub-king known as Kandalanu: an earlier suggestion that Kandalanu was merely the name by which Ashurbanipal was known in Babylonia, as Tiglath-Pileser III took the name Pulu there, has been disproved.

Assyria now intervened again in the royal succession in Elam, marching to Susa in 648 B.C.; but no permanent settlement of the country was secured, and Nabu-bel-shumati, the grandson of Merodach-baladan, was able to use Elam as a base for the activities of the Chaldaean tribes against Babylonia. Between 642 and 639 B.C. the Assyrian army marched through the whole of Elam, devastating all its cities, capturing and looting Susa, and carrying off its deities and all their temple furniture to Assyria. The sanctuaries were desecrated, and the tombs of the Elamite kings violated, in order that punishment might follow them after death, their ghosts being made to suffer the horrors of restlessness and thirst from lack of the accustomed food-offerings and libations. Many senior administrators together with the whole royal family in all its branches were taken prisoner to Assyria, whilst specialized fighting units were incorporated into the Assyrian army. Many of the common population were also taken to Assyria, together with vast herds of cattle and horses. The statue of the goddess Nana of Erech, (not to be confused with the Moon-god Nanna of Ur), which had been captured by Elam a millennium and a half before, was sent back to its original home, no doubt ensuring for Ashurbanipal the subsequent support of the powerful temple administration of Erech, which from this time was virtually the capital for the administration of southern Babylonia.

The reigning king of Elam, Ummanaldash, himself avoided capture by taking to the mountains, and on the Assyrian withdrawal he returned to Madaktu, Susa being now a desolate and uninhabited heap of ruins. He was no longer in a position to protect Nabu-bel-shumati, the Chaldaean leader, and when

Ashurbanipal demanded the surrender of that prince, Nabu-bel-shumati, like king Saul (I *Samuel* xxxi. 4–5), commanded his armour-bearer to kill him. Ummanaldash sent the body, preserved in salt, to Ashurbanipal, who, unable to inflict punishment on the living man, avenged himself on his victim's ghost by refusing the body burial. Ummanaldash himself ultimately fell into Assyrian hands, and a bas-relief in the British Museum shows the captured ruler being sent by chariot to Ashurbanipal.

The other element in the Babylonian revolt, the Arabs, did not constitute a serious problem, and in a series of actions between 641 and 638 B.C. an Assyrian army was able to defeat the tribes and capture the principal leaders, two of whom, as an example, were tied to dog kennels at one of the great gates of Nineveh.

The annals of Ashurbanipal, who reigned till 626 B.C., do not extend beyond 639 B.C. and for information on the events of the remaining thirteen years we have to rely upon allusions in state correspondence, commercial documents and prayers and related compositions addressed to the gods. A penitential psalm of this period laments:

> In the land discord, in the palace strife, depart not from my side.
> Rebellion and evil plotting are continually contrived against me.

The reference is presumably, amongst other things, to disputes concerning the succession. Certainly at the death of Ashurbanipal in 626 B.C. there was an attempted usurpation, and the chosen heir, Ashur-etillu-ili, had to fight his way to the throne. The chronology of the period between the death of Ashurbanipal and the fall of Nineveh in 612 B.C. raises serious difficulties, and the following account can only claim to be an attempt to arrive at the least improbable interpretation of somewhat contradictory evidence.

The evidence has been amplified, but at the same time complicated, by an inscription of the mother of the last king of the Chaldaean dynasty, found at Harran. This good lady, who was high-priestess in the city of Harran and lived to be one hundred and four, specifically states that she lived from the twentieth year of Ashurbanipal, king of Assyria [when she was born] to the forty-second year of Ashurbanipal, the third year of Ashur-etillu-ili his son, the twenty-first year of Nabopolassar, the forty-third year of Nebuchadrezzar, the second year of Amel-Marduk, the fourth year of Neriglissar, during ninety-five years,

till the beginning of the reign of her son. Since this gives a date for the end of Ashurbanipal's reign as 627 or 626 B.C., and as it is known from another source that Nabopolassar assumed the kingship of Babylonia in November 626 B.C., the three years given for the kingship of Ashur-etillu-ili in Babylonia seem to present a problem. If the discrepancy is not to be accounted for as a simple lapse of memory on the part of a person of great age, it must represent an overlap during which Ashur-etillu-ili and Nabopolassar both claimed kingship of Babylonia. Ashur-etillu-ili certainly exercised a substantial measure of control in Babylonia at some time during his short reign, for an inscription shows that he was able to give protection to a sheikh of the Chaldaean tribe of Bit-Dakkuri, whilst he undertook the restoration of a temple at Dilbat, fifteen miles south of Babylon. Equally certainly, the Chaldaean leader Nabopolassar assumed the kingship of Babylonia in late 626 B.C., and the reality of his control is indicated by the fact that commercial documents from Babylon, Erech and Ur are dated by his reign from this time. The explanation of the difficulty is probably that the Assyrian hold on some parts of Babylonia was not yet entirely lost when Nabopolassar first assumed the kingship, and the account of Berossus (a Babylonian priest of the third century B.C. who wrote in Greek on Babylonian history) confirms this by speaking of Nabopolassar as a rebel against Sin-shar-ishkun; this suggests that Assyria still exercised some authority in Babylonia at the accession of the latter. Sin-shar-ishkun, generally taken as the successor of Ashur-etillu-ili, had a reign of at least seven years, as is shown by the dating of contracts. A recently discovered king list now suggests that the reigns of Ashur-etillu-ili and Sin-shar-ishkun overlapped in part, which would indicate that each ruled only a part of the empire formerly governed as a unit by Ashurbanipal: this may point to the existence of tensions coming near to civil war within Assyria itself. It was during the reign of Sin-shar-ishkun that Nabopolassar engaged in the alliance which was finally to overthrow Assyria.

The people with whom Nabopolassar made his alliance were the Medes. The Medes are last met with in the Assyrian annals in the reign of Esarhaddon, when they still consisted of a large number of associated but separate tribes. Probably about the beginning of the reign of Ashurbanipal these tribes began to be welded into a single kingdom by a leader Huvakshatra, known in Babylonian as Ummakishta and to Herodotus as Cyaxares. The date at which he had made the whole Median nation completely independent of Assyria is not certain, but a story told by Diodorus Siculus (a Sicilian contemporary of Julius Caesar who wrote a history of the world), to the effect that Nabopolassar ('Belesys') encouraged Cyaxares to hostility against Assyria, promising him success, suggests that it was not till after the death of Ashurbanipal. In any case, both cuneiform and Greek sources agree that Nabopolassar and Cyaxares were jointly concerned in military action shortly after 621 B.C.

Assyria was not entirely without allies. The Egyptians, although not concerned with territorial expansion, were very much concerned at any development which affected Mediterranean trade or the security of Egypt, and would no doubt not wish to see Syria and north Mesopotamia under the entirely new dispensation which Median control would have represented. Furthermore, there remained the menace of the wandering hordes of the north, the Cimmerians, the Scythians, and various other nomadic tribes of Indo-European origin; and Assyria, with its military prestige won over the centuries, appeared to be the only bulwark against this tide of barbarism. Jeremiah's reference in 626 B.C. to seeing

> a seething cauldron; and the face thereof is from the north (*Jeremiah* i. 13)

is generally taken as referring to an expected invasion by the dreaded nomads of the north. The term 'Scythian' is often used for these peoples, but in fact the Scythian element (for other terms applied to them see page 124) was only a part, and to judge by Assyrian relations with them, a more responsible part.

Of Assyrian provinces and vassal states, whilst some, amongst them the kingdom of Judah, demonstrated hostility to Assyria, others, notably a part of the Mannaeans, gave active support to their suzerain. Even in Babylonia, to judge by datings employing the regnal years of Sin-shar-ishkun, there were in the cities adherents of Assyria till the final fall of Nineveh; this was particularly marked in Erech, where it is thought that a pro-Assyrian rebellion broke out as late as 614 B.C.

There are no details from cuneiform sources of the early stages of Nabopolassar's activities, but it is clear that by 617 B.C. he had cleared Assyrian garrisons out of all Babylonia south of the neck formed where the Tigris and Euphrates come closest together. Nabopolassar now marched up the Euphrates to the Aramaean districts of Suhu and Hindanu, between Hit and the mouth of the Habur, which had been part of the Assyrian empire for over two and a half centuries. Nabopolassar met with some initial successes in this area, the Aramaeans readily submitting and the preliminary Assyrian counter-attack being beaten off. The original strategy planned may have envisaged raising a general revolt in the western provinces to coincide with an attack upon Nineveh from east and west by Medes and Chaldaeans. However, the approach of a combined Assyrian and Egyptian army compelled the withdrawal of Nabopolassar to Babylon. The combined forces of Egypt and Assyria moved eastwards into the province of Arrapkha: it will be recalled (see above, pages 92 and 106) that this province, of which the basis was established by Adad-nirari II, was extended by Tiglath-Pileser III and used by him and his successors as the most successful means of attacking metropolitan Babylonia without the need of running the gauntlet of the easily defensible area at the neck formed by the convergence of the Euphrates and Tigris. At some point south of the Lower Zab the Assyrian forces were opposed and forced to retire by the army brought up by Nabopolassar.

A bold attack upon Ashur, the ancient capital, early the following year (615 B.C.), almost brought disaster upon Nabopolassar, who was forced to flee and take refuge in the citadel of the town known then, as now, as Takrit. The Assyrians were unwilling to press their advantage and withdrew, their intelligence system presumably having information of an incipient Median attack, which was actually made on an unidentified city in the province of Arrapkha later in the year, with the object of establishing advance bases from which to attack Nineveh itself. A Median attack upon metropolitan Assyria was made in 614 B.C., and although Nineveh was too strong to yield to assault, both Tarbisu (modern Sherif Khan, north-west of Nineveh) and Ashur were taken, the latter being completely destroyed. Nabopolassar arrived in the sacked city at the head of his army, and the common action of the Medes and Chaldaeans was sealed by a formal treaty between Nabopolassar and Cyaxares, ratified, according to later tradition, by marriage alliances.

With the province of Arrapkha denied to the Assyrian strategists, the imperial power now attempted to counter-attack Babylonia down the Euphrates. The Suhu tribes, who had made submission to Nabopolassar in 615 B.C., now revolted, and whilst Nabopolassar was undertaking siege operations at Anah an Assyrian army appeared and forced him to retire. It is curious that the Medes, after their spectacular success against Ashur in the previous year, were inactive during 613 B.C., so that Assyria could safely deploy an army at a distance from the homeland; it has been suggested that possibly Assyria was negotiating with the Scythians to procure an attack from the north upon the Medes. The Scythians, whose interests had never directly clashed with those of Assyria, had a tradition of friendly relations with that power going back to their first appearance in the north in the time of Esarhaddon; they constituted a potential ally of great strength. Traditions in later Greek writers suggest that the Medes were at one time seriously threatened by the Scythians but finally induced the leaders to make common cause with them. In the Babylonian sources the northern nomads are referred to not as Scythians but as Ummanmanda, a term about which there has been a good deal of discussion but which seems to mean much the same as 'hordes'. The Ummanmanda undoubtedly contained some Scythian elements, with several other racial components, and it may be that until Cyaxares had met and won over the most influential leaders of this coalition of tribes there was some doubt as to which side it would take. In 612 B.C. Nabopolassar, the Ummanmanda and Cyaxares effected a junction and marched to Nineveh. After a siege of three months the city fell, its last king, Sin-shar-ishkun, dying – according to Greek tradition – in the flames of its destruction. The city was sacked and looted and the survivors enslaved. Traditions in Greek authors and in the *Book of Nahum* (*Nahum* i. 8) assert, credibly, that the capture of this powerfully fortified city was made possible by the flooding of the Tigris, which swept away a section of the defences.

The capital was destroyed, but a nominal kingdom of Assyria still stood. Those of the Assyrian army who could escape from Nineveh fled a hundred miles westwards to Harran, where Ashur-uballit, a junior member of the royal family, was made king, and called upon his Egyptian allies.

5

Neo-Babylonian Empire

LADEN with the loot of the imperial city, the forces of the Medes and the Ummanmanda retired. Nabopolassar's efforts were now directed to getting into his own hands control of as much as possible of the Assyrian empire, and for this purpose he employed his troops to occupy the Nisibin region west of Assyria, as well as central Assyria itself and the provinces along the middle Euphrates, and made strenuous efforts to gain what he could of the north in the Urartian area: however, the Scythians had long-standing interests in the latter region, and Nabopolassar failed to gain permanent control of any part of it except Cilicia. The remnant of the Assyrian army was left unattacked at Harran, possibly because Nabopolassar's most urgent concern was to put himself in effective control of as much of Assyria as possible before the return of the Ummanmanda. This took place in 610 B.C., when they made an attack upon Harran, in which Nabopolassar, to protect his own interests, joined. Ashur-uballit did not attempt to defend the city but fled south-westwards to await his Egyptian allies, leaving Harran to be occupied and sacked by the Ummanmanda. Stiffened by the Egyptian force which now joined them, the remnants of the Assyrian army were now in a position to mount a counter-attack upon Harran, which they did with some initial success. The approach of an army under Nabopolassar compelled the raising of the siege, and the Assyrian and Egyptian forces withdrew to

Carchemish. At this point there succeeded in Egypt Necho II (610–595 B.C.), who decided upon more vigorous measures in support of Ashur-uballit, and hastened to lead the main Egyptian army into Syria (2 *Chronicles* xxxv. 21). It seems that Chaldaean diplomacy had met with a good measure of success in Palestine, for Necho had to put down a rising in Gaza (*Jeremiah* xlvii. 1), whilst Josiah of Judah, the principal remaining native ruler in Palestine, attempted to harry the Egyptian forces on their way northwards and was defeated and killed at Megiddo (608 B.C., 2 *Kings* xxiii. 29), his kingdom temporarily becoming a vassal of Egypt in consequence. Necho had no difficulty in subduing Syria, and made a junction with Ashur-uballit's forces at Carchemish. Under Nabopolassar's son, Nebuchadrezzar, the Babylonians made a direct attack upon the powerful Egyptian army (605 B.C.). There was heavy slaughter upon both sides – 'the mighty man hath stumbled against the mighty, they are fallen both of them together' (*Jeremiah* xlvi. 12) – and according to *Jeremiah* xlvi. 5 ff. the Egyptian army characteristically panicked and bolted in disorder for Egypt. The propaganda effect of the Egyptian defeat was felt far and wide, and the subject peoples recognized that it was too late for further action against the Chaldaeans: 'Pharaoh king of Egypt is but a noise' they said; 'he hath let the appointed time pass by' (*Jeremiah* xlvi. 17). Nebuchadrezzar was able to pursue the retreating Egyptians to their own borders, and might well have continued into Egypt but for the death at this moment of his father Nabopolassar, which demanded his presence in Babylon.

It is unnecessary to emphasize Nebuchadrezzar's ability as a statesman and military commander, for his activities in these spheres have made him one of the most notable figures of the ancient world. His contemporary, Jeremiah, recognized early in his reign that he was the new power in international politics, and estimated the duration of his empire as three generations (*Jeremiah* xxvii. 7). Jehoiakim, the king of Judah appointed by Necho of Egypt, made submission to Nebuchadrezzar at his defeat of the Egyptian army, but returned to allegiance to Egypt when the time appeared opportune. Events proved, however, that Jeremiah had made a wiser appraisal of the situation than the politicians, for Nebuchadrezzar in 597 B.C. sent forces to besiege Jerusalem. Jehoiakim had the good fortune to die during the siege, and it was his son, Jehoiachin, who was taken captive to Babylon, together with the nobility, craftsmen and troops.

With the whole of Palestine and Syria once more in the hands of a hostile power, Egypt's trade, which made considerable use of the Phoenician ports, was bound to be badly affected. This may explain the decision of Hophra (Apries) of Egypt (589–570 B.C., mentioned in *Jeremiah* xliv. 30) to undertake an invasion of Palestine. The Egyptian forces had some preliminary success. They took Sidon, and in Jerusalem and no doubt other cities the Babylonian garrison was forced to retire, leaving the anti-Babylonian statesmen in control. As Jeremiah foresaw, Nebuchadrezzar reacted strongly, dispatching a powerful army to the west. The Egyptians made a hurried withdrawal, leaving their erstwhile vassals to be dealt with piecemeal by the Babylonian forces. Jerusalem was blockaded for eighteen months, and finally starved out (586 B.C.). Zedekiah, the last king of Judah, was blinded and taken captive to Babylon (2 *Kings* xxv. 7), Jerusalem looted, sacked and defortified, the leaders of the anti-Babylonian party put to death, a pro-Babylonian nobleman appointed governor, and a large section of the remaining population deported to Babylonia. Other rebel cities were successively subdued, and the great port of Tyre was put under siege. This latter operation is not only referred to by Menander (342–292 B.C.), who hands on the tradition that it continued through thirteen years, but also referred to several times by the prophet Ezekiel, a contemporary of the event (*Ezekiel* xxvi–xxix). Ezekiel first pictures Tyre as gloating over the fall of Jerusalem: 'I shall be replenished, now that she is laid waste' (xxvi. 2) – a reference to the fact that the trade from Egypt and beyond could pass northwards either by caravan through Palestine or by sea into the Phoenician ports. The trading ventures and the commercial wealth of Tyre are then graphically described:

Tarshish [Tarsus in Asia Minor] was thy merchant by reason of the multitude of all kinds of riches; with silver, iron, tin, and lead, they traded for thy wares. Javan [Greece], Tubal [Tabalu of the Assyrian sources], and Meshech [Mushku], they were thy traffickers: they traded the persons of men and vessels of brass for thy merchandise. They of the house of Togarmah [Til-garimmu of the Assyrian sources] traded for thy wares with horses and war-horses and mules. The men of Dedan were thy traffickers: many isles were the mart of thine hand: they brought thee in exchange horns of ivory and ebony. Syria was thy merchant by reason of the multitude of thy handy-works . . . . . . Haran and Canneh and Eden, the traffickers of Sheba, Asshur and Chilmad . . . . . . were thy traffickers in choice wares, in wrappings of blue and broidered work, and in chests of rich apparel, bound with cords and made of cedar, among thy merchandise (*Ezekiel* xxvii. 12–16, 23–24).

The city of Tyre was finally taken in 571 B.C. and a Babylonian provincial administration set up there.

Meanwhile Cyaxares, with the support of his allies amongst the Ummanmanda, had completely overrun the kingdom of Urartu and pushed into Asia Minor, where he came into contact with the kingdom of Lydia, a flourishing centre of trade. Some initial conflict was settled in 585 B.C. by a treaty mediated by Nabu-na'id (Nabonidus), an officer and later a successor of Nebuchadrezzar, which fixed the boundary between Lydian and Median spheres of influence at the river Halys.

Nebuchadrezzar maintained friendly relations with the Medes, and his main problem in the sphere of foreign politics was Egypt. Nebuchadrezzar's concern in the west had not only military but also economic motives. The unification of the Medes had largely deprived Babylonia of control of the eastern trade routes (though doubtless the difficulty was not felt in the honeymoon period immediately following the sack of Nineveh), whilst the once-thriving Babylonian ports were becoming silted up. For this reason the new Babylonian kings increasingly turned to the west to try to capture the routes coming northwards from Arabia. Egypt, however, its trade damaged by Babylonian control of the Phoenician and Cilician coast, was constantly attempting to weaken the Babylonian hold on the west. 2 *Kings* xxv. 22–26 speaks of the murder, clearly with the approval if not at the

instigation of the Egyptians, of the native governor whom
Nebuchadrezzar had appointed over Jerusalem. At last Nebuchadrezzar undertook, as a fragment of cuneiform tablet shows, an
invasion of Egypt, which is referred to in *Ezekiel* xxix. 19–21.
No details are known. Tradition in *Jeremiah* (xlix. 28) and
Herodotus refers to a successful attack on the Arab tribes of the
desert.

The reign of Nebuchadrezzar was a time of great building
activity in Babylonia, and the extant remains of Babylon (see
plates 4B and 6) are substantially from his period. The fortifications of Babylon were strengthened, an inner and an outer line of
defences being maintained. The rivers on both sides together with
a chain of fortresses north and south of Babylon constituted a
powerful quadrilateral defence round the city.

At the death of Nebuchadrezzar in 562 B.C. he was succeeded
by his son Amel-Marduk (Evil-merodach of 2 *Kings* xxv. 27 and
Jeremiah lii. 31), who after a brief reign of two years was killed in
a revolution. Little is known of him beyond the statement in
2 *Kings* xxv. 27–30 that he showed special favour to Jehoiachin,
one of the two ex-kings of Judah held at Babylon; curiously
enough there is a direct reference to Jehoiachin in some cuneiform
tablets found at Babylon and datable to the reign of Nebuchadrezzar. These tablets are lists of ration issues and the relevant part
of one of them reads:

> For Ya'u-kina king of the land Yahudu, for the five sons of the
> king of the land of Yahudu, (and) for eight Yahudaeans, each $\frac{1}{2}$
> sila (of corn).

Philologically Ya'u-kinu of Yahudu is unmistakably the name
which our Bible translators render Jehoiachin of Judah.

The man who benefited by the death of Amel-Marduk was
Nergal-shar-usur (Neriglissar of the Greek accounts, Nergal-
sharezer of *Jeremiah* xxxix. 3), a son-in-law of Nebuchadrezzar.
It is now known from a Babylonian chronicle that he undertook
a great campaign across the Taurus, probably to anticipate the
Medes' forthcoming thrust across the Halys. After initial success
he suffered a serious defeat and returned to Babylon in 556 B.C.,

dying so soon afterwards that one is tempted to wonder if his personal rivals at home took advantage of his loss of prestige to hasten his end. Certainly his son, Labashi-Marduk, who attempted to assume the throne in succession, was very shortly removed by a rebellion of the chief officers of state, who put on the throne Nabu-na'id (Nabonidus), the diplomatist who had been commissioned by Nebuchadrezzar to assist negotiations between the Medes and Lydians in 585 B.C.

Nabu-na'id was not of the royal family of Nabopolassar but the son of a nobleman and of the high-priestess of the god Sin at Harran: this lady may, however, herself have been of the Assyrian royal house, for she was born in the middle of the reign of Ashurbanipal, and it is well known that before and after this time the high-priesthood of the great shrines was commonly bestowed upon princes and princesses of the royal family.

It was once customary to dismiss Nabu-na'id as a learned antiquary, 'never happier than when he could excavate some ancient foundation-stone', but with the publication of new texts during the past thirty years it has become clear that this king was a statesman of high ability. He recognized the two main problems to be faced, the economic difficulties of the empire and the situation with regard to the ancient religion of Babylonia. On the economic problems more will be said elsewhere: at the moment it is the religious problem which engages our attention. Amongst the Medes and the Jews, with both of whom the Babylonians were now in close contact, new religious ideas and ethical conceptions, implying derision of the ancient polytheistic idolatry, were afoot. It has been credibly suggested that it was in response to this situation, and the inadequacy he recognized in the old polytheism, that Nabu-na'id attempted to make the Moon-god, Sin or Nanna, the tutelary deity both of Ur and of his mother's city of Harran, into the supreme god of the empire. This is not to be dignified by recognition as a movement in favour of monotheism, of which there is no trace, but was rather an attempt to provide a religious unifying force for the whole of the subject peoples. The supreme Babylonian deity, Marduk, an old Sumerian Sun-god with chthonic aspects and specifically associated with the city of Babylon, had no place in the pantheon of the Arabians and Aramaeans: it was otherwise with the Moon-god, who, under various names, was highly honoured by these peoples. The trend of religious reformation had, indeed, probably begun already under Nebuchadrezzar, for the excavations at Ur reveal that during the reign of that king the shrine of the wife of the Moon-god underwent a change in architectural design, implying a change in ritual. It was, however, Nabu-na'id who, according to his own statement as well as the accusations of his enemies at his fall, was mainly responsible for the innovations.

A point at which the economic and religious problems met was the city of Harran. The very name 'Harran' means 'road' and was applied to the place because it was the great meeting point of the routes northwards from Babylonia on the one side and from Egypt, Arabia and Palestine on the other. The place was also one of the great shrines of Sin. Unfortunately the city had remained in the hands of the Ummanmanda since their capture of it in 610 B.C., when they had desecrated and destroyed the temple of the Moon-god. Nabu-na'id relates in inscriptions that in his first year of reign the great god Sin (in another version promulgated in Babylonia he tactfully conjoins the name of Marduk, the god of Babylon) appeared to him in a dream saying: 'Make haste and build Ehulhul ["House-of-great-joy"], the temple of Sin which is in Harran, in view of the fact that all lands are committed to your hands'. In the version promulgated in Babylon Nabu-na'id then points out to Marduk: 'As to that temple which you order to be rebuilt, the Ummanmanda surround it, and their strength is formidable'. Marduk makes the surprising reply: 'The Ummanmanda that you mention, they, their land and the kings their allies no longer exist. In the third year coming I shall make Cyrus king of Anshan [i.e. Persia], his petty servant, expel them. With his few troops he will sweep out the widespreading Ummanmanda'.

The Persians were originally one of the migratory Indo-Aryan tribes, who had ultimately settled in Elam. Their royal family was founded in the middle of the seventh century, after Ashurbanipal had knocked out the old Elamite dynasty, by Achaemenes (Hahmanish), whose son took the title of 'King of Anshan':

Anshan was originally one of the princedoms of the kingdom of Elam, and the new title connoted kingship over that ancient land. The rising power of the kingdom of Persia led the Median king Astyages to give a daughter in marriage to Cambyses I, the third king of Anshan, and from this marriage Cyrus was born.

It seems clear that whatever racial elements the term Umman-manda properly denoted, in the account of Nabu-na'id's dream it referred to a garrison controlled by the Medes. The dream also makes it clear that the old tradition of diplomatic relations between the ruling houses of Babylonia and Elam still continued, since Nabu-na'id and Cyrus were evidently intriguing together for a united effort against the Medes in Nabu-na'id's third year, 553 B.C.

Nabu-na'id ordered a general levy of troops from the western provinces. The Medes, occupied with the insurrection of Cyrus (which, according to Greek accounts, they almost crushed), withdrew from Harran, and Nabu-na'id was able to use his levies to commence the projected work of restoration. This had the effect, however, of promoting a mutiny amongst the people of the great cities of Babylonia: 'The sons of Babylon, Borsippa, Nippur, Ur, Erech, Larsa and the people of the cult-cities of Akkad [northern Babylonia] . . . forgot their duty, and talked treason and not loyalty'. There is evidence that Nabu-na'id had been preparing for something of the kind. The king owned large estates in southern Babylonia, and contracts from the temple archives prove that at the very beginning of his reign he was handing over, in return for a fixed annual payment, control of these to the administrative authorities of Eanna, the great and wealthy temple corporation in Erech. Reforms in the administration of the temples were put under way at this time, and at Erech new appointments were made to all the senior posts in the early years of Nabu-na'id's reign.

Famine now appeared in Babylonia, attributed by Nabu-na'id to the impiety of the people, though more soberly traceable to general economic conditions. The wars and building activities of Nebuchadrezzar and Neriglissar were producing inflation, and the level of prices rose by up to 50 per cent between 560 and

550 B.C. (The trend was not halted by subsequent developments, and the price rise between 560 and 485 B.C. amounted to 200 per cent.) The results are seen in the commercial documents. One such, dated in the first year of Nabu-na'id, relates to a loan of corn made to a herdsman whose cattle were starving. Other texts concern the handing over of children to the temples as slaves, an evident result of extreme indigence. The withdrawal of manpower for years at a time from productive labour on canals to unproductive temple-building or war also contributed to a decline in the land's productivity, whilst the economic situation was further aggravated by the Median control of the routes to east and north. Nabu-na'id's alliance with Cyrus was doubtless intended to have fruitful consequences in the latter respect.

It has been pointed out that in his inscriptions Nabu-na'id scarcely mentions the economic aspects of his undertakings, and it has therefore been doubted whether economic considerations did actually constitute the primary motive for his subsequent actions. However, commercial and administrative documents of the kind already referred to prove beyond doubt, if only incidentally, that Nabu-na'id was *au fait* with economic problems; and in his dedication inscriptions, destined for the gods, it was only reasonable for the king to claim piety rather than economic benefit as the mainspring of his undertakings.

Nabu-na'id's response to the situation in Babylonia was a remarkable attempt to move the centre of gravity of the empire westwards and secure the trade routes from south Arabia. Investing his son Bel-shar-usur (Belshazzar of *Daniel* v. 22, vii. 1, viii. 1) as regent in Babylonia, he led an army through Syria to the oasis of Teima in north-west Arabia, where he executed the native king and made the town his base for the next ten years. During this period of residence in the west he pushed two hundred and fifty miles farther southwards, through a number of places which can be identified, until he finally reached Yatrib [Muslim Medina, the city of Muhammad] on the Red Sea. Nabu-na'id specifically states that he established garrisons in and planted colonies around the six oases which he names. He describes the forces used as 'the people of Akkad and of Hatti-land', that is, both native Babylonians and people from the western provinces, and a fascinating side-issue is that five of the six oases named were, at the time of Muhammad a millennium later, occupied by Jews. The suggestion can hardly be avoided that amongst the troops and colonists accompanying Nabu-na'id was a strong contingent of Jews, though whether from those left in Palestine at the capture of Jerusalem or from those deported to Babylonia cannot at present be said.

This ten-year withdrawal of Nabu-na'id from his capital may well be the basis of the tale of the seven years of madness ascribed to Nebuchadrezzar in the *Book of Daniel* (iv. 28–33). It is a common phenomenon to find in tradition events properly relating to one man being transferred to a more famous person with whom he was historically associated: as an example the killing of Goliath by Elhanan, for which David commonly receives the credit (1 *Samuel* xvii. 50, 2 *Samuel* xxi. 19), leaps to mind. Another form of what is clearly the same Jewish tradition of divine wrath upon a New Babylonian king – though in this case linked specifically with Nabu-na'id instead of Nebuchadrezzar – has appeared amongst the documents from Qumran, the so-called 'Dead Sea Scrolls'.

The document concerned, a fragmentary manuscript of which the larger part was found in 1955, dates from the second half of the first century B.C. and is part of a work written in Aramaic (a language akin to Hebrew and employed for parts of *Daniel* and *Ezra* and a few other verses in the Old Testament). With very heavy restoration (perhaps not in every case justified), the fragment may be translated (closely following J. T. Milik, *Revue Biblique*, 63 (1956), page 408):

> The words of the prayer which Nabu-na'i(d), king of Assyria and Babylon, the great king, prayed when he was smitten with an unpleasant skin-disease by the ordinance of God Most High in the city of Teima: 'I was smitten with an unpleasant skin-disease for seven years. . . . But when I confessed my sins and my faults, He granted me a (favourable) verdict. And there was a Jew from . . ., and he wrote and told (me) to give honour . . . to the name of God Most High. . . .'

At the end of the ten years conditions had so changed that Nabu-na'id, now at least sixty-five and probably more than seventy years old, was able to return to Babylonia, where he met with no more opposition to his scheme for restoring and reforming the great temple at Harran.

The temporary improvement in the position of Nabu-na'id may have been bound up with the fortunes of his erstwhile ally Cyrus. After Cyrus' accession to the throne of the empire of the Medes and Persians, war had again broken out in Asia Minor with Croesus of Lydia. By an unexpected winter campaign Cyrus in 547 B.C. succeeded in capturing the capital of Croesus, Sardes, and in making Lydia into a Persian province, gaining the support of the Greek colonies in western Asia Minor. With his hands now free, Cyrus was able to embark upon preliminary operations against the Babylonian empire, which he did in 547 B.C., gaining control of part of eastern Assyria. In this he may have been anticipating a Babylonian attack upon Media, for the region taken was that which during the Assyrian period had always been used as the base for such attacks, and Herodotus mentions that Croesus had an alliance with both Nabu-na'id and the Egyptians and had called for military assistance before the surprise attack which brought about his downfall. The coincidence of dates makes it reasonable to assume that it was the military threat from the east which produced a temporary unity in Babylonia and a call for the return and active leadership of the king.

Southern Babylonia had always, from its geographical position, been subject to surprise raids from Elam, and it suffered another in 546 B.C. Events now become confused. It was probably after this incident that Nabu-na'id actually returned to Babylon, to direct the defence of his country. The situation was by no means desperate: Erech, the main city of the south, remained securely in Nabu-na'id's hands despite the Elamite raid, Syria and the west gave no evidence of disaffection, and one may infer from Herodotus that Egypt was a potential ally. However, whilst the aged king was fulfilling his long-planned restoration of the temple Ehulhul in Harran, Cyrus was engaged in propaganda work throughout the Babylonian empire. His action towards Croesus, whom he treated with kindness and respect, and towards the Greek oracles of Asia Minor, which he forbore to plunder, gained for him a reputation for clemency and religious tolerance, which is reflected in the *Book of Isaiah*: the anonymous prophet commonly known now as Deutero-Isaiah (*Isaiah* xl–lv) claims to speak for the Lord 'to his anointed, to Cyrus, whose right hand I have holden, to subdue nations before him . . . .', saying 'For Jacob my servant's sake, and Israel my chosen, I have called thee by thy name: I have surnamed thee, though thou hast not known me.' (*Isaiah* xlv. 1, 4.) Similar propaganda must have been fermenting in Babylon, and is reflected in the venomous compositions written upon Nabu-na'id at his fall. The following, based upon Sidney Smith, *Babylonian Historical Texts* (1924), page 87, is a translation of such a text, unfortunately in very damaged condition, referring to Nabu-na'id:

. . . he did not cause justice to proceed from him,
. . . he killed the weak with a weapon;
. . . (in respect to) the merchant, he blocked the road,
. . . . . .
. . . . . .
[At the proper time of the New Year Festival] he advised that there
    be no rejoicing,
. . . a *shedu*-demon altered him,
. . . . . .
. . . he made the non-sanctuary,
. . . . . .
. . . he set [an heretical statue] upon a base,
. . . he called its name 'the god Sin',
. . . . . .
. . . the form of Sin was the eclipse,
. . . . . .
. . . . . .
He used to confound the rites, and upset the ordinances,
He would utter a word against the divinely-ordained order.

Cyrus gradually thrust forward over the mountains of Kurdistan and Luristan until he was in control of the whole of the region east of the Tigris. From here he was able to mount an attack upon Babylonia itself. Cyrus forced a crossing of the Tigris at Opis, and marched upon Sippar, which surrendered. Babylon itself was then attacked, and surrendered with scarcely a struggle. Herodotus attributes this to the Persian strategem of breaching the Euphrates, which constituted one side of the defences of the city, and leading the river into a depression, thereby rendering the main stream temporarily fordable. There is no reason to reject the story, but the real reason for the collapse of the city was not a weakness in its defences but the presence within the city of a 'fifth column'. Nabu-na'id's attempt to question the supremacy of Marduk had, despite the temporary rapprochement claimed in his inscription after his ten years residence abroad, bequeathed him a legacy of discontent. The propaganda of Cyrus had found fertile ground amongst the citizens of Babylon, and they gladly transferred allegiance to the liberal-minded Persian king. He entered the city, which he allowed to be neither sacked nor looted, and without disturbing either the religious institutions or the civil administration appointed a Persian representative as governor. Cyrus' young son, Cambyses, officiated at the New Year Festival in Babylon, whereby the dynasty received investiture from the god Marduk, henceforth exercising kingship over Babylonia not only by the right of conquest but by divine vocation.

So came to an end the last of the ancient native dynasties in Babylonia and Assyria. Achaemenid [Persian] rule continued till 331 B.C., after which for the remainder of the millennium Mesopotamia was successively in the hands of Seleucids [Greeks] and Arsacids [Parthians]. Many parts of Mesopotamia had been under temporary foreign domination before, but the Achaemenid conquest came at a time when new forces were being increasingly felt in the ancient Near East and the two-millennia-old civilization of Babylonia was, irrespective of political considerations, dying. Mention has already been made of the growing sense of the inadequacy of the old Babylonian pantheism and of Nabu-na'id's attempt at reform, and there is ample evidence from the New Assyrian period of what W. von Soden calls a 'secularizing tendency'. Moreover, since the turn of the millennium Aramaean influence had been penetrating Babylonia ever more strongly, both in the social institutions and in the language. In the former, by emphasizing tribal organization, it had tended to weaken the basis of the old city-state system; in the latter, Aramaic had the advantage of being the native tongue of a much more widely-spread ethnic group than was Akkadian, whilst for writing purposes the alphabetic script of Aramaic, with its twenty-two letters, was a far easier vehicle of communication than cuneiform Akkadian, with its six hundred signs. Even whilst Akkadian cuneiform on clay tablets was still the means normally employed for drawing up legal documents, Aramaic writing was sometimes used as a more convenient way of endorsing such tablets for filing purposes. Only the learned could, after many years study, ever master the use of Akkadian cuneiform; and it was amongst the learned that cuneiform writing remained in use for scholarly and esoteric purposes for some centuries more. By 140 B.C. it had completely disappeared except amongst a few priests who employed it for religious purposes for another half century, and amongst astronomers. For astronomical texts cuneiform continued in use right down to the time of Christ.

PART 2

SOCIAL AND CULTURAL

HISTORY

The Foundations of Babylonian Society
and the Babylonian Way of Life

The Pattern of Sumerian Society

AN attempt has been made to show that Sumerian civilization first took characteristic shape in the first half of the third millennium B.C., in what is generally known as the *Early Dynastic* period, and the evidence has been presented for believing that this society arose *via* the *Jemdet Nasr* from the peasant culture known as *Uruk*, which flourished at the end of the fourth millennium B.C. It was, in all important aspects, not a culture imported from abroad but one which arose in the land of the two rivers. Despite development, decay, and changes in many details, especially as a result of successive waves of Semitic immigrants, Sumerian institutions were so well adapted to their *milieu* that in many aspects of life they remained as long as Babylonian civilization survived. To the very end of the period with which we have to deal, Babylonian civilization retained a Sumerian framework and many points of detail characteristic of the earliest times.

It is quite clear that the people of the *Uruk* culture were not the first inhabitants of south Babylonia, for they were certainly preceded by the peoples represented by the *Ubaid* and *Eridu* cultures; the latter, it will be recalled, are regarded by some authorities as proto-Sumerians – that is, as an earlier strand of the racial element responsible subsequently for the *Uruk* culture – and it is they who were the first settlers on the virgin soil of the land which later became Sumer. These people must already have employed some primitive forms of drainage and irrigation, for without this it would be impossible in southern Babylonia to grow barley, their staple cereal. It was, however, with the *Uruk* culture that canal-making and irrigation works on a substantial scale began, with incalculable consequences for human progress. Such works, forced upon these early dwellers of Sumer by climatic considerations, were a vital element in the shaping of the social structure, for they could only be efficiently undertaken by large human units, of which the members were engaged in a common co-ordinated effort; efficient results could not be achieved by the unco-ordinated efforts of individual families in small marsh villages. Once the first steps had been taken, a rapid increase of population ensued as a consequence of the surplus of food supplies which now became available. Thus it was from co-operation of this kind, in large units transcending the family or clan, and operating over a relatively large area of land, that there arose the city-state; and as a corollary it was upon this and not (as in Semitic society generally) on the family or the clan that the social structure was based.

The rise of the city-state, based ultimately on irrigation, led to developments in many other directions, of which some can only be touched upon here. In southern Iraq land is virtually valueless without the right to use irrigation water, and the grant of an allotment of land presupposed the right to irrigate. But the reckless use of irrigation ditches might well wreak havoc on the land of other members of the community, and thus it was necessary to lay down rules for the use of irrigation channels and to ensure that they were observed. Thus this was one of the factors giving rise to written legislation, an administrative system, and the creation of an embryonic police system in the form of the Canal Inspectors later known as *Gugallu*. The bursting of the banks of the rivers at the time of the spring floods, which has been a constant threat to the country right up to the middle of the twentieth century A.D., might obliterate old boundary marks of fields; this was an obvious stimulus to the development of geometry and mensuration. The constant need to struggle against the waters has its influence in mythology, where the primeval being, finally overcome by the great gods her children, is Tiamat, the Sea. The rivers could be beneficent, but their behaviour seemed arbitrary. Their rise, depending on the melting of the snows in the mountains of Armenia and the spring rainfall in the drainage basins of the Zab rivers, was (to the Sumerians) un-predictable, and moreover the time of year at which the floods occurred was not, as in Egypt, well suited to the crops: this element of uncertainty and perennial anxiety about the fruitfulness of the land is reflected in Sumerian religion, and in the whole later Babylonian *Weltanschauung* or way of looking at life. As one final consequence of the city-state it may be mentioned that centraliza-tion made possible large scale architecture, and the ziggurat, or great stepped tower, became, and in some cases remains (see plates 3A and 3B), the most striking landmark of the Sumerian city.

A consequence of improved irrigation technique would be, as an irrigation engineer has pointed out, a shifting of the area of cultivation from the delta region to the river plain. This is precisely what is found. The oldest settlement in Sumer was, as Sumerian tradition and the evidence of archaeology both serve to show, Eridu, on the banks of a lagoon of the Persian Gulf. This site, however, already passed the zenith of its importance by the period known as *Early Dynastic* I (*circa* 2800 B.C.), and in early Sumerian history it was Erech which was the great cultural centre. The shift resulting from the development in irrigation technique is perhaps reflected in the Sumerian myth of Innin's visit to her father Enki (see page 36).

There are few natural barriers to communications in Sumer, and at the very dawn of history there was undoubtedly a striking cultural unity* throughout the land. This is shown not only by a uniform architecture and common political and religious insti-tutions but also by the fact that writing, once invented, was rapidly diffused through all the cities of Sumer, not only as a general principle but in its details: it can be no accident that the lists of

---

* What is under consideration here is cultural unity, not political unification; the latter was hindered by the fact that the cities were mostly, in this early period, enclaves within barren wastes.

signs in the different cities are everywhere basically the same.

Reference has been made above (see page 37) to Jacobsen's widely accepted theory that the earliest form of political organization in Mesopotamia was 'primitive democracy': by this term Jacobsen means a form of society in which 'ultimate power rested with a general assembly of all adult freemen'. This theory cannot be proved directly, since the period to which it is thought to relate came to an end before writing had been adapted to anything beyond the simplest forms of book-keeping; but the institution is deducible from the myths and epics of later Sumerian and Babylonian literature, providing the underlying euhemeristic assumption is accepted that the organization of the gods must be a reflection of the organization of a human society within the memory of the time at which that society crystallized. The myths, though not reduced to writing in their present form before the beginning of the second millennium, certainly reflect a far more ancient period, a time before cities had been provided with defensive walls and organized for siege warfare: on the basis of the archaeological evidence this period may be taken as within a hundred years of 2800 B.C. In the myths, when decisions need to be made, a characteristic procedure is carried out. All the deities, male and female, come to a grand assembly, and after they have drunk freely so that their hearts become expansive, the business is broached by one of the two senior gods. The matter is then open for general discussion, and any deity present may state a view, though it is clear that there is a group of gods whose word carries greater weight. When, as the result of the deliberations, a general view emerges, the two senior gods frame a decision and submit it to the Assembly, whose members, if the senior gods have duly crystallized the feeling of the meeting, respond with a unanimous 'So-be-it'. It is this Assembly which is supposed to reflect the hypothetical national Sumerian Assembly at Nippur postulated by Jacobsen.

The epics reflect circumstances of the slightly later period when the fortifications of the great cities were first being founded, which, according to the archaeological indications, was about 2700 B.C. The increasing size of populations and cities and the growth of large scale trading relations with distant places ultimately resulted in the rise of political and economic rivalries, by opening the way to disputes over irrigated land and the control of trade routes, whilst the colonization of remoter areas contributed to the breakdown of the old system of national consultation. Another potent factor in producing conditions leading to inter-city warfare and the related building of city defences was Semitic immigration. Semitic immigrants were entering Sumer *via* the desert fringe to the west from earliest times, but they must be thought of as trickling in in small isolated family groups, whose members quickly adapted themselves to the higher culture they now enjoyed, rather than as sweeping in as a great wave. These early Semitic immigrants were almost completely assimilated, their permanent effect being seen only in a gradual modification of the whole sociology and not in the appearance of a new stratum. There is no trace of stratification of society into, for example, an indigenous peasant group and an intrusive shepherd group; it is true that an example of Sumerian Wisdom literature with a mythical introduction does show a verbal contest between Shepherd and Farmer (see page 432), but the arguments relate only to the utility of their products and not to social strata or origins. Both woo the goddess Innin, but though one is favoured above the other the story ends in reconciliation between the rivals.

Whilst most scholars now accept that it is wrong to attempt to see third millennium history in terms of a racial struggle between Sumerians and Semites, it does seem to be true that Semitic infiltration introduced ideas in conflict with the basic conceptions of Sumerian society, and this probably had its effect in causing friction between cities with a substantial Semitic element and those shielded from the full pressure of Semitic immigration. The first instance of inter-city warfare is the siege of Erech, under its ruler Gilgamish (so early that he can still be regarded in later times as two-thirds divine); the adversary of Gilgamish was a certain Agga king of Kish, a northern city much more exposed than was Erech to the pressure of Semitic settlers from the west.

War creates a situation in which a leader, or king, has to be commissioned, and in the epics the ruler has already arrived. The myths show that originally the Assembly appointed a king only for the period of the emergency and could withdraw the grant subsequently; there is a reference to the choice of a king by a real human Assembly as late as 2300 B.C. (see pages 359 f.), and although some scholars have denied that this supposed tradition relates to an actual historical event fresh evidence suggests that their scepticism has been misplaced.

Personal rule required the approval of the god, which might be withdrawn at any time. Thus, although in fact dynasties were known from *Early Dynastic* times (hence the name), there was no principle of hereditary succession as such. It is true that the son of the ruler had an obvious and very heavy advantage when the question of the choice of a successor arose: this was so because members of the ruler's family commonly had experience in the administration of minor temples whose gods stood in the same relationship to the chief god of the city as they themselves did to the ruler. None the less, each ruler had to be submitted to the god for approval, and there are exceptions in plenty to what came to be the prevailing custom of hereditary succession. In theory, the temporary nature of kingship was probably recognized to the end in Babylonia (though not in Assyria). This conclusion (which not all scholars now accept) is largely based on the fact that at the New Year Festival each spring the Babylonian king had to surrender his insignia, make a negative confession, and then be re-invested by the god. The limitations in the Epic period on the authority of the *En*, or priest-king, has already been discussed above (see page 39).

The city and its lands, with all its inhabitants, was the estate of the city-god, with the ruler or priest-king (of whom Gilgamish was a prototype) as his steward. The gods created Man to do their service, wherefore the free citizens were technically the servants of the god. Many passages could be adduced to substantiate this statement, but it is strikingly illustrated by a Sumerian myth edited by Th. Jacobsen (*Journal of Near Eastern Studies*, V (1946), pages 136–7). In this myth Enlil separated Heaven from Earth, and bound up Earth's wound at the former point of juncture, which was in the city of Nippur, where the name of the temple area was Duranki, 'Bond of Heaven and Earth'. Then, this done,

> The Lord...drove his pickaxe into the 'flesh-producer' [the ground];
> In the hole (which he thus made) was the vanguard of mankind,
> (And) whilst (the people of) his land were breaking through the ground towards Enlil
> He eyed his Black-headed Ones [humans] in steadfast fashion.
> The Anunnaki [one of the two main groups of gods] stepped up to him,
> . . . . . .
> Black-headed Ones they requested of him [Enlil].

The primary function of the citizens of a Sumerian city-state was thus that they should serve the temple estates, or – what was the same thing in ancient eyes – the human who acted as the god's steward, namely the *Ensi* [governor or city-prince] of the city. In return, each free citizen received an allotment from the god's estates, that is, from the temple lands. The size of the land-holding varied with the status of the tenant, the smallest being about an acre and the largest over a hundred acres, though rights over the larger holdings represent a deviation from the earliest system. Such large private holdings can hardly have been wholly worked by the owner and his family, who must in some cases have employed poor freemen, or, in the later period, slaves. Variations in the size of the plot of land granted existed not only between different professions but also between members of the same profession, and the reason for this different treatment of apparent equals is not clear. It is possible that, apart from other considerations, there may have been a system of family allowances. This possibility (and at present it cannot be considered as more) is suggested by a text which, dealing with the procedure when Martu, god of the Semitic nomads, married a young lady of the city of Kazallu, says:

> Gifts for a married man, he doubled them,
> Gifts for a man with children, he trebled them,
> Gifts for a bachelor, he gave a single lot.

The freeman could own his own house – probably a simply

built mud hut like the *sarifeh* still used by the poorer classes in Iraq – with adjoining it a small garden; the text dealing with Urukagina's reforms just before the time of the Agade dynasty presupposes that, except for the depredations of the wicked and powerful, even the poor would have these.

It is plain that towards the end of the *Early Dynastic* period, when our information becomes relatively abundant, the greater part of the land was owned by the temples, and probable (though some noted Soviet Sumerologists do not accept this conclusion) that at an earlier period the temples were the only owners of land. Urukagina implies this when, in the account of the reforms he attempted to carry through (see page 47), ownership of land by the king, queen and princes is regarded as an injustice against the gods which had to be remedied. Whereas formerly

> The house of the *Ensi* was joined to fields of the *Ensi*, the house of the (*Ensi's*) Wife's Household (was joined to) fields of the (*Ensi's*) Wife's Household, (and) the house of the (*Ensi's*) Offspring (was joined to) fields of the (*Ensi's*) Offspring,

Urukagina took action so that

> in the house of the *Ensi* (and) the fields of the *Ensi* he installed Ningirsu [god of Lagash] as its master; in the house of the (*Ensi's*) Wife's Household (and) the fields of the (*Ensi's*) Wife's Household he installed (the goddess) Bawa as mistress; in the house of the (*Ensi's*) Offspring (and) the fields of the (*Ensi's*) Offspring he installed (the god) Shulshaggana as master.

In keeping with the same conception, the irrigated land between Lagash and Umma, which gave rise to considerable dispute and armed conflict between the two cities, was described as 'the beloved field of Ningirsu'.

The growth of the idea of private ownership of land was one of the points at which the influence of Semitic immigrants was seen. Even before the Agade dynasty, contracts of sale of land are found in the northern cities, where there was a strong Akkadian (Semitic) element, but apart from a few exceptions of this kind, private property in arable land was a very rare thing in early Sumer and unusual until the period of the Third Dynasty of Ur.

A text purporting to be a monument of Manishtusu, third ruler of the Agade dynasty, which appears to show that there existed by that time landed proprietors owning large estates, has been shown by I. J. Gelb to be an Old Babylonian forgery.

The arable land of the temple was divided into three parts, one of which, known as 'the Lord's field', was intended to furnish the needs of the cult and the interior economy of the temple: it amounted, in one case known, to about a quarter of the whole of the arable land of the temple. The rest was distributed to the occupants of the temple estate either as the allotment already mentioned in return for the services given to the god ('Field of maintenance') or as 'Field of Labour', that is, land let out at a rent payable as a proportion of the harvest. In the *Early Dynastic* period this rent was as low as one-seventh or one-eighth of the crop, but by the time of the Third Dynasty of Ur had risen to one-third of the crop. In addition to the arable land and the private gardens there were great areas of marshlands along the rivers and lagoons where cattle might graze and pigs forage, and open country where asses, sheep and goats might find a bite after the winter rains.

The interchange of the terms above may suggest that City-state and Temple were synonymous. This, indeed, probably was the case at the very beginning of urban Sumerian society (though this conclusion would not be accepted by Soviet Sumerologists), but by the time from which our main evidence comes a city normally contained more than one temple estate. Lagash, for example, upon which we are best informed, consisted of four towns or estates, each centred on a temple or group of temples: altogether about twenty temples are known (by name) at the time of the ruler Gudea (nearly twice that number a little later in the period of the Third Dynasty of Ur), but most of these were mere chapels at one of the major shrines. The chief or tutelary deity of the city was Ningirsu, to whom the other deities stood in a family relationship.

The divine wife of Ningirsu was Bawa, and her temple in Lagash comprised a total of about eleven thousand acres of arable land. There were three other main temple estates in the city of

Lagash, and it has been calculated that the temples received considerably more grain from their lands than was usually needed for rations and seed. Much of the surplus would normally be exported, but the temple granaries formed a valuable reserve for the community against shortage in the months before the new harvest or against crop failure at any time: this provides an interesting parallel to the Pharaoh's hoarding of grain against an expected famine in the story of Joseph (*Genesis* xli. 33–36). The temple magazines, which can still be recognized in their ruins at a number of sites excavated, contained a wide range of supplies, and the temple precincts must be thought of as a hive of commercial activity. Here were brought all the products of the temple lands, corn, vegetables and dried fish, cheese, dates, sesame seed for the production of oil, wool, skins for the tanners, and reeds for use in building. Some of these (notably corn, oil and wool) were issued as rations to the people of the god's estate, whilst others were either used in the service of the temple as they were or worked up into manufactured products. Some were destined for export. Sumer lacked three important raw materials: timber (except the date palm), stone and metals; and from earliest days these had to be obtained from abroad, the principal trade routes being opened up in Sumerian times. As early as the period with which the *Epic of Enmerkar* deals (perhaps 2700 B.C.), trading caravans passed between Sumer and the mountains of Iran laden with barley from the surplus of the fertile plains and returning with lapis lazuli and other semi-precious stones for the beautification of the temples. This whole matter is discussed more fully elsewhere: it is sufficient here to note that such imports had to be obtained by trading expeditions, and paid for with the surpluses from the temple estates, particularly grain, wool (either in the raw state or made up into textiles), foodstuffs such as onions and dates, and Sumerian manufactures such as tools, weapons and jewellery. The merchant or caravan leader was a respectable member of society and like other citizens was in the service of the city-god, for he also had his allotment of land on the god's estate.

The network of canals set up during the Sumerian period and

subsequently extended made possible the carriage of large quantities of goods from city-state to city-state, and thus gave shape to the whole pattern of internal Babylonian commerce. Communications between the various parts of a city-state or different city-states was easy by river, and indeed at most times presented little difficulty by land. The *Ensi* Shulgi in a hymn boasts of having given attention to the communications in his land:

> I went through the routes of the land,
> I protected the roads, founded blockhouses there,
> Put gardens by the side, made rest-houses,
> Permitted respectable men to stay there.

Travel could be surprisingly rapid, and Shulgi claims to have celebrated the *Esh-esh* festival in Ur and Nippur on the same day, which would involve a journey of over ninety miles. No doubt, however, this was exceptional, and was presumably made possible by a sailing ship, a strong wind and a steady nerve, since Shulgi refers to a violent storm:

> On that day a storm came shrieking, a tempest-blast beat down, . . .
> Lightning and the seven winds seared the whole heavens; . . .
> Ishkur [the weather god] howled in the heavens,
> The gusts of heaven banked up the waters of earth;
> Hailstones small and hailstones great, beat on my back.

Shulgi's reference to the building of blockhouses brings out another consequence of inter-city trade in Sumer. No one simple city-state was in a position to safeguard the trade routes upon which the prosperity of all depended, and this provided an incentive to political expansion by the wealthier and more powerful states. Thus trade served as a factor in the creation of a unified administrative and political system, and ultimately fostered what is nowadays stigmatized as imperialism, which in the third millennium found its fullest expression in the period of the Third Dynasty of Ur. Trade also, from the earliest period, assisted the diffusion of Sumerian culture far beyond the bounds of Sumer itself. Thus at Tell Brak in northern Syria there was, in the *Protoliterate* period (about 3000 B.C.) a temple built on the same plan as those in Sumer and containing similar objects and decoration, whilst temples of the *Early Dynastic* period have been found both at Ashur and at Mari, containing statues in Sumerian style.

It has been pointed out above (see page 37) that the priest-king, known in earliest times as the *En*, originally lived in the temple of the god, in a chamber called the *Egipar*, and was the immediate representative of the god. As long as there existed a Babylonian (or Assyrian) king he continued in certain respects to be the representative of the god and to exercise some priestly functions. Despite this, the institution of kingship did not develop directly from the office of the *En*. By the middle of the third millennium, when the documents give us detailed knowledge of circumstances and events in Sumer, particularly in Lagash, it was the functionary called the *Ensi* (see page 44) who bore responsibility to the god for the administration of the temples, the temple estates, and the city in general. Whilst each temple estate had its own personnel, known as the 'the people of the god So-and-so', and its own administration, all of them were ultimately controlled by the *Ensi*. The bountiful yields given by the fertile soil of southern Babylonia under the influence of irrigation permitted a substantial degree of specialization and division of labour, and many different types of workers, craftsmen and members of professions are mentioned in the texts. Without giving an exhaustive list one may mention such workers as bricklayers, carpenters, smiths and masons, spinners and weavers, butchers and cooks, brewers and bakers, potters, jewellers and hairdressers, in addition to those engaged on purely agricultural operations on the temple estates. The latter in turn were divided into specialized groups, and besides common labourers there were ploughmen, shepherds, oxherds and swineherds, and gardeners for the date and vegetable plantations. As fish in the early period was an important item of diet, fishermen are found in large numbers amongst the temple personnel, being divided into 'fresh water fishers', 'sea fishers', and 'fishers in salt water', that is, those operating in the tidal lagoons of the delta of the Tigris and Euphrates: the temple of the goddess Bawa alone had more than a hundred fishermen. The same texts show that at the middle of the third millennium the whole working force of the temple estates of this goddess amounted, including workers, to about twelve hundred. Adding wives and children, and making the reasonable assumption that the personnel of the other temples was on the same scale, we arrive at a total not far short of the whole population of the city of Lagash. This is given in a text of the time of Gudea as 36,000, which, though certainly an ideal number ($= 10 \times 60^2$), need not be regarded as other than of the correct order. Thus the working force was in fact the citizens themselves, and there was no large leisure class free from concern in the tasks of everyday life, nor any substantial dependence upon slavery – except in the sense that everyone, the ruler himself included, was technically a slave on the god's estate. As the whole economy of the city-state was based upon irrigation, and as all citizens were equally the slaves of the god and responsible for the due running of his estate, all were subject to the corvée and had to take part in work on dikes and canals and also temple building. This remained true in theory to the end of our period, for even in the middle of the first millennium the kings of Assyria and their sons went through the formal act of carrying the head-basket in connection with such work (see plate 18A for a Sumerian representation of this activity).

Slavery

Slaves (in the ordinary sense) there were, but they were never a majority in the population and the work of the whole community never depended upon them. In the *Early Dynastic* period they were not a very significant social element and consisted largely of prisoners of war. Such slaves as there were, were in the earliest times obtained by raids into the hill country: the ideogram for 'slave girl', accordingly, is basically 'woman of the mountain'.

It is not known precisely at what period it began to be possible for native free citizens to become slaves, but from the period of the Third Dynasty of Ur (*circa* 2100 B.C.) cases are known of free citizens being reduced to slavery either by selling themselves because of debt or hunger, by being seized by creditors, or by being sold as children by indigent parents. Such procedures had become very common by the Larsa period (*circa* 1900 B.C.), probably as a consequence of the economic hardships resulting from the inthrust of Amurrū (Amorites) going on at that time. By the period of the First Dynasty of Babylon, the laws of Hammurabi imply that the main source of slaves was importation from abroad in the way of commerce, rather than as prisoners of war.

In the Sumerian period female slaves seem to have been more numerous than male, and apart from the obvious use for the young and fair their main occupation was in the temple mills and in the workshops where spinning and weaving operations were carried out. In the *Early Dynastic* period almost all slaves were owned by the temples or the palace, being housed in barracks in labour gangs, rather like the unfortunates in Nazi or Soviet labour camps; but private ownership of slaves gradually developed. It has been estimated that the average free household in Babylonia in the first millennium B.C. owned two or three slaves, and the household in Assyria three or four. Female slaves could be used as concubines by the male members of the household, but a girl sold into slavery was sometimes safeguarded from prostitution by the provision being written into the sale contract that she should be married to a husband, normally another slave, though in some cases a freeman. Provision could even be made for remarriage several times if the first and subsequent husbands died.

Slavery in Babylonia was never a caste system, for free men could fall into slavery, or slaves gain their freedom, whilst marriage between a free woman and a slave was by no means uncommon. A slave could acquire property, with which (if his master were agreeable) he could buy his own freedom: at the death of a slave, however, his property passed to his master.

There seems to be no proof that slaves carried any distinctive mark in the early Sumerian period, but from Old Babylonian times and perhaps considerably earlier they were identified (some think) by a distinctive tonsure, or (as others suppose the crucial word means) by the wearing of some kind of chain. There was also often some kind of mark, either tattooed or branded on the face or the back of the hand. Such markings would be more likely on a slave with known runaway tendencies, and such a one could be fettered and have the words 'A fugitive, arrest him!' incised on his face. Mention is also made of a slave who had the name of his owner written in two languages on the back of his hand. Marking was, however, most commonly met with amongst a class of people who became of great importance in Babylonia in the first millennium. These were the persons dedicated to the temples, and included not only state prisoners of war and slaves donated or bequeathed to a temple, but also persons of free birth, such as rescued waifs and children of poor parents handed over in times of famine to save their lives.

Adoption and Child Care

Reduction to slavery was not, however, the inevitable fate of orphans or of the children of the destitute. Often such a child might be adopted by a childless couple as their own heir, and legislation for such a situation is found in the ancient law codes, whilst numerous documents dealing with adoptions of this type have been found. One such document reads:

> Yahatti-Il is the son of Hillalum and of the lady Alitum. He shall benefit by their benefits and suffer ill by their ills. If Hillalum his father or the lady Alitum his mother say to their son Yahatti-Il 'You are not our son', they shall forfeit house and furniture. If Yahatti-Il says to Hillalum his father or the lady Alitum his mother 'You are not my father' or 'You are not my mother', they may shave his head and sell him for silver.
>
> (In respect to) Hillalum and the lady Alitum, however many sons they acquire, Yahatti-Il is the heir. From the house of Hillalum his father he shall receive a double share (at the division of the paternal property) and his junior brethren shall share (the rest) equally.

One does not look in the ancient world for social insurance as we know it, but there are indications (apart from that just mentioned) that the poor and weak might find assistance and protection. As early as the time of Urukagina that ruler set out, according to his own profession, to protect the poor and weak against the rich and strong, and the codes of law of succeeding periods make, either implicitly or explicitly, the same noble claim for the ruler. We find instances of the principle not only in legal codes but in benevolence towards particular persons. Thus there is a letter from Mari in which the young orphan of an old palace servant was recommended to the protection of the sub-king, Yasmah-Adad:

> To my lord Yasmah-Adad say, 'Thus says Hasidanum your servant: "The son of the palace postal official was transferred from Mari and now that man has died. Now he had a son, who is still an infant. Let my lord see the child, and (confirm that) he is an infant and that he has no guardian. May my lord ease the situation for him."'

Holidays

Life for the people of Mesopotamia – even slaves – was not one long unremitting toil. In fact, as in the mediaeval world, holy days were holidays, and all work and business was frequently interrupted by religious festivals, which would occupy several days in each month, though not on a weekly basis like the main Jewish and Christian holy days. The greatest holiday of the year was the eleven (or, at another period, fifteen) days of the New Year Feast, which for the populace, if not for the priesthood, must have been a grand time of merrymaking, pageantry, roistering and wenching. Even on working days there was a limit to the work expected of the workers, and labourers might get a complaint attended to if they felt too much was being put upon them. In a letter of the late seventh century B.C. an official refers to some work being done on a dam by some men for whom he was responsible, and comments:

> The work here is hard. The stint of bricks that we are responsible for is enormous! 110 bricks a day per man!

Another letter actually refers to a threatened strike, occasioned by an unpopular appointment. The official writing the letter reported to the king:

> The king set Nabu-shar-usur . . . over his work-people. The people are not agreeable (to this) and will not do the king's work.

Food and Drink

The diet of the people of Babylonia, slave and free alike, was largely based on barley, which provided the staple drink, beer, as well as the staple cereal food: it was eaten in the form of unleavened bread, probably as thin discs spread and cooked on a hot surface, giving a very palatable food (now known as *khubuz*), still eaten by peasants in Iraq though regrettably despised by the more sophisticated there. Other cereals eaten, in the form of bread or a kind of porridge, were millet, wheat, rye, and (in the first millennium B.C.) rice. Another way of preparing the cereals was to make them into pastry, cakes or biscuits by cooking the flour mixed with honey, ghee, sesame oil, milk or various fruits.

The commonest vegetable was probably the onion, whilst lentils, beans and peas (valuable sources of protein), were also widely used, often in soup. The cucumber and various other cucurbits were eaten, as was the cabbage. The lettuce was grown then as now, and was probably responsible, as it still is, for the transmission of a great deal of waterborne disease. Dates, a valuable source of sugar, were an important part of the common diet, whilst the palm also provided date-wine, as well as a celery-like delicacy cut from the growing heart of the male palm – today sometimes given by Europeans the unworthy name of 'date-cabbage'. Other fruits were the apple, pomegranate, fig, quince, medlar and apricot (see also page 495). Amongst beverages, in addition to beer and date-wine, wine from the grape was known as early as the *Protoliterate* (*Jemdet Nasr*) period, probably as an import from the highlands; it was not in the early period a drink in everyday use. Such beverages, which probably contained a good deal of lees, were in the Sumerian period imbibed through drinking tubes, of which the end was perforated with small holes to form a kind of filter.

Many varieties of beer were known and one of the Babylonian lexical series contains an extensive list of the technical terms for the processes and materials employed in making the different kinds of beer. Down to the time of Hammurabi brewing

Drinking tube

Brewing

seems to have been in the hands of women, for this craft is the only one which was under the protection of female divinities, whilst the alewife is specifically mentioned in the laws of Hammurabi. Occasionally brewing is depicted in art.

Milk was available from sheep, goats and cows, but from the rapidity with which it turns in the climate of south Iraq it was chiefly used, then as now, in the form of yoghurt, butter or cheese. An inlay frieze from the middle of the third millennium (represented below) illustrates the production of milk and milk foods.

The calf is placed at its dam's head; this is well known to have the effect of making the cow let down its milk more readily. The Sumerians thus prove themselves far more acute observers of animal behaviour than the Scythians two millennia later, whose blinded slaves were known, according to Herodotus, to

> use tubes of bone, similar in shape to a flute, which they thrust up the vulva of the mare; some engage in milking the mares, whilst others are busy blowing. They assert that this practice has the object of inflating the mare's veins with air, so forcing the udder down.

In the Sumerian frieze the milker sits on a stool behind the cow, in a position which is not usual but which the writer has seen used in England. A little way off another man sits on a stool rocking the milk in a large stoppered vessel to make the butter-fat

Milking scene

174

coagulate. The scene to the extreme left shows another pair of men apparently straining the resultant product to separate the butter-milk from the butter.

The principal animal protein food apart from milk was, particularly in earlier times, fish, though there was a notable decrease in its use later. Many kinds of fish are mentioned in administrative documents of the third millennium, and up to the period of the First Dynasty of Babylon. There exists from about 2000 B.C. a Sumerian text in which the habits and appearance of many species of fish are described in some detail in the guise of a deity's invitation to enter the house he had prepared for them. Whether this text represented mere scribal erudition or was concerned with charming fish into the fishermen's nets is not yet clear. After the Cassite period the eating of fish became less common, to judge by the texts, and it has been suggested that there was some popular taboo (not accepted into official religion) on fish eating; this is plausible, since a taboo of this kind is attested from Syria in the first millennium B.C., whilst sacred fish are still preserved in a number of places in Iraq. Against this conclusion it may be mentioned that Assyrian bas-reliefs of the first millennium depict the netting of fish in a fish pond, whilst fishing was certainly carried on in the New Babylonian period.

Mutton, and less commonly beef, were eaten at festivals, and in the earliest times offerings of goats were a regular feature of peasant worship and presumably an equally regular part of peasant diet. With increasing urbanization in Sumer, the real goat offered to the god came to be replaced (judging by the evidence of cylinder seals depicting the scene) by a model of a goat, and this probably reflects a diminishing availability of goat meat in the diet of the ordinary townsman. Nevertheless, the gods and the king still received ample meat rations, and some of the cattle destined for food or sacrifice must have been fattened to a huge size, for in one of the letters found at Mari (early second millennium B.C.) there is mention of an ox, intended as a palace offering, which had been made so fat that it could not stand. There was no taboo on the pig, which is still found in large numbers in the marshes of southern Iraq (as, indeed, also in some other parts of the country). In Sumerian times pigs were tended in large herds, the food they could pick up by scavenging being supplemented by barley feed. In many early or primitive communities there tends to be a shortage of fat in the diet, wherefore fat meat is a far greater delicacy than with us. Thus in ancient Babylonia fat pork was a highly prized food, and a Sumerian proverb makes the point that it was too good for slave girls, who had to make do with the lean ham. Cattle were, because of the shortage of suitable pastureland, relatively few in number. Horse-flesh was eaten by humans without involving any religious taboo, at least in the Nuzi area east of Assyria in the fourteenth century B.C., and a lawsuit is recorded in which the defendants had stolen and eaten a horse. Dead asses were used only as dog meat. Of poultry, geese and ducks were kept from early times; the hen did not reach the land till the first millennium B.C.

Many of the foods mentioned were preserved for times of scarcity. Cereals would present no problem, whilst legumes could easily be dried in the sun. Various fruits were kept in edible condition by pressing into cakes. Fish was preserved by salting, a process also used, together with desiccation, for meat.

Housing and House Equipment

Sumerian and Babylonian housing will not, to those accustomed to post-war building standards, appear impressive, and the average citizen's house of the third millennium would hardly be considered more than a thick-walled, almost windowless, mud hut. Rooms were fitted together to suit the site available, generally without reference to a master plan, and the doors between rooms were so low that one would need to stoop to pass from room to room. Often two adjacent houses would have a common wall, and in some such cases contracts are known confirming to both neighbours the right to lay joists on the wall. A superior type of house was also found, made of baked brick. Such houses would be built round a central courtyard, like the older type of better class house still found in Baghdad. These would be, at least in the cities, of more than one storey.

Comparison of Sumero-Babylonian (or modern oriental)

housing with the buildings of western Europe is largely beside
the point. The basic purpose of a house in England is to keep out
the wet and draughts of cold air: the basic purpose of a building in
southern Iraq is to keep out the blasting heat which beats down
twelve hours a day from May to September from the blazing,
pitiless sun. Windows in that climate are not a blessing, and the
misguided folk who attempt to transplant to Baghdad modern
European houses, with relatively thin walls of brick and concrete
and large expanses of glass, find that they can only render their
dwellings tolerable by negating the purpose of the glass with
heavy screening and by installing air-cooling machinery. Houses
in ancient Mesopotamia contained, in the way of windows, at the
most a clay or wooden grille set in the wall: examples from the
third millennium B.C. have been found (see plate 15A) almost
identical with a type still sometimes seen in Iraq today.

The equipment of houses naturally varied a great deal from
period to period, area to area, or class to class. The furnishings of
palaces are obviously not typical, and the ideal way to give an
account of the subject would be to describe the complete contents
of one particular private house. Unfortunately, soil conditions in
Iraq do not favour the conservation of wooden objects and textiles,
whilst more durable utensils of metal or stone are likely to have
been removed from any deserted house in antiquity. Thus it is
not surprising that no private house complete with a full range
of contents has yet been excavated, and the following account
must necessarily be a composite one.

Wooden beds were in common use and are depicted on
Assyrian bas-reliefs. They are also frequently mentioned in
medical texts, where it is often assumed that the patient will be
lying in one. One supposes that the ancient people of Mesopotamia
slept between rugs or blankets, but there seems to be no positive
evidence on this, though a word of fairly common occurrence
in lists of personal possessions has been plausibly taken to mean
'blanket'. As to tables, the gods certainly had them for their meals,
which suggests, in view of human conservatism in things religious,
that the use of tables for meals in Babylonia was of high antiquity.
Well-to-do citizens at least enjoyed the same convenience as the

gods in this respect, for tables are frequently depicted on the Assyrian monuments. Chairs with legs, a back and even arms were common enough in palaces, whilst stools were used even for menial tasks as early as the beginning of the third millennium (see illustration on page 174). Built-in mud benches are also found. The other major pieces of furniture in the house would be a few wooden storage chests.

As to feeding utensils, no doubt fingers were often considered adequate for solids, though single-pronged bone forks have been found in large numbers. Knives were, of course, common. For liquids, spoons made of bitumen or of bone have been found, and ladles of terra-cotta were also in use. Fashions in the shape of eating and drinking vessels changed enormously from time to time, but typically there were platters, bowls and cups made of pottery, wood, stone or metal.

Food would be prepared on an oven, often situated in the courtyard of the house, though indoor hearths are also found. Portable braziers (of the type illustrated in plate 59) could also be used indoors, where they would be a great comfort in the cold season, though the particular specimen illustrated, which was made of copper and ornamented with figures in the form of lions, may actually have been employed in the cult. Amongst cooking utensils, a copper vessel almost indistinguishable from a modern frying pan has been found from the early third millennium (see plate 15B).

Some of the cereal foods and legumes were prepared by pounding, and a pestle and mortar must have been a necessity for any industrious Babylonian housewife. Certainly above the former residential areas of ancient cities – Cuthah, for example – one can pick up, at the cost of a little searching, quite a number of broken pestles and mortars of baked clay or stone. Another necessity would be a mill for the grinding of corn to make bread, and as early as the *Protoliterate* period handmills of imported volcanic stone were found in private houses.

Items of jewellery – ear-rings, beads, pendants, bracelets and anklets (see plate 62 for some examples) – would also have been present in the average house, together with toilet accessories, such as pots of unguents for the anointing of the body and hair, and mirrors and tweezers of copper or even silver or gold. From a palace of about 2300 B.C. beads were found in company with mussel shells containing kohl (eye-shadow) and rouge, leading the excavator to conclude that he was in a lady's apartment. Special bathrooms (of the Turkish type) have been found in palaces, but probably did not exist in private houses, whose occupants presumably bathed in the rivers. Lavatories, consisting of a platform above a pit or drain (see below), have been found from as early as the third millennium, one having a seat of bitumen for added comfort (see plate 13A).

As far as is known, there was no municipal system of sewage disposal for private houses, but government buildings as early as the third millennium had an elaborate system of drainage. In a large building of about 2300 B.C., taken to be a palace, at Eshnunna (modern Tell Asmar) on the Diyala, there were six lavatories with raised seats made of baked brick, and five bathrooms. Except in a wing of the building which was at too low a level and therefore had its own cesspool, all these lavatories and bathrooms were connected with drains which led into a main sewer a yard high and vaulted over with baked bricks (see plate 13B). Each lavatory was equipped with a large water vessel, some of which at the time of excavation still contained the pottery dipper which must have been employed to flush the lavatory after use. Assyrian palaces of the first millennium B.C. also had an elaborate system of drainage, the main drain being five feet in width and having its end covered with a grating to prevent the ingress of burglars. Such drains discharged their contents into the river.

Artificial lighting was provided either by torches, consisting of a bundle of reeds dipped in oil or bitumen, or by lamps. Such a lamp would consist of a small shoe-shaped pot of oil, with a wick protruding through a hole on top. The oil employed for this purpose would be either vegetable oil from sesame seed (olive oil was much less common), or possibly (the matter is still in dispute) crude oil from the deposits upon which much of western Europe now relies.

Various hazards were associated with ancient housing. The

actual collapse of a house, particularly of the type made of sun-dried brick, was by no means uncommon, and there are many references to this problem. The laws of Hammurabi devote five sections to it, laying down, amongst other things, that if a builder builds a house which collapses and kills the householder, the builder himself should be put to death; if it kills the householder's son, the builder's son should be put to death. Sin-iddinam, king of Larsa, did actually meet his death through the collapse of a temple staircase, as we learn from an allusion in an omen text. There were rituals designed to prevent walls from collapsing, and even omens foretelling death through accidents of this kind:

> If (a man in his dream) descends into the underworld and a dead person blesses him, he will die through the collapse of a wall.
> If (a man in his dream) descends into the underworld and eats a dead person, he will die through a falling roof-beam.

Another inconvenience in ancient houses was creeping things. Scorpions still abound in parts of Iraq, even finding their way into modern houses in the centre of Baghdad from time to time. In ancient times they must have been very common in the mud-roofed, mud-brick house of the ordinary man, and a whole group of omens refers to scorpions falling from the ceiling on to a man or his bed. There were also various magical or more practical treatments for scorpion sting. Snakes also, in modern times as well as ancient, sometimes crawl about – presumably in search of rodents – amongst the branches and mud forming the ceiling and roof of mud-brick houses, and there are many references in Babylonian omen texts to snakes falling out of the roof on to a man or his bed: in certain circumstances this was considered lucky (see page 462).

Town Planning; Water supply

Town planning was not unknown in ancient Mesopotamia, especially in the New Assyrian period. In earlier times a town grew up gradually around the temple area, but in several cases in the Assyrian period kings built new towns on a deliberate plan. A notable example is Calah (modern Nimrud), rebuilt by Ashur-nasir-pal in 879 B.C. and populated with about seventy thousand people. Such royal cities were, of course, planned with military needs in mind, and another instance is Dur-sharrukin (Khorsabad), planned and founded by Sargon II as a new capital on the site of a small village. Such cities were provided with main exit roads, well surfaced with cobble-stones for the benefit of the royal armies proceeding on campaign. A road of this kind has been excavated at Nimrud, whilst Sennacherib mentions another when he says, in connection with his re-planning of Nineveh, that anyone encroaching on the royal road will be impaled. Careful attention was also given to the river communications of Assyrian cities: at Nimrud the city was found to be provided with a great quay wall, about thirty feet in depth, composed of dressed stone blocks measuring a cubic yard or more each.

The water supply of ancient cities was always a matter of great concern to rulers, and attention to this was regarded as one of the notable achievements of Hezekiah (2 *Kings* xx. 20). There was little problem in Babylonia, but the matter needed more careful attention in Assyria, for the level of the Tigris is both more variable than that of the Euphrates and lower relative to the adjacent land, so that its employment for irrigation purposes is less easy at most times of the year. Sennacherib made strenuous efforts to bring water to Nineveh to irrigate the orchards and parks he had laid out (see above, page 122), cutting a canal for six miles and bringing water at one point over an aqueduct three hundred yards long. The whole structure was composed of about two million stones weighing a quarter of a ton each. A bed of rough boulders was placed in the bed of the stream which had to be crossed, and a level pavement formed upon these boulders. From this pavement in the stream rose six piers which supported the arches where the aqueduct spanned the stream: the greater part of the three hundred yards of the aqueduct's length was, of course, built on dry land. The top of the aqueduct itself consisted of a level pavement twent-four yards wide, carefully graded for an even fall, and having its sides strengthened with buttresses. A project of the same kind for supplying Arbailu with water has already been referred to.

In Calah there were a number of wells cut down to a depth

of ninety feet to safeguard the city's water supply in case of siege: one of the wells (cleared out in 1952) proved still to have a yield of five thousand gallons a day. In the same well there was found a wooden pulley wheel with the marks of wear caused by rope still clearly visible, whilst there were also several score of pots, some with pieces of rope still round their necks, which must once have constituted an endless chain of vessels worked by a windlass to draw up water from the well. Sennacherib proudly refers to some device of the same kind when he says, with reference to his rebuilding of his capital Nineveh:

> In order to draw water daily, I had ropes, bronze cables and bronze chains made, and I had beams and cross-bars fixed over the wells instead of poles.

Clothing

As to clothing, fashions changed considerably over the two and a half millennia from 3000 B.C. to 500 B.C. Textiles were certainly known from the third millennium, and before textiles came into general use skins and fleeces were employed; garments worn by Sumerians as depicted on the monuments appear to be made of sheepskins or goatskins, but it must be remembered that ancient art was in the service of the gods and not of the art gallery, so that it is primarily scenes connected with the cult, rather than with contemporary daily life, which are illustrated. There is some evidence suggesting that in the *Protoliterate* period the people of south Iraq went naked at their daily work in the fields. Consonant with this is the fact that the *Ensi* is sometimes depicted (from the *Early Dynastic* period onwards) kneeling before the god naked, and this nude state may possibly have represented the habits of Sumer several centuries before; religious conservatism is such that, for the officiant, the garment for divine worship is seldom or never the garment of current fashion, and this probably applied as much to the cult functionaries of Sumer as to our own ministers.

Where textiles are represented, it is clear that in the Sumerian period the common garment was a kind of kilt, clearly shown on plate 8B. An inlaid panel from Ur (see plate 12) shows soldiers wearing such kilts, together with long cloaks draped over the shoulders and fastened in the manner of a duffle coat with a peg. The *Ensi* Gudea, like some other rulers, is depicted wearing some kind of loose-fitting, ankle-length shawl draped over the left shoulder. During the second millennium the typical dress consisted of an undergarment with lengths of cloth draped about it, often belted at the waist. Stitched clothing was introduced into Mesopotamia during this period, and in the first millennium B.C. the typical dress was a tunic, or several tunics, fitted rather than draped.

Texts mention many different qualities of textiles, ranging from cheap materials suitable for servants to those fit to be worn by royalty. The robes of the king and of the nobility were, as the Assyrian bas-reliefs show, heavily decorated with embroidery.

The wool from which most textiles were made was, of course, obtained from sheep, but not necessarily by the method of shearing as practised by us. This was certainly used – the animal being given a bath before shearing – but there were two other ancient techniques as well. One of these alternative techniques was plucking, and the other was washing the animal in a fast-running stream to separate the loose wool from the fleece. It is not certain that the last-mentioned method was used in Mesopotamia. Goat's hair was probably also used for some purposes, as it is still in Iraq. There are extensive records in Sumerian concerning the wool industry, and it is estimated that one-sixth of all Sumerian tablets found at Nippur deal with this subject. From such tablets those able to appreciate the processes involved have succeeded in deriving considerable information about the bleaching, dyeing, spinning and weaving of wool in the third millennium. Linen and cotton were also used for cloth, but less commonly than wool.

Hair Styles

An interesting study on women's hair styles in Mesopotamia in the third and early second millennia B.C. has been made by Agnès Spycket, from whose articles the following brief summary chiefly derives. The evidence comes, of course, almost entirely from representations in art, most commonly cylinder seals.

In the *Jemdet Nasr* period (*circa* 2900 B.C.), both sexes had long hair hanging down in a bunch behind the neck, possibly tied back from the face in some way, though it seems to have covered the ears. In the succeeding *Early Dynastic* period (say, 2800 to 2400 B.C.), the basic style was long hair swept back from the face, done up into one plait and coiled round the head turban-wise. Various modifications of this are attested, some of them allowing for side tresses in front of the ears. The style was also elaborated by the use of frameworks enabling the hair to be built up even more fetchingly. More simply, the hair could be worn hanging down in one mass controlled by a ribbon or in two or more plaits.

In the Agade period (roughly 2370 to 2230 B.C.), unless the now predominant Semites were naturally curly, the hair must have been artificially waved, for wavy or curly hair was certainly the fashion. The hair was parted in the middle, a fringe sometimes being left at the front and over the temples. The mass of the lady's hair was generally done up at the back into a large chignon or bun, which extended from the nape of the neck to the top of the head. Basically the same style was found in the succeeding period (about 2200 to 2000 B.C.), when the chignon, which by that time was very large, had a snood over it, held in place with a head-band.

Head-bands and snoods were not the only accessories employed for their coiffure by the ladies of these ancient times: they certainly also made use of hairpins, for specimens of these have been found, made of bone, copper, silver or gold.

The Sumerian male of the latter half of the third millennium might either have his hair completely shorn, or wear his hair and beard carefully waved. Many statues (those of plates 18B and 20, for instance) are bald and beardless, and though it might be suggested that such statues were originally provided with wigs, this is improbable, since in some cases the statue incorporates a close-fitting head-dress which gave no scope for the fixing on of a wig. Semitic kings, from the beginning of the second millennium right down to the end of the Assyrian empire, are almost always shown with luxurious wavy beards, and often with long wavy hair, clear of the ears, falling loosely, though very tidily, over the shoulders. In Assyrian religious scenes there are often represented, besides the king and warriors with their long hair and full beards, another group of men, also with long hair but beardless and with rather fleshy faces. It has been suggested that these beardless men were eunuchs, but this is not certain. It may be that there was a convention of representing any young man in royal service as beardless: certainly the expression 'you haven't a beard on your chin' was used of an immature man (see above, page 70).

Slaves had a characteristic kind of tonsure, as did also priests and, apparently, doctors. The latter conclusion derives from the fact that in the story *The Poor Man of Nippur* (published by O. R. Gurney of Oxford in *Anatolian Studies*, VI (1956), pages 145–164), the hero, in order to impersonate a doctor, first goes to have his head shaved.

Marriage and Sexual Relations

Marriage (throughout the whole of Sumerian and Babylonian society) was monogamous in the sense that a man might have only one woman who ranked as a wife and enjoyed a social status corresponding to his. On the other hand, no stigma attached to resort to temple prostitutes or to the keeping of concubines, and once slaves had come to occur widely as private property one of the chief uses, if not the chief use, of female slaves was for the latter purpose: concubinage did not alter the status of a slave-girl, who did not automatically receive her freedom, whilst her offspring also had the status of slaves unless the master formally accepted them as his own legitimate children. It was possible for a freeman – presumably a bachelor (if there were any in Babylonian society) or a widower, or perhaps even a married man with a complaisant wife – to make a slave-girl head of his household, but such a course of action is forcefully criticized in a proverb. The principal and subsidiary ladies of the house did not always agree and might make an uncomfortable home of it for the rash or hapless husband: this is indicated by an omen

If . . . wife and wife agree, that household will get on all right,

which suggests that the opposite state of affairs was not unknown. A biblical instance of such discord which springs to mind is that of Sarai and Hagar (*Genesis* xvi. 4–6).

There is even some evidence, from proverbs and omens, about the actual details of love-making: unfortunately the omens are damaged and the proverbs difficult to understand precisely because of their very pithy style. None the less they indicate that both the normal behaviour and the typical perversions (such as sodomy, lesbianism, transvestism and cunnilinctus) were much the same in ancient Mesopotamia as in modern Europe. Maladjustments familiar in modern society, such as impotence and premature ejaculation, were also well known in Babylonia. However, despite all this, and the existence of prostitution, homosexuality and concubinage, married bliss was no rarity: a Sumerian proverb mentions a proud husband boasting that his wife had borne him eight sons and was still ready to lie down to accept his nuptial embrace. The commonest position for intercourse seems to have been face to face with the woman on her back, but other positions are also attested (see plate 51C, which appears to depict intercourse taking place as a cult act). A text refers to the high-priestess permitting intercourse *per anum*.

There is no evidence that circumcision played any part in the religion of the Sumerians, Babylonians or Assyrians, and the practice seems to have been exclusive to the West Semites and the Hamites (Egyptians and their congeners). It is interesting, however, that a stone model of a phallus, evidently used in some cult, found at Tepe Gawra in a stratum datable as contemporary with the *Protoliterate* period, is circumcised. This may be the result of early West Semitic influence at Tepe Gawra, and certainly proves that (*pace* the fundamentalists) circumcision as a religious practice in the ancient Near East long ante-dated Moses or even Abraham.

The status of women generally was certainly higher in the early Sumerian city-state than it subsequently became: they could be in the service of the temples in various capacities, not only as priestesses or temple prostitutes, and like men received grants of rations and allotments from the temples. The wives of some rulers, such as Lugalanda and Urukagina, attained positions of great importance, but too much should not be made of this, for the same could be said of the womenfolk of some Assyrian kings, at a time when the general position of women was by no means high. There are hints that in the very beginning of Sumerian society women had a much higher status than in the heyday of Sumerian culture: this chiefly rests on the fact that in early Sumerian religion a prominent position is occupied by goddesses who afterwards virtually disappeared, save – with the one exception of Ishtar – as consorts to particular gods. The Underworld itself was originally under the sole rule of a goddess, for a myth explains how she came to take a consort (see page 337); and goddesses played a part in the divine decision-making Assembly in the myths. There is even a strong suggestion that polyandry may at one time have been practised, for the reforms of Urukagina refer to women who had taken more than one husband: some scholars have shied away from this conclusion, suggesting that the reference might only be to the remarriage of a widow, but the wording of the Sumerian text does not really support this.

Education

It is obvious that formal education must have been available in Sumer from the time of the invention of writing: the manipulation of the cuneiform script is not a skill which can be acquired without years of diligent application, as more than one modern student has discovered to his grief. Merchants and administrators required some knowledge of writing, and scribes and priests a high degree of competence. However, we have no need to rely on *a priori* argument to deduce the existence of an educational system from the earliest periods: the tablets themselves prove it, since from such sites as Erech, Shuruppak, Nippur and Ur, inscribed exercise tablets have been recovered. That they are school exercises is put beyond doubt by the fact that they may bear the same text copied out several times by different hands, or else may have, for instance, a piece of literary text on one side of a tablet with mathematical exercises on the other. Most of the early examples of such evidence are written in Sumerian, but school tablets in the Akkadian language are known from as early as the third millennium, and one, a legend full of erasures, has been crossed through, apparently by the exasperated teacher.

Our most copious evidence on the educational system, though written in Sumerian and lauding the merits of that language, actually comes from the beginning of the second millennium, when Sumerian as a spoken language was, if not quite extinct, at least on its deathbed. The evidence consists of a series of compositions, still in course of recovery and interpretation, which actually deal with the education of a scribe, and which were evidently composed in the scribal schools themselves, since the whole underlying theme is that the scribal art is the apex of human achievement. The picture of school life which these texts present gives an impression almost of caricature, and has led a modern authority, C. J. Gadd, who has made a special study of these texts, to remark that 'we can scarcely deny that these men [the scribes] had a keen appreciation of the human comedy, and might be considered inventors of ludicrous presentation'. A more detailed account of these texts is given elsewhere (see pages 434 ff.).

The conditions for admission to the scribal schools are not known, but the scholars were probably the sons of the wealthy and influential – that is, there was, as in the English public school system, a self-perpetuating upper class, with its resultant benefits and abuses. Evidence for this comes from the abundant documents of the period of the Third Dynasty of Ur (*circa* 2100 B.C.), which establish that scribes were generally the sons of city or temple administrators, military officers, priests or men who were themselves scribes. In one of the literary texts of the group in question a father wishes to get the headmaster to take a more favourable view of his son, and is clearly in a position to offer sumptuous entertainment. Nothing is said in these texts to suggest that the system was co-educational, though it is known that there were a few female scribes, probably at all periods.

The period of education was long and rigorous, 'from childhood to maturity', as a text puts it. There was no sparing of the rod, and corporal punishment was freely administered, for poor exercises, lack of diligence, improper dress, undignified behaviour outside school hours, or apparently from sheer spleen on the part of any member of the school staff from the janitor upwards. In the event of insubordination the student might be gated or even put in fetters.

The assumption sometimes made that the schools were always located in the temple complex seems to be ill-founded, at least with respect to the early second millennium, though education, like all other activities, is likely to have been centred on the temple in *Early Dynastic* times, and may have been later. However that may be, the principal finds of literary texts in ancient cities have been made not in the temple quarters but in private houses, whilst at Mari, for example, a building with benches which archaeologists have plausibly interpreted as a school, was not part of a temple.

Sports and Pastimes

Amongst the games, sports and pastimes which we can prove were practised by the ancient people of Mesopotamia it is difficult to be sure which had a religious or magical significance and which were purely for fun. The difficulty of making the distinction appears less surprising when we recall that in our own society certain pastimes can be shown to have a religious or magical origin, of which in some instances (as in traditional games at religious festivals in some places) the participants are still sometimes consciously aware.

The best-known sport of the Assyrians, hunting as practised by the king, certainly had strong and fully recognized religious associations. It was a sacred duty of the king to shoot lions and to slay other beasts. Tiglath-Pileser I, for instance, claims that it was 'at the command of Ninurta who loves me' that in the region west of Assyria he killed four wild bulls, ten bull elephants and nearly a thousand lions. At a later period lions were specially caught and brought to Assyria to be released from their cages as required (see plate 40), for the purpose of enabling the king to demonstrate his prowess by shooting them down in a special park. It seems a reasonable supposition that the royal lion hunt was one of the public spectacles of the year, though there is no direct evidence to substantiate this suggestion. Other hunting scenes are depicted in plates 38–39 and 42–44.

Various forms of hand-to-hand fighting were practised as pastimes, possibly with a religious origin. Thus there is a reference in the *Epic of Gilgamish* to a wrestling match between Gilgamish and Enkidu, in which apparently the winner was the combatant who lifted his rival off the ground (see page 393): a copper stand for offerings, excavated at Tell Agrab, takes the form of two vases on the heads of a pair of wrestlers, clearly demonstrating the kind of hold used (see plate 51B). Boxing is also represented in art (see plate 51A), though the actual scene depicted was probably an activity in connection with the cult.

Dancing is mentioned in texts, but, as in the Old Testament (2 *Samuel* vi. 14–21 and elsewhere), it was so intimately related to the cult that it is perhaps not fitting to put it down as a pastime, as it may not yet in any sense have partaken of the nature of an independent activity.

Games played with pieces or counters on a board marked out in squares existed, for several such boards have been found (see plate 9B) though no details of the particular game are yet known. Dice, almost identical with those still used, have also been found.

From at least the *Early Dynastic* period, music was a concomitant of popular and royal festivals, whilst in the cult it had, as in the Old Testament (1 *Samuel* x. 5 and many other places) an important function. There were in use instruments of the percussion, wind and string types, which are mentioned in texts and depicted in art (see plate 52). Examples of some of the instruments have been found in excavations; plate 7 shows one of two harps from Ur. Another object which was probably a harp or some similar stringed instrument was found at Nimrud in 1952 but disintegrated in the course of excavation. A Babylonian baked clay whistle of the ocarina type (see illustration) was found last century, but has since been lost.

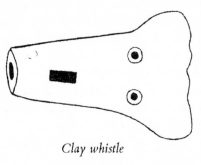

Clay whistle

Probably the most primitive of the musical instruments of Babylonia was the *balag*, a drum of the shape of a sand-glass, used in the temple ritual by the *kalu-*

priest to soothe the heart of the god. A special sacred kettle-drum, the *lilissu*, was set up in the temple courtyard and beaten at the time of an eclipse of the moon.

Health and Psychology

An examination of medical and other texts destroys the popular image of the ancient world as a golden age peopled by a happy, healthy race of mankind, free of inhibitions, free from worry and free from want. Though no statistics are available, mental illness was certainly well known and various neuroses and psychoses are alluded to. For an instance of a psychosis one need only refer to the biblical tradition concerning Nebuchadrezzar, who suffered from lycanthropy (*Daniel* iv. 28–33): whether based on fact about some real king or on theological fancy, it reflects acquaintance-ship in the ancient world with a particular type of mental disease. The royal family of Elam seems to have been particularly subject to mental illness and there are several references to different rulers of this line saying that 'his mind changed', that is, apparently, not that the man concerned altered his policy but that he went off his head. Sexual impotence was one form of psychological maladjust-ment from which some suffered in the ancient world as in the modern, and there are ample references to it in texts. There even existed in Hittite a whole ritual for the treatment of this malady. Nocturnal pollution is certainly no product exclusively of modern tensions and inhibitions; it was well known to the ancients, as omens of the following kind prove:

> If a man is sexually excited during the night and has a pollution in his dream, that man will suffer financial losses.
>
> If a man is sexually excited in his dreams and wakes up during the night and has a pollution, that man will . . . acquire riches.

Amongst other symptoms, syndromes and diseases, headaches and fever were extremely common, and sinusitis, tonsillitis, catarrh, rheumatism, various forms of paralysis, and probably tuberculosis, are mentioned. Eye and ear infections were also of very frequent occurrence. Symptoms are referred to which must relate to various internal complaints, and jaundice and dysentery were very common, as they still are in Iraq. In women breast disorders and miscarriages were no rarity. Gonorrhoea and possibly other venereal diseases are commonly mentioned (see page 463). Reference is also made to varicose veins. Long before nuclear fission could take the blame for such events, the Babylonians were well acquainted with abnormal and monstrous births, which happened to be recorded because of their significance as omens.

The ancient interest in omens also provides us with a fairly detailed knowledge of the kind of things about which the people of Mesopotamia might dream. This fascinating evidence is to be found in scholarly yet readable form in A. L. Oppenheim's *The Interpretation of Dreams in the Ancient Near East* (1956), in which omens drawn from dreams are edited. These omens have the form:

> If a man flies repeatedly, whatever he owns will be lost.

Obviously the ancients, like ourselves, had flying dreams: Sigmund Freud's quite different interpretation of such a dream will be familiar to most readers. They also had nightmares of various kinds: an Old Babylonian omen refers to the man who in his dream had the town – doubtless set on a hill – falling on him repeatedly, with no-one to answer his cries for help. Embarrassing dreams of walking around naked were as well known to the Babylonians as (according to Freud) to modern Europeans. In the ancient world they were considered lucky:

> If in his dream a man walks about naked, . . . troubles will not touch this man.

Many other dreams mentioned in omens shed an interesting sidelight on the mind of ancient man. Thus

> If a man (in his dream) goes in (sexually) to a wild beast, his household will become prosperous.
> If a man (in his dream) goes in (sexually) to his daughter, [apodosis lost].
> If a man (in his dream) goes in (sexually) to his mother-in-law, [apodosis lost].
> If (in a dream) the penis of a man is long, he will have no rival.
> If (in a man's dream) his urine comes out of his penis and fills the streets, his property will be confiscated and given to the town.
> If (in a man's dream) his urine is directed upwards to the heavens,

the son whom that man begets will be important, but his own days will be short.

There are a number of dreams which refer to eating, including references to cannibalism (see above, page 180) and to eating parts of the dreamer's own body. The origin of the interpretation of dreams can in many cases only be guessed at, though in some cases the symbolism is transparent enough. Thus

If (in a dream) someone gives (the dreamer) a wheel, he will have twins. [The connection is that wheels occur in pairs].

If (in a man's dream) someone gives him an empty cup, the poor man will become poorer.

If (in a man's dream) someone gives him a full cup, he will have fame and posterity.

Some interpretations merely depend upon a pun. Thus

If (in a man's dream) someone gives the man *mihru-wood*, he will have no rival [Akkadian *mahiru*].

Social Misfits

Crime was known in the ancient world in as many forms as today. There were young men who attempted to throw off parental authority (see page 202), there were murderers (see page 217) and rapers and common thieves, as well as embezzlers and forgers. An instance of embezzlement is revealed in a letter from one official to another announcing that the writer had been found out by the temple authorities in fraudulently converting to his own use part of the barley which he had been responsible for issuing. The temple authorities had ordered the guilty man to repay the amount embezzled with interest thereon, and in addition to pay the amount of a seemingly illicit gain made on an exchange trans-action, together with his arrears of temple dues and the dues for the current year. Amongst other crimes, as in ancient Egypt so also in Mesopotamia the religious practice of placing valuable goods in graves led to the robbing of tombs: this is obvious from the state in which some tombs have been found when excavated, whilst the possibility of having one's tomb rifled is mentioned in a Babylonian text:

The grave was opened; they took possession of my treasures.

The penalties for crime were generally either death or a fine, though mutilation was sometimes resorted to, especially in Assyria. There was no general system of imprisonment, although a person accused might be taken into custody whilst awaiting trial, or a debtor (or more often one of his household) might be temporarily confined in the house of the creditor or reduced to slavery. This kind of distraint was not, according to Professor A. Goetze (*The Laws of Eshnunna* (1956), page 71) intended to be of long duration, for, as Professor Goetze points out, a period of five months of distraint once mentioned seems to have been 'considered as an outrageously long period'.

Treatment of Animals

There is no reason to suppose that the attitude to animals in ancient Mesopotamia was any more gentle than it is in most parts of the world today. Indeed, one text contains the revealing words: 'I have beaten your body red with a whip like a runaway ass'. However, kings often manifested an interest in wild animals, and were pleased to receive presents of that kind (see, for an example, page 89). We have a letter in which an anxious official reports to the king upon the action he had taken about a lion which had been caught in a barn. He had intended to await further instructions, but those instructions had not been forthcoming. Meanwhile the lion had been kept in the barn for five days, and a dog and a pig thrown in for it to eat. Then, as the official puts it,

> I (said to myself): 'Perhaps that lion will escape'. I was afraid (this might happen), so I got that lion into a wooden cage, and have had it put into a ship and dispatched to my lord.

A tame lion, walking in an orchard with two harpists, is depicted in a frieze (now in the British Museum) from Ashurbanipal's palace at Nineveh.

The horse, which has generally been treated with honour, seems on the whole to have had a high standing in ancient Mesopotamia also. There was an exception to this at Mari, where an official writing to his king pointed out that it was considered, by at least a section of his subjects, rather undignified to ride a horse*:

> Let my lord honour his royal status. You are the king of the Haneans, but you are likewise the king of the Akkadians. My lord should not ride on a horse. Let my lord ride on a chariot or indeed on a mule, and let him honour his royal status.

The horse came into his own with the Cassites later in the second millennium. Amongst them it had not only an honourable reputation but also a pedigree, as we learn from some texts from Nippur, which give lists of horses with their own names and the names of their sires.

* On the interpretation of the text concerned see I. J. Gelb, *Journal of Cuneiform Studies* XV (1961), 37, note 31.

7

Law and Statecraft

ONE of the most marked features of ancient Mesopotamian civilization was its respect for the rule of law. A very large proportion of the cuneiform documents so far recovered – put as high as 95 per cent in the case of those in the Sumerian language, and probably not far short of that in the case of Akkadian – consist of the type of records sometimes referred to loosely as 'contracts', though actually mainly receipts, accounts and records of transactions of various other kinds concerning property. It was generally recognized that a property transaction without written record was not valid, and to alter such a document was a heinous offence.

Many third millennium kings laid claim to having promoted the cause of law and justice, and there is no good reason to doubt that they were active in such matters. Whether in the earlier period their activity involved the promulgation of written laws is less certain. There is, for instance, no proof that the reforms of Urukagina were associated with a public inscription, though such a possibility is not to be excluded, for, as Hobbes points out,

the Law of Nature excepted, it belongeth to the essence of all other Lawes, to be made known, to every man that shall be obliged to obey them, either by word, or writing, or some other act, known to proceed from the Soveraign Authority. (*Leviathan*, chapter 26).

For long the oldest collection of laws known was that of

Hammurabi, of which the greatest part is known from the inscription on a diorite stele, seven feet six inches high, discovered in 1901–2 in French excavations at Susa, the ancient capital of Elam. There at once became obvious certain striking parallels between these laws and those in the Old Testament traditionally attributed to Moses, and for several decades the question was discussed of how much the biblical laws, which even on the traditional view were indisputably some centuries later in date, might owe to the laws of Hammurabi. One school even went so far as to regard the biblical laws as 'borrowed from the earlier Babylonian' laws, and to lay it down as rationalist dogma that 'the Hammurabi Code must have been the immediate or remote progenitor of the Hebrew legal system'. Later discoveries have corrected this impression and put the whole problem in better perspective. There are now known substantial parts of at least three collections of laws ante-dating those of Hammurabi by a century or more, whilst others of a later date have been recovered from the Hittite area and Assyria. Other smaller groups of laws from various *milieux* are also known. All these collections ('codes' is a word at which lawyers shy in this connection, since except in the laws of Hammurabi themselves there is little evidence of any actual codification of the contents) exhibit both common matter and their own peculiarities, and it has become clear that there was in the ancient Near East a large body of common or generally recognized law. Some of this was incorporated in various local collections of laws, with modifications to suit local circumstances, and this fact is adequate to explain the parallels between Hebrew and Babylonian law.

Accumulating evidence now begins to make it appear that written collections of laws were by no means uncommon at the turn of the third millennium B.C.: indeed, it has been suggested, with some probability, that every city-state had such a collection, written, according to local conditions, in Akkadian or Sumerian.

Justice – for which the word used meant literally 'the straight thing' – was an accepted concern of the king. Hammurabi, for example, made the establishment of justice one of his first concerns at his accession; and the formula by which his second regnal year was known was 'the year in which he set forth justice in the land', a formula also employed by certain other rulers. This does not refer to the publication of the famous so-called 'Code', which can be shown to have been published much later in Hammurabi's reign, but rather to certain measures taken for the amelioration of the lot of the citizens. The 'justice' referred to meant, primarily, economic justice, and there is clear evidence that for the king to 'set forth justice in the land' involved some kind of moratorium or general remission of debts. Once the old Sumerian system of state-socialism had begun to break down (and in its economic aspects it was showing evident signs of weakness already by the time of Urukagina's attempted reforms) a situation arrived where it was the individual peasant, holding land as private property or rented land rather than as a fief from the temple, who took the first shock of catastrophes such as flood, drought, blight or sickness. Whereas in the original system the temple, as lord and owner of everything, both land and people, took steps by the issue of rations from the temple granaries to tide the community over such difficulties, the independent land-owning peasant now had to borrow from the temple, and borrow at interest. Over the years this would result in the greater part of the peasantry becoming the victims to a crippling load of debt, and the situation could only be cleared by drastic measures, namely by a general remission and a fresh start. There are traces of the same situation in the Old Testament, and the twenty-fifth chapter of *Leviticus*, which deals with the Year of Jubile, lays down that in the fiftieth year the poor man who had had to pledge property or mortgage land or sell himself into bondage should have restored to him all his former rights.

Although in the case of Hammurabi's year-formula, 'to set forth justice in the land' does not refer specifically to the promulgation of the laws, it may well have been from economic measures of the kind referred to that the issue of specific collections of laws ultimately arose. One of the concerns of the king, to prevent exploitation of the population by the temples and holders of large estates, with consequent economic distress and political instability, involved the issue of decrees fixing prices and wages.

It seems likely that a monument such as the stele of Hammurabi, set up in Babylon or elsewhere to give the text of the royal laws, goes back in origin ultimately to similar but simpler monuments bearing a list of authorized prices. Hammurabi's 'Code' contains sections dealing with rates of hire and wages at the end of the laws immediately before the epilogue, whilst the laws of the state of Eshnunna, ante-dating Hammurabi by at least a century, begin with a list of controlled prices of most of the commodities (barley, oil of various kinds, lard, wool, salt, spices and copper) basic to the economy, followed by clauses fixing the rate of hire of wagons and boats and the wages of various agricultural workers.

Hammurabi and his successors are known to have issued 'royal ordinances' to their officials as guidance in certain matters, such as procedure in lawsuits, breach of contract, and so on, and that these royal ordinances were definite written instructions and do not denote merely Law in the abstract is clear from a passage in a royal letter; in this letter the king, writing to an official, directs him to try a case 'according to the ordinances which are in your presence'. Such royal ordinances, modifying customary law, deciding between variant practices as between two cities, or re-capitulating laws falling into desuetude, may lie behind such an imposing document as the 'Code' of Hammurabi: some scholars go so far as to regard the 'Code' as containing not so much decrees as collections of decisions in particular cases.

The earliest collection of laws now known – which the accidents of archaeological discovery may at any day rob of priority – are those of Ur-Nammu, founder and first king of the Third Dynasty of Ur: these have only been published since 1952. The text (in Sumerian) begins with a brief review of the history of the world and the rise to supremacy of Ur, with its king Ur-Nammu as representative of the city's god, Nanna. After establishing the political and military security of his city, Ur-Nammu turned to economic measures, and rectified a number of abuses: he

> established justice in the land. . . . He did away with the duties, the Big Sailors [whatever that may mean], those who by force seized the oxen, sheep or donkeys,

and ensured that

the orphan was not given over to the rich, the widow was not given over to the powerful, the man of one shekel was not given over to the man of one mina . . .

The remainder of the introduction is broken away, and when the text again becomes legible the laws themselves have begun. Unfortunately they are very badly damaged, but enough remains to enable five laws to be restored with some confidence. These concern respectively, trial by water ordeal, return of a runaway (?) slave to his master, and compensation for injury (which takes up three of the five sections). One of the laws concerning personal injury may be translated approximately

. If a man has broken another man's bones with a weapon, he shall pay one mina of silver,

and the other two are on similar lines. The great interest of these is that they show that already in Sumer the *lex talionis*, or principle of 'an eye for an eye', had – if it ever existed there – been superseded. The same is true in the laws of Eshnunna, possibly under Sumerian influence. The more barbaric principle, found in the laws of Hammurabi, of Assyria and of the Hebrews, reflects the unmodified practice of the less civilized Semites.

There are other laws known which are written in Sumerian. Foremost amongst these are the laws of Lipit-Ishtar king of Isin, who reigned half-way between Ur-Nammu and Hammurabi. These are now known in a text made up from seven fragments of tablets, which bear a partial prologue and epilogue and thirty-seven sections of laws, the whole amounting to about a third of what can be computed as the extent of the original text. Four of the fragments, which show chaotic arrangement and many mistakes, are in fact excerpts of laws from Lipit-Ishtar's 'code' used as exercises for the training of scribes. The other three are pieces of a large tablet which a passage in the epilogue –

When I had established the well-being of Sumer and Akkad I set up this stele –

shows to have been a copy of an original inscribed on a public monument.

The subject-matter of the Lipit-Ishtar laws may be analysed into sections as follows:

1–6 [Fragmentary].
7–11 Related to land, gardens and orchards.
12–14 Slaves.
15–16 Villeins.
   17 [Obscure].
   18 Transfer of fief in event of failure of holder to perform duties.
19–20 [Fragmentary].
21–27 Inheritance.
   28 Bigamy.
   29 A girl may not be given in marriage to the rejected suitor's 'best man'.
   30 Marriage of a harlot. [Provision obscure].
31–33 Division of paternal estate amongst heirs.
33–37 Fines in event of damage to a hired ox.

A few laws may be quoted in full:

8 If a man has given uncultivated land to a man to plant up as an orchard, and (the latter) does not complete the planting up of that uncultivated land as an orchard, (the first man) shall include within the share of the man who planted up the orchard the uncultivated land which he neglected.

11 If next to a man's house there stands someone's uncultivated land which has been neglected, and if the owner of the house has said to the owner of the uncultivated land, 'Someone may break into my house as a result of your land being neglected', and if an agreement on this matter has been ratified by him [i.e. the owner of the uncultivated land], the owner of the uncultivated land shall make good to the owner of the house any of his property that may be lost.

18 If the master or the mistress of an estate has defaulted on the feudal dues of an estate and a stranger has borne them, for three years he [the owner] may not be evicted. (Subsequently), the man who bore the feudal dues of the estate shall take that estate for himself and the (former) owner of the estate shall not raise any claim.

24 If a second wife whom (a man) married has borne him children, the marriage-settlement which she brought from her father's house belongs to her children; the children of the first wife and

the children of the second wife shall divide equally the property of their father.

25 If a man has taken a wife and she has borne him children and those children have survived, and a slave-girl has also borne children to her master and the father has granted freedom to that slave-girl and her children, the children of the slave-girl shall not share the estate with the children of their (former) master.

27 If a man's wife has borne him no children but a prostitute from the street has borne him children, he shall provide for that prostitute her corn, oil and clothing, and the children which the prostitute has borne him shall be his heirs; but as long as his wife lives the prostitute shall not reside in the house with the wife.

29 If a son-in-law has entered the house of his (prospective) father-in-law and he has performed the betrothal procedure, but subsequently they make him go (out of the house) and (propose to) give his wife to his intimate friend; they shall deliver to him his betrothal gift which he brought and that wife shall not be given in marriage to his intimate friend.

35 If a man has hired an ox and damaged its eye, he shall pay half of its price.

A document dealing with legal matters which is certainly in the category of school-texts is the series known, from its initial words, as *ana ittishu*. Though this is only known at present in copies from the first millennium, the internal evidence shows that it must go back in origin to the Isin period (about 1950 B.C.). It contains a collection of Sumerian words, phrases and whole clauses excerpted from contracts, and set down in the form of a list of the Sumerian terms with Akkadian translations alongside. The final tablet of the series seems to incorporate the text of twelve laws dealing with family relationships. Typical examples may be translated as follows:

If a son says to his father 'You are not my father', (the father) may give him a tonsure, put a slave-mark on him and sell him.

If a son says to his mother 'You are not my mother', they shall shave his hair [or 'half his head'; the exact meaning of the term is in dispute], lead him round the city and put him out of the house.

If a wife hates her husband and says 'You are not my husband', they shall throw her into the river. [This does not necessarily imply the death penalty; it could conceivably refer to trial of her guilt by ordeal, if the woman's denial of her husband raised a presumption of adultery].

If a husband says to his wife 'You are not my wife', he shall pay half a mina of silver.

There is a solitary law written in the Akkadian language of the Old Babylonian period which claims, by its heading, to come from Lipit-Ishtar, the king whose Sumerian laws are referred to above. Most authorities agree, however, in rejecting the heading mentioned as an attempt (in ancient times) to give spurious antiquity to the law concerned: forgeries in antiquity were by no means uncommon. Discounting this, the earliest laws in Akkadian are those on two clay tablets found in 1947 at Tell Harmal, a suburb of Baghdad. Tell Harmal represents the ancient town of Shaduppum, which was within the kingdom whose capital was at Eshnunna (modern Tell Asmar on the Diyala); these laws found at Tell Harmal are therefore generally known as the *Laws of Eshnunna*. The tablets do not, as at first imagined, give the name of the legislator as King Bilalama, which would have permitted a fairly close dating, but linguistic and other features of the extant copies show that they derive from a time several generations, probably between one and two centuries, before Hammurabi.

The form of the prologue – a list of prices of basic commodities – has already been mentioned above. This is followed by a number of sections dealing with rates of hire and wages and penalties imposed in certain circumstances in connection therewith. The main points of the remaining forty-eight sections may be analysed thus:

12–13 Penalties for trespass and unlawful entry – by day a fine, by night death.

14–21 Various business transactions. Fee for carriage of money by an agent; brokers not permitted to accept basic commodities or silver from slaves for speculation, nor to make loans to slaves or minors; bride-money handed to girl's father remains property of suitor until the girl enters the suitor's house; if bride dies childless after consummation, husband keeps dowry but does not recover bride-money; repayment of loans.

22–24 Unlawful distraint upon slave-girl or wife.

25–28 Betrothal and marriage. Suitor who serves girl's father in lieu of bride-money and is then defrauded of the girl receives two-fold compensation; penalty for rape of betrothed girl is death; cohabitation without contract does not give a woman married status.

29–30 Husband loses rights over his wife by voluntary desertion but not by absence from *force majeure*.

31 A fine is imposed for deflowering another man's slave-girl.

32–35 Regulations governing foster-parents and ownership of children of slave-girls.

36–37 Liability in event of loss of property deposited for safe-keeping.

38–41 Regulations concerning certain sales and purchases.

42–48 Fines for assaults and injuries; culprit must be tried in more serious cases, before the king in event of death.

49–52 Theft and flight of slaves.

53–58 Responsibility for damage caused by an ox, dog or collapsing wall.

59 Husband who illegally divorces wife who has borne him sons forfeits house and property.

60 [Text badly damaged]. Possibly mentions death as penalty imposed on negligent house-guard.

To give some idea of the style and approach, as well as the contents, of the document, a few of the laws are here translated in full:

25 If a man offers service in the house of a (potential) father-in-law and his father-in-law takes him into service but then gives his daughter to another man, the father of the girl shall refund two-fold the bride-money which he has received (in the form of service). [The situation envisaged is to be compared with the case of Jacob serving Laban seven years for each of his two daughters (*Genesis* xxix. 18-28).]

27 If a man takes a man's daughter without asking her father and her mother and has not made a formal contract with her father and mother, even though she lives a full year in his house, she (has) not the (status) 'wife'.

30 If a man hates his town and his lord and runs away, and a second

man takes his wife, if he [*i.e.* the first man] returns, he shall have no claim to his wife.

31 If a man deflowers a man's slave-girl, he shall pay one-third of a mina of silver; the girl remains the property of her owner.

33 If a slave-girl illicitly hands over her son to a freewoman and when he is grown up his master recognizes him, he may seize him and take him back. [Here the slave-girl attempts to gain free status for her son, whilst the freewoman would presumably be a childless woman wishing to adopt an heir.]

39 If a man becomes insolvent so that he sells his house for money, when the buyer (re-)sells it the original owner shall (be entitled to) redeem (it). [This recalls the provision of *Leviticus* xxv. 29: 'If a man sell a dwelling house in a walled city, then he may redeem it within a whole year after it is sold'. The biblical passage goes on to specify that there is no time limit in the case of a house outside the city. In the Hebrew law the rights of the original owner appear not to be dependent upon the buyer's intention of re-selling.]

42 If a man bites the nose of another man and severs it, he shall pay one mina of silver; an eye, one mina; a tooth, half a mina; an ear, half a mina; (in respect of) a hit on the jaw, he shall pay ten shekels of silver.

54 If an ox is one that gores and the Local Authority has informed its owner, but he does not have his ox *dealt with* [it is not clear whether the verb means 'kept penned' or 'dehorned'], and it gores a man and causes his death, then the owner of the ox shall pay two-thirds of a mina of silver. [This is closely related to section 251 of the laws of Hammaurabi, where a fine is likewise imposed, and to *Exodus* xxi. 29, where the ox and owner are both put to death.]

56-57 If a dog is vicious and the Local Authority has informed its owner, but he does not take precautions with his dog and it bites a man and causes his death, then the owner of the dog shall pay two-thirds of a mina of silver. If it bites a slave and causes his death, (the owner of the dog) shall pay fifteen shekels of silver.

58 If a wall bulges and the Local Authority has informed the owner of the wall, but he does not strengthen his wall and the wall falls and causes the death of a freeman, it is a capital case (for decision by) royal ordinance.

59 If a man divorces his wife after having made her bear sons and

takes a second woman, he shall be expelled from (his) house and from whatever property he has, and shall go off after whoever will accept him.

The Eshnunna laws find many echoes in the longer-known and more extensive 'Code' of Hammurabi, for many years taken as the yardstick for the study of ancient oriental law and still the most valuable single document. A striking difference between Hammurabi's laws and the others so far discussed is that the former show a much more ordered arrangement, and so come much nearer than any of the other documents to deserving the name of 'Code'.

The considerable amount of material common to the Eshnunna laws and the laws of Hammurabi has led to discussion of the problem of whether there is evidence of direct borrowing. Scholars conclude, from a detailed study, that there is no clear evidence of this, and postulate that the basic material of both was ultimately derived from an older common source.

The 'Code' proper is sandwiched between a prologue giving the titles of Hammurabi and a review of his previous achievements, and an epilogue proclaiming the purpose and authority of his laws, and calling upon succeeding rulers, upon pain of his curses,

to pay attention to the words which I have inscribed on my stele, ... that he may thus make straight the way for his Black-headed Ones [humans], that he may judge their causes and decide their decisions, that he may pluck out the evil and the wicked from his land, and make the flesh of his people glad.

The epilogue also lays down the procedure to be observed by an oppressed man. Hammurabi decrees:

Let the wronged man who has a cause go before my statue (named) 'King of Justice' [near which the stele stood], and let him have read out my inscribed stele and let him hear my precious words; let my stele show him his cause, let him see his judgement, let his heart be at ease.

The laws themselves, in which few substantial gaps now remain, at present amount to more than two hundred and sixty sections. Paragraphs of the original stele are in modern editions denoted by numbers, whilst paragraphs discovered subsequently on clay tablets are indicated by letters. The subject matter of these laws may be briefly analysed as follows:

Administration of justice.
1–5 False witnesses; corrupt judges.

Offences against property.
6–14 Theft, including kidnapping of a minor.
15–20 Runaway and stolen slaves.
21–25 Housebreaking, robbery, looting.

Land and houses.
26–41 Tenure of land held as a fief from the king.
42–48 Cultivation of arable land by tenants.
49–52 Regulations governing the financing of tenant-farmers.
53–56 Offences arising from negligent irrigation.
57–58 Trespass of cattle on corn-land.
59 Unauthorized cutting of trees.
60–65 and A Cultivation of palm-plantations.
B–E, G, H Regulations concerning renting, building and repairing of houses.
F, J, K [Fragmentary.]

Merchants and agents.
L–R Loans from merchants; interest rates.
S, T [Fragmentary.]
U Division of profit and loss between partners.
100–107 Regulations governing transactions of merchants' agents.
108–111 Regulations concerning (female) inn-keepers, (who apparently also served as small brokers).
112 Fraud by a carrier.
113–117 Distraint for debt.
118–119 Delivery of dependents into bondage for debt.
120–126 Deposit of goods.

Women, marriage, family property and inheritance.
127 Slander of high-priestess or married woman.
128 Wifehood; cohabitation without contract does not give a woman the status of 'wife'.
129–132 Adultery.

133–136 Remarriage of a wife: this is permitted in the husband's absence only in certain circumstances, though unconditionally for voluntary desertion.

137–143 Divorce.

144–149 Concubinage; and a circumstance in which bigamy is permitted.

150 Inheritance of property settled by husband on wife.

151–152 Liability of spouses for debt.

153 Penalty for wife who murders husband – impalement.

154–158 Incest.

159–161 Breach of contract after betrothal.

162–164 Disposal of dowry after death of wife.

165–167 Division of inheritance amongst sons.

168–169 Disherison.

170 Legitimation of sons of concubine.

171–174 Rights of concubine and non-legitimated sons; widow's property.

175–176 Rights of a free woman married to a slave.

177 Disposal of previous husband's property at re-marriage of a widow.

178–184 Rights of cult women to dowry or paternal inheritance.

185–193 Adoption.

194 Substitution of changeling by wet-nurse.

Assault and personal injury.

195 Assault by a son on his father.

196–205 Penalties for inflicting bodily harm – talion when the victim is a freeman, a fine when he is a villein or slave.

206–208 A man inflicting accidental injury is subject only to a fine or costs, not to talion.

209–214 Assault upon a woman resulting in miscarriage.

Professional fees and responsibilities.

215–225 Fees payable to surgeons and veterinary surgeons for successful operations, and penalties incurred where result of an operation is unfavourable.

226–227 Penalties for excising or procuring the excision of a slave-mark.

228–239 Fees for builders and shipmasters and penalties for negligence.

240 Collision between a galley and a sailing ship.

Agriculture.

241–249 Distraint, hire, death and injury of oxen.
250–252 Responsibility for damage by a goring ox.
253–256 Wrongful conversion by a bailiff.
257–258 Hire of ploughman and ox-herd.
259–260 Theft of agricultural implements.
    261 Hire of stockman or shepherd.

Rates of hire.

268–277 Rates of hire of animals, wagons, labourers, craftsmen, ships.

Ownership and sale of slaves.

278–279 Liability for a slave sold when suffering from sickness or subject to a legal claim.
280–282 Re-claiming of slaves bought abroad and returned to Babylonia.

A good modern English translation of the whole of these laws is available, together with a detailed commentary, in G. R. Driver and J. C. Miles, *The Babylonian Laws*, (2 volumes, 1952 and 1955), but it may be of interest to give translations of a few of the laws as specimens:

    1   If a man has accused a man and has cast against him an accusation of murder and has not proved it against him, his accuser shall be put to death.

22–23   If a man has committed robbery and is arrested, that man shall be put to death. If the robber is not arrested, the robbed man shall certify before the god whatever of his is lost, and the city and the mayor within whose territory or bounds the robbery was committed shall replace the lost thing for him.

   55   If a man has opened his ditch for irrigation and has been slack and has consequently caused the water to carry away his neighbour's field, he shall pay corn corresponding to (the crop of the field) adjoining it.

  117   If a man is in the grip of a bond (for debt) and he has delivered his wife, his son, or his daughter for silver, or has given (them) into bond-service, for three years they shall serve in the house of their buyer or the one who took them into bond-service; in the fourth year their release shall be granted.

128   If a man has taken a wife and has not set down a contract for her, that woman (has) not the (status) 'wife'.

· 153   If a woman has caused the death of her husband on account of another man, they shall set that woman on stakes.

170   If a man's bride has borne him sons and his slave-girl has borne him sons, and the father in his lifetime says to the sons whom the slave-girl has borne to him 'You are my sons', he shall count them with the sons of the bride. After the father goes to his fate, the sons of the bride and the sons of the slave-girl shall share equally in the property of the father's estate. The heir, a son of the bride, shall take (first) choice at the division.

185–186   If a man has taken an infant (to be called) by his name for sonship and brings him up, that adopted child shall not be claimed back. If a man has taken an infant for sonship, and after he has taken it he seeks out its father and its mother, that adopted child may [or(?) shall] return to its father's house. [There is some doubt as to the precise interpretation of the latter law: it is not certain whether it is the child who seeks its parents or the adoptive parent who wishes to cancel the adoption.]

209–210   If a man strikes the daughter of a freeman and causes her to cast that which is within her womb, he shall pay ten shekels of silver for that which is within her womb. If that woman dies as a result, they shall put his daughter to death. [When the woman struck was of the villein or slave class, her death only involved a further fine.]

· 215 and 218   If a surgeon has made a major incision in a freeman with a bronze instrument and saved the man's life, or opened an eye-infection with a bronze instrument and so saved the man's eye, he shall take ten shekels of silver. If a surgeon has made a major incision in a freeman with a bronze instrument and caused the man to die, or opened an eye-infection with a bronze instrument and thereby destroyed the man's eye, they shall cut off his hand.

· 229–230   If a builder has built a house for a man and has not made his work sound, so that the house he has made falls down and causes the death of the owner of the house, that builder shall be put to death. If it causes the death of the son of the owner of the house, they shall kill the son of that builder.

It should be clear from the summary and from the specimens of laws translated that the 'Code' of Hammurabi does not constitute a complete system of law. Hammurabi in his prologue and epilogue makes no claim to having codified the whole of the existing law, and many matters which must at times have needed legal decisions are not included. For instance, there is no reference to parricide, cattle-lifting, or kidnapping a person other than a freeman's son. It therefore has to be concluded that Hammurabi was simply dealing with matters which needed amendment, adoption of one of a number of alternatives found in different cities, or simply recapitulation of regulations liable to fall into desuetude. It has been pointed out that 'there is not a single case in the thousands of legal documents and reports which have been preserved in which reference is made to the wording of the text of the Laws', and this is clear evidence that whatever the Laws were, they were not statute law to be given a verbal interpretation but rather incorporated principles to be observed, or which actually had been observed, in particular cases.

That the principles in question were observed in Babylonia, even more than a millennium after the time of Hammurabi, is clear from a number of records of court cases. One, dating from as late as 527 B.C., may be quoted. Four workmen were arraigned before the Assembly of Erech on a charge of having stolen two ducks belonging to the temple, and the case was heard in the presence of the two principal temple administrators and representatives from the capital. Reference to the laws of Hammurabi sheds light on why the theft of two ducks should set in motion such ponderous legal machinery. Section 6 of the laws decrees that 'if a man has stolen property of a god or the palace, that man shall be put to death', whilst section 8 says 'If a man has stolen either ox, sheep, ass, pig or a boat, if it belongs to a god or the palace, he shall pay thirty-fold'. The distinction between the two cases is that in the more serious case the theft was from within the temple or palace precincts and therefore sacrilegious, whilst in the lighter case the theft was from outside the temple precincts. Clearly the question at issue in the case adduced was whether the offence was a capital one. This is borne out by the nature of the evidence given by the accused, who testified 'On the eleventh of the month Tebet . . . we . . . were digging behind the wall by the river; the two ducks . . . that we killed we buried in the mud'. Clearly the men claimed to be on the river side of the boundary wall of the temple, and thus outside the precincts, at the time of the offence. Their evidence was accepted and the penalty was the lighter one – thirty-fold restitution.

Another collection of laws of great interest to the Comparative Jurist and the historian of the Ancient East is that known as the *Assyrian Laws*. These were discovered in German excavations at the site of the ancient capital of Assyria, Ashur, and are probably to be dated at about the thirteenth century (more accurately between 1450 and 1250 B.C.). Thus, properly speaking, these laws are Middle Assyrian: some fragments of Old Assyrian laws are also known and are mentioned elsewhere. The parts of the Middle Assyrian laws extant are not, like the laws of Hammurabi in the main, from an official stele, but are found on a number of clay tablets, not all from the same hand or even, to judge by the orthography and phonology of the inscriptions, from quite the same date. These laws give no internal evidence as to the compiler, but the indications of subject matter are that they applied to the city of Ashur and the surrounding district.

Jurists have pointed out notable differences between the form of the 'Code' of Hammurabi and that of the Assyrian laws, and have concluded that the latter compilation was the work neither of an original legislator nor of a school of scribes producing a work for use as exercise texts. It is possible to show that the Assyrian laws never contain a mere recapitulation of the subject matter of the laws of Hammurabi (or Eshnunna) but invariably, where there is common matter, introduce some modification. The view usually taken is thus that the Assyrian Laws comprise a series of amendments to the existing law, the latter being basically the common law underlying the 'Code' of Hammurabi, which would not have been wholly appropriate to the more savage condition of Assyrian society in the late second millennium.

The largest and best preserved tablet deals almost exclusively with married women. A few examples may be given. The square brackets enclose summaries or explanatory matter, but otherwise what follows is direct translation of the laws themselves:

2   If a woman, whether the wife of a free man or the daughter of a free man, has spoken blasphemy or sedition, that woman shall bear her guilt; they shall not touch her husband, her sons or her daughters.

4   If a slave or a slave-girl has received anything from the hand of a man's wife, they shall cut off the nose and ears of the slave or slave-girl (and so) requite the theft; the man shall lop his wife's ears. But if the man lets his wife go free and does not lop her ears, they shall not cut those of the slave or slave-girl and shall not requite the theft.

8   If a woman has damaged a man's testicle in a quarrel, they shall   •
cut off one of her fingers; and if a doctor has bound it up but yet the second testicle is subsequently affected with it and takes an infection, or if she has damaged the second testicle in the quarrel, they shall tear out both her ... [the word is missing: 'nipples' has been suggested, but *labia* would seem equally appropriate.]

15   If a man has caught a man with his wife, and a charge is brought   •
and proved against him, they shall kill both of them; there is no guilt for this. If he has caught (him) and brought (him) either before the king or before the judges, and a charge is brought and proved against him, if the husband of the woman puts his wife to death, then he may put the man to death; if he cuts off the nose of his wife, he shall make the man a eunuch and the whole of his face shall be mutilated; or if he lets his wife go free, they shall set the man free.

20   If a man has lain with his male friend and a charge is brought and proved against him, the same thing shall be done to him and he shall be made a eunuch.

26   If a woman still dwells in her father's house and her husband is dead, as to any ornaments which her husband put on her, if there are sons of her husband, they shall take them; if there are no sons of her husband, she herself shall take them.

27   If a woman still dwells in her father's house and her husband habitually goes in (to her there), any marriage-settlement which her husband has handed over to her he himself may take; he may not touch anything from her father's house. [This law, as also the previous one, is proof that a more primitive type of marriage, in

which the wife did not enter her husband's home but remained under the parental roof, was still at this time known in Assyria. There are traces of a similar institution in early Israel, where, for example, Samson had a wife, whom he visited from time to time, living with her father in Timnah, although his own home was at Zorah; see *Judges* xiv. i–xv. 6.]

34 If a man takes a widow but a marriage-contract is not drawn up for her, and she dwells two years in his house, she (becomes) a wife; she shall not go forth. [Except that this appears to apply only in the case of a widow, this is the opposite of the law on the subject contained in the laws of Eshnunna and Hammurabi, which do not recognise marriage by cohabitation. Jewish law agrees in this respect with Assyrian practice against Babylonian, for a passage in the Mishna (*Kiddushin* Ii) reads: 'By three means is the woman acquired. . . . She is acquired by money or by written contract or by intercourse.']

37 If a man divorces his wife, if it is his will he may give her something; if it is not his will he shall not give her anything (and) she shall go forth in her emptiness. [This is harsher than the laws of Hammurabi wherein (§§138–139) a divorced wife receives her dowry plus a minimum of one mina of silver.]

40 [This is a lengthy law dealing with the dress of women in public. Married women must be veiled, as must a concubine accompanying her mistress. But 'a harlot shall not be veiled; her head must be uncovered', and offence in this respect was heavily punished: 'she shall be beaten fifty stripes with rods, and pitch shall be poured on her head.']

41 If a man will veil his concubine, he shall cause five or six of his friends to sit and he shall veil her before them and shall say, 'She is my wife'. She is then his wife. [The remainder of the law emphasizes that the concubine is no wife unless this has been done, and decrees that in the absence of the sons of a veiled wife the sons of concubines are heirs.]

47 If either a man or a woman have performed black magic and (the magical objects) are seized in their hands and charges are brought and proved against them, the workers of black magic shall be put to death. [The rest of the law deals with procedure in connection with evidence in such a case. An exorcist was involved, and provisions made for the case in which evidence was subsequently retracted, no doubt on account of the possibility

that the witnesses might waver because they considered themselves in grave danger from the wizards and witches.]

53 If a woman by her own deed has cast that which is within her
womb, and a charge has been brought and proved against her,
they shall impale her and not bury her. If she dies from casting
that which is within her womb, they shall impale her and not
bury her.

55–56 [In the event of a man raping a virgin, 'the father of the virgin
shall take the wife of the ravisher . . . and deliver her to be
prostituted; he shall not return her to her husband (but) he
(himself) shall take her. The father shall give his deflowered
daughter to her ravisher as a consort'. If the ravisher is unmarried
he must pay bride-money and the father may force a 'shotgun
wedding', though the ravisher acquires no right to the girl by
payment of the bride-money if the father wishes to dispose of her
to another man. On the other hand 'If a virgin has given herself
to a man voluntarily, the man shall take an oath and his wife shall
not be touched. The seducer shall deliver the "third" of silver,
the price of the virgin, and the father shall do with his daughter
as he wishes'.]

59 Leaving aside the penalties for a man's wife which are inscribed
on the tablet, a man may flog his wife, he may pluck her hair, he
may strike and damage her ears. There is no guilt (involved in
this). [This clause, forbidding the Assyrian housewife to suppose
that the punishments to which her misconduct rendered her
liable constituted an exhaustive list, ends the tablet.]

The second in size and importance of the Middle Assyrian law
tablets, extending in the extant form to nineteen sections, deals
with inheritance and sale of land, encroachment on neighbour's
property and rights to irrigation water. Two laws are quoted as
specimens:

8 If a man has encroached upon the great boundary of his neighbour and a charge has been brought and proved against him, he
shall deliver up three times as much land as that upon which he
has encroached, one of his fingers shall be cut off, he shall be
beaten a hundred strokes with rods, and he shall do work for the
king for a full month.

17 If there is water within wells which can be brought for cultivating irrigable land, the owners of the fields (concerned) shall

stand by one another; each man shall do work (thereon) according to the extent of his field and shall (be permitted to) irrigate his field. But if there is not agreement amongst them, he who agrees amongst them shall ask the judges and shall secure a tablet from the judges (stating his rights), and he shall do the work and shall take those waters for himself and irrigate his field. No-one else shall perform irrigation (therewith).

The laws on the remaining sections concern debt (including pledging of persons) and theft of cattle, with fragmentary references to subjects such as assault, wages and irrigation.

As to the manner in which justice was in practice given to the citizen, details varied so widely in the course of the two millennia with which we are concerned that no simple generalizations can hope to be completely accurate. In ancient theory it was a divinely ordained duty of the king, as representing the god, to see that his people received justice, but there seems good reasons for supposing that in the earliest form of Mesopotamian society decisions on private causes, like other decisions, were made in the Assembly; and the Assembly retained a real function in the administration of justice long after the last shadow of its political authority had passed away. In Babylonia, although at some periods and places the king or his official alone might settle a case, this was exceptional, and generally speaking the Assembly retained a concern in cases involving private individuals down to the end of the New Babylonian period. In Assyria, on the other hand, it is common in documents of the first millennium to find decisions made by a single royal officer.

Attendance at the judicial Assembly seems to have been open, in the Old Babylonian period at least, to all free male citizens, to judge by a proverb which, with a notable lack of public spirit, counsels:

> Do not go to stand in the Assembly: do not wander to the place of strife. It is in strife that fate may overtake you, and you may be made a witness for them, . . . to testify in a lawsuit not your own.

A cuneiform account of a murder trial in the Isin period, just before the time of Hammurabi, clearly shows the part played by the king on the one hand, and the Assembly on the other, in the administration of justice. When the charge was made, the case was first brought to the king, as the fountain of justice, who then referred it to the Assembly of Nippur, which heard the evidence and pronounced the verdict. Slightly abbreviated the text reads:

A son of V, B son of W the barber, and C slave of X the gardener, killed D son of Y the *nishakku* official. After D . . . had been killed, they told E, wife of D, that her husband D had been killed. E did not open her mouth, she concealed it.

Their case was brought to Isin before the king, and . . . he ordered their case to be taken up in the Assembly of Nippur.

There F . . ., G . . ., H the villein, J . . ., K . . ., L . . ., M . . ., N . . ., O . . ., addressed (the Assembly) and said: 'They who have killed a man are not (fit to be) alive. Those three men and that woman should be killed in front of the chair of (their victim) D . . .'

P . . . and Q . . . addressed (the Assembly) and said: 'Did E . . . kill her husband, that that woman should be put to death?'.

Then the Assembly of Nippur addressed (them) and said: '(It may be that) a woman who was not loyal to her husband gave information to his enemy, (and the latter) killed her husband. . . . (But) did she herself kill her husband . . . ? They killed the man'.

In accordance with the decision of the Assemby of Nippur, A . . ., B . . ., and C . . . were handed over to be killed.*

There is no mention here of judges, though the existence of men called 'judges' is attested from Sargonid times (*circa* 2370 B.C.) and before. One school of thought on the history of ancient law speaks of judges sitting 'as a college or bench', and the suggestion has even been made that judges could be divided into two types, the secular and the ecclesiastical. The latter suggestion certainly may be rejected, and whilst it is true that judges are often mentioned as a group, they are probably to be regarded in such circumstances as assessors sitting with the Assembly. This is clearly indicated by a section of the laws of Hammurabi, which reads:

If a judge has judged a case, decided details of the decision, caused a

---

* For complete translations of this text see S. N. Kramer, *History begins at Sumer* (Doubleday Anchor edition, New York, 1959), 57–58, and Th. Jacobsen in *Studia Biblica et Orientalia, volumen III, Oriens Antiquus* (Rome, 1959), 136–138.

sealed document to be deposited, and afterwards he changes his judgement, they shall establish that that judge has made alteration in the judgement he judged, and he shall pay twelve-fold the penalty appropriate in the case concerned; moreover, they shall expel him from the seat of his judge-ship in the Assembly, and he shall not return to sit with the judges in a case.

The Assembly is by no means always mentioned in connection with judges in Old Babylonian times, but there are sufficient instances in which it is to support the view that the Assembly was a piece of machinery which still functioned. In some of the cases in which only judges are mentioned they may have been regarded as presidents of the Assembly, which sat passively by, whilst actual physical absence of an Assembly may in some cases have been due not to any official change of procedure but to the lack of public spirit of free citizens too literally following the advice of the proverb quoted above (page 216).

In actual court procedure, where there was a clash of evidence between the parties involved or between witnesses, the Assembly or the judges might order any of those concerned to take an oath at a temple. As an example the following text may be quoted:

> Tablet in connection with the house in New-wall of A daughter of X.
> B daughter of Y made a claim against A . . .
> The judges in the Shamash temple gave judgement that A should take an oath by the life of the god. A took the oath by the life of the goddess Aya her Lady and rebutted her [B's] claim.
> Since she [A] did not turn back (from the oath), B shall make no claim to A's house, paternal inheritance, property, or inheritance from her husband, as much as there may be, from straw to gold.
> She [B] has sworn (to accept this) by (the gods) Shamash, Aya and Marduk and (king) Sumu-la-ilum.
> Judgement of the Shamash temple. C son of D, E son of F. [These are the names of the judges.]
> Before G son of H, J son of K. [These are the names of the witnesses constituting or representing the Assembly.] Before L daughter of M, the lady scribe.

Records of cases are known in which one party recoiled from the oath. The following serves as an example:

> The witnesses of A recounted before the judges, 'B beat A and took oxen away from him'. So the judges said to B, 'Take the oath of the gods against the witnesses'. And this is the declaration of B; before the judges he admitted 'I did strike A': B was afraid of the gods. A won the case and the judges made B pay 30 shekels of silver to A.

When there was a clash of evidence, and neither side admitted guilt by refusing the oath by the life of the gods, the decision would then be handed over to the gods themselves. This was given, as in many other cultures, by the Ordeal. In Babylonia the Ordeal was by the river, and the rule – opposite to that found in mediaeval England – was that the guilty person sank and the innocent was saved. The law of Hammurabi dealing with charges of witchcraft decrees that the accused was to be judged by this means:

> If a man has cast a charge of (operating) black magic against a man and has not proved it, the one against whom the charge of black magic was cast shall go to the Holy River and jump into the Holy River. If the Holy River clutches him, his accuser shall take his estate. If the Holy River clears that man and he comes safely back, he who cast the charge of black magic against him shall be put to death. He who jumped into the Holy River shall take the estate of his accuser.

In the law preceding the one on witchcraft the man who brought a charge of murder and did not prove it was put to death without further ado. The procedure in the case of an accusation of witchcraft probably differed because, as the corresponding law in the Assyrian laws indicates, it was recognized that witnesses might perjure themselves from fear of magical reprisals. The Ordeal was, however, normally reserved as a last resort after the parties concerned had been put to the oath. A text – a letter from the king of Carchemish to the king of Mari – sheds light on the actual practice. The relevant portion of the letter, approximately contemporary with Hammurabi, reads:

Now as to these two men here whom I have sent with A, . . . they have been accused in these terms: 'they have had discussion with B the slave of C; they have knowledge of the affair'. [This must be a reference to some crime committed in their home town in which they were alleged to be implicated.] So now I am duly causing them to be brought to the Holy River. Their accuser is being guarded here under detention. Let one of your servants, a security officer, lead these men, in the company of A, to the Holy River. If these men come safely back, I shall burn their accuser with fire. If these men die, I shall hand over their estates and people to their accuser. Please let me know the result.

An object of Babylonian legal procedure was to secure, as far as possible, a decision accepted by all parties as just and binding. Thus in the case quoted above concerning the dispute between two ladies over the ownership of a house, the loser took an oath to accept the decision. The tablet dealing with a case often specifically stipulates that the case shall not be reopened. The following illustrates this, and also sheds more light on the relationship between the judges and the local Assembly:

In the matter of the orchard of Sin-magir which Mar-Amurrim bought for silver.

Anum-bani made a claim in accordance with a royal ordinance and they went to the judges and the judges sent them to the Bab-Ninmar shrine. Anum-bani took the oath at the Bab-Ninmar shrine before the judges of the Bab-Ninmar shrine. Thus he said: 'I am the son of Sin-magir. He took me for sonship and my official document (of adoption) was never cancelled'. Thus he took the oath, and they [the judges] in pursuance of (the ordinance of king) Rim-Sin established the orchard and house as belonging to Anum-bani.

Sin-muballit [presumably heir of Mar-Amurrim] returned [i.e. re-opened the case]. He claimed the orchard of Anum-bani, and they went to the judges. The judges sent them to the City [i.e. the city Assembly], and the witnesses. They stood in the gate of Marduk (near) the divine *Shurinnu*-emblem of Nanna, the divine Bird of Ninmar, the divine Spade of Marduk, and the Stone Weapon. When the former witnesses of Mar-Amurrim said 'At the Bab-Ninmar shrine they administered to Anum-bani the oath "I am indeed the son"', they established the orchard and house (as belonging) to Anum-bani.

17 Head from Warka (third millennium)

18A (*left*) Bronze foundation depos[it] representing a Sumerian ruler bear[r]ing the head-pad at the building of [a] temple

18B (*above*) Head of a Sumerian i[n] diorite (end of third millennium)

19   A goddess holding vase, for use as fountain (from Mari)

20   A Sumerian official

21A (*left*) Babylonian boundary stone (late second millennium B.C.)

21B (*right*) Cast of the stele of Hammurabi (early second millennium B.C.)

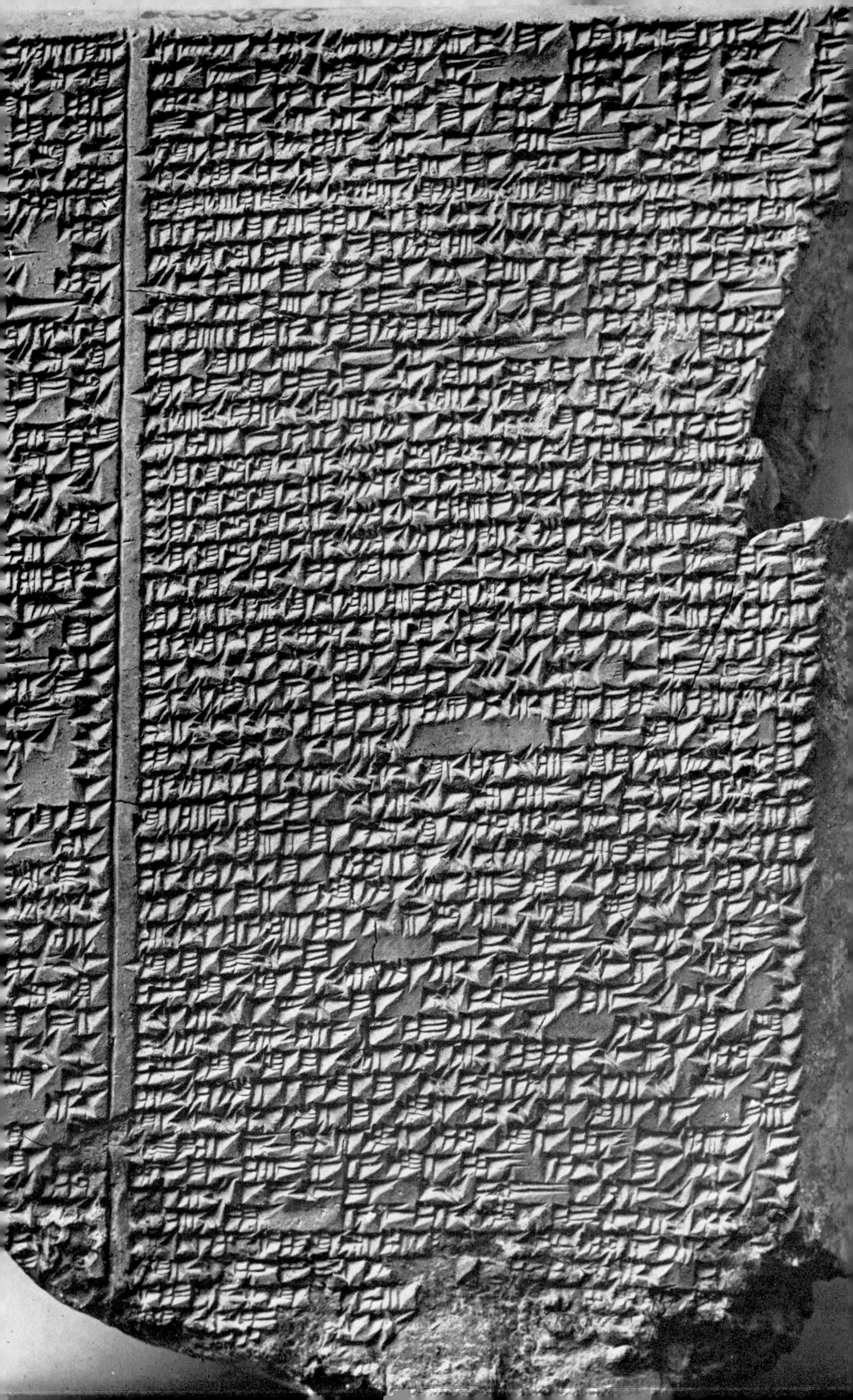

22 (*opposite*) Part of a cuneiform tablet (from Nineveh, first millennium B.C.), bearing the end of the Flood story from the *Epic of Gilgamish*

23 (*above*) Obverse of a cuneiform tablet inscribed with geometrical exercises (early second millennium B.C.)

24 Reverse of a cuneiform tablet inscribed with geometrical exercises
(early second millennium B.C.)

25   Inscribed cone of Ur-Bawa (*circa* 2200 B.C.)

26A Old Babylonian cuneiform tablet and envelope; a contract for the sale of land

26B (*left*) Cuneiform tablet (*circa* 600 B.C.) bearing a map of the world. [The ring represents the ocean supposedly enclosing the earth]

26C (*below*) Cuneiform tablet with Egyptian endorsement

27A Impression of cylinder seal, showing Maltese crosses

27B Inscribed clay model of an internal organ, for use in divination

28 King Ashur-nasir-pal II

29   King Ashur-nasir-pal II

30   An Assyrian god

31   Assyrian religious ceremony of the first millennium B.C. involving
the king [the figure on the left]

32 The Assyrian king in a cult scene before stylized sacred tree

Sin-muballit has (now) sworn by Nanna, Shamash, Marduk and king Hammurabi that he will not return and make a(nother) claim.

Before A the mayor, B, C, D, E, F, G, H, J son of K, L, M the *Redu*-officer, (and) N.

The seals of the witnesses.

The royal ordinance of Rim-Sin referred to is not known, but it seems that by it a son was able to reclaim landed property sold by his father. There is some evidence suggesting that at an early period the original owners of land, or their families, had the right in certain circumstances of resuming ancestral land, and the ordinance of Rim-Sin may have been enforcing a tradition falling into desuetude. Alternatively, it is possible that the orchard and house in question were held by Anum-bani's father as a fief from the king, and section 37 of the 'Code' of Hammurabi lays down that such a holding could not be sold.

Passing to a period a little later, we find from fourteenth century records from Nuzi (a city represented by a site near the modern town of Kirkuk) numerous examples of legal proceedings. Strictly speaking, although these are written in the Akkadian language, they cannot properly be used as examples of Semitic law, since Nuzi was an area in which strong Hurrian (non-Semitic) influence is to be recognized. The texts do, however, show the importance of securing agreement and of preventing the reopening of cases. One cuneiform tablet found gives the record of a trial before the king in which the plaintiff complained that an official had exacted one hundred and eighty sheep from him. The defendant proved, however, that this represented a fine imposed by the judges on the plaintiff's father, and submitted in evidence the tablet relating to the former case. The plaintiff thereupon had to pay a fine of one female slave for reopening a case already decided.

In first millennium Assyria, where administration was highly centralized and an efficient civil service functioned throughout the land, the administration of law also was largely in the hands of royal officials, and many records of legal decisions of the period are introduced by the formula 'The judgement which (such-and-such an official) imposed'. It still remained, however, a general principle that legal decisions should be acquiesced in by all parties. A typical record of a case reads:

> The case which A argued with B over the damage to his house. The damage which B did to the house has been paid in full to A. There is peace between them. One shall not dispute with the other over any further payment due from the other. Whoever transgresses against the other shall pay ten minas of silver: the gods Ashur, Shamash, Bel and Nabu are the lords of his case.

The date and the names of witnesses follow. Similar provisions are made in documents of sale, where heavy penalties are stipulated in the event of one of the parties bringing a lawsuit in an attempt to upset the transaction. Documents of this type are mentioned elsewhere (see page 294) in connection with trade and economics.

Not only was justice between individual men one of the gifts of civilized society provided by the bounty of the gods, but relationships between states, of the kind known to modern man as international law or protocol, was also thought of by the ancients as a system of behaviour which the gods had decreed. Kings and states were subject to the will of the gods: the making of treaties and alliances, the treatment of defeated nations, the relations between vassals and overlords, were not conducted arbitrarily but according to a recognized code supposed to reflect the divine will. In the case of treaties and alliances there was a written contract in which the parties were bound by oath before the gods.

A very large amount of cuneiform material is now available dealing with inter-state relations in the second millennium B.C. from two principal periods. The earlier source consists of the diplomatic archives of the early second millennium excavated by French scholars at Mari. The other main group comes from the half century around 1400 B.C., and was found in central Egypt at El Amarna, being in fact part of the diplomatic archives of the heretical pharaoh Akhenaten. These latter documents make it abundantly clear that Babylonian influence in the development of international law was so pre-eminent that Akkadian came to be the principal language of diplomacy between rulers even where, as between Egypt and the Hittites, it was the mother tongue of neither party. Smaller collections of cuneiform material bearing on inter-state diplomacy in the second millennium come from other sites, amongst which should be mentioned Boghazkoi in Turkey and Ras Shamra (ancient Ugarit) on the coast of north Syria. In the latter case again, although the local language, written in an alphabetic script, was used for most purposes, including religion, in the case of law and international affairs it was Akkadian, written in syllabic cuneiform, which was largely employed.

Certain codes of conduct in inter-state relations were accepted as early as the *Early Dynastic* period, as one may deduce from epics. Thus, in the dispute which developed between Enmerkar, lord of Erech, and the lord of Aratta (a state in the eastern mountains, perhaps in the hills which are now Luristan), there were extensive and detailed (though to us obscure) negotiations between the two parties by means of an ambassador. In the epic dealing with the siege of Erech by the king of Kish, we read that Gilgamish, the ruler of Erech, having defeated his rival did not put him to death nor humiliate him but – possibly because the king of Kish was his nominal suzerain – showed clemency and returned him to his kingdom.

The Mari letters, which give us our clearest glimpse of inter-state diplomacy in the ancient world, come from the period shortly after the beginning of the second millennium, before Hammurabi had finally united Babylonia. This was a time of many small kingdoms, and as most of them were too weak to stand alone, there was a continual grouping and re-grouping of these states, bound to more powerful neighbours either as vassals or allies. This political situation – changing groups of small states – is explicitly referred to in one of the letters (quoted above, see page 67), in which the writer speaks of four different coalitions, each comprising between ten and twenty kings.

The king of a small state who was not within such a coalition would find himself at the mercy of more powerful neighbours, as the following letter, from a lesser ruler to a greater, illustrates:

To Yahdu-Lim say, thus says Abi-Samar: 'Make an alliance! . . .
My towns which have not been captured will be captured now. These
towns have not been lost to the hostile action of the lord of Hashum
(or) Ursum (or) the lord of Carchemish (or) Yamhad; (but) they are
(virtually) lost to the hostile action of Shamshi-Adad [king of
Assyria] . . .'

In a subsequent letter Abi-Samar tells Yahdu-Lim:

If you abandon Abi-Samar, then you abandon your own cities. . . .
Perhaps you are saying 'Abi-Samar is not my son and my estate is
not (involved with) his estate'. (Yet) indeed my estate is your estate
and Abi-Samar is your son.

That is to say, Abi-Samar was offering to accept the status of
vassal to Yahdu-Lim in return for protection; obviously this kind
of situation strengthened the movement towards larger and
larger coalitions.

States entered into such coalitions by the making of treaties,
which would involve the taking of an oath, together with various
ritual or symbolic acts. Amongst such acts was one described as
'the touching of the throat', which may well be an ancient
example of a symbolic action still employed by children in
making a solemn statement. Another action sometimes performed in such circumstances was the killing of the foal of a
donkey, by which a treaty of peace was sealed between former
enemies. This is illustrated by the following extract from a letter,
in which an official writes to his king:

The tablet of Ibal-Adad reached me from (the town) Ashlakku
and I went to Ashlakku for 'killing the donkey foal' between the
men of Hana and the men of Ida-maraz. They brought (in addition)
a puppy and a leafy bough, but I respected my lord('s instructions)
and did not deliver up the puppy and leafy bough; I (only) had the
foal of a donkey killed, (and thereby) established friendship between
the men of Hana and the men of Ida-maraz. . . .

It is clear from the context that there was a further ritual sometimes used in this connection, in which a puppy and a leafy
bough (or, as some think the word means here, a lettuce) were
involved. Yet another symbolic action sometimes performed at

the ratification of a treaty was for the junior member of the coalition or alliance to 'seize the hem of the garment' of the senior.

Each of the coalitions referred to above was headed by a suzerain, who would expect his vassals to accommodate their foreign policy to his, to refrain from having diplomatic relations with his enemies, and also to give him military support in the event of war. Thus we find Shamshi-Adad of Assyria ordering Yasmah-Adad, who was sub-king of Mari as well as Shamshi-Adad's son, to put himself and his troops and staff at Shamshi-Adad's disposal:

> To Yasmah-Adad say, thus says Shamshi-Adad your father: 'I have already sent you a message once or twice to come to Tuttul. Now I have reached Shubat-Enlil and I have had this tablet brought to you. Gather round yourself your officials, your porters, your troops who have gone with Samidahum, and your palace officials, and come to me at Shubat-Enlil.'

When a vassal or ally fulfilled his obligation to send a levy, or a suzerain acceded to a request for military assistance, it was understood that the troops were made available only for the duration of the emergency. Sometimes there was a difference of opinion between two partners as to when the emergency had ended. Thus one finds a certain ambassador, Ibal-pi-El, writing to his king, Zimri-Lim of Mari, about personnel of Mari on loan to Hammurabi:

> To my lord say, thus says your servant Ibal-pi-El: 'In accordance with the instructions of my lord, about which my lord keeps sending me messages, . . . I have now spoken on friendly terms [literally 'good words'] with Hammurabi . . . I spoke in these terms: "Inasmuch as the gods have destroyed the enemy and the days of cold weather have arrived, why do you retain the servants of your brother [i.e. 'your ally of equal rank']? Authorize me that I may go back and that the Officer Commanding may reach his estate before the cold weather". This and many (similar points) I have argued with him. . . .'

The letter becomes damaged at this point, but Hammurabi's reply seems to have been that he had to wait until the tenth of the month to receive a report about the activities of the king of Eshnunna.

There are very frequent references to ambassadors being sent from one court to another, and great importance was attached to their arrival. On one occasion Yasmah-Adad of Mari, always inefficient, received a sharp and sarcastic rebuke from his father, Shamshi-Adad, for holding up the members of an embassy on their way to him from Qatanum in Syria. Yasmah-Adad was in trouble with his father yet again when he reported that another ambassador could not continue his journey beyond Mari because of some mishap, which may have been (if we may slightly emend the French editor's copy of the cuneiform text) the breaking of the axle of his chariot. 'Can't he ride a donkey?', enquired the indignant Shamshi-Adad. Other letters show that omens were taken to obtain some divine guidance as to the reception to be accorded to envoys about to arrive. Diplomatic personnel, then as today, sometimes engaged in activities which made them unwelcome. In one instance known, one sub-king wrote to another to say that a certain person, presumably an agent of the second sub-king, was a liar and *persona non grata*, and that the writer did not wish to see him again.

Hostages were sometimes taken before negotiations between potential allies, and an occasion is known in which, when negotiations broke down, people who seem to have been held as hostages were put to death. In the following letter, which illustrates this, Shamshi-Adad is again writing to his son Yasmah-Adad:

> In the matter of the people of Wilanum who are in your charge, I ordered (you) to detain them in case an alliance came into being. Now there is no question of an alliance with Wilanum. . . . (As to) the people of Wilanum, every single one that is in your charge, give instructions and let them die tonight.

It is, of course, possible that in this case the victims concerned were prisoners whose lives had only been spared in the first place

because of the possibility of an alliance. There is certainly no
suggestion in the letter that they were diplomatic personnel.

If an alliance between rulers were successfully concluded, it
would in many cases be sealed by marriage between members of
the two royal families, a situation illustrated by the following
extract from a letter:

> Ishme-Dagan [senior son of Shamshi-Adad] has made peace with
> the Turukkians. He is taking the daughter of Zaziya [king of the
> Turukkians] for his son Mut-asqur. Ishme-Dagan has had gold and
> silver taken to Zaziya as bridal-gift.

Treaty relations between states involved not only military
alliances but also such matters as extradition of criminals and
international transport. As will be seen, in the treaties later in the
millennium a clause specifically dealing with extradition was
commonly included. No such formal treaties are yet known from
the Mari period, but there are references in letters to demands
for extradition. The following is an example:

> To Yasmah-Adad say, thus says Shamshi-Adad your father:
> 'Ushtan-sharri the Turukkian, who has been deported to Babylon, is
> ... in (the city of) Saggaratum. Now examine the antecedents of
> this man and the place where he is, and let the constables arrest him
> and let them escort him to me in (the city of) Shubat-Enlil. The
> Babylonian Man [i.e. the king of Babylon] has requested (him) from
> me.'

Kings had certain obligations with regard to caravans and
personnel crossing their territory, and a letter is extant in which
Yasmah-Adad, sub-king of Mari, writes to Hammurabi of
Babylon about a caravan which had gone from Mari through
Hammurabi's territory to Tilmun (modern Bahrein) in the
Persian Gulf. On its return journey it had been held up inside
Hammurabi's territory over some question of the use of wells.
Yasmah-Adad was sending a representative to escort the caravan
to Babylon, so that Hammurabi himself might sort the problem
out. In another case Shamshi-Adad writes to his son the sub-king,
Yasmah-Adad (inefficient as always), complaining that some
people from Yamhad had not been able to cross the Euphrates

in Mari territory because there were no boats available. Boats must be provided, said Shamshi-Adad, so that

> as previously, whoever comes along may cross and not be detained.

Rulers were expected to be responsible for the conduct of their subjects outside their own territory, and cases are known of a complaint from one king to another about criminal offences. Yasmah-Adad of Mari complained to Aplahanda of Carchemish that subjects of the latter had kidnapped a young lady in a raid across the border. Aplahanda replied asking for details of the affair, including the names of the lady, the person who had abducted her and the person who was alleged to be holding her at present. In a further letter Aplahanda, whose enquiries seem to have drawn a blank, suggested that the young lady's husband should go to Carchemish himself to see if he could manage to trace the missing person.

Passing to later in the second millennium, we find in Syria in the fourteenth century a situation between suzerain and vassals very similar to that existing in Mesopotamia several centuries before. The following quotations are from documents found at Ras Shamra (ancient Ugarit) in Syria. The situation there at the time mentioned was that the principal suzerain was the king of Hatti (the land of the Hittites), commonly given the title 'the Sun'. In the first document the Hittite king, the great Shuppi-luliuma, urges Niqmanda*, king of Ugarit, to continue his king-dom's traditional relations with Hatti, despite the disturbing influence and threats of aggressors:

> Thus says the Sun, the Great King: Say to Niqmanda: 'Since the lands of Nuhash and Mugish are at war with me, may you, Niq-manda, not fear them. . . . Just as formerly your forefathers were friendly with the land of Hatti and not hostile, now may you, Niqmanda, . . . be hostile to my enemy and friendly to my friend. Now if you, Niqmanda, hearken to these words of the Great King

* For the various spellings of this name, used here in this form because it represents the spelling employed in the letter quoted, see C. F. A. Schaeffer, *Le Palais royal d'Ugarit*, IV (1956), 248.

your lord and observe them, then you, O king, shall see the favour which the Great King your lord shall bestow upon you. . . . (As to) Nuhash and Mugish who have rejected the bond and friendship of the land of Hatti, and are hostile to the Great King their lord, now the Great King will deal with them. . . . And should all those kings release soldiers for aggression against your land, you, Niqmanda, are not to fear them, (but) send your messenger and let him come to me immediately.'

Events transpired as Shuppiluliuma had apparently foreseen; we learn this from an edict of Shuppiluliuma dealing with the situation when the kings of Nuhash and Mugish had invaded the territory of Niqmanda of Ugarit

and had taken spoil from Niqmanda king of Ugarit and had devastated Ugarit.

Niqmanda remained faithful to his suzerain, and as instructed asked at once for aid. So we gather from the document in question, which continues:

Niqmanda king of Ugarit came to Shuppiluliuma and sent a message to the Great King saying, 'May the Sun, the Great King, my lord, save me from the hand of my enemy. I am the servant of the Sun, the Great King, my lord; I am hostile to the enemies of my lord and I am friendly to the friends of my lord. (These) kings are oppressing me'. The Great King hearkened to this saying of Niqmanda, and Shuppiluliuma the Great King sent sons of the king and officers with troops and chariots to Ugarit, and they drove the enemy troops out of Ugarit by force, and all their booty which they had taken they gave as a present to Niqmanda. . . .

The document then proceeds to define the frontiers of Ugarit.

The suzerain was not only an avenger of any vassal who became subject to attack, but might act as an arbitrator in the event of disagreement amongst his vassals. (This is found already in Sumer in the mid-third millennium). Thus in the following case Mursilis II (king of Hatti 1334–1306 B.C.) settled a border dispute between neighbouring states who, after a period of friendship, had begun to drift apart into different political alignments:

Thus says Mursilis the Great King the king of Hatti, son of Shuppiluliuma, the Great King, the hero: 'Of old the king of Ugarit and the king of Siannu were in a state of unity. Now years have passed by and Abdi-Anati king of Siannu has become distant from Niqmepa king of Ugarit and has set his face towards the king of Carchemish. Now Abdi-Anati king of Siannu in the matter of these towns [i.e. towns listed later in the document] has cited Niqmepa king of Ugarit for judgement before the Great King the king of Hatti. . . .'

The Great King then went on to say which towns belonged to Niqmepa and which to Abdi-Anati: Niqmepa came off by far the better of the two. A parallel document dealing with the same piece of arbitration mentions that boundary stones were set up to establish the border between the two states, and concludes with the provision

In future the king of Siannu or his sons or his grandsons shall not re-open the case [literally 'return'] with the king of Ugarit or his sons or his grandsons in the matter of these boundaries.

The latter was a very wise precaution, for minor frontier incidents were liable to give rise to disputes which rapidly grew out of all proportion to the original incident, as the following complaint and threat illustrates:

To the king of Ugarit say, thus says Itur-Lim king of [place-name lost]. 'Greetings to you! . . . (Your people) have come within my borders. . . . Now why have you come within my borders? If your servants, in cultivating the grain, have done as they pleased [i.e. "acted without your authority"], why haven't you said to them "Why have you done (this)? You will raise a dispute between us." . . . If you do something, we also shall do it; . . . may this be known.'

The treaties and edicts so far adduced from the fourteenth century are largely between suzerains and vassals. There are also, however, examples of treaties of friendship between equals, such as the following:

From today Niqmanda king of Ugarit and Aziru king of Amurru have made this oath between them. The claims of Aziru against

Ugarit which existed previously, . . . [and claims of various other people] . . . on the day that the oath is established, shall be abolished. . . .

Another (clause): 5,000 (units) of silver are delivered into the hands of Aziru. . . .

Another (clause): Should there be a king who does a hostile act against the king of Ugarit, Aziru together with his chariots (and) his troops shall fight with my [i.e. Niqmandu's] enemy. If the troops of a hostile king plunder my land, Aziru together with chariots, together with troops, shall fight with my enemy. . . .

International arrangements were also made in treaties for the extradition of criminals or political refugees who had fled from one land to another. Thus in a treaty (written in Akkadian) between Hattusilis III of Hatti (1275–1250 B.C.) and Ramesses II of Egypt, we read:

If a man or two men or three men flee from the land of Hatti and go to Ramesses, beloved of the god Amon, the Great King, king of Egypt, my brother, (then) Ramesses, beloved of the god Amon, the Great King, king of Egypt, shall arrest them and send them to Hattusilis his brother. . . . And if a man or two men or three men flee from the land of Egypt and go to Hattusilis the Great King, the king of the land of Hatti, (then) Hattusilis the Great King, king of the land of Hatti, his brother, shall arrest them and send them to Ramesses, beloved of the god Amon, the Great King, king of Egypt. . . .

Similarly, international arrangements were made for the placing of liability if a subject of one ruler was robbed or murdered in the territory of the other. An instance is provided by the following fourteenth century document:

Ini-Teshub king of Carchemish has made a treaty with the men of Ugarit. If a man of Carchemish is killed in Ugarit, if they who killed him are arrested, they [those arrested] shall pay compensation for the man three-fold and they shall make good three-fold the things of which they robbed him. But if those who killed him are not identified, they [the Ugaritians] shall pay compensation for the life three-fold; they shall repay the things, as much as he was robbed of, (only) at their capital value. And if a man of Ugarit is killed in Carchemish, the compensation is the same.

Many of the points mentioned in connection with international relations could be paralleled from the first millennium, and a number of treaties, sealed by oaths and ratified by symbolic acts, might be adduced. Thus in a treaty between Mati'-Il of Arpad and the king of Assyria (eighth century B.C.), it is provided that

> if Mati'-Il offends against this treaty, then as this ram [the one being sacrificed] is brought up from the flock (and) shall not return to its flock, . . . so shall Mati'-Il, with his sons, daughters, . . . and people . . . ., be brought from his land, and shall not return to his land.
>
> This head is not the head of the ram, it is the head of Mati'-Il. . . . If Mati'-Il offends against this treaty, as my hand cleaves the head of this ram, . . . so may my hand cleave the head of Mati'-Il. . . .

A final example of international negotiations, showing diplomacy in action between kings who (unlike Mati'-Il and the king of Assyria) were more or less equal in status, is provided by a letter, datable to about 710 B.C., in which Sargon of Assyria refers to overtures from Mita of Mushku (that is Midas of Meshech, the country mentioned in *Genesis* x. 2, 1 *Chronicles* i. 5 and 17, *Psalms* cxx. 5, *Ezekiel* xxvii. 13, xxxii. 26, xxxviii. 2 and 3, xxxix. 1). King Sargon was writing to an Assyrian dignitary of high rank, possibly his own son and successor Sennacherib, who had reported that Mita of Mushku in Asia Minor, previously hostile to Assyria or at the best non-committal, had now taken the first steps to a *rapprochement*. The Assyrian king warmly welcomed the new situation and gave certain instructions to assist in the further development of friendly relations. An Assyrian ambassador was to be accredited to Mita, whilst consent was given for an ambassador from Mushku to come to the Assyrian court. In addition, the Assyrian dignitary to whom Sargon's letter was addressed was specifically instructed to inform Mita that the Assyrian king was 'very pleased' about developments; furthermore, the Assyrian dignitary's proposal to make reciprocal extradition arrangements was approved. This letter provides yet another substantiation of the view that Assyrian imperialism owed its undoubted success at least as much to careful administration and diplomacy as to military might.

8

Administration

INCIDENTAL references have been made to matters of administration in the third and the second millennia. This is a subject upon which general statements cannot wisely be uttered, since there were very wide divergences in practice between one period and another, often within a very short span of time. The method of treatment adopted here is, therefore, to give a brief summary of the salient features of each of the main periods, with a longer discussion of administrative developments from the time of the New Assyrian empire. The latter is chosen for special treatment in part because of its particular importance for the subsequent political development of the Near East, and in part because, with the current anti-imperialist fashion of thought, Assyrian imperialism has shared the widespread mis-representation.

End of the Early Dynastic Period (*circa* 2400 B.C.)

At the head of the city-state was the *Ensi*, who, if his dominion extended beyond his own city's territory and he was recognized by the temple of Nippur, would bear the more imposing title *Lugal*, king (literally 'great man'). In the latter case the man ruling for the *Lugal* in each of the dependent city-states would be a *Gir-nita*, governor. Each temple-estate would have its own administration, subject in the first place to the *Ensi* or king and ultimately to the god whose steward he was. The three principal figures in the temple administration were known as the *Agrig* ('superintendent'), the *Nu-banda* ('inspector') and the *Sanga*

233

('priest'): these were responsible for allocating tasks to the temple personnel, for the issue of rations and tools, and for oversight of the herds, fisheries and lands of the temple. There also existed inspectors of various kinds, apparently responsible to the *Ensi*, who took taxes upon cattle, boats, fisheries and the wool-clip, and levied fees for divorce or burial. For further references to the administration of this period see pages 46 f.

Period of the Third Dynasty of Ur (circa 2100 B.C.)

Government under the Third Dynasty of Ur was a highly centralized system, whilst the area controlled from Ur went so far beyond the confines of Sumer that it is not inappropriate to speak of a Third Dynasty of Ur empire. This empire has been described as the most efficiently organized structure of its kind before Assyrian times.

All provincial administrators were civil governors dependent upon the king. The constant internal rebellion which was such a problem under the Agade dynasty (see above, pages 50 and 51) was checked by making the military administration separate from the civil, whilst the independent power of civil governors was further limited by making them liable to transfer from city to city, so that local ties did not develop to make them too powerful. Regular reports from all quarters reached the king through royal messengers, enabling him to keep abreast of all developments in the empire.

The Old Babylonian Period (the kingdoms of Isin, Larsa, Mari and Babylon)

The administrative system of the empire of the Third Dynasty of Ur had already broken down before the capital itself was destroyed. Administration in the small splinter kingdoms which took the place of the old empire was therefore essentially a local matter, in which there was not necessarily any detailed correlation between the systems found in different areas. It seems likely, however, that the administrative practices amply attested (towards the end of the period) from the documents from the kingdom of Mari and Babylon may be taken as fairly typical.

A detailed study has been made by the Belgian scholar J. R. Kupper of the provincial administration of the city of Tirqa, rather more than forty miles north of Mari; in the time of king Zimri-Lim of Mari Tirqa belonged to the territories of Zimri-Lim and was ruled through a governor, Kibri-Dagan.

The territory actually under the jurisdiction of the governor comprised the city itself and the surrounding countryside, which included (as always with major towns in the ancient East) a substantial number of small villages. The actual size of the area has been computed as a sixty-mile stretch along the right bank of the middle Euphrates, probably extending (because of the needs of irrigation) not farther than five miles away from the river. Within this area, in addition to the inhabitants already settled in villages, there were to be found nomads of various tribes. These nomads, and probably also the villagers, who in many cases cannot have been long settled themselves, came into contact with the governor through their sheikhs (*suqaqu*); in the small towns there was a *ḥazannu* (overseer or mayor), whilst the *shibutum* or elders constituted a kind of local Assembly. The governor himself was concerned with the maintenance of order, the execution of justice, and above all, with public works, in particular the canals and irrigation system, for, as Kibri-Dagan says in a letter to the king, 'If the waters are cut off, the land of my lord will die of hunger'. It has to be noted, however, that in all these matters the final responsibility for decisions rested with the king. This made it imperative that governors should make frequent reports not only on political and military matters, but also on everything which concerned the well-being of the territory entrusted to them. Amongst other matters we find such disasters as epidemics, floods and invasion by locust swarms being duly reported to the king. The actual method by which a governor communicated with the king and the governors of other cities was by means of messengers of various kinds, ranging from simple carriers of tablets to confidential agents. The king kept a close eye on his officials, and we have letters in which officials had had to defend themselves to the kings against charges of negligence.

In the event of military emergency there was another method

of communication which could be employed in the kingdoms with which the Mari letters are concerned. This involved the use of fire beacons. By the use of a chain of bonfires, a warning of danger could be transmitted rapidly over the whole land. The only difficulty was that it should be clear in advance what such a signal meant. A letter is extant showing that over this very point the unfortunate Yasmah-Adad, sub-king of Mari, always a muddler, had managed to get himself into trouble. He had apparently set off the whole warning system for nothing more than a local raid, and his helpful and efficient elder brother, Ishme-Dagan, writes to advise him how to extricate himself from his predicament:

> To Yasmah-Adad say, thus says Ishme-Dagan your brother: 'Because you lit two fires during the night, possibly the whole land will be coming to (your) assistance. Have tablets written to all the land, . . . and have your fleet young couriers sent (to deliver them). You should say "A considerable body of enemy came on a raid into the land, and because of this two fires were lit. There is no need to come to (my) assistance".'

For security, inspection of the canals and general police work a governor in the kingdom of Mari would have at his disposal special contingents of troops. Such troops, or at least their officers, would be maintained by grants of land: this system of tenure is at present better known from Babylon than from Mari.

No very wide differences in principle appear to separate the administrative system in Babylonia from that at Mari. The administrative system in the kingdom of Hammurabi is known not only from his laws, but also from a large number of business documents and a considerable volume of the correspondence which passed between the king and his local officials. The general conclusion to be gained from the last-named source is that administration was at the time of Hammurabi highly centralized and that, as in Assyria in the first millennium, no matter was too small to merit the king's personal attention.

The Amorite princes who gradually gathered the fragments of the Third Dynasty of Ur empire and the Isin and Larsa kingdoms into their hands, in the course of doing so were able to bring into their own control much land which at other periods was considered as being temple land. A part of this royal land was allotted to men who held it by virtue of the performance of certain duties to the king, and the laws of Hammurabi specifically proscribed the sale of such land. The officials referred to in the laws as holding land in this way are the *rēdû*, the *bā'iru*, the PA.PA (a Sumerian ideogram sometimes rendered into Akkadian, with doubtful justification, as *dēkû*) and the *labuttû*. All these terms apparently denoted military or police personnel whose titles, if a translation is insisted upon, may be very roughly represented by sergeant, corporal, colonel and adjutant, although their duties were much wider than these terms imply. In addition to these military men it is clear from the letters that a considerable number of professional men and tradespeople, such as merchants, scribes, shepherds, jewellers, smiths and soothsayers, to specify only a few, held land in a similar way. This becomes obvious from letters such as this:

> To Shamash-hasir say thus, thus says Hammurabi: 'When you see this tablet, deliver one *bur* of land to Sin-mushtal, one *bur* to Ili-idinnam, one *bur* to Ili-ishmeani, the three comptrollers of the merchants of Ur, together with their old-standing fields of maintenance.'

'Field of maintenance' is recognized as a term denoting a fief. Registers recording grants and rights in this connection were kept and referred to in case of dispute. Grants were often – as indeed section 28 of the 'Code' of Hammurabi indicates – given in succession from father to son, and the following shows an instance of this:

> To Shamash-hasir say thus, thus says Hammurabi: 'Give to Munawwirum the *rakbu*, as his field of maintenance, three *bur* of land from the land of his father's estate at Dimti-ili.'

The grant of the fief made by the king was administered by the governor, who, as in the kingdom of Mari and elsewhere, was responsible for the threefold duty of security, public works (including canals and royal land) and communications, though in

237

all these matters the governor was closely tied by royal instructions. On occasions the governors did venture to neglect the
king's orders, but such a dereliction of duty would bring a sharp
rebuke. Thus, in one letter, the governor Shamash-hasir is told
by Hammurabi:

> Last year I sent some *rakbu*-archers to you for settlement on the
> land. There were before you (there) for eight months and you didn't
> satisfy a single man.

Detailed instructions follow as to how this matter is to be rectified,
and the king concludes:

> If these *rakbu*-men are not quickly satisfied, . . . you will not be
> pardoned.

The governor's own administrative area was divided into
sectors under subordinate officials. Two terms, *patum and irsitum*,
are known to have denoted areas of this kind under royal officials
(if the *rabianu* or 'mayor' may be properly put into this category),
but the extent of the areas concerned is uncertain. Possibly the
patum included the whole of the cultivated area administered
from a particular city, whilst it has been suggested that *irsitum*
meant a 'quarter' of a city.

New Assyrian Period

Byron's celebrated couplet –

> The Assyrian came down like the wolf on the fold,
> And his cohorts were gleaming in purple and gold –

does little justice to the Assyrian system of military government.
The Assyrians were not simply out for loot. The lands which
came under their control they not only attempted to administer,
but succeeded in administering, by ancient standards, with
admirable efficiency: indeed, Assyrian administration compares
very favourably with the situation which prevailed in much of
the same area a century ago and in some of it at the present day.
That Byron's picture of Assyrian hordes sweeping down on
defenceless valley populations and withdrawing to leave death
and desolation in their wake is a distorted one, even the Old

Testament, written from the point of view of one of the more vocal and nationally conscious subject races, shows. One finds from a detailed examination that in Old Testament prophecy, in those prophecies in which Assyria is condemned, the condemnation is in no case for barbarity nor even for administrative harshness. This is true even of Nahum's gloating prophecy over Assyria's fall. To Nahum, Assyria's offence seems to have been its participation in magic coupled with its commercial success: he proclaims that Assyria is doomed

> because of the multitudes of the whoredoms of the well favoured harlot, the mistress of witchcrafts, that selleth nations through her whoredoms, and families through her witchcrafts (iii. 4),

and casts against Assyria the taunt

> Thou hast multiplied thy merchants above the stars of heaven (iii. 16).

Throughout the other prophets, any condemnation of Assyria that may be expressed is not for any specific aspect of its treatment of subject or conquered races but for what one might best call arrogance, that is, for claiming to exercise as of right power merely delegated by God. By Hosea, indeed, Assyria itself is not condemned at all: it is upon Israel that the condemnation falls, for reliance upon the might of Assyria rather than upon God (xii. 1). Isaiah recognized Assyria – which he described as 'the rod of [God's] anger' (x. 5) – as the instrument of Jehovah, and for him Assyria was doomed not for any specific mis-use of power but for failing to recognize and acknowledge the source of the power it wielded by God's will (*Isaiah* x. 6–16). Zephaniah, in similar strain, foretold the destruction of Assyria not for inhumanity but for pride:

> He will stretch out his hand against the north, and destroy Assyria; and will make Nineveh a desolation, and dry like a wilderness. . . . This is the rejoicing city that dwelt carelessly, that said in her heart, I am, and there is none beside me. (*Zephaniah* ii. 13, 15; Authorised Version).

Biblical reflections on the punishment of Assyria subsequent to

its fall likewise refer not to any particular form of injustice, but
to her arrogance in usurping power belonging properly to God,
and in particular to impiety in swallowing up the Chosen People.
Ezekiel paints a most attractive picture of the Assyrian Empire:

> The Assyrian was a cedar in Lebanon with fair branches, and with
> a shadowing shroud, and of an high stature; and his top was among
> the thick boughs. The waters made him great, the deep set him up
> on high with her rivers running round about his plants, and sent
> out her little rivers unto all the trees of the field. Therefore his
> height was exalted above all the trees of the field and his boughs
> were multiplied, and his branches became long because of the multi-
> tude of waters, when he shot forth. All the fowls of heaven made
> their nests in his boughs, and under his branches did all the beasts of
> the field bring forth their young, and under his shadow dwelt all
> great nations. Thus was he fair in his greatness, in the length of his
> branches: for his root was by great waters. The cedars in the garden
> of God could not hide him . . . nor any tree in the garden of God
> was like unto him in his beauty (*Ezekiel* xxxi. 3–8; Authorised
> Version).

The sin for which the great tree Assyria was felled was Pride, but
Ezekiel felt no vindictiveness in his reflections upon Assyria's fall.
He adds significantly:

> Thus saith the Lord God; In the day when he went down to the
> grave I caused a mourning: I covered the deep for him and I re-
> strained the floods thereof, and the great waters were stayed: and I
> caused Lebanon to mourn for him and all the trees of the field
> fainted for him. (*Ezekiel* xxxi. 15; Authorised Version).

This is not to deny that Assyrian administrative methods were
by modern standards harsh; but the other side of the system must
not be overlooked. Far from being simply a despotic militarism
holding down conquered races by mere brutal harshness, Assyrian
imperialism owed much of its success to a highly developed and
efficient administrative system, and to the attention of an energetic
bureaucracy to the day-to-day trifles of government. Even as
early as the reign of Ashur-nasir-pal II (883–859 B.C.), administrative action in conquered territories was not arbitrary but according to principles which can already be recognized; and from the

time of Tiglath-Pileser III, some hundred and forty years later, in whose reign the Hebrew kingdoms came irrevocably into the Assyrian orbit, a definite pattern in imperial administration may be seen, which was subject to no more than minor developments and differences of detail under succeeding kings.

Political administration is seldom a tidy affair, and there are bound to be exceptions to any general statement, but broadly speaking Assyrian-controlled territory included units of population related to the central Assyrian government in three main ways. Firstly, and most loosely bound, there were those states whose rulers had, from motives of prudence, brought tribute to the Assyrian king as the token of a friendly attitude which, depending upon circumstances, might properly be regarded as lying somewhere between alliance and vassaldom. The rulers of such states would receive in return for their tribute the concrete advantage of an Assyrian guarantee to their states and dynasties against aggression: the Assyrian guarantee, unlike that of Egypt – a power derisively described by an Assyrian Commander-in-Chief as a 'bruised reed, . . . whereon if a man lean, it will go into his hand, and pierce it' (*Isaiah* xxxvi. 6) – was usually implemented, and was so highly regarded that in some cases, of which the best known instance is that of Ahaz of Judah (2 *Kings* xvi. 7–9), a small state would take the initiative in seeking to become an Assyrian tributary. In practice the political status of states in such a relationship with Assyria would vary within very wide limits, according to such factors as geographical position, matrimonial alliances with other states, and particularly the distance away of the nearest Assyrian military forces or officials: in some cases the interests of Assyria might be watched and its influence augmented by an Assyrian adviser or observer permanently attached to a native court.

States which had once accepted – whether of their own seeking or under Assyrian pressure – this kind of relationship with Assyria tended almost inevitably to come in course of time under a closer form of control; for if such a tributary, once having made formal submission, subsequently at any time withheld its annual tribute, the failure to pay its dues was regarded by Assyria as a hostile act, and was liable to call down military action. In some cases, by the good fortune or foresight of the delinquent state, Assyria was fully occupied elsewhere and the tributary escaped immediate retribution, but in many other instances Assyria's response to such a situation was to make an attack on the recalcitrant territory with a small force, pruning it back by annexing the outlying parts to a more reliable subject state or province. The Assyrians would then intervene in the internal affairs of the state to replace the unreliable ruler by another prince acceptable to Assyria, or, where a loyal pro-Assyrian ruler had been removed by internal faction, to reinstate the Assyrian protégé or a member of his family. In any case, the ruler recognized by Assyria would now be bound by oath before the great gods, whilst an Assyrian official, probably backed by a small military force, would be left within his territory to watch local events and the foreign relations of the state and to ensure due payment of tribute. This represented the second or intermediate stage of relationship with Assyria.

Subsequent breaking of the oath of allegiance was an offence, not only against the king of Assyria, but also against the gods by whom the oath had been sworn, and as such was punishable by death. The punishment was not so much revenge against the offender or a warning to others as the expiation of an offence against the gods which, if not suitably dealt with, might bring divine retribution – plague, flood, famine, earthquake or other phenomena by which the god's displeasure was manifested – upon the whole territory. Parallels to this conception of the national ill-fortune likely to result from breaking an oath or otherwise slighting a god are not hard to find in the Old Testament. Achan stole from the booty consecrated to the tribal god: defeat at once befell the Israelites and only gave way to success after the sin had been discovered and the sinner executed (*Joshua* vii). Jonathan, having broken an oath to fast taken by his father Saul on behalf of all the Israelites, faced execution, and only escaped by the popular feeling that the victory just won by Jonathan's leadership demonstrated that God approved his action, Saul's oath not-withstanding (1 *Samuel* xiv). Because of its expiatory nature, the execution in such circumstances might involve tortures, probably with religious or rather magical significance, such as flaying, immuring, pulling out the lying tongue, burning or impaling. It is atrocities of this type which, usually considered without reference to the context of events, have largely been responsible for the indignation expressed against Assyria by modern historians and by commentators on the Old Testament scene. The other two items which give rise to so much indignation amongst modern historians are the heaping up of heads or bodies of the dead, and the holocaust of prisoners, frequently referred to in Assyrian royal annals in words which, translated, read something like 'Their corpses I formed into pillars; their young men and maidens I burned in the fire'. The former, though an offence against religious susceptibilities, was not in itself an atrocity to living men, and moreover it can be directly paralleled from the twentieth century A.D.: Sir Philip Gibbs (*The Pageant of the Years*, page 300) mentions a photograph of 'a Turkish officer sitting on a pile of skulls and smoking a cigarette'. As to the phrase about burning in the fire, whether this means that children were burnt alive is open to question: if it does it was probably a religious, or rather magical, practice parallel to one perpetrated by the Jews throughout the period of the Hebrew kingdoms.

It should be remembered that the actual tortures on living men (see plate 46A), far from being typical of treatment meted out to conquered peoples as a whole, generally affected only a very small number – usually less than a dozen – of the ruling classes: the mass of the population was either fined and left to go about its business, or, with increasing frequency as time went on, dealt with by deportation (see plates 33A and 34), the conquered territory being repopulated from elsewhere and reorganized into a province under direct Assyrian administration. Furthermore, the Assyrian practice should not be considered in the light of the highest Christian ideals – which in the wars of the twentieth century A.D. have been so frequently forgotten – but by comparison with contemporary standards, of which instructive examples may be found in the *Books of Kings*. A few instances from the records of the rulers of the Chosen People at about the same period will make this point clear. Baasha, on taking the throne of Israel from Jeroboam's successor, wiped out, with the approval of the prophets of Jehovah, the whole family of Jeroboam (I *Kings* xv. 25–30); Zimri, also with prophetic approval, did the same to Baasha's family on usurping the throne in his turn (I *Kings* xvi. 8–13), and in this case, as Zimri had a reign of only seven days, the royal assassin can have wasted no time in deliberating on the matter or attempting to contrive a convincing pretext to satisfy public opinion. When one king, Ahab, did show magnanimity to a defeated enemy, he was bitterly denounced by one of the prophets (I *Kings* xx. 30–42). A tradition records, with obvious satisfaction, the fate of forty-two cheeky urchins, cursed by Elisha and in consequence eaten by bears (2 *Kings* ii. 23, 24): whether the events happened as narrated or not, prophetic circles obviously felt it was the kind of thing that ought to happen, and the moral content of the story was acceptable to the prophetic schools not only of the time of Elisha, but much later at the time of the compilation of the *Books of Kings*. Another Israelite monarch, Jehu, having exterminated seventy sons of Ahab and all his surviving relatives, together with forty-two sons of Ahaziah and a great multitude of misguided but otherwise inoffensive followers of Baal, received the enthusiastic approval of influential sections of the worshippers of Jehovah (2 *Kings* x. 1–30). As a final example of ancient standards, Menahem, on capturing a certain district, ripped up all the pregnant women (2 *Kings* xv. 16) without bringing down upon himself any obvious condemnation for this particular atrocity, although the compilers of the *Books of Kings* were ready enough to condemn him for his failures in matters relating to the cult. Judged by the moral standards which accepted such events as normal and justified, Assyria can no longer be indicted for exceptional barbarity. As to comparison with contemporary warfare, there is very little in the more gruesome sections of the Assyrian royal annals that cannot be equalled or exceeded from the records of events in Europe and Africa (black and white) since 1939 A.D.

Although the royal annals of the Assyrian kings, our main quarry for knowledge of Assyrian history in the first millennium, give but scattered and scanty hints of the administrative machinery operating within the imperial provinces, it is fortunately possible to glean a great deal of information on this matter from incidental references in the correspondence between the king and his provincial officials. A large number – now approaching two thousand – of letters of this *genre* have been found in excavations at the old royal capitals of Nineveh and Calah (*Genesis* x. 11,12) and at the provincial city of Guzana on the Habur, the biblical Gozan (2 *Kings* xvii. 6). The great majority of these documents come from archives in the two royal capitals, whence it happens that most of them are letters written to, rather than by, the king, but one may reasonably assume that a corresponding number of royal replies await discovery in still unexcavated, and in many cases unidentified, provincial cities.

These letters cover a wide range of subjects and serve in general to show that the officials we meet in them, whether great or small, were actively administering their territories and not merely grinding wealth from the subjects of the king by a system of tax-farming. Unexpected consideration is sometimes shown to the people governed, and though this was certainly in the first instance in the interests of efficiency rather than of humanity, can any better claim be made for modern philanthropy in industry? In one instance an official named Ashur-matka-gur had received a royal inquiry about some Aramaeans whom he was responsible for re-settling. In his reply he reported: 'They will shortly take the road; I have given them their provisions, clothes, shoes and oil'. But food and equipment did not exhaust the king's arrangements for the settlers: apparently he had also planned to provide wives for them. In this matter, however, the king's project did not meet with immediate success, for in another letter Ashur-matka-gur mentioned that trouble had arisen, apparently because the marriage customs of the Aramaeans differed from those of the ladies. He reported:

> About the Aramaeans of whom the king said 'They are to be married off', the women say, ' We find that the Aramaean men are unwilling to give us money', and 'Not until they give us money!'

It seems that the ladies insisted, in accordance with what is known to have been the normal requirement in Assyrian law, upon receiving money before marriage, as a kind of bride-price, which the Aramaeans were apparently unwilling or unable to pay. Ashur-matka-gur's solution of the problem was to suggest that the ladies' demand should be met and that the Aramaeans should be given the necessary money to enable them to find favour with the ladies. Such details were doubtless planned not for abstract humanitarian considerations but with a view to ensuring the stability of the re-settled populations: none the less, attention to such details must have alleviated many hardships.

In another letter an official, possibly the governor of the city and province of Kakzu in the east of Assyria, had been accused of settling farmers on land subject to flooding, and hastened to defend his record. 'The harvest', he wrote, 'is in fact a very good one', and he went on to give details to justify his claim. No doubt the anxiety of the central government was largely due to concern at the possible loss of revenue, but from the point of view of the ordinary peasant the net result of the central government's attention to this kind of detail was the encouragement of efficient administration and more tolerable working conditions.

Some letters from an official in charge of affairs at Tyre and Sidon are also instructive. The official, Qurdi-Ashur-lamur, in one letter reminded the king (or so the document seems to say) that he had been sent with express instructions to treat the conquered cities with conciliation, and in another provides us with an illustration of how he fulfilled the king's intentions. He mentions that some Assyrian official, whom we may guess was the military governor who had been in charge of operations at the time the cities were taken, had cut the canal carrying Sidon's water supply; he himself, Qurdi-Ashur-lamur reported, had now overruled his predecessor's order and restored the water supply to the city.

In many such letters the writer can be identified as a provincial governor, usually from the occurrence of the writer's name in the *limmu* list (see page 93), and in such cases one can sometimes see the problems confronting the administrator both from the local point of view and in the wider historical context. This is particularly true of governors of areas on the northern frontiers of the empire, who took the immediate impact of the barbarian pressure from the north which menaced the whole civilized world for a century and a half after Tiglath-Pileser III.

An Assyrian governor (Akkadian *bel piḫati*, meaning literally 'lord of the province') appointed to administer a directly ruled province, would, as personal representative of the king, hold a status which in differing circumstances might involve civil, fiscal, military or religious duties. His official residence in the provincial capital was known as 'The Palace', and to this would be attached a sizeable staff including, amongst others, such officials as scribes, messengers, surveyors, accountants, diviners, astrologers, recruiting officers and irrigation controllers, as well as military aides and officers to command the armed forces at the governor's disposal. There must also have been interpreters present in the governor's entourage, and certainly the Assyrian Commander-in-Chief at the siege of Jerusalem (2 *Kings* xviii. 26ff.) must have had a Hebrew-speaking herald on his staff, unless he both spoke Hebrew himself and made his proclamation in person.

As in any colonial administration, the importance of different provinces and the seniority of their governors varied widely. Some of the more ancient provinces were customarily the responsibility of particular high officers of state, who must at frequent intervals have left their provinces to government by deputy whilst they advised the king at the capital or led campaigns; other more recently constituted provinces were governed by officials of lesser rank. There seems, however, to have been no generally maintained distinction between provinces based on seniority. It is true that two distinct terms, *nagu* (literally 'island') and *piḫatu* (originally 'responsibility') were in different cases applied to the region entrusted to a governor, but they do not appear to correspond to a difference in the status of the governors: rather, the former appears to have denoted a natural geographical entity, such as a river valley or a district enclosed by ranges of hills, whilst the latter represented an area divided off more arbitrarily on political considerations.

The province in Assyria was subdivided into a number of smaller areas called *qannu* (perhaps having the literal meaning 'ring'), each centred on one of the large towns of the province and under the control of an officer known as the *rab alani* ('Chief of the Townships') who also, like the governor in the provincial capital, had military forces at his disposal. As will be seen later, in some cases, particularly inside Assyria proper, as well as in Babylonia, the municipal administrations of the great cities retained some measure of autonomy, in certain instances granted or confirmed by royal charter in return for support at times of internal crisis, particularly rebellion or disputed succession, and in such cases the authority of the local *rab alani* would not extend to the city at the centre of his *qannu*. None the less, the presence of a representative of the central government, backed by troops, in the area around the city no doubt sometimes served to remind a truculent city administration of the wisdom of moderation in its demands on the king.

One essential function of the *rab alani* was the collection of taxes, paid in kind, and the forwarding of them to the depot of the central government; and in the event of any shortfall a royal inquiry would quickly be forthcoming. In a typical case an inspector, Ashipa, had been sent to examine suspicious circumstances in Babylonia and to report on deficiencies. He was apparently satisfied that the *rab alani* was not culpable, and wrote to tell the king the explanation of the trouble. The missing grain, he wrote, could not be transported to Sippar (where apparently the royal depot was) before the local canal had been opened: the writer gave his royal master an assurance that work on the canal was being carried on with all possible speed.

A *rab alani* would also obviously be responsible for safeguarding order within the area under his jurisdiction. On occasion, in a border area, it could happen that imperial security would depend on his taking appropriate military action in the face of enemy troop movements on the frontier. There are several references in the royal archives to this type of action. A typical one refers to a clash on the Urartian frontier to the north-east of Assyria, on which the local governor reported:

'I sent troops with the *rab alani*, making them march in battle-line. The *rab alani*'s lieutenant and nine men with him were wounded by bow-shot. Two of the enemy are dead and three are wounded'.

An efficient communication system was vital to the security and smooth functioning of the empire. The letters already referred to show that provincial governors were in constant day-to-day touch with the central government: and the *rab alani* officers were likewise in close touch with the governors of their provinces and, where necessary, with the central government also. Communication was by means of professional messengers, of whom there appear to have been four or five different classes, though it is not yet clear exactly how they differed. The normal method of communication with the central government was (as much earlier) by means of an official called *mar shipri* ('son of the message'), who travelled along the 'royal roads'. These royal roads were the main arteries of the empire, and though they were probably cleared tracks rather than made-up roads in the modern, or the Roman, sense, they were certainly well enough defined to be used as boundaries between provinces, and level enough to permit the rapid passage of large armies accompanied by chariots. Beautifully made and completely level roads of stone blocks and cobble stones have also been found, but these are restricted to the streets of the metropolis or the immediate approaches thereto. Along the roads across the empire, about a day's journey (twenty to thirty miles) apart, were posts permanently manned by government troops, containing a change of horses or mules for the use of the messengers on the next stage. A *mar shipri* would thus travel mounted, from stage to stage, with a small escort of troops, carrying the tablets containing his governor's dispatches or the king's replies. The post-animals were restricted to particular routes, no doubt to ensure that each section should always have beasts available, and this sometimes led to friction. More than one letter is known containing a complaint to the king from the staff of a stage-post, to the effect that some high official had claimed the right to use the last remaining beast on an unofficial route. This could cause dislocation in the communication system, as one agitated official recognized when, caught in this dilemma, he explained to the king:

> 'The king my lord knows that there is no posting stage to Shabirishu; and (post animals) which go (there) do not return'.

One may thus recognize that the famous Persian system of post-roads operating throughout the Persian Empire was not a Persian innovation but the development of a system already employed some centuries earlier by the Assyrians.

The normal system of imperial communications outlined above was not, however, adequate to the needs of all circumstances. Thus, on occasion, in the more remote and mountainous provinces, heavy falls of snow might interrupt the usual means of communication, but the dispatches must still reach the court. We learn what happened in such cases from a letter by an official named Dur-Ashur, probably the governor of the province of Tushkhan up in the mountains of what is now south-eastern Turkey. Dur-Ashur in his letter to the king remarks: 'Perhaps the king will say, "Why did you not send . . . by the agency of a *mar shipri?*" The snow is very heavy: I therefore sent a *dayalu* ["runner"] with a message'. One concludes that the 'runner' was a skilled mountaineer who could find a way over terrain impassable to horses. Another circumstance in which the employment of an ordinary *mar shipri* was impracticable was when news for the private ear of the king or a governor required to be communicated. In such a case use was made of a special envoy, carrying a letter of introduction attested by his principal's seal: his credentials having been presented, he could then pass on his confidential message with the requisite secrecy. The king had a number of such agents, called *qurbuti* ('Intimates'), travelling on his business, and when a complaint was made of the conduct of a senior official, it would normally be one of them who was dispatched to investigate and report to the king. Even a governor was liable to receive a visit of inspection from the king's confidential agent, for such an official was far from being left with a free hand in his territory: not only was the initiative permitted to him relatively circumscribed, since in many cases the governor received, or asked for, instructions from the capital not only on general policy but even on matters of seemingly trivial detail, but at times one governor might be subordinate to the governor of a neighbouring province, whilst complaints against governors were not infrequently entertained and investigated by the king. But who dared to criticize his governor? It seems that such complaints could come either from another official who felt that the governor in question was encroaching on his privileges, or from a private citizen, even possibly a non-Assyrian, who felt that he had been oppressively treated and who appealed to the king for justice. Thus we have the letter of a certain Marduk-shum-usur who appealed to the king for redress because a small estate granted him by the king's predecessor as a fief had been seized by the governor of Barhalzi although, Marduk-shum-usur claimed, he had never failed in the performance of his feudal duty:

> To the king my lord your servant Marduk-shum-usur. May it be well with the king my lord. May the gods Nabu and Marduk bless the king my lord.
>
> The father of the king my lord delivered to me a field of ten homers in the land of Halahhi. For fourteen years I enjoyed the use of the field and no-one disputed it with me. Now the governor has come . . ., mistreated the tenant-farmer, plundered his house, and taken away his field. The king my lord knows that I am a fief-holder and that I keep the watch of the king my lord. . . . Now the king my lord may see that I am deprived of land. Let the king my lord deal with my cause, that I may not die of hunger.

We do not know if Marduk-shum-usur succeeded in his suit. Nor do we know the conditions under which an appeal from a private citizen was likely to reach the king; no doubt officialdom could in many cases prevent a complaint from obtaining effective royal consideration, but the presence of such letters of complaint in the royal archives shows that in at least some cases they reached their destination.

Some of the ancient cities still enjoyed, even at the height of Assyrian imperial power, a considerable measure of autonomy, which the king, whilst often seeking to curb it, was sometimes compelled to recognize. The manner in which such rights arose or were extended (in these cases outside Assyria proper) is shown in some letters written to Tiglath-Pileser III in 731 B.C. The two writers, officials in Babylonia, found themselves in a very difficult situation. They had a rebellion on their hands, the capital Babylon was controlled by rebels, and no adequate Assyrian forces were within reach. In one letter they reported to the king the measures they had taken. They had, they said, taken their stand outside the city gate to attempt to negotiate with the Babylonians within. They had obviously attempted to cause a breach between the rebel Chaldaean leaders and the native Babylonians, and in this respect and others the whole scene is curiously reminiscent of the attempted negotiations between the Rab-shakeh and the inhabitants of Jerusalem (2 *Kings* xviii. 26ff.). 'Why do you behave hostilely to us on their account?', cried the Assyrian officials; 'Fancy Babylon showing favour to tribesmen!' And then they added 'Your city's privileges are already set down in a charter', clearly implying that Assyria was, in return for their assistance, prepared to recognize all their traditional local rights. Another letter describes similar negotiations elsewhere in the same crisis, and here the writer had specifically promised the occupants of the rebels leader's city 'I will free from forced labour and tribute any Aramaeans who desert'.

Within the ancient cities local government was usually still in the hands of the Elders, or a section of them, presided over by the *hazannu*, an official whose title (already mentioned above in connection with Tirqa in the Old Babylonian period), is often for convenience translated 'Mayor', although in Assyria at least his status seems to have been as much religious as civil. The *hazannu* and the Council of Elders in a city such as Ashur could be a constant source of annoyance to the king, and this may account in part for the several changes of capital city. It could also account for the existence in some of the great cities, alongside and closely connected with the *hazannu*, of another official whose title means 'Man over the City'. This office seems by no means to have had the antiquity of that of *hazannu*, which occurred at least as early as the beginning of the second millennium B.C., nor to have carried the religious significance which an ancient office usually involved, and it may well be that the office of 'Man over the City' was deliberately created by the kings of Assyria in the hope that the appointee would counterbalance the *ḫazannu* and be able to safeguard the royal interests within the city. A corresponding method of securing some royal control within powerful temple corporations was employed in Babylonia a little later. As has already been noted, various kings gave cities which had supported them valuable privileges in the matter of exemption from taxes, and the existence of charters incorporating such privileges often embarrassed succeeding rulers. However, unlike the case in Babylonia, where the city lands might extend for thirty or even fifty miles from the city itself, the legal limits of jurisdiction of an Assyrian city seem to have been very circumscribed, and the authority of the *ḫazannu* did not extend far, if at all, beyond the actual city walls. Thus inside Assyria, in the last resort the central government could always overawe a troublesome city by posting troops in the *qannu* surrounding it, and if necessary by interfering thereby with the trade by which it lived. Cases in which this actually happened have come to light. In one letter the *ḫazannu* of Ashur writes to the king complaining that two sheikhs of the Itu'a tribe had pitched camp with their men in the *qannu* in front of the great gate of Ashur, and were interfering with the normal business of the city:

> To the king our lord your servants Mutakkil-Ashur the deputy priest and your servant Ishtar-na'id the *ḫazannu*. May it be well with the king our lord. May the god Ashur and the temple Esharra bless the king our lord.
> 'Bibiya a prefect of the Itu'a people and Tarditu-Ashur a prefect of the Itu'a people, are both of them squatting in the *qannu* of Ashur in front of the Great Gate and are eating and drinking wine together. They are obstructing the exit from Ashur. When I broached the matter with them they arrested (my) officials and laid hands on (them) . . . . I am powerless against them'.

Now Ashur, a settlement of venerable antiquity, was notoriously one of the cities which claimed special chartered privileges, whilst the Itu'a troops were, as we know from numerous references in other letters, tribal levies specially employed by the king for police work in dealing with troublesome city-dwellers: the *hazannu* can therefore hardly have been so naive as to suppose that the Itu'a sheikhs had set up camp in that inconvenient spot purely by chance.

Cities more recently incorporated into Assyrian territory by conquest would not present the same administrative difficulties to the central government as did those of ancient standing. Frequently, where the original native ruler had co-operated with Assyria, or even where submission had followed armed resistance, that ruler might be confirmed in his old position, as an Assyrian agent, with the title 'Lord of the City'. His duties, from the point of view of Assyria, would be mainly concerned with the collection of the tribute for the payment of which his city was liable. In addition he must have been responsible for the maintenance of order within his area, and to this end had at his disposal a small garrison, although when the Assyrian army was operating in the area control of this force seems to have reverted to the regular military officials. Generally speaking, if this limited autonomy broke down, as a result of the truculence of the citizens or the unreliability of the 'Lord of the City', the city would come under the immediate control of the governor of the province in which it lay. In a few cases it seems that cities of such antecedents may have been put under the rule of a 'Man over the City' (an Assyrian appointee quite distinct from the 'Lord of the City'), who was then directly responsible to the king without reference to the local governor.

Three principal tasks were incumbent upon the officials of the Assyrian administration – the safeguarding of communications, the due collection of taxes, and the maintenance of good order. Some account has already been given of the communication system, though many of the details remain to be worked out from the Assyrian documents. As to taxation, considerable attention is paid to this both in the Old Testament references to Assyrian suzerainty and in the Assyrian royal annals, though it must be pointed out that lists of tribute cited by Assyrian kings in their inscriptions give, in many cases, a distorted picture of the actual weight of taxation upon the ordinary citizen of the Assyrian empire. There are several reasons for this: firstly, in some cases the figures may be exaggerated in the interests of royal prestige; secondly, there is usually no indication of the size and wealth of the population upon which the tribute was levied; and thirdly, the goods listed are in many cases not, properly speaking, tribute, but rather war booty, which although an unwelcome burden at the time, was a non-recurrent charge upon a subject people. The actual weight of taxation would be seen in a better perspective by comparing Assyrian demands from their subjects with similar demands made by other rulers of the ancient world. For the purposes of such a comparison the Old Testament figures are the only ones readily accessible.

A number of payments of tribute or taxes are referred to in the Old Testament records: most are related to the reign of Solomon – rather earlier than the period now under consideration – and may well be inflated figures. Certainly the figure of six hundred and sixty-six talents of gold (1 *Kings* x. 14) as the total annual revenue for the reign of Solomon looks suspiciously like an ideal number: whether this is, in fact, a reliable figure, and how it is made up, is not clear, though as the purpose of giving the figure was the glorification of Solomon, it if bears any relationship to reality at all it must be an optimum figure. It might be argued that this figure, if calculated from the records of one particular year, may conceivably have included the whole of the profits of a naval expedition to Ophir, four hundred and twenty talents, which ought to have been spread over three years (1 *Kings* ix. 26–28 and x. 22), or possibly one of the non-recurrent payments of one hundred and twenty talents from either Hiram of Tyre (1 *Kings* ix. 14) or the Queen of Sheba (1 *Kings* x. 10). Against this supposition is the fact that the biblical account does specifically state that the six hundred and sixty-six talents of Solomon's annual revenue was 'beside that which he had of the merchant-men, and of the traffic of the spice merchants, and of all the kings of Arabia, and of the governors of the country' (1 *Kings* x. 15)*,

* The Hebrew original of this verse contains several words which appear to have been technical terms of commerce or administration. Because of our failure to understand these fully, the sense is not completely clear. The rendering of the RV is not necessarily more accurate than that of the AV.

and the present writer therefore accepts the biblical figure as being of the right order, even if representing an ideal maximum rarely if ever attained. It is interesting to estimate what this may have represented in terms of burden upon the average Israelite. Despite 1 *Kings* ix. 22, part of this revenue undoubtedly came from slave trading, since it has long been recognized from the biblical evidence that Solomon obtained chariots and horses from Egypt in exchange for Israelite slaves, whilst ancient Palestine produced very few other commodities, except copper from the Israelite zone of Sinai, suitable for export. The remainder of the royal revenue must have come ultimately from the products of forced labour, and from direct taxation, of both of which a detailed account is in fact given in the *Books of Kings*. It is hazardous to attempt a precise estimate of the size of the population over which this burden was spread, but some indication is given by the quantities of food used for the dedication feast mentioned in 1 *Kings* viii. 63–65. A very similar dedication feast lasting, like that of Solomon (which was apparently in two relays), for a week, was held at the re-founding by Ashur-nasir-pal of the Assyrian capital city Calah; and in the recently discovered account of the latter feast the quantities of sheep and cattle were approximately one-tenth of those consumed at the dedication of Solomon's temple. The Assyrian inscription puts the number present at Ashur-nasir-pal's feast as nearly 70,000, so that in proportion one would expect that a number of people approaching 700,000 shared in the feast at the dedication of Solomon's temple. This estimate agrees fairly well with the biblical statement (1 *Kings* v. 13–15) that Solomon's labour levy amounted to some 180,000 men: the latter figure would be made up by assuming two adult able-bodied males from an average household of eight in a population of 720,000. Thus according to the biblical figures, and accepting the assumptions made as not wildly inaccurate, the maximum annual royal revenue in Israel was six hundred and sixty-six talents of gold from a population of about 700,000, or nearly a talent of gold per thousand of population or (if the ration of the value of gold to silver, which frequently varied between about 8 and 12 to 1, may be taken to be about 10 to 1 at that time) roughly four minas (about 4 lb.) of silver per family, almost all of which must have come directly or indirectly from forced labour. Provided the figures for Solomon's revenues are reasonably reliable and that the population of Palestine did not decrease considerably in the next two centuries, this represents a much heavier annual drain on the country than did the combined payments of Menahem of the northern kingdom to Tiglath-Pileser III (a thousand talents of silver) and Hezekiah of the southern kingdom (three hundred talents of silver and thirty talents of gold), which would, on the figures assumed, amount to about one and a quarter minas of silver per family. Even if the figures of Solomon's revenues are inflated, or if in Solomon's reign gold was cheaper in terms of silver than it later became, the silver value of those revenues still has to be divided by three before the exactions of Solomon from the people of Palestine appear as moderate as those of the Assyrian kings. It is true that the figures are not strictly parallel inasmuch as the revenues of Solomon were to a considerable extent spent on building in Palestine from which some visible satisfaction could be obtained by the ultimate producers of the wealth which made it possible, whilst the later payments disappeared to Assyria, but in terms of the burden on the common citizen they may justly be compared. There are other facts which point to the general conclusion that Assyrian taxation bore less heavily on the Palestinian population than did the demands of Solomon. The burden of taxation in the time of Solomon was so heavy that after his death the northern tribes made a special approach to his successor in an attempt to secure a reduction in the royal demands (1 *Kings* xii. 4), refusal of which led to rebellion; whereas the terms offered by the Assyrian commander besieging Jerusalem at the time of Hezekiah seemed so likely to prove seductive that a special attempt had to be made by the city authorities to ensure that the Assyrian offer should not even be heard by the common people (2 *Kings* xviii. 26–36).

The actual tribute levied upon subject territories could include payments of several kinds. At the time at which it made submission after military operations, a conquered state generally made a payment called *tamartu*, which must have been a kind of war indemnity. Another term probably describes the gift made to the king of Assyria by a client ruler who had received active Assyrian aid on the occasion of rebellion or foreign attack. These two were single payments on particular occasions. There was in addition tribute proper (Assyrian *mandattu*), which was a fixed regular payment which a tributary or client state was expected to send to the Assyrian capital annually (see plate 36).

In addition to tribute from conquered and client states there were also, primarily amongst citizens of Assyria proper though also in some cases amongst tributaries, taxes for the payment of which individuals were liable. Such individual taxes were, as in almost all societies except the most recent, principally those connected with the tenure of land. All the land of Assyria was in theory, and to a large extent in practice, the property of the king, and much of it was granted to army veterans and members of the civil service either as a reward for faithful service or in consideration of the performance of certain specified duties. In the case of some favoured individuals exemption might be granted from the payment of the customary dues, and such exemptions would be specified in a charter. The following is an extract from such a charter:

> I, Ashurbanipal, the great king, the mighty king, king of the civilized world, king of Assyria, king of the four regions, true shepherd, worker of good, king of justice, lover of right, who makes his people prosper, who requites with favour the officials who stand in his presence and serve him well by being respectful and observing his royal orders,
>
> as to Bulta, a chief official of Ashurbanipal king of Assyria, a good and well-disposed man, . . . whose heart is perfect towards his lord, who has stood before me in faithfulness, who has gone about in integrity within my palace, . . . who has kept my royal guard,
>
> by my own pondering and by my own counsel I have considered . . . and I have declared free the fields, orchards, (and) people that he has acquired under my protection . . . and I have written and sealed (this charter) with my royal seal and delivered it to Bulta the chief official. From those fields and orchards no grain shall be levied, no straw shall be levied, the increase of their cattle or their sheep

shall not be requisitioned; they [the lands and their personnel] shall not be liable to levy, temple conscription or militia service; they are clear of quay and ferry taxes . . . .

From charters such as these we are able to build up a fairly full list of the payments to which a holder of land might be liable. These included a 25 per cent tax on grain, a 10 per cent tax on straw, a tax (its rate uncertain at present) on herds, as well as militia service or a money payment in lieu thereof, and a similar service or money payment due to the local temple. The land-holder was also liable to tolls on any produce of his transported by water.

The third principal responsibility of Assyrian officials, maintenance of civil order, is a subject about which little is known, possibly because there is little to be known. It is unnecessary to point out the absence of a police force in the modern European sense, though certainly within the cities of Babylonia, and probably also within Assyria, there was normally a Watch which would serve as a deterrent to crime and civil disorder. More serious disturbances were often dealt with by a special branch of the army. Like all armies up to the time of the Greeks, much of the Assyrian army (though not all of it) was organized on a tribal basis: one tribe, the Itu'a, was very commonly brought into a city to deal with serious rioting. The use of these troops as a precautionary measure has already been referred to in connection with Ashur (see page 253), whilst another official letter (quoted on page 108) mentions an occasion upon which they had had to be employed in Sidon, where the citizens (believers in the policy of direct action) had rioted over a tax on timber which they were accustomed to fell in the Lebanon, and in the excitement had murdered a tax-collector.

It is appropriate at this point to say a word about the organization of the Assyrian army. Inasmuch as the theory was consciously held that the land and its population were the property of the tribal god, acting through his representative the king, every able-bodied man might be called upon to bear arms if the national god at the Fixing of Destinies at the New Year Feast proclaimed war. In practice many of the wealthier citizens could buy exemption from bearing arms. In addition to the national militia there was a small standing army with, as the *corps d'élite* at its centre, shock troops, royal guards, and young noblemen who had the privilege of running by the king's chariot. Obligation to supply militiamen was not confined to Assyria proper but extended to the provinces, and such troops must, for obvious reasons, have been organized largely according to nationality. The native Assyrian army, on the other hand, was organized in a more specialized manner, in units of chariotry, cavalry (see plate 47), archers (see plate 45), storm troops, engineers, and what would correspond in modern times to service corps. The size of such units, and indeed of the army as a whole, is very uncertain: recent estimates of the size of an Assyrian army in the field have been in the range of one to two hundred thousand; but a more accurate figure would be arrived at if all the census lists of the period lying in the museums of the world were available for consideration. These consist of lists of names of persons in various places liable to military service, and in many cases the apparent lack of intrinsic interest of mere lists of names has resulted in an indefinite delay in the publication of such texts.

The command of Assyrian troops in the field could be taken by any governor, since all governors seem to have been military governors. For major operations, however, the army was usually under the supreme command either of the king himself or of one of the great officers of state, either the Rab-shakeh (see 2 *Kings* xviii. 17 etc.) or the Tartan (mentioned in *Isaiah* xx. 1). An officer of high rank beneath the Supreme Commander was the *Rab-mugi*, a title which may have been taken over into Babylonian military administration, and which may be represented by Rab-mag of *Jeremiah* xxxix. 3, 13. The term for one of the major military units was *kiṣru*, and such a unit would be commanded by a 'Chief of the *kiṣru*' (Akkadian *rab kiṣri*). Under the *rab kiṣri* were subordinates known as the 'Officer of Fifty' and the 'Officer of Ten'. Other titles of army officers, besides those mentioned, are known; some of these may have represented grades in the military hierarchy, whilst others probably denoted specialist posts.

New Babylonian Period

The collapse of Assyrian rule which came about between 625 and 612 B.C. did not involve a general breakdown of government throughout the empire: had it done so it would have been impossible for the successor-state, Babylonia, to reorganize the area so rapidly, whereas in fact within thirty years, under Nebuchadrezzar, the empire was outwardly stronger than before. Administrative changes were, however, inherent in the downfall of Assyria: the breakdown of the central government gave the provincial governors a freer hand, and indeed it was one of these governors, Nabopolassar in south Babylonia, who ultimately took over the reins of government. One thus finds in the New Babylonian empire far less concentration of power in the hands of the king, and the domestic history of Babylonia during the succeeding century was in some aspects a struggle for power between the dynasty and the temple corporations, in which the corporations were finally victorious.

The decentralization of power is well shown in the case of the city of Uruk, the biblical Erech, about a hundred miles south-east of Babylon. Under the Assyrian empire this seems, despite the existence of its ancient corporation, to have been fairly firmly under royal control: decisions about canals, about corn supplies, about action against troublesome Chaldaean tribesmen encroaching on lands belonging to Erech, all originated from the Assyrian capital. Contrariwise, in the documents we have from the New Babylonian period the temple authorities prove to have been exercising a large measure of autonomy, which the Babylonian kings attempted, without much success, to check. In Assyria, in theory and to a large extent in practice, all land was part of the royal estates, to be granted as fiefs to the king's tenants, and this conception had its influence in parts of the empire where a different theory may originally have prevailed. At the time of Hammurabi, when Babylonia had been unified and administratively reformed under a powerful conquering dynasty, much the same situation prevailed temporarily in Babylonia. In general, however, and at most periods, most of the land for many miles around a Babylonian city belonged in practice to the temples, the theory, explicitly stated in some cases, being that the land had been the property of the local god since even before the city was built. This difference is related to the difference between the Babylonian and Assyrian conceptions of the status of the king, mentioned elsewhere. As has been pointed out (see pages 100 f.), whilst in Assyria the king was consecrated at the beginning of his reign once and for all (or possibly originally for a renewable period of thirty years), and so was the representative of the gods without limitation, in Babylonia to the very end the king had to lay his insignia humbly before the god each year, submit to personal indignities at the hands of the high priest, make a declaration of good intentions, and only then receive re-investment with the royal authority. Thus in Babylonia the king remained to the end a tenant-at-will of the god and as such was less able to gather temple lands into his own hands and thereby into permanent royal control. For this reason we find the heads of the temple corporations at Erech taking action and directing activities which in Assyria, or even in Babylonia under Hammurabi or an Assyrian ruler, would have been the prerogative of the king.

Eanna, the great temple at Erech, which seems to have owned almost all of the land of Babylonia from Ur in the south to within sight of Babylon to the north, was at the beginning of the New Babylonian empire controlled by three principal administrators, the *Shatammu* (a title possibly meaning 'Guardian of the Precincts'), the *Qipu* ('Warden') and the Scribe. It is probable that the *Qipu* was a royal nominee, but it is clear from his diminishing importance in the documents of the period that he was gradually being elbowed out of any real share in control of temple affairs. The king therefore needed to take measures to reinforce his representative's waning influence in the temple administration. The king had certain privileges in connection with the temple, such as a share of particular revenues, and Nabu-na'id in the third year of his reign, 553 B.C., installed two royal officers (the 'Royal Officer Lord of the Appointment' and the 'Royal Officer over the King's Coffer') ostensibly to safeguard such interests, in fact as a counterpoise to the power of the *Shatammu*. In

Babylon, indeed, it is known that Nabu-na'id actually had his own henchman as *Shatammu*, a highly unpopular state of affairs which helped to bring about his downfall, as we know from the *Persian Verse Account of Nabonidus*, which narrates the events of his reign from the viewpoint of his opponents:

Zeria the *Shatammu* bowed down before him,
Rimut the *Zazakku* bowed down with him;
They established the instructions of the king, they made his word
    stand;
. . . . They took an oath,
'We recognize only what the king says.'

Whether a similar situation prevailed in Erech is not certain (there were four successive occupants of the office of *Shatammu* of Eanna during Nabu-na'id's reign) but it appears that in the first year of his reign he regarded the temple administration as sufficiently reliable to hand over to it the management of a large royal estate at Larsa: this may, however, have been purely a business deal, since the lease secured a large and assured annual revenue for the king.

A full account of all the multifarious activities for which the *Shatammu* and his colleagues, particularly the Royal Officer Lord of the Appointment, were responsible would yield an over-lengthy list. One may summarize by saying that their duties included the hiring and letting of the lands of the huge temple estates, the assignment of rights and obligations in connection with canals, general supervision of the assessment, collection, transportation, use and distribution of the products of the land and canals, and the keeping of the multitude of accounts and records associated therewith.

Goods produced on the temple estates, whatever their ultimate destination, were usually in the first place brought to a depot in Erech. The network of canals made transport a simple matter for any class of goods: an extant letter gives instructions for sending a consignment of sheep. The writer, probably the *Shatammu* of Eanna, orders:

'If the ground is suitable, let them come on the hoof; if not, let them come by ship.'

Ships so employed were probably in most cases temple property, though certainly in some cases they were hired from private shipmasters. Whilst ships might be commissioned by any of the senior temple officials, it seems that as they neared Erech all ships destined for the temple came under the jurisdiction of the *Shatammu*. We find mention here and there of quay-masters along the canals, apparently royal officers empowered to stop passing shipping and levy a toll, but ships plying for the temple seem to have been privileged, and the *Shatammu* could, by providing the ship with an emblem called *ḫutaru*, of which the exact nature is uncertain, obtain toll-free passage for such vessels, as the following letter shows:

> Letter of Iddina and Shamash-eriba to the *Shatammu* our lord. Daily we pray to Bel, Nabu, the Lady of Erech and Nana for the life, breath, happiness and health and length of days of our lord.
>
> We have brought up 200 *kur* of dates from the canal (called) 'Nadin-apli's cutting'. We are being detained by the quay-master in Bit-kasir. Let a missive come from my lord to Nuna the quay-master to let us pass the quay . . . . Half a shekel of silver as the hire of the ship and one shekel of silver as the hire of hired men (is due) against us per day. Our lord ought to know that we have been detained at the quay since the twentieth. Let a *ḫutaru* come with my lord's missive and let it stay on board.

Eanna, the great temple of Erech, was, like the monasteries much later, more than a religious shrine: it was a thriving trading centre, and a substantial part of the goods collected there subsequently went out again to other parts of the land of Babylonia and even abroad. In extant letters there are a number of references to trade in which the products of the temple estates, mainly agricultural, were exchanged for such goods as pottery, alum, sesame, metal, timber or cloth, some of which merchandise came from as far afield as Asia Minor. Erech also produced wine for the capital; since one letter mentions an indignant complaint from some authorities in Babylon that wine had been sent to them in a ship which also contained pitch.

It is interesting to find that whereas the *Shatammu* and the Royal Officer Lord of the Appointment dealt substantially with the same kind of matters, the former acted from the central temple whilst the latter operated to a large extent from the towns and settlements on the temple estates away from Erech. This is not out of keeping with our conception of the Royal Officer Lord of the Appointment as a kind of inspector watching over the interests of the king: his absence from Erech would not damage the king's interests inside the temple itself, since they were safeguarded by the Royal Officer over the King's Coffer, who seems to have been, as a fuller form of his title suggests, permanently stationed there. A good deal of the correspondence between the *Shatammu* and the Royal Officer Lord of the Appointment has been recovered, and it shows that though occasionally one official had a sharp comment to make on the work of the other, on the whole these two worked together with very little friction.

The temple officers mentioned, principally the *Shatammu* and the Royal Officer Lord of the Appointment, were also responsible for the control and disposal of the many thousands of people on the temple estates, who ranged in status from senior officers of the temple with ancient prescriptive rights, such as *mar-bani* (members of patrician families, noblemen with certain duties), down to the lowest type of slave. Between these were the free men who hired themselves out as workmen for a daily wage. There was also a very large class of temple servants known as *shirke* (singular *shirku*). The latter term means 'one bestowed', and the *shirke* were people – of either sex – who had been dedicated to the goddess and were thus technically her slaves. This status was hereditary. At Erech *shirke* were recognizable by the presence of a tattooed star – the symbol of the tutelary goddess Ishtar – on the wrist, and this star mark is frequently mentioned as the decisive evidence in the records of lawsuits dealing with the status of various persons. Thus there is one lawsuit recorded in which a certain Shamash-shum-iddin was brought before a court and claimed as a *shirku* on the grounds that he was 'the son of Silim-Ishtar, the daughter of Harshinana, a female *shirku* of the Lady of Erech [Ishtar]'. The crucial evidence was that given by a woman who had assisted at the confinement of the grandmother of the man concerned. This old lady swore:

'I certainly saw the star and tattoo marks upon the back of the hand of Harshinana, the slave-woman of my uncle Nadina-ahu, the grandmother of Shamash-shum-iddin, whom – before she gave birth – my uncle Nadina-ahu dedicated for *shirku*-ship to the Lady of Erech.'

The status of a *shirku* could be very different from that of an ordinary slave, and some of these people held positions of high responsibility. Their services were not confined to the execution of any particular sort of duty, and in the correspondence between the officials of the temple they are found working in a great variety of crafts and trades both inside Erech and on the temple estates. On the estates they must have come more directly under the control of the Royal Officer Lord of the Appointment, who, as mentioned above, had much closer personal connections with the temple estates than did the *Shatammu*, and it is probably largely through this official that the king gradually acquired rights over the *shirke*. Certainly by the time of Cyrus (539–529 B.C.), although day-to-day control remained with the temple officers, ultimate control of the *shirke* lay not with the *Shatammu* nor with his associates in the temple administration but with the central government.

It is clear from the documents which have come down to us that the king in the New Babylonian period took a share of the temple revenues; and indeed, as we have seen, special royal officers came to be installed in the temples for this purpose. The precise proportion of the temple revenues which ultimately went to the king it is impossible at present to discover, as there were at this time many different kinds of tithe, tax or toll with which the temples were, either as payer or payee, concerned in some way or other, and the king's share of each was not the same. Amongst revenues which certainly went to the temples in the first instance were tithes on date-crops and catches of fish, rents (payable in kind) on corn-land, a cattle tax, customary (though not voluntary) offerings made by farmers at the time of particular festivals, and other dues of a more or less obscure nature. There were also death duties which were levied on rich private citizens and which, like the tolls in certain of the canals, went wholly to the king, even though the temple authorities may have been responsible for their assessment and collection. All in all, it seems probable that in the course of the sixth century B.C. the New Babylonian kings managed to get control of an increasingly large share of the temple revenues: certainly the administrative changes already noted for the beginning of Nabu-na'id's reign worked to the king's advantage, whilst the enthusiasm with which the Persian conquerors were welcomed by the temple administrators in 539 B.C. suggests that internal royal policy was very unpopular. On the other hand it must be borne in mind that, in the light of Nabu-na'id's attempt to usurp for the god Sin Marduk's place as head of the pantheon, the reasons for that king's unpopularity may have been more religious than fiscal.

Despite the agricultural wealth of the temples, the New Babylonian empire was probably in a considerably less healthy state economically than the Assyrian empire had been, at least till about 650 B.C. There seem to have been two main reasons for this. One, which is obvious even from the Old Testament, was that though Assyria was certainly a state organized for war, it did not normally keep a standing army in the field, but limited the strain on its manpower by undertaking campaigns only for a few months each year. Babylonia, on the other hand, from the time of Nebuchadrezzar operated with a standing army which might remain on field operations for years at a time, as in the case of the siege of Tyre, referred to in *Ezekiel* xxix. 17–18, which continued unsuccessfully for thirteen years. The other main reason for the economic inferiority of the New Babylonian empire compared with Assyria was the closing of the trade-routes to the east and north-east. From the time of Ashur-nasir-pal onwards much of the endeavours of the Assyrian kings had been directed to keeping open those routes from the Persian highlands, the exports of which were vital for the advanced civilization in the valley of the Euphrates and Tigris: the latter area, though of phenomenal fertility, was, from the ancient point of view, almost devoid of raw materials except for agricultural products and bitumen. By the time of the New Babylonian kings the routes to the east and north-east were in the hands of the Medes and

Persians, who were rapidly growing in strength. It seems very probable, therefore, that, as said above (page 148), Nabu-na'id's activities of nearly a decade in Arabia, during which he penetrated as far south as Medina, were motivated by the attempt to gain control of the important trade-routes with South Arabia, as a substitute for those lost.

In the provinces of the New Babylonian empire the general lines of Assyrian policy continued to be carried out. Thus, the celebrated deportations by Nebuchadrezzar in 597 B.C. and 586 B.C. of sections of the people of Judah were nothing but a continuation of the policy instituted by Ashur-nasir-pal II and developed by Tiglath-Pileser III to deal with recalcitrant vassals. At the same time Nebuchadrezzar, like the Assyrian government in similar circumstances, appears to have made strenuous attempts to preserve a native administration for the government of the people remaining. After the surrender of Jerusalem in 597 B.C. and the deportation of the young king Jehoiachin along with his nobles, Nebuchadrezzar attempted indirect rule, using Zedekiah as a vassal prince bound to Babylonia: for nine years the experiment was successful. Even after the siege and capture of Jerusalem consequent on Zedekiah's ultimate yielding to the pro-Egyptian party, Nebuchadrezzar still did not abandon the attempt to employ some form of indirect rule, and appointed a Jewish nobleman, Gedaliah, as governor. It was only after Gedaliah's assassination by Jewish patriots (as we in the twentieth century A.D. have learnt to call those who commit murder for political ends) that Judah came under direct Babylonian administration.

9

Trade and Economics

Foreign Trade

MESOPOTAMIA, at the very beginning of the historical period, was far from being a closed economic unit, for our evidence about long-distance trade goes back at least two millennia into pre-history, to the period of Jarmo. Jarmo is a site in the foothills east of Kirkuk, and is datable by radiocarbon analysis to about 5000 B.C. Though the precise place of this settlement in the sequence of cultures of Mesopotamia is a matter of considerable controversy, the points in dispute do not substantially affect the evaluation of the information it yields as to the basic economy. The archaeological evidence indicates that the settlement was economically self-sufficient, with the exception of one commodity. That commodity was the hard stone obsidian which, though utilized on the site, is not obtainable from any nearer source than Armenia, several hundred miles to the north. This indicates, already in 5000 B.C., some form of inter-regional trade in this area, though we have at present no information as to the technical aspects of this trade. The general asumption is that the obsidian was carried by pedlars.

During the next two millennia we find, in the cultures which chronologically succeeded that of Jarmo, that though the economies were still in some respects closed units, inter-regional trade was gradually extending. In the *Hassuna* cultures there appear, in addition to obsidian, the semi-precious stones turquoise and malachite, whilst the presence at sites in northern Mesopotamia of shells which can only have come from the Persian Gulf bears witness to trade relations between the *Hassuna* settlements and people further south, possible in Iran. From the *Samarra* and succeeding periods the wide dissemination of certain art motifs on the pottery, which it has been suggested were borrowed from such materials as carpets, textiles and basketry, may indicate the existence of commerce in these perishable commodities. In view of the pre-scientific treasure-hunting techniques too commonly employed until quite recently by some archaeologists in the Near East, one wonders whether in some cases traces of such perishable objects, which could have been recognized by microscopic examination or chemical analysis, have not been missed by excavators.

Copper begins to appear at sites of the *Halaf* culture: we can only guess at its source, but as no copper ores occur in Iraq this again establishes the existence of inter-regional trade, very probably carried on in the case of metals by itinerant smiths. At a much later period (about 1900 B.C.) smiths of the type postulated are depicted on a painting in an Egyptian tomb, showing a small clan of nomadic metal-workers, whose asses carry bellows and other equipment. The pottery distribution of the *Halaf* culture, which extends across the region bounded to the west by the north Syrian coast and Mersin in Cilicia, to the north by Lake Van and to the south by Samarra, implies widespread cultural links and the possibility of equally widespread trading relations: there is no suggestion, of course, that the pottery itself was manufactured in and distributed from one single site. The lack of evidence for the *Halaf* culture in Iran points to an absence at this time of trading contacts between Iran and Mesopotamia.

The first notable culture in southern Iraq, that of *Ubaid*, had definite affinities with Iran, though the links are not such as to require the assumption of any highly organized trade. It has indeed been suggested that the use of clay tools based on metal forms – a characteristic of the *Ubaid* culture – indicates an inability of the people concerned to organize trade in copper after settling in an area which lacked the ores they had in their earlier habitat (probably Iran) utilized. *Ubaid* pottery, like that of *Halaf*, is found as far away as north Syria: as timber was certainly needed for the temples of the *Ubaid* period, this may well indicate that trade between Syria and Mesopotamia was already beginning on a large scale, the lumber being dragged from the Lebanon overland to Carchemish and then floated down the Euphrates. Certainly other trade routes were coming into use at this time, for a pottery native to the Alalah region (near the Gulf of Alexandretta), produced under the joint influence of *Halaf* and *Ubaid* ware, is found at Mersin in Cilicia: whether this is the earliest evidence for sea transport, or whether the goods concerned went overland, is not clear.

For the period just after 3000 B.C. (in archaeological terms the *Jemdet Nasr* or late *Protoliterate* period) there is substantial archaeological evidence for cultural relations between Egypt and Sumer, or more accurately for Sumerian influence on Egypt, almost certainly in connection with trade. The bare outline of the evidence of such relations has already been given above on page 27, but Egyptological aspects of the matter are beyond the scope of the present work; for details the reader may consult H. Frankfort's *The birth of civilization in the Near East* and the articles of H. J. Kantor noted below in the Bibliography, pages 539 f. However, the suggestion made above that the trading contacts concerned took place in south Arabia or Somaliland does perhaps deserve amplification. Basically the theory rests upon assumptions with regard to the use of incense. Two of the principal gum-resins used as incense, namely frankincense and myrrh, are the products of various species of a genus of tree occurring nowhere but in south Arabia, Somaliland, northern Sudan and Ethiopia. The very common mention of these two substances in Egyptian texts from the Fifth Dynasty onwards establishes trading from the Egyptian side with Somaliland or south Arabia from the middle of the third millennium at latest, though as at present it is only a guess that the Sumerians also used the two gum-resins in question, Sumerian voyages to Somaliland or Aden in the early part of the third millennium cannot be considered more than a reasonable hypothesis. There is, however, good archaeological evidence for Sumerian trading relations eastwards from about

2800 B.C., since there are obvious similarities between an ancient culture found in south Baluchistan, known as the *Kulli* culture, and that of Elam and Mesopotamia. *Kulli* motifs are found on pots from Susa and the Diyala, and stone ointment pots with carved ornamentation of a type found in south Baluchistan are found at a number of sites of this period in Mesopotamia, including the 'royal tombs' of Ur. A carved cup of Sumerian type from the Diyala, a cylinder seal from Ur, and figurines from Susa, all show characteristic Indian humped bulls, in some cases clearly in connection with a cult-scene, which suggests not only Sumerian trading with the Indian area, but also the presence in Mesopotamia of merchants from India who required the consolations of their own religion. Since no traces of *Kulli* culture have been found along the overland route across Iran, this trade link was probably by sea.

Whilst the voyages from Sumer to Somaliland or Aden in the late *Protoliterate* (*Jemdet Nasr*) period are hypothetical, two or three centuries later trading voyages from Sumer to distant places *via* the Persian Gulf indisputably took place, three trading stations in particular being mentioned in inscriptions from the middle of the third millennium onwards. These are Tilmun, Magan (or Makkan), and Meluhha, in that order both in distance from Sumer and in the difficulty they occasion modern scholars. Tilmun, almost everyone now agrees, was probably Bahrein, though the noted Sumerologist S. N. Kramer would place it on the eastern side of the Persian Gulf. Magan is frequently taken, though with less unanimity, as the coast of Oman. The region in which Meluhha is to be sought is still quite uncertain, the main theories placing it either on the coast of Baluchistan or northwest India (West Pakistan in political nomenclature), somewhere in south Arabia, or on the Somali coast. A substantial commerce was carried on between these places and Babylonia, and Sargon of Agade (about 2370 B.C.) was able to refer proudly to ships trading with Meluhha, Magan and Tilmun, moored outside his capital, though there is no indication whether this trade was actually conducted by Sargon or by foreigners. Shortly after the time of Sargon of Agade direct contact with Meluhha was lost.

Direct trading with Magan continued down to the end of the Third Dynasty of Ur (about 2000 B.C.), for we have texts of this period in which a man is issued by the storehouse of the Temple of Nanna (the Moon-god of Ur) with large quantities of garments, wool, oil and leather objects to take by boat to Magan to buy copper: the trading method employed was clearly a developed system of barter. The goods brought back from Magan included, as we learn from lists of deliveries to the temple, not only the main commodity, copper, but also beads of precious stones, ivory, and vegetables called Magan-onions.

Magan, if the identification with Oman is anywhere near the mark, cannot have been the primary source of the ivory and must have served as an international emporium or commercial exchange. With reference to the actual source of ivory at this time it is interesting to recall that in Mesopotamian sites of the period 2370 to 2000 B.C. there have been found a number of engraved seals which are typical of the kind found at Harappa in the Indus valley, whilst cylinder seals – which generally speaking are characteristic of Mesopotamia – have been found at Mohenjo-daro (also in the Indus valley).

After the collapse of the highly-organized bureaucracy of the Third Dynasty of Ur, direct contact with Magan was lost, and in the succeeding centuries it is Tilmun of which we hear as the principal trading station within the Persian Gulf area.

The earliest known records referring to Tilmun are administrative documents of 2500–2400 B.C., and these show that regular trade existed at that time between Sumer and Tilmun, the most usual exports of the latter being dates. It has also been shown that certain plants and animals later acclimatized in Babylonia first reached the country by importation through Tilmun. Other texts from the late third and early second millennia list as imports from Tilmun goods which were certainly not products of the island itself but which must have originated in more remote countries; the goods in question are chiefly copper, precious stones, and ivory, and specimens of all of these have been found in excavations of Bronze Age sites in Bahrein. Tilmun was clearly an important emporium from the late third millennium at least.

Our most detailed knowledge of this maritime trade with Tilmun comes from the time of the Dynasty of Larsa (*circa* 1900 B.C.). At this period the city of Ur seems to have been the main port of entry into Mesopotamia, and from this city we have a group of tablets dealing with the Tilmun trade. The principal imports from Tilmun mentioned are copper (in ingots or as manufactured objects), lapis lazuli, pearls (if this is what the ideogram meaning literally 'fish-eyes' denotes), and certain kinds of wood. It is not necessary to suppose that all these goods originated in the same place, since Tilmun may well have constituted a neutral meeting-place for merchants from many lands, particularly as in Sumerian tradition it was thought of as a holy island of which a characteristic was its lack of strife. Judged simply as a commodity the ivory could have reached Tilmun from either Egypt or the Indus valley, but the mention of ivory combs points rather to the latter, since combs of ivory have been found in the Indus valley.

The principal exports from Sumer to Tilmun were garments and oil, provided by private capitalists. Contracts were drawn up, giving the value of the goods in terms of silver and stating the agreed silver value for the copper to be brought back by the trader. A typical document of this type took the form:

> 2 minas of silver, (the value of) 5 *gur* of oil (and of) 30 garments, Lu-Meshlam-ta-e and Nig-si-sa-nabsa have borrowed (as the) capital for a partnership from Ur-Ninmar-ka, for an expedition to Tilmun to buy copper (there). After safe termination of the voyage, he [the creditor] will not recognize (any responsibility for) commercial losses (encurred by the debtors); they [the debtors] have agreed to satisfy Ur-Ninmar-ka with 4 minas of copper for each shekel of silver as a just (price).

(The translation is, with slight alterations, that of A. L. Oppenheim in *Journal of the American Oriental Society*, 74 (1954), page 8).

This financing by private capitalists is a point of difference from the maritime trade of two hundred years earlier, in which the seafaring merchant was financed not by an individual but by the temple. Superficially the financial organization of the trade

with Tilmun is more like that of the caravan trade with Cappadocia to be referred to subsequently; but there are some important
differences, which in view of the high profits likely in this luxury
trade almost certainly favoured the sea-going merchant as against
the caravan leader. In the caravan traffic, the entrepreneur
financing an agent seems to have been entitled to two-thirds
of the total profits, with a guaranteed minimum return of 50
per cent on his outlay and no risk (in practice) to his capital. In
the sea trade to Tilmun, on the other hand, the entrepreneur
normally received, instead of a share in the profits, a fixed return.
If the investor did become a full partner in the venture, he then
apparently shared the risks as well as any profits. The more
favourable conditions for the sea trader as against the caravan
leader are probably related to the fact that the trade with Tilmun
was likely to be a 'closed shop', admission to which was a matter
of great difficulty; it needed technical skill to undertake the
actual voyage, whilst it may have been necessary for the trader to
have personal ceremonial contacts on the island before he could
trade there at all.

Something is known of the scale of the trade in copper, since
one text mentions thirteen thousand minas (roughly seven or
eight tons) of copper. The metal came in ingots of up to four
talents (roughly two hundredweight) – that is, as one might
expect, in a piece about as large as the average workman can
carry. The administrative authorities in Sumer, acting through
the temples, levied heavy customs on the imported goods.

After about 1800 B.C., though trading relations with Tilmun
continued, the island ceased to be, for over a millennium, an
international emporium, and during this time its exports were
confined to agricultural products. As to the reason for the
diminished importance of Tilmun as a commercial centre, if one
accepts that some of the goods bought at Tilmun in the earlier
period came from Baluchistan or the Indus valley, one could
guess that the evidence of violent change in the latter area
shortly after 2000 B.C. had something to do with it.

We have some evidence as to the technical side of ancient
sea trade, and it would appear that Sumerian and Babylonian

ships were, by modern standards, very small. The ancient records give the size in terms of hold capacity, but with this converted to weight in terms of the specific gravity of grain, it seems that Sumerian ships in the third millennium would hold about twenty-five tons, and Babylonian ships in the first millennium about forty tons. In terms of copper ore, of course, the load would have weighed considerably more. Such ships would, to judge by a model found in the 'royal tombs' of Ur (see plate 2B), be of the same shape as the modern Iraqi *belem* (a king of whaler), and would be equipped with a mast, a sail and a steering oar for use as rudder. Rafts of the *kelek* type, consisting of a wooden platform supported by inflated skins, still found on the Tigris, and the flat-bottomed coracles called *quffas*, also still employed in Iraq, were used for river transport down the Euphrates and Tigris. For internal trade within the Euphrates and Tigris valleys shipping remained important throughout the whole of the period of Babylonian history, and we have innumerable references to the transport by water from city to city of foodstuffs, wine, building materials, metals, wool, leather, and so on. At Nimrud, the capital of Assyria in the early first millennium, a massive quay wall of great blocks of heavy limestone has been found (see page 181), which served shipping on the Tigris.

We now have to return into the third millennium and consider overland trading from Mesopotamia. We have already seen that this was established over a very large area before the dawn of history, and we have references to such trade, largely with Iran, in the Sumerian epic literature which reflects – with what degree of accuracy being in dispute – the social conditions of about 2700 B.C. One such text (very difficult to understand in detail) describes the equipping and dispatching of a donkey caravan carrying sacks of barley from a city in Sumer to a highland site in Luristan; the circumstances of this trading journey, and the social conditions in which it took place, are referred to above on page 40. From just before the middle of the third millennium we get contemporary records of such trade, either in the form of receipts or in references in the dedication inscriptions of rulers of Sumerian city-states. A number of these rulers refer to bringing timber down from the mountains. Others speak of imposing tribute on the peoples from the Persian Gulf to the Mediterranean, but it seems likely that in most such cases what the ruler had actually done was to establish not political dominion but regular and secure trade relations throughout the area.

Sargon of Agade (about 2370 B.C.), who established the first Semitic dynasty in Mesopotamia, presents us with a special problem. Contemporary inscriptions show that he himself claimed control over the Lebanon and the Amanus range, significantly designated, with reference to their commercial importance, as 'the cedar forest' and 'the silver mountains'. There is, however, a literary tradition, referred to above on page 50, which accords Sargon a more extensive commercial empire, and it is not impossible that the wider claim may have had some historical basis; it may well be that there were, before the end of the third millennium, merchant colonies from Mesopotamia in Asia Minor and even, perhaps, Crete. At Tell Brak, on the route from Agade to Asia Minor, a fortified palace built by Sargon's grandson has been discovered, and it is reasonable to regard its purpose as the guarding of a trade route. As for the claim concerning Crete, pottery finds indicate that there were links between the Aegean and Mesopotamia from the fourth millennium, and they were certainly very strong by the early second millennium, since Babylonian cylinder seals of this period have been found in Crete itself, whilst a Babylonian princeling left a dedication inscription on one of the islands (Kithira) between Crete and Greece. Moreover, it is now being claimed with some force that one of the early languages attested in inscriptions in Crete from the first half of the second millennium B.C. was not only Semitic but specifically Akkadian Semitic: the language in question is known as Minoan Linear A, and the inscriptions for which it was employed are datable to between the seventeenth and fifteenth centuries. Furthermore the decoration on a Cretan vase representing a harvesting scene shows the natives in the charge of an official who is apparently clad in Mesopotamian dress. Taken together these facts make it a reasonable suggestion that there may have been Mesopotamian traders in the Aegean in the early second and perhaps even the late third millennium B.C. The Aegean during much of the second millennium must have been a scene of great commercial activity, which was particularly marked between 1400 and 1250 B.C. At that time the island of Crete itself was intersected with good roads suitable for wheeled traffic, with guard-posts along them; at least one artificial harbour is known, although generally speaking ships were small enough to be beached.

For Asia Minor we have noted the possibility that there may have been colonies of merchants from Mesopotamia before the end of the third millennium. From 1900 B.C. onwards the matter is put beyond all doubt by the archives of a colony of Assyrian traders at Kultepe (ancient Kanesh). These prove the existence of a continuous and extensive caravan traffic between Kanesh and Ashur, and the documents have enabled scholars, notably Professor J. Lewy, to work out the commercial and economic system in some detail. The trade was generally by donkey caravan, which might consist of up to two hundred beasts, travelling perhaps twelve to fifteen miles a day; but between certain towns in Asia Minor it might be by wagon, which indicates the existence already of some form of road system. The caravan-leaders were given an allowance on setting out and kept diaries recording their expenses *en route*, rendering an account to the principal at the end of the journey. The chief export from Asia Minor was copper, and we find mention of quantities up to five tons. As to the goods sent from Assyria, these were chiefly textiles and lead or lead ores. Lead ores, containing a high proportion of silver, are found in Assyria near the source of the Great Zab and in the Judi Dagh, and the suggestion has been made that these ores were exported to Asia Minor for smelting where a plentiful supply of fuel was available, as well as technicians. A caravan of eleven tons of lead is once mentioned, and blocks of nearly half a ton have actually been found in the foundations of a temple at Ashur. Other consignments to Asia Minor included olive oil, hides, fleeces, and wool, the last in amounts of up to two tons. A commodity traded in minute amounts (an ounce or less) in Asia Minor was tin, of which the average value was fifty times that of silver.

We know very little about arrangements for security on these journeys. Traders were certainly liable to misadventures of various kinds, since the laws of Hammurabi legislate for some of them, such as loss by brigandage or act of god. Judging by evidence from Mari, a caravan going through foreign territory paid certain toll-charges to local officials and was then entitled to the use of wells and the protection of the local ruler. From a slightly later period we find a royal letter to a customs official giving a certain man immunity from all transit dues for his asses. Later Hittite, Hebrew and Greek laws make special provision for the protection of the foreign trader in the community, and this probably goes back much earlier.

The American economic historian Karl Polanyi (in *Trade and Markets in the Early Empires* (1957)) has argued that the economy of ancient Mesopotamia was not a market economy and has attempted to reinterpret the evidence of this Cappadocian trade to fit such a conclusion. By a 'market economy' is meant an economy in which prices are fixed directly by the interplay of supply and demand. The contention is that this situation did not subsist in ancient Mesopotamia, and that ' "prices" took the form of equivalencies established by authority of custom, statute or proclamation' (op. cit., page 20). Babylonian and Assyrian merchants did not (according to this theory) make their profit from a price differential, and so trading was risk-free. Thus, according to Professor Polanyi, the Assyrian merchants in Cappadocia were merely agents, holding their position by descent, apprenticeship or appointment, and responsible firstly for encouraging copper production by assuring the natives 'that at least a part of the equivalencies, presumably in goods coveted by the people, would be forthcoming in definite amounts' (op. cit., page 20), and secondly for the physical transport of copper and its equivalencies from one place to another. In Professor Polanyi's view, all obligations were registered by the appropriate public authority, which in effect guaranteed them. This, for Professor Polanyi, explains the lack of reference to business profits or loss, and is said to explain 'why apparently no default on debt occurs' (op. cit., page 21), the reason being that 'the account-keeping authority can simply charge the defaulter's account with the amount awarded to the other party' (op. cit., page 21). It is certainly probable that the Cappadocian trade and those engaged in it were ultimately controlled by the municipal or national authority in Ashur, but recognition of this does not commit one to accepting Professor Polanyi's view as a whole. A difficulty confronting Polanyi's theory of ancient Mesopotamian trade is that – in Babylonia if not in Cappadocia – insolvency and default on debt did in fact occur, and these financial mishaps were one of the main paths by which free men or their dependents could fall into slavery. Another objection is that price-fixing by the interplay of supply and demand certainly did occur in ancient Mesopotamia: instances are known of rocketing prices in time of war or famine (see pages 58, 147 f.), whilst when Ashurbanipal had conquered and looted the Arab tribes he specifically mentioned that camels were so numerous that the price fell to a shekel and a half. For these reasons Professor Polanyi's theory, though it does set some features of the Cappadocian trade in clearer perspective, is not accepted as accurately describing ancient Mesopotamian economy as a whole.

The trading arrangements between Asia Minor and Assyria came to an end shortly after 1800 B.C., for reasons not altogether clear, but probably related to racial movements in Anatolia. Shortly after this date the Hittites came into prominence. We find evidence from Hittite documents that in the second half of the second millennium the Hittites had trading relations not only with Mesopotamia but also with Egypt and Ahhiyawa; the latter represents a Mycenaean kingdom either in western Asia Minor, Rhodes, or Greece itself, and the word may be related to the Greek term 'Achaeans'. Copper and silver were produced in large quantities, whilst for part of the second millennium the Hittites had a virtual monopoly of iron, still a relatively rare metal. To judge by a royal letter in which the Hittite king makes an excuse to the king of Assyria for not being able to send iron as requested, the export of iron was a royal monopoly. Some scholars have doubted the validity of this conclusion, and taken the king's excuse as a genuine one, but there certainly is some evidence suggesting that production and export of particular metals of military importance were frequently under tight state control. The best known example is in connection with the Philistines, who when they controlled Palestine at the end of the second millennium would not allow any non-Philistine to work as a smith (1 *Samuel* xiii. 19). In the nineteenth century Assyrian settlement in Cappadocia, it seems to have been illegal to export tin, whilst mention of an Inspector of Bronze, coupled with the uncommonness of references to bronze in the texts – although archaeology shows that it existed, especially as weapons, in the area – suggests that the bronze trade was rigorously controlled.

It is appropriate here to refer to the part played by Syria in international trade, as Syria was for a time in the Hittite orbit, whilst northern Syria always formed a terminal of one of the main trade routes from Mesopotamia. We have already noted that the Alalah district was a terminal of trade routes from both south Mesopotamia and Cilicia as early as the fourth millennium. In the second millennium Alalah had a chequered career politically, coming under the control successively of Egypt, northern Mesopotamia and the Hittites, but this very fact is an indication of its commercial importance. Between 1600 and 1400 B.C. there is evidence from pottery of trade with Cyprus, Palestine and later Nuzi (eastern Assyria) and also the Aegean generally, but a more vivid picture of Syrian trade is provided by an Egyptian source. This is a painting from the tomb of a mayor of Thebes of about 1400 B.C. showing ships of an Egyptian type manned by Syrian crews who were discharging cargo in an Egyptian town (presumably Thebes). Some kind of check was made on the crew, for one detail shows a port official recording names or other particulars of a group of sailors. The main merchandise consisted of large jars of wine or oil, and vases of precious metal, and the picture indicates that these were sold not to private individuals but through a government official, presumably the owner of the tomb, who was in charge of the municipal storehouses. There seems in addition, however, to have been some small scale private trading, for waterside shops are shown, where sandals, textiles and foodstuffs were sold. On one of the ships are two lonely-looking women and a boy, possibly slaves brought as a *douceur* for the high Egyptian official himself.

International trade was facilitated by the presence of colonies of expatriate merchants in various centres of commerce: a well-known biblical instance is provided by 1 *Kings* xx. 34 (ninth century B.C.). There were similar provisions at Ugarit in Syria at about 1400 B.C., when, in addition to a thriving trading colony established by Mycenaean merchants, there were also Assyrian and Egyptian colonists present, to judge by a document listing wine deliveries for people of these nationalities. Foreign trade was encouraged by the king of Ugarit, and thus one finds a royal contract which in explicit terms gives a man exemption from customs duties on his ships returning from Crete. The royal supervision of trade at Ugarit is also attested by another document issued by the same king (about 1400 B.C.), which is a kind of passport issued to a man and his son, authorizing them to use the routes to Egypt and the land of the Hittites. The metal trade was important in the economy of Ugarit, and not only are precious metals (including iron – still very valuable) mentioned in the texts, but also there have been found in the port many remains of copper and bronze, as well as large ingots of lead in the palace. As to values, it is stated in texts that gold was at this time worth three or four times its weight in silver.

At the end of the second and the beginning of the first millennium the old pattern of trade across Mesopotamia and Syria was seriously dislocated by the pressure of the Aramaeans forcing their way into Babylonia and Assyria (see pages 90 f.). The consequent economic difficulties of Assyria were probably one of the factors which led to Assyria attempting to gain military control of the routes to the Mediterranean littoral. Assyria finally succeeded in this task by about 740 B.C., gaining control of all Syria and Phoenicia, including the cities of Tyre and Sidon. Some contemporary letters dealing with the Assyrian control of trade in the latter cities have recently come to light. From these it appears that the Tyrians and Sidonians were permitted to fell timber in the Lebanon, but had to pay a tax on the timber when it came down to the warehouses. This was an unpopular policy and had in fact provoked a riot in which an Assyrian tax-collector had been killed (see page 108). The Assyrians had had to call in troops to restore order, and subsequently they took over control of the trade by export restrictions: the writer of the letter quotes the order he had given:

> Henceforth have timber brought down here; do your work upon (it), (but) do not sell it to the Egyptians or to the Palestinians.

The inference is that the Assyrians were diverting the timber to Assyria. The whole affair is in accordance with the general Assyrian policy of exercising central control over the economy and trade of subject states. The Assyrian capture of Tyre may well be the matter referred to in *Isaiah* xxiii. 1–13, in the course of which Isaiah says:

> 'When the report cometh to Egypt, they shall be sorely pained at the report of Tyre.'

Egypt would understandably have been 'sorely pained' at the loss of the timber from the Lebanon resulting from the Assyrian embargo mentioned above.

North of Assyria, centred on Lake Van, there lay at this time (second half of the eighth century B.C.) another powerful state, Urartu, and much of the history of this period can be interpreted as a struggle between these two powers for vital trade routes. It is certainly noteworthy that the chief points of political or sometimes military conflict between these two major states were not along their common border, but in the extreme west, that is, in north Syria and southern Cilicia, and in the east, in the area south-east of Lake Urmia.

The importance of north Syria as a terminal of several trade-routes has several times been referred to, and both Urartu and Assyria made strenuous efforts by both diplomatic and military means to secure control of this area. In the west, just north of Syria and west of Urartu, and controlling the land routes to the Greek settlements on the western shores of Asia Minor, was the state called Mushku (Meshech), whose king, Mita, was known to the Greeks as Midas and noted for his wealth. Recently published

283

documents, mentioned elsewhere (see page 232) show that the Assyrian king was delighted when he finally secured an alliance with Mita of Mushku. This happy turn of events must undoubtedly have relieved pressure on the north-western sector of the Assyrian empire, and must also (though there is less concrete evidence of this at present) have facilitated trade with Greece and lands beyond.

To the north-east of Assyria, there is good evidence for the existence of another trade route, competition for control of which was probably one of the main causes of conflict between Assyria and Urartu. The terminals of the route in question are not certainly known, but there is a certain amount of evidence bearing upon the matter; this is summarized above, on page 113. There is a further small point which proves the existence of trading contacts at this time between Greece and the regions east of Assyria. It is at this period that the domestic cock is first found painted on Greek vases, and its Greek name (which means 'the Persian bird') shows that it reached Greece from Iran; the route by which it arrived in Europe is likely to have been through Urartu.

In addition to the route across Urartu, the route from Mesopotamia to Carchemish and across to Al Mina near the Gulf of Alexandretta was also flourishing in the late eighth century, and Assyria took strong steps for the security of this region. The actual trade across the Assyrian empire was expedited by the establishment of posting stages and a rapid system of communications, for the introduction of which the Persians have generally received the credit (see page 249).

By 700 B.C. there was a good deal of activity of migrating tribes in Iran, which one would expect to have dislocated trade routes there. The matter cannot at present be proved, but it is interesting that it is at this time that, after a lapse of nearly a millennium, Tilmun is once again heard of in connection with the trade in copper. A possible inference is that whoever was at the eastern end of the trans-Iranian trade had been driven to shift to more southerly routes, perhaps using sea transport, instead of the established overland routes through Iran. Furthermore, although Assyria did indeed have military successes over Urartu, the latter declined much more rapidly than the military situation would seem to warrant. This also would be explicable from the cutting of trade routes through Iran and Armenia, which previously brought wealth to Urartu.

Assyria herself, despite vigorous measures such as the virtual annexation of Elam, by which she made direct contact with the Iranians, also declined very rapidly, probably from the same dislocation of routes; and Babylonia became the leading power in Mesopotamia, with a great increase in economic as well as military activity. This also goes to support the hypothesis that the ethnic movements in Iran had temporarily diverted the old trade routes, so that all westward trade was now flowing across southern Elam, Babylonia and up the Euphrates.

The political unification of the two kingdoms of Media and Persia under Cyrus permitted him to pacify the whole area, making it possible for the old routes across northern Iran to be used again. One would expect this to have had adverse economic consequences on Babylonia, and there are indications that in fact this did occur. There was rapid inflation in Babylonia, prices practically doubling between 560 and 540 B.C. It seems that some of the New Babylonian kings were aware of the problem, and attempted to take appropriate steps. One king, Neriglissar (see page 144), in 557 B.C. made an expedition to Cilicia in an attempt to secure control of the rich route westwards through it from north Syria. However, Cyrus outmanoeuvred the Babylonians and himself quickly gained control of the whole of Asia Minor and its trade. The last New Babylonian king, Nabu-na'id, turned southwards, spending ten years away from Babylon at Teima in north-west Arabia (see page 148), establishing colonies all along the route from Teima to Medina in an attempt to give his kingdom a more secure economy by gaining control of the south Arabian trade routes. Nabu-na'id also attempted internal economic reforms. However, the reforms were either too late or inadequate, and in 539 B.C. the whole of the Babylonian empire fell into the hands of Cyrus. Cyrus at once reversed the policy of deportation of conquered populations; this policy, introduced by the Assyrians and exploited by Nebuchadrezzar, had totally disrupted the economy of some parts of the empire for the temporary advantage of the central government.

A. L. Oppenheim has pointed out (K. Polanyi (ed.), *Trade and Market in the Early Empires* (1957), page 34) that in the New Babylonian period, despite the certain existence of foreign trade, (referred to, for instance, in letters, as well as attested archaeologically), there are very few commercial documents concerned with it. He argues from this that two quite distinct practices in large scale commercial activity in the ancient Near East have to be differentiated. One, exemplified by the Cappadocian trade and the copper importers operating from Ur in the Larsa period (see page 274), employed all the devices of Sumerian bureaucracy including its practice of committing every transaction to writing. The other, to which we must assume that New Babylonian trade conformed, seems, according to Oppenheim, 'to have preferred oral agreements supplemented by a variety of operational devices' (op. cit., page 34).

Internal Trade

The Greek traveller Herodotus (who visited Babylonia in the fifth century B.C.) quotes a certain remark of Cyrus, king of Persia, and explains that this was intended as a criticism of the Greeks, 'because they [the Greeks] have markets where they practise buying and selling; for the Persians themselves are not accustomed to use markets, and indeed have not a single market place in their country'. Professor Polanyi (op. cit., page 16) curiously takes this to prove that the Babylonians had no markets or market-places. This equation of the Persian with the Babylonian economy entirely disregards the differences between the social and economic structure of the Persians, still tribal nomads only two centuries before Cyrus, and the Babylonians, who had over two millennia of urban civilization behind them. The statement of Herodotus cannot therefore be considered relevant to the question of whether or not the Babylonians had markets. Professor A. L. Oppenheim (op. cit., page 31) speaks of the absence of a market-place in ancient Mesopotamian cities, whilst Polanyi (op. cit., page 17) suggests that there were no open spaces in those cities which could have served as markets. The latter suggestion is certainly baseless: beyond doubt there were, in Assyrian cities at least, open spaces large enough for a man to be able to rape a struggling woman without being disturbed, for an Assyrian law legislates for this circumstance. There was in the first millennium B.C. an open space in Nineveh large enough for a victory parade, whilst at Eshnunna in the third millennium the excavators specifically stated that 'for a considerable portion of its length North Road widens into a public square'. There were also the spaces around the gates of cities, where business was often transacted in the ancient east (see *Deuteronomy* xxii. 15, *Ruth* iv. 1ff., 2 *Kings* vii. 1, etc.), whilst both Assyrian and Babylonian documents from the first millennium refer to the *bab* (*ša*) *maḫiri*, 'gate of buying', in one case certainly as the place where goods and silver changed hands. Professor Polanyi's case for denying the existence of markets within ancient Mesopotamia does not appear to have been made out, though it must be admitted that the positive evidence for their existence is not very strong either.

It has been mentioned elsewhere that a good 90 per cent of extant cuneiform texts are economic in content. This makes it impossible to attempt in the space of a few pages to give any useful outline even of the main aspects of trade and commerce in all the various periods, and the account offered must be severely selective. Some features of the economic system in the Sumerian city states of the third millennium have been outlined elsewhere, for which reason this period, though of great importance, will here be largely ignored in favour of the later periods.

In the Old Babylonian period trade was largely the concern of a class known as *tamkarū* (singular *tamkarum*); this term is commonly translated 'merchant', though, as pointed out by the Dutch scholar W. F. Leemans, the word connotes rather more than this, since the *tamkarum* in his various activities might be not only a merchant travelling in goods himself, but also a broker, a merchant banker, a money-lender, or – one might add – a government agent. An attempt has been made by Professor

Polanyi, in the work already mentioned, to re-define the status of the *tamkarum* in accordance with the view that the last-mentioned function subsumes all the others. For Professor Polanyi, the *tamkarum* was a 'public trustee' (op. cit., page 24): the *tamkarum*'s function according to this conception was to take appropriate action when anyone brought a business tablet to him, to advance fares and expenses, to accept pledges, and 'to facilitate transportation by accepting responsibility for money and goods entrusted to carriers' (op. cit., page 24), and so on. Furthermore it is categorically stated by Professor Polanyi that 'the *tamkarum* derived no revenue from the business in hand, although he may have charged small service fees to the traders according to some fixed scale. His living was ensured through the landed property with which he was invested at his appointment' (op. cit, page 24).

Certainly in some respects the *tamkarum* was a government agent, but that he was a 'public trustee' in the rigorous sense required by Professor Polanyi's theory is highly disputable. Certainly the statement that 'the *tamkarum* derived no revenue from the business in hand' is not invariably true, for the laws of Hammurabi (§101, quoted below) make it clear that a *tamkarum* was accustomed to make loans to agents upon which he expected at least 100 per cent profit (see below, page 289).

There are a number of references in the laws of Hammurabi to *tamkarū*, shedding light upon the activities of that class. Their trading was not confined to the homeland, and certainly people of that class engaged in the slave trade abroad, for the laws of Hammurabi envisage the case in which a native Babylonian, captured on royal service, comes into the hands of a *tamkarum*. The slave trade was not of course restricted to foreign lands, and there are many tablets showing that men of the *tamkarum* class dealt in the buying and selling of slaves within Babylonia. Besides dealing in slaves, *tamkarū* also organized trade in such commodities as foodstuffs, wool, timber, garments and textiles, grain, wine and ale, metals, building materials such as reeds and bricks, and cattle and horses. Many letters of the Old Babylonian period refer to internal trade in such commodities, and show that this trade was then, as at all periods in Babylonia, largely river-borne. The trading activity of the *tamkarum* is illustrated by such a letter as the following:

> To Sin-idinnam say, thus says Hammurabi: Ilushu-ibi the *tamkarum* . . . had notified me in these terms, saying thus: 'I delivered thirty *gur* of grain to the governor Sin-magir and I have his tablet (to this effect). For three years I have kept asking him but he will not deliver [*i.e.* repay] the grain to me'. He notified me in these terms.
>
> I have seen his tablet. Let Sin-magir have grain and interest thereon delivered; then deliver it to Ilushu-ibi.

The following letter shows a *tamkarum* having goods sent by river:

> The *tamkarum* Tamlatum son of Kish-nunu hired the ship of the shipmaster Ibbatum and had it sailed downstream to Babylon. That ship, which he has moored, until now has carried bricks . . .

The letter goes on to deal with a dispute which had arisen between the *tamkarum* and the shipmaster.

The *tamkarum* was not only a merchant himself, but also a merchant banker, providing money for others to go on trading journeys for him. Here again the laws of Hammurabi take notice of the situation, laying down provisions regulating the relations between the *tamkarum* and his agents. It appears that on the normal type of loan made by a *tamkarum* to an agent for a trading journey, the *tamkarum* could reckon on a minimum profit of 100 per cent. The relevant paragraphs of the laws read:

> If a *tamkarum* has delivered silver to an agent for selling and buying and has sent him off on a (trading) journey, . . . if he [the agent] sees a profit where he has gone, he shall register the interest of the silver, as much as he has received, and they shall count up his days and he shall pay his *tamkarum*.
>
> If, in the place where he went, he has not seen a profit, he shall double the silver which he received and the agent shall deliver it to the *tamkarum*.

Another type of loan (*tadmiqtum*), is also mentioned, in which, if the agent made a loss on the enterprise, he simply returned the full capital sum to the *tamkarum*. In this type of loan it is likely that any profit was shared in a fixed proportion between the agent and the *tamkarum*.

Loan agreements were a very common feature of Babylonian economic life at all periods. A proverb sums up the attitude to loan transactions in the words:

> The giving of a loan is like making love; the returning of a loan is like having a son born.

The reference is obviously to the interest added at repayment. The religious feeling against usury, so prominent in Hebrew and Islamic law, was entirely absent from the Sumero-Babylonian world, where the payment of interest upon a loan is regarded as a normal and respectable phenomenon and referred to both in laws and in the contracts themselves. Excessive rates of interest were however frowned upon, and the laws of Hammurabi provide that a *tamkarum* who charged more than the legal rate would forfeit his capital:

> If a man who has acquired a debt has no silver to return but has corn, according to the ordinance of the king the *tamkarum* shall take the interest on it in corn, but if the *tamkarum* raises the interest on it above 100 *qa* per *gur* (of corn) . . . he shall forfeit whatever he has delivered (on loan).

The rates of interest payable on loans varied according to the period of Babylonian history and the commodity involved. In the Old Babylonian period it was commonly $33\frac{1}{3}$ per cent on barley and 20 per cent on silver. It is often not very clear in the documents of the Old Babylonian period what the term of the loan is, nor is it explicitly stated whether payment of interest was monthly or annual. Generally the loan would be till after the coming harvest-time or till the conclusion of the trading journey in connection with which it had been made.

One very common type of loan, known as a *ḫubuttatu*-loan, has often been assumed to mean an interest-free loan. However, the Turkish scholar Bilgiç has shown that the term denoted a loan in which the amount received by the borrower was less than the amount entered in the contract, the difference representing the interest payable. If such a loan was not repaid within the period originally agreed, interest on the amount stated in the contract became due in the normal way. The following contract provides an example of such a transaction:

> Shamash-nasir the governor, son of Sin-iqisham, has received from Ilushu-nasir and Nanna-ibni 133 *gur* 1 *pi* 4 *sutu* of grain as a *ḫubuttatu*-loan; for two years there shall accrue no interest. If he has not returned the grain by the third year, then he shall add interest. [The names of witnesses follow, together with the date.]

The odd amount of grain mentioned represents a real loan of 100 *gur* plus interest of exactly 33⅓ per cent over two years, since 1 *gur* = 5 *pi* = 30 *sutu*.

The primary condition for the validity of most commercial transactions (including loans) was the presence of witnesses and a written record in the form of a contract. A letter has been quoted above in which Hammurabi examined the tablet of a creditor before giving judgement in his favour. It is specified in the laws of Hammurabi that loans made without a contract and witnesses could not be recovered. An apparent exception to this general principal occurs at about this time in the Assyrian merchant colony in Cappadocia, where a type of loan called *ebuttu* is known, which could be transacted without witnesses or a contract and which carried no interest. This however was a very specialized situation, as these loans were made between members of the same merchant colony, all of whom presumably knew and trusted each other's credit.

Tablets recording commercial contracts were usually sealed with the impression of the cylinder seals of those concerned, or in the later period with the mark of a finger-nail. The tablet was often then (in the earlier period) enclosed in a clay envelope containing a duplicate text (see plate 26A), whereby falsification was rendered impossible, since the envelope would not be broken unless a dispute arose, when the protected text within the envelope would be taken as the official version of the contract: this practice of using an envelope inscribed with a duplicate text had disappeared by New Babylonian times.

Falsification or forgery of tablets was on occasions attempted, but was a heinous crime. Even though the tablets were normally of unbaked clay, it was not a simple matter to moisten the clay at the appropriate point only, obliterate the old inscription without damage to the remainder, and superimpose the new text. Forgery of a complete tablet was sometimes attempted, but this required the collusion of a competent scribe.

Another door to dishonesty was the fact that there was no unified system of weights and measures, which might vary slightly from place to place within the same country. This obviously opened the way to roguery, for an unscrupulous dealer might lend or buy on one system of weights and receive repayment or sell on another. Dealing of this kind is denounced in *Amos* viii. 4-5:

> Hear this, O ye that would swallow up the needy, and cause the poor of the land to fail, saying, When will the new moon be gone, that we may sell corn? and the sabbath, that we may set forth wheat? making the ephah small, and the shekel great, and dealing falsely with balances of deceit.

Using different sets of weights to one's own advantage is also mentioned in *Deuteronomy* xxv. 13 and *Proverbs* xx. 10 and 23. Roguery of this kind was often forestalled in Mesopotamia by the provision being written into a contract that payment should be made by a particular standard, for example, the mina of Shamash, that is, the system of weights used in the temple of Shamash. None the less, this kind of dishonesty did happen in commercial dealings in Babylonia, as there are references to it, as for example in a magical text directed to releasing a man from the consequences of

> delivering by small measure, receiving by great measure,
> delivering by a small shekel, receiving by a great shekel,
> delivering by a small mina, receiving by a great mina.

Transport of goods within Babylonia was most commonly by ship, and the Euphrates, especially between the great cities, must often have presented a busy scene. On the middle Euphrates Mari seems to have been an important boat-building and ship-building centre, and there are several extant letters in which the sub-king Yasmah-Adad received orders from his father Shamshi-Adad to have boats built. Once sixty are mentioned at one time, though without reference to size, and on another occasion large and small boats were to be made, including thirty large ones. The boatmen, or bargees, navigating these vessels seem to have formed a close-knit group, with – according to a literary text – their own dialect of Sumerian. Also they took their wives with them, as we learn from a letter in which the ruler of Carchemish complained to the sub-king of Mari that

'they have detained at Tuttul thirty sheep, fifty jars full of wine, and the wife of a ship-man'.

There were various other hazards to shipping besides over-zealous officialdom. Weather was sometimes pleaded as an excuse for delay. Thus, in answer to a complaint, we find one official explaining

'These vessels went off, but I detained all of them at Tuttul. From the day that these vessels came (here), the heavens opened and it has been raining continuously'.

Another letter mentions some accident which had occurred to a ship carrying grain for the palace: the ship had had to be beached and the official wanted instructions about the grain now lying on the bank of the river. It is not clear what had happened in this case, but collision between boats on the river were not unknown, and the laws of Hammurabi (§240) deal with a particular case of this.

In addition to documents dealing with the sale or transport of goods, there are many concerning real estate transactions. Documents dealing with the sale of land and houses are very common for all periods from the Third Dynasty of Ur onwards. At the sale of real estate a written record was drawn up and given into the keeping of the purchaser. The following is a simple example:

$1\frac{1}{2}$ *sar* (of land) with a house built on it, next to the house of Kununu and next to the house of Irraya, Arad-Zugal has bought from Arad-Nanna. He has paid him 8½ shekels of silver as its full price.

Arad-Nanna has taken an oath by the king that he will not in the future say 'it is my house'.

[The names of the witnesses, and the date, follow.]

The clause against revendication was a very common one in ancient Mesopotamian contracts, especially, though not only, in contracts dealing with sales of real estate. Sometimes a specific penalty is mentioned in the event of revendication. The following provides an example of this:

> 1 *sar* (of land) with a house built on it, next to the house of Shubisha and next to the house of Bur-Sin, with one long side by the Ishkun-Sin canal and the second long side by the old house of Mishar-gamil, Ilushu-nasir the son of Bur-Sin has bought from Mishar-gamil, the owner of the house. He has paid him silver as its full price. His [Mishar-gamil's] heart is content, the affair is settled [literally 'its word is complete'].
>
> They have taken an oath by Ishtar and by Ibal-pi-El the king that neither will in future return against the other. He who makes a claim (at law) shall pay two minas of silver and his tongue shall be torn out.
>
> [Names of witnesses follow, with the name of the scribe.]

Sale of land was not in all circumstances, even in the Old Babylonian period, a simple and straightforward procedure. The following contract from Mari, though simple in form, was probably phrased in a particular way to get round a legal impediment to the sale of the land concerned:

> Ili-palahum has granted by division (of common property) five *sar* (of land) with a house on to Yarim-Adad. Yarim-Adad of his own free will has granted by division (of common property) half a shekel of silver to Ili-palahum. [Several lines of text are lost] . . . . In the presence of [ten named witnesses]. They have eaten the bread, they have drunk the cup, they have anointed themselves with oil.

The final section is taken to refer to some ceremonial meal, perhaps shared by the witnesses, sealing the sale.

The word translated 'granted by division (of common property)' is not the ordinary word for 'to sell', but refers properly to the allocation of tribal property to members of the tribe. It is in fact identical with the Hebrew verb translated 'to divide (or 'distribute') for inheritance' in *Numbers* xxxiv. 17, 18 and *Joshua* xix. 49. The transaction in the contract was therefore apparently a sale under the fiction of a division of common property, the fiction presumably being necessary because the land in question was technically tribal property and inalienable. In another document from Mari thirteen headman of the tribe of Awin, including representatives of the tribe resident in the town and in the desert, by the same device allotted to a high official – who for the purpose of the transaction was called 'their brother' – about one hundred and fifty acres of tribal land.

All the documents quoted above are from the Old Babylonian period. In the Nuzi area (near Kirkuk) later in the second millennium the sale of real estate took a very different form. In this society, strongly coloured by Hurrian influence, land seems to have been inalienable as a general principle. There were, however, at about 1400 B.C. a number of wealthy men in the Nuzi district engaged in building up large estates. A man of this kind would overcome the legal difficulty by having a document drawn up in which he was 'adopted' by the person from whom he wished to buy the land. He would make to his adoptive father a 'present' which really represented the price of the land, and he would receive as his 'inheritance' from his adoptive father the piece of land he wished to buy. The following is an abridged extract from a typical document of this kind:

> Tablet of adoption which X son of Y duly made for adoption (in connection with) M son of N.
>
> X has given to M as his (inheritance) portion 8 *awiḫari* of irrigated land in Nuzi, on the bank of the Sarae canal. . . . On the same day M has given to X 9 minas of lead as his gift.

As to the first millennium, it is clear that trade flourished in the New Assyrian empire, and that indeed a thriving economy as much as successful warfare was the basis of Assyrian prosperity at this time. A number of Assyrian kings boast of the economic prosperity and favourable price levels in their reigns, though usually this is related specifically to a thriving agriculture rather than directly to trade. Thus Shamshi-Adad I boasts:

> When I built the temple of my Lord Enlil, the prices in my city of Ashur were: two *gur* of grain for a shekel of silver, fifteen minas of wool for a shekel of silver . . . .

Sometimes the reference is to low prices produced by a sudden glut of a commodity (such as camels) from a successful campaign. In one case the relation of economic prosperity to trade is referred to more directly, for Sargon II, speaking of an attack on Egypt at the time of a campaign in Palestine, says

> I opened the sealed (border) of the land of Egypt and mixed the people of Assyria and Egypt together and caused trading to be done.

It is notable also that one of Nahum's chief complaints against Assyria was that it had 'multiplied [its] merchants above the stars of heaven' (iii. 16; see above, page 239).

In Babylonia in the first millennium internal trade seems to have been largely in the hands of the great temple corporations, such as that of Eanna in Erech, and this would seem to provide a situation in which much of Professor Polanyi's views (see above, page 279) about the nature of ancient economy is borne out. However, Oppenheim has pointed out (see above, page 286) that at this period foreign trade was negotiated through operational devices distinct from those which characterized the traditional temple-centred bureaucracy, and it is quite possible that outside the ponderous centralized temple economy of this time there was free trading on market lines between individuals, whose transactions might not have required a written record. Certainly one still finds at this period records of loans for trading journeys, taking the form of the following:

> Three minas of silver of Shum-ukin . . . is in the charge of Zababa-shum-iddin . . . for a (trading) journey. Zababa-shum-iddin shall enjoy an equal share in the profit, as much as there may be in town or country, with Shum-ukin . . . .

References to loans are also very common, though as in most

cases the purpose is not stated these loans may have been for agricultural rather than trading purposes. Another indication of the existence of trading outside the temple system at this time is that one frequently finds contracts in which the temple authorities hire ships from private persons. This implies that there were private ships plying between the cities of Babylonia, and they can hardly have had the transport of temple goods as their sole *raison d'être*, or they would soon have come under direct temple control, as so many other sectors of New Babylonian life (including some royal estates) ultimately did.

However, despite the likelihood that private trading did occur in New Babylonian times, most of our information about New Babylonian commerce relates to that administered by the temples. This type of trade was largely an administrative matter arranged between the appropriate officials of different temples. This is made very clear by such a letter as the following, written in 616 B.C. to the *Shatammu* of Erech (see above, pages 262 ff.) by a man who, as he calls the *Shatammu* of Erech 'brother', must have held corresponding rank in a temple further north:

> Letter of Shuzubu to Marduk-shakin-shum [known to have been *Shatammu* of Eanna in Erech] and Nadin my brothers. May Bel and Nabu decree the wellbeing of my brothers.
>
> I have sent Bel-na'id-shu to the Sealands [south Babylonia] for *shibeshu*-wood. He does not know the territory. Let my brothers send a man with him who knows the way: give him provisions.
>
> Let my brothers send gall-nuts (to the value) of one mina of silver and let your messenger come to me, and I will send white sesame, which is satisfactory to my brothers, (to the value) of one mina of silver . . . .

This letter also provides a very clear instance of the practice of using silver as a standard of values without any silver actually changing hands. This practice was, of course, widespread in the ancient Near East, and an Egyptian document of just after 1300 B.C. presents another good example of it. According to this document (a lawsuit), a merchant had gone from house to house, offering a Syrian slave-girl for sale, until finally the wife of an official bought her. The price was stated in terms of silver, but was actually paid in various cloths, garments and bronze vessels, each item being valued separately.

The movement of goods within Babylonia could be further attested from many other New Babylonian letters between temple officials. As, however, the aspect in which such transactions are viewed in the letters is primarily administrative rather than commercial, the subject is dealt with elsewhere (see page 263 f.).

Religion

'What account of their religion can you suppose to be learnt from savages? Only consider, Sir, our own state: our religion is in a book; we have an order of men whose duty it is to teach it; we have one day in the week set apart for it, and this is in general pretty well observed: yet ask the first ten gross men you meet, and hear what they can tell you of their religion.'

(Boswell's *Life of Johnson*, 29 April, 1776.)

T HOUGH the Babylonians and Assyrians were by no means savages, one does well, in embarking upon a study of their religion, to carry Dr. Johnson's warning in mind. One must decide from the outset whether one is speaking of religion as it was practised and experienced by the common man and his family in the mud hut, or whether one is considering the systematized theology drawn up by the priests. Two distinct lines of approach are possible. The investigator may attempt to describe the pantheon, doctrines and beliefs associated with the religion, or he may attempt to describe the inner experience and world-view of a devotee of the religion. The choice lies between describing the outward and visible sign, which can often be done with considerable confidence, and attempting to catch a glimpse of the inward and spiritual grace, which is fraught with wide possibilities of misunderstanding.

Knowledge of Babylonian religion has never been completely dead, inasmuch as some details of it have been preserved in classical writers and in the Old Testament. From these sources alone enough remains for certain definite assertions to be made: quite clearly Babylonian religion was pantheistic, with features associated with fertility cults strongly represented. In addition, classical sources amplify this information with some details of Babylonian cosmogony, that is, theories concerning the creation of the universe and men, and indeed, of the gods themselves. The principal material of the latter kind comes from the fragments of a work written in Greek by Berossus, a Babylonian priest of *circa* 340–275 B.C. The work of Berossus is not itself extant, but extracts are quoted in other ancient authors.

These scanty and distorted details have been enormously augmented and much clarified by the mass of cuneiform material of religious significance which has come to light since the middle of last century. This material includes epics, myths, hymns, prayers, incantations, exorcisms, ethical treatises and proverbs, omens, ritual directions, lists of god-names, and so on. Even a prosaic business receipt may shed light on the cult when it refers to such matters as the delivery of beasts for sacrifice or equipment for rituals. Even lists of personal names have their significance for the study of religion, in that examination of theophoric elements may show which particular gods were most popular in a given period or place. The documents concerned vary greatly in the ease and extent to which they can at present be understood; and as to language they may be in either Akkadian, Sumerian or both. Occasionally a Hittite or Hurrian text, although originating outside the area with which we are primarily concerned, sheds light on religious practice inside Mesopotamia. There are, in all these languages, texts about the detailed meaning of which there is at present no general agreement, and it is perhaps not superfluous to give a warning that a tendentious writer, or a non-specialist quoting inadequate translations, or a specialist in comparative religion who has made up his mind that Mesopotamian religion conforms to a certain pattern or who has not kept abreast of recent researches in Assyriology, is often able to use texts of the kind mentioned as an apparent proof of very doubtful theories. As an instance, it may be mentioned that general books on the religions of the ancient Near East still give details of Marduk dying and rising again at the New Year Festival in Babylon, despite the fact that one of the most distinguished scholars of Akkadian, W. von Soden of Munster, has already shown that this interpretation of the text concerned, based on an out-of-date translation, is untenable.

In discussing the great monotheistic religions one has the advantage of being able to start from a fairly precise date. This is not possible with non-reformed religions, where such changes of belief and modification of practice as are found arrive by gradual evolution from a system having its roots in prehistory. This is so markedly true of the religions of Babylonia and Assyria that it has been questioned whether, in view of the relatively late arrival of the Semites, the religion may properly be regarded as Semitic at all. Some authorities have categorically denied that it is Semitic, and insisted that its Sumerian origin remained so marked throughout the whole of the period that Babylonian civilization endured that it can best be regarded as a religion of Asiatic type overlaid and coloured by a veneer of Semitic features. The prevailing opinion is, however, that though there was a strong Sumerian substratum, the religious conceptions are pre-dominantly similar to those of the Hebrews before Moses, of the Canaanites, and of the Arabs before Muhammad, and so may be treated as Semitic. The point becomes of some importance in a study of the religion of the Old Testament, in view of the tendency amongst Scandinavian, and to some extent British and German scholars, to see patterns in the religion of the ancient Near East, particularly in connection with kingship, New Year Feasts and fertility cults. It is no difficult task, for example, to find phraseology and conceptions in Old Testament psalms similar to those in Babylonian hymns; from parallels of this kind the conclusion is then very easily drawn that the Old Testament psalms were used in rituals which, although we have no inde-pendent evidence of their existence, must have been similar to those in which the (apparently) corresponding Babylonian hymns were employed. If, however, the Babylonian hymns concerned were Semitic compositions superimposed upon an ancient and specifically Sumerian ritual, the parallel in literary form between the Babylonian and Hebrew would not necessarily imply a parallel in usage. This hypothetical case is given as a warning and not as an attempt to set up or knock down a particular theory.

Although from the time of the earliest written records there existed a developed pantheon, which will be briefly discussed later, Sumero-Babylonian religion was basically, as it affected the ordinary man, animistic. The ordinary man saw himself surrounded by forces which to him were gods and devils. There was a raging demon who manifested himself in the sand-storm sweeping in from the desert, and the man who opposed this demon was likely to be smitten with a painful sinusitis. Fire was a god. The river was a god and at the Ordeal, in which an accused person had to jump into the water, would seize the wicked man who perjured himself. The shimmering light which appeared upon the mountains just before sunrise was the glow from the haloes of the scorpion-men who guarded the sun at his ascent. A host of demons stood always ready to seize a man or a woman in particular circumstances, as, in lonely places, when eating or drinking, in sleep, and particularly in childbirth. The gods themselves were not exempt from the attacks of demons, and the eclipse of the moon was considered as a case of the Moon-god Sin having been temporarily vanquished by these beings, for a myth narrates:

> The Seven Evil Gods forced their way into the vault of heaven; they clustered angrily round the crescent of the Moon-god. . . . By night and day he was dark and did not sit in the seat of his dominion. . . . Enlil saw the darkening of the hero Sin [the Moon-god] in heaven; the Lord [Enlil] called to his vizier Nusku [the Fire-god]: 'O vizier Nusku, take word to the Abyss. Repeat to Ea in the Abyss the report about my son Sin, who has been grievously bedimmed in heaven. . . .' Ea in the Abyss heard this message. He bit his lip and filled his mouth with lamentation. Ea called his son Marduk and instructed him with a message: 'Go, my son Marduk! . . .'

This myth forms the introduction to a ritual apparently designed for the time of an eclipse with a view to protecting the king, and through him the country, from the Seven Evil Gods, who after their temporary victory over Sin 'swept over the land like a hurricane, attacked the land like a whirlwind'.

For protection against perils from demons, or for deliverance in the event of attack, the Babylonian had the consolations of official and popular religion in many forms. As a prophylactic an amulet (as shown in plate 56B) might be worn, and the great gods themselves did not scorn such devices, for Marduk in his combat with the primeval monster Tiamat.

> held in his lips [some object] of red clay, clasped in his hand the venom-quenching plant.

The developed form of amulet bore a portrayal of the devil against whom protection was sought and a magical incantation invoking the great gods against the threatened evil. One such reads:

> *Incantation*. That one which has approached the house scares me from my bed, rends me, makes me see nightmares. To the god Bine, gatekeeper of the Underworld, may they appoint him, by the decree of Ninurta, prince of the Underworld, by the decree of Marduk who dwells in Esagila in Babylon. Let door and bolt know that I am under the protection of the two Lords. *Incantation*.

One common type of amulet was apparently originally worn as protection against the appalling discomfort and even danger of the hot west wind which in summer brings sandstorms from the desert. The form of this amulet was either a grotesque head of the demon carved in the round or a bronze or stone plaque of the whole creature (see plate 57A), showing its bird-like chest, its human arms and legs terminating in talons with one hand holding a thunderbolt aloft, its curled tail and four wings. In either form the inscription on the back of the amulet (see illustration on page 304) reads (with slight variations):

> *Incantation*. I am the god Pazuzu, son of the god Hanbi, king of the evil wind-demons. It is I who rage mightily in the Mountain (of the Underworld) so that they come up. As to those winds which accompany them, the west wind is set at their front – The winds, their wings are broken.

Here the last phrase is apparently the magical formula the

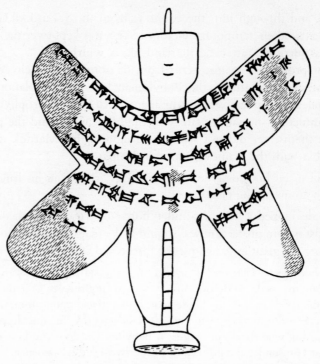

Inscription on Pazuzu amulet

utterance of which, following the identification of the demons concerned, rendered them powerless against the possessor of the amulet. Despite the totally inappropriate inscription, this amulet ultimately came to be used to protect women in childbirth, probably from the general similarity to the Lamashtu amulet, which was directly concerned with the being who threatened women in childbirth and nursing mothers. The most noted example of the latter type bears on one side four registers, of which the lowest and most prominent has as its central figure a monster with a lion's head and woman's body. This monster, who kneels on an ass as she embarks in a boat on the river, is giving suck to two animals, and probably represented Lamashtu herself, who by such magical means was sent on her way. (See plate 54B for a similar representation). In addition to such amulets a whole series of rituals existed for employment against this dreaded being.

When a victim already showed symptoms of demonic possession, the magician was called in to diagnose the malady and to
expel the evil being concerned: this was done by reciting the
proper incantation with the appropriate ritual, after invocation
of a god. Most commonly the god invoked was Marduk, son
of Ea, the god of magic. Any of the gods could intervene to
assist mankind against the demons, and in some contexts long
series of deities are named. Not all deities were, however, equally
willing or potent to assist suffering humanity. Two of the first
triad, Anu and Enlil, were respectively too remote or too iras-
cible to be relied upon always to take the side of mankind, but
the third, Ea, was a reliable and constant friend of humanity.
Ea was a ready help in trouble, always alert to frustrate the anger
of Enlil or the malevolence of demons. This deity, the god of
waters and the god of wisdom, was the supreme authority on
magic, and he freely imparted his knowledge to his son Marduk.
The usual procedure followed by a man in distress was for him
to apply to Marduk, through a priest, for help in his misery.
The typical liturgy for such circumstances then depicts Marduk
going to his father Ea, repeating the problem concerned, and
receiving the courteous answer

My son, what do you not know . . .?

followed by advice on the magical procedure for the case in
hand. As will be seen, a great power against magic and evil
influence was fire, and other gods potent against black magic
were the three Fire-gods, Gira, Gibil and Nusku. These were
regularly invoked against the demons or witches in this manner:

Incantation. Flaring Gira, son of Anu, the hero, you are the fiercest
amongst your brothers. You who judge cases like the gods Sin and
Shamash, judge my case, make a decision concerning me. Burn my
wizard and my witch! O Gira, consume my wizard and my witch!
O Gira, burn them! O Gira, consume them! O Gira, bind them!
O Gira, annihilate them! O Gira, send them away!

The priests concerned with deliverance from evil magical
forces or demons were the exorcists (ashipu and mashmashu) who
performed the appropriate incantations and rituals, and for the

healing of the sick might employ incantations and rituals either alone or in associations with actual surgical or medical techniques. The possible blend of magic and practical measures is illustrated by the following text, giving the treatment for toothache:

> After Anu had made the heavens, the heavens made the earth, the earth made the rivers, the rivers made the canals, the canals made the mud, the mud made the worm. The worm came weeping before Shamash, shed tears before Ea: 'What will you give me for my food ...?' (Ea replied): 'I will give you the ripe fig ...' (The worm said:) 'What is the ripe fig to me? Let me drink among the teeth, and set me on the gums, that I may consume the blood of the teeth and destroy the marrow of the gums'.
> *Fix the peg* [i.e. forceps] *and grip the root.*
> Because you said this, O worm, may Ea strike you with the might of his fist.

The sentence italicized obviously contains the effective direction, whilst the last sentence quoted presumably accompanied the wrench that brought out the tooth beneath which the offending worm lurked. The text concludes with instructions for the preparation of a mouth-wash composed of beer, oil, and some species of herb.

The priests' techniques often rested upon less practical measures, particularly the use of sympathetic (or symbolic) magic. An illustration of this is in a text which first states that

> An evil curse has been put on this man like a *gallu*-demon

and then mentions his symptoms,

> A dazed silence has been put on him,
> An unwholesome silence, an evil curse, a spell, a headache;
> His god has gone away from him,
> His goddess who looks after him has stood aside,
> A dazed silence has covered him like a garment.

Then, says the text, Marduk noticed the man, went to his father Ea, and outlined the situation. Ea, after his usual courteous disclaimer of superior knowledge, gave Marduk instructions for the cure:

Go, my son Marduk,
Take him to the pure ablution-house,
Loose his spell, loose his spell,
That the activating evil of his body,
Whether the curse of his father, or the curse of his mother, or the
   curse of his elder brother, or the curse of the murder of a man he
   does not know,
By the conjuration of Ea,
Let the curse be peeled off like this onion,
Let it be wrenched apart like this date,
Let it be untwined like this wick'.

Separate incantations for each object mentioned (the onion, the
date and the wick) and also for some not previously mentioned
(wads of wool and goat's hair) now follow and show that the
priest performed a symbolic action to dispose of the evil curse:

Incantation. Like this onion which he peels and throws into the
fire, which the fire consumes entirely, . . . whose roots will not
take hold in the soil, whose shoots will not sprout, that will not be
used for the meal of a god or a king, so may oath, curse, : . . sickness,
weariness, guilt, sin, wickedness, transgression, the sickness that is in
my body, my flesh or my limbs, be peeled off like this onion; may
the fire consume it entirely today; may the curse be taken away
that I may see the light.

The mention above of 'the pure ablution-house' suggests that
the ceremony in question was performed at the temple, but
often such magical rites were performed not in the temples but
in a private house, a sickroom, a reed hut, by the river or in the
open steppe land.

Another magical technique employed, distinct from sympathetic magic, was substitution. A good example is provided
by a text from Ashur, of which the following is an abridged
edition:

For making exchange for a man wanted by the Goddess of Death. At
sunset the sick man shall make a kid lie down with him on the bed.
At dawn you [that is, the priest] shall get up and bow (to the Sun-
god). The sick man shall carry the kid in his lap to a house where
there is a tamarisk tree. You [that is, the priest] shall make the sick
man and the kid lie down on the ground. You shall touch the throat

of the sick man with a wooden dagger, and you shall cut the throat of the kid with a bronze dagger . . . . You shall then dress up the kid with clothes, put sandals on it, put eye-black on its eyes, put oil on its head. You shall take off the sick man's turban and tie it on the kid's head. You shall lay the kid out and treat it like a dead man. The sick man shall then get up and stand in the door-way while the priest repeats a charm three times. The sick man shall take off his garment, give it to the priest and go away. The priest shall then set up a howl for the sick man, saying 'So-and-so has passed away!' The priest shall then give orders to institute mourning, . . . and shall bury the kid.

Conjurations, such as those already quoted, go back, in their simplest forms, to the Third Dynasty of Ur (about 2100 B.C.), though it was not until a much later date that collections of such texts were made: the three principal collections are known as *Shurpu*, *Maqlu* and *Utukki Limnuti* ('Evil Spirits'). The titles of the first two (both meaning 'Burning') reveal that fire was the principal agency by which evil influences were driven out, though there were other techniques available, particularly in the case of ghosts. The two kinds of 'Burning' are, though closely related, distinct in their functions. *Maqlu* incantations were mainly for the purpose of foiling the machinations of human wizards and witches: they accompanied official black magic, being uttered whilst wax, wooden, bronze, or tow images of the witch who had wrought the evil were destroyed by fire. *Shurpu* ritual, on the other hand, was a means of getting rid of sins: the sufferer's sins, ritual offences or breaches of taboos, which had offended the god and thereby brought ill upon the sufferer, were made over to some object which was then burnt. *Utukki Limnuti* incantations and rituals were applied to exorcise particular types of evil spirits.

These three types of conjuration were far from being the only ones known and used. There is a text which contains an extensive catalogue of such titles, its purpose being revealed in the first line: 'Headings of the series which are prescribed for learning and study for the exorcist-priesthood'. The succeeding list contains, in addition to those already mentioned, such items as

'Headaches', 'Toothaches', 'Ablution House', 'To loose a curse', 'Evil of all kinds', 'Eye-ache', 'To cure snake-bite', 'To cure scorpion's sting', 'Magical rites for town, house, field, orchard, river'. Such magical works were sought out and collected for his library by Ashurbanipal, as a letter, giving an official a list of the king's desiderata, shows.

The hosts of evil spirits which threatened the Babylonians and Assyrians were of many kinds: these demons, 'children of Anu', 'spawned in the mountains of the west', were often referred to collectively as the 'Seven', though in fact more than seven species can be distinguished and the term probably originally referred to a special group. There was Lamashtu, already mentioned, the dreaded she-spirit who threatened women in childbirth and stole infants from the breast. Equally dreaded was Namtaru, the plague-demon, the messenger of Nergal, god of the Underworld. Rabisu, the Croucher, was to be met in doorways and dark corners. Lilitu, probably the Hebrew Lilith, (though the connection has been denied – see below, page 485), was a succubus who visited men and disturbed their slumbers by lascivious suggestions: born from such unions were creatures such as the *alu* and *gallu*, faceless monsters who would rend those who came into their power, and who – to judge by the corresponding forms in Jewish tradition – clustered round the bedside of a sick man to greet their father after death. In addition to these there were the plain ghosts of dead humans. The ghosts of those who had died by violence or in consequence of infringement of a taboo –

> whether a ghost that was slain by a weapon or a ghost that died of a sin against a god or a crime against a king –

were particularly liable to wander, as was one neglected by its family in the matter of funeral and memorial rites,

> a forgotten ghost, or a ghost whose name is not uttered or a ghost who has no-one to care for it.

Not only could such ghosts strike terror into the hearts of those they haunted, but they might actually harm those to whom they appeared. To deal with this menace incantations and rituals were provided, of which the following is an example.

Unleavened bread was prepared from specified ingredients to the threefold recitation of an incantation:

> Dead folk, why do you appear to me, you whose towns are the ruins, whose houses (?) are bones? As for me, I do not go to Cuthah, the assembly-place of the ghosts: why, then, do you come after me? Be ye exorcised by . . . [names of deities follow].

As the sun was setting the magical bread so prepared was taken to a newly dug hole, into which it, with flour and water, was poured through an ox-horn, a torch then being applied to a censer placed nearby. Whilst the column of incense was rising to the setting sun another incantation was recited, calling upon the Sun-god to exorcise the offending spirit and,

> whether it be an evil spook or an evil *alu* or an evil ghost or an evil *gallu* or a buried ghost or an unburied ghost, or a ghost without brother or sister, or a ghost with no-one to mention its name, or a ghost whose family is nomadic, or a ghost which was left in the desert, . . . appoint it to the keeping of the ghosts of its family.

Finally, in the case where the ghost had actually smitten the man with sickness and might be presumed to wish to see him in the tomb, a wax image of the sick man was made and placed in the family grave together with clay images of the ghosts. This had the two-fold intention of laying the ghosts by token burial, and at the same time deceiving them into believing that their victim had died.

An alternative cure could be effected as follows, but unlike the preceding recipe required definite identification of the ghost. A piece of ground would be made ceremonially pure by rituals and incantations performed over a period of three days, and on the fourth day a clay figure of the offending ghost was prepared there. The image was assimilated to the ghost by inscribing its name on its left hip: the ghost was then rendered helpless by twisting its feet, throwing it down and putting a dog's tooth in its mouth as a gag. A cult stand was placed in position and a libation poured out to the Sun-god Shamash. Then the officiant recited three times:

I conjure you by Shamash at his setting, get clear of the body of so-and-so; depart, begone!

The rubric adds:

Thus you shall say, and you shall bury that image in a hole at the setting of the sun, and as long as he lives that man will not see the dead ghost.

A slightly different technique was involved when the demon was not so much magically identified with as actually trapped in a clay figure, the figure containing the demon then being disposed of in various ways. The following two extracts are from rituals dealing with the dreaded female demon Lamashtu.

Spell for Lamashtu

Its ritual. You shall sanctify the site. You shall take clay from the site and make an image of Lamashtu. You shall set it at the head of the sick man. You shall fill a brazier with ashes and thrust a dagger therein. For three days you shall put it at the head of the sick man. On the third day at close of day you shall bring it forth and smite Her with the dagger and bury Her in the corner of the wall.

Spell for Lamashtu

Its ritual. You shall make an image of the Daughter of Anu [i.e. Lamashtu] from the clay of a ditch. You shall make an ass from the clay of a ditch and you shall provide it with provender. . . . . You shall make a libation of bread and beer and you shall slaughter a young pig and put its heart into the mouth of the Daughter of Anu. For three days, thrice daily, you shall recite the incantation in front of Her. On the third day, at close of day, you shall make Her go forth into the open country.

An elaborate example of a rite to remove an evil spirit by trapping it in some object which was then physically removed is provided by the text of which the following is a slightly abbreviated translation:

For an inhibiting deity who sits on a man and seizes his mouth so that he can neither eat food nor drink water.

They shall tie a full-grown billy-goat at the head of his bed.

They shall cut a staff from the orchard, and twine coloured threads on the staff. They shall fill a cup with water. They shall break off a bough from the orchard. They shall put the staff, the cup of water, and the bough, the three of them, in the city gate . . . .

Then porters shall carry the full-grown billy-goat, the bough, the staff, and the cup into the waste-land. They shall not take them all into one rural district; they shall remove the staff and the cup away from each other. They shall carry the bough and the full-grown billy-goat to the rural district (which lies) on the main road. They shall slaughter the billy-goat and take off the hooves with the skin. They shall cut off the head, (and then) they shall cook the meat. They shall fill bronze vessels with honey and oil and bring (them there). They shall (then) dress the bough in the skin and tie the front legs with snares. They shall dig a pit and pour honey and oil into it. (Then) they shall hack off the forelegs and put them into the pit . . .

The remainder of the ritual is too broken to enable a translation to be offered. The conclusion of the text does however remain. It says:

That man will live. The god who is on him will depart, (whereupon) he will open his mouth and eat food and drink water.

Demons, whose attacks upon a man had brought sickness, might be satisfied or deceived in simpler fashion by the provision of a substitute. The substitute might take the form of an animal, or even an inanimate object such as a reed of the man's height, which was brought alongside the sufferer and identified with him in detail. The text for such a ceremony explains:

An evil *asakku*-demon dwells in the man's body. It covers the man like a garment as he walks about. It holds his hands and feet, it paralyses his limbs.

An obscure mythological reference is then made to Ea, the god of magic, introducing the text for the ritual:

The kid is the substitute for mankind, the kid is given for his life. The kid's head is given for the man's head, the kid's neck is given for the man's neck, the breast of the kid is given for the breast of the man.

This type of belief, that a demon on leaving a man needed to be provided with an alternative home, may be seen underlying one of the New Testament stories, that of the Gadarene swine (*St. Matthew* viii. 28–32, *St. Luke* viii. 26–33). According to the Evangelists' conception of things, those unfortunate beasts were immediately taken possession of by the multitude of devils expelled from a single man. Hitherto, according to the New Testament account, the devils had driven the human victim into the desert, a region particularly favoured by demons, and they feared that after expulsion they would be sent back to the abyss: the conception of the abyss, and the very word itself, both go back to the Sumero-Akkadian *apsu*, the waters of the primeval deep. The idea of the advantage of providing an exorcised devil with an alternative home is also reflected in a New Testament parable:

> . . . the unclean spirit, when he is gone out of the man, passeth through waterless places, seeking rest, and findeth it not. Then he saith, I will return into my house whence I came out; and when he is come, he findeth it empty, swept, and garnished. Then goeth he, and taketh with himself seven other spirits more evil than himself, and they enter in and dwell there: and the last state of that man becometh worse than the first'. (*St. Matthew* xii. 43–45).

Not all demons were ill-disposed to mankind, and indeed some incantations conclude

> Let the evil *utukku* and the evil *alu* go away,
> Let a benevolent *utukku* and a benevolent genie be present.

As well-disposed counterparts of the malevolent powers already mentioned there existed good *utukku*-spirits, good representatives of various other demonic species, and beings such as the *shedu* and *lamassu*. The last two stood at the entrance of Assyrian royal palaces in the form of huge winged lions (see plate 53) and bulls, and were powerful prophylactics against evil. The private house or bedroom might be similarly protected by figures either standing at the doorway or buried under the threshold. Many such figures have been discovered. At Ur, for example, clay figures were found in boxes of burnt brick placed under the floor against the walls: these boxes, which were provided with lids, had one end open, facing into the centre of the room, which the figures thereby watched and guarded. These particular figures at Ur, which in some cases had been given a lime-wash and then painted in black and red, were of various kinds. There were human figures clad in a garment composed of a pointed hat and a long robe painted with scales: these were fish-men, creatures mentioned in the mythology. Other figures had human bodies and the heads and wings of birds, and some represent a benevolent-looking long-bearded long-robed godling (similar in appearance to plate 30), with his closed hands folded across his breast as though grasping some object. Yet others were clay representations of the *mushrushshu* or red dragon, a composite creature with the body of a dog, the head of a serpent, and a long tail. For another form of dragon see plate 56A.

The ritual with which such figures were made and set up for the protection of a house has been largely recovered. It began with an enumeration of possible causes of the misfortune of the house:

> Whether it be an evil ghost or an evil spirit or an evil spook or an evil ghoul or an evil god or an evil Croucher or a *Lamashtu* or a *Labasu* or the Seizer or Lilu, Lilith or a Handmaid of Lilu, or the Hand-of-a-god or the Hand-of-a-goddess, or Epidemic, . . . or Plague-demon or the Bad-luck-demon [literally 'He who offers the bad things of life'] or Death or Heat or Fever or the Killer, . . . whatever there may be . . . which does harm to a man, in a man's house . . . .

Instructions were then given for the preparation of the figures of wood and clay to protect the house:

> You shall sprinkle holy water; set up a cult-stand; offer lambs for sacrifice and bring the hams, lard and roast meat; scatter dates and fine meal; set out a confection of honey and butter; set up a censer with juniper-wood; pour out a wine-libation; do obeisance, purify the censer, torch, holy-water vessel and tamarisk wood, and speak thus before Shamash:
>
> *Incantation:* 'O Shamash, great lord, exalted judge, the one who supervises the regions of heaven and earth, the one who directs

aright the dead and the living, You are . . . the holy tamarisk, the pure wood for the form of the statues which I shall cause to stand in the house of so-and-so for the overthrow of evil beings. I have bowed before you. May the thing which I do be completely efficacious.'

The tamarisk, which had thus been assimilated to the Sun-god, now had to be cut up in the approved manner. The rubric stated:

> You shall say this; then nick the tamarisk with an axe of gold and a saw of silver, and cut it up with a *qulmu*-tool.

Various groups of figures were then to be made from the wood, appropriately dressed and set up, and after this the incantation special to them was to be recited. The next morning at sunrise the figures were put, together with the censer, torch, holy-water vessel, seven grains of silver, seven of gold, and two precious stones, into a container called a *kullatu*. A libation was made to the Sun-god and the incantation *kullatu, kullatu* recited.

Further sets of statues were now made, this time of clay: since modelled clay lasts far longer in moist soil than carved wood, it is this type of figure which has been found at Ur and elsewhere. Many of these clay figures must originally have borne inscribed upon them magical formulae, as the texts suggest. Thus with reference to clay figures of this type in the form of dogs the text reads:

> Name of one dog coated with gypsum: 'Don't stop to think; open your mouth!'. Name of the second one: 'Don't stop to think, bite!'.
>
> Name of one black dog: 'Consume his life!'. Name of the other one: 'Loud of bark'.
>
> Name of one red dog: 'Driver away of the *asakku*-demon'. Name of the other one: 'Catcher of the hostile one'.
>
> Name of one green dog: 'The one who puts the enemy to flight'. Name of the other one: 'Biter of his foe'.
>
> Name of one spotted dog: 'Introducer of the beneficent ones'. Name of the other one: 'Expeller of the malevolent ones'.

In the ritual for the purification of a house, all the statues, both of wood and clay, were now to be taken to the river bank and placed facing east; there, at sunrise, another ceremony of sacrifice and libation was made to the Sun-god and the statues then taken back to the house. At the house followed yet further sacrifices and libations, this time to Marduk, to the three great gods, to the god and goddess of the house, to the protecting spirit (*shedu*) of the house, and to the Queen of the Underworld under one of her many titles. Crucial points of the house – corners, doorways, roofs and air vents – were then touched with various substances and purified, the purifying substances after- wards being brought out to the gate. The evil had now been temporarily removed, and it was for the statues to shoulder their task of keeping the house spiritually clean. Sacrifices were therefore now made to the statues and incantations recited, informing them that

> on account of some evil things which stand and call with malignant purpose in the house of so-and-so the son of so-and-so, . . . I have made you stand at the gate, at right and left, to dispel them from the house of so-and-so the son of so-and-so. Let anything malignant, anything not good, be removed from you a distance of 3600 double-hour journey.

The purification ritual outlined was a lengthy, complicated and no doubt expensive affair, but was efficacious against all types of evil influence, presumably for an indefinite period. A limited range of evil influences could be removed by simpler means, but the period of security guaranteed was limited to one year:

> To cut off the foot of evil from a man's house, you shall pound up, bray and mix in mountain honey the seed of . . . [seven named plants] . . . , divide it into three parts, bury it in the threshold of the gate and to the right side and to the left; and illness, headache, insomnia and pestilence shall not approach that man and his house for one year.

Such evil influences as those against which these rituals were directed did not always seize upon a man by their own volition. Often they were directed by witchcraft. As with most peoples, the Babylonians knew a malevolent and a beneficent witchcraft, and the illicit exercise of the former was proscribed by law as early as the time of Hammurabi (*circa* 1800 B.C.), the wizard being liable to the death penalty. Legislation, however, was in many cases powerless to prevent the evil and of no avail against its dire consequences, to counter which exorcism would be needed. Many texts are known containing exorcisms for this purpose. Such a text would contain first the diagnosis, for instance:

> The witch has wrought her evil bewitchment,
> She has made me eat her no-good spirit,
> She has made me drink her drink, to take away my life,
> She has washed me with filthy washing, for my being a dead man,
> She has anointed me with her bad oil for my destruction,
> She has made me catch a bad illness which is the grasp of a curse,
> She has appointed me to the ghost of a stranger who prowls around,
>   who has no kin.

Treatment then succeeds diagnosis. The god Asar-lu-hi (the great Marduk) takes note of the sufferer's situation and reports to his father Ea, the great god of wisdom and magic. He says:

> My father, who created mankind with your hands,
> The witch has gone to tear away his life,

and repeats to Ea the diagnostic facts already given.

At the end of the recital Ea answers Marduk, giving him instructions for treatment:

> Go, my son Marduk! Give him your pure drink of life, let him eat the plant of life. Let him anoint himself and wash . . . . Reach his witch with the wind of your mouth. Let the wind of your mouth reach her. Let bewitchment, venom, filth, be far from him by the pure incantation of life. Let the curse go forth into the wilderness, let the ghost of the stranger disappear . . . . Let the man live, let the man be right. Let the man be healthy before you for ever. What his witch has done to kill him, may Marduk loose so as to give life to his men.

From the need of the illicit operator to practice secrecy it is only to be expected that we should find little direct trace of their activity. There is, however, no doubt, from the numerous references in exorcisms, that illicit witchcraft was widespread and feared. A typical exorcism includes the passage:

> *Incantation.* My witch, and my bewitcher, sits in the shadow of a heap of bricks. She sits and works bewitchment on me, makes images of me. I send against you the *ḥashu*-plant and sesame. I scatter your magic, I turn your words back into your mouth. The bewitchment which you have wrought, let it be directed against you! The images which you have made, let them apply to you! The water which you have drawn up, let it be used against yourself! Your incantation shall not come near me. Your words shall not reach me. At the command of Ea, Shamash and Marduk and the princess Belit-ili. *Incantation.*

This forms part of the text for a rite whereby the official practitioner for a fee turned back the magical powers which the witch had directed upon his or her victim, and similar texts are quite common. Although original documents employed in the illicit exercise of black magic are much rarer, a few of these are known. One such purports to be a letter to a god asking the deity to destroy and wipe out the writer and the whole of his family and connections. The text begins:

> *Incantation.* Bawa-ah-iddina . . . addresses the great lord Ninurta thus: 'O Ninurta, great lord! Tear out the heart, extinguish the life, kill the wife, annihilate the sons, the relations, the connections, the name, the seed, the offshoot, the descendants of Bawa-ah-iddina. . . . .,

and ends with a great oath, allegedly by the unfortunate Bawa-ah-iddina, assuring the doubtless rather puzzled deity that Bawa-ah-iddina and his relations bore

> the effect, the penalty, the guilt, the sin, the offence of this oath.

Not all afflictions befalling a man were, however, the result of witchcraft, or of ill-disposed demons. The affliction might be brought upon the man by his own action in violating a taboo. Thus it was well known that there were certain foods and certain activities interdicted on particular days, and in a hemerology we read:

In the month of Tashrit, . . .

first day: . . . (a man) shall not eat garlic, or a scorpion will sting him; he shall not eat an onion, or there will be dysentery (in store) for him . . .;

second day: he shall not eat garlic, or an important person in his family will die; . . . he shall not ascend to a roof, or the Handmaid of Lilu will espouse him;

third day: . . . he shall not have intercourse with a woman, or that woman will take away his sexual powers;

fourth day: he shall not cross a river, or his virility will fail;

fifth day: he shall not eat pig-meat, or there will be a lawsuit for him; he shall not eat cooked meat, or the Croucher-demon will strike him; he shall not eat beef, or the *Utukku*-demon will lay hands on him; he shall not bend down to a garden, or the godling Shulak will strike him.

Therefore, when a man was oppressed by sickness or trouble, to trace the cause such matters had to be enquired into. It was only a step from this to enquiring into the other activities of a man, into what we would call his observance of ethical standards. Thus we find an incantation for someone who is 'sick, in danger, distraught, very troubled'. A list of his possible offences is given. It is said that he may, *inter alia*, have

eaten what is taboo to his god, eaten what is taboo to his goddess, . . . divided son from father, father from son, divided daughter from mother, mother from daughter, divided daughter-in-law from mother-in-law, mother-in-law from daughter-in law, brother from brother, friend from friend,

or he may have failed in his duty in that

he did not set the captive free, did not release the man who was bound, . . . (but) said with respect to the captive 'Keep him captive!' and with respect to the man who was bound said 'Bind him well!'.

It may be that

he treated a god with disrespect, neglected a goddess, . . . neglected his father and mother, treated his big sister with disrespect, sold by a small measure and received by a large, said 'there is' when there was not, said 'there is not' when there was, . . . set up a false boundary stone, entered his neighbour's house, lay with his neighbour's wife, shed his neighbour's blood, . . ., dispersed an assembled clan, . . ., did ignoble things, set his hand to magic and sorcery.

Amongst other conceivable offences it is possible that he

> ate something taboo to his city, . . . gave his city a bad utterance-omen, . . ., lay in the bed of a person under a curse, sat in the chair of a person under a curse, ate at the table of a person under a curse, drank from the cup of a person under a curse.

Some of the offences are plainly, from the modern point-of-view, ethical ones. The distinction between ethical sins and the unwitting breaking of taboos was however never clearly drawn, and was meaningless to the ancient Babylonian or Assyrian, who saw his religious duty in terms not of a moral law but of the arbitrary and usually unpredictable will of a pantheon of gods.

Although the decisions of the gods were arbitrary, mankind was not left without indications of the divine will. The intentions of the gods were supposed to be reflected or foreshadowed in events on earth, even the most trivial. The Babylonians saw the universe as a whole, and believed that what happened in one part was mirrored in another. If a certain event succeeded another in time, there was a possible causal connection, and the same result might be expected to succeed the same event on another occasion. In accordance with this view of things, lists of unusual occurrences with the standard consequences were drawn up, and a great pseudo-science arose directed to the interpretation of omens. The types of phenomena from which omens could be drawn were virtually unlimited, but three main divisions may be made, the three groups concerned being

(i) those which employed special techniques, such as liver-divination,

(ii) those which divined from casual phenomena, such as dreams, the movements of animals, or freak births,

(iii) astrology.

Within these main groups it would be possible to make many sub-divisions.

The question of the time of origin of such omens has been widely discussed. Some techniques were certainly very ancient, and there are traditions in the texts of the employment of divination by some prediluvian kings. Certain of the techniques were favoured at particular times and places. Thus hepatoscopy (liver-divination) is well attested from Old Babylonian times, whereas astrology is not, though in Assyria it became of high importance. Likewise dream-omens, though known from the Old Babylonian period both in Babylon and Susa, enjoyed their greatest popularity in later Assyria, chiefly at the time of Ashurbanipal.

The prognostications in the omen-literature fall into two main classes – those which concern the king, high officials and the country, and those which concern private persons. Astrological omens and those concerned with liver-divination relate to public affairs, whilst the other types (dreams, casual meetings, movements of animals and so on) relate to private persons.

Omens had, to ancient man (as still in many cases to his modern successor) a practical use: prediction of misfortune constituted a warning, and by making use of the appropriate ritual the potential victim could avert the danger. The illogicality of supposing that fate could be averted did not, apparently, bother ancient man.

No actual Sumerian omens are yet known, even though there are references in Sumerian literature to the use of omens. The extant Akkadian ones range from the Old Babylonian period onwards, and form a very large proportion of that part of Akkadian literature which is not economic in content; it has been estimated that about 30 per cent of the twenty to thirty thousand extant tablets from the library of king Ashurbanipal at Nineveh come into the category of omen-literature.

Some typical omens may be quoted. The first list contains examples selected from the ancient compilation known, from its opening line, as 'If a town is set on a hill'. The full omen reads:

If a town is set on a hill, it will not be good for the dweller within that town.

This is followed (typically) by the antithesis:

If a town is set in a depression, it will be good for the dweller within that town.

Other omens in this very large collection include:

> If there is seen in a house the dead owner of the house, his son will die,
>
> If there is seen in a house the dead lady of the house, the owner of the house will die.

In building a house,

> If black ants are seen on the foundations which have been laid, that house will get built; the owner of that house will (live to) grow old.
>
> If white ants are seen . . . as to the owner of that house, his house will be destroyed.
>
> If yellow ants are seen . . ., collapse of the foundations; that house will not get built.
>
> If red ants are seen . . ., the owner of that house will die before his time.

Omens were also drawn from the chance behaviour of many other creatures:

> If a snake is aggressive to a man, seizes him, bites him, hard times will reach his adversary.
>
> If a snake passes from the right of a man to the left of the man, he will have a good name.
>
> If a snake passes from the left of a man to the right of a man, he will have a bad name. [This and the preceding omen well illustrate the standard interpretation of the right as lucky, the left as unlucky.]
>
> If a snake appears in a place where a man and wife are standing and talking, the man and wife will divorce each other. [The symbolism is obvious even to the modern man, who, using closely related imagery, could speak of 'a snake in the grass' 'coming between' a man and his wife.]
>
> If a snake keeps threshing about in a man's house, that house will be thrown down or destroyed.
>
> If a scorpion kills a snake in a man's house, that man's sons will kill him; he will die. [The lesser creature unexpectedly destroys the greater.]
>
> If a mongoose kills a snake in a man's house, (this means) the approach of barley and silver.
>
> If a snake falls (from the ceiling) on a man and wife and scatters them, the man and wife will be divorced.
>
> If a scorpion lurks in a man's bed, that man will have riches.

If a scorpion stands on the head of a sick man's bed, his sickness will quickly leave him. [A lizard in the same circumstances implies the same omen.]

If a man unwittingly treads on a lizard and kills it, he will prevail over his adversary.

If ants are numerous at the entrance to the great gate; overthrow of the town.

If ants kill each other, making a battle; approach of the enemy, there will be the downfall of a great army.

If there are black winged ants in the town, there will be pouring rain and floods.

If an ox has its left horn sticking straight out and its right horn set to the right, that cattleyard will become broad [i.e. well-stocked with cattle].

If an ox has tears come into both its eyes, some evil will reach the owner of that ox.

If an ass mounts a man, that man will be sold for money, or (alternatively) hard times will seize him.

If an ass brings forth and (the creature has) two heads, there will be a change in the throne.

If a horse enters a man's house, and bites either an ass or a man, the owner of the house will die and his household will be scattered.

If a nobleman is riding a chariot and falls behind the chariot, it is set down for him as unfavourable; the Government will recall him from his post [literally, 'the palace will make him return'].

If a horse runs of its own accord into the house of a nobleman and breaks a chair, . . . [prognosis unfortunately lost].

If a man sees lizards copulating and grasps them and they do not part and he kills them, a scandalmonger(?) will harry him and he will die of slander.

If a wild ox appears in front of the great gate, the enemy will invest the town.

If a wild ox goes in to a herd of cows and pastures with them daily, it is favourable. If it separates and goes off the same day, it is unfavourable.

If a fox runs into the public square, that town will be devastated. [There is extant a letter to an Assyrian king reporting such an incident, which was obviously regarded as a matter of concern. The letter reads: 'To the king my lord your servant Nabua. May Nabu and Marduk bless the king my lord. On the seventh day of the month Kislimu a fox came into the city Ashur into the park of the god Ashur. It fell into a well. They got it out and killed it'.]

If pigs gnash their teeth, that town will be scattered.

If a sow kindles and brings forth three and their heads are white and their tails black, the furniture of that man's house will be pledged for silver. [Corresponding omens continue through a series of numbers and colour combinations.]

If a black dog cocks its leg before a man and urinates, . . . [significance lost].

If a god lies on his (master's) bed, his [the master's] god is angry with him.

If a white dog urinates on a man, hard times will seize that man.

If a red dog urinates on a man, that man will have happiness.

If a dog mounts a dog, women will commit lesbianism. [Here the modern author – who may be wrong – has assumed symbolism, in postulating a meaning for a rare verb of which the sense is otherwise unknown.]

If a flood comes in the month Nisan and the river is coloured like blood, there will be pestilence in the land. [Although severe floods do in Iraq bring disease and epidemics in their wake if stringent precautions are not taken, the connection in the omen is simply that between the colour of the water and blood and death.]

If fish are numerous in a river, (this portends) quiet dwelling for the land. [The shoals of fish obviously suggest contented crowds in the city streets.]

If in (some) place there is an open well and its water is yellow, fish and birds will not lay eggs in that land.

If in (some) place there is an open well and bitumen appears, that land will be destroyed.

If in some place there is an open well and oil appears, (this portends) the approach of the enemy against the land.

If a falcon eats a bird on the roof of a man's house and puts it down, someone in that house will die.

Another type of omen was what one may paradoxically describe as an accidental omen deliberately sought. The man prayed to his god and then accepted any chance utterance (*egirrû*) as an omen applying to himself. The reliability of the *egirrû* was however affected by the circumstances in which it reached the man:

If the *egirrû* answers the man 'yes!' once, achieving of desire;
If the *egirrû* answers the man 'yes!' twice, bringing about(?);
If the *egirrû* answers the man 'yes!' thrice, this is a firm 'yes!'

Likewise the value of the *egirrû* was affected by whether it came from right or left, or from in front of or behind the man.

Illogically, it was considered possible to prevent the ill consequences of a bad omen, and the lists of omens are followed by the appropriate recipes. For instance, in the case of the ants:

> Loosing of the evil of the ants which are seen in a man's house, so that its evil shall not come near to the man or his house. You shall sprinkle good oil over the ants and their hole. You shall introduce (?) into their hole gypsum and alkali from glasswort plants. You shall mix – with either well water or river water – dust from a boat, clay from the river meadows, and dust from the threshold of the outer gate (of the city), and you shall sprinkle it. You shall put incense burners with juniper and myrrh on the threshold together, and you shall loose its (portended) evil.

This ritual was performed not by the private individual but by the special priest called the *Mashmashu* (see page 346). It should be emphasized that in rituals of this kind the action taken was not designed to get rid of the ants but to avert the evil which their presence portended.

Though magic played such a very great part in ancient Mesopotamian life it would be misleading to give the impression that magic constituted the whole of the Babylonian response to the adversities and problems of life. On the contrary, prayer, the expression of a sense of utter dependence on the deity, was also a common means by which the Babylonian sought solace and aid. He himself possibly did not recognize any essential distinction between the two forms of contact with the spiritual world, (an attitude in which the ancient religion-ridden man and the modern atheist come together), for he headed his magical formulae and his prayers both with the term 'Incantation'. None the less, the difference of approach is to the modern reader unmistakable. A typical prayer begins thus:

> *Incantation.* O Lord, the strong one, the famous one, the one who knows all,

Splendid one, Self-renewing one, Perfect one, First-begotten of
  Marduk,
. . . .
Counsellor of the gods, . . . the one who holds cult-centres firm,
The one who gathers to himself all cults, . . .

and continues in like vein through a series of titles and attributes,
culminating in the phrases:

... You watch over all men,
You accept their supplication,
You bestow upon them wellbeing;
The whole of mankind makes prayer to you.

The worshipper then introduces his personal circumstances:

I, Balasu, son of his god, whose god is Nabu, whose goddess is
  Tashmetum,
On account of the evil of the outbreak of fire in my house
I am afraid, I am troubled, I am very troubled.

The 'evil' referred to is not the damage done by the fire itself but
the disasters which such an event was believed to prognosticate.
This is quite clear from the fact that parallel prayers, intended
for the use of the king on behalf of the nation, often refer to
'the evil of the eclipse of the moon'. The prayer continues:

I am (one liable to be) plundered (or) murdered, one whose punish-
  ment is great,
I am one who is weary, disturbed, whose body is very sick
So that taboo (and) pain have met me; I bow before thee.
Sickness from magic, sorcery, witchcraft has covered me;
. . . .
O Lord, Wise One of the gods, by thy mouth command good for me;
O Nabu, Wise One of the gods, by thy mouth may I come forth
  alive.

The relatively exalted conception of the deity which a prayer
of this kind implies is beyond doubt. Yet it becomes abundantly
clear that the priests representing the main stream of ancient
Mesopotamian religion saw no essential difference between magic
and prayer, for in a later part of the same compilation we find,
after a prayer to the Moon-god Sin, the instructions:

Its ritual. At night you shall sweep the roof before Sin; you shall sprinkle holy water. You shall pile up a pyre; upon the pyre you shall fix seven loaves of emmer. You shall divide up a pure lamb, without blemish. Three measures of flour which a male has milled, one measure of salt, you shall prepare; and seven clay bottles you shall fill with honey, ghee, wine, beer and water, and pile them on the pyre; you shall pour a libation of the concoction and do obeisance. The remainder (?) you shall cast into the river.

Another example, amongst many which could be adduced, of a prayer implying a more noble conception of the relationship between Man and the deity is the following prayer to a goddess:

Incantation. O heroic one, Ishtar; the immaculate one of the goddesses,
Torch of heaven and earth, radiance of the continents,
The goddess 'Lady of Heaven', first-begotten of Sin, first-born of Ningal,
Twin-sister of . . . the hero Shamash [the Sun-god];
O Ishtar, you are Anu [the supreme god], you rule the heavens;
With Enlil the Counsellor you advise mankind;
The Word, creator of liturgies and rituals of 'Hand-washing'.
. . . .
Where conversation takes places, you, like Shamash, are paying attention,
. . . .
You alter the Fates, and an ill event becomes good;
I have sought you amongst the gods; supplications are offered to you;
To you amongst the goddesses I have turned, with intent to make entreaty,
Before you is a (protecting) *shedu* [a genie], behind you a (protecting) *lamassu* [another type of genie],
At your right is Justice, at your left Goodness,
Fixed on your head are Audience, Favour, Peace,
Your sides are encompassed with Life and Well-being;
How good it is to pray to you, how blessed to be heard by you!
Your glance is Audience, your utterance is the Light.
Have pity on me, O Ishtar! Order my prospering!
Glance on me in affirmation! Accept my litany!
. . . .
I have borne your yoke; set tranquillity (for me)!

I have sought your brightness; may my face be bright.
I have turned to your dominion; may it be life and well-being for
me.
May I (too) have a favourable *shedu* like that before you;
May I (too) have a *lamassu* like that which goes behind you.
May I garner the prosperity at your right hand,
May I attain to the favour at your left hand.
. . . .
Lengthen my days, bestow life!
Let me live, let me be well, let me proclaim your divinity.
Let me achieve what I desire . . . .

At the end of the prayer comes the instruction:

> *Wording of the 'hand-raising to Ishtar'.* Before Ishtar you shall set a
> censer with juniper-wood; you shall pour a gruel-libation, you
> shall recite the 'hand-raising' three times, you shall do obeisance.

The hymns and prayers quoted bear suggestions of henotheism
and monolatry. That this was a conscious trend in Assyro-
Babylonian religion is shown by texts of the type in which parts
of the god adored were identified with other gods, as in this
hymn to Ninurta:

> Your two eyes, O Lord, are Ellil and Ninlil . . .
> Anum and Antum are your two lips . . .
> Your teeth are the 'Seven', who overthrow evil,
> The approach of your cheeks, O Lord, is the coming out of the stars,
> Your two ears are Ea [god of wisdom and understanding] and
>   Damkina [his spouse], princes of wisdom . . .
> Your neck is Marduk, judge of heaven and earth . . .

This henotheistic trend has to be viewed, however, in the light of
the extensive polytheism which characterized Assyro-Babylonian
religion. As early as the *Early Dynastic* period, four thousand gods
are known by name. These were systematized and syncretized
by later theologians, but a vast pantheon always remained.

The Pantheon

At the head of the pantheon stood, across the whole three millennia of Sumero-Akkadian religion, the god Anu (Sumerian An),

often rather a shadowy figure. His main characteristic was royalty, and it was primarily from him that mankind and individual rulers received this institution and its insignia: according to the *Epic of Etana* (see pages 423 ff.) there lay before Anu in heaven the sceptre, tiara, royal head-dress, and shepherd's staff. The principal symbol used to represent this god was the horned cap, though this could also be used for the other two members of the first triad of deities. With the supersession of the old world of city-states by national units, there was a tendency for Anu to be replaced in Assyria by the national god Ashur and in Babylonia by Marduk, whilst Anu's even more shadowy consort Antum was often replaced by or assimilated to Ishtar, the great mother-goddess and goddess of love, known in Sumerian as Innin, popularly taken as representing Inanna, 'Lady of Heaven'. Though he had shrines elsewhere, the principal city with which Anu was specifically associated in the period of Sumerian city states was Uruk (biblical Erech), where his consort Inanna was honoured in the great temple of Eanna; subsequently Inanna-Ishtar quite overshadowed her consort in Erech, so that by the New Babylonian period, when the extent and power of Eanna was so extensive that for many purposes it was synonymous with Erech, there is no more than incidental mention of Anu in connection with Eanna.

Alongside Anu was his powerful son Enlil (or Ellil), literally 'Lord Wind', the tutelary deity of Nippur. Though associated with a particular city, he was a national god of Sumer, not a mere local god, and the possession of the whole of Sumer by the ruler of any city-state depended upon recognition by him. A Sumerian text speaks of a time when Shubur (Assyria, or – according to another interpretation – Elam and the other eastern lands), Sumer and Akkad, and Martu (the western nomads) all dwelt in peace and all gave praise to Enlil. Just as Anu was king of heaven, so was Enlil king of the earth. Like Anu, Enlil could be called 'Father of the gods' or 'King of the gods'. Anu and Enlil were often associated as leaders of the gods, and Nisan, the first month of the year, in which the 'destinies' for the year were decided, was sacred to the two of them jointly. To Enlil originally belonged the Tablets of Destiny, by which the fates of men and of gods were decreed, but with the growth of national religion and the syncretistic tendency these, with other aspects of Enlil, were taken over by Marduk. Enlil, though lord of the earth, had an ambivalent attitude towards mankind, and it was through his violent urgings that the Deluge was unleashed upon the world, whilst in another myth he created the monster Labbu to destroy mankind. His consort, Ninlil, was a faint shadow of Enlil, and was ultimately assimilated to Ishtar in one of her aspects.

The third of the great gods at the head of the pantheon is known under various designations, the two principal being Enki 'Lord of the *Ki*' (*Ki* meaning either 'earth' or 'subterranean region'), and Ea '(god of) the house of water': both names were Sumerian, but the latter is principally used in the Semitic *milieu*. Though the term 'triad' is often applied (as it is elsewhere in this book) to the three gods Anu, Enlil and Enki considered together, it can be misleading if 'triad' is to mean anything more specific theologically than three gods of roughly equal rank. In many respects Enki stands apart from Anu and Enlil, and the conception of a triad (in the more precise sense of three deities whose inter-relationship is of the essence of their natures) is certainly not present in Sumerian religion in the earliest stage at which we know it. Enki-Ea was the god of wisdom and the god of waters, and was associated with the primeval deep. It was he amongst gods of the first rank who unfailingly displayed favour to the human race and indeed to fellow gods: when Innin was preparing to face the perils of a descent into the Underworld she directed her vizier, in the event of her non-return, to appeal first to Enlil and then to the Moon-god Nanna for succour: if these did not help her then assuredly Enki would come to her aid. Eridu, the oldest of the Sumerian cities, was the city with which Enki was associated, and the connection of Eridu with the god of wisdom reflects the fact that it was there that the earliest flowering of Sumerian culture took place. As god of wisdom Ea also bore the name Nin-igi-ku, 'Lord of the bright [intelligent] eye', whilst under another aspect he was Nu-dim-mud, 'Begetter of man-kind'. His spouse was variously Ninki (the most primitive form, simply the feminine doublet of Enki), Ninhursag, or Damkina.

Sumero-Akkadian mythology is not consistent as to the precise relationship of the three great gods, but according to the most celebrated account, the *Epic of Creation*, the origin of Anu and Ea was on this wise. The two primeval monsters, Lahmu and Lahamu, were born from Apsu (the Deep) and Tiamat (Ocean) and from them were engendered Anshar and Kishar, the Universe above and below. Then

> The days stretched out, the years multiplied;
> Anu their son, the equal of his forefathers,
> Anshar made him – (that is,) Anu his first-born – like (unto him-self.
> Anu begat his likeness, Nu-dim-mud, . . .
> All-hearing [literally 'wide-eared'], understanding, mighty in power,
> Far stronger than Anshar, the begetter of his father,
> Without equal amongst the gods his brethren.

The origin of Enlil was less clearly defined by the ancient theologians. One text makes him a son of Anu, though elsewhere he himself is considered as father of the gods. Theological spec-ulation makes him (and Anu also) the end-product of a chain of forty-two named ancestors, occurring in pairs like the aeons of later gnostic theology. Enlil probably originally had a prominent place in the *Epic of Creation*, being – it is supposed – in the original conception the splendid son begotten by Ea to vanquish Tiamat, a sphere of action ultimately taken over by the national gods, Marduk in Babylonia and Ashur in Assyria.

A second group of deities was constituted by the Sun, Moon and the planet Venus, whose Sumerian and Semitic names were respectively Utu or Shamash, Nanna or Sin, and Innin or Ishtar. Again it gives a false impression to speak of a 'triad', if 'triad' is to mean anything more specific than 'trio', for on occasions it was Shamash, Ishtar and Adad who occurred together. Of the deities mentioned the greatest was the Moon-god. Sin, controller of the night, of the month and of the lunar calendar, was manifestly a god whose activities intimately concerned mankind; and hymns and rituals for Sin and reports of the moon's appearance and omens drawn from such phenomena are of very common occurrence. Sin himself was the son, according to variant theologies, of either Anu or Enlil: his wife was Nin-gal, 'Great Lady', whilst Shamash and Ishtar were their children. The name Sin, although used by the Semites, was, like the name Ea, not Semitic but a loan-word from Sumerian (Su-en). The city with which Nanna-Sin was principally connected was Ur, whilst Harran in the north was also a city of the Moon-god. As both cities were associated in the biblical narrative with Abraham, there have been attempts to see in the henotheistic worship of the Moon-god the roots of the religion revealed through Abraham. Such a conclusion (popularized by Sir Leonard Woolley) is highly speculative, but certainly at a much later period (sixth century B.C.) the last New Babylonian king, Nabu-na'id, did deliberately attempt a reformation – which proved highly unpopular – based on a cult which placed Sin at the head of the pantheon. The symbol of Sin was, as one might expect, the crescent moon (which has left its legacy in Islam, just as the old sun-symbol of the cross was taken over by Christianity); since in Mesopotamia the crescent moon commonly appears with its convexity at the bottom, the idea arose of the crescent as a boat, carrying the Moon-god across the skies.

Utu-Shamash, in his daily course across the heavens, dispelled all darkness and could see all the works of man: thus, by being the 'one from whom no secrets are hid' he was the god of justice, and it was he who is portrayed on the stele of Hammurabi as symbolically handing over the just laws to that king (see plate 21B). As the god of justice Shamash is commonly represented with the rod and ring, denoting straightness and completeness, that is, right and justice. (Other deities also on occasions carry the rod and ring). His symbol was in Assyria the winged disk, in Babylonia a disk with a four-pointed star and rays, as in plate 49. The principal cities with which Shamash was associated were Sippar and Larsa.

Innin-Ishtar held a position of vast significance in Sumero-Babylonian religion, particularly after the Semites had become predominant, when she remained as virtually the only female deity, assimilating the personality and functions of other goddesses,

33A Scenes from the bronze gates of Shalmaneser III (ninth century B.C.)

33B Scenes from the bronze gates of Shalmaneser III (ninth century B.C.)

34   Assyrian forces and [bottom register] prisoners-of-war

35 Relief on an obelisk of Shalmaneser III showing [top section] Jehu of Israel offering tribute

36   Foreigners bringing tribute to Assyria (from an Assyrian bas-relief)

37 Esarhaddon with captive Egyptian kings

38 Wild horse hunt (from an Assyrian bas-relief)

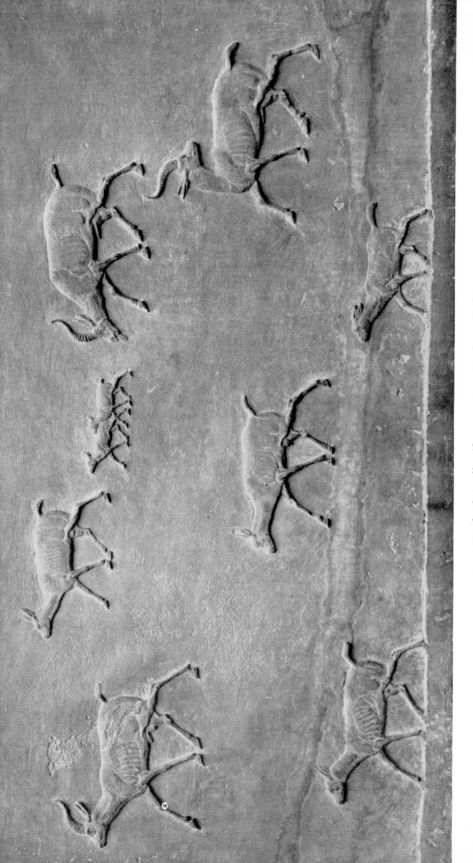

39 Herd of gazelles (from an Assyrian bas-relief)

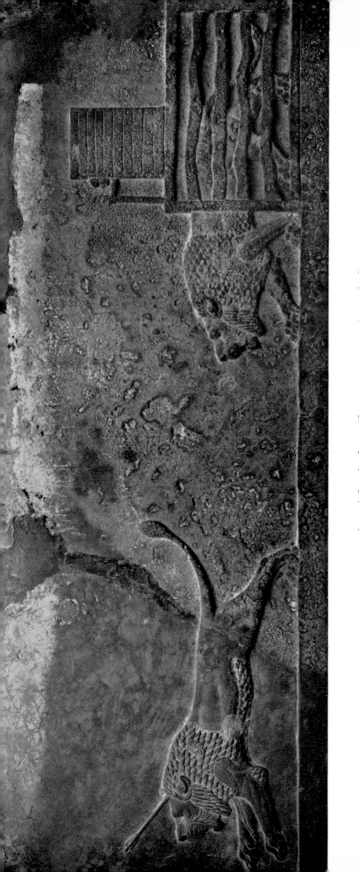

40   Lions released for the hunt (from an Assyrian bas-relief)

41   Hunting dogs, and man with nets (from an Assyrian bas-relief)

42   The deer hunt (from an Assyrian bas-relief)

43A Dying lion (from an Assyrian bas-relief)

43B Paralysed lioness (from an Assyrian bas-relief)

44A Hunting dogs (from an Assyrian bas-relief)

44B Hunting scene (from an Assyrian bas-relief)

45   Assyrian archer and squire (from an Assyrian bas-relief)

46A Assyrian tortures (from an Assyrian bas-relief)

46B (*below*) Assyrian siege craft, showing prototype of the military tank (from an Assyrian bas-relief)

47 (*opposite*) Battle scene (from an Assyrian bas-relief)

48 Assyrian slingers
(from an Assyrian
bas-relief)

so that the word *ishtar* became used as the term for 'goddess'.
A Sumerian religious text says of her:

... she is sovereign, she is the lady of lands,
In the Apsu of Eridu she has received (authority to make) decisions,
Her father Enki has given it to her,
The high-priesthood of kingship he has put in her hand.
With Anu, in the great shrine, she has set a dwelling (for herself),
With Enlil in his land [Sumer] she fixes destiny.
Monthly at the new moon, in order to make proper the divine order,
The gods of the Land [Sumer] assemble before her,
The great Anunna [major gods] do reverence to her,
My Lady pronounces the judgement of the Land [Sumer] in their
   presence.

As with Our Lady in the Catholic Church (and no suggestion is
made that the parallel extends further) Ishtar existed under many
local manifestations, felt by worshippers to be in some way
distinct, so that one finds Ishtar of Nineveh, Ishtar of Arbela,
and Ishtar of Bit-kitmuri mentioned together. Little is known
from Assyria about the goddess under her form of Ishtar of
Nineveh, and although she was certainly one of the great deities
not one ritual has been found in Assyria connected with her.
It has been suggested that this is because her worship in Assyria
had the nature of a mystery cult. She was highly honoured
outside her homeland amongst the Hurrians (in one of whose
myths she played an important part) and the Hittites; furthermore,
in the period around 1400 B.C. (in circumstances mentioned above
on page 79) she was certainly on one occasion, and possibly on a
second, sent as far afield as Egypt, for the benefit of the Pharaoh.

The two predominating characteristics of Innin-Ishtar were
her aspects as goddess of war and goddess of sexual love and
procreation. The union in one deity of these two disparate
conceptions is paradoxical to the modern mind, but it is probably
to be explained as crystallizing the idea that whenever life was
cut off in the violence of battle or created in the fervour of the
sexual act, there Ishtar was manifest. As goddess of war, Ishtar
marched before Assyrian armies and on one celebrated occasion
granted a theophany of herself to the whole army. Normally she

revealed herself to man as the Morning Star and Evening Star, that is, the planet Venus; and her two aspects – goddess of love and goddess of war – have been related to her manifestation respectively as Evening and Morning Star. Like Shamash, she was the child of the Moon-god Sin; the goddess was worshipped in most periods and places, from at least *Protoliterate* times in Erech down to the century before the Christian era in Babylon.

This goddess was frequently represented in art, especially on cylinder seals, either anthropomorphically or in the form of certain symbols. On monuments from Erech from the *Protoliterate* period onwards, the symbol of the goddess, in the Sumerian form Innin, is what is commonly known as a 'gate-post with streamers' (see illustration below).

This originally represented the bundle of reeds forming the gatepost of a reed hut: the connection between the reed hut and Innin was that a building of this type was concerned in a very early fertility cult in Erech, in which the goddess was a central figure. Under her Semitic form of a sky-deity, this goddess, as Ishtar, was often represented by an eight-pointed star.

Ishtar symbol

Not only Innin-Ishtar but also many of the other deities had both an astral and a chthonic aspect. This was a consequence, probably, of syncretism between Sumerian religion, which was primarily a fertility religion of chthonic aspect, and Akkadian religion which, like all Semitic religions, had a marked astral character. A god who retained markedly chthonic aspects to a late period was Nergal, god of the Underworld (see below, page 337). Another chthonic fertility deity was Dumuzi (Tammuz), who was closely associated with Innin. This god, who occupied a position of vast significance in popular religion, is briefly discussed in the following chapter (see pages 377 ff.).

A deity often associated with Shamash and Ishtar was Adad, the Weather-god. His manifestations were the lightning and thunder, and the ideogram used to represent his name was also the ideogram for the wind. A Weather-god Ishkur was known to the Sumerians, but had no particular prominence, whereas amongst the Semites, particularly the West Semites, the cult of the Weather-god was very marked. His Akkadian name Addu or Adadu (where the final -u is simply the case ending) represents the West Semitic Hadad, well known from such names as Benhadad and Hadad-rimmon (the latter meaning 'Hadad is the thunderer') in the Old Testament (I *Kings* xv. 18 and elsewhere, *Zechariah* xii. 11). For the West Semitic peoples who founded the kingdoms of Mari and Babylon at the beginning of the second millennium B.C. this deity was amongst the gods of first rank, and in the documents from Mari Adad is by far the most frequently occurring god-name in theophoric personal names, being well over twice as common as any other, the next in frequency being Sin, Shamash, and Dagan (the god mentioned as Dagon in *Judges* xvi. 23), which are approximately equal. Hammurabi mentions Adad in his stele, in the prologue and epilogue as well as in the laws themselves. These references leave no doubt as to the function of this god, for the laws speak of the legal consequences if 'Adad inundates' a field, that is, if the field is flooded through a cloudburst, whilst in the epilogue to the laws Adad is described as 'the lord of abundance, the controller of the floodgates of heaven and earth'. In Assyria also, Adad was amongst the greatest of the gods. From the Assyrian area there remains at Maltai a rock relief showing a line of Assyrian deities: at the head is Ashur and his consort, and those following him are Enlil, Sin, Shamash, Adad and Ishtar. In this relief and elsewhere Adad is identified by his symbol, the forked lightning: the form shown here is that which the symbol took on Cassite boundary stones.

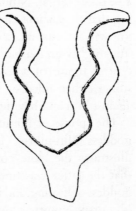

Adad symbol

Like Jehovah (*Isaiah* xix. 1), Adad rode the clouds and the thunder was his voice (compare I *Samuel* ii. 10, vii. 10, *Job* xxxvii. 4, 5, xl. 9, and so on). He

335

was also a fighting god, and in the myth explaining lunar eclipses he was, together with Shamash, won over by the hostile forces.

Another deity who bore some characteristics of a god of the storm was Ninurta (whose name is sometimes transcribed as Enurta and in older books as Ninib). One of his manifestations in the Sumerian period was Ningirsu, tutelary deity of Girsu, a quarter of the city of Lagash, whilst this god shows a number of affinities with Enlil and in some respects appears to have been assimilated to him. This is indicated by the numerical symbol for this god. Each of the gods could be designated by a symbolic number, according to the following system: Anu, head of the pantheon, was 60 (the perfect number in the sexagesimal system), Enlil 50, Ea 40, Sin 30 (with references to the days of the lunar month), Shamash 20, Ishtar 15 and Adad 10. In this system the number 50 could represent not only Enlil but also Ninurta, whilst the temple of Ningirsu at Lagash bore the name E-Ninnu, 'House of Fifty'.

As the warrior god, it was Ninurta who granted to such a king as Hammurabi 'the exalted weapon' which gave victory, and it was he who was the champion of Enlil in certain myths. Ninurta, as the great warrior and god of hunting, achieved special prominence in the Middle Assyrian period, and his cult was particularly prominent at Calah (mentioned in Genesis x. 11, 12). Like Nergal, Ninurta was a god of hunting, and it is interesting that the ancient city of Calah, specially sacred to him, is now known as Nimrud, a name which clearly represents Nimrod, 'the mighty hunter before the Lord' of Genesis x. 9. Ninurta is the central figure of a myth which tells how in his wars various stones either aided or opposed him, flint in particular rebelling against him and having inflicted upon it the penalty of flaking.

The spouse of Ninurta was Gula, who was assimilated to the goddess Nin-nibru, 'Lady of Nippur', a fact which further illustrates the close connection between Ninurta and Enlil, in that the latter was tutelary deity of Nippur. Gula herself was a goddess of healing, and is associated in art with a dog. The spouse of Ningirsu (Ninurta's local form at Lagash) was Bawa (whose name is sometimes alternatively transliterated as Babu, Baba or Bau).

A powerful and much feared god was Nergal, the god of pestilence and the Underworld and the great patron deity of Cuthah: his city Cuthah (mentioned in 2 *Kings* xvii. 24, 30) is called in magical texts 'the assembly-place of ghosts' (see above, page 310). As patron deity of Cuthah, Nergal had as consort a goddess called Laz, but as Lord of the Underworld his spouse was Ereshkigal. The goddess Ereshkigal, elder sister of Innin, was the original mistress of the Underworld, and an Akkadian myth tells how it was that Nergal came to be king in that realm. The gods made a banquet, and as Ereshkigal was unable to leave the Underworld to come up to partake, she was invited to send her messenger to receive her portion. Accordingly Ereshkigal sent her messenger to the Assembly of the gods, and in such awe was she held that on his arrival the gods stood up out of respect to his mistress. One god, however – Nergal – withheld this tribute of respect, and was ordered to go down to the Underworld, presumably to make amends. He was given detailed instructions by Ea (the god of wisdom) on how to conduct himself, being specially warned not to accept food or drink, nor to succumb to the seductions of Ereshkigal. Nergal did his best to comply, but eventually the charms of Ereshkigal were too much for him, and Nergal lay with the Queen of the Underworld in her bedchamber for six days. On the seventh day he persuaded Ereshkigal to allow him a temporary return to the upper world, to allay alarm about his safety. When Nergal had gone, Ereshkigal had a strong yearning for him, wanting him as her husband. She therefore sent up her messenger, demanding Nergal, employing as the sanction to enforce compliance with her demands her power to blight all earthly fecundity, fertility and life. Nergal returned, went up to Ereshkigal, took her by the hair and pulled her from her throne. The pair then lay together for a further six days. Finally a message came from the gods above giving permission for Nergal to remain in the Underworld, where henceforth he reigned as king.

Although the name and conception of Nergal are both Sumerian, this myth probably reflects Semitic sociology, in which leadership by a female is an unacceptable situation. (The same psychology of Semitic religion is seen in Saint Paul and the modern Church in the prejudice against women priests). The elevation of Nergal in semitized religion was also assisted by the fact that, like Marduk, he represented a hypostasis of the Sun-god, in the case of Nergal the killing sun of the Mesopotamian summer.

Many other gods could be named, but most of these had only local or seasonal significance, rather like minor saints in the Catholic Church (though it is not implied that the parallel extends further). Amongst minor gods the Fire-gods are worth mentioning in that they were commonly invoked in magical texts, being, under the names of Gibil and Gira, the destroyers of witchcraft and black magic. Under the name Nusku the Fire-god manifested himself in the sacrificial flame, consuming sacrifices and sending up incense to the great gods; his symbol in art was the lamp, though this occurs relatively rarely.

In the later period, probably beginning in the second half of the second millennium, the national gods, Marduk in Babylonia and Ashur in Assyria, achieved a position of supremacy in the pantheon. In the Sumerian period each city-state had its own god, or rather, to look at the matter from the Sumerian point-of-view, each god had a farm which took the form of a city-state, or (in some cases where neighbouring villages had grown together into one city) of a section of a city-state. Such local city-gods were not in all cases major deities in the pantheon, nor did they in all cases ultimately assimilate the personalities of major deities. Generally speaking, if the city-state extended by conquest the territory it controlled, the domain of the city-god tended to spread out coterminously, though there were factors, in particular the local loyalties of the priesthoods of the great ancient shrines, mitigating against this. The leadership of the divine Assembly, and thus in theory the political control of Babylonia, was in the hands of the two gods Anu and Enlil, and because of the remoteness of Anu, the leadership of the divine assembly often virtually belonged to Enlil, tutelary deity of Nippur. This view of things would conform with an old theory which held that the beginning of the process by which the obscure Marduk of Babylon rose to ascendancy was Hammurabi's gaining control of Nippur. Against this it has been pointed out that there is no trace of a deliberate overt attempt by Hammurabi to elevate Marduk to the rank of Anu and Enlil. It is clear that when in the 'Code' of Hammurabi Enlil gave Marduk *enlilutu kishshat nishe* 'Enlil-ship over the whole of the people (of Babylonia)', he gave it to him as to a governor, the highest authority still remaining with Anu and Enlil. In the prologue Marduk is formally subordinated to Anu and Enlil, whilst the shrine of Marduk is only mentioned after the shrines of Enlil and Ea in Nippur and Eridu. In the epilogue Hammurabi claims no relations with Marduk beyond those he enjoyed correspondingly with other deities, whilst in the reliefs at the top of the stele it is from Shamash and not from Marduk that he receives the rod and ring symbolizing justice. Moreover, in building inscriptions of Hammurabi Marduk stands after Enlil, Ninurta and Shamash, or after Anu, Enlil and Shamash, and the building inscriptions of Hammurabi's successors to the end of the dynasty show the same picture. All this gives no evidence of a deliberate elevation of Marduk at this period, and this view is borne out by an examination of the year-formulae. During the First Dynasty (as earlier) each year was given a designation, known as a year-formula (see page 57, footnote), referring to some work carried out in that year; often, since the work might be the erection of a statue or the restoration of a temple, the formula would contain the name of a god. In the god-names in these year-formulae Marduk takes the leading place only in the reign of Hammurabi's third successor, Ammi-ditana, in whose reign Marduk is concerned eleven times in forty years; however, even this seems to have been accidental and to have no great significance, for the trend does not continue in the reign of the next king. It seems that despite the political eminence of Babylon and the consequent tendency for its god to achieve an elevated rank in the pantheon, Hammurabi and his successors could not, in view of the vested interests of the priesthoods of Nippur, Ur, Sippar and Larsa, exalt Marduk to supremacy (even supposing they wished to do so). The rise of Marduk to supremacy can therefore not have taken place till the dark centuries after the fall of the Hammurabi dynasty.

In his original Sumerian form Marduk (in etymology Amar-utu-(k), meaning 'young bull of the sun') was a chthonic aspect of the Sun-god. Some consider that he was originally associated with the most ancient Sumerian city of Eridu, of whose god, Enki-Ea, he was the son. Certainly the name Esagila, 'House of the Exalted Head', later used to denote the great temple complex sacred to Marduk in Babylon, was originally applied to a temple in Eridu, as we learn from one of the creation myths. In consequence of his connection with Eridu and Enki-Ea, Marduk (commonly under the name Asar-lu-hi or Asalluhi) was a god of magic: in practice he was the god of magic *par excellence*, though theologically he always remained in this respect subordinate to his father, and the magical rituals always contain a phrase which refers to Marduk asking his father Ea for guidance on the magical procedure required (see pages 305, 306, 317).

By the time of the final recension of *Enuma Elish* (the *Epic* – or more properly *Myth* – *of Creation*, the great myth of cosmogony which was recited at the New Year Feast), Marduk had become in Babylonia the leader of the pantheon. It has commonly been held that *Enuma Elish* in its existing form dates from the Old Babylonian period, but the difficulties in the way of accepting Marduk as the supreme god at this period constitute a weighty objection, whilst the grounds for placing the origin of the existing form of *Enuma Elish* in that period are but slight. The myth makes clear the circumstances in which Marduk was promoted to supremacy. Marduk, 'created in the pure Apsu', whose 'father Ea begat him', whose 'mother Damkina gave birth to him', whose 'form was inscrutable, transcendent, passing understanding', who had four eyes and four ears, who 'when his lips moved, the fire flashed forth', appeared before Anshar, the proto-deity, and offered his services to destroy the primeval monster Tiamat:

'Lord of the gods, Destiny of the great gods,
 If I am he who is to wreak vengeance for you,
 If I am to bind Tiamat and give you life,

Set an Assembly! Make my destiny surpassing and proclaim it!
Sit together in the assembly-chamber in gladness!
Let the utterance of my own mouth fix destinies, like you'.

The Assembly of the gods was duly called, and granted to Marduk the pre-eminent power he asked for:

They set for him a great throne,
For him to take his place in counsel before his fathers:
'It is you', (they proclaimed), 'who are the honoured one among
 the great gods,
Your destiny is unrivalled, your utterance is Anu;
O Marduk! You are the honoured one among the great gods . . .
We have given you kingship over everything'.

At the end of the sixth tablet of *Enuma Elish* and in the seventh (and final) tablet, the gods in assembly proclaimed the 'fifty names' of the victorious Marduk. He was 'Son of the Sun-god', 'Marduk the god who creates everything', Marutukku the support of his land and people', 'Lugaldimmirankia' (which is Sumerian for 'King of the gods of heaven and earth'), 'Asaru, who bestows fertile land, . . . who creates corn and plants and makes greenery come forth', 'Tutu', as to whom 'no-one among the gods is like him'; he was 'Shazu, who knows the hearts and sees the inward parts of the gods', and 'Adununna, counsellor of Ea' (the god of wisdom). In his visible manifestation he was Nibiru, the planet Jupiter. Ea even assimilated Marduk to himself:

Ea heard and his heart rejoiced;
He said: 'He whose names the gods have made splendid,
Let him be like me, let his name be Ea'.

Finally, in making the last of his fifty names 'Fifty', the assembly of the gods formally assimilated him to Enlil, to whom that numerical designation belonged, and Marduk is indeed called the 'Enlil of the gods'.

This deliberate assimilation of Marduk to many of the other major gods of the pantheon has been regarded by some scholars as indicating a monotheistic tendency. However, to use the term 'monotheistic' in this connection puts the matter too strongly. A henotheistic tendency is the most that should be postulated. It is hardly necessary to emphasize the difference between this Babylonian theological trend and the emergence of monotheism in Israel. In the latter, although the Baalim may earlier have been accepted as having a real existence, they were always, in religion as revealed through the prophets, considered as differing from Jehovah ('The Lord') not only in degree but also in their essential nature. The assimilation of the supreme god to other deities, attested for Babylonia, was one of the main things against which the prophets in Israel were fighting.

As the 'Lord' *par excellence*, Marduk received the title Bel, 'Lord', just as Ishtar was often called simply Belit, 'Lady', and under this name he is mentioned in the Old Testament (*Isaiah* xlvi. 1) and in the amusing book of *Bel and the Dragon* in the Apocrypha.

The spouse of Marduk was Sarpanitum 'The shining one', who had little independent importance, though by a pun on her name, which was taken as Zer-banitum, 'Creatress of seed', she was assimilated to a Creatress-goddess Aruru.

Closely associated with Marduk was Nabu, the god of Borsippa, whose connection with the god of Babylon is referred to in the Old Testament (*Isaiah* xlvi. 1; Nebo is the Hebrew form of Nabu). Theologically Nabu was the son of Marduk, and was closely associated with him in the New Year Festival at Babylon. It has been plausibly suggested that just as Marduk supplanted Enlil in supremacy in the pantheon, and just as Enlil himself had pushed the original supreme god Anu into the background at a much earlier period, so, when Babylonian civilization finally died under competition from the new ideas from Persia, Greece and Palestine, Nabu was on the point of supplanting Marduk.

In addition to his direct relationship with Marduk, Nabu also played the part of patron god of the scribal art, and like Ea and Marduk was a god of wisdom. His spouse bore the name 'Tashmetum', which means 'Hearing', and was virtually a personification of a quality of this beneficent deity, who is described as 'wide of ear', that is to say, ready to hear prayer.

In Assyria as in Babylonia an elevation of the national deity took place, the god in this case being Ashur. The land, the old capital, and the deity all bore the same name, and it is still uncertain to which of the three the name 'Ashur' was first supplied. If the god-name could be proved to have had priority it would suggest that Ashur was originally a tribal rather than a city god, in the same way as Yahweh (Jehovah) amongst the Hebrews.

In a version of *Enuma Elish* found at the city of Ashur, the Babylonian text is faithfully reproduced, except that the name Ashur is substituted for that of Marduk. In corresponding manner, during the Sargonid period, the ideogram for Anshar, who was properly one of the aeons or proto-divinities existing before the great gods came into being, was applied to Ashur.

In the city Ashur, which was the cult-centre of the god Ashur, the god dwelt in a temple called E-shar-ra. His spouse was Ninlil, originally the feminine counterpart and consort of Enlil, whose personality Ashur is thus seen to have adopted, as he also adopted his title *Kur-gal*, 'great mountain'.

In Assyrian historical inscriptions, almost without exception, Ashur has indisputably the first place, preceding Anu, Enlil and Ea. A famous example is contained in a letter written by Sargon II to the gods, giving a detailed account of his successful campaign against Urartu and its allies in 714 B.C.; the relevant part is quoted below, on page 370, where it will be seen that Ashur takes precedence. Likewise in several friezes sculptured on the rocks in parts of Assyria, representing processions of deities, Ashur occurs at the head.

Ashur was represented in art bearing, like Shamash and Enlil, the rod and ring, and holding in his right hand the curious curved weapon commonly described by the Greek term *harpé*. He stands upon two mythical beasts, the dragon and the horned lion. Like Marduk, Ashur had assimilated many of the characteristics of the leaders of the pantheon, and – again like Marduk – had a solar aspect. In connection with the latter, it is generally considered that one form of the winged sun-disk specifically represents Ashur, though this interpretation of the symbol has been questioned.

The consort of Ashur originally was a Creatress-goddess bearing the name Sherua, but in the later period, as a consequence of the syncretism by which Ashur absorbed the leadership of the pantheon properly belonging to Enlil, his consort, as has already been pointed out, was normally Ninlil.

Another god of some interest, who may in a sense be treated as a national god, was Dagan, who was of particular (though not paramount) importance in the kingdom of Mari. This god is familiar to us from the Old Testament (*Judges* xvi. 23, 1 *Samuel* v. 2–5 and 7, 1 *Chronicles* x. 10), but was known in Babylonia long before the period referred to in the biblical passages, being found in personal names which show evidence of the West Semitic inthrust during the Isin-Larsa period; the element Dagan is also found in names of about the same period in Assyria, under similar influence. The god is also met with in the Ugaritic myths as the father of Baal: these myths are documents of the fourteenth century B.C. found at Ras Shamra on the Syrian coast, and represent ancient Canaanite religious literature.

A revealing cuneiform letter from Mari shows the manner in which Dagan once made a direct intervention in the politics of the kingdom of Mari. A certain man had had a dream, which was considered of sufficient importance to be reported to the king, Zimri-Lim. The dreamer dreamt he was on a journey and in the course of it entered the temple of Dagan in Tirqa to prostrate himself before the god. The god asked him if peace had yet been concluded between Zimri-Lim and the sheikhs of the troublesome Benjamina tribes*, and was told that this had not yet been achieved. Dagan was not a bit surprised and commented:

'Why do the messengers of Zimri-Lim not present themselves regularly to me and deposit his full reports before me? Were that done, I would long ago have delivered the sheikhs of the Benjamina tribes into the hands of Zimri-Lim'.

The dreamer was instructed in his dream to pass on the hint, and

* There is nothing beyond the name to point to any connection between these tribes and the biblical tribe of Benjamin, and – as some scholars (most recently I. J. Gelb in *Journal of Cuneiform Studies* XV (1961), 37–38) have pointed out – even the reading of the name in the Mari documents as 'Benjamina' is not certain; it might instead be 'Mar-jamina' or simply 'Jamina'.

had dutifully done so. The account indicates the national status of Dagan as able to bestow victory.

The Service of the Gods

The gods, as the original lords of the temple estates and cities, received from the human inhabitants, who were their tenants, the rents and services which were their due. Service of the gods was not an optional extra: in ancient Mesopotamian theology, explicitly stated in more than one creation story, humans were specifically created in order to relieve the gods from the tedium of doing work (see above, pages 162 f.). In order to obtain their rights, as well as to mediate their beneficent powers to the people, it was necessary for the gods to appoint human representatives in their estates. In the original social scheme, so far as we can at present penetrate into the shadows of proto-history, the god's human representative was known as the *En*, who must have been a priest-king and fertility figure in the manner of the priest-kings of Frazer's *Golden Bough*, and like them may originally have met a ceremonial death, of which the so-called 'royal tombs' of Ur (of the *Early Dynastic* III period), may contain the willing victims (see below, pages 372 ff.). The *En* in the earliest period, as the immediate representative of the deity, actually lived in the temple, in an apartment known as the *Giparu*; Gilgamish represents a notable early example of this personage.

Still at a very early period in Sumerian society a development took place in which the *En* moved out from the temple into a separate palace, and related to this was the division of functions. The temporal ruler (who still however continued to play a part in a vast area of religious and temple matters) became the *Ensi*, whilst within the temple a priest attended to the immediate day-to-day needs of the god. Later, with the coalescence of several city-states into one political unit (particularly if it included Nippur), the *Ensi* of the predominant city became a *Lugal* or king. Throughout the whole of Babylonian and Assyrian history, however, the *Ensi* or *Lugal* remained ultimately the direct representative of the god, and was responsible for ensuring the fertility of the land by participation in New Year rituals. Meanwhile in the temples an elaborate priestly administration developed. The sphere of activity of this priestly administration covered the economic as well as the sacerdotal sphere, and the distinction between the two would not necessarily have been accepted as valid in the ancient world: for convenience, however, the sacerdotal aspects of the priesthood is treated here as far as possible separately.

A term employed from Old Babylonian times for those priests who were admitted to all parts of the temple is *Erib-biti* (literally 'temple entrant'): sometimes it means the entire priesthood of a temple, though in New Babylonian times it generally denoted specifically priests below those of highest rank. The *Erib-biti* priests appear to have carried out the ordinary ceremonials for the regular offerings to the gods and to have assisted other classes of officials in special kinds of ceremonies, as when we read that

> the chief *Erib-biti* will lead the torch from the ziggurat, with the *Mashmashu* priests, *Kalu* exorcists and singers . . .

or

> the king and the *Erib-biti* go to the sanctuary, and the *Erib-biti* extends the water basin for hand-washing to Ishtar.

The *Mashmashu* and the *Ashipu* (a term used either of the *Mashmashu*'s assistant or of a specialized counterpart) were classes of priests concerned with incantations; it is a word related to *Ashipu* which is used in the *Book of Daniel* (ii. 10 and elsewhere) for 'enchanter'. Incantations of the type employed by the *Mashmashu* have already been adduced, and the curriculum for the training of this class of priest has been referred to; see above, pages 308 f.

Many of the rituals and incantations mentioned above were conducted by the *Mashmashu* not in the temple area but in the home of the afflicted man. The *Mashmashu* did however have tasks to perform in the regular running of the temple, and it was he who performed the purification rites before the temple rituals.

The *Kalu* (Sumerian *Gala*) was an exorcist, part of whose

task was to calm the heart of the god by his music. The text of a ritual exists, giving details of the preparation of the sacred drum employed by this type of priest.

The *Naru* (another term of Sumerian origin) was the 'chanter', and there were female as well as male members. These were closely connected with the *Kalu* exorcists, and the two classes took part together in singing laments.

In the cult of the temple the chief director was the *Sheshgallu* (from the Sumerian *shesh-gal*, 'great guard'). He it was who, at a late period, officiated in Babylon at the New Year Feast and bestowed upon the king his insignia. Sacrifices were performed by priests called *Shangu* (Sumerian *Sanga*), at the head of whom was the *Shangamahhu* ('Supreme *Sanga*'): originally the title *Sanga* belonged to the king, but was assumed by a separate priest in the mid-third millennium. Two classes of official employed for certain practical aspects of the temple rituals were the *Mari-ummani* ('Craftsmen') and *Nash-patri* ('Swordbearer'). The former dealt with such tasks as preparing images required in the rituals, whilst to the latter fell the duty of actually slaughtering the sacrificial beasts; other rituals in which the *Nash-patri* was concerned involved the symbolic cutting off of the head of certain images.

There were other classes of priests (called respectively *Ramku* and *Pashishu*) who dealt with washing and anointing rituals. Washing rituals took place in a part of the temple or palace called the *Bit-rimki* 'Ablution house'.

The great science of omen-interpretation required its own technologists. These were the *Baru* priests ('Observers'). Their influence on affairs of state could be enormous, for in their hands was the interpretation of the signs when the king brought a problem of statecraft before them. Often the *Baru* diviner used lecanomancy, working with his *makeltu* or divining-cup: the reader will not fail to notice the parallel with the magical technique favoured by Joseph (*Genesis* xliv. 5). The *Baru* might accompany the army, and would win great honour by successful prediction, and contrariwise disgrace by failure. In their interpretation of omens the *Baru* priests made use of commentaries, which were arranged in sections under the technical terms relating to the organs, particularly the liver, of the sacrificed beast. The first sacrifice had to be followed by a second as a check, and in certain conditions by a third. The basic theory seems to have been that the god, when properly approached before the sacrifice and informed of the problem under consideration, 'wrote the oracle in the body of the victim'.

Specialized classes of omen interpreters were the *Sha'ilu* priests, who are often mentioned beside the *Baru* priests, though the latter seems to have had higher status. Female members of the class (known as *Sha'iltu*) are also found, and the texts suggest that it was women in particular who made use of the *Sha'iltu* diviners to ascertain the will of the gods; the *Sha'iltu* was apparently outside the official religion centred on the temple. The *Sha'ilu* priest is in one hymn described as the one who solves dreams, and this seems to have been his primary function, though it does not appear that the services of his female counterpart in popular religion were restricted to this. The *Sha'ilu* seems to have applied for a solution of the dream to the deity who sent it, but the actual technique employed is not clear: it has been suggested that it may have been performed by observation of the smoke from burning incense.

Other classes of male personnel found in the temple were the *Kurgarru* and *Assinnu* (or *Issinnu*), probably eunuchs, who took part as actors, possibly in female dress, in cultic performances: there is a text referring to

> the *Kurgarru* and the *Issinnu* whose virility Ishtar has changed into femininity to wear the mask before the people.

Both classes carried certain objects (weapons or tools) as their insignia. Professor A. L. Oppenheim has suggested that the mythical precursors of these sexless beings were created to circumvent a curse of Ereshkigal: the latter, Queen of the Underworld, at the time Ishtar was her prisoner banned any deity or creature, male or female, from entering and leaving the Underworld to save the captive. It was the clever god Ea who got round this curse by creating sexless beings, so rescuing Ishtar.

In addition to the classes mentioned there were associated with the temple a number of female officiants, some of whom might properly be called priestesses, others temple-prostitutes. At the head of them was the *Entu* (a feminine form of the noun from the Sumerian *En*), whose status might reasonably be rendered as 'high-priestess' and who was, according to her Sumerian ideogram, 'the wife of the god', or (according to an alternative interpretation) 'the lady (who is) a deity'. The ideogram for *Entu* might also denote a class of priestess called *Ugbabtu*, of lower social standing but of related function in the cult. The *Entu* was of very high rank, and kings might make their daughters the *Entu* of a god, as did Nabu-na'id his daughter in the temple of the Moon-god in Ur. In the earliest period the *Entu* was the female counterpart of the *En* in the Sacred Marriage upon which the fertility of the land depended, and in this sense was truly the human 'wife of the god'. This was the basis of the report in Herodotus (I 181–2) that on top of the eight decks of the stepped temple [the ziggurat] at Babylon

> stands a great temple with a sumptuously-equipped couch in it. . . . No-one spends the night there except one Assyrian woman, chosen by the god himself; or so say the Chaldaeans who are the priests of Bel. These Chaldaeans also say – not that I believe them – that the god himself comes into the temple and takes his rest on the couch. The Egyptians tell a similar story about Thebes in Egypt . . . . Both women, we are told, are forbidden intercourse with men.

The *Entu* lived in a part of the temple called the *Giparu* (or *Egipar*), which was also originally the term applied to the residence of the *En*. To judge by the two qualified terms – 'great *Entu*' and 'little *Entu*' – which sometimes occur, there seem to have been *Entu* priestesses of greater or lesser importance. It is clear from various omen texts, predicting disaster if a man had intercourse with an *Entu*, that (as Herodotus says) these women were expected to live in chastity. An *Entu* could, we gather from the laws of Hammurabi, under certain conditions marry, though the general assumption in the texts is that any son she may have will be adopted. This probably indicates that she had to remain virgin until after the age of child-bearing, when perhaps she retired from the god's service, as did the vestal virgins of Rome after thirty years. It has been alternatively suggested that either such women were sterilized (for which there is little convincing evidence) or that in the case of an inconvenient conception, abortion (certainly practised in Assyria, where it was a capital offence) was resorted to. The mother of Sargon of Agade was by tradition a woman of this class, who disposed of her unwanted child by exposing him.

The *Entu* is mentioned in connection with many of the ancient sacred cities (Ur, Erech, Larsa, Lagash, Isin, Sippar, Nippur, Kish and Ashur). The office seems to have passed largely into desuetude some time after the Old Babylonian period, and Nabu-na'id in the sixth century B.C., describing how the god Nanna 'expressed a wish for a high-priestess' refers to the fact that 'the office of *Entu* had been forgotten [at Ur] since distant days'.

A second class of temple woman, related to the *Entu* but rather lower in rank, was the *Naditu* (or *Naṭitu*; the exact transliteration is uncertain). Like the *Entu* she might have a husband, but the Babylonian laws do not envisage her, any more than the *Entu*, as bearing children, and conventions for the two classes of women in this respect were probably the same.

Many – though not all – of these temple-women lived within the temple precincts in an area called the *gagu*, 'cloister', a complex of buildings having its own administration and land. A great part of our knowledge of them comes from the laws of Hammurabi, and it has been suggested that the frequent mention in these laws of classes of temple-women indicates that they were in danger of becoming a depressed class, for whose protection Hammurabi, with his avowed purpose of succouring the weak, found it necessary to legislate.

A class of woman whose name at least is found in the Old Testament is the *Qadishtu*: the Hebrew equivalent *Qadeshah* is translated in the Revised Version (*Deuteronomy* xxiii. 17) as 'harlot' alongside the male counterpart 'sodomite', which latter was certainly found at one period within the temple cult (2 *Kings*

xxiii. 7). There is good reason for supposing that the *Qadishtu*, like her Hebrew counterpart, was dedicated to ritual prostitution. An Old Assyrian marriage contract stipulates that the man concerned shall not take another woman in the country but may have intercourse with a *Qadishtu* in the Town (that is, the city of Ashur). From the fifth century B.C. Herodotus in a much-quoted passage states (I 199) that in Babylon

> every woman must once in her life go and sit in the temple of Aphrodite and there have intercourse with a stranger. . . . Most seat themselves in the temple precincts wearing a band of plaited* cord round their heads. . . . Gangways are marked off in every direction through the crowds of women, by which the men may pass along and make their choice. Once a woman has taken her seat she may not return home until some stranger has cast a silver coin into her lap and taken her outside the temple to lie with her. As he throws the coin, the stranger has to say 'In the name of the goddess Mylitta'. [The word represents Akkadian *Mu'allitu* 'the one who brings to birth', a title of Ishtar.] The piece of silver may be ever so small, but it may not be refused, and that coin is considered sacred. The woman is not allowed to be choosy – she must go with the first man who throws her the money. When she has surrendered herself, her duty to the goddess has been rendered and she may return home; from that time it will be impossible to seduce her, no matter how large a sum you offer her'.

Though it is generally agreed that the statement of Herodotus is misleading as it stands and that the historian was under a misapprehension, it seems likely that the basis of the story was in the customs connected with *Qadishtu* women. The *Kulmashitu* may have been a similar class of woman.

Offerings to the Gods; Sacrifices

On early cylinder seals worshippers are commonly represented as bringing an offering of a goat to the deity. This illustrates the conception that high amongst the services the gods required from their worshippers was the provision of food, drink, and

---

* This mention of plaiting is reminiscent of 2 *Kings* xxiii. 7, in which it is said that the women associated with the Sodomites 'wove hangings'.

oil for anointing. Thus, for instance, we find oil mentioned in account tablets, which contain such entries as

> 5 *qa* of best Mari oil for anointing the throne of Shamash

or

> ½ *qa* of best Mari oil for Nergal

or

> 1 *qa* of *diqaratum* oil for anointing the gods.

The gods enjoyed regular meals, two or – at some places in the late period – four a day, a 'great' and a 'little' meal morning and evening placed on tables before the divine images. Rimush of Agade in the third millennium already dedicated bread and beer for the daily offerings for the table of Shamash, and a text from the Seleucid period gives details of the provisions for the gods at Erech, which amongst other things included a daily total of about ten hundredweight of bread (made from flour which was three-quarters barley and the rest wheat), fifty sheep, two oxen, one calf, eight lambs, and fifty-four containers of beer of different kinds and of wine. This recalls the details of the story of *Bel and the Dragon*, in which

> the Babylonians had an idol, called Bel, and there were spent upon him every day twelve great measures of fine flour, and forty sheep, and six firkins of wine. [*Bel and the Dragon*, verse 3].

Amongst other foods provided for the meals of the gods were honey, ghee, fine oil, milk, dates, figs, salt, hydromel, cakes, poultry, fish, vegetables, and 'golden fruit' – perhaps some kind of citrus. Certain animals and other foods were taboo to particular deities: thus it is specified that mutton must not come near one god, beef near a second or poultry near a third.

The meal of the god was technically a banquet to which other deities were invited, and at which the human worshippers and even the dead might be present. The gods themselves received specified parts of the animals, both in the daily offerings and special sacrifices, the remainder going to the king, the priests and the temple staff.

The regular daily offerings to the gods were called *sattukku* or *ginu* (terms which were almost synonymous), whilst *guqqu* denoted some kind of monthly offering. A distinction was made between vegetable sacrifices (*nindabu*) and animal sacrifices, the latter including many rituals and feasts in which sheep, goats or cattle were slaughtered. As in Israel (compare *Isaiah* i. 11, *Exodus* xxix. 16), the blood was poured out before the deity, for which reason the term applied to the animal sacrifice was *niqu*, properly 'pouring'. The choice of the victim, most commonly a sheep, was as carefully made as in the Old Testament (compare *Exodus* xii. 5), conditions being specified as to age, colour, virginity, whether entire, whether grass-fed or corn-fed, and so on. The throat of the animal was cut by the *Nash-paṭri* ('sword bearer'), who recited an incantation the while, the welling blood itself being a libation. The decapitated head was placed near an incense-burner and aspersed with holy water, to the accompaniment of another incantation. The actual sacrifices were offered on special altars or on the roofs of temples, by a *Shangu* priest.

There are texts which enumerate different types of offerings and sacrifices, such as one mentioning 'the *niqu* of the king, the *niqu* of the worshipper, *ginu* offerings, offerings for *eshsheshu* days, for night offerings, and 'greeting-of-the-house' [that is, early morning ceremonies]'. There were special sacrifices on particular days of the month, notably the day of the new moon and the day of the full moon, that is, the first and the fifteenth days of the month in the lunar calendar. (The day of the full moon bore the name *shapatu*, from which comes the Hebrew term Sabbath; the latter, later applied to the last day of the week, originally had this same meaning of 'day of full moon', as is still evident, for example, in 2 *Kings* iv. 23, *Isaiah* i. 13). The *eshsheshu* was the name given to the festival which originally fell on the first, seventh and fifteenth days (that is, it subsumed the feasts of the new and full moon): later the *eshsheshu* festivals were shifted and celebrated more frequently – up to eight days in the month in the case of Erech. We read in the cuneiform tablets of meat 'which is served upon the table of Bel on the day of the *eshsheshu* festivals', and there is also mention of various kinds of cakes for these feasts, recalling the passage in *Jeremiah*

vii. 18, in which 'the women knead the dough, to make cakes to the queen of heaven'. (See also *Jeremiah* xliv. 19).

Another aspect of the cult was the libation (incidentally mentioned above), which was distinct from the drinks given to the gods at their meal-times. Libations were poured out to the gods from early Sumerian times, in the form of water, beer or wine, oil, or the blood of a sacrificial animal. (There is a striking instance of a water libation in 2 *Samuel* xxiii. 16, in which it is recorded that David, receiving the water that had been brought to him, 'would not drink thereof, but poured it out unto the Lord'). The libation in Mesopotamia is frequently represented in art, and the scene has been formally sub-divided into six types, according to such details as whether the liquid is poured over an altar, into a vessel, on to the ground or over an animal; it is not, however, clear in what fundamental ways the various ritual actions differed from one another. A famous Assyrian frieze represents Ashurbanipal as making a libation over the lions he has killed in the chase, but the accompanying text, although confirming our view as to what is actually happening, adds nothing to our understanding of the underlying purpose of this libation. In the earliest period the officiant is sometimes represented naked, suggesting an association amongst the Sumerians of nudity with the libation ritual, but this is very rare after the Agade period, and ceases altogether after the period of the Third Dynasty of Ur.

The incense-burner was a very common feature of the temple ritual, and the burning of aromatic woods could be applied either as a purification rite or as a service to the deity, for the gods delighted in sweet odours. Herodotus states that about two and a half tons of frankincense was burnt annually in the temple of Bel in Babylon, but this cannot yet be confirmed from cuneiform sources, in which the burners used in the cult are generally stated to contain aromatic woods such as cypress and cedar, rather than the gum resins, imported from South Arabia, to which the name 'frankincense' properly belongs.

The Temple Complex

Man was created for the service of the gods and the gods had themselves prescribed the rites, ceremonies and services which were due from man. It was within the temple complex that most of these took place.

The great temple complexes have in some cases been traced back by archaeological investigation to their earliest beginnings, showing that the original temple was a very modest shrine, whereas in its final form the temple complex might cover an area of many acres, and would include buildings of numerous types. The main single feature in the temple area was the ziggurat, the great stepped tower of three to seven stages which dominated the city. The size of the ziggurat varied from city to city, but its base would be up to a hundred yards square and the whole structure perhaps as much as fifty yards high. On the top stood a small 'high temple', probably covered in blue glazed tiles. The precise religious function of these towers is still in dispute, but it can with assurance be said what they were not. They were not (at least primarily) observatories, and they were not tombs of kings: the ziggurats were in no sense parallel in function to the pyramids of Egypt and any external similarities between examples of the two were accidental.

The idea that a ziggurat represented the cosmic mountain as the tomb not of a king but of a dying and resurgent god may not be rejected with quite the same confidence. Substantial (though by no means conclusive) evidence has been adduced in favour of this theory. Amongst such evidence, it is significant that the same technical term, *gigunu*, was applied to the ziggurat and to some structure at a lower level. The suggestion has been made that in the latter sense *gigunu* referred to some kind of subterranean burial chamber, but this has not been proved and, indeed, now seems unlikely. A strong argument against interpreting ziggurats as tombs of dying and resurgent gods is that not all gods associated with ziggurats did die and rise again, whilst it is now far from certain (see pages 381 and 385) that even Marduk and Tammuz – the two gods formerly supposed to have this characteristic beyond doubt – were in official religion actually thought to do so.

Other scholars have seen the ziggurat as the throne of the

deity, and have pointed to such passages as *Isaiah* xiv. 13 for a parallel to the conception. The ziggurat has also been regarded as an immense altar, an idea for which *Ezekiel* xliii. 13 to 17 – which describes an altar in the form of a miniature ziggurat – has been adduced in support.

The line of interpretation of the ziggurat most commonly accepted today is basically the theory of W. Andrae, though various scholars have modified it in a number of respects. Andrae pointed out that in connection with a ziggurat there were two temples closely associated, one on top of the ziggurat and the other at its foot. The 'high temple' was, according to Andrae, the residence proper of the deity, who at appropriate times came down to the 'low temple'. Critics point out that this theory, based primarily on architectural considerations, does not do full justice to the texts, which in some cases specifically speak of the 'low temple' as the dwelling-place of the deity. Some scholars have therefore modified the theory by regarding the 'high temple' as a temporary resting place for the god on his way between heaven and his 'low temple'. The stages of the ziggurat are then taken either as a mere means of attaining a suitable elevation for the 'high temple', or as a kind of ladder set up to heaven from earth. In connection with the latter theory one may consider the story of the tower of Babel in *Genesis* xi. 3–5, which undoubtedly is related to a Mesopotamian ziggurat, or the mention in Jacob's dream (*Genesis* xxviii. 12) of the ladder of which we are told that it was 'set up on the earth, and the top of it reached to heaven: and behold the angels of God ascending and descending on it'.

H. Lenzen, the leading authority on the ziggurat, points out certain difficulties in the way of accepting Andrae's theory in its totality as an explanation of the origin of the ziggurat, since in the early stages of Mesopotamian civilization there seems in some cases to have been only a 'high temple' and no 'low temple'. Lenzen emphasizes that the 'high temple' was not a mere resting place for the deity, but that an actual cult was practised there: in this sense the ziggurat was, therefore, indeed a giant altar.

Inside the temple near the foot of the ziggurat was the cella of the principal god and a number of smaller chapels sacred to associated deities, whilst outside these main shrines was a great courtyard where the populace assembled at the time of festivals. There were rooms for housing the equipment (such as garments, musical instruments, tools and vehicles) employed in the cult, and there would also be a temple library (*girginakku*), generally associated with a temple of Nabu, the god of the scribal art. Special quarters for the priests and priestesses existed, the latter living in an area called the *gagu*, of which the *bit ashtammi* ('brothel') seems to have been a part. There would be workshops for the artificers, and the temple complex would have its own quay and its warehouses and barns for storing the products of the temple lands and the goods obtained by trade.

The god himself stood, represented by his image or symbol, in the long chamber which was the focal point of the temple. The statue might stand on a podium, possibly in a niche behind a curtain to protect him from profane eyes, The main entrance to this long cella was variously on the short side opposite to the god at the far end, or in the long side, in which latter case the view through the open doorway would not fall upon the deity: the difference is related to a different attitude to exposure of the deity to the public gaze. In the kingdom of Mari, it appears, a traveller passing through a city might without much ceremony go into the temple to offer worship to the deity (see above, page 344), but there is no evidence that such public access to the god was commonly the case in Babylonia or Assyria.

The divine image itself would be carved from a piece of wood, and ornamented with metals and precious stones, a fact of which *Isaiah* (xliv. 12–20) made merry play. For the Babylonians there was a definite point in the manufacture of the idol at which the deity took up his dwelling therein, and a ritual is known for the 'opening of the mouth'. Two pots of holy water were provided in the workshop and a preliminary 'washing of the mouth' of the newly-made image performed. The officiant then recited incantations, one of which announced to the god: 'From this time forth you shall go before your father Ea'. The god was then led at night by torchlight to the river bank, and seated on a reed-mat facing east. Offerings and libations were made, incantations recited, and the washing of the mouth repeated. The god was then turned to the west and further offerings, libations, incantations and washings of the mouth performed. In the morning, after further offerings and incantations, each doubtless making magically perfect some part of the statue, a ram was sacrificed, and then came the incantation 'Holy image that is perfected by a great ritual'. The priest then 'opened the eyes of the god' by touching them with a twig of the magical tamarisk, and the god was then led by the hand, to the accompaniment of the incantations 'Foot that advances' and 'When he goes in the street', to his temple. After offerings had been made at the gate the god was led in, brought to his shrine, and placed on his throne. After a fourteenth and final mouth-washing the insignia of divinity were brought and placed upon the god at night.

Within the temples, as early as Sumerian times, the gods might enjoy the company both of divine courtiers and of statues of worshippers: thus the king might install a statue representing him praying to the god, and texts state explicitly that such a statue would continually serve as a reminder to put the king's prayer before the god.

The gods were not permanently confined to the temples. At particular festivals they came forth, richly clad and borne in honour on the shoulders of the priests to be displayed to the adorants. Chance movements of the image on such occasions, giving an apparent nod to a worshipper or a start away from him, were loaded with ominous significance. The god might also pay ceremonial visits to other deities on the occasion of the great festivals; thus Nabu of Borsippa regularly visited his father Marduk at the New Year Festival in Babylon.

II

The King

IN Mesopotamia kingship was one of the underlying concepts of civilization: it was one of the gifts won by Innin (Inanna) from Enki to bestow upon the people of the Sumerian civilization of which the centre was at Erech (see above, page 36). Kingship, the *Sumerian King List* tells us, was lowered from heaven; at the time of the Flood it must have returned to heaven, for it was lowered again subsequently. Thus, for the Sumerians and their successors, kingship as an institution, and even its insignia, existed before, and independently of, the human king. In the *Epic of Etana* we read

At that time no tiara had been worn, . . .
Sceptre, headband, tiara and staff were deposited in heaven before
   Anu;
There used to be no (royal) direction of her [the goddess's] people;
Kingship (then) came down from heaven . . . .

The king himself was chosen by the gods and invested with the attributes of kingship by them. Enlil, from early times the national god of Sumer, is himself called 'king of the lands', and he was later recognized as 'king of the gods' even in Assyria, where the Assyrian national god Ashur was assimilated to him.

Historically the king was originally elected by the Assembly, and a memory, and possibly an actual example, of this is found as late as the Agade period (*circa* 2300 B.C.). A text, which some would regard as incorporating a genuine historical tradition, reads:

> In the 'common of Enlil', a field belonging to Esabad, the temple of Gula, Kish assembled; and they raised to kingship Ipkhur-kish, a man of Kish . . . .

Originally the king was no more than *primus inter pares*, a temporary leader elected in time of war, but this situation had been superseded before the end of the *Early Dynastic* period. The Sumerian term translated 'king' (*Lugal*) basically means merely 'great man' and was originally used not only of the political head of the state but also of a master in relation to his slaves.

Inasmuch as a great deal of attention has been paid by students of comparative religion to a supposed pattern in the ancient Near Eastern conception of kingship, it is worth pointing out that there are significant divergences between the Sumerian and the Hebrew theories of kingship. When kingship finally arose in Israel, it evoked severe religious disapproval in some quarters, where it was felt that the Lord alone was king (1 *Samuel* viii. 7). The institution of kingship was in fact not a native Hebrew institution at all but one introduced in imitation of foreign practice, as is explicitly recognized in *Deuteronomy* xvii. 14 and 1 *Samuel* viii. 5. Kingship in Israel was thus in the main stream of official religious thought considered a specifically human institution, though the man appointed had to be chosen or at least approved by the Lord. Except in the sense that the Lord himself was king, kingship was certainly not one of the basic concepts of Hebrew civilization.

The extensive discussion of the idea of 'divine kingship' in Mesopotamia and the rest of the ancient Near East has resulted in the general conclusion that it is wrong to speak of the king in Mesopotamia as divine. Later in this chapter there is employed at one point the expression 'the king as god': this is correct in the context, which refers to a point in a ritual at which the king had been identified with the god for the Sacred Marriage, but it is wrong to speak of the king as a god outside the context of this ritual. Certain kings, notably all but the first of those of the Third Dynasty of Ur, on some occasions had their name written with the cuneiform sign DINGIR (the determinative indicating that the following name is that of something in the class of the divine), and it has been argued from this that the particular kings concerned were in fact regarded as gods. Against this it has been pointed out that even the kings who had their names written in this manner did not necessarily do so from the beginning of their reigns, nor in every city of the kingdoms over which they ruled, and it has been suggested with plausibility that the apparent apotheosis of the kings in question derived from the deity having chosen them, in some way yet unknown, as fitted to represent the god at the Sacred Marriage. Even in the period of the Third Dynasty of Ur there were significant differences between so-called 'divine kings' and gods proper. It is true that the names of such kings occur on the lists of food-offerings with the names of gods, but food-offerings have to be distinguished from sacrifices, and sacrifices proper were made only to gods and never to kings. Furthermore, a supposedly divine king might build temples to the gods 'for the king's own life', indicating acceptance of a primary difference in status between gods and divine kings.

The king was, from the religious point of view, primarily the link between the gods and the people whom they had created to do them service. He represented the people before the gods, and in turn was the pipe-line through which the gods regulated the affairs of the state for the people.

As the welfare of the nation depended upon the welfare of the king, any danger threatening the king was a matter of grave import. When omens and portents announced such impending dangers, special measures had to be taken. In certain circumstances a man would be chosen as substitute for the king and even (according to one interpretation) put to death in his place. This institution is best known from Assyrian letters of the reign of Esarhaddon, though it is also attested for other periods. The earliest occurrence known is from the Old Babylonian period, when (circa 1860 B.C.) a king of Isin died whilst eating hot porridge at a time when a substitute king had been appointed temporarily: the substitute remained permanently on the throne.

The actual procedure for appointing a royal substitute in Assyrian times seems to have been set in motion by the fear of an eclipse, which threatened dire disaster to the king. It seems likely that the substitute was chosen by the gods through an inspired priestess. In the period of Esarhaddon the substitute was enthroned for a hundred days and enjoyed all the privileges of royalty, whilst the real king and his sons were strictly confined to the palace. The role of the substitute king was to take to himself all the evil forebodings that threatened the king: a letter reports of such a substitute that 'he has taken upon himself all the omens of heaven and earth', a statement which might refer to a special ritual, though this has not been proved. Once the substitute had taken upon himself the evil omens threatening the king, he died, or so many scholars, on an interpretation supported by an account handed down in Greek by the Babylonian priest Berossus, suppose. The French scholar R. Labat, however, has acutely pointed out that the actual phrase used in the letter speaking of the outcome of the substitution is that the substitute 'went to his fate'. Now 'to go to one's fate' is certainly a common euphemism for 'to die', but it generally refers specifically to a natural death, and – as Labat reminds us – an untimely death is sometimes described by the phrase 'he died in a day not of his fate'. This makes it less likely that the statement that the sub- stitute king 'went to his fate' meant that he died a violent death by execution. Labat for this reason takes the phrase to mean that the substitute placed himself in readiness for any possible death awaiting the king: the implication of the phrase would then be that it was in the hands of fate whether the substitute king died or not, but whatever misfortune was to befall would occur to the substitute and not to the real king.

It may be noted that the institution of the substitute king (whether it involved ultimate execution or not) was quite dis- tinct from the widely attested practice in primitive religion of destroying the king himself when his powers began to fail: this latter practice certainly occurred in Egypt in prehistoric times, whilst some authorities argue that it survived far into historical times. The institution of the substitute king is not, however, known from Egypt, where no mere human could have taken the place of the god-king who was the Pharaoh.

The various Babylonian stories of creation, differing though they do in detail, have this in common, that the creation of man was intended to provide for the service of the gods. Prominent amongst the consequent duties of the king was, therefore, his responsibility for the house of the god. In a Sumerian creation story the goddess Nintu says

'We will make mankind to dwell in their settlements,
That he may build cities . . .,
That he may cast the brickwork of our houses in a clean spot'.

Thus it was not only a mark of piety but an absolute duty for the king to give attention to the building or restoration of the temples of the gods. There exist many representations of kings and princes carrying out this pious duty: plate 18A offers one example, and one may also instance a stele showing Ur-Nammu, founder of the Third Dynasty of Ur, bearing on his shoulder the implements with which he was going to lay the foundations of a ziggurat. This conception, of the duty to provide a house for the god, is not unknown to us from the Old Testament, since it was a matter of concern to king David, who

said unto Nathan the prophet, See now, I dwell in an house of cedar, but the ark of God dwelleth within curtains (2 *Samuel* vii. 2).

In one of the ancient Canaanite myths (*circa* 1400 B.C.) found at Ras Shamra (ancient Ugarit) in Syria, it was likewise a matter of concern that the god Baal had no proper house. In the Babylonian *Epic of Creation*, when Marduk had won victory over Tiamat for the gods, they themselves declared:

'Now O Lord, who has established our deliverance,
What can we bestow upon you as a favour?
Let us make a shrine . . .'

This, however, was before the creation of mankind, which by the generous impulse of Marduk was subsequently undertaken to relieve the gods of just such tasks.

Attention to the restoration of temples had important practical consequences, for if a temple fell into disrepair or was destroyed the gods might leave it. Esarhaddon relates that because of his anger with events in Babylonia, Marduk allowed

Babylon to be devastated, whereupon 'the gods who dwelt therein flew off like birds and went up to heaven'.

The restoration of a temple or the building of a new temple was an undertaking requiring the most complicated rituals, as well as the most precise investigations to ensure that the god's will was properly understood and carried out. The decision to rebuild a temple was actually made by the god, who informed the king of what was required. One of the best known instances of divine instructions for the building of a temple is found in the celebrated dream of Gudea. In the words of Gudea's inscription:

> In the dream there was a man, who was as huge as heaven, as huge as earth. As to his upper part he was a god, as to his wings he was the Imdugud bird,* as to his lower part she was the hurricane. At his right and left there crouched a lion. He commanded me to build a temple, but I did not (fully) understand his intention. The sun rose before me from the horizon. There was a woman – who could she have been? – . . . . She held a stylus of gleaming metal and inscribed on a tablet the 'Star of the propitious heavens' and meditated thereon. A second hero was present. He had his arms bent and held a slab of lapis lazuli in his hands and set down thereon the ground-plan of the House (to be built). He put before me the (ceremonially) pure hod, arranged the pure brick-mould for me (and) fixed the 'brick of decision of fate' in the brick-mould.

Gudea had therefore betaken himself to the temple of the goddess chiefly concerned with dreams to have the meaning of his dream confirmed and amplified.

Nearly two millennia later the New Babylonian king Nabu-na'id similarly received instructions through a dream about the rebuilding of the temple of the god Sin at Harran. He records:

> At the beginning of my eternal(ly ordained) reign (the great gods) made me see a dream. Marduk the Great Lord and Sin the Luminary of Heaven and Earth were standing together. Marduk said to me: 'Nabu-na'id, king of Babylon, bring bricks in your horse-drawn processional wagons and build Ehulhul [the temple of Sin in Harran], and let Sin, the Great Lord, set up his dwelling in

* See plate 10.

its midst'. Reverently I said to Marduk, Chief [literally 'Enlil'] of the gods: '(As to) the House of which you command the (re)building, the Ummanmanda [see page 138] surround it and their strength is formidable'. Marduk however said to me: 'The Ummanmanda of whom you speak, he, his land, and the kings who go at his side no longer exist. . . .'

Explicit instructions of the kind quoted might be amplified or even in some cases entirely replaced by the revelation of the divine will through omens. Sometimes this was very direct in form, for on occasions the winds would blow away all the accumulated sand from a ruined temple, indicating that

they wanted the ground plan to become visible.

Commonly, however, the omens would be drawn from the examination of the liver of a sacrificial animal, and indeed Nabu-na'id lists a whole series of such omens taken to ensure that the time was ripe for the rebuilding of the temple of Sin at Harran.

Once it was beyond doubt that the gods had really ordained the rebuilding of a temple, the site had to be cleared. This was a solemn matter and an undertaking which involved special rituals and lamentations, as texts of the following type decree:

> When the walls of a temple fall into ruins, in order to pull down and rebuild that temple, . . . in a favourable month, on a good day (of the month), at night, a fire shall be lit for Ea and Marduk, and a sacrifice shall be made for Ea and Marduk. The Kalu-priest shall sing a lament, the Singer shall make lamentation. In the morning, on the roof of the temple, you shall set up three cult-stands for Ea, Shamash and Marduk. The Kalu-priest shall make music with a flute before Marduk. . . . The Kalu-priest shall raise his hands and do obeisance before the god, then he shall recite a penitential psalm . . .

Excavations had then to be made into the foundations to recover the original divinely-approved pattern of the temple and its brickwork. If this were not done with scrupulous care the temple might well collapse in consequence. This happened with the Ebabbara temple of the Sun-god in Sippar, which, says Nabu-na'id,

Nebuchadrezzar the former king made; he sought out its ancient foundation-platform but did not (manage to) see (it), and (none the less) made that House. Within the forty-five years of that House its walls collapsed.

Nabu-na'id himself did the job more thoroughly at his restoration of that temple:

> I sought out its ancient foundation-platform and I went down into the soil (to a depth of) eighteen cubits, and the Sun-god, the Great Lord of Ebabbara, the Dwelling of His Heart's-ease, showed me personally the foundation-platform of Naram-Sin son of Sargon, which for 3200 years no king preceding me had seen.

When the foundations had been laid bare, the site had to be ceremonially purified in preparation for the new building. This was performed with appropriate rituals by the king himself. The ceremonial purification was however not limited to the temple foundations but affected the whole town, and a kind of saturnalia took place. Thus, at the time when Gudea of Lagash was about to build a temple,

> The city-prince gave his town instructions as though it had been just one man, Lagash unanimously followed him like a child its mother. ... The mother did not scold the child, the child said nothing to upset its mother; the master did not strike the head of the slave who had offended him, the mistress did not slap the face of the slave-girl who had done something wrong. No-one brought a law-suit before the city-prince, Gudea, who was building the temple. The city-prince cleansed the town, purified it with fire, put away from the town all that was unclean. ...

Finally came the moulding of the first brick. This was the direct responsibility of the king. Like all other solemn undertakings of the king, it might only be performed on a lucky day in a favourable month: the suitability of the day was declared by *ad hoc* omens as well as traditional lists of lucky and unlucky days. One month, Siwan (approximately late May and early June) is actually described in a hemerology as 'the month of the king's brick-mould; the king moulds the brick-mould'. There are many references to this undertaking, and Gudea describes it at length, telling how it was preceded by a night of spiritual preparation:

In the evening he [Gudea] went to the old House in prayer,
. . . .
The day had passed; he washed himself,
He performed everything adequately according to rule;
(Next morning) the Sun-god shone forth splendidly on him,
Gudea went . . . to the holy city,
Offered cattle and goats without blemish,
Went to the House, performed (the ritual gesture of) 'hand to the
    face'.
He took for E-Ninnu [the name of the temple] the pure head-pad,
    the true brick-mould of 'decision of fate'.
. . . .
He poured luck-bringing water into the frame of the mould;
While he did so drums were beaten.
He smeared (the mould) with honey, best quality oil, fine best
    quality oil;
. . . .
He raised the holy hod, went to the mould,
Gudea worked the mud in the mould,
Performed completely the proper rites,
Splendidly brought into being the brick for the House.
. . . .
He struck on the mould, brought the brick to the light.
. . . .
Over the brick, that he [Gudea] had put in the mould, the Sun-god
    rejoiced.
. . . .
He [Gudea] brought (the mould) into the House,
He took the brick out of the frame of the mould.

The mould itself was a holy object and had to be made of
specified woods, and afterwards preserved within the temple. It
was, as narrated by Gudea, filled with clay by the king (or city-
prince) to the accompaniment of prayers, music and sacrifices.
This successfully done, the actual building operations had to wait
until the first brick had dried out (referred to by Gudea as the
Sun-god rejoicing over it) and the others had been made; then,
when another favourable day arrived, the actual building could

commence. In one case known the interval between the ceremonial brick-moulding and the actual building was about two months. Gudea describes the scene when the first brick, having dried and hardened, had been taken from its mould:

> Gudea prepared the brick, brought it to the House,
> Put (it) down (to establish) the ground plan of the House.
> . . . . . .
> Gudea, who built the House,
> Took the head-pad for the House on his head, as though it had been a holy crown;
> He laid the foundation. . . .

The 'head-pad' referred to was a shallow-sided basket in which building workers carried clay for building: it was supported on the head. The same device, employed in the same way, is still used in Iraq. Ancient kings and city-princes had figurines made (like the one illustrated in plate 18A) showing them engaged in this pious work; these were buried in the temple foundations. Other members of the royal family also had to assist in the sacred task of building the temple, and a number of rulers record that their sons duly did this. The actual building operation, accompanied by appropriate rituals at various stages, was a time of festivity and extra rations for the citizens.

The temple having been finally completed and consecrated with appropriate rites, the statue of the god to whom it belonged was brought from wherever (in some other temple) it had been given hospitality, and re-installed by the king in the sacred House now made fit for use as a divine residence. Once again, for this solemn occasion, all strife, ritual uncleanness and whatever might displease the god was set aside from the city. Gudea describes the occasion of bringing the god to his newly-adorned earthly home. He informs the gods:

> 'I, the shepherd, have built the House; I want to introduce my King into his House.
> Anunna-gods [the great gods collectively], pray for me about this!'

The narrative then goes on to describe how Gudea

Goes to the Lord in E-Ninnu and prays to him:
'My King, Ningirsu,
Lord who restrains the wild flood-waters,
Lord whose word is supreme beyond everything,
Son of Enlil, the Hero, you have given me orders,
I have truly fulfilled them for you,
O Ningirsu, I have built your House for you,
May you enter therein in joy'.

Gudea likewise informed Bawa, Ningirsu's spouse, that her shrine was waiting to receive her:

'My (lady) Bawa, I have established your chapel for you;
Take up there (your) pleasant abode!'

The narrative goes on to say that

His [Gudea's] cry was heard;
The Lord Ningirsu, his King, accepted the offerings and prayer of
    Gudea;
The year was past, the months were complete,
A new year had arrived in the heavens,
The month of this House had arrived,
Of this month three days had passed,
(Then) Ningirsu came from Eridu.
. . . . . .
(Gudea), having spent the day in offerings, the night in prayer, . . .
    introduced the hero Ningirsu into his House.
The King [i.e. Ningirsu] went to the House;
He was (like) an eagle, that casts its glance upon a wild bull;
As the Hero entered the House,
He was (like) a storm, that summons to battle.
Ningirsu went into his House. . . .

The king was not only the representative of humankind to the god, and so responsible for the due maintenance of the god's abode: he was also the god's steward, and as such responsible to the god for the welfare of his land. Accordingly it was to the gods, and not to the people, that the king had to make his reports. The early foundation inscriptions of the Sumerians were inscribed upon clay cones (see plate 25) or bricks, which were buried out of sight of man. It was, indeed, from these simple dedications, bearing merely the statement that such-and-such a ruler built the temple for such a god, that the Assyrian historical inscriptions evolved. This came about by two steps. First, a note was prefixed, relating the building of the temple to some point of time, in the form: 'When so-and-so had done such-and-such, he built. . . .' Further historical matter was then introduced before the account of the building operation, until this preface could contain a complete account of the king's military campaigns. The technical purpose of such inscriptions remained, however, the same as that of the simple building inscription: they were intended for the eye of the god and were either in the form of foundation deposits buried under the building, or in the form of reports placed before the divine statue. The foundation deposits would only be seen again by a man if some later prince, in restoring the temple, came upon them anew, and such a finder was instructed simply to anoint them and leave them in place.

The most notable royal inscription in the form of a report to the gods is the letter of Sargon II to the god Ashur, reporting a major military operation against enemies east and north of Assyria. It begins:

> To Ashur, father of the gods, the great lord, who dwells in his great temple Ehursaggal-kurkurra, may it be very very well!
> To the gods of Fates and the goddesses who dwell in their great temple Ehursaggal-kurkurra, may it be very very well!
> To the gods of Fates and the goddesses who dwell in their great temple of the city of Ashur, may it be very very well!
> To the city and its people may it be well! To the palace situated in its midst may it be well!
> It is very very well with Sargon, the pure priest, the slave who reverences your great god-head; and (likewise with) his camp.

The king had a recognized responsibility not only to report to the god about affairs of state, but also to consult him directly about them. Provisional decisions on all major matters of state, such as a foreign campaign or the appointment of senior officials, were submitted to the god for approval. The proposal would be inscribed on a tablet and placed before the god, Shamash (the Sun-god and god of justice) being particularly favoured for this purpose at certain periods. The documents would take some such form as 'O Shamash, shall I appoint the man whose name is inscribed on this tablet to the governorship of such-and-such a province?'. An animal was then ceremonially slaughtered, and its internal organs examined. The Sun-god was believed, if the correct ritual for slaughter had been used, to inscribe his oracle on the liver; and examination by the priestly experts, using an inscribed clay model (see plate 27B) as a key, would show whether the decision of Shamash was favourable or unfavourable. (Here there was clearly the possibility of intervention by some of the most intelligent and well-informed members of the hierarchy to prevent the execution of an ill-advised or unpopular plan).

Another responsibility of the king as the god's steward was the maintenance of the irrigation work upon which the fertility of the land depended, and many rulers describe their concern for the pious work of excavating or clearing canals. Hammurabi mentions in the prologue to his laws that he was

> the lord who made Erech live, who established the waters of abundance for its people, ... the one who set grazing-places and watering-places for Lagash and Girsu, ... the one who caused there to be an abundant water supply for Cuthah.

Canals, like temples and all other major works, could only be begun on a favourable day, and work on them required to be accompanied at all stages by appropriate rituals.

As representative or steward of the god, the king was also the 'shepherd' of his people, and this title was very commonly used by kings, or of them. An official writing to an Assyrian king in the first millennium B.C. quotes a song as saying

> All the people rely on you, O Shepherd, in connection with the propitious (utterance of) your mouth.

The king's task as shepherd was to guide his people, and in one text the simile is used that king Lipit-Ishtar (see page 63) may guide the people of his land 'as a ewe guides her lamb'. This guidance largely took the practical form of the king giving his people the benefits of just law, protecting the weak, and attempting to control prices. Many rulers from the third millennium

371

onwards speak of their activities directed to the end 'that the strong may not oppress the weak', whilst the royal insignia granted to the king by the gods actually included 'a sceptre of justice'. Reference has been made elsewhere to the reforms of the Sumerian ruler Urukagina (see page 47), and Hammurabi in turn proclaims in the prologue to his laws that

> When Marduk commissioned me to set right the people of the land and to cause them to have government, I set truth and justice throughout the land, and made the people prosperous.

The economic aspect of this kind of claim is emphasized by the fact that a number of kings set up lists of standard exchange rates in their cities.

The king's status as guarantor of justice is further evidenced by the fact that oaths could be taken either by the gods alone, jointly by the gods and the king, or by the king alone.

Some highly controversial evidence on Sumerian religion at a very early period, possibly relevant to an understanding of the institution of kingship in early times, comes from the so-called 'royal tombs' of Ur. These tombs, excavated by C. L. Woolley in the years following 1927, were designated 'royal' by him largely because of the long and complicated rites obviously associated with the burials, as well as because of the splendour of the contents of the tombs, which contained a great many ornaments and vessels in lapis lazuli and gold. In fact there is no conclusive evidence that these tombs were of royal personages, and the view has been disputed.

Nearly two thousand graves were excavated in the cemetery at Ur, but of these only sixteen are included in the category 'royal'. They are distinguished by being solid stone or brick constructions of one to four chambers, by containing evidence of long and complicated burial rites, and by being accompanied by the bodies of people, in numbers between three and seventy-four, who had been the victims of what we may for the moment call human sacrifice.

Woolley's excavations indicate that the 'royal tombs' were made in the following fashion. First a rectangular shaft was dug down to a depth of eleven yards or more, producing a pit with a size at the bottom of up to fourteen yards by ten. The sites of the shaft were as near vertical as the nature of the soil permitted. The bottom of the pit thus formed was levelled, and another shaft dug into one side to form an entrance passage with a sloping or stepped floor, leading into the pit from ground level. The actual tomb was then built of stone or brick in the bottom of the pit: it would consist of one to four rooms, and might, but need not, occupy the whole area of the pit.

At the appropriate time a number of people, predominantly women, some carrying stringed instruments of music, filed into the pit. Ceremonial carts drawn by oxen or donkeys were then backed down the entrance passage: presumably these contained the body of the principal burial and the tombs furniture and ornaments. One may reasonably assume (though there is no concrete evidence for this) that whilst the principal body was being placed in the tomb some kind of ceremony, accompanied by music, took place in the tomb or in the courtyard formed by the rest of the pit. Then came the mass suicide. Each of the people in the pit or along the entrance passage was provided with a little cup of clay, stone or metal, and with this cup he or she dipped into a great bowl of poison. The people willingly drank the narcotic and then composed themselves for death: the bodies were in neat rows and even the delicate head-dresses of the women were not disturbed, showing that the deaths had taken place in a scene of calm and that the bodies had not required to be moved after death. After the suicide of the human victims the animals harnessed to the carts were slaughtered, falling on top of their grooms, where Woolley found them. The excavated earth was then thrown back into the pit over the victims. When the filling of the shaft had reached a certain level, further libations were poured out, together with a ritual meal of which the traces as described by Woolley look very much like the funeral meal for the dead, known elsewhere in the ancient Near East. Woolley assumes, though admittedly with no support whatever from archaeological evidence, that when the pit had been completely filled in some kind of chapel or monument was built from ground level directly above the tomb.

In most cases where the evidence is clear, someone subsequently dug down into the tomb – generally through the roof – and plundered the 'royal' coffin and its immediate surroundings: in Woolley's view, this was the work of tomb robbers, though a quite different interpretation of the evidence has been proposed by another scholar. One tomb which was found undisturbed had as its central figure a woman, whose name is given by an inscription on a cylinder seal as Shub-Ad: she has generally been referred to as Queen Shub-Ad, though there is in fact no conclusive evidence that she was a queen. There was in the floor of this tomb, concealed by a wardrobe chest, a hole broken through into the tomb below. Woolley took this as having been made at the time of the preparation of Shub-Ad's tomb by rogues who wanted to plunder the lower and earlier tomb beneath. He points to the fact that the bones in the lower tomb were scattered, indicating that the bodies there had already decayed to skeletons at the time of the plundering. This would, according to Woolley, require the assumption that the burial of the 'king' took place some years before that of the 'queen', so that the two tombs do not form part of the same ceremony. No 'royal' body was found in the lower tomb, and this, though simply explained by Woolley as the consequence of the grave robbers scattering everything in their haste, has great significance for supporters of another theory.

The actual date of the tombs is placed, according to which chronological system one accepts for third millennium history, between 2700 and 2500 B.C. (As Woolley's *Ur of the Chaldees* is still widely read, it may be useful to mention that the date there given for these 'royal' tombs (*circa* 3500 B.C.) was later abandoned by Woolley himself). The tombs can be archaeologically equated with the earliest Ur dynasty mentioned in the *Sumerian King List* (see page 34), and therefore known as the First Dynasty of Ur.

The facts as to the sixteen 'royal' tombs have been explained in several ways. The basic theories (which have been subject to many variations in detail) are as follows:

(1) The king (or queen), regarded as a deity, had died, and the

interment of the courtiers represents a human sacrifice (albeit a voluntary one), whereby the rest of the court accompanied their divine master (or mistress) into the next world.

(2) The tombs represented not part of the funeral rites of a dead royal personage but a primitive fertility cult. The chief male and female participants were not necessarily royalty but primarily priestly personnel who were put to death after representing the god and goddess in the Sacred Marriage upon which the fertility of the land was thought to depend. A variant of this theory would consider the chief male personage as the king himself (or the king's substitute), who had celebrated the Sacred Marriage.

The basic objection to the first theory is that nowhere in ancient Mesopotamia does there seem to be any certain trace of human sacrifice: a Sumerian text dealing with the death of Gilgamish has been taken to speak of the sacrifice of his entourage to accompany him, but despite the great authority of S. N. Kramer who proposes it, this interpretation does not appear to be certain. Woolley, the original proponent of the 'burial of the god-king' theory, meets the objection by pointing out that in fact the king, being a god, was not considered to die; he was merely transferring his place of abode to another world, and it was fitting that his whole court should accompany him. Something is known, from references in letters as well as from religious texts, about funeral rites at a much later time in Mesopotamia, namely, in Assyria in the first millennium B.C. Part of this evidence concerns the burial of a 'substitute king' (see pages 361 f.). We learn of a case in which, during the period for which he had taken the place of the king, such a man had died (whether by execution or in the course of nature being a matter of controversy). The funeral rites with which the man was buried were therefore, because from the religious point of view he actually was king, those appropriate to a king. These rites are referred to in a letter, unfortunately in poor conditions and subject to different interpretations in point of detail. The relevant part of the letter says (following mainly the interpretation of W. von Soden of Munster):

We have made a tomb. He and his palace-lady have been properly prepared and put in place. . . . They have been buried and lamentation has been made over them.

The mention of the 'palace-lady', who also suffered death, could well be taken to support the view that even as late as the first millennium it was not unknown for the king to be accompanied in death by certain people close to him. The letter is, however, far from necessitating this interpretation, for the death of the 'palace-lady' could be explained in a number of other ways.

Objections can also be raised to the opposing theory that the 'royal' tombs represent a ritual death of the participants after the Sacred Marriage. It is known that the Sacred Marriage was celebrated annually at other periods of Mesopotamian history, so that one would expect to find one tomb for each year, instead of sixteen covering a period of at least a century. Furthermore, if both god and goddess were represented by human participants in the sacred marriage ritual, both being put to death, we should expect to find two principal bodies in each tomb: this is never the case. If, on the other hand, the principal god of Ur was believed to go to his waiting human bride in person, or if the king representing the god slept with her, only the woman being put to death, then none but female bodies should have been found as the central burials of the tombs, whereas (according to Woolley) there were more men than women as principal burials. Furthermore, Woolley makes the point that, for the 'Sacred Marriage' theory, 'the bride chosen for the god would be a virgin, probably good-looking, certainly young; Shub-Ad was a woman of forty'.

Woolley is unjust to women of forty: he is also unjust to the facts. The view that there were more men than women as the central burials may be true, but is it not soundly based on archaeological evidence. There were in fact only four of the sixteen series of burials in which the principal body was recovered by Woolley; in two cases (the tombs PG/800 (Shub-Ad's tomb) and PG/1054) the principal body was that of a woman, and in two cases (PG/1618 and PG/1648) that of a man. In one of the tombs in which a man's body was the principal burial (PG/1618) there were some odd features, and Woolley himself remarks that the evidence was 'not easy to understand'. Of the other twelve series of burials, three concern pits only in which the tomb with the principal burial was not identified, whilst in the other nine the principal burial and its immediate surroundings had been plundered in antiquity. In one of these latter tombs a cylinder seal bearing the name 'A-kalam-dug king of Ur' was found: this could, but need not, identify the principal burial.

The German scholar A. Moortgat, basically accepting the 'Sacred Marriage' theory to explain the phenomenon of the 'royal' tombs of Ur, presents an elaborate and in many ways attractive theory by which he relates them to a Tammuz cult.

With the mention of Tammuz (Sumerian Dumuzi) we come to one of the main cruxes of ancient Mesopotamian religion. Tammuz was a chthonic deity who, whilst in the official theology no more than one of the two door-keepers guarding the entrance to the chamber of the great gods, held in popular religion, widely diffused throughout all its aspects, a place of special regard as (it is commonly supposed) a dying god of fertility: the cult, originating in Sumer early in the third millennium B.C., spread far beyond its homeland, and by the middle of the first millennium B.C., was even found in Jerusalem, where Ezekiel saw the women weeping for Tammuz (*Ezekiel* viii. 14). The widespread occurrence of fertility features in the cults of the great gods has been explained in two opposing ways. According to one view, there was, in Mesopotamia as in Israel, an active opposition between official and popular religion: the Tammuz cult is taken to represent popular religion, and fertility elements in the cults of the great gods are supposed to derive from a consequent syncretism, in which some of the characteristics of Tammuz have been assimilated to official city-gods. The other view (which is the one accepted by the present writer) is that many, if not all, of the Sumerian city-gods had from the beginnings a chthonic and fertility aspect.

There is some evidence even from the first millennium that the king at his death may have been assimilated to the (supposedly) dying god Tammuz; Moortgat's interpretation of the First

Dynasty 'royal' tombs from Ur connects them with this idea.

Professor Moortgat points out certain facts about the 'king's' tomb adjacent to that of Shud-Ad, and claims that these were not adequately explained by Woolley. Firstly, the body of the principal burial is not, as Woolley's description might be taken to suggest, simply scattered: it is completely lacking from the tomb. Tomb robbers might have stolen jewellery, but hardly a complete royal body or skeleton. Secondly, the supposed robbers had left behind certain conspicuous and valuable objects, such as a silver boat over two feet long and eight inches high (see plate 2B), which could hardly have been missed, however hurried the looting. Thirdly, the ornaments in the tomb are rich in examples of motifs which (according to Professor Moortgat) all belong specifically to the Tammuz cult.* Finally, considering the immense ritual importance obviously attached to Shub-Ad's interment, and recalling the scrupulous priestly control of every small detail in the preparations leading up to any major ceremony, it is scarcely reasonable to imagine workmen being left to their own devices, digging in the sacred necropolis, long enough to be able to locate and rifle a royal tomb. This is particularly so when (on Woolley's own theory) not only was the presence of the tomb well known but it was actually being deliberately uncovered with a view to putting the new tomb of Shub-Ad in physical contact with it.

The very close association between Shub-Ad's tomb and that of the 'king' did not escape Woolley: he explained it, however, as due to the sentimental desire of 'Queen' Shub-Ad to be buried as close as possible to her late-lamented husband. Moortgat, however, regards the two tombs as having a more intimate connection.

Professor Moortgat points out the unlikelihood of tomb robbers going to the trouble of removing the king's body from his tomb whilst they left behind such treasure as the silver boat. The absence of the body requires explanation, however, and Moortgat concludes that the tomb was in fact not plundered but rather that the dead body was released from its chamber through the ceiling. He emphasizes the presence in the tomb of a golden

* For examples of such motifs see plate 11B and the colour plate opposite.

Ram from Ur (first half of third millennium) in gold foil, shell and
lapis lazuli. [Related to a Sumerian fertility cult (compare plate 11B,
top frame) but not to the 'ram caught in a thicket' of *Genesis* xxii.
13.]

saw and golden chisels. These, he points out, can have had no practical use (gold is too soft) and their presence must have been symbolic, in connection with some ritual:* Moortgat's specific suggestion is that the ritual was that of releasing the dead king, identified with the risen Tammuz, from the tomb. A motif found on Akkadian and Old Babylonian seals shows a god (generally taken as the Sun-god at his rising) emerging from a mountain holding a saw (see plate 50A). Moortgat suggests that this motif actually represents the god (probably the Sun-god in a chthonic aspect, and so parallel to Tammuz) rising from the Mountain of the Underworld, which was his grave.

Professor Moortgat therefore explains the evidence of the two tombs, that of Shub-Ad and the one adjacent to it, as follows. The one which was found without a body in the burial place was indeed the tomb of a king – a king who at the New Year Feast had played the part of Tammuz, celebrating the Sacred Marriage upon which the fertility of the city depended. He was then put to death and buried as Tammuz, to rise again as that god (through the symbolic withdrawal of his body through the roof of the tomb). Shub-Ad was the king's partner in the Sacred Marriage: she was either the high-priestess or the queen, and had been identified with the mother-goddess Innin as counterpart to the king as Tammuz. The death of Shub-Ad may have occupied the same place in the ritual as did the descent of Innin into the Underworld in the later myth of that name (see page 419 ff.).

Two of Woolley's objections to the 'Sacred Marriage' theory which do not appear to be specifically answered by Professor Moortgat are, the fact that Shub-Ad was a woman of about forty, and the fact that whilst the Sacred Marriage was an annual event in the period for which we have it certainly attested, there is by no means one 'royal' tomb for each year. These are not fatal objections to Moortgat's theory. It is known from other ancient and primitive cultures (including ancient Egypt; see page 362) that the divine king was put to death not at the end of a year but when he had passed his prime and his physical powers (upon which the fertility of his land depended) began to fail.

* Compare the ritual use of a golden axe mentioned above, page 315.

Thus it is possible that the king was normally (as in later times) identified not primarily with Tammuz but with the city-god proper; only when his powers began to fail was he identified either with the dying god Tammuz or with the city-god in his hypostasis as Tammuz. If the divine king and his female counterpart, the high-priestess, were put to death in such circumstances, a new couple in the prime of their vigour would have to be chosen to represent the god and goddess in the annual fertility ceremony: to be specific one would expect (bearing in mind the differing rates of sexual development in the human male and female) the man chosen to be about twenty and the woman about fifteen. Thus the male and female partners in the fertility ceremony would always be of approximately the same age. Thus, as one could expect the king to show signs that he was past his prime just after forty, it should not be surprising that his female counterpart was at that time a woman of about forty.

It may be mentioned that at the beginning of the second millennium, when the king and the high-priestess were certainly no longer put to death, there is evidence (see pages 349 f.) that the high-priestess remained in office until she reached the menopause, when she retired and could marry. This is a clear indication (against Woolley's baseless hypothesis that gods preferred young virgins) that the high-priestess left the god's service in her forties: this may be a relic of an earlier custom by which she left the god's service at that age through a splendid death.

It should be added that Moortgat develops his theory to embrace certain evidence of royal burials from the Third Dynasty of Ur (end of the third millennium). This will not be discussed here, though it may be noted that Moortgat's explanation has the great advantage over Woolley's that it does not make the 'royal' tombs of the First Dynasty of Ur appear as something completely outside the religious conceptions of all other periods of ancient Sumer. Some scholars, basically accepting Woolley's theory of a human sacrifice, have been so struck by the oddness of it in Sumer that they have been driven to postulate a foreign invasion by some race (possibly the ancestors of the Scythians) amongst whom such barbarities are known (at a later period) to have taken place.

Moortgat's theory in turn has been criticized, the main points made against it being

(1) the difficulty of understanding why the body had to be removed furtively through a hole in the roof rather than through the main entrance. (There is an equal and corresponding difficulty in understanding why in certain oriental Christian sects the greater part of the Mass is performed in secret behind curtains, but the difficulty does not cancel out the fact. In a lighter vein, but quite relevantly, one may point out that in modern mythology Father Christmas is believed to come down the chimney even though the front door is available. It is also worth noting that the use by Baby-lonian priests of a secret hole in the floor, hidden by a table as the hole in the floor of Shub-ad's tomb was hidden by a chest, is attested – or, at least, alleged – in *Bel and the Dragon*, verse 13).

(2) the possibility that some of the tombs containing a woman's body as the principal burial also had deliberately-made holes in the roof.

(3) a general non-acceptance of Moortgat's view of a widely-diffused cult of Tammuz as the dying god who rose again.

The last-mentioned is the weightiest objection. Texts have recently been found, and others have come to be better under-stood, serving to cast doubt upon the view generally taken of Tammuz as a dying god restored to life again by the Great Mother. Thus, although Innin (Ishtar) certainly went down into the Underworld, it has now become clear that her purpose in doing so was not to release Tammuz. What her actual purpose was is doubtful: it may have been to give temporary release to the shades of the dead, but this is an hypothesis which must wait for proof or disproof until the rest of a certain Sumerian text is found.

That the 'royal' tombs of the First Dynasty of Ur represent the culmination of the Sacred Marriage seems to the present writer (despite a few residual difficulties in Moortgat's theory) the best explanation of the facts. The details of the Sacred Marriage are fairly well known from later in the third millennium, from texts of the period of Shulgi, one of the rulers of the Third Dynasty of Ur, as well as much earlier from glyptic art. It is the central element of the New Year Festival, in the ritual of which the king played, under the name Ama-ushumgal-anna, the part of the god Tammuz (Dumuzi): Ama-ushumgal-anna, possibly meaning 'the one great source of the date-clusters' and representing the productivity of the date-palm, may originally have been the name of a real ruler of Sumer. A hymn sets the scene:

> In the palace . . . of the king of the land. . . .
> A chapel has been raised for the goddess Nin-egal.
> The king as god is present within it.

The whole New Year ceremony in the Sumerian period may be analysed into five elements; the introduction scene, the ritual bath, love songs, the Sacred Marriage, and the determination of destiny. The central part played by the king is proclaimed in a hymn of Shulgi referring to the activities of the New Year Festival:

> Goddess! I will perform perfectly for you the rites which constitute my royalty. I will accomplish for you the divine pattern. Whatever sacrifices appertain to the day of the New Moon and the day of the New Year, I will do them for you.

Another text of Shulgi shows this king actually performing the ritual. The king goes by boat to the temple, and leading a sheep and holding a kid makes his entry before Inanna in the sanctury of Eanna. The king is received with acclamation, and great joy fills the city. On seeing the 'good shepherd Shulgi', clad in his magnificent ceremonial robe and splendid headgear, Inanna falls into ecstasy, and, in the person of the high priestess representing the goddess, sings a love song for the king representing the god:

> For the king, for the lord,
> When I shall have washed myself,
> When I shall have washed myself for the shepherd, the true son,*
> When my body is charmingly (?) clad,
> When my face takes on a glow from amber,
> When the mascara has been put on my eyes, . . .
> When the lord who sleeps with the pure Inanna,

---

* Possibly 'Dumuzi' rather than 'the true son' (Sumerian du_5-mu-gi plus dative postposition). The cuneiform signs zi and gi are very similar and liable to confusion.

The shepherd Dumuzi, shall have said:
'I will open the bosom', . . .
When he shall have made love to me on the bed,
Then I in turn shall show my love for the lord;
I shall fix for him a good destiny, . . .
I shall fix for him as destiny
To be the shepherd of the land.

Yet another text describes how these things took place, giving details of how Inanna had a ritual bath, and then dressed herself in her trinkets and finery in readiness for the god-king her lover. A text of the Old Babylonian period (*circa* 1850 B.C.) gives an extensive list of the dress and ornaments of Ishtar (the Semitic equivalent of Inanna) in one city. It includes two finger-rings of gold, one vulva of gold, nineteen fruit-shaped beads of gold, two breast-ornaments of gold, two ear-rings of silver, six cylinder seals, six breast-ornaments of ivory, one great ring of carnelian, two skirts, three outer garments of linen, six woollen ribbons, a silver mother-figurine, and two loin-cloths. These particular objects were used for dressing a statue, but the priestess playing the part of the goddess must have been similarly equipped.

Sexual intercourse between the incarnate god and goddess then took part in the sacred chamber of the temple known as the *Egipar*.

After the Sacred Marriage the goddess – as the text has already stated – 'fixed the destiny' of the king for the coming year, investing him with divine power to ensure fertility and security to the land. This done, there followed great popular rejoicing, including a banquet and music. There were probably also games in which the king took part.

As in many other societies, in Mesopotamia some festivals which were originally distinct finally became interfused; thus, the New Year Festival centred on the Sacred Marriage ultimately came to assimilate the rituals and even the name of the *Akitu*-festival.

The term *Akitu*, which is often applied to denote the whole New Year Festival, actually applies only to a part of it and in the third millennium was quite distinct. The *Akitu*-festival (spelt in

Sumerian *A-ki-ti*, though no plausible etymology can be offered from Sumerian any more than from Akkadian and the word may be foreign to both languages) was known in the city of Ur in the pre-Sargonic period, and in Nippur, and possibly also in Lagash and Umma, by the end of the third millennium B.C. By Old Babylonian times the *Akitu*-festival was widely disseminated amongst the principal shrines of Babylonia and Assyria.

Originally in Ur, as also in Nippur, the *A-ki-ti* feast took place twice in the year, in the twelfth and in the sixth or fourth month, the two feasts being differentiated as 'the *A-ki-ti* of seed-time' and 'the *A-ki-ti* of barley-cutting'. The evidence points to the celebration of the feast being originally an event of autumn which was later, with a change in the calendar, transferred to the spring.

The details of what happened at the *Akitu*-festival are not yet known. The event centred around a visit to the *Akitu*-house, which was some kind of temple built on or near a canal in the open country outside the wall of the city. A procession took place, in which the god's statue left the city temple, embarked on a ship, and made a journey to the *Akitu*-house, returning afterwards to his temple by the same means of transport. The participation of the king in the ceremony was essential and it is clear that the populace joined in and found it a period of great joy and feasting, for Utnapishtim, the hero of the Babylonian Deluge story, in building his ship in preparation for the flood relates:

> I slew bullocks for the people,
> I killed sheep every day,
> I gave the workmen must, red wine, oil, and white wine,
> As freely as though it were river water;
> They made a feast as though it were the day of *Akitu*.

It has been suggested that the *Akitu*-festival, originally connected with the open country in the autumn, goes back to the practice, arising from an obvious psychological compulsion in an agricultural society, of the populace going out to inspect the country-side at the end of summer, when the cooler air brought relief from the blazing heat which envelops Mesopotamia between

May and September, and announced again the coming of the time for tilling and sowing the land.

It seems certain that the *Akitu*-festival had originally nothing to do with the other central feature of agricultural religion discussed above, namely, the Sacred Marriage. However, by the first millennium B.C. the two had come together into one great feast revolving round the king, and taking place in spring in the eleven days of the New Year ceremony. This ceremony, in the form it finally took in the first millennium, has been studied and written about by many scholars, but the basic work remains *The Babylonian Akitu Festival* (1926) by the Danish scholar S. A. Pallis, though this is subject to correction in many details; in particular the text, on the basis of which Pallis concludes that Marduk was a dying god who rose again, has been shown not to require this interpretation. The New Year Festival, in the form it took at Babylon in the first millennium, may be briefly summarized as follows:

The feast took place in the first eleven days of Nisan, the month which included the spring equinox, March 20th. The ritual for the first day has not yet been found. On the second day the *Sheshgallu* priest (see page 347), having arisen before sunrise and performed ceremonial ablutions, went in before the statue of the god Marduk, to whom he made a long prayer, referring to the god's triumph over his enemies and asking his favour towards the city, the people and the temple. The doors were then opened, and the other priests admitted to bring the daily offerings before Marduk and his consort. The ritual for the third day began in similar manner. Afterwards materials were given to craftsmen who made two puppets of wood, gold and precious stones, and clothed them in red. One grasped a snake in his left hand and held his right hand extended; the other held a scorpion in his right hand. These figures were for use on the sixth day. On the fourth day the *Sheshgallu* rose three hours and twenty minutes before sunrise, and after special prayers before the god and goddess went out into the temple courtyard, where he awaited the rising of a group of stars known as the 'Acre', sacred to Babylon. He greeted the appearance of this with a special incantation. In the evening of the fourth day the whole of the *Epic of Creation*, *Enuma Elish* (see pages 409 ff.) was recited: some scholars think that to the accompaniment of the recitation the events narrated were acted as a cult drama, rather like a mediaeval mystery-play.

On the fifth day, after the routine prayers and food-offerings as before, a special purification ceremony was carried out, from which the *Sheshgallu*, to avoid accidental ritual contamination, had to absent himself. The temple was sprinkled with holy water and holy oil, and after this a special magical ceremony was performed with a sheep. The animal was beheaded, and an incantation priest then went round rubbing the bleeding headless body against the walls of the temple, presumably to absorb all evil. The incantation priest and the sword-bearer who had cut off the head then went with their burdens to the river, hurling the head and body of the sheep into the water. They themselves were considered to be in a state of ritual impurity and had to remain in the open country until the whole New Year Festival was over.

Also during the fifth day, a special canopy called the 'golden sky' was erected in association with a certain chapel in the temple, in preparation for the coming of the god Nabu from Borsippa. The gods were also asked to cast out all evil in readiness for his coming.

The king now made his appearance, being introduced by the priests before the statue of Marduk, where he was left alone. The *Sheshgallu* then joined him, and took from him his royal insignia, which he lay down before Marduk. The king knelt down before the god, and recited a negative confession in which he claimed not to have offended against the god in certain specified ways:

I have not sinned, O Lord of lands, I have not been negligent in
    respect to your godhead;
I have not destroyed Babylon, I have not ordained (anything) to
    disrupt it;
I have not disturbed Esagila [the temple complex in Babylon], I
    have not been oblivious of its rites;
I have not smitten the cheek of the people under (your) protection,
I have not occasioned their humiliation;
I have cared for Babylon, I have not destroyed its walls.

The *Sheshgallu* then struck the king's face and pulled his ears: the more painful the treatment for the king, the better for Babylon; for if tears came into the king's eyes Marduk was considered to be well pleased with his land. The *Sheshgallu* then restored to the king his insignia of kingship.

That evening at nightfall the king took part in a ritual in the courtyard. A trench was dug, and into it was placed a sheaf of forty reeds bound with a palm branch. A white bull was tethered beside the trench. Then the king, in the company of the *Sheshgallu*, set fire to the reeds and sacrificed the bull. The king and *Sheshgallu* then joined in an incantation beginning:

Divine Bull, splendid light that illumines the darkness.

On the sixth day the principal event was the arrival of Nabu, the son of Marduk, from the neighbouring city of Borsippa. The two puppets made on the third day had been set up in such a way that as Nabu approached they were pointing at him; at his arrival these two figures were decapitated by a sword-bearer and cast into a fire. The meaning of the ritual act is obscure but clearly the two figures represented some evil force or evil beings overcome by Nabu.

The ritual for the remainder of the eleven days of the New Year Festival at Babylon is lost, but there are so many references to this feast in Babylon and elsewhere that we know in general terms a good deal of what took place. Firstly, it is clear that for whatever happened the presence of the king was indispensable: in a few instances, notably during the reign of Nabu-na'id, the inability of the king to officiate prevented the feast from taking place at all. Secondly, we know that in the remaining days there must have taken place the procession to the *Akitu*-house, the Sacred Marriage, the 'Fixing of Destinies' for the year, and dramatic representation of myths.

Something is known about the procession to the *Akitu*-house from excavations at Babylon itself. There the German archaeologists (a brilliant and devoted team) found remains of the Sacred Way used for this ceremony. Made of stone paving, it passed through a splendid gateway, called the Ishtar Gate (see plate 6), and along walls decorated in enamelled bricks upon which the figures of bulls and dragons appeared in relief. The king himself 'took the hand' of Marduk to lead him from his shrine, and the divine statue then passed along the Way to the *Akitu*-house, being transferred where necessary to a ceremonial barge. Hymns and other texts have been recovered touching upon the divine journey to the *Akitu*-house: the procession was gravid with ominous significance. What happened when the god reached and entered the *Akitu*-house is not known: it has been suggested that a ritual combat took place between Marduk and the primeval monsters whom he anciently challenged and defeated, as narrated in the *Epic of Creation*.

The details of the manner in which the Sacred Marriage was celebrated at Babylon in the first millennium B.C. are not known. It probably differed substantially from that already described for Shulgi in the third millennium, for the account of Herodotus from the fifth century B.C. (see page 349) indicate that the high-priestess spent the night not with the king, but in a lonely vigil in the sacred bridal-chamber, where the god himself came down to possess her*.

There is another fertility rite, quite distinct from the Sacred Marriage, in which the king was the primary participant. This is the rite which we may call 'cone-smearing' – a rite frequently represented on the monuments (especially Assyrian bas-reliefs of the first millennium B.C.) and subject to a variety of interpretations. An example of the scene is shown in plate 31, which, however, shows only a part of the complete frieze. In the original frieze the king has facing him a second winged eagle-headed figure, placed antithetically to the one shown in the plate, and

---

* It may be mentioned that a parallel to the idea of the intercourse of a god with a human bride occurs in Jewish tradition. The Jewish scholar Rashi (eleventh century A.D.), commenting on the ancient myth preserved in *Genesis* vi. 1–2, writes: Rabbi Yudan said, '. . . when they had made (a bride) look good as she was adorned to enter the bridal chamber, a *Gadol* [a 'Great One', used of a supernatural being] used to go in and possess her first'. It is in no anti-Christian spirit that the present writer points out the possibility of the same idea having underlain the story of the annunciation of the Blessed Virgin Mary. Furthermore, St. Paul's ordinance that a woman ought 'to have a sign of authority on her head, because of the angels' (1 *Corinthians* xi. 10) may relate to the same idea.

the whole group is in front of a sacred tree. The most common explanation of the rite has been that it relates to the pollination of the date-palm. This explanation, however, will hardly stand, since the tree depicted is not usually a palm, whilst the cones, supposed to be the male date spathes, are applied not to the female flower but (as seen in plate 31) to the king and his weapons. It seems most probable that in fact the tree is the Tree of Life, for it is frequently overspread with the winged disk; the purpose of the ceremony was thus (on this view) magically to identify the king with the Tree of Life and so to invest him with the fertility and longevity of the tree.

Finally it may be pointed out that of all that has been said about the place of the king in ancient Mesopotamian religion (and what has been said is only a small part of what is now known) there is very little than can be paralleled convincingly from the institution of kingship amongst the ancient Hebrews. The attempt has, indeed, been made to see parallels, but the arguments do not (in the present writer's view) compel conviction. In particular, though there were cult prostitutes in the temple at Jerusalem at one period, there is no proof whatever that the rite of the Sacred Marriage was officially practised in the Israelite New Year Festival at any time. We have seen that insofar as the king in Mesopotamia was divine, his divinity derived from his assimilation to the god in the Sacred Marriage. If there was no tradition in Israel of the king's participation in a Sacred Marriage, there is no reason why the king should ever have been considered (even in the limited Mesopotamian sense) as divine.

12

Literature

THE standard works on Babylonian and Assyrian literature normally include in their scope such topics as omens, hymns, royal annals, building inscriptions, and medical, chemical and philological texts, as well as such works as myths and epics. This is fully justified, since (with the possible exception of myths and epics and some of the Wisdom texts) there was in the ancient conception no class of text corresponding to literature in our narrower sense. It is, however, convenient to make the distinction and to divide off for separate consideration those works which might properly be called 'literature' according to our modern categories. It should be made quite clear that, although from their interest such works are amongst the best known of cuneiform texts, quantitatively they form only a small fraction of all extant cuneiform writing. No attempt is made in what follows to distinguish rigidly between Sumerian and Akkadian literature.

In the restricted modern sense of the word 'literature', the greatest, and certainly the longest, work in Akkadian is the *Epic of Gilgamish*, called in Akkadian, from its first line, *ša naqba imuru*, 'who saw the deep'. The work is principally known from the extant remains in Ashurbanipal's library at Nineveh, but enough fragments remain from other sites and earlier periods to indicate that as an Akkadian epic the work dates from the Old Babylonian period: some fragments from Boghazkoi in

Turkey show that the work had even been translated into Hittite and Hurrian. Some elements in the work can, however, be traced back beyond that time, for it has been conclusively proved that beyond the Akkadian *Epic of Gilgamish* there lie at least four separate Sumerian stories, which the Old Babylonian poet in masterly manner has woven into a unified narrative. The last of the twelve tablets into which the Akkadian epic is divided, though an almost verbatim translation of yet another Sumerian poem, is no part of the original Old Babylonian composition but a clumsy later addition.

The story is called an epic rather than a myth as the main participants are human beings rather than deities. In archaeological terms the story comes from the *Second Early Dynastic* period, when walled fortifications were first being made in Babylonia; Gilgamish himself was the builder of the fortifications of Erech. He was described as one-third human and two-thirds divine, his mother being the goddess Ninsun and his father the high priest (or priest-king) of Kullab, a tradition which reflects the Sacred Marriage, in which the priest or priestess of the city lay with the goddess or god to ensure the fertility of the soil and the fecundity of the human and animal population of the state. Gilgamish, himself an *En* or priest-king, doubtless incorporates a shadowy memory of some real ruler or series of rulers in the dawn of history.

The epic begins by briefly summarizing the exploits of Gilgamish, and then goes on to set the scene. Gilgamish was oppressing Erech, taking the son from the father, the maiden from her lover. The gods heard the consequent complaint of the people of Erech and commissioned the goddess Aruru to make a rival to Gilgamish. This rival, Enkidu, Aruru made from clay. He was a wild man, a creature of the steppe,

His whole body is covered with hair . . .
The locks of hair on his head grow abundantly like barley,
He knows neither people nor country . . .
He eats grass with the gazelles, . . .
His heart is glad at water with the wild creatures.

The existence of Enkidu was discovered by a hunter, who,

terrified, reported to his father that the wild man was destroying his traps and preventing him from catching the wild beasts. His father recommended him to inform Gilgamish, who should send a temple-harlot to ensnare the wild man with her charms:

> Let her strip off her garment; let her lay open her comeliness;
> He will see her, he will draw nigh to her.

His innocence lost, says the old man, Enkidu will find that the wild beasts will no longer accept him among them.

The plan was carried out with success:

> The prostitute untied her loin-cloth and opened her legs, and he took possession of her comeliness;
> She used no restraint but accepted his ardour,
> She put aside her robe and he lay upon her.
> She used on him, the savage, a woman's wiles,
> His passion responded to her.
> For six days and seven nights Enkidu approached and coupled with the prostitute.

The honeymoon over, Enkidu tired of his new plaything and turned again to his gazelles. But now they shunned him and fled. Enkidu, no longer able to pace them, returned to the harlot, who, as he sat at her feet, Delilah-wise said:

> 'O Enkidu, you are wise, you are godlike;
> Why run with beasts of the field?
> Let me conduct you to Erech . . .'.

Enkidu accepted, perforce, the advice of the courtesan and she brought him to civilization, where for the first time he learnt to eat the normal food of mankind:

> He was accustomed to suck the milk of wild animals;
> When they placed bread before him, he was puzzled, he looked and stared.
> Enkidu did not know about eating bread; he had not been taught about drinking strong drink.

However, he trusted his woman, and ate and drank until his heart was merry and his face glowed. Then he, formerly a naked savage, anointed himself and dressed himself like a man, and helped the shepherds to protect the flocks. This continued until a messenger came summoning them to Erech, apparently to the feast of the Sacred Marriage in which Gilgamish would 'fertilize the woman of destiny'. As Enkidu arrived in the city, he was recognized by the assembled people as a match for Gilgamish, and combat ensued between the two heroes. The basic theme may go back to the well-known practice of the priest-king, upon whom the fertility of the land depended, having to defend his ritual position against all comers. This custom may be exemplified from *The Golden Bough*, in which (abridged edition, page 1) Sir J. G. Frazer graphically describes the priest in the sacred grove, prowling, sword in hand, awaiting the adversary who was sooner or later to murder him and succeed to the priesthood, as he himself had gained that office by slaying his predecessor.

At the encounter of Gilgamish and Enkidu the two heroes wrestled until the walls shook; cylinder seals depict such wrestling matches, in which apparently the aim was not to throw the opponent but to get his feet off the ground. Finally it was Enkidu who was defeated:

It was Gilgamish who leant over, his foot (still being) on the ground.

Having defeated his rival, Gilgamish bore no malice, and the two heroes became fast friends. They now undertook an expedition together against an ogre, warden of the cedar-forest, named Huwawa (or Humbaba), whose voice was the hurricane, whose mouth was the Fire-god, whose breath was death, who was strong and never slept. (For a representation of the face of Humbaba see plate 54A). Equipped with great axes and daggers, weighing nearly two hundredweight apiece, the friends, regardless of the dissuasion of the elders of Erech, set out for the cedar-forest, Gilgamish having placed himself under the protection of the Sungod Shamash. Reaching the cedar-mountain, Gilgamish was for a while overcome with fear, but was encouraged by his friend and by dreams which the gods sent him:

Gilgamish leant his chin on his knees,
Sleep, which is poured out upon mankind, fell upon him;
In the middle watch he ended his sleep,

He got up and told his friend,
'My friend, you did not call me yet I am aroused,
You did not touch me and yet I am bemused;
A god did not pass by and yet my limbs are benumbed.
My friend, I have seen a third dream,
And the dream that I saw was very confused'.

The two former dreams had already been described. The first is
lost to us and in the second a mountain fell over and trapped
Gilgamish by the feet. But there appeared a man of great beauty
to save him, to pull him out from beneath the mountain, and to
give him water to drink. In the yet more terrifying third dream,
Gilgamish related to his friend:

The mountain stood stark and still; it became overcast with gloom;
The lightning flashed, it caught fire,
. . . . it rained down death,
. . . . and that which fell turned to ashes.

Enkidu listened to his friend and then 'made him accept (the
omen of) his dream' and so continue in the enterprise. In consequence Gilgamish proceeded to cut down a cedar, so bringing
himself to the notice of Huwawa. Aided by the Sun-god, Gilgamish attacked the monster, who was rendered powerless by
eight winds sent by Shamash. Huwawa offered surrender, but
Enkidu insisted that Huwawa must be put to death.

Gilgamish returned victoriously to Erech, washed his flowing
locks, and donned clean raiment and head-dress. Seeing him in
his full virile beauty, the goddess Ishtar, goddess of love and
fertility, offered herself to the hero:

Bestow your fruit upon me as a gift;
You be my husband, and I will be your wife;
I will have a chariot of lapis lazuli and gold harnessed for you,
With wheels of gold and trappings (?) of precious stone;
You shall harness to it storm-winds as though they were giant mules;
. . . .
. . . . . . steppe and homeland shall bear tribute for you,
Your goats shall bring forth triplets, your sheep twins;
Your pack-ass shall be able to overtake the wild ass;
Your chariot-horses shall be famed for their running.

Gilgamish insolently rejected the honour offered by the goddess: he vilified her as:

A back-door which does not keep out the wind or draught,
. . . .
Pitch which fouls the man who carries it,
A water-skin which leaks over the man who carries it,
. . . .
A shoe which throws its owner down.

He pointed out her fickleness:

What lover did you ever love constantly? . . . . . .
Come! I will enumerate your lovers . . . . . .
For Tammuz, the lover of your youth,
You have brought about repeated weeping year upon year;
You used to love the pied *allalu*-bird,
Yet you struck him and broke his wing,
And he stands in the woods and cries 'my wing!'.
You used to love the lion, perfect in strength,
Yet you have dug innumerable pits for him.
You used to love the horse, renowned in battle,
Yet you have assigned to him the whip, the goad and the lash . . .
You used to love the herdsman,
Who regularly heaped up *tumri*-cakes for you,
And daily slaughtered kids for you,
Yet him you struck and turned into a wolf,
So that his own shepherd lads chase him,
And his dogs snap at his shanks,

and, says Gilgamish,

You would love me too, and then make my fate like theirs.

The furious Ishtar went raging to her father Anu to enlist his help to avenge the insult. Under pressure from Ishtar Anu finally created the heavenly bull, which came down to earth to punish Gilgamish. After destroying by the hundred the first humans it met, the bull made a rush at Enkidu, but

Enkidu sprang and seized the heavenly bull by its horns, ...
He seized it by the thick of its tail, ...

and Gilgamish

Thrust his dagger between the neck and the horns.

Thereupon,

> When they had killed the heavenly bull, they tore out its heart,
> And set it before Shamash.

As a final insult to Ishtar, Gilgamish tore out the thigh-bone (possibly a euphemism for 'genitals') of the heavenly bull and threw it at the goddess, taunting:

> 'And as for you, if I could get you,
> I would do the same to you as to him'.

There followed popular rejoicing and feasting. That night, Enkidu had a dream, which he related to Gilgamish:

> Anu, Enlil, Ea and Shamash took counsel together,
> And Anu said to Enlil,
> Because they have killed the heavenly bull and killed Huwawa,
> One of the two must die . . .
> Enlil said, 'Enkidu must die;
> Gilgamish is not to die'.
> But Shamash retorted to Enlil the hero:
> 'Was it not at my command that they killed the heavenly bull and
>   Huwawa?
> And is the innocent Enkidu to die?'.
> But Enlil was enraged at Shamash . . .,

and the decision of Anu and Enlil had to stand.

Enkidu thereupon became sick, even unto death, to the great grief of Gilgamish:

> Enkidu lay (dying) before Gilgamish,
> And as his tears streamed down,
> (Gilgamish lamented): 'My brother, my dear brother, why do
>   they exonerate me instead of you? . . .
> Shall I never again see my dear brother with my eyes?'.

Enkidu, regretting the fate in which his leaving the steppe had ended, cast curses upon the gate of Erech, the hunter and the courtesan; but when Gilgamish had pointed out the advantages of civilized life and the splendid burial rites of civilized society,

Enkidu became calm and turned his curses to a blessing upon the courtesan:

> 'Kings, princes, and nobles shall love you . . .
> For you the virile man shall desert his household,
> . . . For you he shall loose his girdle,
> He shall bestow on you lapis lazuli and gold, . . .
> For love of you the senior wife, the mother of seven, shall be
>   forsaken'.

Now there came to Enkidu a dream telling of the condition of the dwellers of the Underworld. Then, after twelve days on his sickbed, he died. Gilgamish raised a lament over his lost friend:

> 'Now what is the sleep which has seized you?
> You have become an object of fearfulness, for you do not hear me!'
> . . . Yet he could not take [his eyes from him].
> He touched his heart, and since it did not beat, he veiled his friend
>   like a bride.
> He cried out like a lion,
> Like a lioness robbed of her cubs . . . . . .
> He kept turning towards his friend . . . . . .

The dread of death for himself then entered into Gilgamish:

> Gilgamish runs about in the steppe-land,
> Weeping bitterly for Enkidu his friend.
> 'I myself shall die; shall not I be like Enkidu too?
> Sadness has entered my bowels.
> I fear death, and I run about in the steppe-land.
> I propose taking the path to Utnapishtim son of Ubar-tutu,
> And I shall go there quickly'.

Gilgamish therefore set out to consult his ancestor, the deathless Utnapishtim. He passed the mountain of Mashu at the edge of the world, over which the sun passes night and morning. Here he came upon

> The scorpion-people who keep watch at its gate,
> Whose radiance inspires terror, a glance at whom is death,
> Whose lambent halo spreads out over the cosmic mountain,
> Who at sunrise and sunset stand guard over the sun.

But the scorpion-people recognized Gilgamish as two-thirds divine and allowed him to pass through the gate of the mountain and to follow the path the sun takes when not visible on earth. Through the darkness he travelled for eleven leagues, till the first rays of the sun appeared. Presently it was fully light, and Gilgamish found himself in a garden of shrubs bearing precious stones. Here he spoke with the sympathetic Sun-god, who warned him however:

'To what purpose are you wandering around, Gilgamish?
You will not find the Life you are yearning after'.

Proceeding on his way, Gilgamish came to the abode of the lady Siduri, the innkeeper who lived by the edge of the Abyss. She looked out and saw Gilgamish coming along

Clothed in skins, ...
Though the flesh of the gods is in his body,
There is grief in his bowels;
His countenance is like that of one who has walked a path from distant places.

Siduri was alarmed at the appearance of the stranger:

She reflected within herself
'Perhaps this man is a raper (?), . . .'
When the innkeeper saw him, she locked her door,
She then locked her outer gate and shot the bolt.

Gilgamish, however, threatened to break down the gate and door, wherefore, having received some explanation of the strange visitor, Siduri admitted him. Gilgamish related his exploits, and Siduri asked him,

'If you have [done all these things],
Why is your face sad? Why are your features anguished?
Why is there grief in your bowels?'.

Gilgamish told her of the loss of his friend, of how he refused to face the fact of his death until the maggots were actually crawling on his face, of his dread at the thought of his own ineluctable death, and of his determination to consult Utnapishtim. 'Tell me,' he said, 'the way to Utnapishtim', and

'If it is possible, I will even cross the Abyss,
But if it is not possible, then I will roam about the steppe-land'.

Siduri said to Gilgamish:

'At no time, O Gilgamish, has there been a crossing
And whoever since olden times has reached this point has not been
    able to cross the Abyss;
The valiant Sun-god does indeed cross the Abyss, but who but the
    Sun-god can cross it?
The crossing is arduous; the way is very arduous
And in the middle part the waters of death are channelled on its
    surface'.

Siduri tells Gilgamish, however, of the existence of Urshanabi,
Utnapishtim's ferryman, and of the whereabouts of some
enigmatic objects called 'those-of-stone'. Precipitately Gilgamish
goes off and apparently smashes the latter. Then he finds Urshanabi and is again called upon to account for his unusual appearance
and remarkable journey. Urshanabi tells him that because he
has smashed 'those-of-stone' – which apparently had some
magic power to enable their bearer to cross the waters of death –
he has made attainment of his object more difficult. Nevertheless,
said Urshanabi, he was to

'Go down to the forest, cut punting poles, each thirty yards long,
Paint them with bitumen, put on a tip and bring them to me'.

Gilgamish followed these instructions and he and the ferryman,
thus equipped, boarded the boat, which sped along at a miraculous
pace, at fifteen times the normal speed. Thus they arrived at the
waters of death, where Urshanabi instructed Gilgamish to use
his poles for punting. The purpose of the large number taken
now becomes clear. Not a drop of the water of death might
touch the hands of Gilgamish, and each pole, when Gilgamish
had made his thrust with it, had to be dropped into the waters
of death. Finally Gilgamish had exhausted the hundred and
twenty poles he had brought aboard. Now they were within
sight of the further shore, where Utnapishtim watched in wonder-
ment:

Utnapishtim gazes into the distance
He reflects within himself, he makes a comment
As he takes counsel within himself:
'Why are the "those-of-stone" of the ship smashed?
And why is someone other than its master riding on it?
The man who is coming is not mine'.

Finally Gilgamish reached Utnapishtim and as in his previous encounters gave an explanation of his distraught appearance and strange mission. In reply Utnapishtim pointed out the transience of all human activity and all nature:

'Do we make a house (to last) for ever? Do we seal (a document that it my hold good) for ever?
Do brethren divide (paternal property that the division may last) for ever?
Does hatred continue in an enemy for ever?
Does the river raise a flood and bear it up for ever?
. . . .
The Anunnaki, the great gods, are assembled, . . .
They set out death and life,
But do not reveal the days of death'.

Gilgamish was not, however, satisfied. He pointed out to Utnapishtim that the latter appeared to be no different in nature from Gilgamish himself, yet he could lie at ease, without the gnawing anxiety of thoughts of death. 'Tell me', he asked, 'How is it that you have acquired eternal life?'. In reply Utnapishtim related to Gilgamish the celebrated story of the Deluge:

'I will reveal to you, O Gilgamish, a secret matter;
Yes, I will tell you a secret of the gods.
Shurippak, a city that you know yourself,
That was set on the bank of the Euphrates,
That city was ancient, and within it were the gods.
The great gods felt driven to make a Deluge'.

The principal deities are enumerated. Amongst them was the wise and benevolent god Ea – called Nin-igi-ku, 'Lord of the bright eye', that is, the 'Intelligent' – who recognized the folly of extinguishing all mankind. He devised a stratagem whereby, without breaking the confidence of the gods, he could warn one favoured mortal:

> He repeats their words to a reed hut,
> 'O reed hut! reed hut! Wall! wall!
> Reed hut, hear! Wall, pay attention!
> Man of Shurippak, son of Ubar-tutu,
> Pull down your house, build a ship!
> Leave your goods, seek life! . . .
> Make every kind of living creature go up into the ship'.

When Utnapishtim understood his instructions, he promised to obey Ea, but was concerned as to how to explain his conduct to the other people of his city. The clever Ea taught him a punning answer which was to deceive those who heard without involving Utnapishtim in an actual lie. He was to say:

> 'I have become aware that Enlil hates me,
> So that I cannot continue to live in your city . . .
> I must go down to the Abyss and dwell with my lord Ea',

'Then when I have gone', he was to continue,

> 'Enlil will make showers of *kibati* rain down upon you',

where *kibati* is ambiguous in that it can mean either 'wheat' or 'grave misfortune'.

The construction of the ship or ark is now described in detail. It was a remarkable vessel, built in seven decks, with the area of the base almost an acre, and the height of the vessel equal to the length of a side. It has therefore been taken by some to have been a perfect cube, but this is not a necessary conclusion, for the decks may have been stepped, in which case the ark would have looked, in dimensions as well as shape, like a floating ziggurat. The workmen were feasted without thought of expense until the vessel was completed. Then Utnapishtim loaded it with his silver and gold, with livestock, with his family and connections, with wild creatures, and with craftsmen, and at a warning from the Sun-god, went abroad himself and battened down the ship. Then he handed over control of the vessel to Puzur-Amurri, the pilot.

In the morning the storm began:

> There came up from the horizon a black cloud,
> Adad [the storm-god] kept thundering within it,
> The gods Shullat and Hanish precede (him),
> They come as heralds over hill and dale (?);
> Irragal [Nergal, god of the Underworld] tears out the (retaining)
>   posts (of the dam of the waters beneath the earth),
> Ninurta comes, and allows the dykes to flow;
> The Anunnaki raise their torches,
> They set the land aglow with their flashing.

Darkness succeeded, and as the cataclysm continued it became so terrifying that

> Even the gods became fearful of the deluge,
> They retreated and went up to the heaven of Anu.
> The gods cowered like dogs and crouched in corners (?)
> Ishtar cries out like a woman in travail,
> The sweet-voiced Lady of the gods calls out:
> '(Mankind of) olden times has, alas, turned to clay,
> Because I myself decreed evil in the Divine Assembly;
> How came I to decree evil in the Divine Assembly,
> To destroy my people? . . .
> (And now) they fill the sea like fish fry'.
> The gods – that is, the Anunnaki – wept with her;
> The gods were humbled, they sat in tears.

After seven days the storm abated, and Utnapishtim was able to look out upon the watery desolation. In every direction all was sea. Then there emerged a number of islands, which were the mountain peaks. On one of these – mount Nisir – the ark grounded. After seven days, as the waters declined, Utnapishtim sent forth a dove, but the dove found no resting-place and returned. Likewise a swallow was released, but that too found no resting-place and returned. Finally a raven was released. The raven found that the waters were now falling back into their accustomed bounds, and Utnapishtim saw that the raven

> Was eating, flying about, cawing – and did not return.

Thereupon Utnapishtim was able to release everything from the ark, and he himself prepared to make a sacrifice to the gods on the top of the mountain. The gods smelled the odour of the aromatic woods, and

> The gods clustered like flies round the lord of the sacrifice.

Ishtar arrived, still lamenting the folly of the universal destruction. She was followed by Enlil, who was furious to find that his decision had not been fully implemented:

> Enlil saw the ship and was furiously angry,
> He was full of wrath against the high gods:
> 'Has some living thing come out (safety) (?); no human was to survive the destruction'.

His son and counsellor Ninurta spoke to him:

> 'Who can perform anything without Ea?
> For Ea it is who understands every kind of business'.

Ea then addressed Enlil in propitiatory tones, pointing out both the injustice and the unreasonableness of indiscriminate destruction of mankind as a whole:

> 'On the sinner impose his sin, on the transgressor impose his transgression,
> . . . .
> Instead of causing a deluge, let a lion come and reduce mankind;
> Instead of causing a deluge, let a wolf come and reduce mankind;
> Instead of causing a deluge, let a famine be instituted and let it reduce the land;
> Instead of causing a deluge, let plague come and smite the people.

Enlil, appeased by the words of the wise god, went up into the ship and took the hand of Utnapishtim. He made Utnapishtim and his wife bow down in obeisance; he touched their foreheads, he stood between the pair and blessed them, announcing their apotheosis:

> 'Formerly Utnapishtim was human,
> Now Utnapishtim and his wife shall indeed become gods like us,
> Verily Utnapishtim shall dwell far away, at the mouth of the rivers!'

Thus concluded Utnapishtim's account of the deluge, which served only to emphasize the uniqueness of the happy lot of

Utnapishtim and his wife: Gilgamish could expect no similar deliverance from the common fate of mortals, for, asked Utnapishtim,

'Who is going to assemble the gods on your particular account,
That you may find the Life that you seek?'.

To emphasize how little Gilgamish would be able to bear immortality Utnapishtim challenged him to remain awake for six days and seven nights, but at once, as Gilgamish squatted there,

Sleep wafts over him like a mist.

The wife of Utnapishtim had compassion on the weary hero, and urged her husband to awaken him, that he might return in peace on the road to Erech. But Utnapishtim had planned to bring fully home to Gilgamish his frailty:

'Humanity is deceitful; he would seek to deceive you.
Come then! Bake his bread rations and keep setting them at his head,
And mark up on the wall the days that he sleeps!'.

Day by day she did this, and had just set down the newly baked bread for the seventh day when Utnapishtim roused Gilgamish. Gilgamish quickly excused himself; he had been taking a nap:

'Scarcely had sleep poured over me,
When you quickly touched and roused me'.

Utnapishtim commanded him:

'Gilgamish, count your bread-rations,
So that the days you have slept are known to you!'.

Gilgamish, dismayed, did so: he found bread-rations ranging from newly-baked bread, through bread that was sour and mouldy, to the dried-up remains of bread which had stood a week in the open sun. Perforce he acknowledged that he had utterly failed in his test, and accepted death as his lot:

'The "Snatcher" has hold of my flesh,
Death sits in my bedchamber,
And wherever I set my feet there is Death'.

Utnapishtim now prepared Gilgamish for the return to his

city. He instructed Urshanabi to wash him, to replace the filthy skins he had been wearing with a fair new garment, and to put a new turban upon his head. Just as Gilgamish and Urshanabi had embarked and begun to move out to sea for the return journey, the wife of Utnapishtim prevailed upon her husband to give Gilgamish some reward for his wearisome journey. Utnapishtim called out to Gilgamish the secret of a magic plant, a plant with thorns, found beneath the sea, a wonderful plant called 'The old man becomes young', which would restore to an ageing man his youth and virility. Gilgamish tied heavy stones to his feet and sank down into the sea, where despite the thorns he obtained the plant. Casting off the weight from his feet, he was thrown up by the sea upon a shore, where Urshanabi rejoined him. They walked on for fifty leagues, until they stopped for the night. There

> Gilgamish saw a pool whose waters were cool,
> He went down into it and bathed in the waters.
> A snake smelled the scent of the plant,
> It came up . . . and took the plant,
> And on its return sloughed its skin.

Gilgamish, finding the loss of the plant to gain which he had so greatly wearied himself, sat down and wept. He had obtained nothing for himself: it was the snake, which he called the 'earth-lion', which had won the reward of renewing its youth, by its annual casting of its skin.

Empty-handed, Gilgamish and Urshanabi reached Erech: Gilgamish took his guide up upon the walls of Erech and pointed out to him the magnificent city. The brickwork was not mere sun-dried clay but burnt brick, and the city itself was in three equal parts, the built-up area, the orchard lands and the open fields, to say nothing of the lands belonging to the great temple of the patron goddess Ishtar. To show Urshanabi all this splendour, for fortifying which he himself was responsible, was the one consolation remaining to Gilgamish.

It has been demonstrated by Professor S. N. Kramer that a number of Sumerian stories underlie the *Epic of Gilgamish* in its existing Akkadian form. In addition there are certain other epics in Akkadian which have evident connections with the *Epic of Gilgamish* either in theme or content. Thus the epic known to us as *Atrahasis* and to the Babylonians as *inuma ilu awilum*, which is extant in Old Babylonian and New Assyrian fragments, centres round a flood story: it is in three tablets, of which the first has not yet been identified. This epic is in some respects fuller than the flood story in the *Epic of Gilgamish*, for it makes clear the motivation of Enlil's decision to destroy mankind utterly. A comparison of *Atrahasis* with the *Epic of Gilgamish* suggests that the former was one of the sources utilized by the editor of the latter.

The fear of over-population and its evil consequences is nothing new: in the *Atrahasis* epic we are introduced to a situation in which the human race had already increased in Sumer to such an extent that it was causing annoyance to the gods:

> The land became wide, the people became numerous; . . .
> The god was depressed by their uproar;
> Enlil heard their noise,
> He exclaimed to the great gods,
> 'The noise of mankind has become burdensome,
> On account of their uproar I am losing sleep'.

Thereupon the gods decided to create a famine. Adad withheld the waters and Nisaba, goddess of grain, let the land grant no yield of corn. On the parched fields appeared salt crystals, as often happens still in Iraq. For six years the famine became progressively worse, until finally the unfortunate people sank to cannibalism:

> When the sixth year arrived, they would prepare a daughter for a meal,
> They would prepare a child for food, . . .
> One house devoured another.

Finally the benign god Ea gave counsel to the man Atrahasis (whose name means 'the exceedingly wise'), and Atrahasis accordingly did something (not at present clear because of the broken state of the text) to cancel the curse and produce rain.

However, the increase of mankind, with its consequent inconvenience to the gods, recurred, and a second time the gods took action. This time the penalty took the form of a plague. Enlil, having formulated his complaint as before, told the gods:

'The plague will stop their noise!
It will blow aches, vertigo, chills and fever over them like a storm'

So it came about, but Atrahasis appealed to Ea, who told him the measures to take to bring the plague to an end.

Once again mankind increased, and for the third time the gods, under Enlil's persuasion, decided upon action. This time the destruction was to be complete, by means of a flood. Enki (Ea) interposed, undertaking himself to create (or rather to 'beget') the Flood, which must have been thought of in personified form as some kind of monster. By himself taking control of the operation, it has been plausibly suggested, Enki was able by his superior intelligence to institute measures within the framework of his mandate to preserve (unknown to Enlil) a few of the human race. There follows the account, strikingly similar to that in the *Epic of Gilgamish*, of how Enki warned the favoured man to pull down his house and build a ship. The rest of the tablet, which is not extant, is presumed to have contained an account of the Flood, with the story of the escape of Atrahasis and his apotheosis.

A work which, though not directly connected with the *Epic of Gilgamish*, has a theme in common with it is that known as the *Epic of Adapa*, which has a reference to the possibility of mankind acquiring immortality. This work is known from fragments from the library of Ashurbanipal at Nineveh and from a piece found in the fourteenth century cuneiform archives at El Amarna in Egypt. Adapa (whose name, it has been suggested, may be related to the biblical Adam) was a votary of the cult at Eridu in the most ancient times. He was out in his boat one day fishing when the south wind came and capsized him. Infuriated, Adapa caught the south wind and broke its wing. Thus for seven days the wind failed to blow. The high god Anu noted this and in perplexity called his vizier for an explanation.

His vizier Ilabrat answered him: 'My Lord,
Adapa, son of Ea, has broken the wing of the south wind'.

Thereupon Adapa was summoned to appear before Anu. Ea, however, stood by Adapa, advising him what course to take for his own safety. He was to go with his hair dishevelled and dressed as a mourner. On reaching the gate of Anu he would find there two gods as guards, who would ask him why he was in mourning. He was to reply:

'Two gods have disappeared from our land,
For that reason I am thus'.

The guards would ask:

'Who are the two gods who have disappeared from the land?'

and Adapa was to reply

'Tammuz and Gizzida'.

These were in fact the two watchmen themselves, and the flattery would gain their goodwill and secure a favourable introduction to Anu. At the interview, Ea warned, Adapa would be offered bread and water of death: he was not to eat or drink:

'As you stand before Anu,
When they offer you bread of death, you shall not eat it.
When they offer you water of death, you shall not drink it'.

Adapa secured favourable admission to Anu as planned, and gave Anu the explanation of the circumstances of his offence. Tammuz and Gizzida spoke on his behalf, and Anu was won over and his anger appeased. Then said Anu:

'Fetch bread of life for him that he may eat it'.

But Adapa recalled Ea's advice: whether that advice was given with the intention of preventing Adapa from gaining immortality or from incomplete knowledge of the intentions of Anu is not clear, but as a consequence of it

When they brought him the bread of life, (Adapa) would not eat it,
When they brought him the water of life, he would not drink it.

At Adapa's refusal Anu looked at him and laughed:

'Well then, Adapa! Why would you neither eat nor drink?
You will therefore not obtain (eternal) life'.

Adapa, his chance of immortality lost, was sent back to earth.

Alongside the *Epic of Gilgamish* a second great work which from our modern point of view may be treated as a literary composition is the myth known as the *Epic of Creation*, or, from its initial words in Akkadian, *Enuma Elish*. This work, consisting of seven tablets, was recited at Babylon on the fourth day of the New Year Festival, and in Assyria was correspondingly employed with appropriate substitution of the Assyrian national god Ashur for the Babylonian national god Marduk.

The date of composition of the work is uncertain, though many scholars would attribute it to the Old Babylonian period. But this has not been conclusively proved, and since none of the extant texts belonging to it is earlier than the first millennium it has been suggested that in fact this work arose only in the Cassite period, a time now known to have been one of intense literary activity, when a process of canonization of Babylonian religious literature was going on. In agreement with such a standpoint would be the view (which has been propounded on other grounds) that Marduk – the god exalted in the Babylonian form of the myth – did not achieve a national pre-eminence until substantially later than the Old Babylonian period; see pages 339 f.

The myth gives an account of the origin of the existing world order, in which the universe is governed by a pantheon of gods amongst whom Marduk is supreme, mankind existing only to serve the gods. It had not always been so. Once, according to the myth, there existed only the primordial beings. Initially there were only Apsu, the primeval Sweet Waters or Abyss, and Tiamat, Ocean, representing the male and female principles respectively. There also occurs at this stage a term Mummu, which occasions much difficulty. Some modern writers (following Damascius) see Mummu as the third component in a primeval Father–Mother–Son triad, but this view is untenable. The term actually occurs, as will be seen below, in two different contexts. In one it is prefixed to the name Tiamat, whilst in the other it represents some being or principle with which Apsu took counsel. Theologically it probably connoted something like 'Creative Life-Force', the conception being rather like that of the Holy Spirit in Neo-Platonism.

The state of affairs before Creation is described at the beginning of the myth:

When on high the heavens had not been named,
And below the land had not been called by name,
When only Apsu the primeval, who spawned them,
And Mummu-Tiamat, who gave birth to them all,
Mingled their waters as one;
When marsh-flats had not consolidated, canebrakes were not to
  be found,
When no god at all had been made manifest,
When they had not been given a name, when there had been no
  fixing of the(ir) destiny,
Then were the gods created inside them [*i.e.* inside the mingled
  waters of Apsu and Tiamat].
Lahmu and Lahamu were made manifest, they duly received names.
The aeons grew great and burgeoned.
Then were created Anshar and Kishar, who exceeded them [i.e.
  the former pair];
The days stretched out to great length, the years added up.
Anshar made in his likeness Anu his first-born – Anu their son,
  rivalling his father.
Anu begat as his likeness Nu-dim-mud [*i.e.*, Ea].
Nu-dim-mud it was who was Creator [literally 'Begetter'] for his
  fathers;
Perceptive, wise, of outstanding intelligence,
Much more powerful then Anshar, his father's creator,
He had no equal amongst the gods his brethren.

These new and junior gods now proceeded to give annoyance to the primeval beings by their tumultuous and noisy conduct.

Then Apsu who spawned the great gods,
Cried out and called to Mummu his vizier,
'O Mummu, my vizier, who gladdens my heart,
Come and let us go to Tiamat!'.

They went and sat in front of Tiamat;
They took counsel together in the matter of the gods their first-
    born.
Apsu opened his mouth
And said forcibly to Tiamat:
'Their comings-and-goings are hurtful to me,
By day I cannot rest, by night I cannot sleep;
Let me destroy, yes, let me make away with their comings-and-
    goings,
That silence may be re-established and that we may rest'.

Tiamat, however, strongly dissented, and angrily asked:

'What! Should we destroy what we ourselves have created?
Their comings-and-goings are certainly very hurtful, but let us
    continue on good terms'.

On the other hand, Apsu's vizier Mummu – that is, theologically,
the personification of the divine force of Apsu's utterance –
favoured destroying the mutinous gods, and the two together
plotted action. This came to the knowledge of the junior gods,
and Ea, 'who understood everything', took action. He cunningly
devised a powerful incantation, recited it and caused it to dwell
in the waters. By this means he 'poured out sleep' over Apsu and
paralysed Mummu. Apsu he slew, founding his dwelling-place
and shrine over his slain body (wherefore Ea is lord of the Apsu,
the cosmic waters) and Mummu he made his prisoner.

Within the Apsu Ea dwelt with his spouse Damkina, and there
a god was begotten. It was Marduk, described as wisest and most
powerful of the gods. The poem details the splendour of the
new god:

His dimensions were cunningly devised and incomprehensible,
Impossible to understand, difficult even to see;
His eyes were four, his ears were four,
When his lips moved, fire flashed out . . . .
He was tall indeed; among the gods his stature was pre-eminent.

All this contributed to the disturbance wrought by the junior
gods and consequently to the discomfort occasioned to Tiamat.
Tiamat's advisers reminded her of the fate of Apsu and Mummu,

and urged her to avenge them. Their words found favour in her sight, and she prepared a series of monsters to fight against the young gods:

> Mother Hubur [a title of Tiamat], who fashions everything,
> Added an irresistible weapon; she gave birth to dragons
> – Their teeth were sharp, their fangs unsparing –
> She filled their bodies with venom for blood;
> She made them bear haloes; she made them like gods . . . .
> She caused to be there the poisonous serpent, the red dragon, and
>   the *laḫamu*-monster,
> The great-lion, the mad-dog and the scorpion-man,
> Fierce storms, the fish-man, the bison,
> Bearing unsparing weapons, not fearing battle.

Tiamat created eleven monsters of such kinds, and at their head she placed Kingu, her firstborn among the gods. In her Assembly she told Kingu:

> 'I have cast an incantation for you, I have made you great in the
>   Assembly of the gods,
> I have placed fully in your hand the power of counselling all the
>   gods;
> You are indeed very great; you alone are my consort!'.

The younger gods learned that Tiamat was preparing for battle. Ea heard of it and for a while was struck dumb. Finally he went to his ancestor Anshar and told him what he had heard:

> 'My father, Tiamat who bore us now hates us,
> She has put the Assembly into session, she is furiously angry;
> The gods, all of them, have assembled round her;
> Even some which you yourselves created go at her side'.

Anshar was much troubled at the tidings, and after giving vent to his distress proposed that Ea, who had dealt with Mummu and Apsu, should take action against Kingu. Ea's reply is broken, but it seems that he was unable to accept the challenge. Anshar then turned to Anu. Anu set out to deal with the enemy, but on coming within sight of Tiamat's mighty forces his heart failed him and he returned to Anshar. The Anunnaki (the younger high gods) sat in silent despair, and finally Anshar proposed that

Marduk should be their champion. Marduk, who was apparently too young and junior to be at the divine Assembly, was called by his father Ea, and instructed to present himself before Anshar. This he did, to the great joy of Anshar. Marduk, however, made a condition:

'If indeed I, your avenger,
Am to bind Tiamat and give life to you,
Then put in session an Assembly, proclaim my destiny pre-eminent.
Sit joyfully together in the Hall of Assembly,
Let me determine destinies by the utterance of my mouth, like you;
So that whatever I myself create shall be unalterable,
So that the word of my lips shall neither turn about nor be changed'.

Anshar thereupon sent his vizier Gaga to his own progenitors Lahmu and Lahamu, who with the other gods came to the Hall of Assembly:

The great gods, all of them who determine destinies,
Entered before Anshar; they filled the Hall of Assembly.
They embraced each other in the Assembly,
They held conversation, they sat down to a banquet,
They ate bread, they drank wine,
They made the sweet liquor flow through their drinking-tubes,*
As they drank the strong drink, they became elated,
They were very carefree, their anxiety left them,
For Marduk, their avenger, they determined his destiny.
They set for him a princely throne,
In front of his fathers he sat down for (the purpose of) giving
    counsel.

The Assembly of gods then proclaimed his pre-eminent status:

'You are the most honoured one among the great gods,
Your decree is unequalled, your utterance is Anu . . .
From this very day your command shall be unalterable,
To exalt or to bring low, this is verily in your hand,
What comes forth from your mouth shall come true, your utterance
    shall not prove false;

* Because of the thick lees, alcoholic beverages in early Sumerian times were imbibed through a tube with a strainer fixed on the end; see illustration on page 173 for the use of such drinking-tubes. Strainers of the kind mentioned have been found in excavations.

No-one among the gods shall overstep your bounds . . .
We have given you kingship over the whole universe;
Sit in the Assembly and let your word be supreme!'.

There followed a naive experiment to test the efficacy of the
pronouncement by which special power was granted to Marduk.
A cloth was put down in the Assembly and Marduk had to order
it first to disappear and then to reappear. This was done successfully and the gods were delighted at the effectiveness of their
enactment:

They rejoiced and gave blessing: 'Marduk is king!'.
Then they added to him the sceptre, the throne and the *palu* [the
insignia of royalty].

Then they armed him and sent him off to destroy Tiamat. He
took a bow and arrows, and in his right hand grasped a mace,
and set off.

He set the lightning in front of him,
His body he filled with blazing fire,
He made also a net to enmesh Tiamat within it,
He posted the four winds that nothing of her should get away,
The south wind, the north wind, the east wind, the west wind.
The net, the gift of his father Anu, he held close by his side.
He created Bad-wind, Whirlwind, Hurricane,
Four-wind, Seven-wind, Cyclone, Unrivalled-wind;
Then he let the winds which he had created go forth, all seven of
them;
They followed after him to disturb the inside of Tiamat.
Then the Lord took up the *Abubu* [hurricane or flood], his great
weapon,
He rode the storm-chariot, irresistible, awe-inspiring,
Harnessing and attaching to it a team of four, (named)
Murderer, Unsparing, Ravager, Winged-one;
Sharp were their teeth, laden with poison.

Marduk, surrounded by the other gods, approached the raging
Tiamat, holding in his lips a magical red amulet, and clutching
in one hand a magical plant that was a prophylactic against
poison. As the hordes of Marduk and Tiamat met, the two threw

taunts at each other, and Marduk challenged Tiamat to single combat:

> When Tiamat heard this,
> She became like a mad person, she went out of her senses,
> She cried out aloud in temper,
> Her legs trembled together down to the roots,
> She recited an incantation, she kept casting her spell.

Then Tiamat and Marduk joined in battle:

> The Lord spread out his net to enmesh her,
> He let loose Bad-Wind . . . at her face;
> When Tiamat opened her mouth to eat him up,
> He made Bad-Wind go in so that she could not close her lips;
> The furious winds inflated her belly,
> Her inside was held in grip, her mouth was held open.
> He shot an arrow, thereby breaking open her belly,
> It cut open her inside, it split her middle apart.
> He bound her and then extinguished her life.
> He threw down her corpse, he stood upon it.

The victorious Marduk then proceeded to deal with all the auxiliaries of Tiamat. He took them prisoner, amongst them their leader Kingu, from whom he took the Tablets of Destiny, fastening them upon his own breast. Marduk then returned to the body of Tiamat, and with it created heaven and earth:

> The Lord rested and proceeded to inspect her corpse,
> He would divide the monster and bring clever works into existence;
> He broke her into two parts like a shell-fish,
> One half of her he set up and stretched out as the sky,
> He shot a bolt, he posted guards,
> He instructed them not to let her waters come out.

Thus the physical heaven and earth were created, and in the myth the next section has reference to astronomical phenomena, mentioning the fixing of the constellations and the stations of certain heavenly bodies. With the heavens made perfect, Marduk now had the idea of creating a creature, to be known as Man, for the purpose of performing the service of the gods, that they themselves might be at ease. He put forward his scheme to his

father Ea, who approved the scheme but considered it necessary
for one god to perish in order that Man might be created:

> Ea answered him, he spoke a word to him,
> For the sake of the repose of the gods he detailed a plan to him,
> 'Let one of their brethren be handed over,
> Let that one be destroyed in order that mankind may be manufact-
> ured.
> Let the great gods assemble
> So that the guilty one may be handed over and they themselves
> may endure (?)'.

The Assembly was duly called, and Marduk asked for a
decision upon who it was who had led Tiamat into hostilities
against the gods. The great gods replied with an accusation
against Kingu. Marduk thereupon bound the captive and led
him before Ea:

> They imposed on him the penalty of his guilt, they spilt his blood;
> From his blood they created mankind;
> He [Ea] imposed service (on mankind) and let the gods go free.

Marduk now divided six hundred Anunnaki gods into groups
based in heaven and on earth: the theological reference of this
is not clear and it is difficult to relate it to the other division of the
gods into Anunnaki and Igigi gods.

In gratitude for their deliverance the Anunnaki now exerted
themselves to make a worthy shrine for Marduk. For a full year
they laboured, and by the second year they had created the great
temple complex of Babylon, Esagila – 'House of the Exalted
Head' – with its ziggurat, which was thought of as a mirror
image of the Apsu which lay beneath the earth.

There follows a passage dealing with the dedication and cult
of Esagila. The remainder of the passage, whilst containing
many obscure mythological allusions, is in its present form
primarily an elaborate theological work in which Marduk is
proclaimed and exalted under his fifty names (see page 341).

Enuma Elish, though the longest and best preserved, is not the
only myth of creation extant from the Babylonian *milieu*. The
motif of making mankind from the blood of a slain god recurs

in another myth, in which mankind was created by a female
deity: this myth, of which an Old Babylonian fragment exists,
came to be used as part of a ritual for use in childbirth. In the
Old Babylonian version the gods address the wise goddess Mami:

> You are the primeval womb, creatress of mankind;
> Create then Lullu [possibly 'Savage' or 'Weakling'] and let him
> bear the yoke . . .
> Nintu [another name of the creatress-goddess] opened her mouth
> And said to the great gods: 'With me is the doing of everything
> that is fitting.
> . . . Let Lullu come into being!
> . . . Let him be moulded from clay, let him be animated with
> blood.'
> Enki opened his mouth and said to the great gods ' . . . .
> Let them slaughter one god . . . .
> With his flesh and his blood let Ninhursag mingle clay . . .'.

The later Assyrian version relates the details of how the goddess
Mami pinched off fourteen pieces from the clay,

> Fourteen pieces she pinched off, seven pieces she put on the right,
> Seven pieces she put on the left; between them she cast a brick.
> . . . .
> The seven and seven wombs: seven gave origin to males,
> Seven gave origin to females;
> The primeval womb, creatress of destiny,
> Perfected them in pairs;
> She perfected them in pairs in front of her;
> Mami formed them into the forms of actual people.

The brick referred to was clearly used in a magical rite at childbirth, for the text continues:

> Let the midwife be glad in the house of the woman in labour,
> As the Bearing One [i.e. the Mother Goddess] gives birth,
> Let the mother of the baby constrict (?) herself [meaning of verb
> uncertain; possibly a reference to the appropriate muscular move-
> ments to assist the midwife.]

Another creation myth (this time a Sumerian one from the
third millennium) gives an explanation of the origin of a group of

eight gods. The action of the myth is set in the land of Tilmun, which is to be identified geographically either with Bahrein or, according to the Sumerologist S. N. Kramer (upon whose *Sumerian Mythology* (1944), pages 54 ff., the following account of the myth depends), with the land on the eastern side of the Persian Gulf. Tilmun was in Sumerian literature thought of as an ancient centre of civilization, earlier even than Eridu, and it may have marked an early settlement of the Sumerians before they migrated to Mesopotamia. In the myth the land of Tilmun enjoys the characteristics of a golden age:

> The land of Tilmun is pure, the land of Tilmun is clean, . . .
> The lion does not kill, the wolf does not touch the lamb, . . .
> Birds which come down to devour the corn are unknown, . . .
> There is no old woman to say 'I am an old woman',
> There is no old man to say 'I am an old man' . . .

Thus the land was happy and fertile. Here it was that the god Enki impregnated the goddess Ninhursag and made her conceive.

> She accepted in the womb the semen of Enki
> One day as her one month,
> Two days as her two months, . . .

so that in nine days she fulfilled the nine months of pregnancy, and gave birth to a daughter, Ninmu. Enki's wandering eye then fell upon Ninmu, and he cohabited with her in turn. In nine days she brought forth a daughter Ninkurra, and with her also Enki cohabited. Ninkurra bore a daughter Uttu, but when Enki attempted to impregnate her Ninhursag intervened, and apparently Enki had first to bring a present of cucumbers, apples and grapes. When this had been done Uttu gladly accepted Enki's advances, and in consequence ultimately gave birth to a number of plants. Enki went out with his vizier to examine the plants and to decree their magical destiny, and in order fully to comprehend their inwardness he had to eat them. For this Ninhursag cursed Enki, who at once fell grievously sick, at which the Anunnaki were grievously troubled. Only Ninhursag could cure Enki and she had disappeared. However, the fox, on promise of rewards, undertook to bring Ninhursag to Enlil, the leader of the pantheon, and this was duly done, and Ninhursag, in some way that is not yet clear, persuaded to heal Enki. For this purpose Enki was placed in or by her vulva, whilst she gave birth to eight gods to cure the eight maladies which the plants eaten by Enki had caused.

> Ninhursag placed Enki at her vulva . . . .
> 'My brother, what hurts you?' 'My tooth hurts me.'
> 'I have caused Ninsutu to be born for you.'
> 'My brother, what hurts you?' 'My mouth hurts me.'
> 'I have caused Ninkasi to be born for you.'
> 'My brother, what hurts you?' 'My rib hurts me.'
> 'I have caused Ninti to be born for you.'

A corresponding formula is used for the eight different pains. It has been plausibly suggested that the reference to the rib may have affinities with the biblical story of the creation of woman from a rib. In Hebrew there is no connection at all between the word for 'rib' and the name of the woman created, whose name 'Eve' means 'Life'. In the Sumerian story, on the other hand, there is a word play: the name Ninti can mean both 'Lady of the rib' and 'Lady of Life', the latter corresponding precisely to the Hebrew name of the woman who was made from a rib.

A substantial number of other myths are known in more or less complete form. The myth *Nergal and Ereshkigal*, known only from the cuneiform archives of the fourteenth century B.C. found at El Amarna in Egypt, and from a late Assyrian version discovered at Sultantepe in Turkey, gives an account of how Nergal became king of the Underworld and spouse of Ereshkigal. It has already been outlined above (see page 337). Another myth connected with Ereshkigal and the Underworld is extant in both Sumerian and Akkadian forms; the Akkadian form of this myth, known as the *Descent of Ishtar*, is clearly a borrowing and adaptation of the older Sumerian *Descent of Inanna (Innin) to the Underworld*, and it is the latter which is here summarized.

For some reason which has not yet become clear Inanna wished to go down to the Underworld: it was formerly assumed, on the basis of a particular interpretation of the Akkadian version, that the purpose was to release the captive Tammuz (Dumuzi), the dying fertility god, but the Sumerian version shows that this was not so. As an alternative it has been tentatively suggested that her intention may have been to release the spirits imprisoned in the Underworld, in a kind of Feast of All Souls.

To make her journey, Inanna put on her jewels and insignia and left the cities of Sumer and Akkad to go down to the Land of No Return. Her vizier Ninshubur was with her and to him she gave instructions what to do if she should fail to return. Ninshubur was to make lamentation and weeping, put on a mourning garment, and go to Ekur, the shrine of Enlil in Nippur, to explain the danger in which Inanna stood. If Enlil took no action, Ninshubur was to go to Ekishnugal, the temple of Nanna the Moongod in Ur. If Nanna took no action Ninshubur was finally to present himself to the god Enki in Eridu. Enki, 'who knows the food of life, who knows the water of life', would certainly render assistance.

Inanna then presented herself at the first gate of the Underworld, saying that she wished to witness the funeral rites of Gugalanna, husband of her elder sister Ereshkigal, queen of the Underworld. The gatekeeper reported this to his mistress, and received his instructions. Inanna was permitted to proceed upon surrendering her crown.

> Neti, head porter of the Underworld, obeyed the word of his queen;
> He opened the seven gates of the Underworld.
> . . . .
> He said to the pure Inanna, 'Come, Inanna, enter.'
> As she entered, (her) *sugurra*-crown . . . was removed.
> 'What, now, is this?'
> 'Silence, Inanna! The decrees of the Underworld are befitting.
> O Inanna, do not question the customs of the Underworld.'

A like procedure followed at each of the six other gates, Inanna losing her lapis lazuli necklace, her breaststones, her gold ring, her breast-plate, and her garment. Thus she entered the Underworld defenceless and naked. Here Ereshkigal took her seat upon her throne, and the seven Anunnaki judges of the Underworld cast upon Inanna the glance of death. Inanna became a corpse, and for three days and nights her body hung from a stake. Then her vizier Ninshubur, true to his trust, set up mourning and applied himself to Enlil. But

Father Enlil stood not by him in this affair; he therefore went to Ur.

In Ur the Moon-god Nanna likewise failed to offer assistance, so Ninshubur betook himself to Enki in Eridu. Enki was, as Inanna had foreseen, disturbed at the matter.

Father Enki answered Ninshubur:

'What a thing to happen to my daughter! I am troubled.
What a thing to happen to Inanna! I am troubled.'

He scraped dirt out of his finger-nails and then proceeded to make from it two sexless creatures called the *kurgarru* and the *kalaturru:* from the Underworld, 'the Land of No Return', no-one born of a womb, whether male or female, could come back to earth, but these sexless creatures created by Enki in his wisdom did not fall within the terms of the prohibition. He gave the *kurgarru* the food of life and the *kalaturru* the water of life, and sent them off to restore Inanna. They reached her and sprinkled upon her corpse the food of life and the water of life. Inanna revived and ascended from the Underworld surrounded by a crowd of demons: their object can at present only be inferred from the subsequent part of the myth, which is not complete, but it is usually assumed that they were seeking a substitute for their erstwhile victim Inanna. Risen from the Underworld, Inanna was met by her vizier Ninshubur. The demons at once wished to seize him and carry him off, but Inanna restrained them, relating his faithful service to her. The party then proceeded to the temple of the city Umma where the tutelary deity Shara threw himself in the dust before Inanna, who thereupon restrained the demons from seizing him. At a second city, Bad-tibira, a similar thing happened. Inanna and her ghastly entourage then made their way to Inanna's own city Erech, to the district Kullab. Here the god Dumuzi (Tammuz) remained sitting on his throne and failed to do obeisance to Inanna. Inanna accordingly handed him over to the demons, who seized him, presumably to take down to the Underworld. The end of the myth has not yet been recovered.

A myth known from a considerable number of fragments and allusions is the *Myth of Zu*. Zu was a bird-god who stole the Tablets of Destiny (the objects containing the magical power which gave the wearer control of the universe) from the god Enlil. It is by no means clear what the position of Zu in the Sumero-Akkadian pantheon was, nor is the theological meaning of the myth plain. It possibly relates to a stage of religious development at which the older chthonic fertility gods were being subordinated to sky gods at a time in the shadows of pre-history when a new stratum of population was imposing its religious conceptions in Mesopotamia. In the myth, Zu for some reason is sent to be with Enlil. Envy and ambition overcome him:

> His eyes gaze at the exercise of Supreme Rule [literally 'Enlilship,]'
> Zu keeps glancing at the crown of his dominion, the robe of his divinity, his Tablets of Destiny,
> Yes, he keeps glancing at the father of the gods, the god of Duranki [*i.e.* at Enlil]
> He conceives in his heart the taking away of Supreme Rule . . .
> 'Yes, I myself will take the Tablets of Destiny of the gods,
> I will gather to myself the commands of the gods, all of them,
> I will establish my throne, I will govern the rites,
> I will direct the whole host of the Igigi gods.'

The opportunity for the theft came when Enlil was washing himself.

> When Enlil was washing himself with pure water,
> Having descended from the throne and put his crown down,
> Zu snatched the Tablets of Destiny in his hand,
> He thus took away the Supreme Rule . . .
> Zu flew away and took refuge (?) in his mountain.

The gods were distressed at this occurrence and Anu called for a volunteer to go to slay Zu. Whoever would slay Zu should become the greatest in the Assembly of the gods. The Weather-god Adad [a West Semitic god, which may be relevant to the origin of the myth] was called upon, but he refused. He said to Anu his father:

'Who is like Zu among the gods your sons? . . .
He has snatched the Tablets of Destiny in his hand,
And thereby taken Supreme Rule . . .
His word is now (like) that of the god of Duranki,
He who goes against him will become like clay.'

A second god was approached but he likewise refused. Finally a champion of the gods did appear, though his identity was not fixed, and in different sources it is variously Shara, Marduk, Lugalbanda or Ningirsu who filled this role. The precise details of the defeat of Zu await discovery.

Another Akkadian myth, best known to us from the version found in the library of Ashurbanipal but also extant in Old Babylonian and Middle Assyrian fragments, is that of *Etana*. Etana is referred to in the *Sumerian King List* as a post-diluvian king of Kish, the city which was the northern cultural centre corresponding to Erech in the south.

After the Flood had covered the earth, when kingship came down again from heaven, kingship was (first) in Kish . . . [There follows a list of twelve kings, each ruling between 600 and 1200 years.] . . . Etana, a shepherd, he who ascended to heaven and who makes firm all lands, was king and ruled 1560 years.

The myth of *Etana* begins with a very broken reference to the gods sending kingship to the earth. When the text becomes fully intelligible it is giving an account of the relationship between the eagle and the serpent. These two take an oath of friendship before the Sun-god Shamash:

Before the hero Shamash they swore an oath, (saying):
'Whoever transgresses the bounds of Shamash,
May Shamash smite him! . . .'

In consequence of their pact the eagle and the serpent used to go hunting together and share their catch:

They arose and went up to the mountain; . . . .
When the eagle happened to catch a wild ox or a wild ass,
The serpent would eat, then withdraw and his young would eat;
When the serpent happened to catch a mountain goat or a gazelle,
The eagle would eat, then withdraw and his young would eat.

423

So it continued until the young eagles had grown large; then the eagle began to think of betraying his friend:

> The eagle received food, the eagle's young grew and thrived;
> When the eagle's young had grown and thrived,
> The eagle plotted evil in his heart. . . .
> He fixed his attention upon eating the offspring of his friend.
> The eagle opened his mouth and said to his young:
> 'I myself will eat the young of the serpent. The serpent will (?)
>   not (?) catch (?) me (?)
> (For) I will go up to heaven and dwell there,
> And will come down and eat fruit in the crown of the tree.'

One of the young eagles warned his father against the danger of such treachery:

> A young one, exceedingly wise, uttered advice to the eagle his father,
> 'Don't eat, my father! The net of Shamash will catch you,
> The traps of the curse of Shamash will give way under you and
>   catch you.'

But the eagle

> Did not hearken to them, he did not hearken to the word of his son,
> He went down and then ate up the young of the serpent.

The serpent returned and found his young missing. He went weeping before Shamash with his complaint, asking to be avenged on the eagle, whom he designated as 'the evil-doer Zu':

> 'I have trusted in you, O brave Shamash,
> I for my part bestowed goodwill on the eagle,
> I have feared and honoured the oath by you.
> I have maintained no evil against my friend.
> He, his nest is whole, but my nest is scattered . . .
> His young are safe, my children are not there.
> He came down and ate up my offspring.
> You know, O Shamash, that he goes after evil . . .
> From your net may the eagle not escape . . .'

Shamash agreed to avenge the injured serpent, and gave him instructions to enable him to catch the eagle himself:

Shamash opened his mouth and said to the serpent:
'Take the path, cross over the mountain,
I will bind a wild bull for you.
Open its inside, tear its belly,
Make your dwelling in its belly.
Every kind of bird of the heavens will come down to eat the meat;
The eagle will eat the meat with them.
Since he does not know his peril,
He will hunt about for the way into the meat, . . .
When he comes into the inside, you seize him by his wing,
Tear off his wings, his pinions and his talons,
Pluck him and throw him into a pit . . .
Let him die a death of hunger and thirst.'

The serpent did as Shamash ordered, catching the wild bull and concealing himself within it. The eagle found the dead animal and called his young to come and eat. One young eagle, exceedingly wise, gave a warning to his father:

'Don't go down, my father; perhaps the serpent lies coiled within this wild bull',

but the eagle

Hearkened not to them, he would not hearken to the word of his son.

Accordingly the eagle put himself within the power of the serpent and was caught. He begged for mercy, but the serpent did as Shamash had ordered and cast the eagle into the pit.

From the pit the eagle cried for mercy to Shamash. Shamash replied that because of his grievous offence he himself would not come to him, but yet he would send a man to him who would come to the eagle's side and help him.

The myth now introduces us to the man Etana. Daily Etana prays to Shamash, asking that he shall be given a son:

Etana kept presenting himself daily before Shamash:
'O Shamash, you have eaten my fat sheep, the earth has drunk the blood of my lambs,
I have honoured the gods and respected the ghosts . . .

> O Lord, let (the command) come forth from your mouth; give me
> the plant of birth;
> Show me the plant of birth; strip away my burden and establish
> a name [*i.e.* progeny] for me.'

In reply to his prayers Shamash directed Etana to the pass over
the mountain leading to the pit wherein was the eagle. The eagle
would show Etana the plant of birth. Etana found his way to
the pit and released the grateful eagle. Learning of Etana's quest,
the eagle undertook to carry him up to the highest heaven,
the heaven of Anu:

> 'Come, I will bear you up to the heaven of Anu;
> Place your breast upon my breast,
> Place your palms against the feathers of my wings,
> Place your arms upon my sides.'

Etana did as he was instructed.

> He [the eagle] was very strong, for his burden was great: for one
> double hour he bore him upwards.
> The eagle spoke to him, to Etana,
> 'Observe, my friend, how the land is.
> Notice the sea at the sides of the Cosmic Mountain.
> The land is circumscribed by a mountain, the sea has turned (in
> appearance) into the waters of a channel.'
> For two double hours he bore him upwards.
> The eagle spoke to him, to Etana,
> 'Observe, my friend, how the land is . . .' [text broken] . . .
> He bore him upward three double hours.
> The eagle spoke to him, to Etana,
> 'Observe, my friend, how the land is.
> The sea has turned (in appearance) into a gardener's ditch.'

Finally they reached the heaven of Anu, and came to the gate
of Anu, Enlil and Ea. At this point the story breaks off, and
whether the quest met with success or not is in doubt. Certainly
the *Sumerian King List* indicates that Etana did have, as he sought,
a son and heir, but on the other hand another fragment of the
epic seems to refer to the eagle, and Etana with it, falling back
to earth.

The formal distinction between myths and epics is that the former concern gods whilst the latter recount the exploits of human heroes. This distinction cannot always be rigidly maintained in the literature of ancient Mesopotamia, since such a protagonist as Gilgamish, or even Dumuzi (Tammuz), whilst in many contexts treated as a god, may have originally represented a real historical personage. There are, however, some epics or legends in rather a different category in that, whilst not to be taken as history in the proper sense, they grew up around real historical people in a definite historical setting. There is a term *naru* which properly denotes a stele engraved by a king with a record of the events of his reign; legends of the type referred to have been called *naru*-literature from the fact that they represent apocryphal *naru*-inscriptions drawn up in the early second millennium B.C. in the name of famous kings of ancient times. The most celebrated story of this kind is the legend of Sargon of Agade. The story begins:

> I am Sargon the mighty king, king of Agade,
> My mother was a high-priestess, I did not know my father . . .
> My city was Azupiranu, set on the banks of the Euphrates.
> My priestess-mother conceived me, and bore me in secret,
> She put me in a basket of rushes, she caulked my lid with bitumen,
> She put me into the river, which did not rise over me.
> The river took me away and brought me to Akki, the irrigator.
> Akki the irrigator drew me out as he dipped his pail;
> . . . .
> Akki the irrigator took me as his son and brought me up.
> Whilst I was a gardener, the goddess Ishtar loved me,
> And for . . . years I exercised kingship.

Another king of Sargon of Agade's dynasty around whom legends grew up was Naram-Sin, Sargon's grandson, the supposed events of whose reign are often allusively referred to in omens. The principal legend of Naram-Sin is largely known, like the greater part of the ancient literature of Mesopotamia, from Ashurbanipal's library at Nineveh, but there also exist Old Babylonian fragments, a well-preserved section from Sultantepe in Turkey, and a piece in Hittite from Boghazkoi.

After the introduction, still fragmentary, in which Naram-Sin introduces himself as a pious ruler, reference is made to an invasion by a great horde of warriors with ravens' faces.

> Warriors with bodies of birds-that-live-in-holes, people with
> ravens' faces,
> The great gods created them, and . . . Tiamat gave them suck . . .
> In the midst of the mountain they grew up, they became virile,
> they acquired stature . . .
> 360,000 was the number of their troops.
> The king their father was Anubanini, the queen their mother was
> named Melili.

The names of seven brothers, acting as leaders, are now given. This horde, coming from the northern mountains, first overran Burushkhanda, an Akkadian trading station in what is now Turkey. They then thrust on into Subartu (Assyria), Gutium (central Kurdistan) and Elam (south-western Iran), finally reaching the Persian Gulf and going on to devastate Tilmun (Bahrein), Magan (Oman) and Meluhha (perhaps Baluchistan or the Indus valley). Naram-Sin did not know if these hordes were men or devils, but sent an officer to make an experiment:

> 'Touch them with the *luddu*-weapon, prick them with the lance!
> If blood comes out they are men like ourselves,
> If blood does not come out, they are devils, plague-demons,
> Ghosts, evil Croucher-fiends, the work of Enlil.'

The officer returned his report:

> 'I touched them with the *luddu*-weapon,
> I pricked them with the lance, and blood came out.'

Naram-Sin thereupon consulted the gods by omens to obtain permission to attack the invading hordes, but this was not forthcoming. Despite this he decided to take action on his own initiative. The result was disastrous. In three successive years he sent out large armies (120,000, 90,000 and 60,700 men), only to have them utterly annihilated. In addition there came upon his land all the horrors of drought, famine, plague and flood. In the fourth year, it seems, Ea persuaded the great gods to relent and to give Naram-Sin a favourable omen at the New Year Festival, in consequence of which he was enabled to do something (possibly mount a successful offensive, but the passage is broken) which resulted in his taking twelve prisoners. He took omens as to whether these men should be executed, but the sentence of the gods was that they should be spared, for, as the planet Venus (that is, Ishtar) explained:

'In after days Enlil will take note of them for evil,
They are waiting for the angry heart of Enlil.
The city of those warriors will be destroyed,
Its dwellings will be set fire to and besieged;
The (men of the city) will pour out their blood,
The earth will make small its yield of corn, the date-palm its crop,
The city of those warriors will die.
City will show hostility to city, house to house . . .'

The point seems to have been that if the twelve prisoners remained as a permanent memorial to Enlil, in due course he would ponder upon the evil that their race had done, and wipe out their cities by warfare, famine and civil strife.

All the myths and epics so far mentioned come, like most of the religious literature, ultimately from Babylonia (or, earlier, Sumer). There is one important epic which is a native Assyrian work, and this is known as the *Epic of Tukulti-Ninurta*. It gives an account from the Assyrian viewpoint of how the pious Assyrian king Tukulti-Ninurta I (1244–1208 B.C.) was enabled by Enlil, who had placed him third in the divine hierarchy after himself and Ninurta, to overthrow Kashtiliash IV, the Cassite king of Babylonia, who had broken his oaths and been deserted by the gods. This epic has been aptly described as a propaganda work.

Wisdom Literature

English readers are well acquainted with ancient Wisdom literature from the Old Testament books of *Proverbs*, *Job* and *Ecclesiastes*, besides isolated passages such as *Judges* ix. 8–15. Generally speaking, Wisdom literature tends to be cosmopolitan rather than national in character. This is clearly demonstrated in the Old Testament, where the queen of Sheba (the kingdom of Saba in south Arabia) visited Solomon specifically on account of his 'wisdom', whilst Edom (*Obadiah* 8, *Jeremiah* xlix. 7), Egypt (*Isaiah* xix. 11, 12) and the 'children of the East' (1 *Kings* iv. 30) were noted for this in Israel. It is clear that certain works of Wisdom literature (as indeed certain myths and epics) were translated from one language into another in antiquity.

In Mesopotamia Wisdom literature certainly goes back, in its written form, to the Larsa period (about 1900 B.C.), or more precisely to the period between the reign of Rim-Sin of Larsa and the time of Ammi-saduqa of Babylon. From this period there is extant a large amount of Wisdom literature in Sumerian. How much earlier such texts arose is not certain, but it has been pointed out that as we have no evidence for the existence of this type of literature from the period before Semitic influence was being strongly felt, it cannot be actually proved that any part of it is purely Sumerian in conception.

This Sumerian Wisdom literature has been formally divided into between five and eleven main categories, the difference in numbering depending upon whether one includes such literary forms as maxims, precepts, bywords and apothegms under the general heading of 'proverbs' or considers them as separate classes. No attempt is made below to give an example of every class which can be distinguished.

The most common type of Wisdom literature in Sumerian is the proverb. From the hundreds known a few may be quoted:

> Pleasure from liquor; weariness from a journey. [There is parono-masia in the Sumerian between *kash* 'liquor' and *kashkal* 'journey'].

The value of alcohol in relaxing tension was well recognized:

> He who doesn't know liquor, doesn't know what is good; liquor makes the house pleasant. [It may be recalled that one of the marks of Enkidu's savagery was that he was unacquainted with bread and liquor].

> Flatter a young man, he'll give you anything you want;
> Throw a scrap to a puppy, he'll start to wag his tail at you.

The man who supports neither wife nor child,
His nose has never borne a tether.

To keep on having wives is (a matter) for a man (himself),
(For him) to keep on having sons is (a matter) for the god.

The penis of the adulterer is on a par with the vulva of the adulteress.

Conceiving is nice, being pregnant is irksome.

It is the poor men who are the silent men in Sumer.

Resembling the proverbs in spirit but formally distinct from them are what one may call precepts and maxims. The 'precepts' consist of series of pithy sentences bearing exhortations on moral behaviour, and introduced as the advice of a parent to a son. This type of composition is well-known from the Old Testament, for example from *Proverbs* xxxi., which is introduced as the precepts delivered to king Lemuel by his mother. The *genre* is also known in Egyptian, whilst another good instance of it is the Aramaic *Words of Ahiqar*. Not more than two or three of these 'precept' texts are at present known in Sumerian. Some sections of one of these texts read:

Pay heed to the word of your mother as to the word of a god!

In a place of quarrelling, don't let your own face appear angry;
When quarrelling consumes someone like a fire, make sure you know how to extinguish (the flame) . . .
Should he say something unfriendly to you, don't say the like to him; this (involves) serious (consequences).

When you pronounce judgement, don't accompany it with a (personal) comment of disapproval.

As an example of the type of text which we may call 'maxims', which are better represented in Akkadian than in Sumerian, one may quote the following, as tentatively translated by Professor Th. Jacobsen of Chicago (*Bulletin of the American Schools of Oriental Research*, 102, 15):

'The king who loves righteousness . . . (will impose penalties on the guilty party) . . . when he has straightened out the relevant testimonies and seen the relevant decision, but he will not burden (the guilty person) with the wages of a grave sin.'

(This occurs in a text which praises the goddess Nanshe as guarantor of the moral order.)

Another example, this one from a bilingual text in Sumerian and Akkadian, is the following extract:

> He who sleeps with [Akkadian version 'impregnates'] a man's wife, his guilt is grave;
> He who swears to (do) unworthy things, he who slanders,
> He who points the finger of evil behind his fellow,
> He who casts unseemly words at his family [Akkadian version 'brothers'],
> He who oppresses a subordinate,
> He who hands over the weak to the strong, . . .
> Such a one is blameworthy (?).

More extensively represented in Sumerian Wisdom literature is what the Sumerians themselves called *adaman-du₁₁-ga*. (The $_{11}$ after *du* simply means that this sign in the eleventh in frequency of the Sumerian signs pronounced 'du'). The ideogram *adaman* is composed of the sign for 'man' written together twice, in this form – MANNVW. *Du₁₁-ga* means 'a word' or 'speaking', so that *adaman-du₁₁-ga* should mean 'speaking between two people opposite to each other'. The term is in fact used of the tenson or verbal contest between two parties with distinct characteristics, for instance Summer and Winter, Shepherd and Farmer, Copper and Precious Metal, Pickaxe and Plough, who argue as to their respective merits: it has been suggested that such compositions were devised for recitation or performance for the entertainment of the court at festivals. These compositions have a stereotyped form: there is first a mythological introduction, setting the scene at some particular point of time in the origin and development of the cosmos, introducing the disputants and showing how they fit into the world order, and then giving the particular grounds for the argument. Then follows the contest proper, in which each party extols his own merits or points out the disadvantages and demerits of his adversary. Finally the two have recourse to a god, who pronounces the judgement between them, which they accept, becoming friends again. Seven such contests (by no means all complete) are now known in Sumerian.

The longest of them is *Summer and Winter*, of which a summary, making considerable use of the work of S. N. Kramer of Philadelphia, follows.

The god Enlil decided to establish agriculture in the land and with it the blessings of plenty, and to this end created two brothers, Summer and Winter, to whom were assigned certain duties. Winter brought about the birth of lambs, kids and calves, he gave abundance of milk, he brought greenness to gardens and caused the trees to come into fruit, he made the fish spawn and he caused the grain to sprout. Summer on the other hand filled the farms with crops, brought on the harvest and loaded the granaries with corn, and caused houses, temples and cities to be built. (The attribution of building to Summer refers to the fact that summer always was, as it still is, the time of brick-making in Iraq). Having performed their allotted tasks, the two brothers made their way to Nippur to give thanks to Enlil, bringing with them their gifts. The exact translation is open to doubt, but it seems that Winter brought various vegetables, whilst

Summer, son of the hero Enlil,
Brings as an offering to E-nam-tila [the House of Life], the house
  of Enlil,
A kid and a goat and a mountain sheep.

In consequence the two became jealous of each other and began to quarrel:

Summer shunned Winter like an enemy, wouldn't walk at his side,
Then Winter, the 'Mountain', lost his temper and began to quarrel
  with Summer, (saying):
'Summer, my brother . . .'

This marks the beginning of the contest proper, and each of the two contestants now proceeds to argue his own superiority. Winter points out the important part he plays in the cult:

Summer, my brother, . . .
When the king, . . . the divine Ibbi-Suen, . . .
Is clad in his ceremonial garment and his royal robe,
To officiate at the feast of the gods, . . .

And when in the House of Life, the splendid royal abode which
  Anu created,
. . . the stringed instruments play for him . . .
Then it is I who am concerned in preparing the sweet butter.

Summer makes a sharp retort on the discomforts that Winter
represents:

. . . Summer answered Winter,
'Winter, my brother, in your season the thick clouds roll up, . . .
Inside the town (people's) teeth are chattering,
No-one ventures out in the streets even at midday,
Both slave and master, enjoying the fire-place, wait for the
  evening . . .'

Finally the two contestants appeal to Enlil for a decision between
them. Both state their case, Summer beginning with flattery of
Enlil, Winter speaking more directly. At last Enlil states his
decision:

Enlil replied to Summer and Winter:
'Winter controls the waters which give life to the lands,
He, farmer of the gods, heaps up all the crops;
O Summer, my son! How can you compare yourself with your
  brother Winter?'

The verdict is accepted and reconciliation follows:

The exalted word of Enlil, . . . the judgement pronounced by
  him, . . . who would venture to transgress it?
(Therefore) Summer did obeisance to Winter, made supplication
  to him;
Summer gives gold and silver to Winter,
Brings into his house *ulushin*-beer and wine . . .

Another important class of Sumerian Wisdom literature
comprises the *Edubba* compositions. *Edubba* means literally
'tablet-house', in effect 'scribal school', and a number of characteristic compositions, narrated in rather satirical vein, relate specifically to the education of a scribe. Contrary to an assumption
which has been widely held in the past, scribal schools were (at
least after the decline of the theocratic Sumerian city-state, and
nothing is known about them before) associated specifically

neither with the priests nor with the temples, and most literary texts have been found not in temples but in private houses, whilst archaeology shows that in the Old Babylonian period the scribal schools were usually physically separate from the temple area (see page 189).

In the Old Babylonian period, when Sumerian as a spoken language was rapidly dying, the scribal schools flourished, largely to the end of educating scribes in the writing of Sumerian, still dominant in literature and religion. The texts enable us to glean an outline of the organization of such a school. At the top was the Headmaster or Dean, (Sumerian *ummia*, a word which means something like 'expert' or 'authority'). Next in rank came the form-master, known in Sumerian as *adda edubba* 'father of the tablet-house'. For particular subjects there were specialist teachers, such as the *dubshar nishid* ('the scribe of counting', that is, the Mathematics master), the *dubshar ashaga* ('the scribe of the field', that is, the Geometry master, possibly identical with the former). The most important teacher of the lot, like the Classics master in Grammar and Public schools until recently, was the *dubshar kengira* ('the scribe of Sumerian'). Much of the actual teaching was carried out by a pupil-teacher known as 'Big Brother', who tended to throw his weight around amongst his juniors. Administration was in the hands of the School Secretary, who also had a hand in maintaining discipline.

The text from which most of the above information is derived was first edited fully by S. N. Kramer (*Journal of the American Oriental Society*, 69 (1949), pages 210 ff.). It gives an amusing account of the routine for a pupil in his first year. The composition begins with the student being asked:

'Son of the tablet-house, where did you go in your early days?'

He replies:

'I went to the tablet-house; . . .
I read my tablet, ate my meal,
Prepared my tablet, inscribed it, finished it.
When the tablet-house opened, I went home.
I entered (my) house, my father was sitting there.'

The lad gave his father some account of his day and then prepared for an early supper and bed.

> 'I am thirsty, give me drink;
> I am hungry, give me food.
> Wash my feet, make (my) bed, I want to sleep.
> Rouse me early in the morning;
> I mustn't be late, or my Headmaster will whack me.'

The next morning the mother gave her boy two loaves and he hurried off to school; but it was his unlucky day. Despite everything he was late, and got into trouble. The form-master caned him for the poor quality of his tablet of the previous afternoon. The lad was further caned for his other subjects as well as for his general behaviour. So disastrous did the day prove that the lad mooted to his father a proposal for entertaining the Headmaster. This was done, the father putting on a sumptuous entertainment for the Headmaster, who was provided with a fine new garment, given a gift and fittingly regaled. The boy was accordingly taken into favour, the flattered Headmaster prophesying a great future for him.

Another tablet from the same text, edited by C. J. Gadd (*Teachers and Students in the Oldest Schools*, (1956), pages 28 ff.), gives an account of the later history of the once-timid new boy. In this new text the boy is in his second year and has turned, as Professor Gadd puts it, 'into a bold unbiddable youth, whose unbridled conceit brings him into deliberate conflict with authority'. The speakers in this dialogue are the student and the 'Big Brother'. The student is invited to suggest what he should write for an exercise. He answers that he is not going to do routine exercises:

> 'I am determined to write something of my own; I'll give the instructions.'

The Big Brother rebukes the conceited young man:

> 'If you are to give the instructions, I am not your Big Brother;
> Where does my Big Brother status come in (in such a case)?

In the scribal art conceit [literally 'an excessive name'] destroys a
Big Brother relationship.'
O massive intelligence! Prime member of the tablet-house! . . .
Your hand may be skilful; but is it a hand not (very) skilful at
(using) a stylus (on) a tablet.'

The student's inefficiency is listed in detail:

'He inscribes a tablet – he doesn't bring it off effectively;
He writes a letter – he gets the wrong address (?);
(If) he goes to divide an estate, he won't (be able to) divide the
estate.'

There is more in the same vein, the scornful Big Brother finally
asking:

'O man without praise amongst the scribes,
What are you skilful at? . . .'

The student does not, however, take this passively, but after
defending his own technical ability turns the attack upon the
Big Brother's skill, criticizing his arithmetic, his geometry, and
the accuracy of his copying of religious texts. The abuse and
counter-abuse grew more heated until finally (to judge by the
sequel, for the relevant passage is missing) the quarrel developed
into a stand-up fight. Another tablet gives the conclusion of the
affair. The headmaster himself appears and thunders at the
delinquent student:

'Why is it that you two are behaving so?
One man knocks down another . . . !
. . . . . .
Why is it that your Big Brother exists?
(It is) because he is more learned than you in the scribal art.
. . . . . .
The Headmaster can do anything,
He is exceedingly respected whatever he does;
But if you do whatever you please
A person acting like you will come into conflict with his Big Brother.
There is a cudgel in the store-room (?), I will beat such a one with it;
I will put a copper chain on his foot;
He will (be able to) go around the house, but he shall not go outside
the tablet-house for two months.'

Then, says the text, the Headmaster, having uttered this grim threat, took the two young men by the hand in token of reconciliation.

A further type of Wisdom literature, well known to the Jewish and Christian world from the *Book of Job*, is that in which the problem of evil and suffering is considered. It has been convincingly argued by the Dutch scholar J. J. A. Van Dijk that, contrary to an earlier view, this problem did arise in Sumerian thought. However, this type of composition is at present represented in Sumerian only by two texts which are very difficult to interpret, and this *genre* will therefore only be instanced with examples from Akkadian in which it is very clearly represented.

A new convenient edition of all the Wisdom literature at present known in Akkadian is to be found in W. G. Lambert's *Babylonian Wisdom Literature* (1960), which by the kindness of the author in lending the manuscript before publication, it was possible to utilize extensively in the following summary account.

One of the most striking works is that known from its first line as *Ludlul bel nemeqi* ('I will praise the lord of wisdom') or alternatively, from the general trend of its subject matter, '*The Poem of the Righteous Sufferer*' or '*The Babylonian Job*'. The last-mentioned title is, however, hardly merited, for though this poem does, like the biblical *Book of Job*, deal with the problem of suffering, the biblical work by its spiritual insight and beauty of imagery soars so high above the Babylonian that the two can scarcely be compared.

The Poem of the Righteous Sufferer, probably originally consisting of four tablets, is a monologue of five hundred lines allegedly spoken by some Babylonian nobleman. Its literary characteristics indicate that it was originally a product of the Cassite period. In the poem the pious narrator was deserted by all the gods, so that the king became angry with him, the courtiers plotted against him, and he became an outcast. The diviners and magicians were unable to help him. He recalls his former exemplary piety and sadly concludes that man does not know what satisfies the gods:

Would that I knew that these things found favour with the god.
That which is good to oneself is an insult to the god;
That which is of ill repute in a man's own heart is good to the god.
Who knows the opinion of the gods in the midst of heaven?

The unfortunate man was then smitten with sickness, a whole series of devils coming up from the Underworld to seize upon him, giving him apparently the symptoms of paralysis, dysentery, tuberculosis and malaria.

The sufferer now had three dreams. In the first a fine-looking young man appeared, but the text containing his message is broken. In the second a young man appeared as an exorcist, who performed rites over the sufferer on the instructions of a god. In the third there appeared a woman like a queen or a goddess, giving promise of delivery, and succeeding her came a bearded incantation priest, bearing a tablet from Marduk with a promise of prosperity. With Marduk once more favourably disposed to the sufferer, his miseries quickly departed. The devils were sent back to the Underworld and the man recovered his health and his respectability and proceeded to the temple of Marduk. The end of the work is in doubt: it has been proposed by some scholars to see the missing fourth tablet in some fragments which deal with the triumphal entry into the temple of Marduk of the once-rejected man.

The second major work of Wisdom literature, possibly a little later in its date of composition than the foregoing, is that known as *The Babylonian Theodicy*. This has the form of a dialogue between a sufferer and his friend. It is from the point of view of literary structure an elaborate composition, consisting originally of twenty-seven stanzas, each of eleven lines all beginning with the same syllable. The twenty-seven syllables constitute an acrostic which yields a sentence meaning 'I am Saggil-kinam-ubbib the incantation priest, worshipper of the god and the king'. The contents of the work may be summarized as follows, the sufferer and his friend speaking in alternate stanzas:

Sufferer: I was a posthumous child and my mother died in childbed,
  leaving me an orphan.
Friend: Death is the lot of all people.

Sufferer: I am in bad health physically, miserable and not well off.

Friend: The gods finally reward the pious.

Sufferer: There are cases of people prospering without piety; I have been pious without prospering.

Friend: We do not understand the ways of the gods. The impious who prosper temporarily will finally get their deserts.

Sufferer: According to my observation this has not been the case.

Friend: It is blasphemy to dispute the decisions of the gods. [Four stanzas are missing or badly damaged at this point].

Sufferer: There are advantages in living like a beggar without obligations to society.

Friend: This is madness.

So the dialogue continues, setting the theory of divine retribution against the divergent experience of actual life. The two speakers finally agree upon the conviction that men are unjust, and that they are so because the gods made them so.

To give some flavour of the original a translation of one stanza is offered: the elaborately courteous introduction of the speech quoted is a characteristic of the whole composition.

> My friend, your mind is a spring whose source is unfailing,
> (It is) the accumulation of the mighty sea of which there is no diminution.
> I will pose a question to you; heed my saying!
> Pay attention for a moment! Listen to my words!
> My bodily grace is hidden, distress overclouds me;
> My luck has passed (me) by, my luxury has passed;
> My vigour has turned to weakness; my splendour has come to an end;
> Lamentation and grief have disfigured my face.
> Rations from my farm are far from adequate for me;
> (My) wine, the life of mankind, is a long way from satisfying (my need).
> Is there a time of favour arranged for me? I would like to know the way (to get) it.

Another work in dialogue form, but of a very different character, is that commonly known as the *Dialogue of Pessimism*. This recounts a series of exchanges between a master and his slave, the master each time proposing some course of action, to the propriety of which the slave at once offers glowing testimony. At once there follows a *volte face* on the part of the master, matched by the succeeding speech of the slave, who is equally ready to recommend the opposite course. Only at the end does the slave offer an independent opinion, when, directly asked what course of action really is worthwhile, his answer is that

'To have my neck and your neck broken
And us thrown into the river – that is good!'

It can hardly be denied that the work has a humorous intent, and is to be regarded as a satire. This is not, however, to deny that there was, underlying the humorous treatment, serious considera- tion of a philosophical problem, namely, What is the purpose of life? A section will give some idea of the tone of the work:

'Slave, make yourself agreeable!' 'Yes, sir, yes.'
'Fetch water for my hands straightaway and give it to me,
So that I may make a sacrifice to my god.' 'Do so, sir, do so!
That man who makes sacrifices to his god, his heart is content;
He makes investment upon investment.'
'No, slave, I will not make a sacrifice to my god at all.'
'Don't do so, sir, don't do so!
As to a god, you can train him so that he keeps trotting behind
    you like a dog,
Whether (it is) rites he wants from you . . . or anything else.'

Precept texts are represented in Akkadian as in Sumerian (see page 431). A typical example is the *Counsel of Wisdom*, which takes the form of advice from a father – possibly a vizier, certainly a highly placed gentleman – to his son. The date of compilation is uncertain: the Old Babylonian and the Cassite periods have been variously suggested.

The kind of precepts given constitute good practical down- to-earth advice, based like that of Lord Chesterfield to his son on pragmatic considerations rather than on an ethical system. The son is exhorted to shun bad companions; lest

(Departing) from good habits you become associated in their view(s);

441

(Whereby) you will diminish the value of your service, forsake
  your path,
(And) allow your opinion, which was profound and sensible, to
  become distorted.

The son is also advised to speak guardedly, avoiding blasphemy,
falsehood and slander, and to avoid getting mixed up in lawsuits.
He should not make a slave-girl mistress of his house, nor marry
a temple-prostitute, who besides being accustomed to accepting
other men would prove an unsympathetic and intractable wife.
If put in charge of his prince's treasure-house he must eschew the
opportunity of embezzlement, not, be it noted, for moral reasons
but because of the risk of being found out. Above all, he should
worship the gods regularly and give them the offerings due, when
they in turn would reward him:

> Prayer, supplication and adoration
> You shall give each day: your emolument will be heaped up (?),
> . . . . . .
> Sacrifice prolongs life
> And prayer absolves guilt.

Contest literature, corresponding to the Sumerian *adaman-
du₁₁-ga*, is well represented in Akkadian, six examples being
known at present. The best preserved, represented by a number
of fragments of recensions of which the oldest is from the Old
Babylonian period, is the contest between the tamarisk and the
palm tree. As in the Sumerian examples, the work begins with a
mythological introduction, setting the time and circumstances in
which the two contenders were created. Then it continues:

> The king planted the palm tree in his palace,
> With it *ditto* [so in the original] . . . the tamarisk.
> In the shade of the tamarisk a banquet was held . . .

The two then fall to arguing. The palm tree urges:

> You, O tamarisk, are one of the trees which are useless.
> What are your branches? Wood without fruit! . . .
> The gardener says nice things about me,

In respect to (my) being a benefit to slave and city dignitary (alike) . . .

The tamarisk, on the other hand, points out the utility of its timber:

Think of the equipment in the royal palace!
What of mine is there introduced into the royal palace?
The king eats from my table,
The queen drinks from my goblet . . .

There is much more – unfortunately badly damaged – in this vein. It seems that as in the Sumerian examples the contestants finally betook themselves to a temple for decision.

Proverbs, and various associated categories such as maxims, precepts, and what some scholars call 'miniature essays', are represented in Akkadian as well as in Sumerian. Most proverbs in Akkadian actually occur in bilingual texts alongside a Sumerian original, but there are a few instances of collections of proverbs written solely in Akkadian, as well as some quoted appositely in letters. Some examples of the various categories are offered.

Proverbs

A hungry man will dig into a brick-built house.

Would you hand a lump of mud to someone throwing things around?

At the gate of the judge's house the mouth of a sinful woman is mightier than her husband's.

Precepts

Do no crime, (then) fear of the god will not worry you.
Utter no evil statement; grief will not drag at your heart.
Do no evil; you will not receive permanent hardship.

Maxims

When you are provident, your god is for you;
When you are improvident, your god is not for you. [The spirit is that of 'Trust in God and keep your powder dry.']

Miniature Essays (or 'Humorous stories')*

When a stallion came up and mounted a she-ass,
As he was riding her he whispered in her ear:
'The foal which you bear, let it be a courser like me;
Don't make it like an ass that has to carry a pannier.'

A mongoose went into a culvert out of the way of a dog.
When the dog jumped in, it stuck in the mouth of the culvert,
And let the mongoose get away.

A gnat, as it sat on an elephant,
Said, 'Blood-brother, do I bother you? (If so), I'll be off to the
    watering-place.'
The elephant answered the gnat:
'I didn't know you were sitting there – What are you, anyway? –
And I shan't know about it when you get off.'

---

* Examples from this last category provide another indication that the Babylonians did in fact enjoy a sense of humour. No doubt our rather wooden
renderings of ancient Sumerian and Akkadian texts, of which we must often fail
to catch the finer nuances of meaning, sometimes totally miss flashes of Babylonian
wit or humour; but there are times when we are able to share the joke. We meet
such a case in a letter from a Babylonian official to his superior. He writes in
effect (the translation is not quite literal): 'There is here neither doctor nor mason.
The wall is beginning to fall down and there is no one to deal with it. A tumbling
stone may hit someone. . . . May my lord be pleased to send either a doctor or a
mason.'

49 The high-priest and goddess escort the king to the
Sun-god sitting in his shrine behind the sun-disk (first
millennium B.C., probably copied from a more ancient
monument)

50A The rising of the Sun-god; a cylinder seal impression

50B Mythical hero [Gilgamish?] with lion; a cylinder seal impression

51A Boxing, possibly as a cult act (from a plaque)

51B Copper stand in the form of wrestlers (third millennium)

51C Cult scene of questionable nature (from a plaque)

52 (*opposite*) Musicians (from an Assyrian bas-relief)

53 (*above*) Colossal human-headed lion, representing a good genie guarding an Assyrian palace

54A Face of Humbaba, an ogre mentioned in the *Epic of Gilgamish*

54B Lamashtu, a dreaded female demon (from an amulet)

55 (*opposite*) A Babylonian devil

56A (*above*) Babylonian monster (*circa* 1900 B.C.)

56B (*left*) Amulet, showing gods associated with mythical beasts

57A The wind-demon Pazuzu, with [top register] exorcist priests in animal head-dress (an alabaster amulet from Babylon, first millennium)

57B (*below*) Detail from reredos by Jacques de Baerze (*circa* 1300 A.D.), showing astral symbols and demons possibly deriving ultimately from ancient Mesopotamia

58A Rein-ring from Ur (third millennium)

58B Weight in form of a lion (first millennium B.C.)

59 Brazier (from Nuzi)

60A A carved ivory; a lady [perhaps a cult-woman] at her window

60B A carved ivory

61B Bronze dragon's head from Babylon (sixth century B.C.)

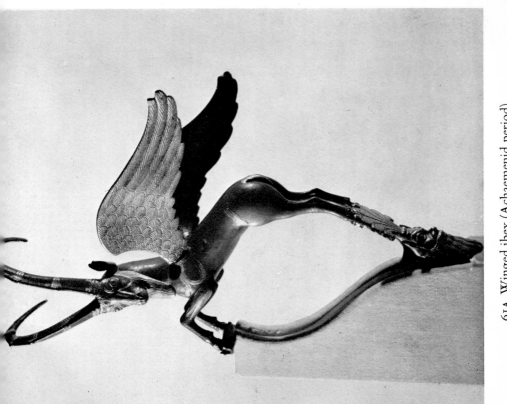

61A Winged ibex (Achaemenid period)

63   Carved limestone floor from doorway of an Assyrian palace

64   The Gebel el-Arak knife, with carved handle showing ship of Mesopotamian type

Mathematics and Astronomy; Medicine; Chemical Technology; Art

'What, amongst other fine discourse, pleased me most, was Sir G. Ent [President of the College of Physicians], about respiration; that it is not to this day known, or concluded on, among physicians, nor to be done either, how the action is managed by nature, or for what use it is.'

(Samuel Pepys, *Diary*, January 22nd, 1665–6.)

Numeration and Mathematics

ONE of the surprises which met Assyriologists when cuneiform texts other than the common run of historical, ritual and economic material began to become available and intelligible, was the advanced stage of development which Babylonian mathematics had reached at an early period.

The origin of writing was, as pointed out elsewhere, not related to literature in the narrow sense but to the practical need of keeping records of temple property and produce. For this purpose number symbols were also required, and these are found from the beginning of writing in Mesopotamia. The cuneiform signs for the numerals were basically very simple, the single vertical wedge Y (in the earliest period $\triangleright$, an elliptical impression produced by a slanting thrust with the rounded end of the stylus) denoting, reasonably enough, the numeral 1. For the higher units groups of wedges were used, thus:

10 was denoted by a broad diagonal wedge ⟨ (in the earlier period a circular impression) and multiples of 10 up to 50 by groups of broad diagonal wedges, thus:

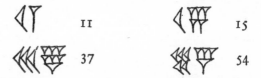

Numbers up to 59 which were not exact multiples of 10 were represented by a group of broad wedges for the tens followed by a group of vertical wedges for the units, thus:

⟨𝖸   11   ⟨𝖶   15

⟨⟨⟨𝖶   37   𝖶𝖸   54

At 60 complications arose. There were two systems of numeration, a decimal and a sexagesimal, in use in Babylonia from the very beginning of Sumerian civilization. The decimal system, employing powers of 10, requires no explanation. The sexagesimal system used powers of 60 (that is, multiples of 1, 60, and 3600, corresponding to the decimal system's units, tens, and hundreds) and enjoyed a certain advantage over the decimal system in that calculations involving fractions were facilitated by the fact that 60 has a large number of divisors (1,2,3,4,5,6,10, 12,15,20,30). It was seldom that either system was used with complete consistency, the only cases of a consistent and exclusive usage of the sexagesimal system being in mathematical or astronomical calculations. Elsewhere the two systems occur side by side, just as in Great Britain a decimal system is used alongside a system based on powers of 12, whilst the sexagesimal system continues in use for geometry and for the measurement of time.

As 60 was itself a unit in the sexagesimal system, it could be denoted by a vertical wedge, originally distinguished by its greater size from the wedge representing 1, though the distinction in size later disappeared. Correspondingly we find for numbers between 60 and 99 such groups as

（symbols） 70   （symbols） 80

（symbols） 90   （symbols） 94

On this system 100 would be （symbol）, and indeed was often written in that way. Alternatively, however, 100 could be represented either (in the early period) by a specially big circle (implying a purely decimal system, in which 100, the large circle, is considered as a higher power of 10, the small circle), or by a special sign （symbol） (pronounced ME), which in origin represents the actual pronunciation in Semitic of the word for 100. There are further modifications and combinations available to denote higher numbers. Thus 120 could be represented as

（symbol） = 2 × 60 (the wedges originally being larger than the wedge for 1)

or (in the early Sumerian period) （symbols） = 100 + 10 + 10 or

（symbols） = one ME + twenty.

1000, significant in the decimal system, had the special sign （symbol）, compounded of （symbol） and （symbol）, and thus denoting 10 × 100. In the sexagesimal system the significant high number was 3600, the square of 60. This was denoted originally by a very big circle (also used, as already noted, for the square of 10 in the decimal system); and finally by the sign （symbol）.

It will be seen from the examples given that the germ of a place-value notation (a system in which the value of a number-symbol depends upon its position relative to other symbols) was

447

already present in the numerals used in Babylonia from an early period. For the less mathematically-minded, it may be pointed out that our own system is a place-value notation: thus in the numbers written 15 and 51, in the former the '5' symbol means 'five' whilst in the latter the identical symbol means 'fifty'. The use of Roman numerals illustrates a system which is not a place-value notation: thus although the groups iv and vi have different values, the symbol 'v' in whatever position it occurs means 'five' and nothing else. In cuneiform writing 𒐕 is quite distinct from 𒁹𒐕, since in the former the 𒁹 means 'sixty', whilst in the latter it means 'one', so that the two groups of which it is a part denote respectively 'seventy' and 'eleven'. King Esarhaddon made ingenious political use of the fact that these two numbers differ in cuneiform only in the position of the two constituent symbols; for the details see above, page 125.

This place-value system was developed and extensively employed by Babylonian mathematicians, initially under the influence of the scale of weights which occurs in economic documents from Sumerian times onwards. The basis of the Sumerian and Babylonian weight system was the mina: this weight, in the region of one to two pounds, was sub-divided into 60 shekels, whilst 60 minas made a larger unit, the talent. Thus the Babylonians were familiar with a numeration X-Y-Z in which the units of X were 60 times those of Y and the units of Y 60 times those of Z. From this conception arose the possibility of an elaborated place-value notation, based on a sexagesimal system, in which X-Y-Z could mean either

$$(X \times 60 \times 60) + (Y \times 60) + Z$$

$$\text{or } (X \times 60) \quad \times (Y) \quad + \left(\frac{Z}{60}\right)$$

$$\text{or even } (X) \quad + \left(\frac{Y}{60}\right) + \left(\frac{Z}{60 \times 60}\right)$$

Such a system has two obvious disadvantages, both of which arise from the absence of a zero sign or a symbol corresponding to a decimal (or rather one should say here 'sexagesimal') point. In our own decimal system a number like 538.4 is unambiguous because of the convention that the first symbol to the left of the point represents units, the second to the left tens, and the third hundreds, whilst the first symbol to the right of the point represents tenths. The mathematically-minded will perhaps excuse elaboration of something which to them is obvious; but there may be readers for whom it will be useful or even surprising to emphasize that this decimal system of ours is no part of the nature of number itself but a mere (even if a very useful) convention. In the writing 538, 'three tens' is in fact simply represented by a 3 and 'five hundreds' simply by a 5, in each case made unambiguous by its position. Ambiguity could arise if there were either no tens or no units in the number: in such an instance this ambiguity is removed in our system by placing a zero sign in the appropriate position. If there are respectively no tens or no units, then to represent five hundred and eight or five hundred and thirty, we generally do not write 5 8, or 53 , which could be ambiguous, but use the symbols 508, 530. (One often finds exceptions to this convention in the marginal working of decimal multiplication or division sums, where a number in the form 53 may represent either 5.3 or 530, without, in many cases, involving the operator himself in any error.)

Applied to Babylonian numerals, ambiguities of the two types referred to could appear in the following forms. In a writing like ⟪symbol⟫ the vertical wedges could be intended to represent either the 'units' or the 'sixties' column, and the four broad wedges either the 'sixtieths' or the 'units' column. Thus such a writing (generally transcribed in the form 2,40) could denote in our terms either

$$(2 \times 60) + 40, \text{ that is, } 160$$

$$\text{or} \quad 2 + \frac{40}{60}, \text{ that is, } 2\tfrac{2}{3}$$

The second ambiguity is that the two groups of wedges might not denote consecutive powers of the sexagesimal system; that is, in the cuneiform writing instanced above, if the four broad wedges represented simply forty units, the two vertical wedges might have represented not 'two sixties' but 'two' in the next higher power, namely, 'two times sixty squared', that is, 2×3600;

𝖸𝖸 𐎣 would then represent 7200+40=7240. In the earlier period this ambiguity was sometimes avoided by writing a number with the two elements spaced widely apart when they did not represent successive powers of 60. Thus 7240, which equals

$$(2\times 60\times 60)+(0\times 60)+(40\times 1)$$

might have been written as 𝖸𝖸   𐎣

very widely spaced: this was not, however, consistently applied. In the Seleucid period a special sign for zero (𐎣) was used in such cases.

It is obvious that errors could arise in such a system, and quite certainly occasionally they did. It is worthy of mention, however, that Neugebauer, the greatest modern authority on Babylonian mathematics, confessed that he made more errors in checking the ancient computations than did the scribes in the original documents.

The mathematical texts with which we are acquainted belong to two distinct periods separated by well over a millennium. The earlier and larger group comes from the Old Babylonian period, the remainder from the Seleucid period, after 300 B.C.

It has generally been assumed that behind the relatively advanced Old Babylonian mathematics there lay a long period of gradual development. There is however no concrete evidence in favour of such a supposition, and Neugebauer points out that in all instances of periods of mathematical advance of which we actually know the antecedents, the fact has been a century or so of rapid progress set as an island between two long periods of stagnation.

It may be well to re-emphasize at this point that the vast majority of the hundreds of thousands of cuneiform tablets so far known are economic in content, dealing with prosaic matters such as receipts, loans and ration issues. The number of purely mathematical cuneiform texts known amounts only to hundreds, comprising about a hundred 'problem texts' and two hundred 'table texts'. The problem texts are concerned with algebraical or geometrical problems, whilst the table texts contain tables for multiplication and division and the calculation of reciprocals, squares, square roots, cubes, cube roots and so on. Many of these table texts, coming largely from the city of Nippur, were evidently school exercises. This is clear from the fact that on some tablets the same table is repeated in different hands, whilst on others one finds mathematical tables written on one side and vocabularies (one of the items much used in the training of scribes) on the other. Nippur is now known to have been a flourishing centre of scribal education in Old Babylonian times, and mathematics was obviously a part of the scribal curriculum.

As to the actual level of mathematical achievement in Babylonia in the Old Babylonian period (about 1800 B.C.), Neugebauer compares it with that of the early Renaissance. It was basically algebraical, but the properties of elementary sequences, such as arithmetic and geometric progressions, were known, as well as a certain number of geometrical relationships. It is now clear that the substance of what is known to us as the Pythagoras theorem – that in a right-angled triangle the sum of the squares of the sides about the right-angle equals the square of the hypotenuse – was known to the Babylonians as a practical fact: there is however no evidence that the Babylonians could formally prove such a theorem, and though some authorities have supposed one Old Babylonian tablet covered with geometrical diagrams (see plates 23 and 24) to be concerned with theoretical proofs of the relationship between areas of different figures, Babylonian mathematical procedures (like all Babylonian science) generally rested on empirical knowledge rather than formal proof. The value of π was fairly accurately known as $3\frac{1}{8}$, which is correct to about 0.6 per cent: this may be contrasted with the situation in Israel in the time of Solomon nearly a millennium later when, as I *Kings* vii. 23 shows, π was inaccurately taken as exactly 3. Quadratic equations involving terms up to the eighth degree are known, and, as already mentioned, there are tablets of square roots and cube roots.

A brief account of two simple examples of Old Babylonian problems follows. The first is an example of a quadratic equation. It is set down initially in a literal translation, then with (it is hoped) sufficient explanation to make it intelligible to the reader who has at some time mastered elementary algebra.

> I have added the surface-area and the side of the square: 45′
> You shall put down 1, the unit.
> You shall break (it) in halves: 30′
> You shall cross-multiply 30′ and 30′: 15′
> You shall add 15′ to 45′: 1
> That is the square of 1
> You shall take away the 30′, which you have multiplied by itself, from 1: 30′, the side of the square.

When one takes into account that the sexagesimal system was in use in mathematical problems, this becomes much clearer.

45′ then represents $\frac{45}{60}=\frac{3}{4}$, 30′ represents $\frac{30}{60}=\frac{1}{2}$, and 15′ represents $\frac{15}{60}=\frac{1}{4}$. The sum may then be stated as follows:

> Area of square plus side of square $=\frac{3}{4}$
> Take coefficient (of the linear measurement) as unity.
> Half of coefficient $=\frac{1}{2}$
> Square of $\frac{1}{2}$ $=\frac{1}{4}$
> $\frac{1}{4}$ plus $\frac{3}{4}$ $=1$
> Square root of 1 $=1$
> 1 minus $\frac{1}{2}$ $=\frac{1}{2}$

Finally, set out in modern symbols, the processes may be expressed as follows:

$$x^2+x \qquad =\tfrac{3}{4}$$
$$x^2+x+(\tfrac{1}{2})^2 =\tfrac{3}{4}+\tfrac{1}{4}$$
$$(x+\tfrac{1}{2})^2 \qquad =1$$
$$x+\tfrac{1}{2} \qquad =\sqrt{1}=1$$
$$x \qquad =1-\tfrac{1}{2}=\tfrac{1}{2}$$

(The Babylonian mathematician did not, it will be observed, concern himself with the negative value of x).

An Old Babylonian tablet dealing with geometrical relationships is illustrated in plates 23 and 24. The text is divided into sections, each of which consists of a figure with beneath it a note of the construction. The student was apparently required to calculate the area of the various shapes constructed. One section goes as follows:

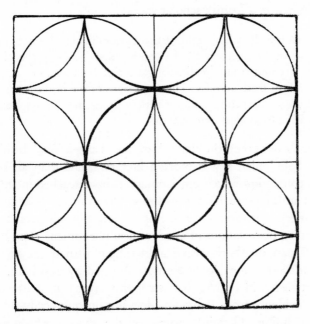

A square, the side is 1. Inside it (are) 4 quadrants, (and) 16 boat-shapes. I have drawn 5 regular concave-sided tetragons. This area, what is it?

Astronomy

Comparatively few Western Europeans with any pretensions to culture are able to live far from a city, with all that that involves in atmospheric pollution and bright street-lighting, both of them factors which seriously obscure the clarity of the night sky. In much of Iraq, however, these two factors are largely absent, whilst furthermore for much of the year it is very pleasant to sit outside after dark to enjoy the cool of the evening after the heat of the day. Thus it often happens that the European tourist or archaeologist, transported to Iraq and changing his habits accordingly, virtually sees the night sky for the first time, and is amazed by what he sees. As an interesting consequence of this, books by Assyriologists and others tend to contain extravagant statements about the brilliance of the night sky in Babylonia. As an instance, a Danish scholar states:

> Modern travellers have told of the extraordinarily distinct appearance to the human eye of the constellations, notably the planets, in the dry and cold, cloudless, night air of Mesopotamia, accounts I can affirm from autopsy. The silent signs of the heavens naturally compelled observation from the earliest times, and the ziggurats . . . must have been ideal observatories.

Neugebauer points out that this supposed exceptional 'brilliance of the Babylonian sky is more a literary cliché than an actual fact', a conclusion which other observers have reached independently. The difference of opinion is more than a matter of aesthetics, for it affects our estimate of the actual and possible accuracy of Babylonian observations of astronomical phenomena close to the horizon, particularly the rising and setting of planets, the accurate observation of which could be much affected by dust haze.

It has been widely held that astronomy arose out of astrology, but the evidence from Babylonia does not unequivocally support this conclusion. Certainly some of the earliest astronomical observations may have been taken to provide material for omens, but a distinction must be made between omens drawn from the behaviour of celestial bodies as conspicuous phenomena, and astrology, based on the theory of a correspondence between the earth and the sky. Astrology itself is divisible into two types. Astrology in the modern sense, that is, horoscopic astrology, involving the belief that the fortunes of an individual are related to the positions of celestial bodies at the moment of his birth, was certainly (in terms of Mesopotamian history) of late origin, and did not arise until the second half of the first millennium B.C. However, preceding this there did exist a more general type of astrology, generally called 'judicial' astrology (as distinct from the horoscopic type), which purported to predict from celestial or meteorological phenomena the immediate future of the king and country in relation to such matters as harvest, floods and invasions. The following may serve as examples of judicial astrology:

> If the sun stands in the station of the moon, the king of the land will be secure on the throne. If the sun stands above or below the moon, the foundation of the throne will be secure. The king of the land will stand in his justice. If the sun and the moon are invisible, the king of the land will make broad the ear [i.e. will show wisdom].

> In the night Saturn came near to the moon. Saturn is the 'star' of the sun. This is the solution: it is favourable to the king, (for) the sun is the king's star.

> If there is an earthquake in the month Nisan, the king's land will rebel against him.

> If in the month of Ab it thunders [literally 'the Thunder-god casts his mouth'], the day is dark, the heavens rain down, and lightning flashes, (then) water will be poured out in the rhines. If it thunders [literally 'the Thunder-god calls'] on a cloudless day, there will be gloom in the land. If the heavens rain down in Ab, there will be a slaughter of people. If a whirlwind comes from the west, there will be a slaughter of the people of the west. If it thunders twice, the land which sent you a message of hostility will send you a message of peace.

Earlier than reports of this type there occur astrological omens, of which individual examples go back to the beginning of the second millennium B.C. and even, some scholars would say, to the time of Sargon of Agade (circa 2370 B.C.). These were subsequently grouped in collections (known as 'Series') of which the most important is called Enuma Anu Enlil, which reached its final form in the late second or early first millennium B.C., most probably in Cassite times. The following extract serves as an example:

> If an eclipse occurs in the month of Siwan on the fourteenth day, and the (Moon-)god in his darkening darkens at the east side above

and brightens on the west side below, a north wind gets up in the first
night-watch and abates (?) in the middle night-watch, the (Moon-)
god who in his darkening darkens at the east side above and brightens
at the west side below . . . will give therein a decision for Ur and the
king of Ur: the king of Ur will see famine, the dead will be numerous.
(As to) the king of Ur, his son will do violence to him, but as to
the son who does violence to his father, (the Sun-god) Shamash
will catch him, and he will die for the impiety (concerning) his
father. A son of the king, who has not been proclaimed for kingship, shall take the throne.

There is no evidence at present for the taking of systematic
astronomical observations in the third millennium B.C., and the
earliest recorded examples of such observations are from the reign
of Ammi-saduqa, one of the kings of the First Dynasty of Babylon.
These records relate to the rising and setting of the planet Venus,
and they were probably taken to serve as the basis for omens, though
they could conceivably have been related to the fixing of the calendar in connection with religious festivals. The position of Venus on
given dates can of course be extrapolated for the second millennium B.C., and thus these Babylonian observations of Venus,
dated to certain years in the reign of Ammi-saduqa, serve as one
of the keys to ancient chronology: the matter is complicated by
the fact that Venus repeats its cycle over a period of years, so that
the same observations could relate to more than one series of
dates, whilst the Babylonian observations themselves are not of a
high order of accuracy.

Apart from these records of the heliacal rising and setting of
Venus, the oldest astronomical documents extant from Mesopotamia are the so-called astrolabes. These are clay tablets inscribed
with three concentric circles divided by twelve radii. In each of
the thirty-six divisions thus made is the name of a constellation
together with some numbers. The purpose of these astrolabes is
not altogether clear, but it is evident that they formed a kind of
celestial map and that they were probably related to the origin of
the zodiac. The numbers mentioned in the astrolabes are related
to each other in an arithmetical progression.

In copies themselves dating from about 700 B.C. but based on older material, we have two texts called ^{mul}APIN. In these the fixed stars are classified in three 'roads', and these texts in fact constitute a simple descriptive account of basic astronomical conceptions, divorced from mythology.

By 700 B.C. we also find the systematic reports of astronomical observations to the court, which have already been referred to. The actual practical purpose of these reports was certainly related primarily to judicial astrology, and not only do they not imply any mathematical treatment of astronomical phenomena, but they even fail to distinguish between astronomical and meteorological phenomena. None the less they do show that it was already recognized that solar eclipses could only occur at the new moon, and lunar at the full, which indicates the systematic recording of such events. Consistent with this is the report of the Greek astronomer Ptolemy (who lived in Alexandria in the second century A.D.) that records of eclipses were available to him from 747 B.C. onwards. Thus although the original purpose of observations of this type was astrological, such systematic observations from 700 B.C. onwards provided data from which could be derived fairly accurate average values for the various periodic phenomena. In other words, on the basis of such series of observations extending over centuries, it was possible to calculate average apparent movements of the sun, moon and planets. Neugebauer argues that this knowledge did not develop into a systematic mathematical theory before 500 B.C. The grounds on which he bases this view are that up to 480 B.C. there was only haphazard intercalation. Throughout Babylonian history the calendar was lunar, the month beginning (as still in Judaism and Islam) with sunset on the evening upon which the new moon was visible shortly after sunset: twelve lunar months amount only to approximately 354 days, which is $11\frac{1}{4}$ days short of the solar year. Thus an additional month was required roughly once in three years to bring the lunar calendar into step with the solar year. By the fourth century B.C. this was certainly being done on a mathematical basis, the rule of seven intercalations in nineteen years being apparently in use. The actual order of intercalation in the nineteen-year cycle was as follows, the asterisks denoting a year containing an intercalary month:

1*	2	
3*	4	5
6*	7	8
9*	10	
11*	12	13
14*	15	16
17*	18	19

In the first year of this cycle the intercalation was in the middle of the year, in other cases at the end.

Once values for the principle periodic phenomena had been worked out, the next major development, applied originally and principally to the moon, was to consider the complicated movement of celestial bodies as compounded of a number of simpler periodic effects, and to apply the periodic deviations as corrections to the average movement. That is to say, if the sun and moon moved in the sky with apparently constant velocity, it would be simple to calculate their relative positions at any time and hence to arrive at the moment of new or full moons. In fact the actual apparent movement of the moon varies from the ideal (or average) apparent movement: such variations were recorded, found to be amenable to treatment as periodic phenomena and applied in this form as corrections to the ideal (or average) movement of the moon. Neugebauer concludes, from the details of the manner in which this method was applied in astronomical texts, that it was invented by a single individual in the fourth or third century B.C.: it was certainly in existence by 250 B.C. The method was applied not only to the moon but also to the movements of the planets. Cuneiform texts from the last two or three centuries B.C. make it clear that the methods used by the Babylonians for calculating the movements of the moon were – as Neugebauer puts it – 'among the finest achievements of ancient science, comparable only to the works of Hipparchus and Ptolemy'. The Babylonians had only very crude equipment for observation – there is certainly no trace from texts or archaeology of such a thing as a telescope, although lenses of rock-crystal have been found – and individual observations were undoubtedly of no high order of accuracy. Thus the high achievements of late Babylonian astronomy were the result of the application of the relatively advanced mathematical techniques, developed over a millennium earlier, to a long series of fairly rough observations, to give results more accurate than could be obtained from any single observation.

The texts referred to, containing tables of the positions of the sun, moon and planets calculated for regular time intervals, are known as ephemerides, and their practical purpose was to predict new moons, eclipses, and probably the rising and setting of planets: closely related to the ephemerides are 'procedure texts' giving the rules for calculating an ephemeris. About three hundred texts of these types are known, a hundred from Erech and the remainder from Babylon. The periods covered by these computations extend altogether from about 230 B.C. to 49 A.D. Some of these texts are provided with a colophon giving the date of writing, and this shows that the tablets were usually written at a date near the beginning of the period covered by the computation. Thus the latest text in this class, of which the period of fifty-six years covered ends with 49 A.D., was probably written early in the first decade B.C. The latest astronomical text of all – and the latest of all known cuneiform texts – has a date of 75 A.D.

Finally it may be pointed out that, even in the latest period, although the methods and aims of the ephemerides texts were scientific, the computations concerned may have been thought to involve some religious or magical consequences. This is suggested by some of the colophons, such as one which says:

> He wrote it for the life of his soul, for length of days, for the well-being of his seed, for the establishment of his foundation, in order that there should be no ill-fortune for him.

Medicine

In Iraq before the revolution of 1958 Baghdad contained about one-fifth of the population of the country but about three-quarters of the physicians. The situation between the capital and the rest of the country cannot have been wildly different in ancient Babylonia. There, although physicians certainly existed, the availability to the man in the street (the phrase being literal in this case) was such that Herodotus in the fifth century B.C. was misled into writing of the Babylonians:

> They bring out all their sick into the streets, for they have no regular doctors. People that come along offer the sick man advice, either from what they personally have found to cure such a complaint, or what they have known someone else to be cured by. No-one is allowed to pass by a sick person without asking him what ails him.

In fact, from at least the end of the third millennium there were medical practitioners who employed, alongside a certain amount of humbug, methods of healing that were strictly rational. The antiquity of the medical profession in Babylonia, as well as its antecedents, is indicated by the term denoting 'physicians'. This word, *asu* in Akkadian, derives from the Sumerian *a-zu* or *ià-zu*, which terms mean 'the man who knows water (*or* oil)', the implication being that the *asu* was originally a man who divined by water or lecanomancy, presumably with the aid of the water-god Ea. Medicine was under the particular protection of the goddess Gula. There was also a god actually called Ninazu 'Lord Doctor', whose son Ningizzida had as his symbol the rod with intertwined serpents, still accepted as a symbol of the healing profession.

Medical practitioners and aspects of the medical profession are referred to in legal codes, letters and other texts, whilst magical texts and omens are full of references to diseases. Our main knowledge of Babylonian medicine comes, however, from the large number of medical texts extant. Most of these are from the seventh century library of Ashurbanipal at Nineveh (Kuyunjik), but there are other earlier ones from Ashur, from the thirteenth century archives at Boghazkoi (in Hittite translations), and from the Cassite period. A Sumerian example of medical prescriptions has now been identified from the period of the Third Dynasty of Ur.

There were two main classes of texts which one could call medical. In one class there is an account of symptoms, in the other a list of prescriptions for various complaints. The two classes are not however completely separate, and one may find prescriptions in the diagnostic texts, or diagnoses amongst the prescriptions.

The tablets giving diagnoses (and prognoses) have particular interest, in that they shed light on the basic notions behind the medical theories of the ancient Babylonians, and confirm, as one could equally deduce from magical and religious texts, that illness was generally thought to be due either to the 'hand' of a deity or to possession by a devil. It was in accordance with this view that a sick man might be treated either by rational medicine (or possibly surgery) to reduce the symptoms, or by magical procedures (efficacious then as now with cases of hysterical illness) to expel the supposed evil influence.

The texts dealing in codified form with symptoms and maladies have been ably edited by the French scholar R. Labat (*Traité Akkadien de Diagnostics et Pronostics Médicaux*, I (1951)). These texts are known not only from a number of cities in Babylonia and Assyria, but even from the Hittite area. The dates of most of the extant copies which (in that they belong to one standard tradition) we may call 'canonical', range between 721 B.C. and 453 B.C., though there are three texts not belonging to the main tradition which are earlier in date. One assumes by analogy with other technical compilations that the origin of the canonical tradition in these texts goes back to the Cassite period, but this is not yet actually proved.

The work in question originally contained forty chapters, and was divided into five sections. The general kind of contents of these sections are noted below, with a few extracts from each of them.

The first section, comprising two tablets or chapters, is not strictly medical at all, although it was regarded by the ancient scribes as part of the series. It actually contains omen texts concerning the interpretation of signs seen whilst the exorcist or some other person was on the way to the patient's house:

If the door of someone's house, where the sick man is lying, cries out [*i.e.* creaks] like a lion, he has eaten the taboo of his god; he will drag out and then die.

If [the exorcist] sees either a black dog or a black pig, that sick man will die.

If [the exorcist] sees a white pig, that sick man will live . . .

If [the exorcist] sees pigs which keep lifting up their tails, (as to) that sick man, anxiety will not come near him.

If a raven croaks plaintively in front of a man, he will experience tears; if a raven croaks plaintively behind a man, his adversary will experience tears.

If a snake falls on the sick man's bed, that sick man will get well.

The second section consists of twelve tablets which go through symptoms visible in the body, grouping them according to different organs and parts of the body; it is the symptoms themselves rather than the disease which are the interest of these tablets.

If (the sick man) keeps crying out 'My skull! My skull!', (it) is the hand of a god.

If he is beaten in his head [perhaps meaning 'if his head throbs'] on the right side, it is the hand of Adad.

If he is beaten in his head and he coughs up blood, it is the hand of the Twins; he will die.

If he is beaten in his head and if the muscles of his brow, his hands and his feet are affected together, being red and burning, it is the hand of a god; he will live.

If from his head to his feet he is full of red pustules, and his body is white, he has been attacked when in bed with a woman; hand of the god Sin.

If from his head to his feet he is covered with black pustules, and his body is red, ditto; hand of the god Shamash.

If he is puffy as to the temples, and his ears do not hear, the hands of his god are put upon him; he will die.

If his brow is white and his tongue is white, his illness will be long, but he will recover.

If he grinds his teeth, and his hands and feet shake, it is the hand of the god Sin; he will die.

If the sick man's right ear throbs, his illness is serious but he will live. If his left ear throbs, (cause for) anxiety. If both his ears throb, he will die.

If his face is red and yellow and he gets up, then he will have a relapse.

If his face is white, he will live.

If his face is white and overcast with yellow, and his mouth and lips are full of ulcers, and his left eye twitches, he will die.

If his neck keeps turning to the left, his hands and feet are stretched out, his eyes are wide open to the sky, spittle runs out of his mouth, he makes a croaking noise, he is delirious [literally 'doesn't know himself'], and at the end of a seizure he . . . [meaning of the next words is uncertain]; it is epilepsy (?); hand of the god Sin.

If his neck throbs and his head keeps falling, and his hands and feet keep swelling up and he rubs (them) against the ground; the demon Handmaid of Lilu has seized him.

The treatise continues in like vein through symptoms of the throat, gullet, arms, hands, fingers, chest, breasts, loins, back, abdomen (in various sub-divisions), hips, anus, penis, urine, testicles, thighs, feet and other parts of the body. Thus:

If blood flows out of his penis, (it is) the hand of Shamash; sign of Land-of-no-return [*i.e.* the Underworld].

If his penis and testicles are inflamed, the hand of the goddess Dilbat [Venus] has reached him in his bed.

If his testicles are inflamed, if his penis is covered with sores, he has gone in to the high-priestess of his god.

In the third section (containing ten tablets) the prognoses are grouped according to the progress of the disease from day to day; at the end of this section groups of symptoms are listed as indicating specific diseases. The texts in this section have contents typically of the form 'If, when a man has been ill so many days, such-and-such a symptom is (*or* is not) visible, then his fate will be so-and-so', the period referred to increasing from one day up to a month or so. The following are examples:

If, having been ill three days, he gets up; in the night, easing [literally 'loosing'] of the illness. . . .

If, having been ill four days, he keeps putting his hand on his belly and his face is overcast with yellow, he will die.

If, having been ill for four or five days, sweat keeps coming over him, easing of the illness: if he has been ill for four or five days, hand of Ahhazu [name of a demon, literally 'the Seizer'].

If, having been ill for five days, blood comes out of his mouth on the sixth day, his illness will be eased; it is *setu*-fever.

If, having been ill for five days, his flesh is overcast with yellow (and) his eyes are full of blood, he will die. . . .

If, having been ill for five or ten days continuously, he suffers from chronic difficulty in breathing (?), he will die . . .

If, having been ill with a severe illness for five or ten days continuously, a steady (trickle of) blood comes out of his mouth for five days [or possibly 'on the fifth day'] and (then) stops, his illness will be eased; it is the *setu*-fever; he is cured; there is no 'hit'. . . .

If, having been ill for five or ten days, there is neither fever nor sweat, it is the hand of Sin; he will die. . . .

If, for five, ten, fifteen or twenty days the fingers of his hands and (the toes of) his feet stay contracted and he cannot open (them) nor separate (them), it is the Hand of Ishtar; she will however set (him) free; he will get on all right and will live.

If his illness keeps coming upon him in the middle watch (of the night), he has had sexual relations with someone's wife; hand of the deity Urash.

If, when he is ill, his body is very cold, his illness will be prolonged and he will die. If, when he is ill, he cannot keep in his stomach the food which he eats and cannot keep sustenance in his mouth but casts (it) out of his mouth, he will die.

If he is ill in the morning, and his illness leaves him in the afternoon, but returns to him quickly, abatement of his illness; he will get up and be well on

the second day some time before midday,
the third day at some time in the afternoon,
the fourth day before twilight,
the fifth day before the end of the day,
the sixth day before the (first) watch,
the seventh day before the middle watch,
the eighth day before the dawn (watch),
the ninth day before day-break,
or the tenth day.

As examples of the type of text at the end of the third section, in which specific syndromes are described, one may instance the following:

If a man's body is yellow, his face is yellow, and his eyes are yellow, and the flesh is flabby, it is jaundice.

If grief falls upon him, his throat is tight, when he eats food or drinks water it doesn't agree with him, he says 'Oh, my heart!' and keeps on sighing, he is sick with love-sickness; it is the same (diagnosis) for a man or a woman.

If a man's penis and the top of his stomach are burning, if he has a glowing fever, the bottom of his stomach troubles him and his stomach is disturbed, if he is burning in his arms, feet and belly, that man is suffering from a venereal disease; hand of the goddess Ishtar.

The fourth section of the work, originally comprising ten tablets, is very badly damaged and little of it remains. Amongst other things the remaining fragments refer to treatment in specific cases, as well as giving the description of various syndromes:

If something like sleep keeps taking him, if his limbs are unsteady, his ears sing, his mouth is gripped and he cannot speak; it is the hand of a malevolent *alu*-demon. If, after washing with water, as he comes up from the river he is taken with convulsions and falls down, the Croucher-demon of the river has struck him.

If grief falls upon him, and he begs for everything he sees, if he is burning, has sweating (fits) daily, keeps having furies of desire (for things) and coughs up (his) stomach until they bring (them) to him, and then when they bring (them) to him he sees but doesn't comprehend; it is the hand of a ghost which struck him in the water.

If the 'hand of Ishtar' turns (in) him to epilepsy, (this indicates) hand of the god Sin – (alternative diagnosis) hand of Ishtar. To save him: human semen, sea fruit, a *hulu*-mouse of the canebrake which is sparsely covered with hair, the tip of the ear of a black dog, hair of a black riding-ass, tail of a black dog, with the hair of a virgin kid, white and black, ditto. [Apparently, in view of the preceding paragraphs, 'ditto' here indicates 'you shall put at his neck and he will get well']. If the hand of Ishtar turns (in) him to Bel-uri [some unidentified malady], (it is) 'hand of Shamash'. To save him: root of caper, root of thorn, root of fennel, seed of henbane, the bloody cloth of a woman, and *euphorbia*, in the skin of a virgin kid, ditto.

The final section, consisting of six tablets, relates to women and small children. The following extracts are typical of the part dealing with pregnant women:

> If the top of a pregnant woman's forehead glows white; that which is within her womb is a daughter; she will be rich. If it is red, that which is within her womb is a man-child; he will die.
>
> If the nipples of a pregnant woman are yellow, that which is within her womb will be miscarried.
>
> If the womb of a pregnant woman lies on her stomach, she will bear a deaf child.
>
> If the womb of a pregnant woman is thrown down upon the right side of her stomach, she has conceived a man-child.
>
> If the pregnant woman keeps vomiting, she will not bring to completion.
>
> If the pregnant woman discharges matter from her mouth, she will die together with that which is within her womb.
>
> If blood comes out of the mouth of the pregnant woman, she will not survive her confinement.

Other prognoses foretell the birth of twins, and various other details of the well-being of mother and child. Other sections refer to the woman having sexual intercourse at various times during her pregnancy: thus, for intercourse between five months and three days and five months and ten days the prognosis is 'Life' except at five months and eight or nine days, when (respectively) the lady will be seized by *mamitu* [a word often meaning 'a curse' but here perhaps a specific disease] or will die.

The other part of this section concerns babies:

> If a baby takes the breast but is not satisfied and screams a lot, it is injured internally [literally 'its inside is broken'].
>
> If a baby has its stomach inflamed and when the breast is offered to it it does not feed, a witch has picked that baby out.
>
> If the baby keeps being cold and grinds his teeth, his illness will be long; it is a seizure of the god Kubu.

It will be seen from these diagnostic and prognostic texts that whilst some sections might be considered purely rational and others purely superstitious, the general approach of these texts to sickness was a tangle of crude supersitition* and acute practical observation. Supposed magical cures were, as one might gather from the chapter on Religion (see pages 311 ff.), common in Babylonia, and frequently messy. As an instance, the ritual might require the priest to tear the heart out of a kid and thrust the still quivering organ into the hand of a sick man whilst a spell was recited. None the less, rational methods employing drugs were also in use; these are known principally from the prescription texts, which are numerically the most important group of medical texts.

There is now known – as mentioned above – a prescription text going back at least to the Third Dynasty of Ur (2000 B.C.). This text is completely rational and, unlike some later examples of this class, contains no reference at all to spells to accompany the preparation or administration of the drugs prescribed. In the prescription texts in the Akkadian language there are generally three sections:

(1) a note of the symptoms,
(2) a list of pharmaceutical materials,
(3) instructions for the preparation and application of the remedy.

In the Sumerian text the first element appears to be lacking. The fifteen prescriptions on the tablet are classified according to the manner of application. The treatments employed included (a) poultices, (b) potions, (c) bathing with hot infusions: twelve out of the fifteen prescriptions involved external applications. An example of each type of prescription follows:

(a) Having brayed the roots of [such-and-such plants] together with dried river bitumen, and poured beer thereon, and having

---

* Superstition in connection with the symptoms and treatment of illness is, however, not limited to the ancients or to the unlearned. One need only quote the clergyman of the Church of England who noted in 1791: 'The Stiony on my right Eye-lid still swelled and inflamed very much. As it is commonly said that the Eye-lid being rubbed by the tail of a black Cat would do it much good if not entirely cure it, ... a little before dinner I made a trial of it, and very soon after dinner I found my Eye-lid much abated of the swelling and almost free from Pain.' The reverend gentleman did not hesitate to scoff at superstition, for he added: 'Any other Cats Tail may have the above effect in all probability – but I did my Eye-lid with my own black Tom Cat's Tail...' [Parson Woodforde's Diary, 11 March, 1791].

massaged (the affected place) with oil, you shall put (the preparation) on as a poultice.

(b) When you have brayed the seed of [such-and-such plants] and put (the mixture) into beer, the patient shall drink (it).

In the third type of prescription the reader is instructed to take various ingredients, including dried figs and some kind of salt, and

(c) having heated (them), you shall wash (the affected place) with the liquid. [There is a further instruction of which the meaning is not clear. It is just possible that it may have referred to the administration of an enema through a tube].

Apart from this Sumerian text the oldest prescription texts are some fragments from the Old Babylonian period. After this come some Cassite pieces and an important group from Boghazkoi. The great bulk, however, comes from the New Assyrian period, from which there are series of texts classifying prescriptions according to the parts of the body. Thus a whole group of texts prescribes for afflictions of the stomach:

If a man's stomach is hot, and will not accept food or drink, you shall take the seed of tamarisk, and mix (it) with honey and curd. He shall eat and recover.

To remove heat in the stomach, you shall bray together the seven drugs elder, sweet reed, . . . [the names are missing], *asa foetida*, dates, and fir-turpentine. You shall strain, steep in beer, heat in an oven, take out, strain and cool. You shall add thereto husks (?) of barley, and on the top you shall put rose-water. You shall put this into his anus and he will recover.

As the preceding text indicates, the use of the enema was certainly known in the New Assyrian period (before 612 B.C.). In another prescription twenty-four drugs (mostly woods and wood resins) were mixed in beer, left to stand, boiled up and strained. The operator was then instructed to add honey and pure oil, after which

whilst it is still warm you shall pour it into his anus. He will evacuate and recover.

Another method of administration of drugs is indicated by

the following. A preparation was made from various plants, and the instruction then given:

> . . . he shall swallow it with his mouth and he shall suck it up into his nostrils, and he shall recover.

Yet another method was available:

> If pain seizes on a man, you shall put . . . gum of Aleppo pine, gum of galbanum and turmeric on the fire and shall fumigate his nostrils (therewith); you shall fill your mouth with oil and shall blow into his nostrils, and he will recover.

Sometimes there is a reference to reciting a charm at the same time as the practical measure was performed.

Another group of tablets deals with lung and chest troubles:

> If a man is sick of a cough, you shall beat up styrax in strong beer, honey, and refined oil: you shall let his tongue take it without a meal; let him drink it steaming hot in beer and honey. You shall make him vomit with a feather. Afterwards he should eat a mixture of honey and curds and drink sweet wine, and he will recover.

Inhalation was another method of treatment. A number of vegetable ingredients were prepared and infused in oil, beer and curds. Then, say the instructions,

> You shall prepare a great . . . pot, stop up its sides with wheaten dough, boil the brew (therein) over a fire, put a reed tube into it, let him draw the steam up so that it strikes against his lungs, and he shall recover.

It will be clear, particularly from the diagnostic texts, that no very advanced knowledge of anatomy or physiology can be claimed for the Babylonians. They did not know the functions of most internal organs, which were simply regarded as the seat of various emotions. Thus the ear was the seat of the understanding, and the heart the centre of creative intelligence. Though variations in the pulse rate were known, and the fact that blood flowed through the veins was recognized, the Babylonians did not go further and deduce the circulation of the blood. Knowledge of anatomy and physiology was certainly hindered by the religious taboo upon dissection of a dead human body, but this impediment could have been overcome by the intelligent observation of animal anatomy. Although, however, careful observation of certain features of animal anatomy was commonly carried out, this was done only in the interests of the pseudo-science of liver-divination or lung-divination, so that no useful scientific observations were attempted. Moreover, as only beasts in good condition would be sacrificed for this or other purposes, the Babylonian officiants were prevented by the very means of selection of sacrificial animals from gaining wide experience of animal organs in heavily diseased conditions, with the possibility of connecting this with externally visible symptoms of sickness. An even greater hindrance than the taboo upon dissection was the theory that illness was due to demonic possession. Holding such a view, a Babylonian would have considered it mere idle curiosity to attempt to learn more of the functioning of particular organs in sickness and health: the two points to be attended to in illness were the demon who lay at the bottom of the trouble and the external symptoms.

In such a state of affairs one does not expect an advanced stage of surgery. Surgeons of a kind there certainly were, as early as the time of Hammurabi, for the 'Code' of Hammurabi lays down the fees payable in the event of successful treatment, together with penalties to which the operator rendered himself liable by failure.

> If an *asu* has made a serious incision in a gentleman with a bronze lancet and has brought about the man's recovery, or has opened a *nakkaptu* in a man with a bronze lancet and has brought about the recovery of the man's eye, he shall receive ten shekels of silver. [The meaning of *nakkaptu* is in dispute; the reference may be to opening a caruncle or to making an incision in the temple.]

Payment was proportionately less if the patient was of a lower social class. The surgeon's profession was not without risk, for if he caused the death or blindness of a patient of the gentleman class, his hand was cut off. Three other sections of the laws of Hammurabi refer to the *asu* mending broken limbs.

Despite these relatively early references to surgery, there is no text known amongst the hundreds of later medical texts which deals specifically and systematically with the subject. This at first suggests that surgical methods were virtually unknown in the later period, but another possible interpretation of the lack of texts has been pointed out. Surgery is pre-eminently a matter in which techniques are learned by observation and practice: there is no place for the correspondence course in surgery. Thus it is highly probable that the apprentice surgeon in Babylonia acquired his knowledge and skill by watching a master of the profession at work, and nothing was to be gained by attempting to commit the details of the techniques to writing.

There are one or two broken texts in which there *may* be a reference to surgical operations. Eye disease, possibly cataract, is not infrequently referred to in phrases which speak of the eye of a man being covered with a shadow, and one damaged text does say:

If a man's eye is covered with a shadow, with a lancet . . .

Did the remainder of the sentence refer to a surgical operation? At present we cannot tell. Another text, which mentions the use of a cutting instrument and later says

If the sickness has reached the inside of the bone, you shall scrape and remove,

has been taken to refer to a deep incision, but could be otherwise interpreted. There are other passages mentioning the use by a doctor of a cutting instrument, but these probably only refer to the lancing of an abscess, a technique which can scarcely be dignified with the name of surgery.

Chemical Technology

Technical knowledge was, like religious rituals, a closely guarded secret. One finds as a colophon to texts dealing with either matter such instructions as

Let the initiate show the initiate; the non-initiate shall not see it. It belongs to the tabooed things of the great gods.

For this reason some processes known to the technologists of ancient Mesopotamia may never have been committed to writing, whilst others were written in a manner which was deliberately obscure and may well defeat the attempts of modern scholars to understand the texts concerned.

One instance of a text written in cryptogram is a recipe (not later than the sixteenth century B.C.) for glaze-making, though in this case two modern scholars, C. J. Gadd and R. Campbell Thompson, did succeed in deciphering it. They found that the ancient technologist had employed devices of the following kind to conceal his meaning. The word for 'stone' – *aban* – would normally either be written with an ideogram or spelt out with the signs for the three syllables *a-ba-an*. The technologist, however, wrote the three syllables *ha-bar-an*, which to those in the secret would be understood as (*h*)*a-ba*(*r*)-*an* but to outsiders would give the meaningless word *ḫabaran*. Much of the text is written according to this principle. Once the cryptogram had been broken the text proved detailed enough for modern chemists to perform the operations described and duly produce glaze, although some of the magical operations essential to the ancient technologist for placating the spirits of the dead could safely be dispensed with.

An interesting study of early chemical apparatus in Mesopotamia has been made by Martin Levey in his *Chemistry and Chemical Technology in Ancient Mesopotamia* (1959). Professor Levey shows that archaeological finds attest, in addition to pestles and mortars, mills and strainers (any of which could have been for domestic use), such things as crucibles, filtering apparatus, distillation and extraction apparatus, and drip bottles. The drip bottle mentioned was found at Nuzi (a site near modern Kirkuk which flourished *circa* 1400 B.C.), and is regarded by Levey as having been particularly suitable for the preparation of colloidal pharmaceutical preparations. The distillation apparatus referred to consisted of double-rimmed earthenware pots dating from 3000 B.C. A related vessel, but with a drainage hole in the inner rim, is regarded by Levey as an extraction apparatus. The raw material would be placed between the two rims, and a lid put over the vessel. A solvent (water or oil) would be boiled in the bottom of the pot: the vapour would condense on the lid, run down over the raw material, extract the ingredient sought, and drip back into the bottom of the pot. The principle was in fact that of the coffee percolator.

As sources of heat for chemical processes different types of furnace were employed: they are sometimes represented in art, whilst actual examples have been found in excavations. Fire was, in the first millennium B.C., produced by the striking of flint against steel to light tinder. It is even possible, according to R. Campbell Thompson (*A Dictionary of Assyrian Chemistry and Geology* (1936), page 39), that the sulphur match was known: this possibility is revealed by a text which reads

You shall light the brand [match (?)] in a fire of sulphur.

A discussion of the chemicals and some of the chemical processes known to the ancient people of Mesopotamia is to be found in R. Campbell Thompson's *Dictionary of Assyrian Chemistry and Geology*. Amongst acids, the Assyrians in the first millennium B.C. could already produce fuming sulphuric acid and possibly *aqua regia* (a mixture of nitric and hydrochloric acids). The latter Campbell Thompson deduces from the fact that the Assyrians employed gold to give a red colour to glass, and for this process the gold must first be dissolved in *aqua regia*. Various salts were in use, amongst them borax, common salt, saltpetre, washing soda, sal ammoniac and copper sulphate, whilst other elements and compounds employed, in addition to the common metals and metallic oxides, were mercury and its sulphide cinnabar, sulphur and the sulphides of different metals, and various compounds of arsenic.

The chemical processes in use in ancient Mesopotamia are described so clearly by Martin Levey (op. cit.) that only a brief summary of some of the better attested is given here. Amongst such processes mention may be made of the tanning of leather, which goes back at least to the third millennium B.C. The skins were first soaked in water or a saline solution and then scoured and scraped to remove adhering flesh, fat and hair. According to Levey, 'bating' with dung would then be carried out to improve the texture of the skin. The actual tanning was then performed by soaking the skin in a solution prepared from alum and the extract from gall nuts: both alum and gall nuts were important items in the commerce of ancient Mesopotamia. Tanning with oil could be combined with the alum-and-tannin method or employed as an alternative.

The prepared leather was frequently subject to the subsequent process of dyeing. Dyeing was another well-known and ancient technique, and was employed for wool from at least the third millennium, though at present we have no detailed information about the methods used. Apart from natural shades, red, yellow, blue, black and purple are all attested as colours of wool.

Soaps, prepared from a vegetable oil and a vegetable alkali, sometimes medicated by the addition of sulphur or resins, were certainly known from 2000 B.C., though Levey points out that there is no evidence for the deliberate production of true soap (that is, a soap made by boiling an oil with a caustic alkali). It is possible however, according to Levey, that in some processes in which salts were boiled up with oils the presence of sodium hydroxide as an impurity would in fact yield some true soap.

Art

The art of ancient Mesopotamia, one of the concrete manifestations through which we can gain some insight into Mesopotamian civilization and above all into its religion, is known to us in many media. Perhaps most widespread across the whole period are the cylinder seals, originating in the *Protoliterate* [Uruk V] period and continuing down to the second half of the first millennium, when they were replaced by stamp seals. Sculpture in the round is well represented, along with reliefs and that intermediate form between the two utilized for such objects as the Assyrian winged human-headed bulls. From certain periods chance has preserved masses of carved ivory (see plate 60A, B for two examples), often beautiful by our canons as well as instructive for ancient religion. Other categories represented are metal-work, jewellery and amulets, and wall-decorations in painted tiles or the coloured ends of clay cones embedded in plaster. Even a few paintings are known, on plastered walls. Carpets and tapestries are not known directly from ancient Mesopotamia, but an example of a Scythian rug of the type which would have been known in Mesopotamia has been miraculously preserved further north in U.S.S.R. Though Assyrian carpets are not themselves extant, the patterns of the carpets used in Assyrian palaces are known to us from designs on limestone slabs (see plate 63). These slabs, set around the doorways of palaces, presumably matched the design of the carpets covering the floor of the rest of the room.

An appraisal of the style and techniques employed by the artists in ancient Mesopotamia is the work of an Art Historian, which the writer does not claim to be: for the reader interested in this aspect of the matter the account in H. Frankfort's *The Art and Architecture of the Ancient Orient* (1954) is recommended. The brief account offered below is descriptive and not analytical.

Throughout the whole two and a half millennia with which we are concerned all works of art were anonymous. Almost all art was purely functional, and the function with which it was associated was the service of religion. Thus the Sumerian examples of sculpture in the round were not created to perpetuate the subject of the piece before his fellowmen, but so that the piece could be placed with its message of intercession by the ear of the god, thereby giving the prince or nobleman represented by it all the advantages of access to the god twenty-four hours a day. The elaborate necklace, or perhaps more properly pectoral, found in one of the 'royal tombs' of Ur, almost certainly had a function other than its decorative one, being probably a prophylactic against devils.

Another general consideration is that much ancient art was the work of what we should regard as craftsmen rather than artists. At some periods cylinder seals were virtually mass-produced, whilst even the magnificent Assyrian bas-reliefs were, as some unfinished patches indicate, carved out in rough by competent masons, only the fine touches being worked in by skilled artists.

The earliest art known to us from Mesopotamia is decorated pottery, coming from the *Hassuna, Samarra, Halaf, Hajji Muhammad, Eridu* and *Ubaid* periods. Many of these designs have great beauty, even for the modern eye. It is an odd fact that these fine examples of decorated pottery occurring in prehistoric times had no successors in the historic period; it has been suggested that the reason for this is that after the *Ubaid* period technical achievements permitted the production of fine vessels of stone or metal. These were then employed for any purpose for which fine ware was required, pottery generally being retained only for humbler purposes which would in any case not merit decorated ware.

Another branch of art which had no direct successor in later periods was the *Protoliterate* device for decorating columns and walls. The walls and columns were plastered with wet clay, into which were pressed small cones of baked clay about four inches long. These cones had been dipped into various pigments, so that their flat tops were black, red or buff. By appropriate arrangement of the cones coloured patterns were formed on the walls and columns, giving both an agreeable decorative effect and a weather-proof covering (see plate 2A).

Sculpture in the round, another form of representation also found from the *Protoliterate* period onwards, is known in this earliest phase in the form of animals carved in stone for the purpose of being attached to temple walls by wire; other examples are freestanding and represent figures of humans, or human heads. Some of these may have been deities, but others certainly represented human worshippers and must have been intended to stand, as the characteristic attitude of adoration (see Frankfort, op. cit., plate 9B) shows, before the god. This latter point becomes increasingly evident, and examples to illustrate it increasingly plentiful, in the *Early Dynastic* period, whilst from the time of Gudea of Lagash onwards there are statues inscribed with a message which might thereby be perpetually rendered to the god. The principal god of a sanctuary would in ancient times have been represented by a statue standing on a dais in a niche in one wall of the shrine, but from the fact that such statues would usually be covered in gold or other precious materials few of them have come down to us. Frankfort points out that the *Early Dynastic* statues of humans are reduced almost to geometrical forms: thus the chest-muscles are represented by the line of intersection of two planes, whilst the head and neck may be a sphere resting on a short cylinder with the chin, lips and nose as a series of wedges set upon the sphere. There seems to have been no attempt in this period at naturalistic representation of the original figure.

Steles are known from the *Early Dynastic* period, a fine example being one of Eannatum of Lagash, generally known as the Stele of the Vultures. This much-damaged monument, now in the Louvre, shows, in four registers, supposed scenes from a battle between the cities of Lagash and Umma, depicted from the point of view of Lagash. One sees the tight phalanx of Sumerian soldiers led by the king; vultures devour the corpses of the dead. In another register Eannatum himself is shown in his war chariot. On the reverse Ningirsu, tutelary deity of Lagash, is capturing the enemy forces in his net.

Another art form widely found in *Early Dynastic* times is work in inlay. The famous Standard of Ur uses this technique. It is in six registers, comprising a war panel and a peace panel, and showing the story of a battle and the triumphal feast which followed it. In the war panel (see plate 12) the battle itself is represented by the 'strip cartoon' method, the action being shown in its successive stages. The panel is to be read from the bottom register upwards. The bottom register shows, taking it from left to right, first a war-chariot with the draught animals walking and the chariot crew not yet engaged. Next the animals are shown breaking into a trot, whilst the squire is handing his charioteer a javelin for action. In the third section the charioteer has discharged his weapon, more victims have been claimed from the enemy, and the draught animals are in furious motion. The fourth section shows the chariot crew preparing to discharge another javelin. The middle register depicts naked prisoners being driven along under guard, whilst the top register shows such prisoners being brought before the city ruler, represented as bigger than anyone else present.

Steles corresponding to the *Early Dynastic* examples are known from the Agade period, but by the time of Naram-Sin the different registers had been reduced to one for artistic unity. One example has been cut high up in a rock in a pass in the Kurdish mountains (see plate 16A), whilst another, known as the Stele of Victory, is in the Louvre (see plate 16B). Here the warriors are ascending a mountain in pursuit of the enemy: Naram-Sin, depicted half as large again as his men and wearing the head-dress of a god, goes at the head of his troops.

The Neo-Sumerian period succeeding the Dynasty of Agade utilized, as Frankfort puts it, 'the technical achievements of the [Agade] period' without a trace 'of the aspirations of that time'. Certainly to the layman's eye Neo-Sumerian sculpture appears proficient but dead (see plate 20).

In the Isin-Larsa period one finds mass production of clay figurines and reliefs on plaques, turned out from moulds for the religious use of private persons. From Ashur, Mari and other cities at this period come a number of statues of local rulers or deities: one of the most striking, both technically and artistically, is the statue from Mari of a goddess holding a vase (see plate 19). There is a channel through the vase and goddess which made it possible to feed water into the statue to emerge by way of the vase as a fountain. It is interesting to note that when seen in the round the statue of this goddess gives a distinctly erogenic impression: she really does personify the forces of fertility. There are a number of works which represent or have been taken to represent Hammurabi. The principal example is a head in black granite, which, employing what Frankfort calls 'an almost impressionistic rendering of the face', imparts a sense of great majesty and power. The best known representation of Hammurabi is the relief on the top of his code of laws (see plate 21B), but as a work of art this over-heavy relief falls well below the delicate calligraphy employed for engraving the laws beneath it.

Apart from the cylinder seals plentiful at all periods, the extant works of art most characteristic of the Cassite period which followed the collapse of the First Dynasty of Babylon are the *kudurrus*, sculptured boundary stones marking grants of land and the boundaries of fields; although most common under the Cassites they were not actually limited to this period. Typically the stone is irregular in shape and a foot or two high, and bears the emblems of the deities under whose protection the boundary or grant of land is placed; sometimes the ruler making the grant of land is also depicted. From the modern point of view these Cassite *kudurrus* are curious, and of interest for the religious conceptions they illustrate, rather than significant as works of art (see plate 21A).

Quite otherwise are some of the examples of Assyrian art of the first millennium, which from their subject-matter, style and vigour can still be enjoyed by the average European. Assyrian art is represented from the fourteenth century onwards by sculptured monuments, both in relief and in the round, but the most striking examples come from the first millennium. The first great period is in the reign of Ashur-nasir-pal (the re-founder of the capital Calah) and of his son Shalmaneser III, that is, in the period 883 to 824 B.C. The second phase covers the final period of Assyrian greatness, from the accession of Tiglath-Pileser III (745 B.C.) to the end of the reign of Ashurbanipal: Frankfort divides this latter into two divisions on stylistic grounds.

Within the first millennium Assyrian sculpture in the round is not of great importance artistically: there are examples, representing kings or gods (see plates 28, 30), but whilst the figures carry a certain dignity they appear to lack life.

Objects which most people would consider as characteristic of Assyria at this period (though related objects are found also in the Hittite area and Syria) are the great winged human-headed bulls and lions, cut out of a slab of rock weighing many tons, and designed to protect the gateways to royal palaces. These massive figures are worked in a technique which is midway between relief and sculpture in the round, so that although not freed from the original block of stone they give the impression of independent existence. Many who marvel at them in our museums fail to notice that these creatures are provided with five legs each (see plate 53) – a device to ensure a naturalistic appearance when viewed either from front or side.

The great artistic achievement of the later Assyrian period is, however, the reliefs. Relief carving was employed as early as the third millennium, but with the limitations imposed by the use of a single stele. The single stele form still remained in use even with the Assyrians to represent particular cult acts of mythological conceptions, and some of the reliefs in this form are very impressive. The real importance of the Assyrian employment of reliefs was that they developed the old technique and brought it to the service of narrative. A whole wall or chamber would be lined with stone slabs and the whole covered with a series of scenes related in such a way that a narrative was built up. The technique was also applied in metal, as for example on the famous bronze gates of Balawat (now in the British Museum), where bands of metal eight feet long were embossed with two registers five inches high showing scenes from the king's campaigns; for specimen sections see plates 33 and 34.

The scenes on the stone reliefs are of two main types: they may show incidents in the royal campaigns (see plates 46B, 47, 48), or hunting scenes, wherein the king may be depicted slaughtering big game Traces of colour originally used to emphasize the figure of the king and his courtiers still survive.

In these reliefs the most noted mastery is found in the rendering of animals (see, for example, plate 39). In the frieze of the wild horse hunt (see plate 38), the horses seem really in motion, whilst the dying lion and lioness (plate 43A, B) in the famous lion hunt scenes in the British Museum are amongst the most vivid examples of sculpture of all time. The fact that there is no developed conception of perspective and little attempt to represent spatial depth does not hinder the modern appreciation of these powerful reliefs. As G. K. Chesterton once pointed out, 'perspective is really the comic element in everything' and 'is always left out of dignified and decorative art'.

Another aspect of Assyrian art which has considerable appeal to modern taste is carving in ivory. Carved ivory, often overlaid with gold (see the colour plate opposite, was employed as decoration on furniture – and indeed a throne of ivory overlaid with gold is mentioned as a possession of Solomon (1 Kings x. 18), whilst Ahab built an 'ivory house' (1 Kings xxii. 39). The actual craftsmen both in Palestine and Assyria were probably Syrians. When the ancient palaces of Calah were looted, the ivory panels were stripped off the furnishings for the sake of the gold overlay,

Carved ivory embellished with gold and precious stones, from Nimrud
(eighth century B.C.)

and the discarded ivory heaped up on a bonfire, where much of it was exposed to heat just sufficient to preserve it without carbonizing it. Such are the antecedents of the carved ivories which have been recovered in such quantities in the brilliant excavations of Professor M. E. L. Mallowan at Nimrud (Calah).

As to ancient painting little can be said, even though throughout the whole of antiquity in Mesopotamia plastered walls may often have been covered with murals. After the collapse of the buildings bearing them works of art of this kind would have a very poor chance of survival in the wet earth, but by good fortune a few actual examples do survive. The earliest known is from the temple of Tell Uqair, which belongs to the *Protoliterate* period. Large scale mural paintings are then not found again until the early second millennium, but whether this results from a neglect of the technique or from the accidents of preservation and discovery is not clear. In the palace (early second millennium) of the kings of Mari were found a number of fragments of this kind: they comprise traditional designs, war scenes, cult scenes in which a priest or king is leading a sacrificial bull, and a mythological scene. Later in the millennium, large scale mural paintings from the Cassite period (*circa* 1400 B.C.) have been found at Aqarquf. From the first millennium there are a few instances of wall paintings known from the Assyrian period; such paintings, which were in red, blue, black and white, have been found at the sites of Nimrud, Til Barsip and Khorsabad. Much of the composition in the Assyrian examples consists of geometrical figures or mythological beings regularly repeated to give a pattern: such a pattern commonly forms the setting or framework for the principal panels, in which cult scenes are depicted.

Metal-work, being executed in a material which can be melted down and used again, or which if by chance left in the earth is likely to corrode, must have been much better represented in Mesopotamia than one might suppose from the extant remains (see plate 58A for an early example): if there were any doubt as to the validity of this conclusion, one could refer to the historical texts of the Assyrian kings, which frequently speak of the looting of large hoards of metal objects, including metal vessels and furnishings.

Figures cast in copper or bronze are known from the *Early Dynastic* II period onwards. The commonest type in the earliest period typically represents a human (or perhaps divine) figure either standing on or supporting some kind of holder, and evidently formed some kind of cult-stand for use in the service of the gods. There has also been found from the *Early Dynastic* II period a copper foot which must once have belonged to a statue of almost life size: there is, of course, no evidence that the whole statue was of metal, as the body may well have consisted merely of metal plating over a core of some other material, like the head of plate 5, from Ubaid.

Frankfort points out that in the *Early Dynastic* II period the statuary in stone and in metal are quite independent of each other, whereas in later Mesopotamia metal-work seems to have enjoyed the greater prestige and to have influenced the style of work created in stone by imposing modelling techniques which were less appropriate to carved stone than to cast metal-work.

It was in the period of the Dynasty of Agade that the finest examples of Mesopotamian metal-work were created. A bronze head of this period (see plate 14) is thought to represent Sargon of Agade himself. The head is of three-quarter size and of a vigour and dignity unsurpassed in all examples of Mesopotamian art known to us from later times. The eyes must originally have been inlaid with precious stones, for the bronze mask shows the scar where one has been gouged out.

Metal work of the later period is known chiefly from vessels and holders of various kinds, weights in the form of animals (see plate 58B), bronze bands on gates (see pages 100 and 480), and images a few inches high representing demons or monsters (as plate 61B). On the development of the *cire perdue* metal-casting process, see above, page 123. Some of the finest work from the first millennium B.C. came from the peripheral regions, especially Urartu to the north and Persia to the east, both of them owing much to Assyrian influence: the winged ibex of plate 61A is Achaemenid work of between the sixth and fourth centuries B.C.

14

Legacy and Survival

'The grand object of travelling is to see the shores of the Mediterranean. On those shores were the four great Empires of the world; the Assyrian, the Persian, the Grecian, and the Roman. – All our religion, almost all our law, almost all our arts, almost all that sets us above savages, has come to us from the shores of the Mediterranean.'
(Boswell, *Life of Johnson*, Thursday, 11 April 1776).

THERE was a time, not long past, when it was possible to write all that was known of ancient Mesopotamia in a few pages of mangled history and garbled legend. Now that we have, during the past century, gained some first-hand knowledge of that civilization – sketchy, inadequate, misunderstood and distorted though our knowledge still is at many points – it is possible to see what a great debt our own civilization owes to that of ancient Mesopotamia. Ancient Sumerian and Babylonian ideas and techniques have come down to us through a number of sources. Transmitted and often transmuted through the Bible come a number of ancient myths, as well as ideas connected with magic and witchcraft, whilst other myths and epics have become part of our own literature through the Greek tradition. Through Greece and Rome, Byzantium and the Arabs, there have come to us Mesopotamian elements in our numeral systems, and in our calendar. Astrology has been transmitted through the same channels, as has knowledge of various food plants and drugs, as well as certain chemical processes. Above all, the science of astronomy itself and many astronomical

483

conceptions are a direct legacy from ancient Mesopotamia: this has been dealt with above (see pages 457 f.). Ancient Mesopotamian elements probably lie at the bottom of some of our law and commerce, whilst long-distance overland communication systems certainly have their roots in Mesopotamia (see page 249). The superiority of the literate man – not always accepted in the Middle ages – is an idea taken over at the Renaissance from the classical tradition, and probably linked there with the honour in which literacy was held in Mesopotamia (see page 188). If the modern world has yet learnt anything from Rome about international administration and the maintenance of order, this too is in part a debt to the ancient Near East, for Rome in turn benefited by its contacts with Greece and Persia, and the latter certainly took over a great deal in connection with administration from Assyrian practice. Some motifs in Christian art come by an unbroken tradition through Byzantium from Sumer, whilst more controversially one might argue that certain features of Christian ritual, such as the mystical significance of the East in worship and burial, had their origins in Babylonian paganism.

Mesopotamian elements in the Bible

Any attempt to exercise literary criticism upon the Bible or to suggest that anyone other than God had a hand in its production is likely to arouse strong passions in the hearts of certain readers. To these the writer makes a preliminary apology, pointing out that he himself accepts the spiritual value of the Old Testament as the message of God. It is beyond doubt, however, that certain of the stories in *Genesis*, in particular the stories of Creation and the story of the Flood, have some relationship – in the case of the Flood story a close relationship – to Babylonian or Sumerian myths, of which some account has already been given. No Mesopotamian original has plausibly been postulated for the actual story of the garden of Eden (despite claims made in some older books), but Professor E. A. Speiser has shown that the geographical details given in *Genesis* ii. 6–14 require it to be conceived of as a part of the Near East closely connected with Mesopotamia.

Less commonly recognized than the Mesopotamian elements in *Genesis* is the presence in the Old Testament, especially in *Psalms*, of references to magic and witchcraft. It is true that even if their presence is admitted in the Old Testament the conclusion need not at once be drawn that these ideas came from Mesopotamia, for witchcraft is a monopoly of no one section of mankind. Yet the details of such references do point strongly to direct Mesopotamian influence. The most commonly accepted instance is the passage translated in the Revised Version

> If thou doest well, shalt thou not be accepted? and if thou doest not well, sin coucheth at the door. (*Genesis* iv. 7).

The word translated 'coucheth' is in Hebrew *rōbeṣ*, which, allowing for vowel changes (ā>ō, i>e) known to have occurred in the development of the Hebrew language, is the exact equivalent of *rābiṣu*, the name of a well-known Babylonian demon. The Hebrew word translated 'sin' could be otherwise explained. and the translation of the end of the passage quoted would then be

> the Croucher-demon is lurking at the door.

In *Isaiah* xxxiv. 14 there occurs a phrase, in the curse upon Edom, translated in the Revised Version as

> the night-monster shall settle there, and shall find her a place of rest.

The Hebrew word rendered 'night-monster' is *Liliṯ* (Lilith), which is remarkably like the Akkadian *Lilitu*, a well-known and much-feared female demon. Lilith has indeed commonly been identified with Lilitu, but Professor G. R. Driver objects to this (*Palestine Exploration Quarterly*, 1959, pages 55–58) on the ground that all the other creatures mentioned in the passage are either real 'or may be such'. However, Driver's qualification 'may be such', referring to the term translated 'satyr' (which might otherwise mean 'he-goat'), admits the possibility 'may be otherwise' and robs the argument of its main force. Even apart from this, there is no reason to suppose that in a non-scientific society demons were considered as less real members of the fauna than what we accept as real beasts. The writer recalls the nervous anxiety of his police escort when, as he was on a visit (before the resumption of the German excavations) to the site of Erech, night began to fall: it was clear that there was no well-marked distinction in the minds of the peasant policemen between the danger from prowling wild beasts which had their lairs amid the ruins and that from lurking *jinn*. Both stood together as hazards from which those in their charge should be removed as soon as possible. So likewise there is no reason to assume that a rigid distinction was maintained in the *Isaiah* passage between fauna and fauns.

Two whole books of the Bible, as well as isolated chapters or verses, have, by certain modern scholars, been related to Mesopotamian religious ideas. The two books are *Nahum* and *The Song of Songs*, both of which have been related to the Tammuz cult (see above, page 377). The Scandinavian scholar A. Haldar argues for instance (in his *Studies in the Book of Nahum*) that the passage *Nahum* ii. 3–4 has reference to ceremonial races which took place at the New Year Festival. The present writer would not go as far as that, but accepts (see *Journal of Theological Studies* XI (1960), pages 318–329) that there are references in *Nahum* and elsewhere in the Old Testament to a fertility cult with Mesopotamian associations. *The Song of Songs* is a much clearer case than *Nahum*, and although some theologians have shown uneasiness over the matter, no-one has been able substantially to refute the case made out by T. J. Meek ('Canticles and the Tammuz Cult' in *American Journal of Semitic Languages*, XXXIX, pages 1–14) that this was originally part of a fertility cult. (This need not prevent the Christian from finding a spiritual value in *The Song of Songs*; see *Acts of the Apostles* xvii. 23).

The belief in demonic possession, which ultimately goes back to the Babylonian view of the world-order, still persists amongst some educated and intelligent people*. As late as 1960 a rural dean in the Church of England was able to state publicly the view, as reported in a local newspaper, that

there are opportunities today for evil spirits to be exorcised. . . .

---

* These people and the Babylonians may of course be in the right, even though the current twentieth century opinion is against them.

Fewer people were possessed by demons in this country than in Africa, because of the existence in every parish of a Christian community, centred on a church in which the Sacraments were resolved. There were, however, occasions when medicine was powerless. When doctors could not discover the cause of a disorder, a priest might seek the consent of his bishop, who would obtain expert advice. If the consent was given the evil spirit might be exorcised. It might enter into the priest, for which reason two priests were always posted, having undergone thorough spiritual preparation.

The doctrinal basis for such beliefs is a literal interpretation of certain passages in the New Testament referring to devils, such as the incident in the country of the Gadarenes (see above, page 313) in which a host of devils were supposedly sent into a herd of pigs. There is also the parable (as this writer takes it to be) of the exorcised devil who returned to find his old habitation, his erstwhile human host, swept and garnished, and so took up his abode there again in company with seven other devils worse than himself (*St. Matthew* xii. 43–45, *St. Luke* xi. 24–26). Such ideas, however, simply reflect the current of thought of later Judaism, in which demons loom large simply because of the strong Babylonian influence to which it was subjected during the Exile. This is not to say that pre-exilic Hebrew religion positively rejected the conception of demons, but the idea of demons – though a general Semitic one – played little part in pre-exilic Hebrew thought. Most of the pre-exilic references to supernatural beings not described as gods refer to ancient gods who had been reduced, under the pressure of Mosaic religion, to demons: such demoted gods still had a cult amongst the ignorant (*Leviticus* xvii. 7, *Deuteronomy* xxxii. 17) but are never mentioned as threatening to possess a man. *Genesis* iv. 7, mentioned above, is – if the proposed interpretation is accepted – an exception to the general statement, but an exception manifestly due to early Mesopotamian influence.

Although the Old Testament makes surprisingly little reference to demonic possession, there are probably in the original Hebrew text more allusions to witchcraft than has commonly been recognized. This does not imply deliberate concealment on the part of the translators of the Authorized and Revised Versions, but merely unfamiliarity with rare Hebrew words or usages which have since become clearer in the light of comparative Semitic philology. Thus *Psalm* xciv. 20, which reads very oddly in the Authorized and Revised Versions, is probably, in the light of the convincing researches of Professor A. Guillaume (*Journal of the Royal Asiatic Society*, 1942, pages 117f.), to be translated

> Can he that binds spells charm Thee,
> He that devises mischief against the (divine) statute?

Likewise *Proverbs* x. 3 probably meant in the original Hebrew

> The Lord will not allow the soul of the righteous to be spellbound,
> And the binding curse of the wicked He shall thrust away.

whilst *Proverbs* x. 11 is to be translated

> A fountain of life is (the product of) the mouth of the righteous,
> But the mouth of the wicked utters baneful spells.

A substantial number of further related instances occur in the Hebrew text of the Old Testament. Not a few such passages use the very same technical vocabulary found in Akkadian magical texts, and all show a close similarity in thought with Babylonian magic. Since such passages were not recognized by the English translators at the Reformation they have had no direct effect on our religious thought, but there is the possibility that they did none the less operate indirectly on the western world. In Judaism there was a traditional belief in witchcraft, of which the details were such that they may well have derived ultimately from passages of the kind referred to. Thus contact with Jews, themselves ultimately influenced by Mesopotamia in this or other ways, is one channel through which the religious superstition already firmly rooted in Mediaeval and Reformation Europe (and certainly not to be blamed on the Jews in its origin) may have been given the particular shape it finally took.

A religious conception which has come down to us by unbroken tradition from the ancient Near East, partly mediated through the Bible, is the idea of coronation. As Professor C. J.

Gadd puts it (*Ideas of Divine Rule in the Ancient East* (1948), pages 48 f.), in the ancient Near East 'the crown was not merely a symbol but an amulet with its own magical powers, and so was the oil with which kings were anointed'. These conceptions remain clearly visible in the coronation service used for English monarchs in the present century.

Astrology, Astronomy, Numeration, and Time Division

There is one aspect of Babylonian superstition which, though certainly known to us through the Bible, was principally transmitted through Greek and Roman agency. The superstition in question is astrology, a folly which, to judge by the space devoted to it in certain daily newspapers and women's magazines, is still far from eradicated from our own civilization. Omens were drawn from many types of event in Babylonia, and the prognoses fell into two main classes. On the one hand were those affecting particular individuals, drawn from events – such as a snake dropping from the mud ceiling on to a man's bed – which by ancient logic obviously applied to a particular person. On the other hand there were those, not obviously in direct connection with a particular individual, which were thought to refer to the land as a whole or to its mystical representative the king. The latter type of omen is commonly designated 'judicial', and originally astrology fell into this class. In the light of Babylonian cosmological theory it was quite clear that events in heaven and on earth were related: the *Epic of Creation* specifically states that the earth is the counterpart of heaven, and therefore any event in the sky must have its equivalent on earth. As there was in the earlier period no obvious relationship recognized between celestial phenomena and any particular person, celestial portents were necessarily thought of as relating to the nation as a whole.

The final step to horoscopic astrology could not be made until some technique had been devised which enabled celestial phenomena to be specifically related to a particular individual. A possible means of doing this was to note which planets were visible and which invisible at the time of the individual's birth, and there is a cuneiform text which suggests that this was prac-

tised before the fifth century B.C. However, the final systematiza-
tion of the procedure into a 'science' had to await the invention
of the zodiac. The zodiac was not invented for astrological
purposes, but once it had been invented it was only a step – albeit
a big one – to proceed from the idea of making general predictions about the future on the basis of the heavenly bodies, to
making predictions about an individual, on the basis of the
position of the planets in the zodiac at his birth. The details of
how this last step came to be made remain very obscure. It was
formerly much in dispute whether this development came about
in Greece, Egypt or Mesopotamia: each land has had its cham-
pions, but two considerations combine to give priority to Babylonia. There is the theoretical consideration that the idea can only
have arisen in a *milieu* where celestial bodies were regarded as
divinities affecting the life of mankind, and there is the practical
fact that much earlier examples of horoscopes are known from
Babylonia than from Greece or Egypt. It is now generally agreed
amongst historians of science that the conception did in fact first
arise in Mesopotamia.

B. L. Van der Waerden points out that there are two conceptions to be distinguished in discussing the origin of the zodiac.
One is the zodiacal belt, that is a belt of 12 degrees breadth in
which the sun, moon and planets move. The zodiacal constellations or 'signs of the zodiac' lie in this belt. As early as 700 B.C.
the Babylonian text mulAPIN (see above, page 457) refers to
this belt and mentions fifteen constellations lying in it. A number
of the names of constellations listed are identical with those
still used for the zodiacal signs, as the Bull, the Twins (Gemini),
the Lion, the Scorpion, the Archer (Sagittarius), and Capricorn.
The other conception was that of the ecliptic, defined by Van der
Waerden (*Archiv für Orientforschung*, XVI, 216) as 'a line in the
middle of the zodiacal belt, the sun's orbit and locus of moon
eclipses, divided into twelve zodiacal signs of thirty degrees each'.
Van der Waerden shows that this also was a Babylonian invention, employed by 419 B.C. at the latest, which arose ultimately
from the schematic year, employed in the text mulAPIN, of
twelve months of thirty days each. By the device of twelve

zodiacal signs of equal breadth, the sun dwelt in each of these signs for one schematic month.

There are no very early Greek horoscopes: of about a hundred and seventy Greek horoscopes known, on papyri and graffiti and in astrological literature of the Roman period, the earliest is from 62 B.C. and the others from 4 B.C. or later. Demotic horoscopes so far known from Egypt go back no further than the first half of the first century A.D. In contrast to this there is a cuneiform text now known in which a horoscope is cast relating to a child born on 29th April, 410 B.C., whilst there are four further examples from the third century B.C. An example from 263 B.C. has been translated by Professor A. Sachs (*Journal of Cuneiform Studies* VI, page 57):

> (In the) year 48 (of the Seleucid era, month) Adar, night of the twenty-third (?), the child was born. At that time the sun was in 13;30° Aries, the moon in 10° Aquarius, Jupiter at the beginning of Leo, Venus with the sun, Mercury with the Sun, Saturn in Cancer, Mars at the end of Cancer. . . . He will be lacking in wealth. . . . His food will not satisfy his hunger. The wealth which he has in his youth will not remain (?). For thirty-six years he will have wealth. His days will be long. [There are five more lines, of difficult and doubtful interpretation.]

Astrology is a part of the Babylonian legacy which Europe could well have been spared. There are in compensation many valuable conceptions deriving ultimately from Babylonian astronomical procedures.

The week ultimately goes back to Mesopotamian influence, though this is not the same thing as saying that the week was a Mesopotamian institution. From an early period religious rites were observed for the first day of the moon, the day at which it was at the full and the day of its disappearance, that is to say, the 1st, 15th and 28th (or 29th) days. Later the days of half-moon were introduced as feast-days, and the resultant division of the lunar month into four seems to have been the model for the week as used by the Jews and later by Christians and Moslems. (There is another quite different theory as to the origin of the Jewish week: this postulates that Mosaic religion were strongly under Kenite

491

influence, and that the Kenites were a tribe of smiths who had an ancient taboo on the use of fire on the seventh day. This theory ignores some of the facts and involves several unproven theories.)

Not only in the calendar but in numerical method, particularly in connection with the measurement of time, Mesopotamian procedures have left traces which are still evident in our own civilization. The old Sumerian sexagesimal system is still plainly seen in the division of the circle into 360 degrees and the division of the hour into 60 minutes and 3600 seconds: this represents an unbroken tradition handed on through ancient and mediaeval astronomers. The most important feature of the Babylonian numeral system, its place-value notation, has also probably reached our own civilization by an unbroken tradition. In this place-value notation, which has already been described in more detail (see page 447 ff.), a number written as

$$\text{𝗬𝗬𝗬 \quad 𝗬𝗬} \quad i.e., 3, 2$$

would mean three times sixty [the sexagesimal unit] plus two. It seems likely that the principle of the Babylonian place-value notation was never entirely lost and that it was transmitted into early Hindu astronomy, through which intermediary it came in the first millennium A.D. into Islamic civilization and then into our own, in the so-called Arabic numerals, in which, analogously with the Babylonian system, 32 means three times ten [the decimal unit] plus two.

The division of the day into hours also goes back in part to Mesopotamia, the final result being the consequence of the crossing of Egyptian and Babylonian influence. The Egyptian and Babylonian astronomers used different systems of dividing the day. The Egyptians divided the period from sunrise to sunset into twelve parts, thus obtaining hours of which the length depended on the season. The people of Mesopotamia did much the same in ordinary life, so that, for example, the night from sunset to sunrise was divided into three watches, each comprising two *beru* – a word commonly translated 'double hour', though in terms of our hours such periods would vary in length with the season. The Babylonian astronomers, however, took the whole of the day and night, dividing it into six sub-divisions of equal and constant length. At a later period the Hellenistic astronomers adopted the Babylonian astronomers' device of dividing day and night into equal parts, but further sub-divided the twelve *beru*, giving twenty-four sub-divisions of day and night, as in the Egyptian system, but of equal length. Thus arose our twenty-four-hour day.

Not only these by-products of astronomy, but astronomy itself – defined by O. Neugebauer (*Journal of Near Eastern Sudies*, IV, 2) as 'those parts of human interest in celestial phenomena which are amenable to mathematical treatment' – is a legacy from Babylonia. Indeed, it is the most direct legacy of all, being, as Neugebauer points out, 'the only branch of the ancient sciences which survived almost intact after the collapse of the Roman Empire'. Some account has already been given of the zodiac (see page 490) and of the Babylonian discovery of methods for predicting the positions of heavenly bodies (see page 457 ff.).

Vocabulary

The evidence of classical authors appears to indicate that Greek medical practice, and so ultimately that of the modern world, owed much more to Egypt than to Babylonia. Yet certainly knowledge of a number of the drugs (of vegetable and mineral origin) utilized by the Greeks must have come from Mesopotamian sources, for several of the Greek names are manifestly loan-words from Akkadian. Amongst names in this category which have reached our own language (mostly by way of Greek) may be mentioned the following:

English	Greek	Akkadian
carob	charrouba	kharuba
crocus	krokos	kurkanu
cummin	kuminon	kamanu
gypsum	gypsos	gaṣṣu
hyssop	hussopos	zupu
ladanum	ledanon	ladanu
myrrh	murra	murru

493

English	Greek	Akkadian
naphtha	naphthos	naptu
saffron	———	azupiranu [through Arabic zaᶜfaran]

Amongst words of other classes which have come from Akkadian or Sumerian, not many examples can be adduced from English or other modern languages. There are persistent attempts to find Sumerian words in unlikely places, particularly at the present time in Hungarian, but these may be ignored as always resting on an inadequate knowledge of Sumerian and generally on a faulty understanding of the historical development of the language compared with it. Words in European languages which either certainly or probably have some connection with ancient Mesopotamia include the following:

'Alcohol', through Arabic *kohl* from Akkadian *guhlu*. According to R. J. Forbes (*Studies in Ancient Technology* III (1955), page 18) the term *kohl* came to mean first 'a finely divided powder' and was subsequently applied to volatile substances and then specifically to what in consequence we call alcohol.

'Alkali' comes through Arabic from Akkadian *kalati* 'burnt things' (with reference to the ashes of plants which were burnt to make potash).

'Cane', through Greek from Akkadian *kanu* 'reed'. 'Canon' comes from the same word in its derived sense of 'measuring rod', 'standard.'

Greek *chrusos* 'gold' and its modern derivatives beginning with 'chrys-' (such as 'chrysalis', originally 'golden thing'; 'chrysanthemum', 'golden flower') are probably related to Akkadian *khurasu* 'gold'; possibly both the Akkadian and the Greek word has a common origin which is neither Semitic nor Indo-European.

'Dragoman' comes through Arabic and Aramaic from Akkadian *targumanu*.

'Horn' (Latin *cornu*, Greek *keras*) is possibly connected distantly with Akkadian *karnu*, which has the same meaning; this may be another word of which the prehistoric original was neither Semitic nor Indo-European.

'Jasper' derives through Greek *'iaspis* from Akkadian *iashpu*.

French 'mesquin', Italian 'meschino', denoting 'poor, mean', are forms of an Arabic word considered to derive ultimately from the Akkadian *mushkinu*, meaning 'a lower-class freeman'.

'Mina' comes ultimately from Sumerian MA.NA, or if (as seems likely) the latter is a false ideogram representing a genuine Semitic word based on the verb *manû* 'to count', from Akkadian. Not only was the name 'mina' taken over into Greek, but the actual unit was adopted into the Greek weight system, sixty minas making, as in Babylonia, one talent.

'Plinth' comes from the Greek *plinthos* 'a tile or brick', which in turn derives from Akkadian *libittu* (etymologically *libintu*), meaning 'a moulded (*i.e.* sun-dried) brick'.

The name 'Rachel' comes from Hebrew *raḥel* 'ewe-lamb', which, with two consonants transposed, ultimately goes back to the Sumerian LAḤRA, the name of a deity concerned with sheep.

'Shekel' comes through Hebrew from the Akkadian *shiḳlu*.

Two fruits possibly derive their European names from Mesopotamia, suggesting that they reached Europe from cultivation in Mesopotamia. One of these is the apricot. This fruit is known in Latin as *armeniaca*, which was formerly taken to indicate that it came from Armenia. However, as the apricot was well known to the Assyrians and Babylonians under the name *armanu*, it could well be that the Latin name was ultimately a loan-word from the Akkadian term, and that the fruit and tree reached Europe by way of Mesopotamia. Other fruit-trees with which the people of Mesopotamia were acquainted were the cherry, pistachio, fig, apple, pomegranate, peach, medlar, quince, citron, lemon and mulberry: the evidence for this comes from texts or – in the case of the last two – from remains found in excavations. Which, if any, of these were first brought into cultivation in Mesopotamia it is at present impossible to say, but certainly several Assyrian kings showed keen interest in botany and introduced exotic trees and other plants into their parks. The cherry (Akkadian *karshu*, which actually refers to a scented variety of cherry-tree which the Assyrians met in the Kurdish mountains) is the only fruit besides the apricot of which the European names (Greek *kerasos*, German *Kirsche*, etc.) appear to come from the Akkadian.

Architecture

An instance of an architectural legacy from ancient Mesopotamia, transmitted through Greece, is the Ionian column. This is
the type of column which has deep fluting and is surmounted
by a capital with lateral volutes. The basic shape, of which this
can be recognized as a development, was used as a religious
symbol in the art of the *Protoliterate* period. It was clearly originally
a bundle of tall reeds tied together with the heads tied over,
used as a post in the building of a cult-hut. The original device is
still employed in hut-making amongst the marsh-Arabs of south
Iraq.

Ionian column [right] *and its ancestor*

Symbols in Religious Art

Substantial Mesopotamian influence is traceable in the art of
both Christianity and Islam, though it cannot be assumed that
every symbol or motif common to the ancient and more recent
religions necessarily represents a direct borrowing. The simpler
the form of the symbol, the harder it is to prove a relationship.
Cases in point are the cross and the crescent. Both were well

known religious symbols in ancient Mesopotamia, the crescent being very common, the cross less so, though still adequately attested. Howbeit, the simple Greek cross might well arise independently as a religious symbol in different *milieux*. With the more elaborate Maltese cross the case is different, and the fact that it already occurs as a religious symbol in the *Jemdet Nasr* period (*circa* 2900 B.C.) in precisely the form in which it is met with in oriental Christian art can hardly be a coincidence. Almost certainly the cross in its Maltese form (see on plate 27A) was an ancient religious symbol later taken over by Christianity. There are also two Jewish symbols which can be traced back to the religious art of ancient Mesopotamia. These are the *menorah*, or ritual lamp, and the *magen Dawid*, or shield of David, which occur together on an Old Assyrian seal of the early second millennium B.C.

In some cases the similarity between complicated motifs in ancient Mesopotamian and Christian art is very striking, and some Mesopotamian in- fluence is generally accepted by historians of Christian art: the main point of contention amongst such authorities con- cerns not the recognition of this influence but the channels through which it flowed from ancient Mesopotamia to Byzantium and mediaeval Europe.

A religious symbol which undoubtedly comes by un- broken tradition from the ancient east is the Tree of Life. This is found in some of the

Assyrian sacred tree

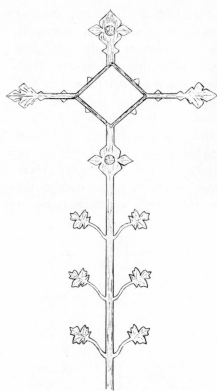

Cross in form of sacred tree, after a brass in an English cathedral

earliest Sumerian art, and continues throughout Mesopotamian history, being very prominent in the Assyrian friezes of the first millennium B.C. (see plate 32). The mythological conception of the Tree of Life is also found in *Genesis* iii. 22. The symbol is represented in oriental rugs, and occurs throughout Christian art from the earliest times.

There are a number of other motifs which art historians commonly accept as occurring in Christian art by transmission from ancient Mesopotamia, either through Parthian mediation or through the monks of Edessa and Nisibis who, according to O. M. Dalton (*East Christian Art*, [1925], page 9) 'from the fifth century ... determined Christian iconography, and imparted to its artistic expression the un-Hellenic qualities . . .'

A number of these symbols were in ancient Mesopotamia associated with Tammuz. The writer would warn non-Christian readers against glibly concluding from this that either historically or doctrinally Christianity was a development of the cult of Tammuz: that role fell to Mithraism, a contemporary and rival of early Christianity. Christianity accepted Tammuz symbols – commonly presumed to be the symbols of a dying Saviour who rose again – as it has always accepted any pre-Christian conceptions which represent a striving in the dark after the revelation finally given in Christ. (See *Acts of the Apostles* xvii. 23).

Plate 57B, a detail of a reredos of the crucifixion by Jacques de Baerze (*circa* A.D. 1300), is full of motifs which show Mesopotamian affinities, and there is no reason to suppose that these were introduced in a restoration known to have been carried out in 1825. The sun symbol (the rays on the crucifix), and the symbols of the moon and a star are indisputable, whilst the little winged devil snatching the soul of the unrepentant thief shows striking points of similarity with the Babylonian demon known as Pazuzu (on which see the present writer in *Archiv für Orientforschung* XIX (1960), pages 123-127).

Not only individual motifs but also points of style appear in Christian art by transmission from ancient Mesopotamia. There are two features of style in particular which come into this category. One is the use of vertical perspective, that is, of placing background scenes above foreground scenes. The other is the device of variable scale, in which the principal figure in a scene is disproportionately large compared with the other figures. Even the manner in which Christ is represented in Christian art sometimes shows Mesopotamian influence. Professor D. Talbot Rice points out (*Byzantine Art* (revised edition, 1954), page 81) that in Byzantine art there are two traditions found. Under Hellenic influence Christ is depicted as charming and youthful, but in the oriental presentation he is bearded and mysterious, with the numinous majesty characteristic of the old Mesopotamian deities.

According to K. A. C. Creswell, the authority on Islamic architecture, a few early Muslim minarets and other towers show Mesopotamian influence. The most striking is the spiral minaret at Samarra, built between 849 and 852 A.D. and still standing: the sketch gives a rough idea of its appearance.

The form of this minaret is, according to Creswell (*Early Muslim Architecture*, II, page 261), directly based on the ziggurat, even though the plan of the tower is circular

Mosque of Samarra

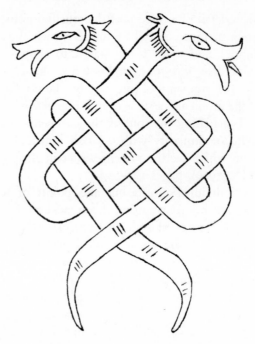

Intertwined Serpents in Islamic Art

instead of square. The use of this spiral type of tower subsequently spread from the Islamic world to China, where the same architectural form was employed between the eleventh and thirteenth centuries.

An attempt has been made to establish that many motifs in Islamic art are survivals from ancient Mesopotamia. On the whole the writer does not find this very convincing (perhaps from ignorance of Islamic art), but there is one striking similarity: the intertwined serpents drawn above (from an Islamic basin of the eleventh century A.D.) strikingly recall the serpents of plate IIA, which represents a lamp cover from the end of the third millennium B.C.

The symbol of the intertwined serpents is certainly one that has been transmitted from the ancient to the modern world, since in both *milieux* it is a symbol of healing. In Babylonia it was associated with Ningizzida, son of the divine patron of healing (see page 460), whilst in the modern world it is connected with the apothecary.

Literature, Literary Forms, and Folk-Lore

Amongst literary forms, the fable is one that may be traced back to ancient Mesopotamia, though it is the 'Elephant and Gnat' type of story and not the tenson which must be regarded as the ancestor of the Aesopian fable. Mr. C. S. Mundy, Senior Lecturer in Turkish in London University, kindly informs the writer that a story almost identical with that of the 'Elephant and Gnat' (see above, page 444) is represented in the folk-lore of modern Turkey.

There are many aspects of folk-lore and folk-sayings where it is usually impossible either to prove or to disprove that there has been a transmission of ideas. Where there is common material, it may be explained in one of two ways: it may be taken to result from a similarity in mode of thinking (which itself might be a consequence of a cultural tradition which has never quite died) or it may be taken as a direct continuous tradition. A few instances of similarity are adduced, though no opinion is offered upon the question of whether there is any connection beyond a similar psychological make-up of mankind ancient and modern.

In modern folk-lore the principle that 'dreams go by opposites' is well-known. The Assyrians thought the same:

> If (in a dream) the god utters a benediction before the man . . ., he will experience the wrath of the god. If the god utters a curse against the man, his prayer will be accepted.

In the ancient Mesopotamian conception the character of various animals was the same as with us. The eagle was the king of birds and, as with us, had a quite undeserved reputation for high flying. The fox already had a reputation for slyness. The snake was believed never to grow old, a belief still found in many parts of Europe. The creature called by us the 'praying mantis' suggested a similar imagery to the Babylonians, who called it 'the sha'ilu-priest of the countryside'.

Besides the stories of Mesopotamian origin (notably the Flood story) which have come to us through the Bible, there are others known to us through Greek literature. Most famous are the stories of Heracles, who is generally accepted as owing much to the Sumero-Babylonian Gilgamish. The details of the parallelisms between Gilgamish and Heracles are listed by Robert Graves in *The Greek Myths*, (1955), vol. II, page 89, though some of the parallels proposed there probably do not exist. Besides the figure of Heracles himself, there are many other features of Greek mythology which appear to be echoes of the *Epic of Gilgamish*. There is, for example, the snake with the magic life-giving herb (*The Greek Myths*, vol. I, page 304), reminiscent of the serpent which stole the plant 'The old man becomes young' (see above, page 405) from Gilgamish. The giant scorpion responsible for the death of Orion after his journey to the place of sunrise recalls the scorpion-men found by Gilgamish at the edge of the world on the way to his ancestor (see above, page 397).

A less well-known Greek myth which may have a distant connection with Mesopotamia is that related by Hesiod about Ouranos (Sky). Ouranos lay with Gaea (Earth) but would not allow the Titans with whom she became pregnant to be brought to birth. Finally, as Ouranos approached Gaea, one of the Titans, at her instigation, castrated Ouranos with a flint knife. This rebellion against Ouranos by means of a flint tool may be a faint echo of the Babylonian myth in which Flint rebelled against the god Ninurta, for which impiety it was decreed that it should flake. This myth (as also possibly the others mentioned) was probably mediated from Babylonia to Greece by the Hittites, with whom there occurred a myth of a god biting off the genitals of the deity corresponding to Ouranos.

It has been said that the two leading features of modern western thought is that it is scientific and that it is historical. Mesopotamia, though it gave us much of our technology and the rudiments of our mathematics and astronomy, can by no means take the credit for the scientific basis of modern life; but one strand in our modern historical habit of thought may ultimately derive from Mesopotamia. Where one looks for the beginning of history depends upon what one understands by the term. If one thinks of it as an interest in the origins and development of human society, one can see it already in the Sumerian and early Babylonian myths. If, on the other hand, we mean by 'history' something more specific, namely the conscious bringing of the present into connection with the past, then, as an American scholar (H. Lewy at the *Rencontre Assyriologique Internationale* held at Geneva in June 1960) has pointed out, history was originally an Assyrian creation – though, of course, it may also in some cases have arisen independently outside Mesopotamia, as possibly in the court records of David which are taken to underlie much of the *Books of Samuel*.

In Mesopotamia royal inscriptions were originally building inscriptions, which they remained in Babylonia until the end. In the typical inscription the king gave his name and titles and a hymn of praise to the god, a brief reference to the time and circumstances in which the building work was put in hand, and then the account of the building operation itself. In Assyria in the second millennium at about 1300 B.C., the kings began to elaborate the note of time, giving not only a reference to the event immediately preceding and leading up to the building operation, but also a summary of all the king's military exploits to date. This shortly afterwards came to be arranged systematically according to the yearly campaigns, and ultimately this developed into the elaborate annal form so well known in the records of the Assyrian rulers of the first millennium. Such annals in many cases were not limited to the recountal of raw fact, but offered statements of motive, criticisms of courses of action, appraisals of character, notes of political changes, generalizations about the history of a region or the characteristics of a race, as well as matters which though not essentially history are generally associated with history – such as geographical, topographical, strategical and tactical aspects of campaigns. Thus the Assyrians may justly be regarded as the first historians, though whether our own historians may properly be considered related to them in an unbroken tradition, linked by the Greeks, is another matter. Yet the possibility that the Greek historians were directly influenced by the Assyrian attitude to history is a very real one. It is not insignificant that the Greek famed as 'the Father of history', Herodotus of the fifth century B.C., himself travelled in Mesopotamia; though Assyria at that time no longer existed as a political unit, habits of thought are less easily destroyed, and Herodotus may well have come, through later Babylonian scholars inheriting the tradition, under the influence of the Assyrian philosophy of history.

There are many other attitudes, practices and ways of thought in which one can see resemblances between modern life and that of ancient Mesopotamia, but so few scholars have an adequate knowledge of the cultural history of the whole of the two and a half millennia spanning the gulf, that little research has been done on specific points. For instance, an authority on the history of Law informs the writer that, though it has not been formally established by published research, the law dealing with mortgage almost certainly goes back ultimately, through the practice of monasteries and mediaeval Jewish money-lenders, to the ancient Near East. There are many similar instances of probable, though not finally established, debt to Mesopotamia. Even the very structure of our family life is set in a Mesopotamian framework. Unlike many oriental peoples, including the Jews to the twelfth century A.D. and the Moslems to the present day, the ancient Mesopotamians were (except in the special case of the king) legally monogamous: as in our western civilization, however, women were in practice expected to be rather more monogamous than men.

Bibliography

In this bibliography an attempt has been made to do two things. These are, to give some idea of the principal sources employed in preparing this book, and to mention some of the most important works available to the student wishing to proceed further in particular aspects of the subject. A number of specialized works utilized in the writing of this book, such as articles on points of grammar, lexicography or chronology, most excavation reports, and certain publications (and in some cases editions) of cuneiform texts, have been omitted; any reader equipped to utilize such specialist works is unlikely to require guidance in tracing the sources employed. A few works drawn upon, in particular certain books dealing with theories of Sumerian origins, have been deliberately omitted as being potentially misleading to non-specialist readers unable to check the primary sources.*

The symbol † is placed before a number of works which, being largely complete in themselves, are likely to be found specially useful by readers wishing to follow up particular topics without much specialist knowledge. It is not necessarily implied that items not so marked are either on the one hand more advanced or on the other less reliable.

Titles of books, periodicals and series are given in italics, whilst titles of articles from periodicals are in roman type.

General

†ALBRIGHT, W. F.: *From the Stone Age to Christianity* (Doubleday Anchor Books, New York; 2nd edition, 1957).

ANDRAE, W.: *Babylon, die versunkene Weltstadt und ihr Ausgräber Robert Koldewey* (Walter de Gruyter & Co., Berlin, 1952).

†BUDGE, E. A. W.: *The rise and progress of Assyriology* (Martin Hopkinson, London, 1925).

†BURROWS, M.: *What mean these stones?* (New Haven, 1941).

†BURY, J. B. and others (editors): *The Cambridge ancient history*, volumes I-III (University Press, Cambridge, from 1925). [Volume I in particular is now very antiquated and a completely new edition, with the relevant section under the editorship of C. J. Gadd, is on the point of publication].

---

* Bibliographies which aim at completeness in works relating to Assyriology have been published from time to time in the periodicals *Archiv für Orientforschung* and *Orientalia;* for the period from 1954 onwards there is also the *Bibliographie Analytique de l'Assyriologie et de l'Archéologie du Proche-Orient* edited by L. Vanden Berghe and B. A. van Proosdij and published by E. J. Brill of Leiden, of which three volumes (two dealing with Archaeology and one with Philology) have so far appeared.

BIBLIOGRAPHY

†CAMERON, G. G.: *History of early Iran* (University of Chicago Press, 1936).

†CHIERA, E.: *They wrote on clay* [Edited by G. G. Cameron] (Phoenix Books, University of Chicago Press, 1959).

†CORY, I. P.: *Ancient fragments of the Phoenician, Chaldaean, Egyptian . . . and other writers* (London, 1832). [Of interest in reflecting the little that was known of Assyro-Babylonian civilization before the beginning of excavations just before the middle of the nineteenth century].

†DRIVER, G. R.: *Semitic writing from pictograph to alphabet* (University Press, Oxford; revised edition, 1954).

DUSSAUD, R.: *La pénétration des Arabes en Syrie avant l'Islam* (Paris, 1955).

EBELING, E. and others (editors): *Reallexikon der Assyriologie* (Walter de Gruyter & Co., Berlin, from 1932). [Volumes I and II appeared before the Second World War. Publication was resumed in 1957, and two parts of volume III have now appeared, a third part being under preparation].

EHRICH, R. W.: Culture area and culture history in the Mediterranean and the Middle East (=page 1-21 in Weinberg, S.S. (editor): *The Aegean and the Near East*, 1956).

†FINEGAN, J.: *Light from the ancient past* (Princeton University Press, Princeton; Oxford University Press, London; 2nd edition, 1959).

†FRIEDRICH, J.: *Entzifferung verschollener Schriften und Sprachen* (Springer-Verlag, Berlin/Göttingen/Heidelberg, 1954).

GELB, I. J.: *A study of writing and the foundations of Grammatology* (Routledge and Kegan Paul, London, 1952).

HOMMEL, F.: *Ethnologie und Geographie des alten Orients* (Munich, 1926).

KRAUS, F. R.: *Wandel und Kontinuität in der sumerisch-babylonischen Kultur* (Leiden, 1954).

KRAUS, F. R.: Altmesopotamisches Lebensgefühl (*Journal of Near Eastern Studies* 19 (1960), 117-132).

†MALLOWAN, M. E. L.: *Twenty-five years of Mesopotamian discovery* (British School of Archaeology in Iraq, London, 1956).

MEISSNER, B.: *Babylonien und Assyrien* (Two volumes. Carl Winters Universitätsbuchhandlung, Heidelberg, 1920 and 1925).

MEYER, E.: *Geschichte des Altertums* (Five volumes in nine. Stuttgart and Berlin, 1925–58).

MOSCATI, S.: *Ancient Semitic civilizations* (Elek Books, London, 1957).

†MOSCATI, S.: *The Semites in Ancient History* (University of Wales Press, Cardiff, 1959).

†OLMSTEAD, A. T. E.: *History of Assyria* (New York, 1923).

PALLIS, S. A.: *The antiquity of Iraq* (Copenhagen, 1956).

†PARROT, A.: *Archéologie mésopotamienne; les étapes* (Albin Michel, Paris, 1946).

†PARROT, A.: *Archéologie mésopotamienne; technique et problèmes* (Albin Michel, Paris, 1953).

†PRITCHARD, J. B. (editor): *Ancient Near Eastern texts relating to the Old Testament* (Princeton University Press, 2nd edition, 1955).

†SCHMÖKEL, H.: *Geschichte des alten Vorderasien* (Brill, Leiden, 1957).

†SEMPLE, E. C.: *The geography of the Mediterranean region; its relation to ancient history* (Constable, London, 1932).

SODEN, W. VON: *Der Aufstieg des Assyrerreiches als geschichtliches Problem* (Leipzig, 1937).

SODEN, W. VON: *Herrscher im alten Orient* (Berlin, 1954).

SODEN, W. VON: Aufstieg und Untergang der Grossreiche des Zweistromgebietes (Sumerer, Babylonier, Assyrer) (=page 37–64 in W. F. Mueller (editor): *Aufstieg und Untergang der Grossreiche des Altertums [circa 1958]*).

SPEISER, E. A.: Ancient Mesopotamia (=pages 35–76 in Dentan, R. C. (editor): *The idea of history in the ancient Near East. American Oriental Series* 38; Yale University Press, New Haven and Oxford University Press, London, 1955).

STAMM, J. J.: *Die akkadische Namengebung (Mitteilungen der vorderasiatisch-aegyptischen Gesellschaft* 44, 1939).

UNGER, E.: *Babylon; die heilige Stadt nach der Beschreibung der Babylonier* (Walter de Gruyter, Berlin, 1931).

UNGER, E.: Vom Weltbild der Babylonier, (*Kosmos*, Jahrgang 53, Heft 12 (1957), 588–593).

Weinberg, S. S. (editor): *The Aegean and the Near East* (J. J. Augustin, New York, 1956).

Wright, H. E.: Geological aspects of the archaeology of Iraq (*Sumer* 11 (1955), 83–91).

Maps of Iraq with notes for visitors (Government of Iraq, 1928).

Prehistory and Protohistory

BRAIDWOOD, R. J.: Earlier prehistory of highland Iraq (*Archiv für Orientforschung* 17 (1956), 428–429).

BRAIDWOOD, R. J.: Reflections on the origin of the village-farming community (=pages 22–31 in S. S. Weinberg (editor): *The Aegean and the Near East*, 1956).

BRAIDWOOD, R. J. and others: *Prehistoric investigations in Iraqi Kurdistan* (Studies in Ancient Oriental Civilization 31; University of Chicago Press, 1960).

†BROOKS, C. E. P.: *Climate through the ages* (Benn, London, 2nd edition, 1950).

†BURINGH, P.: Living conditions in the lower Mesopotamian plain in ancient times (*Sumer* 13 (1957), 30–46).

†CHILDE, V. G.: *New light on the most ancient East* (Routledge & Kegan Paul, London, rewritten edition, 1952).

†COLE, S.: *The Neolithic Revolution* (British Museum (Natural History), 1959).

FALKENSTEIN, A.: *Archaische Texte aus Uruk* (Harrassowitz, Leipzig, 1936).

†FRANKFORT, H.: *The birth of civilization in the Near East* (Doubleday Anchor Books, New York, 1956).

GARROD, D. A. E.: The Palaeolithic of Southern Kurdistan (*Bulletin of the American School of Prehistoric Research* 6 (1930), 13–23).

GARROD, D. A. E. and BATE, D. M. A.: *The Stone Age of Mount Carmel*, I (Clarendon Press, Oxford, 1937).

KANTOR, H. J.: The early relations of Egypt with Asia (*Journal of Near Eastern Studies* i (1942), 174–213).

KANTOR, H. J.: Further evidence for early Mesopotamian relations with Egypt (*Journal of Near Eastern Studies* 11 (1952), 239–250).

†KENYON, K. M.: *Digging up Jericho* (Benn, London, 1957).

LEES, G. M. and FALCON, N. F.: The geographical history of the Mesopotamian plains (*Geographical Journal* 118 (1952), 24–39). [For a criticism of the arguments of Lees and Falcon see *Geographical Journal* 120 (1954), 394–397].

McCOWN, D. E.: The material culture of early Iran (*Journal of Near Eastern Studies* i (1942), 424–449).

McCOWN, D. E.: *The Comparative stratigraphy of early Iran* (*Studies in Ancient Oriental Civilization* 23, University of Chicago Press, 1942).

MOORTGAT, A.: *Die Entstehung der sumerischen Hochkultur* (Leipzig, 1945).

PERKINS, A. L.: *The comparative archeology of early Mesopotamia* (*Studies in Ancient Oriental Civilization* 25, University of Chicago Press, 1949, reprinted 1959).

SPEISER, E. A.: *Excavations at Tepe Gawra*, I (University of Pennsylvania Press, Philadelphia, 1935).

SPEISER, E. A.: The Sumerian problem reviewed (*Hebrew Union College Annual* 23 (1950–51), I, 339–355).

SPEISER, E. A.: The rivers of Paradise (=pages 473–485 in Kienle, R. von and others (editors): *Festschrift Johannes Friedrich;* Carl Winter, Heidelberg, 1959).

VOÛTE, C.: A prehistoric find near Razzaza (Karbala liwa). Its significance for the morphological and geological setting of the Abu Dibbis depression and surrounding area. (*Sumer* 13 (1957), 135–148).

History and Institutions of the Third Millennium

CORNWALL, P. B.: Two letters from Dilmun (*Journal of Cuneiform Studies* 6 (1952), 137–145).

CORNWALL, P. B.: On the location of Dilmun [With appendix by A. Goetze] (*Bulletin of the American Schools of Oriental Research* 103 (1946), 3–11).

DIAKONOFF, I. M.: Sale of land in pre-Sargonic Sumer (*Papers presented by the Soviet delegation at the XXIII International Congress of Orientalists; Assyriology*, 19–29).

DIAKONOFF, I. M.: Some remarks on the 'Reforms' of Urukagina (*Revue d'Assyriologie* 52 (1958), 1–15). [Students able to read Russian should note that several important works on Sumerian institutions and economics have been produced in Russian by this scholar and his colleagues.]

EVANS, G.: Ancient Mesopotamian Assemblies (*Journal of the American Oriental Society* 78 (1958), 1–11, 114–115).

FALKENSTEIN, A.: Die Ibbīsîn-Klage (*Die Welt des Orients* 1950, 377–384).

FALKENSTEIN, A.: La cité-temple sumérienne (*Cahiers d'Histoire Mondiale*, I (Paris 1954), 784–814).

GELB, I. J.: Hurrians at Nippur in the Sargonic period (=pages 183–194 in Kienle, R. von and others (editors): *Festschrift Johannes Friedrich;* Carl Winter, Heidelberg, 1959).

GELB, I. J.: New light on Hurrians and Subarians (*Studi orientalistici in onore di Giorgio Levi Della Vida* [Rome, 1956], I, 378–392).

JACOBSEN, TH.: The assumed conflict between Sumerians and Semites in early Mesopotamian history (*Journal of the American Oriental Society* 59 (1939), 485–495).

JACOBSEN, TH.: *The Sumerian King List* (*Assyriological Studies* 11, University of Chicago Press, 1939).

JACOBSEN, TH.: Primitive Democracy in ancient Mesopotamia (*Journal of Near Eastern Studies* 2 (1943), 159–172).

JACOBSEN, TH.: The reign of Ibbī-Suen (*Journal of Cuneiform Studies* 7 (1953), 36–47).

JACOBSEN, TH.: Early political development in Mesopotamia (*Zeitschrift für Assyriologie*, neue Folge 18 (1956), 91–140).

JESTIN, R.: Übungen im Edubba (*Zeitschrift für Assyriologie*, neue Folge 17 (1955), 37–44). [Finally proves that, as had been supposed before, the living Sumerian language was tonal.]

KRAELING, C. H. and ADAMS, R. M. (editors): *City invincible. A symposium on urbanization and cultural development in the ancient Near East.* (*Oriental Institute Special Publications*, University of Chicago Press, 1960.)

KRAMER, S. N.: New light on the early history of the ancient Near East (*American Journal of Archaeology* 52 (1948), 156–164).

KRAMER, S. N.: Sumerian historiography (*Israel Exploration Journal* 3 (1953), 217–232).

†KRAMER, S. N.: *History begins at Sumer* (Doubleday Anchor Books, New York, 1959).

KRAUS, F. R.: Le rôle des temples depuis la troisième dynastie d'Ur jusqu'à la première dynastie de Babylone (*Cahiers d'histoire mondiale* i (Paris, 1953–54), 518–545; English summary xxx–xxxii).

KRAUS, F. R.: Provinzen des neusumerischen Reiches von Ur (*Zeitschrift für Assyriologie*, neue Folge 17 (1955), 45–75).

LAMBERT, M.: La période présargonique. Essai d'une histoire sumérienne (*Sumer* 8 (1952), 198–216).

LAMBERT, M.: Une histoire du conflit entre Lagash et Umma (*Revue d'Assyriologie* 50 (1956), 141–146).

SCHMÖKEL, H.: *Das Land Sumer* (W. Kohlhammer Verlag, Stuttgart, 1956).

SIEGEL, B. J.: Slavery during the Third Dynasty of Ur (*American Anthropologist*, New Series 49 (1947), No. 1, Part 2).

SOLLBERGER, E.: Sur la chronologie des rois d'Ur et quelques problèmes connexes (*Archiv für Orientforschung* 17 (1954–56), 10–48).

SPEISER, E. A.: *Mesopotamian origins* (Philadelphia, 1930).

THUREAU-DANGIN, F.: *Die sumerischen und akkadischen Königsinschriften* (Vorderasiatische Bibliothek, 1. Band, Abteilung 1, Leipzig, 1907).

WEIDNER, E.: Das Reich Sargons von Akkad (*Archiv für Orientforschung* 16 (1952), 1–24).

History of the Second Millennium

BAUER, TH.: *Die Ostkanaanäer. Eine philologisch-historische Untersuchung über die Wanderschicht der sogenannten 'Amoriter' in Babylonien* (Leipzig, 1926).

[Though Bauer's general position has been generally abandoned now, this work is still of importance in that it has formed the starting point for much of the later discussion of the subject.]

DOSSIN, G.: *Archives Royales de Mari, I. Correspondance de Šamši-Addu* (Imprimerie Nationale, Paris, 1950).

DOSSIN, G.: *Archives Royales de Mari, IV. Correspondance de Šamši-Addu* (Imprimerie Nationale, Paris, 1951).

DOSSIN, G.: *Archives Royales de Mari, V. Correspondance de Iasmaḥ-Addu* (Imprimerie Nationale, Paris, 1952).

DUPONT-SOMMER, A.: Sur les débuts de l'histoire araméenne (=pages 40–49 in *Supplements to Vetus Testamentum*, volume I, *Congress Volume, Copenhagen*, 1953; Brill, Leiden, 1953).

EBELING, E., MEISSNER, B., WEIDNER, E. F.: *Die Inschriften der altassyrischen Könige* (*Altorientalische Bibliothek*, 1 Band; Quelle & Meyer, Leipzig, 1926).

EDZARD, D. O.: *Die 'zweite Zwischenzeit' Babyloniens* (Harrassowitz, Wiesbaden, 1957).

FINE, F. A.: Studies in Middle Assyrian chronology and religion (*Hebrew Union College Annual* 24 (1952–53), 187–273 and 25 (1954), 107–168). [These two articles were also published as a book, Cincinnatti, 1955.]

GARSTANG. J. and GURNEY, O. R.: *The geography of the Hittite empire* (British Institue of Archaeology at Ankara, London, 1959).

GELB, I. J.: *Hurrians and Subarians* (University of Chicago Press, 1944). [See also the two related articles by I. J. Gelb listed in the preceding sub-section.]

GELB, I. J.: The name of Babylon (*Journal of the Institute of Asian Studies* i (1955), 1–4).

GELB, I. J.: The early history of the West Semitic peoples (*Journal of Cuneiform Studies* 15 (1961), 27–47). [A valuable review article.]

GOETZE, A.: An Old Babylonian itinerary (*Journal of Cuneiform Studies* 7 (1953), 51–72).

GOETZE, A.: *Kleinasien* (C. H. Beck'sche Verlagsbuchhandlung, Munich, 2nd edition, 1957).

†GURNEY, O. R.: *The Hittites* (Penguin Books, London, 1952).

HALL, H. R.: Minoan fayence in Mesopotamia (*Journal of Hellenic Studies* 48 (1928), 64–74).

HALLO, W. W.: The last years of the kings of Isin (*Journal of Near Eastern Studies* 18 (1959), 54–72).

JEAN, CH.-F.: *Archives Royales de Mari, II. Lettres diverses* (Imprimerie Nationale, Paris, 1950).

KANTOR, H. J.: The Aegean and the Orient in the second millennium B.C. (*American Journal of Archaeology* 51 (1947), 1–103).

KNUDTZON, J. A.: *Die el-Amarna-Tafeln* (Two volumes. *Vorderasiatische Bibliothek*, 2. Stück; Hinrichs, Leipzig, 1915). [This is generally considered to be better than another later edition of the same texts.]

KUPPER, J.-R.: *Archives Royales de Mari, III. Correspondance de Kibri-Dagan* (Imprimerie Nationale, Paris, 1950).

KUPPER, J.-R.: *Archives Royales de Mari, VI. Correspondance de Baḥdi-Lim* (Imprimerie Nationale, Paris, 1954).

KUPPER, J.-R.: *Les nomades en Mésopotamie au temps des rois de Mari* (*Bibliothèque de la Faculté de Philosophie et Lettres de l'Université de Liège*, no. 142; Paris, 1957).

LEWY, J.: Šubat-Enlil (*Annuaire de l'Institut de Philologie et d'Histoire Orientales et Slaves* 13 (1953), 293–321).

LEWY, J.: On some institutions of the Old Assyrian empire (*Hebrew Union College Annual* 27 (1956), 1–79).

LEWY. J.: Amurritica (*Hebrew Union College Annual* 32 (1961), 31–74).

†LUCKENBILL, D. D.: *Ancient records of Assyria and Babylonia*, I (University of Chicago Press, 1926).

O'CALLAGHAN, R. T.: *Aram Naharaim. A contribution to the history of Upper Mesopotamia in the second millennium B.C.* (Pontificium Institutum Biblicum, Rome, 1948).

OPPENHEIM, A. L.: The archives of the palace of Mari (*Journal of Near Eastern Studies* 11 (1952), 129–139 and 13 (1954), 141–148).

SCHAEFFER, C. F. A. (editor): *Le palais royal d'Ugarit*, III (Imprimerie Nationale, Paris, 1955).

SCHAEFFER, C. F. A. (editor): *Le palais royal d'Ugarit*, IV (Imprimerie Nationale, Paris, 1956).

SMITH, S.: *Early History of Assyria to* 1000 B.C. (Chatto and Windus, London, 1928).

SMITH, S.: *The statue of Idri-mi* (British Institute of Archaeology in Ankara, London, 1949).

SMITH, S.: The chronology of the Kassite dynasty (*Compte Rendu de la deuxième Rencontre Assyriologique Internationale* (1951), 67–70).

SPEISER, E. A.: Ethnic movements in the Near East in the second millennium B.C. (*Annual of the American Schools of Oriental Research*, vol. 13 for 1931–32, 13–54).

SPEISER, E. A.: The Hurrian participation in the civilizations of Mesopotamia, Syria and Palestine (*Cahiers d'Histoire Mondiale* i (Paris, 1953–54), 311–327).

WEIDNER, E.: Hof- und Harems-Erlasse assyrischer Könige aus dem 2. Jahrtausend v. Chr. (*Archiv für Orientforschung*, Sonderreihe H.1; Wiesbaden, 1956).

WEIDNER, E.: Die Inschriften Tukulti-Ninurtas I und seiner Nachfolger (*Archiv für Orientforschung*, Beiheft 12; Graz, 1959).

History of the First Millennium

ANSPACHER, A. S.: *Tiglath-Pileser III* (*Columbia College Contributions to Oriental History and Philology*, No. 5, 1912).

BARNETT, R. D. and WATSON, W.: Russian excavations in Armenia (Karmir-Blur) (*Iraq* 14 (1952), 132–147).

BARNETT, R. D.: The Archaeology of Urartu (*Compte Rendu de la troisième Rencontre Assyriologique Internationale* (1954), 10–18).

BAUER, TH.: *Das Inschriftenwerk Assurbanipals. I. Teil: Keilschrifttexte. II. Teil: Bearbeitung* (Hinrichs, Leipzig, 1933).

BAUMGARTNER, W.: Herodots babylonische und assyrische Nachrichten (*Archiv Orientální* 18,1–2 (1950), 69–106).

BIBLIOGRAPHY

BORGER, R.: *Die Inschriften Asarhaddons Königs von Assyrien* (*Archiv für Orientforschung*, Beiheft 9; Graz, 1956).

BOUDOU, R. P.: Liste de noms géographiques (*Orientalia* [old series] 36-38 (1929)).

BUDGE, E. A. W. and KING, L. W.: *Annals of the kings of Assyria*, I (British Musuem, 1902). [No further volumes were published.]

CAVAIGNAC, E.: Mushki et Phrygiens (*Journal Asiatique* 241 (1953), 139-143).

DELITZSCH, F.: *Die babylonische Chronik* (Leipzig ,1906).

DOUGHERTY, R. P.: *Nabonidus and Belshazzar. A study of the closing events of the Neo-Babylonian empire* (*Yale Oriental Series, Researches* XIV, New Haven, 1929).

FREEDMAN, D. N.: The Babylonian Chronicle (*The Biblical Archaeologist* 19 (1956), 50-60).

FRIEDRICH, J., MEYER, G. R., UNGNAD, A. and WEIDNER, E.: *Die Inschriften vom Tell Halaf. Keilschrifttexte und aramäische Urkunden aus einer assyrischen Provinzhauptstadt* (*Archiv für Orientforschung*, Beiheft 6; Berlin, 1940).

GADD, C. J.: The Harran inscriptions of Nabonidus (*Anatolian Studies* 8 (1958), 35-92).

HALLO, W. W.: From Qarqar to Carchemish. Assyria and Israel in the light of new discoveries (*The Biblical Archaeologist* 23 (1960), 34-61).

LANDSBERGER, B.: *Sam'al. Studien zur Entdeckung der Ruinenstätte Karatepe*, I (Ankara, 1948). [No further volumes were published.]

LANE, W. H.: *Babylonian problems* (John Murray, London, 1923).

LANGDON, S.: *Die neubabylonischen Königsinschriften* (*Vorderasiatischen Bibliothek*, 4. Stück; Hinrichs, Leipzig, 1912).

LUCKENBILL, D. D.: *The annals of Sennacherib* (*Oriental Institute Publications* II; University of Chicago Press, 1924).

†LUCKENBILL, D. D.: *Ancient records of Assyria and Babylonia*, II (University of Chicago Press, 1927).

MALAMAT, A.: The historical setting of two biblical prophecies on the nations (*Israel Exploration Journal* i (1950-51), 149-159).

MELIKICHVILI, G. A.: Études de l'épigraphie ourartou et certaines questions de l'histoire d'Ourartou (*Rapport presenté au XXIV Congrès International des Orientalistes*, Moscow, 1957).

MILIK, J. T.: 'Prière de Nabonide' et autres écrits d'un cycle de Daniel (*Revue Biblique* 63 (1956), 407-415).

NYBERG, H. S.: Das Reich der Achämeniden (*Historia Mundi* III (1954), 56-115).

OLMSTEAD, A. T. E.: *Western Asia in the days of Sargon of Assyria* (*Cornell Studies in History and Political Science*, No. 2, 1908).

OLMSTEAD, A. T. E.: Assyrian historiography (*University of Missouri Studies. Social Science Series* III,1 (1916), 1-66).

OPPENHEIM, A. L.: The city of Assur in 714 B.C. (*Journal of Near Eastern Studies*, 19 (1960), 133-147).

PALLIS, S. A.: The history of Babylon 538-93 B.C. (*Studia Orientalia Ioanni Pedersen septuagenario . . . a collegis discipulis amicis dicata* [Einar Munksgaard, Copenhagen, 1953], 275-294).

RIGG, H. A.: Sargon's 'Eighth Military Campaign' (*Journal of the American Oriental Society* 62 (1942), 130–138).

SMITH, S.: *Babylonian historical texts* (Methuen, London, 1924).

SMITH, S.: *Isaiah chapters XL–LV* (*Schweich Lectures* for 1940; British Academy, 1944).

SPEISER, E. A.: Southern Kurdistan in the annals of Ashurnasirpal and today (*Annual of the American Schools of Oriental Research* 8 (1928), 1–42).

STRECK, M.: *Assurbanipal und die Letzten assyrischen Könige* (*Vorderasiatische Bibliothek*, 7. Stück; Leipzig, 1916).

TADMOR, H.: The campaigns of Sargon II of Assur: a chronological-historical study (*Journal of Cuneiform Studies* 12 (1958), 22–40, 77–100).

THUREAU-DANGIN, F.: *Une relation de la huitième campagne de Sargon* (714 av. J.-C.) (Geuthner, Paris, 1912).

VOGELSTEIN, M.: Nebuchadnezzar's reconquest of Phoenicia and Palestine and the oracles of Ezekiel (*Hebrew Union College Annual* 23 (1950–51), II, 197–220).

WATERMAN, L.: *Royal correspondence of the Assyrian empire* (Four volumes, University of Michigan Press, Ann Arbor, 1930–36).

WEIDNER, E.: Jojachin, König von Juda, in babylonischen Keilschrifttexten (*Mélanges Syriens offerts à Monsieur René Dussaud*, [Geuthner, Paris, 1939], tome 2, 923–935).

WEIDNER, E.: Hochverrat gegen Nebukadnezar II (*Archiv für Orientforschung* 17 (1954–56), 1–9).

WETZEL, F.: Babylon zur Zeit Herodots (*Zeitschrift für Assyriologie*, neue Folge 14 (1944), 45–68).

WISEMAN, D. J.: *Chronicles of Chaldaean kings* (626–556 B.C.) (British Museum, London, 1956).

WRIGHT, E. M.: The eighth campaign of Sargon II of Assyria (*Journal of Near Eastern Studies* 2 (1943), 173–186).

Chronology

[A very large number of contributions to the problems of ancient chronology have been published. The few works listed below are intended only to introduce students to certain of the principal points under dispute. The forthcoming contribution of M. B. Rowton on chronology in the new edition of the *Cambridge Ancient History* will presumably contain a comprehensive bibliography.]

ALBRIGHT, W. F.: Further light on synchronisms between Egypt and Asia in the period 935–685 B.C. (*Bulletin of the American Schools of Oriental Research* 141 (1956), 23–27).

BRAIDWOOD, R. J.: Jericho and its setting in Near Eastern History (*Antiquity* 31 (1957), 73–81).

GELB, I. J.: Two Assyrian King Lists (*Journal of Near Eastern Studies* 13 (1954), 209–230).

LEWY, J.: Apropos of a recent study in Old Assyrian chronology (*Orientalia* 26 (1957), 12–36).

LIBBY, W. F.: *Radiocarbon dating* (University of Chicago Press; 2nd edition, 1955).

MEER, P. VAN DER: *The chronology of ancient Western Asia and Egypt* (Brill, Leiden; 2nd edition, 1955).

PARKER, R. A. and DUBBERSTEIN, W. H.: *Babylonian chronology 626 B.C.–A.D. 75* (*Studies in ancient oriental civilization* 24, University of Chicago Press, 1956).

PARROT, A.: Chronologie mésopotamienne (=pages 332–438 in Parrot, A.: *Archéologie mésopotamienne; technique et problèmes;* Paris, 1953).

ROWTON, M. B.: The date of Hammurabi (*Journal of Near Eastern Studies* 17 (1958), 97–111).

SMITH, S.: *Alalakh and chronology* (Luzac, London, 1940).

TADMOR, H.: Historical implications of the correct rendering of Akkadian *dâku* (*Journal of Near Eastern Studies* 17 (1958), 129–141).

Everyday Life

[This section is very brief as most of the facts incorporated in the chapter dealing with the *Babylonian Way of Life* are incidental deductions from sources properly to be classified as historical, religious, literary, legal or economic.]

BARNETT, R. D.: An Assyrian helmet (*British Museum Quarterly* 18 (1953), 101–102).

BUREN, E. D. VAN: Some archaic statuettes, and a study of early Sumerian dress ([*Liverpool*] *Annals of Archaeology and Anthropology* 17 (1930), 39–56).

†CONTENAU, G.: *Everyday life in Babylon and Assyria* (Arnold, London, 1954).

GORDON, C. H.: The status of Woman reflected in the Nuzi texts (*Zeitschrift für Assyriologie*, neue Folge 9 (1936), 146–169).

GORDON, C. H.: Belt-wrestling in the Bible world (*Hebrew Union College Annual* 23 (1950–51), 1, 131–136).

KINAL, FÜRUZAN: Die Stellung der Frau im alten Orient (*Belleten* 20 (1956), 367–378).

†LAMBERT, W. G.: Morals in ancient Mesopotamia (*Ex Oriente Lux* 15 (1957–58), 184–196).

MÜLLER, V.: Types of Mesopotamian houses (*Journal of the American Oriental Society* 60 (1940), 151–180).

†SPYCKET, A.: La coiffure féminine en Mésopotamie (*Revue d'Assyriologie* 48 (1954), 113–129, 169–177, and 49 (1955), 113–128).

Law, Statecraft and Administration

BIROT, M.: *Archives Royales de Mari, IX. Textes administratifs de la salle 5 du palais* (Imprimerie Nationale, Paris, 1960).

BOYER, G. and SZLECHTER, É.: Introduction bibliographique à l'histoire du droit suméro-akkadien. II (1939–55) (*Revue Internationale des Droits de l'Antiquité*, 3ᵉ serie, 3 (1956), 41–79).

BOYER, G.: *Archives Royales de Mari, VIII. Textes juridiques* (Imprimerie Nationale, Paris, 1958).

BOYER, G.: Nature et formation de la vente dans l'ancient droit babylonien (*Archives d'Histoire du Droit Oriental, Revue Internationale des Droits de l'Antiquité* 2 (1953), 45–85).

CARDASCIA, G.: L'adoption matrimoniale à Babylone et à Nuzi (*Revue historique de droit français et étranger*, 4ᵉ ser., 37 (1959), 1–16).

CROSS, D.: *Movable property in the Nuzi documents* (*American Oriental Series* 10 New Haven, 1937).

DOUGHERTY, R. P.: The Babylonian principle of suretyship as administered by temple law (*American Journal of Semitic Languages* 46 (1929), 73–103).

†DRIVER, G. R. and Miles, Sir J. C.: *The Assyrian Laws* (Clarendon Press, Oxford, 1935).

†DRIVER, G. R. and MILES, Sir J. C.: *The Babylonian laws. Volume I; legal commentary* (Clarendon Press, Oxford, 1952).

DRIVER, G. R. and MILES, Sir J. C.: *The Babylonian laws. Volume II; transliterated text, translation, philological notes, glossary* (Clarendon Press, Oxford, 1955).

EBELING, E.: *Neubabylonische Briefe aus Uruk*, 1.–4. Heft (Ebeling, Berlin, 1930–34).

EBELING, E.: *Neubabylonische Briefe* (Munich, 1949).

FALKENSTEIN, A.: Das Gesetzbuch Lipit-Ištar von Isin. I. Philologisches zum Gesetzbuch (*Orientalia* 19 (1950), 103–111).

FALKENSTEIN, A.: *Die neusumerischen Gerichtsurkunden* (Three Parts. Munich, 1956–57).

FEIGIN, S.: The Babylonian officials in Jeremiah 39³, ¹³ (*Journal of Biblical Literature* 45 (1926), 149–155).

FIGULLA, H. H.: Lawsuit concerning a sacrilegious theft at Erech (*Iraq* 13 (1951), 95–101).

FOLLET, R.: 'Deuxième Bureau' et information diplomatique dans l'Assyrie des Sargonides (*Rivista degli Studi Orientali* 32 (1957), 61–81).

FORRER, E.: *Die Provinzeinteilung des assyrischen Reiches* (Hinrichs, Leipzig, 1920).

GOETZE, A.: *The laws of Eshnunna* (*Annual of the American Schools of Oriental Research* 31; New Haven, 1956).

GORDON, C. H.: Nuzi tablets relating to theft (*Orientalia* 5 (1936), 305–330).

JACOBSEN, TH.: An ancient Mesopotamian trial for homicide (*Studia Biblica et Orientalia*, volumen III, *Oriens Antiquus* [Rome 1959], 130–150).

KLAUBER, E.: *Assyrisches Beamtentum nach Briefen aus der Sargonidenzeit* (Leipzig, 1910).

KLÍMA, J.: New discoveries of legal documents from pre-Hammurapian time (*Archiv Orientální* 19 (1951), 37–59).

KOHLER, J. and UNGNAD, A.: *Assyrische Rechtsurkunden* (Eduard Pfeiffer, Leipzig, 1913).

[KOSCHAKER, P.], (in honour of —): *Symbolae ad iura orientis antiqui pertinentes Paulo Koschaker dedicatae* (Brill, Leiden, 1939).

KRAMER, S. N. and FALKENSTEIN, A.: Ur-Nammu law code (*Orientalia* 23 (1954), 40–51).

KRAUS, F. R.: *Ein Edikt des Königs Ammi-ṣaduqa von Babylon* (Brill, Leiden, 1958).

KRAUS, F. R.: Ein Zentrales Problem des altmesopotamischen Rechtes: Was ist der Codex Hammu-rabi? (*Genava*, n.s. 8 (1960), 283–296). [An article of the highest importance.]

KUPPER, J.-R.: Un gouvernement provincial dans le royaume de Mari (*Revue d'Assyriologie* 41 (1947), 149–183).

LAMBERT, M.: Les 'Réformes' d'Urukagina (*Revue d'Assyriologie* 50 (1956), 169–184).

LAMBERT, M.: Documents sur le §3 des 'Réformes' d'Urukagina (*Revue d'Assyriologie* 51 (1957), 139–144).

LANDSBERGER, B.: Die babylonische Termini für Gesetz und Recht (*Symbolae . . . Koschaker dedicatae* [Leiden, 1939], 219–234).

LIEBESNY, H.: The oath of the king in the legal procedure of Nuzi (*Journal of the American Oriental Society* 61 (1941), 62–63).

LIEBESNY, H.: Evidence in Nuzi legal procedure (*Journal of the American Oriental Society* 61 (1941). 130–142).

LIEBESNY, H.: The administration of justice in Nuzi (*Journal of the American Oriental Society* 63 (1943), 128–144).

MANITIUS, W.: Das stehende Heer der Assyrerkönige und seine Organisation (*Zeitschrift für Assyriologie* [alte Folge] 24 (1910), 97–149, 185–224).

†MUNN-RANKIN, J. M.: Diplomacy in Western Asia in the early second millennium B.C. (*Iraq* 18 (1956), 68–110).

NOUGAYROL, J.: Le prologue du Code Hammourabien, d'après une tablette inédite du Louvre (*Revue d'Assyriologie* 45 (1951), 67–79).

NOUGAYROL, J.: Un fragment oublié du Code (en) sumérien (*Revie d'Assyriologie* 46 (1952), 53–55).

†OPPENHEIM, A. L.: On an operational device in Mesopotamian bureaucracy (*Journal of Near Eastern Studies* 18 (1959), 121–128).

†PRAAG, A. VAN: *Droit matrimonial Assyro-Babylonien* (Amsterdam, 1945).

PURVES, P. M.: Commentary on Nuzi real property in the light of recent studies (*Journal of Near Eastern Studies* 4 (1945), 68–86).

PURVES, P. M.: Additional remarks on Nuzi real property (*Journal of Near Eastern Studies* 6 (1947), 181–185).

SAGGS, H. W. F.: Two administrative officials at Erech in the sixth century B.C. (*Sumer* 15 (1959), 29–38).

SAGGS, H. W. F.: The Nimrud letters, 1952—Part V. Administration (*Iraq* 21 (1959), 158–179).

SAN NICOLÒ, M.: *Babylonische Rechtsurkunden des ausgehenden 8. und des 7. Jahrhunderts v. Chr.* (Munich, 1951).

SAN NICOLÒ, M.: *Beiträge zu einer Prosopographie neubabylonischer Beamten der Zivil- und Tempelverwaltung* (Munich, 1941).

SCHOTT, M.: *Urkunden des altbabylonischen Zivil- und Prozessrechts* (Vorderasiatische Bibliothek, 5. Stück; Hinrichs, Leipzig, 1913).

SNYDER, J. W.: Babylonian suretyship litigation; a case history (*Journal of Cuneiform Studies* 9 (1955), 25–28).

SPEISER, E. A.: Authority and Law in the ancient Orient (Mesopotamia) (*Journal of the American Oriental Society*, supplement 17 (1954), 8–15).

STEELE, F. R.: *Nuzi real estate transactions* (American Oriental Series 25, Philadelphia, 1943).

STEELE, F.R.: The code of Lipit-Ishtar (*American Journal of Archaeology* 52 (1948), 425–450).

Szlechter, É.: Le code d'Ur-Nammu (*Revue d'Assyriologie* 49 (1955), 169–177).

Szlechter, É.: Le code de Lipit-Ištar (*Revue d'Assyriologie* 51 (1957), 57–82, 177–196; 52 (1958), 74–90).

Szlechter, É.: La saisie illégale dans les lois d'Ešnunna et dans le code d'-Hammurabi (*Studi in onore di Petro De Francisci* [Milano 1956], I, 271–281).

Ungnad, A.: *Babylonische Briefe aus der Zeit der Hammurapi-Dynastie* (Vorder-asiatische Bibliothek, 6. Stück; Hinrichs, Leipzig, 1914).

Weidner, E. F.: *Politische Dokumente aus Kleinasien. Die Staatsverträge in akkadischer Sprache aus dem Archiv von Boghazköi* (*Boghazköi-Studien*, 9. Heft; Hinrichs, Leipzig, 1923).

Trade, Economics, Communications and Transport

Bottéro, J.: *Archives Royales de Mari, VII. Textes économiques et adminis-tratifs* (Imprimerie Nationale, Paris, 1958).

Cardascia, G.: Les villes de Mésopotamie: Leurs institutions économiques et sociales (*Recueils de la Société Jean Bodin* 7 (1955), 51–61).

†Clay, R.: *The tenure of land in Babylonia and Assyria* (Institute of Archaeology, London, 1938).

Deimel, A.: *Šumerische Tempelwirtschaft zur Zeit Urukaginas und seiner Vor-gänger* (*Analecta Orientalia* II; Rome, 1931).

Delagneau, R.: La batellerie. Son évolution en Mésopotamie du IVe au Ier millénaire avant J.-C. (*Positions des thèses des élèves de l'École du Louvre*, 1944–52 [Paris, 1956], 122–126).

Dossin, G.: Signaux lumineux au pays de Mari (*Revue d'Assyriologie* 35 (1938), 174–186).

Dougherty, R. P.: Cuneiform parallels to Solomon's provisioning system (*Annual of the American Schools of Oriental Research*, vol. 5 [New Haven, 1925], 23–65).

Dougherty, R. P.: *The Shirkûtu of Babylonian deities* (*Yale Oriental Series; Researches*, vol. V[2]; New Haven, 1923).

Dubberstein, W. H.: Comparative prices in later Babylonia (*American Journal of Semitic Languages* 56 (1939), 20–43).

Faulkner, R. O.: A Syrian trading venture to Egypt (*Journal of Egyptian Archaeology* 33 (1947), 40–46). [Provides the Egyptian material referred to on pages 281 f.]

Gardiner, Sir A. H.: A lawsuit arising from the purchase of two slaves (*Journal of Egyptian Archaeology* 21 (1935), 140–146). [Provides the Egyptian material referred to on pages 297f.]

Gordon, C. H.: Colonies and enclaves (*Studi orientalistici in onore di Giorgio Levi Della Vida* [Rome, 1956], I, 409–419).

†Heichelheim, F. M.: *An ancient economic history*, volume I (Sijthoff, Leiden, 1958).

Jacobsen, Th.: On the textile industry at Ur under Ibbī-Sîn (*Studia Orientalia Ioanni Pedersen septuagenario . . . a collegis discipulis amicis dicata* [Einar Munks-gaard, Copenhagen, 1953], 172–187).

Johns, C. H. W.: *Assyrian deeds and documents recording the transfer of property* (Four volumes. Deighton Bell, Cambridge; G. Bell, London; 1898–1924).

[The discussions in volumes III and IV, though in some respects antiquated, are still of value. Many of the cuneiform texts published in volumes I and II have been edited, with emphasis upon the juristic rather than the economic aspects, in Kohler and Ungnad: *Assyrische Rechtsurkunden, q.v. sub* previous section.]

KÖNIG, F. W.: Gesellschaftliche Verhältnisse Armeniens zur Zeit der Chalder-Dynastie (9-7 Jahrhundert) (*Archiv für Volkerkunde* 9 (1954), 21-65).

LAMBERT, M.: La période presargonique. La vie économique à Shuruppak (*Sumer* 9 (1953), 198-213, and 10 (1954), 150-190).

LAMBERT, M.: Textes commerciaux de Lagash (époque presargonique) (Parts I and II in *Revue d'Assyriologie* 47 (1953), 57-69 and 105-120; part III in *Archiv Orientální* 23 (1955), 557-574).

LAUTNER, J. G.: *Altbabylonische Personenmiete und Erntearbeitverträge* (Brill, Leiden, 1936).

LEEMANS, W. F.: *The Old Babylonian merchant* (Brill, Leiden, 1950).

LEEMANS, W. F.: *Legal and economic records from the kingdom of Larsa* (Brill, Leiden, 1954).

LEEMANS, W. F.: *Foreign trade in the Old Babylonian period* (Brill, Leiden, 1960).

LEHMANN-HAUPT, C. F.: [Summary of paper given at Leiden in 1931.] (*Actes du XVIIIᵉ Congres International des Orientalistes;* Brill, Leiden, 1932).
[The source of the suggestion on page 113 of a possible connection between China and Urartu in the eighth century B.C.]

LEWY, J.: Some aspects of commercial life in Assyria and Asia Minor in the nineteenth pre-Christian century (*Journal of the American Oriental Society* 78 (1958), 89-101).

LUTZ, H. F.: *Legal and economic documents from Ashjâly* (*University of California Publications in Semitic Philology*, vol. 10, No. 1, 1-184; Berkeley, 1931).

†MENDELSOHN, I.: *Slavery in the ancient Near East* (Oxford University Press, New York, 1949).

OPPENHEIM, A. L.: A fiscal practice of the ancient Near East (*Journal of Near Eastern Studies* 6 (1947), 116-120).

OPPENHEIM, A. L.: The seafaring merchants of Ur (*Journal of the American Oriental Society* 74 (1954), 6-17).

†OPPENHEIM, A. L.: A bird's-eye view of Mesopotamian economic history (=pages 26-37 in Polanyi, K., *Trade and market in the early empires*, 1957),

†POLANYI, K.: *Trade and market in the early empires* (Free Press, Glencoe, Illinois and The Falcon's Wing Press, 1957).

PRICE, I. M.: Transportation by water in early Babylonia (*American Journal of Semitic Languages* 40 (1923), 111-116).

SAARISALO, A.: New Kirkuk documents relating to slaves (*Studia Orientalia* [Helsinki] 5/3 (1934), 1-101).

SALONEN, A.: Die Wasserfahrzeuge in Babylonien (*Studia Orientalia* [Helsinki] 8/4 (1939), 1-199).

SALONEN, A.: Nautica Babylonica (*Studia Orientalia* [Helsinki] 11/1 (1942), 1-118).

SALONEN, A.: Die Landfahrzeuge des alten Mesopotamien (*Annales Academiae Scientiarum Fennicae*, ser. B, tom. 72, 3; Helsinki, 1951).

SALONEN, A.: *Hippologica Accadica* (*Annales Academiae Scientiarum Fennicae*, ser. B. tom. 100; Helsinki, 1956).

SAN NICOLÒ, M. and UNGNAD, A.: *Neubabylonische Rechts- und Verwaltungs-Urkunden* (Hinrichs, Leipzig, 1935).

SAN NICOLÒ, M.: Materialien zur Viehwirtschaft in den neubabylonischen Tempeln. I-V (*Orientalia* 17 (1948), 273-293; 18 (1949), 288-306; 20 (1951), 129-150; 23 (1954), 351-382; 25 (1956), 24-38).

SMITH, S.: A pre-Greek coinage in the Near East? (*Numismatic Chronicle*, fifth series 2 (1922), 2-11).

SMITH, S.: The Greek trade at Al Mina (*Antiquaries Journal* 22 (1942), 87-112).

STEPHENS, F. J.: Notes on some economic texts of the time of Urukagina (*Revue d'Assyriologie* 49 (1955), 129-136).

Religion; Magic and Divination

(a) Primarily editions or translations of texts

BERNHARDT, I. and KRAMER, S. N.: Enki und die Weltordnung (*Wissenschaftliche Zeitschrift der Friedrich-Schiller-Universität Jena*, Jahrgang 9, Heft 1/2 (1959-60), 231-256).

CASTELLINO, G.: Rituals and prayers against 'Appearing Ghosts' (*Orientalia* 24 (1955), 240-274).

CASTELLINO, G.: Urnammu three religious texts (*Zeitschrift für Assyriologie*, neue Folge 18 (1957), 1-57).

DOSSIN, G.: Un ritual du culte d'Ištar provenant de Mari (*Revue d'Assyriologie* 35 (1938), 1-13).

DOSSIN, G.: Une revelation du dieu Dagan à Terqa (*Revue d'Assyriologie* 42 (1948) 125-134).

EBELING, E.: Beschwörungen gegen den Feind und den bösen Blick aus dem Zweistromlande (*Archiv Orientální* 17/1 (1949), 172-211).

EBELING, E.: Ein babylonisches Beispiel schwarzer Magie (*Orientalia* 20 (1951), 167-170).

EBELING, E.: Kultische Texte aus Assur (*Orientalia* 20 (1951), 399-405); 21 (1952), 129-148); 22 (1953), 25-46; 23 (1954), 114-128; 24 (1955), 1-15).

EBELING, E.: *Die akkadische Gebetsserie 'Handerhebung'* (Akademie-Verlag, Berlin, 1953).

EBELING, E.: Ein neuassyrisches Beschwörungsritual gegen Bann und Tod (*Zeitschrift für Assyriologie*, neue Folge 17 (1955), 167-179).

EBELING, E.: Beiträge zur Kenntnis der Beschwörungsserie Namburbi (*Revue d'Assyriologie* 48 (1954), 1-15, 76-85, 130-141, 178-191; 49 (1955), 32-41, 137-148, 178-192; 50 (1956), 22-33, 86-94).

FALKENSTEIN, A.: Sumerische religiöse Texte (*Zeitschrift für Assyriologie*, neue Folge 15 (1950), 80-150; 16 (1951), 61-91; 18 (1957), 58-75).

FRANK, C.: *Lamaštu, Pazuzu und andere Dämonen. Ein Beitrag zur babylonisch-assyrischen Dämonologie* (*Mitteilungen der altorientalischen Gesellschaft* XIV/2; Harrassowitz, Leipzig, 1941).

FRANKENA, R.: *Tākultu, de sacrale maaltijd in het Assyrische ritueel* (Brill, Leiden , 1954).

BIBLIOGRAPHY

FALKENSTEIN, A. and SODEN, W. VON: *Sumerische und akkadische Hymnen und Gebete* (Artemis-Verlag, Zürich/Stuttgart, 1953).

FRANK, C.: *Kultlieder aus dem Ischtar-Tamuz-Kreis* (Harrassowitz, Leipzig, 1939).

GOETZE, A.: *The Hittite ritual of Tunnawi* (*American Oriental Series* 14; American Oriental Society, New Haven, 1938).

GURNEY, O. R.: Babylonian prophylactic figures and their ritual ([*Liverpool*] *Annals of Archaeology and Anthropology* 22 (1935), 31-96).

†HEIDEL, A.: *The Babylonian Genesis. The History of the Creation* (University of Chicago Press; 2nd edition, 1952).

JASTROW, M.: *Die Religion Babyloniens und Assyriens* (Two volumes in three. Giessen, 1905-12).

JESTIN, R.: Textes religieux sumériens (*Revue d'Assyriologie* 35 (1938), 158-173; 39 (1944), 83-97; 40 (1946), 47-54; 41 (1947), 55-66; 44 (1950), 45-71).

LABAT, R.: *Le poème babylonien de la Création* (Adrien-Maisonneuve, Paris, 1935).

LAMBERT, W. G.: Divine love lyrics from Babylon (*Journal of Semitic Studies* 4 (1959), 1-15).

†LANGDON, S.: *The Babylonian Epic of Creation* (Clarendon Press, Oxford, 1923).

LANGDON, S.: An incantation for expelling demons from a house (*Zeitschrift für Assyriologie*, neue Folge 2 (1925), 209-214).

LEEMANS, W. F.: *Ishtar of Lagaba and her dress* (Brill, Leiden, 1952).

MEIER, G.: *Die assyrische Beschwörungssammlung Maqlû* (*Archiv für Orientforschung*, Beiheft 2; Berlin, 1937).

MEIER, G.: Ein Kommentar zu einer Selbstprädikation des Marduk aus Assur (*Zeitschrift für Assyriologie*, neue Folge 13 (1942), 241-246).

MYHRMAN, D. W.: Die Labartu-Texte (*Zeitschrift für Assyriologie* [alte Folge] 16 (1902), 141-200).

NÖTSCHER, F.: *Haus- und Stadt-Omina der Serie*: Šumma âlu ina mêlê šakin (*Orientalia* [old series], vols. 31, 39-42 and 51-54; 1928-30).

†OPPENHEIM, A. L.: *The interpretation of dreams in the ancient Near East. With a translation of an Assyrian dream-book* (Philadelphia, 1956).

OPPENHEIM, A. L.: A new prayer to the 'gods of the night' (*Studia Biblica et Orientalia*, volumen III, *Oriens Antiquus* [Rome 1959], 282-301).

REINER, E.: *Šurpu. A collection of Sumerian and Akkadian incantations* (*Archiv für Orientforschung*, Beiheft 11, Graz, 1958).

ROST, L.: Ein Hethitisches Ritual gegen Familienzwist (*Mitteilungen des Instituts für Orientforschung* 1 (1953), 345-379).

†SACHS, A.: Babylonian Horoscopes (*Journal of Cuneiform Studies* 6 (1952), 49-75).

SAGGS, H. W. F.: Pazuzu (*Archiv für Orientforschung* 19 (1960), 123-127).

SODEN, W. VON: Ein neues Bruckstück des assyrischen Kommentars zum Marduk-Ordal (*Zeitschrift für Assyriologie*, neue Folge 18 (1957), 224-234).

Thompson, R. C.: *The reports of the Magicians and Astrologers of Nineveh and Babylon.* Vol. II. *English translation and transliteration* (Luzac, London, 1900).

THOMPSON, R. C.: *The devils and evil spirits of Babylonia* (Two volumes. Luzac, London, 1903).

THUREAU-DANGIN, F.: Rituel et amulettes contre Labartu (*Revue d'Assyriologie* 18 (1921), 162–198).

THUREAU-DANGIN, F.: *Rituels accadiens* (Paris, 1921).

VIEYRA, M.: Ištar de Nineve (*Revue d'Assyriologie* 51 (1957), 83–102, 130–138).

WITZEL, M.: *Tammuz-Liturgien und Verwandtes (Analecta Orientalia* 10; Rome, 1935).

ZIMMERN, H.: Zu den 'Keilschrifttexten aus Assur religiösen Inhalts' (*Zeitschrift für Assyriologie* 30 (1915–16), 184–229).

(b) Primarily discussion

†BOTTÉRO, J.: *La religion babylonienne* (Paris, 1952).

BUREN, E. D. VAN: The God Ningizzida (*Iraq* 1 (1934), 60–89).

BUREN, E. D. VAN: Fish offerings in ancient Mesopotamia (*Iraq* 10 (1948), 101–121).

BUREN, E. D. VAN: The Rod and Ring (*Archiv Orientální* 17/2 (1949), 434–450).

BUREN, E. D. VAN: *Symbols of the gods in Mesopotamian art* (Pontificium Institutum Biblicum, Rome, 1945).

BUREN, E. D. VAN: Foundation rites for a new temple (*Orientalia* 21 (1952), 293–306).

BUREN, E. D. VAN: The building of a temple-tower (*Revue d'Assyriologie* 46 (1952), 65–174).

BUREN, E. D. VAN: An investigation of a new theory concerning the Bird-man. (*Orientalia* 22 (1953), 47–58).

BUREN, E. D. VAN: The Sun-God rising (*Revue d'Assyriologie* 49 (1955), 1–14).

DANMANVILLE, J.: La libation en Mésopotamie (*Revue d'Assyriologie* 49 (1955), 57–68).

†DHORME, E.: *Les religions de Babylonie et d'Assyrie* (Presses Universitaires de France, Paris, 1949).

FALKENSTEIN, A.: *Die Haupttypen der sumerischen Beschwörung* (*Leipziger semitistische Studien*, neue Folge 1; Hinrichs, Leipzig, 1931).

FALKENSTEIN, A.: Was sagen die schriftlichen Quellen über das Tammuz-Problem aus? (*Compte rendu de la Rencontre Assyriologique Internationale* 3 (1954), 41–65).

FALKENSTEIN, A.: akiti-Fest und akiti-Festhaus (=pages 147–182 in *Festschrift Johannes Friedrich*; Carl Winter, Heidelberg, 1959).

FRANKFORT, H.: *The problem of similarity in ancient Near Eastern religions* (Clarendon Press, Oxford, 1951).

†GADD, C. J.: Babylonian myth and ritual (=pages 40–67 in Hooke, S. H. (editor): *Myth and ritual*; University Press, Oxford, 1933).

†HOOKE, S. H.: *Babylonian and Assyrian religion* (Hutchinson, London, 1953). [For those able to read French, the works by Bottéro and Dhorme are to be preferred.]

†JACOBSEN, TH.: Mesopotamia (=pages 137–234 in Frankfort, H., and others: *Before philosophy;* Penguin Books, Harmondsworth, 1949).

JEAN, CH.-F.: *La religion sumérienne* (Geuthner, Paris, 1931). [This is badly out-of-date but is included because at present there is no other work which attempts to cover the same ground.]

KRAUS, F. R.: Tammūz (*Compte rendu de la Rencontre Assyriologique Internationale* 3 (1954), 69–74).

LEWY, J.: The late Assyro-Babylonian cult of the Moon and its culmination at the time of Nabonidus (*Hebrew Union College Annual* 19 (1945–46), 405–489).

MOORTGAT, A.: *Tammuz* (Walter de Gruyter & Co., Berlin, 1949).

OPPENHEIM, A. L.: Akkadian *pul(u)ḫ(t)u* and *melammu* (*Journal of the American Oriental Society* 63 (1943), 31–34).

OPPENHEIM, A. L.: Mesopotamian Mythology (*Orientalia* 16 (1947), 207–238; 17 (1948), 17–58; 19 (1950), 129–158).

PALLIS, S. A.: *The Babylonian Akîtu festival* (Copenhagen, 1926).

ROUX, G.: Adapa, le vent et l'eau (*Revue d'Assyriologie* 55 (1961), 13–33).

SMITH, S.: A Babylonian fertility cult (*Journal of the Royal Asiatic Society* 1928, 262–268).

SMITH, S.: The face of Humbaba ([*Liverpool*] *Annals of Archaeology and Anthropology* 11 (1924), 107–114).

SMITH, S.: Notes on 'The Assyrian Tree' (*Bulletin of the School of Oriental Studies* 4 (1926–28), 69–76).

SODEN, W. VON: Gibt es ein Zeugnis dafür, dass die Babylonier an die Wiederaufstehungs Marduks geglaubt haben? (*Zeitschrift für Assyriologie*, neue Folge 17 (1955), 130–166).

SODEN, W. VON: Licht und Finsternis in der sumerischen und babylonisch-assyrischen Religion (*Studium Generale*, 13. Jahrg., Heft 11 (1960), 647–653).

SODEN, W. VON: Religiöse Unsicherheit Säkularisierungstendenzen und Aberglaube zur Zeit der Sargoniden (*Studia Biblica et Orientalia*, volumen III, *Oriens Antiquus* [Rome, 1959], 356–367).

TALLQVIST, K.: *Akkadische Götterepitheta* (*Studia Orientalia* ([Helsinki] 7 (1938), 1–521).

(c) Texts and Studies on the Underworld and ideas of the Afterlife

BÖHL, F. M. TH. DE LIAGRE: Hymne an Nergal, den Gott der Unterwelt (*Bibliotheca Orientalis* 6 (1949), 165–170).

CURTIS, J. B.: An investigation of the Mount of Olives in the Judaeo-Christian tradition (*Hebrew Union College Annual* 28 (1957), 137–177).

EBELING, E.: *Tod und Leben nach den Vorstellungen der Babylonier*, 1. Teil: *Texte* (Walter de Gruyter & Co., Berlin und Leipzig, 1931).

EBELING, E.: Eine Beschreibung der Unterwelt in sumerischer Sprache (*Orientalia* 18 (1949), 285–287).

JESTIN, R.: La conception sumérienne de la vie post-mortem (*Syria* 33 (1956), 113–118).

KRAMER, S. N.: The death of Gilgamesh (*Bulletin of the American Schools of Oriental Research* 94 (1944), 2–12).

KRAMER, S. N.: 'Inanna's descent to the Nether World' continued and revised (*Journal of Cuneiform Studies* 5 (1951), 1–17).

LEWY, H.: Origin and significance of the *Mâgên Dâwîd* (*Archiv Orientální* 18/3 (1950), 330–365).

†SAGGS, H. W. F.: Some ancient Semitic conceptions of the Afterlife (*Faith and Thought* 90 (1958), 157–182).

SODEN, W. VON: Die Unterweltsvision eines assyrischen Kronprinzen (*Zeitschrift für Assyriologie*, neue Folge 9 (1936), 1–31).

TALLQVIST, K.: Sumerisch-akkadische Namen der Totenwelt (*Studia Orientalia* [Helsinki] 5, part 4 (1934), 1–46).

VANDEN BERGHE, L.: Réflexions critiques sur la nature de Dumuzi-Tammuz (*La Nouvelle Clio* 6 (1954), 298–321).

(d) Temples and Ziggurats

Amiet, P.: Ziggurats et 'Culte en Hauteur' des origines à l'époque d'Akkad (*Revue d'Assyriologie* 47 (1953), 23–33).

BUSINK, T. A.: De Babylonische tempeltoren (Brill, Leiden, 1949). [In Dutch, with a short summary in English.]

EBELING, E.: *Stiftungen und Vorschriften für assyrische Tempel* (Institut für Orientforschung, Berlin, 1954).

LENZEN, H. J.: *Die Entwicklung der Zikurrat von ihren Anfängen bis zur Zeit der III. Dynastie von Ur* (*Ausgrabungen der Deutschen Forschungsgemeinschaft in Uruk-Warka* 4; Harrassowitz, Leipzig, 1941).

LENZEN, H. J.: Mesopotamische Tempelanlagen von der Frühzeit bis zum zweiten Jahrtausend (*Zeitschrift für Assyriologie*, neue Folge 17 (1955), 1–36).

†PARROT, A.: *Ziggurats et Tour de Babel* (Albin Michel, Paris, 1949).

(e) Kingship and the Sacred Marriage

BERNHARDT, K.-H.: *Das Problem der altorientalischen Königs-Ideologie im Alten Testament, unter besonderer Berücksichtigung der Geschichte der Psalmenexegese dargestellt und kritisch gewürdigt* (Brill, Leiden, 1961). [This contains, *inter alia*, a very useful bibliography.]

BUREN, E. D. VAN: The Sacred Marriage in early times in Mesopotamia (*Orientalia* 13 (1944), 1–72).

DIJK, J. VAN: La fête du nouvel ans dans un texte de Šulgi (*Bibliotheca Orientalis* 11 (1954), 83–88).

ENGNELL, J.: *Studies in divine kingship in the ancient Near East* (Uppsala, 1943).

†FRANKFORT, H.: *Kingship and the gods* (University of Chicago Press, 1948).

FRANKFORT, H.: State festivals in Egypt and Mesopotamia (*Journal of the Warburg and Courtauld Institutes* 15 (1952), 1–12).

†GADD, C. J.: *Ideas of divine rule in the ancient East* (*Schweich Lectures* for 1945; British Academy, 1948).

GRAY, J.: Royal substitution in the ancient Near East (*Palestine Exploration Quarterly* 1955, 180–182).

HALLO, W. W.: *Early Mesopotamian royal titles; a philological and historical analysis* (*American Oriental Series* 43; New Haven, 1957).

LABAT, R.: *Le caractère religieux de la royauté Assyro-Babylonienne* (Adrien-Maisonneuve, Paris, 1939).

LAMBERT, W. G.: A part of the ritual for the substitute king (*Archiv für Orientforschung* 18 (1957), 109–112).

MÜLLER, K. F.: Das assyrische Ritual, Teil I: Texte zum assyrischen Königs-ritual (*Mitteilungen der vorderasiatisch-aegyptischen Gesellschaft* 41/3, 1937).

SCHMÖKEL, H.: *Heilige Hochzeit und Hoheslied* (Wiesbaden, 1956).

SMITH, S.: The practice of kingship in early Semitic kingdoms (=pages 22–73 in Hooke, S. H. (editor): *Myth, Ritual, and Kingship* (Clarendon Press, Oxford, 1958).

WIDENGREN, G.: *The king and the Tree of Life in ancient Near Eastern religion* (Uppsala, 1951).

Literature (narrowly defined) and Literary Texts

(a) primarily editions or translations of texts

BÖHL, F. M. TH. DE LIAGRE: Der babylonische Fürstenspiegel (*Mitteilungen der altorientalischen Gesellschaft* 11/3, 1937).

BÖHL, F. M. TH. DE LIAGRE: Die Myth von weisen Adapa (*Die Welt des Orients* 2 (1959), 416–431).

EBELING, E.: Eine neue Tafel des akkadischen Zû-mythos (*Revue d'Assyriologie* 46 (1952), 25–41).

GELLER, S.: Die sumerisch-assyrische Serie Lugal-e ud me-lam-bi nir-gal (*Altorientalische Texte und Untersuchungen* 1/4, 1917).

†GORDON, E. I.: *Sumerian proverbs* (University Museum, University of Pennsylvania, 1959).

GÖSSMANN, P. F.: *Das Era Epos* (Würzburg, 1955).

GURNEY, O. R.: The Sultantepe tablets (*Anatolian Studies* 2 (1952), 25–35; 3 (1953), 15–25; 4 (1954), 65–99 [in collaboration with W. G. Lambert]; 5 (1955), 93–113; 6 (1956), 145–164; 7 (1957), 127–136; 10 (1960), 105–131).

JACOBSEN, TH. and KRAMER, S. N.: The myth of Inanna and Bilulu (*Journal of Near Eastern Studies* 12 (1953), 160–188).

JENSEN, P.: Assyrisch-babylonische Mythen und Epen (*Keilinschriftliche Bibliothek* VI/I; Berlin, 1900).

KRAMER, S. N.: Man's golden age: a Sumerian parallel to Genesis xi 1 (*Journal of the American Oriental Society* 63 (1943), 191–194).

KRAMER, S. N.: Schooldays: a Sumerian composition relating to the education of a scribe (*Journal of the American Oriental Society* 69 (1949), 199–215).

KRAMER, S. N.: *Enmerkar and the Lord of Aratta. A Sumerian epic tale of Iraq and Iran* (University Museum, University of Pennsylvania, 1952).

LAESSØE, J.: The Atrahasis epic: A Babylonian history of mankind (*Bibliotheca Orientalis* 13 (1956), 90–102).

†LAMBERT, W. G.: *Babylonian Wisdom literature* (Clarendon Press, Oxford, 1960).

LAMBERT, W. G.: Three unpublished fragments of the Tukulti-Ninurta epic (*Archiv für Orientforschung* 18 (1957–58), 38–51).

LANGDON, S.: *The legend of Etana and the eagle* (Geuthner, Paris, 1932).

NOUGAYROL, J.: Un chef-d'oeuvre inédit de la littérature babylonienne (*Revue d'Assyriologie* 45 (1951), 169–183).

NOUGAYROL, J.: Ningirsu, vainqueur de Zû (*Revue d'Assyriologie* 46 (1952), 87–97).

REINER, E.: Deux fragments du mythe de Zû (*Revue d'Assyriologie* 48 (1954), 145–148).

SCHEIL, V.: Fragment de la légende du dieu Zû (*Revue d'Assyriologie* 35 (1938), 14–32).

THOMPSON, R. C.: *The epic of Gilgamish. Text, transliteration and notes* (Clarendon Press, Oxford, 1930).

(b) primarily discussion

DIJK, J. J. A. VAN: *La sagesse suméro-accadienne* (Brill, Leiden, 1953).

EBELING, E.: *Die bablonische Fabel und ihre Bedeutung für die Literaturgeschichte* (*Mitteilungen der altorientalischen Gesellschaft* 11/3, 1937).

FALKENSTEIN, A.: Zur Chronologie der sumerischen Literatur (nach altbabylonische Stufe) (*Mitteilungen der Deutschen Orient-Gesellschaft* 85 (1953), 1–13).

FISH, T.: The Zu bird (*Bulletin of the John Rylands Library* 31 (1948), 162–171).

†GADD, C. J.: *Teachers and students in the oldest schools* (School of Oriental and African Studies, University of London, 1956).

GÜTERBOCK, H. G.: Die historische Tradition und ihre literarische Gestaltung bei Babyloniern und Hethitern bis 1200 (*Zeitschrift für Assyriologie*, neue Folge 8 (1934), 1–91; 10 (1938), 45–149).

JACOBSEN, TH.: The investiture and anointing of Adapa in heaven (*American Journal of Semitic Languages* 46 (1929), 201–202).

JORDON, F.: *In den Tagen des Tammuz. Altbabylonische Mythen* (Munich, 1950).

KRAMER, S. N.: Dilmun, the land of the living (*Bulletin of the American Schools of Oriental Research* 96 (1944), 18–28).

†KRAMER, S. N.: *Sumerian Mythology* (American Philosophical Society, Philadelphia, 1944).

KRAMER, S. N.: The Epic of Gilgameš and its Sumerian sources. A study in literary evolution (*Journal of the American Oriental Society* 64 (1944), 7–23 and 83).

†KRAMER, S. N.: Mythology of Sumer and Akkad (=pages 95–137 in Kramer, S. N. (editor): *Mythologies of the ancient world*; Doubleday Anchor Books, New York, 1961).

LAESSØE, J.: Literacy and oral tradition in ancient Mesopotamia (*Studia Orientalia Ioanni Pedersen septuagenario . . . a collegis discipulis amicis dicata* [Einar Munksgaard, Copenhagen, 1953], 205–218).

LAMBERT, W. G.: Ancestors, authors and canonicity (*Journal of Cuneiform Studies* 11 (1957), 1–14).

LANDSBERGER, B.: Babylonian scribal craft and its terminology (*Proceedings of the XXIII International Congress of Orientalists* (1954), 123–126).

MEISSNER, B.: *Die babylonisch-assyrische Literatur* (Wildpark, Potsdam, 1930).

REINER, E.: Le char de Ninurta et le prologue du mythe de Zû (*Revue d'Assyriologie* 51 (1957), 107–110).

SODEN, W. VON: Das Problem der zeitlichen Einordnung akkadischer Literaturwerke (*Mitteilungen der Deutschen Orient-Gesellschaft* 85 (1953), 14–26).

SPEISER, E. A.: The case of the obliging servant (*Journal of Cuneiform Studies* 8 (1954), 98–105).

WILLIAMS, R. J.: The literary history of a Mesopotamian fable (*The Phoenix* [Toronto] 12 (1956), 70–77).

BIBLIOGRAPHY

Mathematics and Astronomy

BAQIR, T.: An important mathematical problem text from Tell Harmal. (On a Euclidean Theorem) (*Sumer* 6 (1950), 39–54).

BAQIR, T.: Another important mathematical text from Tell Harmal (*Sumer* (1950), 130–148).

BERRIMANS, A. E.: A new approach to the study of ancient metrology (*Revue d'Assyriologie* 49 (1955), 193–201).

BRUINS, E. M.: On the system of Babylonian geometry (*Sumer* 11 (1955), 44–49).

CARATINI, R.: Quelques aspects de la mathématique babylonienne (*Semitica* 2 (1949), 3–15).

CARATINI, R.: Quadrature du cercle et quadrature des lunules en Mesopotamie (*Revue d'Assyriologie* 51 (1957), 11-20).

CORNELIUS, F.: Die Venusdaten des Ammisaduga (*Zeitschrift für Assyriologie*, neue Folge 14 (1952), 146–151).

GADD, C. J.: Forms and Colours. 1—Forms (*Revue d'Assyriologie* 19 (1922), 149–158).

HUBER, P.: Zur täglichen Bewegung des Jupiter nach babylonischen Texten (*Zeitschrift für Assyriologie*, neue Folge 18 (1951), 265–303).

KILMER, A. DRAFFKORN: Two new lists of key numbers for mathematical operations (*Orientalia* 29 (1960), 273–308).

LEWY, H.: Studies in Assyro-Babylonian mathematics and metrology (*Orientalia* 20 (1951), 1–12).

LEWY, H.: Origin and development of the sexagesimal system of numeration (*Journal of the American Oriental Society* 69 (1949), 1–11).

†NEUGEBAUER, O.: The history of ancient astronomy; problems and methods (*Journal of Near Eastern Studies* 4 (1945), 1–38).

NEUGEBAUER, O.: Studies in ancient astronomy VIII. The water clock in Babylonian astronomy (*Isis, an international review devoted to the History of Science and Civilization* 37 (1947), 37–43).

†NEUGEBAUER, O.: *The exact sciences in antiquity* (Brown University Press, Providence, Rhode Island; 2nd edition, 1957).

NEUGEBAUER, O.: The alleged Babylonian discovery of the precession of the equinoxes (*Journal of the American Oriental Society* 70 (1950), 1–8).

†NEUGEBAUER, O.: Ancient mathematics and astronomy (=pages 785–804 in Singer, C., and others (editors): *A history of technology*, vol. 1; Clarendon Press, Oxford, 1954).

NEUGEBAUER, O.: Babylonian planetary theory (*Proceedings of the American Philosophical Society* 98 (1954), 60–89).

NEUGEBAUER, O.: *Astronomical cuneiform texts. Babylonian ephemerides of the Seleucid period for the motion of the sun, the moon, and the planets*, vols. I–III (Institute for Advanced Study, Princeton and Lund Humphries, London, 1955).

NEUGEBAUER, O. and SACHS, A.: *Mathematical cuneiform texts* (with a chapter by A. Goetze) (*American Oriental Series* 29; New Haven, 1945).

SACHS, A. J.: A Late Babylonian star catalog (*Journal of Cuneiform Studies* 6 (1952), 146–150).

SACHS, A. J.: Babylonian mathematical texts II–III (*Journal of Cuneiform Studies* 6 (1952), 151–156).

SACHS, A. J.: Sirius dates in Babylonian astronomical texts of the Seleucid period (*Journal of Cuneiform Studies* 6 (1952), 105–114).

SACHS, A. J. and NEUGEBAUER, O.: A procedure text concerning solar and lunar motion: BM 36712 (*Journal of Cuneiform Studies* 10 (1956), 131–136).

SAGGS, H. W. F.: A Babylonian geometrical text (*Revue d'Assyriologie* 54 (1960), 131–146).

†SARTON, G.: Chaldaean astronomy of the last three centuries B.C. (*Journal of the American Oriental Society* 75 (1955), 166–173). [A useful review article.]

SCHOTT, A.: Marduk und sein Stern (*Zeitschrift für Assyriologie*, neue Folge 9 (1936), 124–145; 10 (1938), 205–210).

THUREAU-DANGIN, F.: La méthode de fausse position et l'origine de l'Algèbre (*Revue d'Assyriologie* 35 (1938), 71–77).

†THUREAU-DANGIN, F.: *Textes mathématiques babyloniens* (Brill, Leiden, 1938).

UNGER, E.: Die Milchstrasse Nibiru, Sternbild des Marduk (*Die Welt des Orients* 2 (1959), 454–464).

†WAERDEN, B. L. VAN DER: History of the Zodiac (*Archiv für Orientforschung* 16 (1952–53), 216–230).

WAERDEN, B. L. VAN DER: Babylonian astronomy, I (*Jaarbericht Ex Oriente Lux*, Deel III (Nos. 9–10) (1944–48), 414–424); II (*Journal of Near Eastern Studies* 8 (1949), 6–26).

†WAERDEN, B. L. VAN DER: *Science awakening* (Noordhoff, Groningen, 1954; reprint 1961).

Medicine

CIVIL, M.: Prescriptions médicales sumériennes (*Revue d'Assyriologie* 54 (1960), 57–72).

GOETZE, A.: An incantation against diseases (*Journal of Cuneiform Studies* 9 (1955), 8–18).

HORGAN, E. S.: Medicine and surgery in the most ancient East (Babylonia and Egypt) (*Sudan Notes and Records* 30; Supplement (1949), 29–46).

LABAT, R.: *Traité akkadien de diagnostics et pronostics médicaux*, I (Academie Internationale d'histoire des Sciences, Paris and Brill, Leiden, 1951).

LABAT, R.: *La médecine babylonienne* (Paris, 1953).

LABAT, R.: À propos de la chirurgie babylonienne (*Journal Asiatique* 242 (1954), 207–218).

LABAT, R.: Une nouvelle tablette de pronostics médicaux (*Syria* 33 (1956), 119–130).

LABAT, R.: Remèdes assyriens contre les affections de l'oreille, d'après un inédit du Louvre (AO.6774) (*Rivista degli studi orientalia* 32 (1957), 109–122).

NOUGAYROL, J.: Présages médicaux de l'haruspicine babylonienne (*Semitica* 6 (1956), 5–14).

OPPENHEIM, A. L.: On the observation of the pulse in Mesopotamian medicine (*Orientalia* 31 (1962), 27–33).

SODEN, W. VON: Die Hebamme in Babylonien und Assyrien (*Archiv für Orientforschung* 18 (1957), 119–121).

THOMPSON, R. C.: Assyrian medical presciptions for diseases of the stomach (*Revue d'Assyriologie* 26 (1929), 47–92).

THOMPSON, R. C.: Assyrian prescriptions for the 'Hand of a Ghost' (*Journal of the Royal Asiatic Society* 1929, 801–823).
THOMPSON, R. C.: Assyrian prescriptions for treating bruises or swellings (*American Journal of Semitic Languages* 47 (1930), 1–25).
THOMPSON, R. C.: Assyrian prescriptions for diseases of the chest and lungs (*Revue d'Assyriologie* 31 (1934), 1–29).

Chemistry, Botany, Geology, Metallurgy, Technology

BAUMGARTNER, W.: Untersuchungen zu den akkadischen Bauausdrücken (*Zeitschrift für Assyriologie*, neue Folge 2 (1925), 29–40, 123–138, 219–253).
†COGHLAN, H. H.: *Notes on the prehistoric metallurgy of copper and bronze in the Old World* (Pitt Rivers Museum, Occasional Papers on Technology 4; Oxford, 1951).
†COGHLAN, H. H.: *Notes on prehistoric and early iron in the Old World* (Pitt Rivers Museum, Occasional Papers on Technology 8; Oxford, 1956).
EBELING, E.: Mittelassyrische Rezepte zur Herstellung von wohlriechenden Salben (*Orientalia* 17 (1948), 129–145, 299–313; 18 (1949), 404–418; 19 (1950), 265–278).
EISLER, R.: Die chemische Terminologie der Babylonier (*Zeitschrift für Assyriologie*, neue Folge 3 (1927), 109–131). [See also *op. cit.*, 205–214, 273–282.]
†FORBES, R. J.: *Metallurgy in antiquity* (Brill, Leiden, 1950).
FORBES, R. J.: *Studies in ancient technology*, I–VI (Brill, Leiden, 1955–58).
GADD, C. J. and THOMPSON, R. C.: A Middle-Babylonian chemical text (*Iraq* 3 (1936), 87–96).
†HARTMAN, L. F. and OPPENHEIM, A. L.: *On beer and brewing techniques in ancient Mesopotamia* (Supplement to the Journal of the American Oriental Society, No. 10; Baltimore, 1950).
†JACOBSEN, TH. and LLOYD, SETON: *Sennacherib's aqueduct at Jerwan* (Oriental Institute Publications 24; University of Chicago Press, 1935).
LABAT, R.: Les sciences en Mésopotamie (*Revue de la Mediterranée* 17 (1957), 123–158).
LAESSØE, J.: Reflexions on modern and ancient oriental water works (*Journal of Cuneiform Studies* 7 (1953), 5–26).
†LEVEY, M.: *Chemistry and Chemical technology in ancient Mesopotamia* (Elsevier Publishing Company, London/New York, 1959).
LIMET, H. *Le travail du métal au pays de Sumer au temps de la IIIᵉ dynastie d'Ur* (Bibliothèque de la Faculté de Philosophie et Lettres de l'Université de Liège, Fascicule CLV; Paris, 1960).
MOORE, H.: Reproductions of an ancient Babylonian glaze (*Iraq* 10 (1948), 26–33).
NORTH, R.: Metallurgy in the ancient Near East (*Orientalia* 24 (1955), 78–88). [A valuable review of Forbes, R. J.: *Metallurgy in antiquity*.]
SAFAR, F.: Sennacherib's project for supplying Erbil with water (*Sumer* 3 (1947), 23–25).
†SINGER, C., HOLMYARD, E. J. and HALL, A. R.: *A history of technology*, vol. I; *From early times to fall of ancient empires* (Clarendon Press, Oxford, 1954).

THOMPSON, R. C.: *A dictionary of Assyrian chemistry and geology* (Clarendon Press, Oxford, 1936).

THOMPSON, R. C.: *A dictionary of Assyrian botany* (British Academy, 1949).

Art and Architecture

BACHMANN, W.: *Felsrelie s in Assyrien, Bawian, Maitai und Gundük* (Hinrichs, Leipzig, 1927).

BARNETT, R. D.: Early Greek and Oriental ivories (*Journal of Hellenic Studies* 68 (1948), 1–25).

BARNETT, R. D.: *A catalogue of the Nimrud ivories with other examples of ancient Near Eastern ivories in the British Museum* (British Museum, 1957).

DEBEOISE, N. C.: The rock reliefs of ancient Iran (*Journal of Near Eastern Studies* 1 (1942), 76–105).

†FRANKFORT, H.: Cylinder seals (MacMillan, London, 1939).

FRANKFORT, H.: *Stratified cylinder seals from the Diyala region* (Oriental Institute Publications 72; University of Chicago Press, 1954).

†FRANKFORT, H.: *The art and architecture of the ancient Orient* (Penguin Books, Harmondsworth and Baltimore, 1954).

†GÜTERBOCK, H. G.: Narration in Anatolian, Syrian and Assyrian Art (*American Journal of Archaeology* 61 (1957), 62–71).

†PERKINS, A.: Narration in Babylonian art (*American Journal of Archaeology* 61 (1957), 54–62).

SCHÄFER, H. and ANDRAE, E.: *Die Kunst des alten Orients* (Im Propyläen, Berlin, 1925).

Music

FOLLET, R. and NOBER, P.: Zur altorientalischen Musik (*Biblica* 35 (1954), 230–238).

†GALPIN, F. W.: *The music of the Sumerians and their immediate successors the Babylonians and Assyrians* (Heitz, Strasbourg; 2nd edition, 1955).

POLIN, C. C. J.: *Music of the ancient Near East* (New York, 1954).

WEGNER, M.: *Die Musikinstrumente des alten Orients* (Aschendorffsche Verlagsbuchhandlung, Münster in Westfalen, 1950).

Legacy

ADOLF, H.: The ass and the harp (*Speculum; a Journal of Mediaeval Studies* 25 (1950), 49–57).

BARNETT, R. D.: Ancient oriental influences on archaic Greece (=pages 212–238 in Weinberg, S. S. (editor): *The Aegean and the Near East*, 1956).

CRESSWELL, K. A. C.: *The evolution of the minaret* (Reprint from the *Burlington Magazine*, March, May, June, 1926; London, 1926).

CRESSWELL, K. A. C.: *Early Muslim architecture*, II (Clarendon Press, Oxford, 1940).

DALTON, O. M.: *East Christian art* (Clarendon Press, Oxford, 1925).

DRIVER, G. R.: Lilith (*Palestine Exploration Quarterly*, 1959, 55–57).

GUILLAUME, A.: Magical terms in the Old Testament (*Journal of the Royal Asiatic Society* 1942, 111–131). [See also *Journal of the Royal Asiatic Society* 1943, 6–16, 251–254; 1944, 165–171; 1946, 79–80.]

BIBLIOGRAPHY

LANDSBERGER, B. *Der kultische Kalendar der Babylonier und Assyrier* (*Leipziger semitistische Studien* VI/1, 2; Hinrichs, Leipzig, 1915). [Despite the date this remains an important work.]

McCOWN, C. C.: *Man, morals and history. Today's legacy from ancient times and biblical peoples* (Harper and Brothers, New York, 1958).

†RICE, D. T.: *Byzantine art* (Penguin Books, London; revised edition, 1954).

†SPEISER, E. A.: Ancient Mesopotamia, a light that did not fail (*National Geographical Magazine* 49 (1951), 41–105).

WEIDNER, E.: Die astrologische Serie *Enûma Anu Enlil* (*Archiv für Orient-forschung* 14 (1941–44), 172–195, 308–318; 17 (1954–56), 71–89).

CHRONOLOGICAL TABLE I

Principal Prehistoric and Protohistoric Cultures of Mesopotamia

DATE B.C.	NORTH MESOPOTAMIA	SOUTH MESOPOTAMIA
5000	Jarmo	
4500	–Hassuna	
	–Samarra	–Eridu
4000	–Halaf	–Hajji Muhammad
		–Ubaid
	–Northern Ubaid	
3500		–Uruk
		–Early Protoliterate (Uruk IV)
3000		
	–Tepe Gawra VII	–Late Protoliterate (Jemdet Nasr)
2800	–Tepe Gawra VI	–Early Dynastic I
	–Tepe Gawra V	–Early Dynastic II
		–Early Dynastic III
2400		–end of Early Dynastic III

CHRONOLOGICAL TABLE II

From the rise of the Dynasty of Agade to the fall of the Third Dynasty of Ur

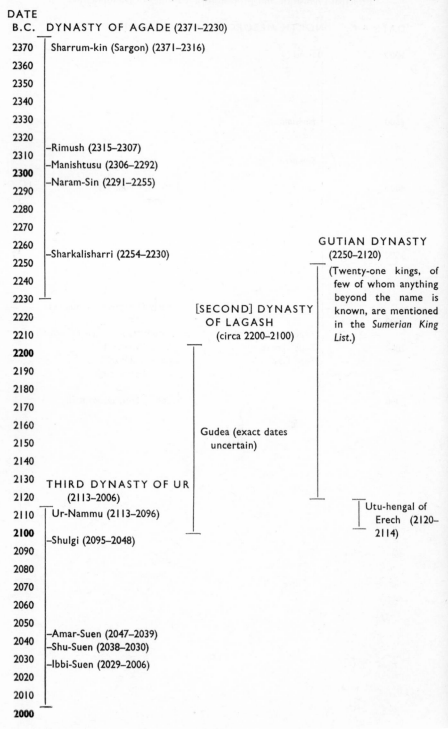

DATE
B.C.   **DYNASTY OF AGADE (2371–2230)**

2370   Sharrum-kin (Sargon) (2371–2316)

2360

2350

2340

2330

2320

2310   –Rimush (2315–2307)

2300   –Manishtusu (2306–2292)

2290   –Naram-Sin (2291–2255)

2280

2270

2260   **GUTIAN DYNASTY**
       –Sharkalisharri (2254–2230)   **(2250–2120)**
2250

2240   (Twenty-one kings, of
                                                              few of whom anything
2230   beyond the name is
                           [SECOND] DYNASTY   known, are mentioned
2220   **OF LAGASH**   in the *Sumerian King*
2210   (circa 2200–2100)   *List*.)

2200

2190

2180

2170

2160   Gudea (exact dates
2150   uncertain)

2140

2130   **THIRD DYNASTY OF UR**
2120   **(2113–2006)**
2110   Ur-Nammu (2113–2096)   Utu-hengal of
                                                              Erech (2120–
2100   –Shulgi (2095–2048)   2114)

2090

2080

2070

2060

2050

2040   –Amar-Suen (2047–2039)
       –Shu-Suen (2038–2030)
2030   –Ibbi-Suen (2029–2006)

2020

2010

2000

CHRONOLOGICAL TABLE III

Principal Dynasties of Babylonia and Assyria from the fall of the Third Dynasty of Ur to the end of the First Dynasty of Babylon

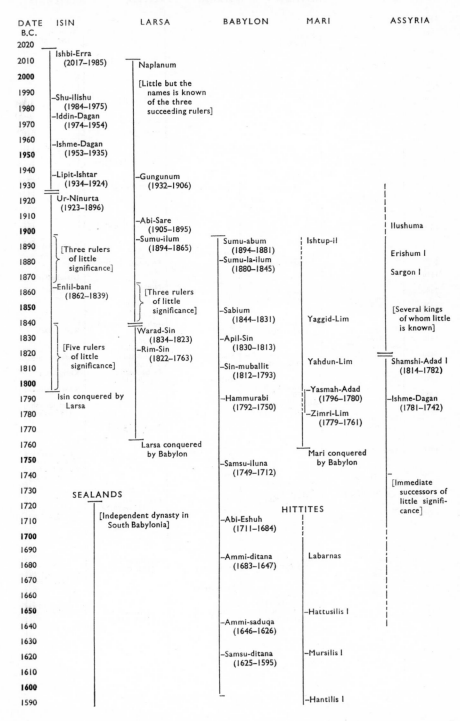

DATE B.C.	ISIN	LARSA	BABYLON	MARI	ASSYRIA
2020					
2010	Ishbi-Erra (2017–1985)	Naplanum			
2000		[Little but the names is known of the three succeeding rulers]			
1990	–Shu-ilishu (1984–1975)				
1980	–Iddin-Dagan (1974–1954)				
1970					
1960	–Ishme-Dagan (1953–1935)				
1950					
1940	–Lipit-Ishtar (1934–1924)	–Gungunum (1932–1906)			
1930					
1920	Ur-Ninurta (1923–1896)				
1910		–Abi-Sare (1905–1895)			
1900					Ilushuma
1890	[Three rulers of little significance]	–Sumu-ilum (1894–1865)	Sumu-abum (1894–1881)	Ishtup-il	
1880			–Sumu-la-ilum (1880–1845)		Erishum I
1870					Sargon I
1860	–Enlil-bani (1862–1839)	[Three rulers of little significance]			
1850			–Sabium (1844–1831)		[Several kings of whom little is known]
1840				Yaggid-Lim	
1830	[Five rulers of little significance]	Warad-Sin (1834–1823)	–Apil-Sin (1830–1813)		
1820		–Rim-Sin (1822–1763)		Yahdun-Lim	Shamshi-Adad I (1814–1782)
1810			–Sin-muballit (1812–1793)		
1800					
1790	Isin conquered by Larsa		–Hammurabi (1792–1750)	–Yasmah-Adad (1796–1780)	–Ishme-Dagan (1781–1742)
1780				–Zimri-Lim (1779–1761)	
1770					
1760		Larsa conquered by Babylon			
1750			–Samsu-iluna (1749–1712)	Mari conquered by Babylon	
1740					[Immediate successors of little significance]
1730	SEALANDS				
1720			HITTITES		
1710	[Independent dynasty in South Babylonia]		–Abi-Eshuh (1711–1684)		
1700					
1690			–Ammi-ditana (1683–1647)	Labarnas	
1680					
1670					
1660					
1650				–Hattusilis I	
1640			–Ammi-saduqa (1646–1626)		
1630					
1620			–Samsu-ditana (1625–1595)	–Mursilis I	
1610					
1600					
1590				–Hantilis I	

CHRONOLOGICAL TABLE IV

Principal Kingdoms of the Near East from 1595 to 1250 B.C.

DATE B.C.	EGYPT	HITTITES	MITANNI	ASSYRIA	BABYLONIA
1600					
1590		–Hantilis I (1590–1560)			Agum II (Agukakrime)
1580	XVIII DYNASTY				
1570	⌐Amosis (1575–1550)				
1560					
1550	–Amenophis I (1550–1528)			–Erishum III	
1540				–Shamshi-Adad II	
1530	–Tuthmosis I (1528–1510)			–Ishme-Dagan II	
1520					[About nine rulers]
1510	–Tuthmosis II (1510–1490)			–Shamshi-Adad III	
1500		[Eight rulers of little importance]			
1490	–Tuthmosis III (1490–1436)		Parattarna	–Ashur-nirari I	
1480					
1470				–Puzur-Ashur III	
1460		Tudhaliyas II (1460–1440)	Saussatar		Kashtiliash III
1450				–Enlil-nasir I	–Ulamburiash
1440	–Amenophis II (1436–1413)	–Arnuwandas I (1440–1420)		–Nur-ili	Agum II
1430				–Enlil-nasir II –Ashur-nirari II	
1420		–Hattusilis II (1420–1400)		–Ashur-bel-nisheshu	
1410	–Tuthmosis IV (1413–1405)		Artatama	–Ashur-rim-nisheshu	–Kara-indash
1400	–Amenophis III (1405–1367)	–Tudhaliyas III (1400–1385)	Shuttarna II	–Ashur-nadin-ahhe II –Eriba-Adad I (1392–1366)	Kadashman-harbe
1390			–Tushratta		Kurigalzu I
1380		–Arnuwandas II (1385–1375)			Kadashman-Enlil I
1370		–Shuppiluliuma (1375–1335)		–Ashur-uballit I (1365–1330)	–Burnaburiash II (1375–1347)
1360	–Akhenaten (1367–1350)				
1350	–Smenkhkare' –Tut'ankhamun (1347–1339)		–[Throne claimed by usurper Artatama] –Mattiwaza		–Kara-indash? –Nazi-bugash –Kurigalzu II (1345–1324)
1340	–Ay –Haremhab (1335–1308?)	–Arnuwandas III –Mursilis II (1334–1306)			
1330				–Enlil-nirari (1329–1320)	–Nazi-maruttash (1323–1298)
1320				–Arik-den-ili (1319–1308)	
1310	XIX DYNASTY				
1300	⌐Ramesses I ⌐Sethos I (1308–1291)	–Muwatallis (1306–1282)	Shattuara I	–Adad-nirari I (1307–1275)	–Kadashman-turgu (1297–1280)
1290	–Ramesses II (1290–1224)		Wasashatta		
1280		–Urhi-Teshub (1282–1275)			–Kadashman-Enlil II (1279–1265)
1270		–Hattusilis III (1275–1250)	Shattuara II	–Shalmaneser I (1274–1245)	
1260					
1250		–		–	

Assyria 1250-746 B.C., with principal contemporaries

DATE B.C.	EGYPT	PALESTINE	ASSYRIA	BABYLONIA
1250	DYNASTY XIX		–Tukulti-Ninurta I (1244–1208)	–Kashtiliash IV (1242–1235)
1240				
1230				
1220				
1210			–Ashur-nadin-apli(1207–04)	
1200			–[Two minor rulers] –Enlil-kudur-usur (1197–1193) –Ninurta-apal-Ekur (1192–1180)	
1190				⎰Ten rulers
	DYNASTY XX			
1180	–Ramesses III (1182–1151)	Philistines	–Ashur-dan I (1179–1134?)	
1170				
1160				
1150				
1140			–Ninurta-tukulti-Ashur –Ashur-resh-ishi (1133–1116)	
1130				–Nebuchadrezzar I (1124–1103)
1120			–Tiglath-Pileser I (1115–1077)	
1110				⎱Three rulers
1100				
1090	DYNASTY XXI			–Marduk-shapik-zer-mati (1080–1068)
1080			–Asharid-apal-Ekur II –Ashur-bel-kala (1074–1057)	
1070				–Adad-apal-iddinam (1067–1046)
1060				
1050			⎰Five rulers of little	
1040			importance	
1030				
1020		David	–Ashur-rabi II	
1010			(1010–970)	
1000				
990				
980		Solomon	–Ashur-resh-ishi II	
970			–Tiglath-Pileser II (966–935)	
960				
950	DYNASTY XXII			⎰Fifteen rulers
940	JUDAH	ISRAEL	–Ashur-dan II (934–912)	
	Rehoboam	Jeroboam I		
930	(931–915)	(931–910)		
920			–Adad-nirari II (911–891)	
910		⎰Four kings		
900			–Tukulti-Ninurta II (890–884)	
890		–Omri (885–874)	–Ashur-nasir-pal (883–859)	
880		–Ahab (874–853)		
870				Nabu-apal-iddin
860		⎰Two kings	–Shalmaneser III (858–824)	
850	⎰Eight kings	–Jehu (841–814)		
840				
830			–Shamshi-Adad V (823–811)	
820			–Adad-nirari III	
810			(810–783)	⎰Five rulers
800		⎰Five kings		
790			–Shalmaneser IV (782–772)	
780			–Ashur-dan III (771–754)	
770	–Azariah (766–740)			
760				
		–Menahem	–Ashur-nirari V (753–746)	
750		(752–741)		–Nabu-nasir (746–734)
740				

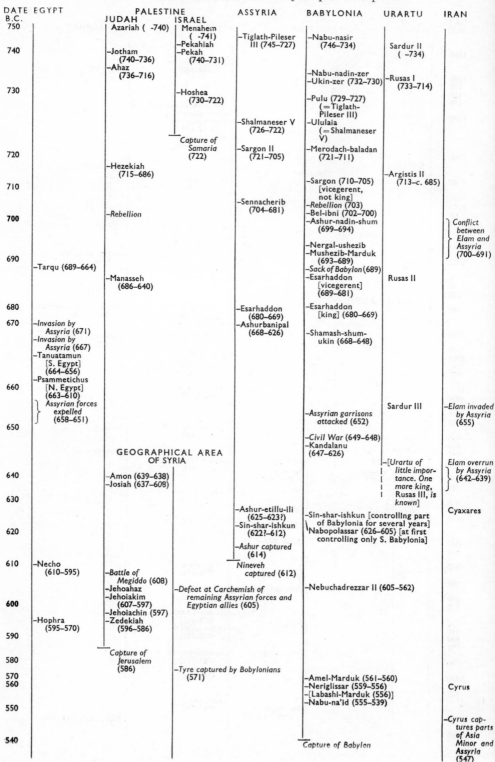

DATE B.C.	EGYPT	PALESTINE — JUDAH	PALESTINE — ISRAEL	ASSYRIA	BABYLONIA	URARTU	IRAN
750		Azariah (-740)	Menahem (-741)	-Tiglath-Pileser III (745-727)	-Nabu-nasir (746-734)		
740		-Jotham (740-736) -Ahaz (736-716)	-Pekahiah -Pekah (740-731)		-Nabu-nadin-zer -Ukin-zer (732-730)	Sardur II (-734)	
730			-Hoshea (730-722)			-Rusas I (733-714)	
				-Shalmaneser V (726-722)	-Pulu (729-727) (=Tiglath-Pileser III) -Ululaia (=Shalmaneser V)		
720		-Hezekiah (715-686)	Capture of Samaria (722)	-Sargon II (721-705)	-Merodach-baladan (721-711)		
710					-Sargon (710-705) [vicegerent, not king]	-Argistis II (713-c. 685)	
700	-Rebellion			-Sennacherib (704-681)	-Rebellion (703) -Bel-ibni (702-700) -Ashur-nadin-shum (699-694)		Conflict between Elam and Assyria (700-691)
690	-Tarqu (689-664)	-Manasseh (686-640)			-Nergal-ushezib -Mushezib-Marduk (693-689) -Sack of Babylon (689) -Esarhaddon [vicegerent] (689-681)	Rusas II	
680				-Esarhaddon (680-669)	-Esarhaddon [king] (680-669)		
670	-Invasion by Assyria (671) -Invasion by Assyria (667) -Tanuatamun [S. Egypt] (664-656)			-Ashurbanipal (668-626)	-Shamash-shum-ukin (668-648)		
660	-Psammetichus [N. Egypt] (663-610) Assyrian forces expelled (658-651)					Sardur III	-Elam invaded by Assyria (655)
650				-Assyrian garrisons attacked (652)	-Civil War (649-648) -Kandalanu (647-626)		
640		-Amon (639-638) -Josiah (637-608)	GEOGRAPHICAL AREA OF SYRIA			[Urartu of little importance. One more king, Rusas III, is known]	Elam overrun by Assyria (642-639)
630							Cyaxares
620	-Necho (610-595)			-Ashur-etillu-ili (625-623?) -Sin-shar-ishkun (622?-612) -Ashur captured (614)	-Sin-shar-ishkun [controlling part of Babylonia for several years] Nabopolassar (626-605) [at first controlling only S. Babylonia]		
610		-Battle of Megiddo (608)		Nineveh captured (612)			
600	-Hophra (595-570)	-Jehoahaz -Jehoiakim (607-597) -Jehoiachin (597) -Zedekiah (596-586)		-Defeat at Carchemish of remaining Assyrian forces and Egyptian allies (605)	-Nebuchadrezzar II (605-562)		
580		Capture of Jerusalem (586)					
570			-Tyre captured by Babylonians (571)		-Amel-Marduk (561-560)		
560					-Neriglissar (559-556) -[Labashi-Marduk (556)] -Nabu-na'id (555-539)		Cyrus
550							
540					Capture of Babylon		-Cyrus captures parts of Asia Minor and Assyria (547)

Index of Biblical References

GENESIS
ii. 6–14 . . 484
iii. 22 . . 498
iv. 7 . 485, 487
vi. 1–2 . . 388
x. 2 . . 232
x.3 . . . 136
x. 9 . . 336
x. 10 . . 19
x. 11, 12 . 245, 336
xi. 3–5 . . 356
xiv. 6 . . 77
xvi. 4–6 . . 185
xxviii. 12 . . 356
xxix. 18–28 . 204
xli. 33–36 . 166
xliv. 5 . . 347

EXODUS
xii. 5 . . 353
xxix. 16 . . 353

LEVITICUS .
xvii. 7 . 487
xxv. . . 198

NUMBERS
xxxiv. 17, 18 . 295

DEUTERONOMY
ii. 12 . . 77
xvii. 14 . . 360
xxii. 15 . . 287
xxiii. 17 . . 350
xxv. 13 . . 292
xxxii. 17 . 350, 487

JOSHUA
vii. . . . 242
xix. 49 . . 295

JUDGES
ix. 8–15 . . 429
xiv. 1–xv. 6 . 214
xvi. 23 . 335, 344

RUTH
iv. 1ff. . . 287

I SAMUEL
ii. 10 . . 335
v. 2–5, 7 . . 344
vii. 10 . . 335
viii. 5, 7 . . 360
x. 5 . . 190
xiii. 19 . . 281
xiv. . . 242
xvii. 50 . . 149
xxxi. 4–5 . . 134

2 SAMUEL
vi. 14–21 . . 190
vii. 2 . . 363
xxi. 19 . . 149
xxiii. 16 . . 354

I KINGS
iv. 30 . . 430
v. 13–15 . . 256
v. 18 . . 99
vii. 13 . . 99
vii. 14 . 99, 100
vii. 23 . . 451
viii. 63–65 . 256
ix. 14 . . 255
ix. 22 . . 256
ix. 26–28 . 255
x. 10, 14, 15 . 255
x. 18 . . 480
x. 22 . . 255

xii. 4 . . 257
xv. 18 . . 335
xv. 25–30 . 244
xvi. 8–13 . 244
xx. 30–42 . 244
xx. 34 . . 282
xxii. 39 . . 480

2 KINGS
ii. 23, 24 . . 244
iv. 3 . . 353
vii. 1 . . 287
viii. 15 . . 99
x. 1–30 . . 244
xiii. 24, 25 . 103
xiv. 25–28 . 104
xv. 16 . . 244
xv. 19–22 . 108
xvi. 5–9 . . 109
xvi. 7–9 . 106, 241
xvii. 3–5 . . 110
xvii. 4 . . 112
xvii. 6 93, 111, 245
xvii. 24, 30 . 337
xviii. 8 . 108, 119
xviii. 13ff. . . 119
xviii. 17 . . 260
xviii. 17–36 . 109
xviii. 21 . . 112
xviii. 26ff. 247, 252, 257
xix. 9 . . 127
xix. 36–37 . 123
xx. 12–17 . 111
xx. 20 . . 181
xxiii. 7 . . 350f.
xxiii. 29 . . 141
xxv. 7 . . 142
xxv. 22–26 . 143
xxv. 27–30 . 144

I CHRONICLES
i. 5, 17 . . 232
x. 10 . . 344

2 CHRONICLES
xxviii. 16–21 . 109
xxviii. 18 . . 108
xxxv. 21 . . 141

JOB
xxxvii. 4, 5 . 335
xl. 9 . . 335

PSALMS
xciv. 20 . . 488
cxx. 5 . . 232

PROVERBS
x. 3, 11 . . 488
xx. 10, 23 . 292
xxxi. . . 431

DANIEL
ii. 10 . . 346
iv. 28–33 149, 191
v. 22 . . 148
vii. 1 . . 148
viii. 1 . . 148

ISAIAH
i. 11, 13 . . 353
x. 5 . . 239
x. 5–6 . . 112
x. 6–16 . . 239
xiii. 19–22 . 52
xiv. 13 . . 356
xix. 1 . . 335
xix. 11, 12 . 430
xx. 1 . . 260
xx. 1–6 . . 112
xxiii. 1–13 . 283
xxiii. 5 . . 108

xxx. 1–5 . . 119
xxxiv. 14 . . 485
xxxvi. 6 . . 241
xxxix. . . 118
xxxix. 1 . . 110
xliv. 12–20 . 357
xlv. 1, 4 . . 151
xlvi. 1 . . 342

JEREMIAH
i. 13 . . 136
vii. 18 . . 353f.
xxvii. 7 . . 141
xxxix. 3 . 144, 260
xxxix. 13 . . 260
xliv. 19 . . 354
xliv. 30 . . 142
xlvi. 5 ff., 12, 17. 141
xlvii. 1 . . 141
xlix. 7 . . 430
xlix. 28 . . 144
li. 27 113, 124, 136
lii. 31 . . 144

EZEKIEL
viii. 14 . 25, 377
xxvi. 2 . . 142
xxvi–xxix. . 142
xxvii. 12–16, 23–24
143
xxvii. 13 . . 232
xxix. 17–18 . 267
xxix. 19–21 . 144
xxxi. 3–8, 15 . 240
xxxii. 26 . . 232
xxxviii. 2, 3 116, 232
xxxviii. 6 . 116
xxxix. 1 . . 232
xliii. 13–17 . 356

HOSEA
xii. 1 . . 239

AMOS
i. 5 . . 91
viii. 4–5 . . 292

OBADIAH
8 . . . 430

NAHUM
i. 8 . . . 139
ii. 3–4 . . 486
iii. 4 . . 239
iii. 8–10 . . 129
iii. 16 . 239, 296

ZEPHANIAH
ii. 13, 15 . . 239

ZECHARIAH
xii. 11 . . 335

BEL AND THE DRAGON
3 . . . 352
13 . . . 381

ST. MATTHEW
viii. 28–32 . 313
xii. 43–45 313, 487

ST. LUKE
viii. 26–33 313
xi. 24–26 . 487

ACTS OF THE APOSTLES
xvii. 23 151, 486, 498

I CORINTHIANS
xi. 10 . . 388

Subject Index

(*Where possible, subjects are entered as sub-sections under more general headings. Thus 'medical texts' occurs as a sub-heading under 'cuneiform tablets and texts, classes of'. Where there are several references to a subject and one reference may be considered as more important than the others, this is given in bold type.*)

abortion, 215, 350
administration, 50 f., 56, 66, 72, 79, 85, 105 f., 108, 125, 158, **233–268**, 484
  Agade dynasty, 50 ff., 234
  Assyria, empire of, 105, 221, **238 ff.**
  Early Dynastic period, **233 f.**, 391
  Hittite kingdom and empire, 75 f.
  New Babylonian period, **261 ff.**
  Old Babylonian period, 67, 72 f., **234 ff.**
  temples, 133, 262 ff.
  Ur, Third dynasty of, 55 ff., 65, 234
adoption, 171, 210, 220, 349
adultery, 213, 431, 464
aeons, 331, 410
Afterlife, 11 ff., 133
agriculture, 6 ff., 10, 73, 433
algebra: *see sub-heading under* 'mathematics'
alliances: *see sub-heading under* 'diplomacy'
ambassadors: *see sub-heading under* 'diplomacy'
amulets, 11, 18, 178, 303 ff., 414
animals, treatment of, 194 f.
animism, 302
Apocrypha, 342
apotheosis, 46, 403, 408 f.
aqua regia, 473
aqueduct, 122, 181

archaeological periods
  Aurignacian, 4
  Early Dynastic 30, **34 ff.**, 68, 157, 159, 162, 168 f., 223, 233 f., 328, 482
  Eridu, 10, **15 ff.**, 32, 147, 157
  Hajji Muhammad, 16
  Halaf, 12 ff., 15 ff., 25, 68, 269 ff.
  Hassuna, 9 ff., 14, 269 f.
  Jemdet Nasr, **26 ff.**, 30 f., 39, 42 f., 157, 173, 183, 272
  Kulli, 272
  Mousterian, 5
  Natufian, 7
  Neolithic, 5 ff.
  Palaeolithic, 4 f., 15
  Pleistocene, 15
  Predynastic [= *Protoliterate*, q.v.]
  Protoliterate, **21 f.**, **26 ff.**, 36, 167, 173, 178, 272
  Samarra 11 f., 15 f., 18, 269 f.
  Ubaid, 12 f., **16 ff.**, 31, 34 f., 68, 147, 157, 270 f.
  Uruk, **19 ff.**, 31, 157
architecture, 12 f., 40 f., 159, 496
  Ionian column, 496
  Islamic, 499 f.
ark, 401
army
  Assyrian, 95, 133, 260
  New Babylonian, 147 f.
  Sumerian, 477

539

art, 18, 41, 66, **474 ff.**
  Achaemenid, 482
  Assyrian, 388
  Byzantine, 499
  Christian, 497 f.
  Islamic, 500
  Sumerian, 476 ff.
Assembly, 126, 162, 211, **216 ff.**, 220,
    337, 359 f., 413, 416
  composition of, 37
  divine, 337 f., **341**, 402, 413 f.
  functions of, 162, 211, **216 f.**, 359 f.
astrolabes, 456
astrology, 320, 453 f., **489 f.**
  horoscopic, 455, **489 ff.**
  judicial, 454 f., 457, 489
astronomy, **453 ff.**, 483 f., 492 f.
  Hindu, 492
  [*For types of astronomical texts see
    under* 'cuneiform tablets and
    texts, classes of']

Babylonian captivity, 142, 144
Babylonian cities, attitude to Assyria,
    111, 116, 137
bas-reliefs, 479 f.
bathrooms, 179
battle, description of, 121
Beduin (the term anachronistically
    employed), 63
Bel, taking the hands of, 111, 116
betrothal, 204
Big Brother, 435 ff.
board games, 190
boundaries, 229 f.
boundary stones, 319, 335, 478 f.
boxing, 190
brewing, 173 f.
bribery, 73
brickmaking, 433
bride-money: see *under* 'marriage'
bronze gates (of Balawat), 100, 480,
    482
building, 118, 122, 144
buildings, collapse of, 180, 205, 210
burial: *see* 'dead, cult of the'

calendar, 73, 331, 384, 456 f., 483, 491 f.

intercalation, 73, 457 f.
canals: *see* 'irrigation and canals'
cannibalism, 132, 180, 193, 406
carbon-14 dating, 5, 7 ff., 269
carpets, 474 f.
castration: *see* 'mutilation'
cavalry, 95
chariots, 12, 43, 226, 229, 394, 477
charters, 79, 252 ff., **258 f.**
chemistry
  chemical apparatus, 472 f.
  chemical technology, 471 ff.
  dyeing, 474
  tanning, 473 f.
childbirth, 302, 417, 466
chronology, 93 f., 134
circumcision, 186
cire perdue process, 123, 482
city-states, 158
  breakdown of economy of: *see
    sub-heading under* 'economy'
clothing: *see* 'dress'
coalitions: *see sub-heading under* 'diplo-
    macy'
colonization, 15, 96, 98, 148 f., 285
  [*See also* 'merchant colonies']
communications, 159, 234 ff., **249 ff.**,
    484
  river, 167
  road, **105 f.**, 181, 249 f., 278
concubines, 185, 214
coronation, 115, 488 f.
cosmetics, 382
Cosmic Mountain, 33, 355, 426
cosmogony, 300
  [*See also* 'Creation']
craftsmen, 168, 480
Creation, **417 ff.**, 484
  [*See also* 'Man, purpose of creation
    of' *and* 'myths and epics']
cremation, 78, 132
crime, 193 f., **213 ff.**, 231
  assault, 193, 205, 213
  blasphemy, 213
  embezzlement, 193, 442
  forgery, 165, 203, 292
  jerry-building, 210
  kidnapping, 207, 228

murder, 193, 209, **216 f.**, 231
parricide, 123, 208, 210
penalties for, 194
rape, 193, 204, 215
robbery, 193, 209, 231
sedition, 213
theft, 193, 204, 209, 211, 216
[See also 'trial']
cultures, prehistoric: see under
    'archaeological periods'
cuneiform tablets and texts, classes of,
    22 ff., 300
annals, 106 f., 120
archaic texts (not strictly cunei-
    form), 22, 42
astronomical procedure texts, 459
astronomical texts, 153, 456 f., 490
building inscriptions, 339, 503
chronicles, 144
commentaries, 347
economic texts, 43, 45, 66, 196,
    291, 293 ff.
ephemerides, 459
El Amarna texts, 76, 78, 80, 222
foundation inscriptions, 369 f.
Hurrian texts, 77, 300
imperial and royal correspon ence,
    107 ff., 131, 199, 245 f.
incantations, 303, 305, 307, 318,
    325, 327 f.
letters to gods, 114, 343, 370
lexical texts, 43
literary texts, 43, 45, 187
Mari letters, **66 f.**, 223
mathematical problem texts, 451 f.
mathematical table texts, 451
medical prescriptions, 460, **467 ff.**
medical texts, 460 ff.
myths and epics: see this as main
    heading
Old Assyrian texts, 68
royal inscriptions [See also 'annals'
    above], 370, 503
Series, 455
temple records of property, 445
Wisdom literature: see this as main
    heading
cuneiform texts, titles of (other than

'myths and epics' and 'Wisdom
    literature', q.v.)
ana ittishu, 202 f.
Assyrian King List, 68, 70, 86
Enuma Anu Enlil, 455 f.
Maqlu, 308
ᵘⁿᵘˡAPIN, 457, 490
Poor Man of Nippur, 185
Shurpu, 308
Sumerian King List, 34 ff., 41, 45 f.,
    48, 54 f., 359, 374, 423, 426
Synchronous History, 93
Utukki Limnuti, 308
cuneiform writing, 187
end of, 153
origin of, 22 f., 159 f., 445
Ugaritic form of, 76 f., 223
curse(s), 307, 317, 320
cylinder seals, 8, **25 ff.**, 175, 183, 291,
    334, 351, 377, 474 f., 478
[See also 'stamp seals']

dancing, 190
dead, cult of the, 6, 11
[See also 'Afterlife', 'cremation']
Dead Sea scrolls, 149
death
bread of, 408
water of, 408
waters of, 399
Death
goddess of, 307 f.
debt, 209, 216
remission, 198
Deluge: see 'Flood'
demons, 19, **302 ff.**, 421, 428, 461,
    470, 486 ff.
alu, 309 f., 465
asakku, 312, 315
Croucher [= Rabisu, q.v.]
gallu, 306, 309 f.
Hanbi, 303
Handmaid of Lilu, 314, 319
Labasu [Labaṣu], 314
Lamashtu, 304, 309, 311
lamassu, 313
Liliṭ, Lilith, Lilitu, 309, 314, 485
Lilu, 314, 319

Namtaru]Namṭaru], 309
Pazuzu, 303, 499
Rabisu [Rabiṣu], 314, 319, 471, 485
Seizer [=Aḫḫazu], 314, 463
shedu, 151, 313, 316
utukku,313, 319
[See also 'ghosts']
deportation, 84, 108, 268, 285
Destiny, Fixing of, 259, 329, 382 f.,
    387, 413
Destiny, Tablets of, 329 f., 415,
    422 f.
devils: see 'demons'
diet, 172 ff.
diplomacy, 66 f., 147, 228 f.
    alliances, 71, 132, 147, 232, 284
    ambassadors, 67, 223, 226
    arbitration, 229 f.
    archives, 66, 78
    coalitions, 67, 223 ff.
    treaties, 117, 126 ff., 227, 230 ff.
diseases, 191 f., 462 ff.
divination, 320, 347 f., 470
    liver, 320 f., 348, 370 f.
    [See also 'omens']
divorce, 203 ff., 208, 322
doctors: see 'physicians'
dogs, 314, 324, 462
dragon, 314
drainage, 158
    [See also 'irrigation and canals']
drains, 19, 179
dream(s), 147, 192 f., 320, 344 f.,
    348, 356, 364 f., 393 f., 397, 439,
    501
    of Gudea, 364
    [See also 'nightmares']
dress, 182 f., 382 f., 405
drink: see 'diet'
drinking tubes, 173, 413
drunkenness, 413

eagle, 423 ff., 501
earthquake, 455
Ecclesiastes, Book of, 429
eclipse, 362, 459
    lunar, 151, 191, 455 ff.
    solar, 457

economy, 94, 104, 143, 145, 267 f.
    city-state, ~of, 165 f.
    city-state, breakdown of, ~of, 198
    economic development, 94
    economic distress, 147 f., 169 f., 198
    economic reforms, 47 f., 143, 147 f.,
        164, 198 ff., 266 f., 285
    inflation, 58, 147 f., 285
    markets, 286 ff.
    prices and price control, 198 f.,
        279 f., 296, 371 f.
    wage fixing, 209
    [See also 'trade' and 'trade routes']
education, 187 ff.
empire
    Assyrian, 83 ff., 233, 238 ff.
    Hittite, 74 ff.
    New Babylonian, 140 ff.
    of Sargon of Agade, 50, 68, 277
enema, 468
enemy, treatment of, 129, 244
epics: see 'myths and epics'
equinox, 385
ethical standards, 319
eunuchs, 185, 348
Evil, problem of, 438 ff.
evil spirits: see 'demons'
execution, 242 f.
exorcists, 305 ff., 346, 439
    training of, 308 f.
extradition, 227, 231 f.

false measures, 292, 319
family allowances, 163
famine, 58, 147, 406, 428 f., 456
feasts: see 'festivals'
felons, 193
    [See also 'crime']
ferry, 228, 399
fertility cults, 12 f., 300, 334, 375 ff.,
    388, 486
festivals, 97, 396, 433, 456
    Akitu (in some contexts, but not all,
        synonymous with 'New Year
        Festival') 388 ff., 387
    esh-esh (or eshsheshu) 167, 353
    New Year 28, 118, 152, 162, 172, 259,
        342, 358, 381 ff., 385 ff., et passim

figurines, 11, 13, 18 f., 313 ff., 340, 478
fines, 204, 219, 221 f.
fire beacons, 236
fire-gods, 305, 338
    [*See also* Gigil, Gira, Nusku *in* Index of Proper Names]
fishing, 168, 175, 407
fish-men, 314
Flood 32, 41, 330, 400 ff., 407, 423, 484, 502
flood, 139, 246, 324, 335
food: *see* 'diet'
forgery: *see sub-heading under* 'crime'
fortifications, 39, 100, 391
fox, 418, 501
frontiers, defined, 230
    [*See also* 'boundaries']
fruits, 495
funeral rites, 310, **372 ff.**
    [*See also* 'dead, cult of the']
furnaces, 473

Gadarene swine, 313, 487
gardens, 97, 122, 181
Genesis, Book of, 484
geometry: *see sub-heading under* 'mathematics'
ghosts, 309 f., 317, 425, 472
    laying, **309 ff.**
goddesses, position of in early Sumer, 187
gods
    access to, 357
    national, 331, **338 ff.,** 343 ff.
    numerical symbols of, 336
    reports to, 343 f., 370
    (supposedly) dying and resurgent, 355, **377 ff.,** 385, 419 f.
Golden Bough, The, 393
golden sky, 386

hair styles, 183 ff.
'hand-raising', 328
headmaster, 435 ff.
health, 191 f.
heaven, 426
hemerology, 318 f.

henotheism, 328, 332, 342
hepatoscopy: *see* 'divination, liver'
holidays, 172
homosexuality: *see* 'sexual abnormalities and perversions'
horoscopes: *see* 'astrology, horoscopic'
horse, 194 f., 323, 480
hostages, 226
housing, 6, 10, 163, 176 f.
humour, 441, 444
hunting, 97, 189
Hurrian influence, 221

immortality, 408 f.
imperial and royal correspondence: *see sub-heading under* 'cuneiform tablets and texts, classes of'
imperialism defended, 167, 232 f., 238 ff.
incense, 271, 348, 354
inheritance, 201 f., 207 f., 210, 215, 237
inflation: *see sub-heading under* 'economy'
intelligence reports, 107, 114, 116
intercalation: *see sub-heading under* 'calendar'
irrigation and canals, 19, 64, 72 f., 94, 97, 122, 158 f., 166 f., 181, 209, 215 f., 235, 332, 371
ivory, carved, 480 f.

jewellery, 178 f., 383
Job, Book of, 429, 438
judges, 217 f., 220 f.
Judges, Book of, 92
justice, 72 f., 197
    administration of, 216 f., 221 f.
    [*See also* 'law', 'laws']

Kenite hypothesis, 491 f.
kidnapping: *see sub-heading under* 'crime'
king, 197 f., 302 f., **359 ff.,** *et passim*
    as shepherd, 371 f.
    election of, 162, 359
    investment of, by the god, 100, 162

priestly function of, 168
substitute, 361 f., 375 f.
in cone-smearing ceremony, 388 f.
Kings, Book(s) of, 99, 111, 243
kingship, 100, 262, 329, **359 f.**, 423
divine, 360 f.
divine, in Old Testament?, 360, 389
insignia of, 329, 359, 372, 386 f., 414

lamps, 179
land
sale of, 293 ff.
redemption of, 205, 221
tenure, 46, 61, 164 ff., 215, 221,
236 ff., 258, 261 ff., 295
languages
Akkadian, 76 *et passim*
Aramaic, 149, 153, 431
Hurrian, 77
Minoan Linear A, 277
Sumerian, 24, 435 *et passim*
Ugaritic, 76
Urartian [Urarṭian], 77
lapis lazuli, 40, 364, 397
lavatory, 179
law, 72, 196 ff., 371, 484, 504
international, 222 ff.
law-giving, 63, 196 ff.
laws
ana ittishu: see sub-heading under
'cuneiform texts, titles of'
of Assyria, 197, 212 ff.
of Eshnunna, 200, 203 ff.
of Hammurabi, 72, 196 f., 199,
206 ff., 237, 279, 288 f., 317, 332,
339, 349 f., 372, 470, 478
of Lipit-Ishtar, 63, **200 ff.**
of Ur-Nammu, 199 f.
lawsuits, decision in, 220 ff.
legacy and survival, 483 ff.
letters: *see* 'intelligence reports', *and*
sub-headings 'El Amarna texts',
'imperial and royal correspondence', letters to gods' *and* 'Mari
letters' *under* 'cuneiform tablets
and texts, classes of'
Leviticus, Book of, 198
lex talionis, 200, 208, 210, 213

libations, **353 f.**, 358
library, 357
Life, bread of, 408
limmu lists, **93 f.**, 101
lion, 194
literature, **390 ff.**, 501
loans, 289 ff., 296 f.
loan-words from ancient Mesopotamia, 493 f.
love-making: *see* 'sexual relations'
love-sickness, symptoms of, 465

madness, 191
magic, 12, 303, 309, 325, 461, 483, 485
black, 214 f., 308, 316 ff., 338
substitution as technique of, 307 f.,
312 f.
sympathetic, 306 f.
[*See also* 'witchcraft']
Man, purpose of creation of, **162 f.**,
345, 354 f., 363, 415 f.
Marduk, fifty names of, 341, 416
marriage, 185, 201 ff., 213 f.
bride-money at, 202 ff.
types of, 213 f.
Marriage, Sacred, 28, 349, 360,
375 ff., 379, 382 f., 388 f., 391,
393
matches?, 473
mathematics, 187, **445 ff.**
algebra, 451 f.
cube roots, 451
decimal system, 446 f.
geometry, 158, 437, 451, 453
numeration, 445 ff.
π, 451
place-value notation, **447 ff.**, 492
progressions, 451, 456
Pythagoras theorem, 451
quadratic equations, 451 f.
sexagesimal system, 446, 448 ff., 492
square roots, 451
zero sign, 449 f.
[*For types of mathematics texts see*
sub-headings under 'cuneiform
tablets and texts, classes of']
medicine, **459 ff.**, 493
anatomical knowledge, 469 f.

medical techniques, 468 f.
merchant colonies, 50, **68 f.**, 74, 77, 277, 282, 291
metals, 10, 12, 17, 21, 29, 54, 85, 88, 96, 100, 104, 107, 116, 128, 142 f., 218, 256, 270, 273 ff., 278, 282, 481
monopoly of, 280 f.
metallurgy and metal technology, 123, 270, 278, **481 f.**
midwife, 417
military tactics and strategy, 92 f., 110 f., 116, 129, 133, 137, 140 f., 150, 152
Assyrian attack on Babylonia, 85, 98, 110 f., 116, 119 ff., 124, 132, 138, 429
Assyrian sea-attack on Elam, 120
Mishna, 214
Mithraism, 498
mongoose, 322, 444
monogamy, 185, 504
monotheism, 145, **341 f.**
Moon-god: see 'Nanna' and 'Sin' in Index of Proper Names
Mother-goddess, 8, 11 ff., 26
mortgage, 504
music, **190 f.**, 347, 373
mutilation, 194, 213, 502
mystery cult, 333
myths and epics, 36, 160 f., 336, 432, 483
Atrahasis, 406 f.
Canaanite myths: see sub-heading 'Ugaritic myths'
Creation of Man, Sumerian myth concerning, 162 f., 363
Descent of Inanna, 419 ff.
Descent of Ishtar, 419
Enuma Elish: see sub-heading 'Epic of Creation'
Epic of Adapa, 407 ff.
Epic of Creation, 331, 340 ff., 363, 385, 388, **409 ff.**
Epic of Enmerkar, 40, 166
Epic of Etana, 329, 359, 423 ff.
Epic of Gilgamish, 189 f., **390 ff.**, 407, 502

Epic of Tukulti-Ninurta, 85, 429
flint, myth concerning [=Lugale u melambi Nergal], 336
Inuma ilu awilum [=Atrahasis, q.v.]
legend of Naram-Sin, 427 ff.
legend of Sargon of Agade, 427
Myth of Zu, 422 f.
Nergal and Ereshkigal, 337, 419 f.
ša naqba imuru [=Epic of Gilgamish, q.v.]
Ugaritic myths, 344, 363

Nahum, Book of, 486
nakedness
in connection with religion, 182, 354
in dreams, 192
nightmares, 303

oath (in lawsuits or treaties), 218 f., 224, 231, 242, 372
'Old man becomes young'; mythical plant, 405
omens, 180, 186, 192, **320 ff.**, 348, 361 f., 365 f., 427, 429, 455 f., 461 f., 489
[See also 'astrology' and 'divination']
'opening of the mouth'; ritual, 357 f.
orchards, 181
Ordeal, trial by, 200, 219 f., 302
organization, social and political
Hittite, 75 f.
Mitannian, 78 f.
Sumerian, 44 ff.
[See also 'administration']
oxen, 323

paintings, 474, 481
pantheon, 73, 90, 267, 302, **328 ff.**, 338 ff., 418
leadership of the, 338 ff.
position of Marduk in the, 338 ff.
parks, 181, 495
physicians, 185, 459 f.
piety, 438 ff.
polyandry, 187
polytheism, 145, 328 f.

poor, protection of, 197 f., 372
population, 160 f., 168 f., 180 f., 256
  problems of, 406
pottery, 10 ff., 476
prayer, prayers, **325 ff.**, 342, 368
priestesses and associated temple per-
    sonnel, 186, 349 ff.
  Entu, 349
  high-priestess [=*Entu*, q.v.]
  Kulmashitu, 351
  Naditu [or *Naṭitu*], 350
  Qadeshah, 350
  Qadishtu, 350 f.
  Ugbabtu, 349
priest-king: *see sub-heading* 'En' *under*
  'Titles'
priests and associated temple person-
    nel, 305, 325, **346 ff.**
  [*Some borderline cases are entered
  under* 'Titles', *q.v.*]
  Ashipu, 305, 346
  Baru, 347 f.
  Erib-biti, 346
  Gala [=*Kalu*, q.v.]
  Kalu, 190, 346 f., 365
  Mashmashu, 305, 325, 346
  Mari-ummani, 347
  Naru, 347
  Nash paṭri, 347, 353, 387
  Pashishu, 347
  Ramku, 347
  Sanga [=*Shangu*, q.v.]
  Sha'iltu, 348
  Sha'ilu, **348**, 501
  Shangu or *Sanga*, 233, 347
  Sheshgallu, 347, 385 ff.
  Sword-bearer [=*Nash paṭri*, q.v.]
primitive democracy, 37 f., 160
propaganda, 84 f., 150 ff., 429
prostitutes, 185 f., 201 f., 215, 349,
  351, 389, 392, 397, 442
proverbs: *see sub-heading under* 'Wis-
  dom literature'
Proverbs, Book of, 429
Psalms, Book of, 485
punishment, 536 f.
  [*See also* 'crime, penalties for' *and*
  'trial']

quay wall, 94, 181

racial conflicts (supposed), 49, 60, 161
racial movements, 69, 73 f., 77, 85,
  88 f., 101 f., 113, 129, 131, 136,
  138, 280, 285 *et passim*
radio-carbon analysis: *see* 'carbon-14
  dating'
reed hut, 334, 401
religion, 299–358
  Canaanite, 344
  Halaf, 12 f.
  Hassuna, 11
  popular, 377
  at Uruk [Erech], 25 f., 334
  of Neolithic man, 6 f.
religious reforms, 145 f., 332
religious symbols, 484, **496 ff.**
resettlement of population: *see* 'colonization'
revendication, 220 f., 294
ritual combat, 388, 393
'Ritual Pattern' theory, 300 ff., 360
ritual(s), 302 f., 311 f., **345 ff.**, 357 f.,
  382 ff.
  against toothache, 306
  concerned with childbirth, 417
  concerned with temple restoration,
    365 ff.
  for purification of a house, 314 ff.
roads: *see sub-heading* 'road' *under*
  'communications'
rod and ring (divine symbols), 339,
  343
royal letters: *see sub-headings* 'El
  Amarna texts, 'imperial and
  royal correspondence' *and* 'Mari
  letters' *under* 'cuneiform tablets
  and texts, classes of'

Sabbath, 353
Sacred Marriage: *see* 'Marriage,
  Sacred'
sacrifices, 102, 338, 352 f., 367, 403 f.
  foundation, 11
  human, 373, **374 f.**, 380
sailors, 120
satire, 441

saturnalia, 366
schools, 187 ff., **434 ff.**
  [*See also* 'education']
scorpion-men, 302, 397 f., 502
scorpions, 180, 319, 322 f., 502
sculptures, 476 ff.
  [*See also* '*Stele of the Vultures*']
secularizing tendency, 152
Semitic infiltration, 14, 39, 41, 49, 58,
  60, 66, 69, 84, 88 ff., 161, 282
serpent (in a myth), 423 ff.
sewers: *see* 'drains'
sexual love, goddess of, 333 f.
sexual perversions and abnormalities,
  186, 191
  homosexuality, 213
  impotence, 191
  lesbianism, 324
  transvestism, 186, 348
sexual relations, normal, 185 f., 383,
  463
shearing, 183
ships, 120, 167, 276, 281 f., 292 f., 384
siege warfare, 93, 110 f., 138 f.
slander, 432, 442
slavery, slaves, 63, 148, **169 ff.**, 202,
  209 f., 297, 434, 441
snakes, 180, 322, 405, 462, 489, 500
soap, 474
social organization: *see* 'organization,
  social and political'
Song of Songs, The, 486
songs, 371, 382
sports and pastimes, 189
stamp seals, 25, 474
  [*See also* 'cylinder seals']
Stele of the Vultures (sculpture), 45, 477
sterilization, 350
strikes, 172
substitution: *see sub-heading* 'substitution as technique of' *under*
  'magic'
succession, royal, 126 f.
suicide, 132, 139, 373
sulphuric acid, 473
Sumerian civilization, **31 ff.**,
  157 ff. *et passim*
Sun-disk, 343

Sun-god: *see* 'Shamash' *and* 'Utu' *in*
  Index of Proper Names
surgery, 208, 210, **470 f.**
syncretism, 330, 341 f., 344

Tablets of Destiny: *see* 'Destiny,
  Tablets of'
taboo, 18, 175 f., **318 ff.**, 326, 461,
  469 f., 492
taxation, 46, 48, 79, 108, 234, **254 ff.**,
  259, 266 f., 279, 282 f.
technology, chemical: *see sub-heading*
  'chemical technology' *under*
  'chemistry'
temple(s), 20 f., 56, 165 ff., 307, 340,
  343 f., 357 f.
  architectural form of, 24 f.
  building and resoration of, 55 f.,
    80, 135, 146, 150, 363 ff.
  excavation of ancient, 355, 365 f.
  high, 356
  'House of Life': *see* 'E-nam-tila' *in*
    Index of Proper Names
  lands of, 46 f.
  low, 356
  records of, 445
  'White Temple' at Erech, 24
textiles, 12, 29, 143, 182 f., 270, 475
theology, 299 f.
theophany, 333
'those-of-stones' (magical objects),
  399 f.
time divisions, 489 ff.
titles
  [*Terms denoting specific classes of
    priests or priestesses will be found
    under* 'priests [*or priestesses*] and
    associated temple personnel'.
  *Some terms denoting personnel, but
    not strictly to be classes as titles,
    are placed in* Index of Sumerian,
    Akkadian, . . . words
  Agrig, 233
  bel pihati, 247
  Elders, 39, 235, 252
  En, 37 ff., 162, 168, 345, 349, 391
  Ensi, **44**, 46 f., 86, 163 f., **168**,
    233 f., 345

Gir-nita, 233
Gugallu, 158
hazannu, 235, 252 ff.
Ishshaku, 86
Lord of the City, 254
Lugal, 38 f., 44, 233, 345, 360
Man over the City, 252 ff.
Mar shipri, 249 f.
Nu-banda, 233
Qipu, 262
qurbuti, 250
Rab alani, 248 f.
Rabianu, 238
Rab-mag, 260
Rab-mugi, 260
rab-kiṣri, 260
Rab-shakeh, 112, 252, 260
Rakbu, 238
Royal Officer Lord of the Appoint-
    ment, 262 ff.
Royal Officer over the King's
    Coffer, 262, 265
Shatammu, 262 ff., 297
Shibutum [=Elders, *q.v.*]
Tartan, 260
Zazakku, 263
toothache, 306
tombs, desecration or robbing of,
    133, 193 f., 373, 378
tonsure, 170, 185, 202
tortures, 95 f., 112, **243 f.**
town planning, 180 f.
trade, 9, 13, 27, 40, 50 f., 54, 62,
    68 f., 102, 104, 136, 142 f., 166 f.,
    264, 277, **269–298** *et passim*
trade routes, 66, 88, 90 f., 94, 98 f.,
    102, 110 f., 117, 128, 143, 161,
    167, 267 f., 281, 283, 285 *et
    passim*
trading colonies: *see* 'merchant colon-
    ies'
transport, 227 f., 248, 264, 271, 284,
    289, 292 f.
    [*See also* 'communications']
treaties: *see* sub-heading *under* diplo-
    macy'
tree, sacred *or* Tree of Life, 338 f.,
    497 f.

triads, 305, **330**, 409
tribal movements: *see* 'racial move-
    ments'
tribute, 51, 93, 107, 109, 241, 255 ff.

Underworld, 303, 309, 334, 337, 348,
    379, 381, 397, **419 ff.**, 439, 463
Ur, 'royal tombs' of, 46, **419 ff.**, 439,
    463
Ur, Standard of, 182, 477

vassals, status of, 103, 107, **240 ff.**
veil, 214

war, goddess of, 333 f.
warfare: *see* 'army', 'battle, descrip-
    tion of', 'fortifications', 'mili-
    tary tactics and strategy' *and*
    'siege warfare'
water supply, 181 f.
week, 353, **491 f.**
weights, 448, 482
    [*See also* 'false measures']
wells, 181 f., 227
winds, 414 f.
wine, 434
Wisdom literature, 429 ff.
    Babylonian Job, The [imaginative
        misnomer for *Ludlul bel nemeqi*,
        q.v.]
    Babylonian Theodicy, The, 439 f.
    Copper and Precious Metal, 432
    Counsel of Wisdom, 441 f.
    Dialogue of Pessimism, 440 f.
    humorous stories, 444
    Ludlul bel nemeqi, 438 f.
    maxims, 431 f., 443
    miniature essays: *see* 'humorous
        stories'
    Pickaxe and Plough, 432
    precepts, **431**, 441, 443
    proverbs, 176, 185, **430 f.**, 443
    Righteous Sufferer, The Poem of the
        [=*Ludlul bel nemeqi*, q.v.]
    Shepherd and Farmer, 161, 432
    Summer and Winter, 432 ff.
    Tamarisk and Palm Tree, 442 f.
    tenson, **432 f.**, 442 f.

Words of Ahiqar [Aḥiqar], 431
witchcraft, 214 f., 219, 316 f., 338, 483, 485, 487 f.
[*See also* 'magic']
witches and wizards, 305, 317
wizards: *see* 'witches and wizards'
woman,
dress of [*See also main heading* 'dress'], 214
hair styles of: *see main heading* 'hair styles'
status of, 186 f., **213 ff.**, 504
wool industry, 183

wrestling, 190, 393
writing,
origin of: *see sub-heading under* 'cuneiform writing'
alphabetic [*See also sub-heading* 'Ugaritic form of' *under main heading* 'cuneiform writing']

year-formulae, 57, 197 f., 339

ziggurat (*or* ziqqurrat), 24, 33, 55, 80, 159, 349, **355 ff.**, 401, 451, 499
zodiac, 456, 490

Index of Proper Names

(*Titles of literary works are excluded from this index, as are names of demons. Entries for these classes will be found in the* Subject Index *under 'cuneiform texts, titles of', 'myths and epics' and 'demons'. Also excluded are (i) names of modern authors, (ii) modern place names other than important archaeological sites, (iii) names occurring only incidentally or in quoted documents.*)

Abbreviations:

[c] town or city
[d] deity
[h] temple or associated building
[l] land, province or state

[p] personal name (not of a ruler or deity)
[r] ruler
[s] archaeological site
[t] tribe or nation

Abdi-Anati [r], 230
Abi-Eshuh [Abi-Ešuḫ] [r], 74
Abi-Samar [r], 224
Abyss: see Abzu
Abzu, Apsu, Abyss,
  [primeval Being *personifying the sweet waters, then the* Cosmic Sweet Waters, *and so the* abode of the god Ea-Enki], 36, 302, 313, 331, 333, 340, 398 f., 401, 409 ff.
Achaemenes [r], 146
Achaemenid dynasty, 152, 482
Adab [c], 45
Adad [Addu *or* Adadu, *and so in personal names containing this element*] [d], 331, 334 ff., 402, 406, 422, 462
Adad-apal-iddinam [r], 90
Adad-idri [r], 98 f.
Adad-nirari I [r], 82, 84
Adad-nirari II [r], 92 f., 95, 137
Adad-nirari III [r], 103 ff.
Adad-shum-usur [Addu-šum-usur][r], 86
Adapa [p], 407 ff.
Agade [c], 49, 51 f., 72

Agade [dynasty *or* empire], 48 ff., 68, 164 f., 184, 217, 234, 359 f., 477 f., 482
Agga of Kish [r], 39, 42, 45, 48, 161
Agukakrime [= Agum II, *q.v.*]
Agum II [r], 76
Agum III [r], 80
Ahab [r], 99, 480
Ahaz [r], 106, 109, 241
Ahaziah [r], 244
Ahlamu [Aḫlamu] [t], 84, 88
A-kalam-dug [r], 377
Akhenaten [r], 81, 222
Akkad (defined) [l], 3
Alalah [Alalaḫ] [c], 77, 271
Aleppo [c], 74 f.
Amar-Suen [r], 57
Ama-ushumgal-anna, 381 f.
Amel-Marduk [r], 135, 144
Amenophis III [r], 79 f.
Ammi-ditana [r], 74, 339
Ammi-saduqa [Ammi-ṣaduqa] [r], 74, 430, 456
Ammon [l], 98
Amon [d], 231
Amorites [t], 58, 60, 66, 68, 70, 170, 236

551

Amurru [l], 90
Amurru [t] [=Amorites, q.v.]
An, Anu(m) [d], 25, 305, 311, 328 ff.,
    336, 338 f., 359, 395 f., 407 ff.,
    413, 422, 426
Anah [c], 138
Anshan [l], 54, 146 f.
Anshar [d], 331, 340, 343, 410, 412 f.
Antum [d], 329
Anubanini [r], 52
Anunna(ki) [group of deities], 333,
    368, 402, 412, 416, 418, 420
Aplahanda [Aplaḫanda] [r], 228
Apries [=Hophra], q.v.]
Apsu [=Abzu, q.v.]
Aqarquf [s], 80, 95, 481
Arabs [t], 49, 125, 132, 134, 143, 483
Aramaeans [t], 84, 88 ff., 93, 96, 102,
    106, 111, 118, 120, 137, 146, 245 f.
Ararat [biblical form of Urartu, q.v.]
Aratta [c], 40, 223
Arbailu [c], 101, 123, 181
Arbela [=Arbailu, q.v.]
Argistis [r], 116 f.
Arik-den-ilu [r], 84
Arpad [c,l], 104, 232
Arrapkha [Arrapḫa] [c,l], 62, 77, 92,
    106, 121, 137 f.
Artatama [r], 78 ff.
Artatama [p], 81
Aruru [d], 342, 391
Arwad [c], 89
Asalluhi [Asalluḫi] [=Asar-lu-hi, q.v.]
Asar-lu-hi [Asar-lu-ḫi] [d], 317, 340
Asharid-apal-Ekur II [r], 90
Ashdod [c], 112
Ashguzaya ⎫ [Forms of the name of
Ashkenaz ⎬ the people known from
Ashkuz ⎭ classical sources as
             Scythians, q.v.]
Ashur [Aššur or Assur, according to
    dialect, and likewise in personal
    names containing this element], [d],
    324, 329, 338, 343, 350, 359, 409
Ashur [c], 68 f., 72, 101, 137 f., 168,
    252 f., 259, 307, 324, 335, 351,
    370, 478

Ashur [l], [Form of the name of the
    state Assyria, q.v.]
Ashur-ban-apli [=Ashurbanipal, q.v.]
Ashurbanipal [r], 126 ff., 145 f., 258,
    321, 390, 407, 423, 427, 460, 479
Ashur-bel-kala [r], 90 f.
Ashur-dan I [r], 86 f.
Ashur-dan II [r], 92
Ashur-dan III [r], 106
Ashur-danin-apli [r], 101
Ashur-etillu-ili [Aššur-etillu-ili] [r],
    134 f.
Ashur-matka-gur [p], 245 f.
Ashur-nadin-apli [r], 120
Ashur-nadin-shum [r], 120
Ashur-nasir-pal II [Assur-naṣir-apli]
    [r], 95 ff., 180, 240, 256, 267 f.,
    479
Ashur-nirari V [r], 104
Ashur-rabi II [r], 91 f.
Ashur-resh-ishi [r], 88, 92
Ashur-uballit I [Aššur-uballiṭ] [r], 82 ff.
Ashur-uballit [p], 139 ff.
Asshur [biblical spelling of Ashur, q.v.]
Assyria (defined) [l], 3
Astyages [r], 147
Atrahasis [Atraḫasis] [p], 406 f.
Aya [d], 218
Azariah [r], 108

Baal, Baalim [d], 244, 344, 363
Baasha [r], 243 f.
Babel, tower of [h], 24
Babylon, First Dynasty of, 64 ff., 76
Babylonia (defined) [l], 3
Bad-tibira [c], 34 f., 421
Balawat [s], 100, 480
Bawa [d], 164 f., 168, 336, 369
Bel [d], 111, 118, 342, 353 f.
Belesys [name under which a classical
    source refers to Nabopolassar, q.v.]
Bel-ibni [r], 119 f.
Belit [d], 342
Belit-ili [d], 318
Bel-shar-usur [Bel-šar-uṣur] [p, not r],
    148
Belshazzar [biblical form of Bel-shar-
    usur, q.v.]

Ben-hadad [*biblical form of the name entered above as* Adad-idri, *q.v.*]

Benjamina [t], 344

Berossus [p], 34, 135, 300, 362

Beth-Eden [*biblical form of* Bit-Adini, *q.v.*]

Bilalama [r], 203

Bit-Adini [l], 91, 96 ff.

Bit-Amukkani [t], 109 f.

Bit-Dakkuri [t], 124, 135

Bit-Halupe [Bit-Halupe] [l], 96

Bit-Sa'alli [t], 110

Bit Shilani [t], 110

Bit-Yakin [t], 111, 116, 120, 124

Boghazkoi [s], 223, 390, 427, 460, 468

Borsippa [c], 72, 91, 124, 132, 147, 342, 358, 386 f.

Burnaburiash II [r], 81 ff.

Burushkhanda [Burushhanda] [c], 50, 75

Burushkhatum [= Burushkhanda, *q.v.*]

Calah [c], 84, 97, 99, 104, 117, 180 f., 245, 256, 336, 479 ff.

Cambyses I [r], 147, 152

Canaanites, East: *see* Amorites, *for which it was previously used as an alternative term*

Carchemish [c], 12, 96 ff., 117, 141, 219, 228, 231, 271

Cassite Dynasty, 76, 79 f., 84, 86 f., 175

Cassites [t], 73 f., 76 ff., 88, 102, 195

Chaldaeans [t], 102, 109, 111, 116, 118, 120 f., 124, 128, 132 f., 135, 137 f. 141, 252, 261

Cilicia [l], 10, 140, 143, 270 f., 285
   [*See also* Que, *the name applied to the Assyrian province in this area*]

Cimmerians [t], 116 ff., 122, 124, 126, 129 f., 283

Crete [l], 277 f., 282

Croesus [r], 150 f.

Cuthah [c], 72, 119, 178, 310, 337, 371

Cyaxares [r], 136, 138 f., 143

Cyrus [r], 147 f., 150 ff., 285 f.

Dagan [*biblical* Dagon] [d], 335, 344

Damascius [p], 409

Damascus [c, l], 98 f., 103 f.

Damkina [d], 328, 331, 340, 411

David [r], 149, 354, 363, 503

Der [c, l], 61, 63, 69, 111, 121

Dilbat [c], 72, 77, 135

Diodorus Siculus [p], 136

Dravidians [t], 33

Dumuzi [*see also* Tammuz] [d], 25 f., 28, 35, 334, 382, 421, 427

Duranki [h], 163, 422 f.

Dur-Ashur [p], 250

Dur-kurigalzu [c], 95

Dur-sharrukin [c], 117 f., 181

Ea [d], 302, 305 ff., 312, 317, 328, 330, 336, 340 f., 348, 357, 365, 396, 400 f., 403, 406 ff.

Eanna [h], 147, 263, 296, 329

Eannatum [r], 45 f., 48, 477

Ebabbara [h], 365 f.

Edom [l], 109, 112, 430, 485

Egypt [l], 89, 99, 112, 119, 127, 129 f., 136 f., 141 ff., 146, 193, 222 f., 241, 256, 282 f., 362, 430, 493

Ehulhul [Ehulhul] [h], 146, 150, 364

Ehursaggal-kurkurra [Ehursaggal-kurkurra] [h], 370

Ekallatim [c], 70

Ekishnugal [h], 420

Ekron [c], 119

Ekur [h], 52, 420

El Amarna [s], 76, 78, 80, 222, 407, 419

Elam [l], 102, 106, 111, 118, 120 f., 124, 131 ff., 146, 150, 191, 272

Ellil [= Enlil, *q.v.*]

Eltekeh [c], 119

E-nam-tila [h], 433

E-Ninnu [h], 367, 369

Enki [d], 32, 36, 159, 330, 333, 340, 359, 407, 417 ff., 421

Enkidu [p], 190, 391 ff.

Enlil [d], 38, 52, 302, 305, 327 ff., 335 f., 338 f., 341, 343, 359, 369, 396, 401, 403, 406 f., 418, 420 ff., 426, 429, 433 f.

Enlil-kudur-usur [Enlil-kudur-uṣur]
  [r], 85 f.
Enlil-nirari [r], 84
Enmerkar [r], 223
Entemena [r], 45
Erbil [=Arbailu, q.v.]
Erech [c], 19 ff., 36 f., 39 ff., 48, 54 f.,
  64, 72, 79 f., 133, 135, 137, 147,
  150, 161, 187, 211, 223, 261,
  296 f., 329, 350, 352, 359, 371,
  391, 394, 405, 421, 423, 459, 486
Ereshkigal [d], 337, 348, 419 f.
Eriba-Adad [r], 86
Eridu [c], 16 ff., 32, 34 ff., 55, 72,
  80, 159, 330, 333, 339 f., 369, 418,
  420
Erzerum [c], 113
Esagila [h], 340, 416
Esarhaddon [r], 123 ff., 129 ff., 136,
  138, 361 f., 363
E-shar-ra [h], 343
Eshnunna [c, l], 61, 66, 70 f., 179,
  199 f., 203, 206, 212, 226
Etana [p], 423, 425 f.
Eve [p], 419
Evil-merodach [biblical form of Amel-
  Marduk, q.v.]

Fara [c], 42 f.

Gaga [d], 413
Gaza [c], 110, 112, 141
Gebal [=Gubla, q.v.]
Gedaliah [p], 268
Gibil [d], 305, 338
Gilgamish [r], 40, 42, 161, 189, 223,
  391 ff., 427
Gimirraya [cuneiform form of the name
  of the people known from classical
  sources as Cimmerians, q.v.]
Gira [d], 305, 338
Gizzida [a form of the name Ningizzida,
  q.v.]
Gomer [biblical form of the name of the
  people known from classical sources
  as Cimmerians, q.v.]
Gozan [biblical form of Guzana, q.v.]
Gubla [c], 89, 99

Gudea [r], 54, 169, 183, 364, 366 ff.,
  476
Gugalanna [d], 420
Gula [d], 336, 360
Gungunum [r], 64
Gurgum [l], 103
Gutians [t], 52 ff.
Gutium [l], 76, 428
Guzana [l], 93, 111, 245
Gyges [r], 129 f.

Hadad [biblical form of Adad, q.v.]
Hadad-rimmon [r], 335
Hadrach [biblical form of Hatarikka,
  q.v.]
Haldi [Ḫaldi] [d], 115
Halule [Ḫalule] [c], 121
Hamath [c, l], 103, 112
Hammurabi [Ḫammurabi] [r], 65 ff.,
  75 f., 170, 173 f., 180, 197 ff.,
  206 ff., 219, 221, 223, 225, 227,
  236 ff., 261, 279, 288 f., 293, 317,
  332, 335, 338, 349, 371 f., 470
Hana [Ḫana] [c, l], 76, 85, 224
Hanigalbat [l], 82, 84, 93
Hanigalbat [Ḫanigalbat] [l], 82, 84, 93
Hanish [Ḫanish] [d], 402
Hantilis [Ḫantilis] [r], 76
Haran [biblical spelling of Harran, q.v.]
Hatarikka [Ḫatarikka] [c, l], 104
Hatti [Ḫatti] [l], 74, 87, 228 ff.
Hattians [t], 74
Hattusas [c], 75
Hattusas [Ḫattusas] [c], 75
Hattusilis I [Ḫattusilis] [r], 75
Hattusilis III [r], 231
Hazael [r], 99
Herodotus [p], 130, 136, 144, 150,
  152, 174, 286, 349, 351, 354, 460,
  504
Hesiod [p], 502
Hezekiah [r], 109, 118 f., 181, 257
Hilakku [Ḫilakku] [l], 124, 129
Hindanu [Ḫindanu] [l], 137
Hiram of Tyre [p, not r], 100
Hittites [t], 69, 74 ff., 80, 88, 281 f.,
  502
Hophra [r], 142

Horims [*form employed in Authorised Version for* Horites, *q.v.*]
Horites [t], 77
Hoshea [r], 109 f.
Humbaba [= Huwawa, *q.v.*]
Hurrians [t], 53
Huwawa [Ḫuwawa] [d?], 393 f., 396

Ibbi-Suen [r], 57 ff., 62, 433
Igigi [group of deities], 416
Ilabrat [d], 408
Ila-kabkabu [p], 70
Ilushuma [r], 69
Imdugud [d], 364
Inanna [=Innin, *q.v.*]
Innin [d], 25, 28 f., 36, 159, 329, 331 f., 337, 359, 381, 420 f.
Ipkhur-Kish [Ipḫur-Kiš] [r], 360
Iraq, geological history of, 14 f.
Irishum I [r], 69
Ishbi-Erra [r], 58 f., 61 f., 64, 66
Ishkur [d], 335
Ishme-Dagan [r], 62 ff., 67, 71, 227, 236
Ishtar [d], 327 f., 331 ff., 342, 348, 381, 383, 394 ff., 402 f., 429, 465
Ishtar of Arbela [d], 333
Ishtar of Bit-kitmuri [d], 333
Ishtar of Nineveh [d], 79, 333
Isin [c], 58, 217, 350
Isin, First Dynasty of, 58, 61 ff., 66, 200, 202, 216, 236, 478
Isin, Second Dynasty of, 87
Israel [t, l], 98 f., 103, 106, 108, 110
Israel, lost tribes of, 111
Itu'a [t], 108, 253, 259

Jacob [p], 204, 356
Jamina: *see* Benjamina
Jarmo [s], 7 ff., 269
Jehoash [r], 103
Jehoiachin [r], 142, 144, 268
Jehoiakim [r], 141 f.
Jehovah [*conventional but false vocalization of the* divine name *represented by the Hebrew consonants* YHWH, *probably to be read* Yahweh] [d], 244, 335, 342

Jehu [r], 99, 244
Jemdat Nasr [Jamdat Naṣr] [s], [*see sub-heading under* 'archaeological periods' *in* Subject Index]
Jericho [c, s], 7
Jeroboam II [r], 104, 244
Jerusalem [c], 109, 119, 142, 252, 268, 389
Jews, as military colonists, 149
Josiah [r], 141
Judah [l], 106, 108 f., 112, 119, 137, 141 f., 144, 241, 268

Kakzu [c, l], 246
Kaldu [*see also* Chaldaeans, *the biblical form of this name; the two terms are not synonymous in all contexts*] [l, t], 92, 96, 102 f.
Kalhu [Kalḫu]: *see* Calah, *the biblical form of this name*
Kandalanu [r], 133
Kanesh [c], 68, 74, 278
Kara-hardash [*alternative form of the name of* Kara-indash the younger, *q.v.*]
Kara-indash [r], 80
Kara-indash the younger [p, r?], 82 f.
Kashtiliash III [r], 79
Kashtiliash IV [r], 84, 429
Kazallu [c], 41, 58, 65, 163
Khorsabad [*the site of* Dur-Sharrukin, *q.v.*] [s], 481
Kibri-Dagan [p], 235
Kingu [d], 412, 415
Kish [c], 41 f., 44 f., 48, 63, 119, 223, 350, 360, 423
Kishar [d], 331, 410
Kudurmabuk [r], 65
Kullab [c], 391, 421
Kultepe [*the site of* Kanesh, *q.v.*]
Kummuh [Kummuḫ] [l], 89, 96
Kurigalzu I [r], 80, 82
Kurigalzu II [r], 84
Kussara [c], 75

Laban [p], 204
Labarnas [r], 75
Labashi-Marduk [r], 145

Lagash [c], 31, 38, 44 ff., 48, 54 f., 72, 165 f., 168 f., 336, 350, 366, 371, 384, 476 f.
Lahamu [Laḫamu] [d], 331, 410, 413
Lahmu [Laḫmu] [d], 331, 410, 413
Larsa [c], 72, 147, 332, 339, 350, 478
Larsa, kingdom and dynasty of, 64 ff., 70 f., 169, 236, 274, 286, 430
[Laz d], 337
Lipit-Ishtar [Lipiṭ-Ištar] [r], 63 f., 200 f., 203, 371
Lugalanda [r], 186
Lugalbanda [d], 423
Lugalzagesi [r], 48 f., 54
Lullu [t, l], 52
Lullubi [t, l], 87 f.
Lumma-girnun canal, 44
Lydia [l], 129 f., 143, 150

Madaktu [c], 131, 133
Magan [l], 272 f., 428
Maltai [s], 335
Mami [d], 417
Manishtusu [r], 165
Mannaeans [t], 113 f., 125 f., 137
Marduk [see also Asar-lu-hi, another name applied to this god] [d], 72 f., 85, 87, 91, 110, 121, 125, 145 f., 152, 218, 220 f., 267, 300 ff., 305 ff., 316 f., 323, 326, 328 ff., 338 ff., 355, 363 ff., 385 ff., 409, 411, 413 ff., 423, 439
Marduk-apal-iddina: see Merodach-baladan, the biblical form of this name
Marduk-balatsu-iqbi [Marduk-balatsu-iqbi] [r], 102
Marduk-shapik-zer-mati [r], 90
Marduk-shum-usur [Marduk-šum-uṣur] [p], 251
Mari [c, l], 41, 48, 58, 66 f., 72, 74 f., 85, 168, 172, 175, 189, 194, 219, 222 f., 225, 227 f., 234 ff., 279, 292 ff., 335, 357, 478, 481
Mar-jamina: see Benjamina
Martu [d], 41
Martu [t], 329

Mati'-Il [r], 232
Mattiwaza [r], 81 f.
Medes [t], 101, 113, 126, 128, 136 ff., 143, 144 f., 147, 150, 267
Media [l], 126, 150, 285
Medina [c], 148, 268, 285
Megiddo [c], 141
Melid [l], 103
Meluhha [Meluḫḫa] [l], 272, 428
Memphis [c], 127, 129
Menahem [r], 108, 244, 257
Menander [p], 142
Merodach-baladan [r], 110 f., 116, 118 ff., 122, 133
Mersin [s], 270 f.
Meshech [biblical form of Mushku, q.v.]
Me-silim [r], 45
Mesopotamia (defined), 3
Metatti [r], 114
Midas: see Mita, the Assyrian form of this name
Minni [biblical form of Mannaeans, q.v.]
Mita [r], 232, 283 f.
Mitanni, land and dynasty of, 76, 78 ff.
Moab [l], 112
Moses [p], 186, 197, 301
Mummu [d], 409 ff.
Mursilis I [r], 74 ff., 80
Mursilis II [r], 229 f.
Musasir [Muṣaṣir] [c], 115 f.
Mushezib-Marduk [r], 120
Mushku [l], 88 f., 95, 116 f., 232, 283 f.

Nabonidus [=Nabu-na'id, q.v.]
Nabopolassar [Nabu-apal-uṣur] [r], 135 ff.
Nabu [d], 91, 323, 326, 342, 358, 386 f.
Nabu-apal-iddin [r], 96
Nabu-bel-shumati [p], 133 f.
Nabu-na'id [r], 143, 145 ff., 263, 267 f., 285, 349, 364 ff., 387
Nabu-nadin-zer [r], 109
Nabu-nasir [Nabu-naṣir] [r], 106, 109
Nairi [l], 84, 95, 102, 108
Namri [l], 102, 107

Nana of Erech [=Innin, q.v.] [d], 133
Nanna [d], 55, 57, 62, 64, 133, 145, 199, 220 f., 273, 330 f., 420 f.
Nanshe [d], 432
Naram-Sin of Agade [r], 50 ff., 366, 427 ff., 477 f.
Naram-Sin of Eshnunna [r], 70
Nazi-bugash [r], 83
Nazi-maruttash [r], 84
Nebo [biblical form of Nabu, q.v.]
Nebuchadrezzar I [Nabu-kudur-usur] [r], 87
Nebuchadrezzar II [also occurs in the Bible in the form Nebuchadnezzar] [r], 135, 141 ff., 147, 149, 191, 261, 267 f., 285, 366
Necho II [r], 141
Necho of Sais [r], 127, 130
Nergal [d], 334, 336 ff., 352, 402, 419
Nergal-sharezer [biblical form of the name entered under Nergal-shar-usur and Neriglissar, q.v.; it is probable, though not certain, that the person of this name mentioned in Jeremiah xxxix. 3 was the man who later became king]
Nergal-shar-usur [Nergal-šar-usur] [references are entered under the Greek form of the name, Neriglissar, q.v.]
Nergal-ushezib [r], 120
Neriglissar [r], 135, 144, 147, 284
Neti [d], 420
Nimrud [s], 94, 97, 99, 180 f., 190, 276, 336, 481
Ninazu [d], 460
Nin-egal [d], 382
Nineveh [c], 51, 72, 101, 120, 122, 126, 130, 134, 137 ff., 143, 181 f., 194, 245, 321, 390, 407, 427, 460
Ningal [d], 332
Ningirsu [d], 164 f., 336, 369, 423, 477
Ningizzida [d], 408, 460, 501
Ninhursag [Ninḫursag] [d], 331, 417 ff.
Ninib [false reading of the name Ninurta, q.v.]
Nin-igi-ku [d], 330, 400
Ninkasi [d], 419

Ninki [d], 331
Ninkurra [d], 418
Ninlil [d], 328, 330, 343 f.
Ninmu [d], 418
Nin-nibru [d], 336
Ninshubur [d], 420 f.
Ninsun [d], 391
Ninsutu [d], 419
Ninti [d], 419
Nintu [d], 363
Ninurta [d], 189, 318, 336, 402 f., 502
Ninurta-apil-Ekur [r], 86
Ninurta-tukulti-Ashur [r], 87
Nippur [c], 38 f., 48 f., 52, 54 f., 57, 62 ff., 69, 72, 147, 160, 163, 167, 183, 187, 195, 233, 329, 338 f., 350, 384, 420, 451
Niqmanda [r], 228 ff.
Niqmepa [r], 230
Nisaba [d], 406
Nisibin, Nisibis [c], 93, 95, 124, 140
Nisir, Mt. [Niṣir], 402
No-amon [c], 129
Nu-dim-mud [d], 330 f., 410
Nusku [d], 302, 305, 338
Nuzi [not to be read Nuzu] [c], 77, 176, 221, 281, 295, 472

Oannes [d?, p?], 32
Opis [c], 152

Padi [r], 119
Parattarna [r], 78
Parthians [t], 152
Pekah [r], 109
Pekod [biblical form of Puqudu, q.v.]
Persians [t], 131, 146, 150, 267 f.
Philistines [t], 108n., 281
Philistine cities, 108 f., 119
Phrygia [classical name of the kingdom known in the New Assyrian period as Mushku, q.v.]
Psammetichus [r], 130
Ptolemy [p, not r], 457 f.
Pul(u) [name applied in certain contexts to Tiglath-Pileser III, q.v.]
Puqudu [t], 106
Puzur-Amurri [p], 401

Qarqar [c], 98, 112
Qatanum [c], 226
Qatna [identified by some scholars with Qatanum] [c], 67, 77
Que [l], 99, 103, 117
Qumran [s], 149
Qurdi-Ashur-lamur [p], 246
Quti [t], 87n., 88

Ramesses II [r], 231
Ramesses III [r], 89
Rapihu [Rapiḫu] [c], 112
Ras Shamra [site of Ugarit, q.v.]
Rim-Sin [r], 65, 67, 70 ff., 220 f., 430
Rimush [r], 352
Rusas I [r], 114 ff.

Saba: see Sheba, the biblical form of this name
Saggaratum [c], 227
Sam'al [l], 103
Samaria [c, l], 110 f.
Samarra: see sub-heading under 'archaeological periods' in Subject Index
Sammu-ramat [r?], 103
Samsu-ditana [r], 74
Samsu-iluna [r], 73 f.
Sanduarri [r], 124 f.
Sapia [c], 110
Sardes [c], 150
Sardur [r], 107 f., 113
Sargon of Agade [r], 48 ff., 69, 88, 272, 277, 350, 366, 427, 455
Sargon I of Assyria [r], 69
Sargon II of Assyria [r], 111 ff., 122, 128 f., 181, 232, 296, 343, 370
Sarpanitum [Ṣarpanitum] [d], 342
Saussatar [r], 78
Scythians [t], 124, 126, 136, 138, 174, 380
Sealands [l], 74, 80, 92, 120 f., 124, 297
Sealands dynasty, 74, 79
Seleucid dynasty, 152
Semiramis [Greek form of Sammu-ramat, q.v.]
Sennacherib [r], 118 ff., 128, 181 f.
Shabirishu [c], 250

Shaduppum [ancient city now represented by Tell Harmal, q.v.]
Shalmaneser I [r], 82, 84
Shalmaneser III [r], 97 ff., 479
Shalmaneser IV [r], 103
Shalmaneser V [r], 110 f.
Shamash [d], 218, 221, 293, 305, 314, 327, 331 f., 334 ff., 339, 343, 352, 370 f., 393 f., 396, 423 ff., 462, 465
Shamash-hasir [Šamšu-ḫaṣir] [p], 237 f.
Shamash-shum-ukin [r], 126 ff.
Shamshi-Adad I [r], 67 f., 70 f., 83, 225 ff., 292, 296
Shamshi-Adad V [r], 101 ff.
Shara [d], 56, 421, 423
Sharkalisharri [r], 52
Shattuara I [r], 82
Shattuara II [r], 82
Sheba [l], 90, 255, 430
Sherua [d], 344
Shirpurla [=Lagash, q.v.]
Shub-Ad [p], 374, 376, 378 f., 381
Shubat-Enlil [c], 225, 227
Shubur [l], 329
Shulgi [r], 56 f., 167, 382, 388
Shullat [d], 402
Shuppiluliuma [r], 80 f., 228 ff.
Shupria [l], 124
Shuruppak [also spelt Shurippak] [c], 34, 43, 187, 400
Shu-Suen [r], 56 f.
Shuttarna II [r], 79 ff.
Sidon [c], 89, 99, 108, 120, 124 f., 142, 246, 259, 282
Siduri [d], 108, 398 f.
Sin [d], 145 f., 151, 267, 302 f., 326 f., 331, 335 f., 364 f., 462 ff.
Sin-iddinam [r], 180
Sin-muballit [Sin-muballiṭ] [r], 66
Sin-shar-ishkun [r], 135 ff.
Sippar [c], 34, 72, 95, 152, 332, 339, 350, 365
So [p, r?], 112
Solomon [r], 255 ff., 430
Subartu [l], 428
Suhu [Suḫu] [t], 96, 137 f.
Sumer (defined) [l], 3

Sumu-abum [r], 64 f.
Sumu-ilum [r], 64
Sumu-la-ilum [r], 218
Suru [c], 96
Susa [c], 131, 133, 272
Sutu [t], 83 f.

Tabal [l], 99, 116 f., 124, 129
Takrit [c, s], 138
Tammuz [d], 355, 377 ff., 395, 408, 419 f., 486, 498
[See also Dumuzi]
Tanuatamon [r], 129
Tarbisu [Tarbiṣu] [c], 138
Tarqu [r], 127 ff.
Tashmetum [d], 342
Teima [c], 148 f., 285
Tell Agrab [s], 190
Tell Ahmar [Tell Aḥmar] [site of Til-Barsip, q.v.]
Tell Asmar [site of Eshnunna, q.v.]
Tell Brak [s], 27, 51, 77, 167, 277
Tell es-Sultan [site of the ancient city of Jericho, q.v.]
Tell Halaf [s], 93
[See also sub-heading Halaf under 'archaeological periods' in Subject Index]
Tell Hariri [s], 66
Tell Harmal [s], 203
Tello [site of Lagash, q.v.]
Tell Uqair [s], 19, 24, 42, 481
Temanites [t], 93
Tepe Gawra [s], 186
Thebes [c], 127 ff., 281
Tiamat [d], 159, 331, 340, 363, 409 ff., 428
Tiglath-Pileser I [Tukulti-apal-Ešarra] [r], 88 ff., 92, 189
Tiglath-Pileser II [r], 92
Tiglath-Pileser III [r], 104 ff., 113, 128, 133, 137, 241, 247, 251, 257, 268, 479
Til-Barsip [c], 96, 481
Tilmun [or Dilmun] [l], 54, 62, 102, 227, 272 ff., 284, 418, 428
Tirhakah [biblical form of Tarqu, q.v.]
Tirqa [c], 235, 252, 344

Trebizond [c], 113
Tubal [biblical form of Tabal, q.v.]
Tukulti-Ninurta I [r], 84 f., 87, 429
Tukulti-Ninurta II [r], 95
Turushpa [c], 114 f.
Tushkhan [Tušḫan] [l], 96, 108, 250
Tushratta [r] 79, 81f.
Tuthmosis III [r], 78
Tuthmosis IV [r], 78
Tuttul [c], 225, 293
Tyre [c], 97, 99, 108, 120, 127 f., 142, 246, 267, 282 f.

Ubaid [Properly Tell El-'Ubaid; see sub-heading Ubaid under main heading 'archaeological periods' in Subject Index]
Ubar-Tutu [p], 397, 401
Ugarit [c], 76 f., 223, 228 ff., 282, 344, 363
Ukin-zer [r], 109 ff., 128
Ulamburiash [r], 79
Ullusunu [r], 114
Umma [c], 44 f., 48, 54, 56, 384, 421, 477
Ummanaldash [r], 133 f.
Ummanigash [r], 132
Ummanmanda [t], 138 ff., 143, 146 f., 365
Ur [c], 24, 33, 42, 48, 56, 62 f., 64, 69, 72, 79 f., 135, 145 ff., 167, 182, 186, 190, 199, 272 f., 276, 286, 313, 332, 339, 349 f., 384, 420 f., 456
Ur, First dynasty of, 46, 374, 380 f.
Ur, Third dynasty of, 55 ff., 57, 62, 64 f., 68, 77, 164 f., 167, 186, 199, 234, 236, 273, 293, 308, 354, 360 f., 363, 380 f., 460, 467
Urartu [Urarṭu] [l], 84, 90, 97, 100 ff., 105 f., 112 ff., 122 ff., 140, 143, 169, 248, 283 f., 343
Urkish [c], 77
Ur-Nammu [r], 55 f., 199 f., 363
Ur-Nanshe [r and dynasty], 44, 47
Urshanabi [p], 399, 405
Uruk [=Erech, q.v.]

Urukagina [r], 47 f., 164, 171, 186 f.,
196, 198
Uruatri [= Urartu, q.v.]
Utnapishtim [p], 384, 397 ff.
Uttu [d], 418
Utu [d], 331 f.
Utu-hengal [Utu-ḫengal] [r], 55

Warad-Sin [r], 65
Warka [site of Erech, q.v.]

Yaggid-Lim [r], 70
Yahdu-Lim or Yahdun-Lim [Yaḫdu-
Lim, etc.] [r], 70, 224
Yahweh: see Jehovah
Yamhad [Yamḫad] [l], 67, 70 f., 75,
227

Yarim-Lim [r], 67
Yasmah-Adad [Yasmaḫ-Addu] [r],
67, 70 ff., 172, 225 ff., 236, 293
Yatrib [c], 148
Ya'u-kina [cuneiform form of Jehoia-
chin, q.v.]

Zamua [l], 95, 107, 114
Zarzi [s], 4
Zedekiah [r], 142, 268
Zenjirli [or Zinjirli] [s], 127
Zer-banitum [= Sarpanitum, q.v.]
Zikirtu [l], 113
Zimri [r], 244
Zimri-Lim [r], 70 ff., 75, 225, 244,
344
Zu [d], 422 ff.

Index of Sumerian, Akkadian, Hebrew and Greek words

(The following are excluded and will be found in the Subject Index *or the* Index of Proper Names: *titles of officials; terms denoting priests, priestesses or associated temple personnel; words occurring as proper names or titles of works.)*

Abbreviations:

[a] administrative term
[c] cult object
[e] economic term
[m] mythical object or character

[p] term, not properly a title, referring to persons
[s] type of sacrifice
[t] part of a temple or other sacred building

aban, 472
Abubu [m], 414
adaman-du₁₁-ga, 432, 442
adda edubba [p], 435
A-ki-ti, 383 f.
Akitu, 383 f.
Akitu-house [t], 384
allalu-bird, 395
Assinnu [m, p], 348
asu [p], 460, 470
a-zu [p], 460
bab (ša) maḫiri [e], 287
bā'iru [a, p], 237
balag [c], 190
beru, 492 f.
bit ashtammi [t], 357
dēkû [=PA.PA, q.v.]
dubshar ashaga [p], 435
dubshar kengira [p], 435
ebuttu [e], 291
Edubba, 434
Egipar [t], 37, 168, 345, 349, 383
egirrû, 324 f.
gagu [t], 350, 357
gigunu [t], 355
ginu [s], 353
Giparu [=Egipar, q.v.]

girginakku [t], 357
guqqu [s], 353
harpé [c], 343
ḫubattatu [e], 290
ià-zu [p], 460
irṣitum [a], 238
Issinnu [=Assinnu, q.v.]
kalaturra [m], 421
Ki, 330
kibati, 401
kiṣru [a], 260
kitru [a], 109
kudurru, 478 f.
kullatu [c], 315
kurgarru [m, p], 348, 421
labuttû [a, p], 237
laḫamu [m], 412
lilissu [c], 191
limmu [a, p], 93 f., 101
luddu-weapon, 428
lullu [m], 417
magen Dawid, 497
makeltu [c], 347
mamitu, 466
mandattu [a, e], 258
menorah, 497
mushrushshu [m], 314

nagu [**a**], 247
nahiru, 89
nakkaptu, 470
naru, 427
nindabu [**s**], 353
niqu [**s**], 353
palu [**c**], 414
PA.PA [**a, p**], 237
patum [**a**], 238
pihatu [**a**], 247
qannu [**a**], 248, 253
qulmu [**c**], 315
rēdū [**a, p**], 237
rōbes [*See also sub-heading* 'Rabisu'

under main heading 'demons' *in*
Subject Index], 485
sattukku [**s**], 352
shapatu, 353
shirku [**p**], 265 f.
sugurra [**c**], 420
suqaqu [**p**], 235
tadmiqtum [**e**], 289
tamartu [**a, e**], 257
tamkarum [**e, p**], 287 ff.
tholoi [**t**], 13, 18
tumri–cakes, 395
ulushin–beer, 434
ummia [**p**], 435

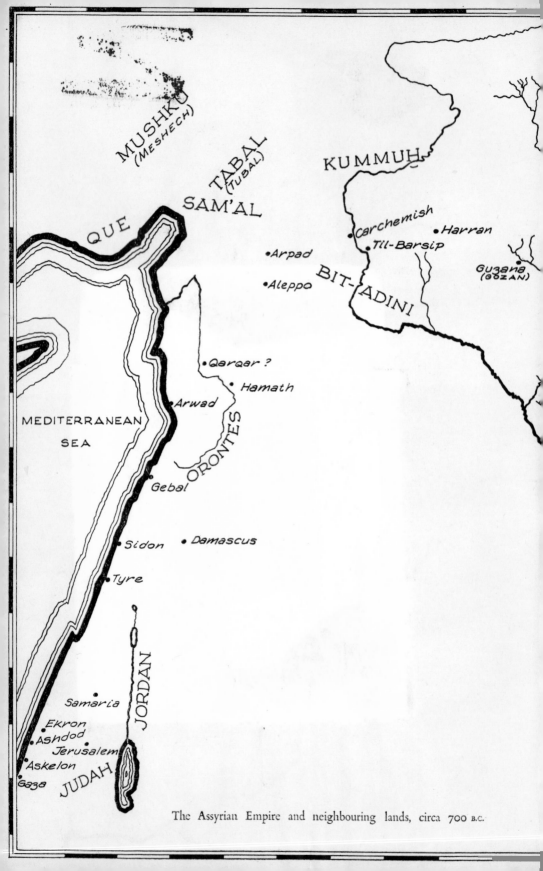

MUSHKU
(MESHECH)

TABAL
(TUBAL)

SAM'AL

QUE

KUMMUH

Carchemish
Til-Barsip
Harran

Guzana
(GOZAN)

BIT-ADINI

•Arpad

•Aleppo

•Qarqar ?

•Hamath

•Arwad

ORONTES

MEDITERRANEAN
SEA

Gebal

•Sidon   • Damascus

•Tyre

JORDAN

Samaria

Ekron
Ashdod
Jerusalem
Askelon
Gaza   JUDAH

The Assyrian Empire and neighbouring lands, circa 700 B.C.